NARRATIVE COMPREHENSION AND FILM

...e is one of the fundamental ways we organize and understand
...rld. It is found everywhere: not only in films and books, but
...everyday conversations and in the nonfictional discourses of
...ists, historians, educators, psychologists, attorneys and many
...s.

...ward Branigan presents a telling exploration of the basic concepts
...arrative theory and its relation to film – and literary – analysis,
...ging together theories from the field of "narratology" along with
...as from linguistics and cognitive science, and applying them to the
...een. Individual analyses of classical narratives form the basis of a
...mplex study of every aspect of filmic texts exploring, for example,
...bjectivity in *Lady in the Lake*, multiplicity in *Letter from an Unknown
...oman*, post-modernism and documentary in *Sans Soleil*.

Through this examination of film, Branigan develops a method of
analysis which reveals narrative as a distinctive strategy for recognizing,
isolating and articulating our responses to the world as a whole.

This book will be essential reading for students and teachers of film,
media and communication studies, and literary studies.

Edward Branigan is Professor and Chair of the Film Studies Program
...t the University of California, Santa Barbara. He is the author of *Point
of View in the Cinema* (Mouton, 1984), as well as general editor (with
Charles Wolfe) of the American Film Institute Readers series
(Routledge).

SIGHTLINES

Edited by Edward Buscombe, The British Film Institute and Phil Rosen, Center for Modern Culture and Media Studies, Brown University, USA

Cinema Studies has made extraordinary strides in the past two decades. Our capacity for understanding both how and what the cinema signifies has been developed through new methodologies, and hugely enriched in interaction with a wide variety of other disciplines, including literary studies, anthropology, linguistics, history, economics and psychology. As fertile and important as these new theoretical foundtions are, their very complexity has made it increasingly difficult to track the main lines of conceptualization. Furthermore, they have made Cinema Studies an ever more daunting prospect for those coming new to the field.

This new series of books will map out the ground of major conceptual areas within Cinema Studies. Each volume is written by a recognized authority to provide a clear and detailed synopsis of current debates within a particular topic. Each will make an original contribution to advancing the state of knowledge within the area. Key arguments and terms will be clearly identified and explained, seminal thinkers will be assessed, and issues for further research will be laid out. Taken together the series will constitute an indispensable chart of the terrain which Cinema Studies now occupies.

Books in the series include:

CINEMA AND SPECTATORSHIP
Judith Mayne

GENRE AND HOLLYWOOD
Steve Neale

NEW VOCABULARIES IN FILM SEMIOTICS
Structuralism, Post-structuralism and Beyond
Robert Stam, Robert Burgoyne and Sandy Flitterman-Lewis

UNTHINKING EUROCENTRISM
Towards a Multi-cultural Film Critique
Ella Shohat/Robert Stam

NARRATIVE COMPREHENSION AND FILM

Edward Branigan

London and New York

First published 1992
by Routledge
11 New Fetter Lane, London EC4P 4EE

Simultaneously published in the USA and Canada
by Routledge
29 West 35th Street, New York, NY 10001

Reprinted 1996, 1998, 2001

Routledge is an imprint of the Taylor & Francis Group

Printed and bound in Great Britain by
T.J. International Ltd., Padstow, Cornwall

British Library Cataloguing in Publication Data
Branigan, Edward
Narrative comprehension and film.
I. Title
809.923

Library of Congress Cataloguing in Publication Data
Branigan, Edward
Narrative comprehension and film/Edward Branigan.
p.   cm.
Includes bibliographical references and index.
1. Motion pictures and literature.   2. Narration (Rhetoric)
3. Motion picture plays – History and criticism.   I. Title.
PN1995.3.B73   1992
791.43'75–dc20   91–25883

ISBN 0–415–07511–4 (hbk)
ISBN 0–415–07512–2 (pbk)

To Carol and Will, and
to the memory of my sister Lorel

CONTENTS

FIGURES

PREFACE

In recent years the study of narrative has acquired a new and prominent role in theorizing about film. Since at least 1907 narrative has been the dominant mode of filmmaking as well as the principal source of examples for writers exploring the ontology, epistemology, aesthetics, and ideology of film. Even so, it has only been within the last decade that writers have fully recognized the formative power of narrative and begun the task of integrating sophisticated theories of narrative with theories of the general nature of film and film style. Indeed it was discovered that classical film theories were often premised on a tacit and fragmentary view of the nature of narrative.

The current situation is the result of two trends. In the mid-1960s film theory began to stress epistemological and psychological questions, developing, first, an object-centered epistemology (where the goal was to present numerous methods by which to segment and analyze the parts of a film) followed by a shift toward a subject-centered epistemology (where the goal was to investigate the actual methods employed by a human perceiver to watch, understand, and remember a film). Feminist theory, for example, shifted from identifying cultural stereotypes in film to concentrating on the role of sexuality and gender in a perceiver's ongoing encounter with film. At about the same time, a second trend appeared in which narrative began to be explored as a discourse in its own right, apart from its manifestation in any particular medium. This study came to be called "narratology." Its goal was also epistemological: at first descriptive and objective, but more recently focused on a perceiver's "competence" – on the conditions that govern and make possible both the comprehension and creation of narrative texts. Today narrative is increasingly viewed as a distinctive strategy for organizing data about the world, for making sense and significance. As the features of narrative came to be specified more precisely, it was detected in a bewildering number of places: not just in artworks, but in our ordinary life and in the work of historians, psychologists, educators, journalists, attorneys, and others. It became clear that narrative was nothing less than one of the fundamental ways used by human beings to think about the world, and could not be confined to the merely "fictional."

The aim of this book is to examine various approaches to narrative in order to isolate a set of basic issues and problems which must be addressed by any new theory of narrative. These approaches to narrative will cast light on the general epistemological issues addressed by specific theories of film and, to some extent, theories of literature, since both film theory and narratology often rely on literary studies. My method will draw upon an interdisciplinary field known as "cognitive science" that emerged in the mid-1970s and whose effect is beginning to be felt in film study. Cognitive science poses questions about how the human mind functions and how we are able to think. Its answers are framed through the concepts of linguistics, cognitive psychology, artificial intelligence, ethnography, literary theory, and philosophy of language. I believe that film theory, even in its classical formulations, has something to contribute to cognitive science, and equally that cognitive science has something important to contribute to film theory.

My examples of narrative principles will be taken mainly from films, but always with the idea that the principles illustrated extend to the narrative organization of literary and other kinds of material. I will not present a historical account of the development of narrative analysis in film, but rather present an interpretation of theoretical claims arranged as a logical account of how different theories construct answers to certain, but not all, issues of narrativity. I will be concerned primarily with *classical* narrative, with Hollywood films and their near relatives. These narratives are prototypical cases against which some other kinds of narrative organization may be measured. It will be seen that classical narrative is a remarkably complex phenomenon.

The emphasis in the book will fall upon narrative fiction, though I will touch upon some types of narrative in nonfiction. I will illustrate concepts with close analysis and small-scale examples, rather than analyses of entire films. I have not assumed that the reader of this book is familiar with any of the films that are discussed nor have I assumed that the reader has any prior familiarity with the methods of cognitive science. Although some knowledge of film structure is presumed, this should not cause any difficulty for a student who has had an introductory course in film, or for a professional trained in another field with an interest in narrative.

My argument in the book develops along the following lines. I first examine a number of theories about the nature of the patterns, or structures, that are created in consciousness when we read a text as a narrative. Here I draw heavily on recent experimental studies of narrative comprehension.

In chapter 2, I introduce the basic concepts of space, time, and causality, and their analysis in terms of data on the screen and in an imagined story world. It will be seen that the process of understanding a narrative arises from an unsteady, sometimes volatile competition among a variety of perceptual mechanisms.

Chapters 3 and 4 consider a pair of issues generally overlooked in experimental studies, but conspicuous in literary and film theory: narration and point of view. If these issues are to escape fuzzy conjectures concerning the psychology of characters, narrators, and authors, they must be stated more concretely in terms of the actual mental processes initiated by readers and spectators. Which aspects of consciousness are relevant to our comprehension of an object being narrated and depicted "under a view"? What kind of knowledge is at stake, of what use is it, and how does it complement story, character, and plot? These questions lead to an analysis of how diverse epistemological boundaries are inscribed, explicitly or implicitly, within a narrative text in order to guide the processing and construction of global patterns. Whether complementary or antagonistic, such boundaries exert powerful effects on our comprehension of narrative events. I conclude by offering an extended definition of all aspects of narrative and a sketch of five broad types of narrative theory.

The next two chapters illustrate how the five broad types of theory engage several basic problems of narrative organization. What is the nature of first-person narration? What does it mean to talk about objective, factual representation in narrative? And what happens when a reader or spectator is confronted by uncertain mixtures of subjective and objective narration – when a text actively challenges us to assess how knowledge of the world is possible at all within symbols and language?

In the final chapter I separate fiction from narrative. A study of the fictional reference of narrative is concerned with how a given narrative pattern may be *connected* to a world or worlds, how we come to believe in its truth and find a value in it. I briefly survey some theories of fiction and offer one account of how a cognitive theory might deal with the psychology of fictional reference. I conclude by analyzing a film which tests many of the concepts and boundaries associated with our ordinary comprehension of narrative.

The book seeks to draw together three basic modes of analysis. Certain concepts from cognitive psychology (e.g., schema, top-down/bottom-up processing, declarative/procedural knowledge) will be joined to concepts from narratology (e.g., diegesis, focalization, levels of narration). This combination, in turn, will be interpreted as a way of thinking about temporal structure; here, linguistics will become my model because of its carefully worked out logic of time and tense. We will discover that perceiving the world narratively is intimately tied to our ways of arranging knowledge (schemas), to our skills of causal reasoning, and hence to our judgments about temporal sequence. Thus – to take one example – the spectator's recognition of a "scene" in a narrative film will be analyzed as a complex temporal event (expressed through the historical present tense) that is being generated by a level of narration which is presenting *one* (past, now made present) time but from the perspective of *another* (later, and still future) time. Not only is the "end" of the story already known at its beginning, but in its telling there is the implicit assertion that the story will be important and worth the time. The spectator's recognition of such a complex time (and causality) in a film narrative can be explained by top-down mental processes and schemas that are not dependent upon the actual time during which data appears on a motion picture screen. Although somewhat surprising, we will discover that the purest instance of a narrative scene may be found in the classical documentary film which seeks to make the past immediate for the spectator by compressing and reducing the levels of narration. It is my belief that many other analytical terms besides narrative "scene" will yield new meanings when considered through the methods of cognitive psychology, narratology, and linguistics.

Books are not written in a vacuum. I would like to acknowledge the many persons who have provided an atmosphere within which to work, have circulated ideas to me, and read drafts.

The National Endowment for the Humanities provided a 1987 Summer Stipend and the American Council of Learned Societies awarded me a 1987–8 Fellowship. These monies, along with the tangible and intangible support of my parents, Evelyn and Henry Odell, made the writing of this book possible.

None of the material written for this book has been previously published. I am grateful to Marvel Entertainment Group for permission to reprint a sequence of panels from the comic book *Nick Fury, Agent of SHIELD* and equally grateful to the story's writer and illustrator, Jim Steranko, for his assistance.

I would like to thank David A. Sprecher, Provost, College of Letters and Science, for his support as well as past and present colleagues at Santa Barbara who have contributed on a regular basis: Anna Brusutti, Kathryn Carnahan, Mary Desjardins, Manthia Diawara, Dana Driskel, Willis Flachsenhar, Victor Fuentes, Naomi Greene, Paul Hernadi, Lea Jacobs, Harry Lawton, Paul N. Lazarus, Suzanne Jill Levine, Marti Mangan, Constance Penley, Michael Renov, Laurence A. Rickels, Jonathan Rosenbaum, Alexander Sesonske, Janet Walker, and Mark Williams.

Special help and encouragement at particular moments during the project were offered by the following: Rick Altman, Dudley Andrew, David Alan Black, Dave Cash, Donna S. Cunningham, Thomas Elsaesser, Ronald Gottesman, Christopher Husted, Henry Jenkins III, Vance Kepley, Jr., Russell Merritt, Mark Smith, Vivian C. Sobchack, Janet Staiger, and Kristin Thompson.

I have been fortunate to have had thoughtful commentaries on my arguments by Edward Buscombe, Nataša Durovičová, and Marsha Kinder. Particularly close and detailed readings were offered by Sabine Gross, Garrett Stewart, and Charles Wolfe. I have appreciated the comradeship since, as the philosopher Heraclitus noted, the trail up the mountain is the same as the one down.

David Bordwell is the most indefatigable friend and generous scholar one could ask for. I have benefited enormously from his teaching, his work, and his reactions to my work. The keenness and wit of his writing has been my model.

I have been excellently well-served by the editorial and production staff at Routledge: Jane Armstrong, Rebecca Barden, Philippa Brewster, Stephanie Horner, Sarah Pearsall, Maria Stasiak, and Penny Wheeler. Philip Rosen has provided me expert advice. He is a superlative editor as sensitive to syntax and organization as he is to argumentative detail. Fortunately for me he is also possessed of patience and humor. I have used many of his ideas.

Finally, I wish to acknowledge the continuing energy and companionship of my nine-year-old son Alex and, since I last penned a preface, second and third sons, Evan and Liam, loved just as dearly. I'm indebted also to Roberta Kimmel who has taken part in all my projects.

The book is dedicated to my sister and brother, Carol and Will, and to the memory of my sister Lorel. Their enthusiasm and earnestness are a permanent inspiration.

Santa Barbara, California
November 1991

1

NARRATIVE SCHEMA

PSYCHOLOGICAL USE VALUE

Narrative has existed in every known human society. Like metaphor, it seems to be everywhere: sometimes active and obvious, at other times fragmentary, dormant, and tacit. We encounter it not just in novels and conversation but also as we look around a room, wonder about an event, or think about what to do next week. One of the important ways we perceive our environment is by anticipating and telling ourselves mini-stories about that environment based on stories already told. Making narratives is a strategy for making our world of experiences and desires intelligible. It is a fundamental way of organizing data.[1]

Recently narrative principles have been found in the work of a wide range of professionals, including attorneys,[2] historians,[3] biographers, educators, psychiatrists, and journalists.[4] This demonstrates that narrative should not be seen as exclusively *fictional* but instead should merely be contrasted to *other (nonnarrative) ways of assembling and understanding data*. The following kinds of document exemplify some *non*narrative ways of organizing data: lyric poetry, essay, chronology, inventory, classification, syllogism, declaration, sermon, prayer, letter, dialectic, summary, index, dictionary, diagram, map, recipe, advertisement, charity solicitation, instruction manual, laundry list, telephone directory, birth announcement, credit history, medical statement, job description, application form, wedding invitation, stock market report, administrative rules, and legal contract. The relevance and connection of narrative, or nonnarrative, to our world – how it may be used in that world to accomplish a goal – is a separate issue concerning its "mode of reference" as either fiction or nonfiction.

As a starting point and for simplicity, then, I will divide texts into four basic types: narrative fiction (e.g., a novel); narrative nonfiction (e.g., history); nonnarrative fiction (e.g., many kinds of poetry); and nonnarrative nonfiction (e.g., essay). The boundaries among these types are not absolute but relative to the questions one wishes to ask

1

about the data that has been organized. The fact that certain poetry, for example, is nonnarrative does not mean that, considered at a fine grain, it may not also exhibit some aspects of narrative organization (e.g., defining a scene of action and temporal progression, dramatizing an observer of events). One should not allow the usefulness of broad categorizations (poetry, novel) to obscure the ways in which a narrative strategy may be applied successfully by a reader in comprehending certain aspects of some texts; or, for that matter, to obscure the ways in which nonnarrative reading strategies may penetrate narrative texts at certain levels.

It is also important to distinguish between two broad fields in which a given narrative may function. In one context, it can be said that a narrative must be consumed as a material and social object, and must respond to an agenda of community issues. In this context, a narrative acquires labels of immense variety in order to arouse the interests of community members. These labels are the pathways on which it moves through society by being bought and sold, or exchanged. In a second context, however, a narrative can be said to exist for only one person at a time. Engaging intimately with a perceiver, narrative enters thought itself, competing and jostling with other ways of reacting to the world. Thus narrative, at least initially, may be analyzed in two different ways. From one angle it appears as a social and political object with an *exchange* value arising from its manufacture as an object for a community; from another angle it appears as a psychological object with a *use* value arising from perceptual labor – from the exercise of the particular skills possessed by a member of that community. Ultimately, of course, these two values are not independent. One may study the psychological dimension of exchange (e.g., commodity fetishism) and the social dimension of use (e.g., propaganda). The particular social ground which defines an individual's language and horizon of action cannot be completely divorced from that individual's language competence and abilities. Narrative depends on an unspoken, permanent agenda of topics in a community which, in turn, justifies the community activities for which abilities must be found and developed in individuals.[5] In studying how a narrative is assigned labels in order to be exchanged and used, one is studying basic human proficiencies: skills employed in manufacturing and selling a material object as well as perceptual skills employed in realizing a use for the object.

In spite of the copresence of exchange value and use value, I will tentatively separate the two contexts in order to better highlight the nature of a *relative* autonomy where each value provides a ground for the other. This will also enable me to limit the terms of discussion so as to begin to talk about how narrative functions in our world. It is the aim of this book to examine the use value of narrative, specifically the *psychological* dimension of use. I wish to examine how we come to know that something is a narrative and how a narrative is able to make intelligible our experiences and feelings. I will argue that it is more than a way of classifying texts: *narrative is a perceptual activity that organizes data into a special pattern which represents and explains experience.* More specifically, narrative is a way of organizing spatial and temporal data into a cause–effect chain of events with a beginning, middle, and end that embodies a judgment about the nature of the events as well as demonstrates how it is possible to know, and hence to narrate, the events.

Although it will often be convenient to use the word "narrative" to refer to an end result, or goal, one should not forget that this final product ("here is a narrative") arises from a particular and ongoing (narrative) method of organizing data. Thus the word "narrative" may refer to either the product of storytelling/comprehending or to its process of construction. The first four chapters will begin to specify narrative in both these senses while chapter 7 will consider how a narrative relates to the real world in a "fictional" or "nonfictional" manner.

If narrative is to be considered as a way of perceiving, one still needs to specify the way. Further, one needs to specify what is meant by "perceiving." In general, my approach will be to allow the notion of "perceiving" to remain quite broad and elastic, capable of referring to any one of a range of distinct mental activities. When sharp lines must be drawn, I will use special concepts. Thus the word "perception" will be used in this book to point toward any of the following: a "percept" derived from reality; a preconscious assumption being made about reality; or an acknowledged fact of physical reality. The word "perception" may also be used to refer to an intuition (e.g., perceiving that color seems to be intrinsic and permanent to an object while sound appears to come from an object, to be created and contingent); or, it may refer to a propositional conclusion that a perceiver has reached about sensory perception through a process of reasoning; or, it may simply refer to an *attitude* we adopt when confronted by something that is a *representation* of something else. Some theories would classify the latter as cognition rather than perception. As we shall see, particular theories of narrative will divide up the operations of human consciousness in various ways to emphasize different abilities. Thus the word "perception" in this book will earn its exactness only through the finer discriminations made by particular theories. In the next chapter, for example, I will begin to refine the notion of "perception" by introducing a fundamental distinction between "top-down" and "bottom-up" modes of perceiving.

LOGICAL TRANSFORMATIONS IN NARRATIVE

What way of arranging data is characteristic of narrative perception? We readily distinguish narrative from other experiences even if we cannot say how the judgment is being made, just as we may not be able to say why something counts as a "game" or a "grammatical" sentence.[6] Intuitively we believe that a narrative is more than a mere description of place or time, and more even than events in a logical or causal sequence. For example, an account of the placement of objects in a room is not a narrative. Similarly, though a recipe involves temporal duration and progression ("bake until golden brown . . . "), it is not normally thought of as a narrative (the story of a pie). Nor does a sequence of actions become a narrative by being causal, completed, or well-delineated; for example, a planet orbiting the sun, the construction of a syllogism, the recitation of an alphabet, or the actions of departing, traveling, and arriving do not by themselves form a narrative. Instead, narrative can be seen as an organization of experience which draws together many aspects of our spatial, temporal, and causal perception.

In a narrative, some person, object, or situation undergoes a particular type of change and this change is measured by a sequence of attributions which apply to the thing at different times. Narrative is a way of experiencing a group of sentences or pictures (or gestures or dance movements, etc.) which together attribute a beginning, middle, and end to something. The beginning, middle, and end are not contained in the discrete elements, say, the individual sentences of a novel but signified in the overall relationships established among the totality of the elements, or sentences. For example, the first sentence of a novel is not itself "the beginning." It acquires that status in relationship to certain other sentences. Although being "physically" first in some particular way may be necessary for a "beginning," it is not sufficient since a beginning must also be judged to be a proper part of an ordered sequence or pattern of *other* elements; the elements themselves are *not* the pattern. Narrative is thus a global interpretation of changing data measured through sets of relationships. We must now consider the nature of this overall pattern of relationships.

Tzvetan Todorov argues that narrative in its most basic form is a causal "transformation" of a situation through five stages:

1 a state of equilibrium at the outset;
2 a disruption of the equilibrium by some action;
3 a recognition that there has been a disruption;
4 an attempt to repair the disruption;
5 a reinstatement of the initial equilibrium.[7]

These changes of state are not random but are produced according to

4

principles of cause and effect (e.g., principles which describe possibility, probability, impossibility, and necessity among the actions that occur). This suggests that there are two fundamental kinds of predication in narrative: *existents*, which assert the existence of something (in the mode of the verb "to be"), and *processes*, which stipulate a change or process under a causal formula (in the mode of such verbs as "to go, to do, to happen").[8] Typical existents are characters and settings while typical processes are actions of persons and forces of nature. But there is more: the changes of state create an *overall pattern* or "transformation" whereby Todorov's third stage is seen as the "inverse" of the first and fifth stages, and the fourth stage the "inverse" of the second (since it attempts to reverse the effects of the disruption).[9] The five stages may be symbolized as follows: A, B, −A, −B, A. This amounts to a large-scale pattern (repetition, antithesis, symmetry, gradation) among the causal relationships and is temporal in a new way; in fact, some theorists refer to such patterns as a "spatial" form of narrative.[10] This emergent form, or transformation, is a necessary feature of narrative because, as Christian Metz observes, "A narrative is not a sequence of closed events but a closed sequence of events."[11]

Consider as an example the following limerick:

> There was a young lady of Niger
> Who smiled as she rode on a tiger.
> They returned from the ride
> With the lady inside
> And the smile on the face of the tiger.[12]

Analyzing the limerick as a narrative using Todorov's transformations, results in the following global structure:

There was [once upon a time]:

A	smile
B	ride
−A	[swallowed: a horrible pleasure?]
−B	return
A	smile

[which goes to show that . . .]

The limerick illustrates several important points about Todorov's transformations. First, the structure does not represent directly the actual processing of the narrative by a perceiver but only its conceptual or logical form after it has been interpreted. The reader discovers that the narrative did not begin with "lady," or "youth," or the place of "Niger," as its initial term ("A") because none of those beginnings will yield a macro-description of the required kind. Taking "smile" as an initial term, however, produces a sequence of transformations that will

5

embrace the limerick as a whole (A, B, −A, −B, A). Nevertheless, this does not yet explain why a reader may smile at the limerick. The humor of the limerick resides in the sudden realization of what must have happened, of what was *omitted* from its proper sequence *in the telling*. The absence of the woman at the end answers to a gap in the chrono-logical structure of the telling of the event. Todorov's middle stage – a "recognition" of the disruption – already hints that the *actual process* of moving from ignorance to knowledge will be of central importance to our experience of narrative. Not only characters and narrators, but readers are caught up in ways of perceiving and knowing. These crucial issues will need to be addressed in more detail and will be the topic of chapters 3 and 4.

Second, Todorov's structure does not represent the entirety of our comprehension of the narrative aspects of the limerick. The reader must supply an epilogue or moral to the story which justifies its being told (which goes to show that . . .). This involves a rereading and a reassignment of some of the meanings – a process facilitated in the first line by assuming that reference will be partially indeterminate in the manner of a fiction (once there was *a* time . . .). Eventually the reader must rationalize how he or she might know such an exotic world within his or her preconceptions of an ordinary world.

Finally, although this narrative is arranged to focus attention on what Todorov calls the inversion of the initial equilibrium (the middle cause which is the opposite of smiling, i.e., being swallowed, −A), the logical structure cannot account for all of the inferences that the reader must draw in discovering the nature of the "inversion" which turns out to have an unexpected literal dimension (ingestion) as well as a number of metaphorical dimensions. What qualifies the inversion *as* an inver-sion? The reader must make inferences in spite of (and also because of) being misled by the verse. Consider, for instance, the deception of the phrase "they returned" in line 3; and the fact that the lady's ride is enlarged by the word "returned" to mean that she had departed on a *trip*, even if only a short trip; and the semantic play with the preposition "on" and with the definite article of "the smile": at the end only her smile "rides on" the tiger and the smile is not hers but a smile of the tiger. (We will examine more fully the significance of deception in relation to perceiving and knowing a narrative in chapters 3 and 4.) The implications of the use of causation and metaphor in the narrative extend at least to the reader's knowledge and beliefs about female sexuality, pleasure, oral gratification, desire, risk and trust; and perhaps also to the consequences of being "away from the home."[13] It is far from clear how the logical form of the limerick is able to summon these forms of knowledge. Would a reader, for example, be able to list all possible "inversions" of a given initial state? Or is there instead a sense in which an inversion must be *discovered* to be appropriate through the operation of processes which are not all "logical" in the same ways?

Before expanding our idea of narrative form, it may be useful to contrast the above limerick with a poem which is nonnarrative:

> Roses are red
> Violets are blue
> Sugar is sweet
> And so are you.

For reasons to be made clear shortly, I will refer to the structure of this poem as a *catalogue*, not a narrative. For now it is enough to notice that the verb "to be" has been used four times in an attributive and atemporal sense (as in the extreme case of identity, "a rose is a rose"). The reader does not interpret the poem as implying one or more temporal adverbial complements, such as, "Roses are red at noon, violets are blue at two." No temporal logic connects the redness of roses with the blueness of violets and the sweetness of sugar and "you." Instead the reader constructs a pair of categories which have no "tense": one which contains two flowers, and another which contains both sugar and the reader himself or herself ("you"). The "causation" at work in the poem – producing the conclusion signaled by "and so" – is asserted to be as logical, natural, and timeless as grouping roses and violets together as flowers (or, perhaps, as objects having color). The rhyme (blue–you) brings together the two categories and implies that the logic of forming the flower category is as certain as the logic of grouping sugar and "you." Thus although both the poem and the limerick compare a person's desirable qualities to something which may be tasted or eaten, the poem is not a narrative because its conceptual structure does not depend on a definite temporal progression which ultimately reveals a global pattern (e.g., A, B, −A, −B, A). Instead the poem is based on forming simple pairs of things with the final intimation – an epilogue of sorts – that "you," the reader, and an implicit "I," the author, should also form a pair.

I would now like to imagine for a moment something incredible. Suppose that the limerick that tells the story of the woman riding on the tiger contains an interlude where the tiger sings for the woman the poem, "Roses are red." In one sense, the narrative has been interrupted by a nonnarrative, catalogue sequence. In another sense, however, there has been no real interruption, for both the narrative limerick and the nonnarrative poem develop a connection between taste and beauty in which the sexual drive is represented as an appetite that devours. Is the limerick-poem then a hybrid? Does the narrative dominate the catalogue, or is the narrative merely an excuse for a clever song? I believe that there is no definitive answer to what it really is. Rather, the answer will depend upon the purpose in asking the question: within what context must an answer be framed, how narrowly must the text be construed, which meanings are most important, and so forth. Recognizing the complexity and dynamism of a text is usually more important than assigning a final, decisive label to it.

Rick Altman has drawn attention to the importance of certain catalogue systems within narrative texts. He speaks of narrative as possessing a "dual focus" where one focus is composed of a chronological and causal progression (the "syntagmatic") while the other is composed of a multitude of binary oppositions among elements that are "static" and that exist outside the time of the causal progression (the "paradigmatic"). A textual element (shot, scene, aspect of style, character attribute, theme, etc.) that is functioning paradigmatically makes a pair not by calling forth its "effect" in a linear fashion, but by suggesting a *parallel* with something else, a similarity or contrast. Paradigmatic pairing (or, what I have described as a "catalogue") creates collections of objects organized according to "conceptual" principles. Altman finds that in the genre of the American musical film, a special kind of paradigmatic focus, designed to show that opposed sets of categories are not mutually exclusive, overwhelms the causal, frame story.[14]

For present purposes, I am less interested in reaching a definitive judgment about the precise nature of a text than in describing the different types of organization that underlie a reader's experience moment by moment. Accordingly, I will construe Altman's notions of "duality" and "focus" more narrowly and shift them to a new realm. I will also introduce new terms that divide up the field of study in a somewhat different way, allowing for finer distinctions.[15] As we shall see, the reason for such a shift in terminology is correlated with a change in the object of study: an attempt to specify the formal logic of narrative gives way to an examination of the interaction of narrative with a perceiver – a pragmatics of comprehension.

PRAGMATIC FORMS IN NARRATIVE

The notion of narrative as a sequence of logical "transformations" brings together two concerns: an awareness of pattern as well as purpose. These concerns may be seen in the double meaning of the English word "design," which may signify either a formal composition, an "arrangement" of elements (e.g., "The *design* utilized bright colors"), or an "intention" (e.g., "Her letter ended in mid-sentence by *design*," "He has *designs* on her property"). The importance of the transformations for Todorov would seem to be the suggestion that some (designing) forces have *intervened* in the five stages of narrative to shape the final pattern (design) which turns out to be a reshaping of the initial state. Thus something more than describing categories, and more even than labeling cause and effect, is needed to create a narrative; however attenuated, an element of choice, probability, or purpose must be seen by the reader to promise through its transformations an answer as to "why" or "when" something is or could be other, and "how" it returns to being the "same." One might say that the reader's discovery of this overall process at work in narrative is a mode of causal reasoning about human affairs which is distinct from merely labeling a cause, or assessing the probabilities of a local action. In this way, one may think of narrative as a mechanism that systematically *tests* certain combinations and transformations of a set of basic elements and propositions about events ("A" and "B" in my examples). The aim is not simply to enumerate causes, but to discover the causal efficacy of an element – its possibility for being, and for being other, as the reader may desire.

Many writers have argued that the logic underlying narrative is more complex than Todorov's pattern (A, B, −A, −B, A). A central concept like "transformation" may be understood in different ways, or new concepts may be developed in an attempt to interrelate narrative pattern and purpose.[16] Claude Lévi-Strauss, Claude Bremond, and A.J. Greimas claim to be extending and refining the insights of Vladimir Propp, who defined the logic of the Russian wondertale in terms of seven basic "spheres of action" (character roles), thirty-one "functions" (types of action), certain "moves" (fixed strings of functions), and "auxiliaries" (transitions).[17] Lévi-Strauss defines pairs of opposed "mythemes" while Greimas tightens narrative logic even further by defining its elements in terms of the "square of opposition" used in traditional logic to classify categorical propositions. For Greimas, narrative becomes a special working through of contraries, subcontraries, converses, and contradictories.[18] Like Todorov's five-part scheme, the goal of these methods is to describe the large-scale symmetries that draw together and unify the parts of narrative.

All of these approaches have been influential and have produced important results with certain texts. Nevertheless, the linguistic theories from which they have drawn many concepts have in the intervening years been modified or superseded. Also, formal logic has been shown to have limitations as a descriptive model for human thought. More recent models of human language emphasize the dynamics of a perceiver's interaction with a text – i.e., pragmatic situations – by studying a perceiver's use of "fuzzy" concepts, metaphorical reasoning, and "frame-arrays" of knowledge. Correspondingly, there has been a general tendency to move away from the linguistics of Ferdinand de Saussure as well as away from an exclusive reliance upon formal and logical schemes, such as Noam Chomsky's deductive rules which in many cases do not seem flexible enough to capture the wide-ranging, often speculative aspect of interpretation.[19] The stakes remain high, however, as Wallace Martin reminds us: "Identification of universal narrative patterns would seem to tell us not just about literature but about the nature of the mind and/or universal features of culture."[20] The goal of a pragmatics of narrative is to achieve a psychological description that can explain how a perceiver is able to interpret a text as a narrative moment by moment.[21]

One might begin to relax a strictly logical definition of narrative so as to include pragmatic aspects by pursuing the definition offered by Stephen Heath in his analysis of Orson Welles's film, *Touch of Evil* (1958):

> A narrative action is a series of elements held in a relation of transformation such that their consecution determines a state S' different to an intitial state S; thus: S–x–x–x–x–x–x–x–x–x–S'. . . . A beginning, therefore, is always a *violence*, the violation or interruption of the homogeneity of S. . . . The narrative transformation is the resolution of the violence, its containment – its *replacing* – in a new homogeneity. "Replacement" there has a double edge: on the one hand, the narrative produces something new, replaces S with S'; on the other, this production is the return of the same, S' re-places S, is the reinvestment of its elements. Hence the constraint of the need for exhaustion: every element must be used up in the resolution; the dispersion the violence provoked must be turned into a re-convergence – which is the action of the transformation, its activity. Ideally, a narrative is the perfect symmetry of this movement.[22]

In *Touch of Evil* the initial violence is literal as a car explodes in flames interrupting a kiss between lovers. Heath notes that when those lovers kiss at the end of the film, it is "the same kiss, but delayed, *narrativised*."[23] For Heath, narrative is a precise series of displacements, often driven by the logic of the disclosure of an enigma that acts to replace an initial situation by returning to it. For Raymond Bellour the search for such a "perfect symmetry" in the form of repetitions and near repetitions ("rhymes") in the text becomes almost obsessive, extending from global patterns (where one is reminded of Todorov's precise transformations) down to the smallest micro-sequence of action.[24]

But symmetries are not Heath's primary concern in defining narrative. He is anxious to show how some elements inevitably *escape* the tight narrative structure and become a residuum, an "excess," revealing hidden psychic and ideological processes at work in the text. Narrative exists because of these hidden processes and is an explicit attempt to master them. For Heath, the causality of narrative events in a plot is merely a pretext for larger transformations which point to our *everyday beliefs* about ourselves and our world, and the ways in which we formulate (or repress) those beliefs. Heath is less interested in discovering a stable logical structure than in uncovering symptoms of belief, modes of persuasion, and values which are not at all logical in the way conceived by Todorov and Greimas. Narrative thus acquires the form of an *argument*, leading to such definitions of it as the following:

a connected sequence of . . . *statements*, where "statement" is quite independent of the particular expressive medium.[25]

(Seymour Chatman)

A closed *discourse* [i.e., a sequence of predicative statements] that proceeds by *un*realizing a temporal sequence of events.[26]

(Christian Metz)

a . . . recounting [of] a chrono-logical sequence, where sequence is taken to be a group of non-simultaneous topic-comment structures the last one of which constitutes a modification of the first.[27]

(Gerald Prince)

Still more generally, Sergei Eisenstein envisioned an "intellectual cinema" in which filmic "reasoning" would enrich narrative and produce a synthesis of art and science.[28]

Prince's notion above of "modification" is quite broad and seems to include spatial, temporal, causal, and "zero" modifications as well as operations of inversion, negation, repetition, manner, and/or modality. The notion of narrative as a series of argumentative "statements" (i.e., propositions analyzable as a comment on a topic) that are suitably modified and independent of their manifestation in words, pictures, gestures, or other materials does capture something important about the phenomenon. Still, the notion of a narrative "statement" may have relinquished important detail for a generality bordering on vagueness. What, for example, are the limits of a "modification" to a "proposition"?

A similar problem of vagueness attends the almost obligatory discussion of the so-called "minimal narrative" which takes as its starting point E.M. Forster's distinction between chronology and causality. The following sentences illustrate the grounds of the debate, though theorists give different reasons for their conclusions:[29]

These do not qualify as narratives:
    (1a)   The king died and then the queen died [chronology].
    (2a)   Mary ate an apple.
These are narratives:
    (1b)   The king died, and then the queen died of grief [causality].
    (2b)   Shirley was good then she drifted into a life of crime.

11

In this debate there is an implicit belief that narrative is built up from a small set of basic units, or particles (e.g., topics, comments, and modifications), by addition and subtraction. The approach is reminiscent of the attempt by "analytic structuralism" in the field of psychology to account for human perception by positing certain basic "sensations" together with simple laws of combination.[30] The idea of narrative has become so impoverished by the search for minimal, logical conditions in a single sentence that it is unclear what qualities might attach to the more typical narratives which are exchanged and used in social arenas. Some writers, perhaps impressed by the pervasiveness of narrative thinking in everyday life and despairing of the attempt to find a bright line between narrative and nonnarrative, conclude that virtually everything is narrative. For instance, the following is deemed by one writer to be a narrative:

(3)   Once upon a time there was a person. The End.[31]

Another writer concludes that "even mathematical proofs, with one step following another toward an inevitable conclusion, exhibit something of the dynamics of plot and closure."[32]

I believe that what is needed is a description of narrative which avoids a strictly "logical" definition of minimal conditions even if supplemented by more expansive mechanisms like Todorov's transformations. Such a new description must also be more precise than discovering a set of "statements" which reveal pragmatic beliefs, or make arguments. One way to accomplish this goal is to concentrate on the cognitive processes active in a perceiver during his or her comprehension of narrative in an actual situation. The issue then focuses on how an overall narrative pattern may be discovered, or imposed, in the very act of perceiving. How do we manage to learn from narratives, moment by moment, and how do we learn to make our own narratives?

For Dan Lloyd the study of narrative comprehension is the study of a primary mode of thought quite distinct from other modes, such as "rational logic." He argues that the use of a "narrative logic" in solving problems explains why persons routinely fail certain tests of deductive and inductive reasoning. Thinking narratively has important advantages in the world and Lloyd calls for a new science – "psycho-narratology" – to examine the psychological foundations of narrative reasoning. The new science would be built upon concepts derived from the general study of narrative – "narratology" – and would include the work of such writers as Todorov, Bremond, Greimas, and Prince.[33]

COGNITIVE SCHEMAS AND OTHER WAYS OF ASSOCIATING DATA

In order to focus on mental processes working in real time, one must begin with the fact that there are rather severe capacity limitations both on an individual's transient memory, which registers sensory information, and on his or her short-term memory, which is able to sort and classify only recent information. Short-term memory can manipulate only about five to nine "chunks" of data. (The word "red" will count as one chunk of data whereas the letters "rde" will count as three.) Thus it is primarily intermediate-term memory (sometimes called "working" memory) and long-term memory that must be carefully studied, for these are the sites of special mental operations that play decisive roles in redescribing data and recognizing global relationships, whether narrative or otherwise. Moreover, these special operations of working and long-term memory are not directly experienced by a perceiver, since "consciousness" has many of the limitations of short-term memory.

The use of working and long-term memory by a perceiver are notable examples of the fact that sensory perception (transient memory) cannot be considered apart from other types of mental processing. Experiments have demonstrated that what perceivers remember from a narrative, as well as what they forget, is not random but dictated by the specific method used in searching for global properties. This method of search guides the acts of encoding, comprehending, storing, retrieving, and "remembering" the features of narrative. These experiments support a basic premise of cognitive psychology, namely, that the classifications which a person imposes on material at the time of its processing will limit the ways in which the material can be subsequently accessed and used in problem-solving.[34] (Much of a person's childhood experience is lost because it is classified in ways that are incompatible with the classifications used by an adult to sort and retrieve experience.) I will refer to the specific method which searches for a narrative pattern as a narrative *schema*.

The notion of a schema is basic to much of cognitive psychology. A schema is an arrangement of knowledge *already possessed* by a perceiver that is used to predict and classify new sensory data. The assumption underlying this concept is simply that people's knowledge is organized. The fact that one often knows immediately what one *does not know* testifies to the structured nature of our knowledge. As Jean Mandler states, "when we know something about a given domain our knowledge does not consist of a list of unconnected facts, but coheres in specifiable ways."[35] A schema assigns probabilities to events and to parts of events. It may be thought of as a graded set of expectations about experience in a given domain. What we implicitly know about a

13

"room," for example, is much more than either the "connotations" of that word or the properties of an actual room that we may remember. We know still more about a "living room." The vague sort of mental pictures that we may summon of a "room" or a "living room" are not unlike the operation of a schema in representing an ordered set of associations and expectations that are used to judge certain experiences. A schema, of course, is more complex than a given word because it interacts with the environment. A schema tests and refines sensory data at the same time that the data is testing the adequacy of the (implicit) criteria embodied in the schema. The interaction of schema and data creates a perceiver's recognition of global patterns characteristic of that data. "Meaning" is said to exist when pattern is achieved.

A schema does not determine its object through necessary and sufficient conditions. It is a hierarchical arrangement which ranges from tentative and contingent conclusions about data (including "default" specifications) at one extreme to increasingly general and invariant specifications governing a class of data at the other extreme. Thus when "meaning" has been attributed to something through the use of a schema, the meaning has a probabilistic quality which incorporates assumptions and expectations rather than an absolute quality defined by necessary and sufficient conditions.

A schema is only one type of mental structure and a narrative schema is only one of many types of schema used to solve a wide range of everyday problems. Nonnarrative types of schema (some of which will be discussed shortly) may be applied to a narrative text; conversely, a narrative schema may be applied quite generally to process data and (as we shall see) may even be used to generate sense from "nonsense" data.

What sort of schema is responsible for the recognition of narrative patterns?[36] Nearly all researchers agree that a narrative schema has the following format:

1 introduction of setting and characters;
2 explanation of a state of affairs;
3 initiating event;
4 emotional response or statement of a goal by the protagonist;
5 complicating actions;
6 outcome;
7 reactions to the outcome.[37]

Such a schema helps to explain some remarkable facts about narrative comprehension.

One of the most important yet least appreciated facts about narrative is that perceivers tend to *remember* a story in terms of *categories of information stated as propositions, interpretations, and summaries* rather than

14

remembering the way the story is actually presented or its surface features. It requires great effort to recall the exact words used in a novel or the exact sequence of shots, angles, lighting, etc. used in a film. The reason is that features of the "surface structure" of texts are typically stored only by recency in so-called "push-down" stacks where new elements are continually being added at the boundary, pushing the older elements farther away.[38] When we say we remember a film, we do not normally mean that we remember the angle from which it was viewed in the movie theater, or the exact angles assumed by the camera in a scene. Rather, when we speak of comprehending something, we mean that our knowledge of it may be stated in several equivalent ways; that is, our knowledge has achieved a certain independence from initial stimuli. In comprehending a visual object in film, for example, our knowledge of the object is such that we might imagine moving about within the space and assuming various angles of view, without thereby altering the object known. We know the object when we know how it may be seen regardless of the position from which it was actually seen. The object thus acquires an "ideal" or "abstract" quality. It should be mentioned that knowing how the object may be seen is very nearly imagining an object that is not in view at all.[39] This suggests that a theory of narrative comprehension will be incomplete without parallel theories of metaphor (because something new may be standing in for an original experience), and of fiction (because what is new may refer initially to the nonexistent).[40]

There are many other remarkable facts about narrative comprehension. Information from a text is sorted and measured by a schema against other kinds of knowledge base. The result is that certain information in a narrative is elaborately processed and assigned to a hierarchy in working memory according to relative importance while much else is discarded. The "value" of information increases according to its *im*probability so that typical and probable elements – so-called "unmarked" elements of a paradigm – carry the least amount of information. The more typical the information is for a perceiver, the less well it is recalled for it is already implicit in a guiding schema. Events in a text are therefore marked as salient and acquire special significance because of expectations defined by the internal order of a schema.

Furthermore, complex propositions tend to be formed in memory (and reading time slows) when "boundaries" in the text are perceived to correspond to the segmentation provided by a schema. The reason is that story comprehension involves the continuous generation of better-specified and more complicated expectations about what might be coming next and its place in a pattern. Thus a perceiver will strive to create "logical" connections among data in order to match the general categories of the schema. This will involve a mental rearrangement of temporal sequences in a text. These new macro-propositions concerning global relationships among data are stored in memory and represent the "gist" of the narrative. In this manner a perceiver uses a schema to automatically fill in any data that is deemed to be "missing" in the text.[41]

There are many ways that a text may disrupt a perceiver's expectations. Unclear character "goals" and "inverted" order in a text require increased processing time because of a necessity to experiment with various classifications of the data within a schematic framework. Also, unexpected information can cause a reorientation of the schema in order to reclaim the important from the superficial. Comprehension slows when explicit propositions constructed earlier must be reactivated (cf. the notion of "retrospective" temporal order in chapter 2); or when previous inferences are indirectly disconfirmed (e.g., by a *pattern* of events rather than by explicit statement); or when a perceiver must make novel inferences. Finally, the limitations of working memory may be exploited in order to accentuate the so-called "fluctuating existence" of diegetic off-screen space in film.[42]

In short, it has been amply demonstrated through many psychological experiments that an individual's attention does not spread equally through a narrative text but works forward and backward in an uneven manner in constructing large-scale, hierarchical patterns which represent a particular story as an abstract grouping of knowledge based on an underlying schema. Furthermore, a narrative schema may be applied in many situations. It has been shown that

> even with meaningless nonsense figures moving in abstract paths, viewers were able to describe and remember a much longer series of events, by generating a simple story, and attributing anthropomorphic qualities to the figures and the motions they perform, than they could handle in purely physical terms.[43]

Especially important is the way a perceiver infers the purposes, intentions, and goals of the constructed anthropomorphic entities. Thus it would seem that a narrative schema is always an option in processing data even when there are no human characters or the events are essentially "nonsense" data.[44]

Although narrative is a powerful and general way of organizing information, it is essential to realize that the concept of a schema addresses only some of the issues concerning narrative.[45] A narrative schema does not directly address such problems as a perceiver's fascination, emotional reaction, or participation in a story; the effect on a perceiver of manipulations of point of view; nor the effect of actually experiencing a story in a community setting. Also, presumably, the nature of the medium and the "style" of the story will exert pressure

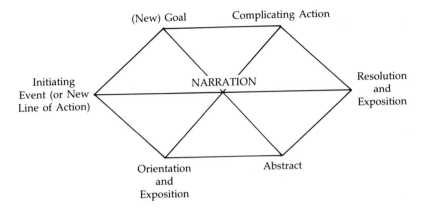

Figure 1 Narrative schema
Elements of a narrative schema displayed as a hexagon. A narrative is constructed by moving through the hexagon to create patterns at the levels of action, scene, episode, sequence, etc.

on comprehension. There is even a question about the nature of the "macro-propositions" generated through a schema: are they verbal, pictorial, or something else?[46] This range of issues is a reminder of the complexity of the narrative phenomenon. Still, it does not rule out addressing problems one at a time and then attempting to integrate various theories about human capability and performance.

I believe that by studying comprehension as a constructive activity (encompassing much more than the mere retrieval of images or words stored in the order received), one bypasses the now vexed film-theoretical question of whether film is like a "language."[47] Indeed, one almost bypasses the question of whether film is like a "communication." There is, in fact, good reason to believe that both film and natural language are special subsets of more general cognitive enterprises. One of these general enterprises is our ability to construct a narrative out of experience; that is to say, our ability to use a narrative schema to model a version of the world. In this view, both film narrative and written narrative express temporal relationships because both are mental constructions, not because film reduces to language.

A PROPOSAL FOR A NARRATIVE SCHEMA

It may be helpful to construct a narrative schema in somewhat more detail and to illustrate its application to a particular film. The elements of the schema I will present are derived primarily from Mary Louise Pratt's interpretation of the work of the sociolinguist, William Labov, who studied narrative patterns in the everyday conversation of inner city minority groups.[48] I will represent the relationships among the elements as a hexagon (see fig. 1) because, in general, simple hierarchical tree diagrams, and other standard patterns, are not powerful enough to capture the complex semantic relationships generated by narrative.[49] Using a hexagon, then, is a way of leaving open the interrelationships among the elements of a narrative. It is important to note that one can apply the schema at many different levels – to a camera movement, composition, shot, sequence of shots, scene, sequence of scenes, etc. – depending on the size of the units that have been chosen for analysis. Narrative is a recursive organization of data; that is, its components may be embedded successively at various micro- and macro-levels of action.

The schema contains the following eight components, or functions, which may be repeated in various patterns to model our understanding of a given story; that is, one can move through the hexagon in a myriad of ways and any number of times.

1 An *abstract* is a title or compact summary of the situation which is to follow.[50] If an abstract is expanded, it becomes a *prologue*.
2 An *orientation* is a description of the present state of affairs (place, time, character) while an *exposition* gives information about past events which bear on the present.
3 An *initiating event* alters the present state of affairs. A narrative which delays orientation and exposition and begins with an initiating event, or a complicating action (see below), is said to begin *in medias res*.
4 A *goal* is a statement of intention or an emotional response to an initiating event by a protagonist.
5 A *complicating action* (linked to an antagonist) arises as a consequence of the initiating event and presents an obstacle to the attainment of the goal.
6 The climax and *resolution* end the conflict between goals and obstacles and establish a new equilibrium or state of affairs.
7 The *epilogue* is the moral lesson implicit in the history of these events and may include explicit character reactions to the resolution.
8 The *narration* is constantly at work seeking to justify implicitly or explicitly (1) why the narrator is competent and credible in arranging and reporting these events and (2) why the events are unusual, strange, or worthy of attention. In other words, how is it possible to possess the knowledge and why should it be possessed?

The study of how children acquire a narrative schema has been a fertile area of investigation and has greatly contributed to an understanding of mental schemas in general.[51] The basic comprehension represented by a narrative schema is apparently not operative in most children until about the age of seven. Complex forms of narrative utilizing psychological causation, point of view, multiple plots, and temporal complexity are not acquired until much later. Prior to the age of 7, there are partial realizations of the schema along with certain nonnarrative organizations of experience. In order to put the schema into context, I will briefly describe one researcher's attempt to sketch the stages of cognitive development leading up to the acquisition of narrative skills. The following stages of development may also be thought of as strategies by which to collect and associate data generally, ranging from creating a virtually random list through a chronology and finally to the causality and closure of a basic narrative. Although the essence of narrative is a presentation of systematic change through a cause and effect teleology, there is no reason that an actual narrative may not also contain some of these other ways of organizing data.[52]

1 A *heap* is a virtually random collection of data or objects assembled largely by chance. Objects are linked to one another only through an immediacy of perception, a free-association of the moment.[53]

2 A *catalogue* is created by collecting objects each of which is similarly related to a "center" or core. For example, a list of objects that belong in a particular room; or are used by a particular person; or are recorded in a particular time span (which yields a *chronology*). A list of personality traits in a novel helps define a "character." And, as shown in an earlier example, roses and violets may be collected together as flowers as well as placed in the category of what is only natural like sugar, sweetness, and "you."

One could perhaps think of the 180 degree rule in film as a catalogue of three-dimensional spatial fragments with a fixed relationship to a given hypothetical plane such that left–right orientation is preserved in all of the spatial fragments. The center also may be phonic,[54] or may be a particular action, such as, A does X to N; B does X to O; C does X to P (which yields the catalogue: A, B, C, N, O, P, with X as the "center" which justifies the list).[55]

3 An *episode* is created by collecting together the *consequences* of a central situation: for example, collecting everything that happens to a particular character in a particular setting as well as everything that the character does in that setting. Unlike a heap or a catalogue, an episode does not simply grow longer, it shows change; it develops and progresses. Because the parts of an episode are defined through cause and effect, it is easier to *remember* an episode than to remember the miscellaneous parts of a heap or a catalogue.[56]

4 An *unfocused chain* is a series of cause and effects but with no continuing center. For example, character A is followed for a time, then character B, then character C. (Consider, for example, Max Ophuls's *La Ronde*, 1950; Luis Buñuel's *The Phantom of Liberty*, 1974; and Jim

Jarmusch's *Mystery Train*, 1989. On a smaller scale, consider certain elaborate camera movements by, for example, Ophuls, Renoir, Welles, Mizoguchi, Godard, and Jancsó.

5 A *focused chain* is a series of cause and effects with a continuing center. For example, the continuing adventures of a character, the events surrounding an object or place, or the elaboration of a theme.

6 A *simple narrative* is a series of episodes collected as a focused chain. Not only are the parts themselves in each episode linked by cause and effect, but the continuing center is allowed to develop, progress and interact from episode to episode. A narrative ends when its cause and effect chains are judged to be totally delineated. There is a reversibility in that the ending situation can be traced back to the beginning; or, to state it another way, the ending is seemingly entailed by the beginning. This is the feature of narrative often referred to as *closure*.[57]

Without attempting to overly simplify these six ways of associating data, one can discern at least four different notions of time at work. The "heap" and "catalogue" primarily exploit two types of time: an atemporal, descriptive time[58] where elements are deemed to be simultaneous, and/or a chronological time of duration where elements are deemed to be merely consecutive. From "episode" to "simple narrative," however, time becomes increasingly consequential (implications, probabilities) and thus directional ("effects" never precede "causes").[59] And finally, time comes to exhibit a large-scale configuration (symmetry, reversal, parallelism, cycle, closure, unity) comparable, say, to the action of Todorov's transformations in creating principles of order out of local causation. The spectator's experience of duration and causality is forward in time while the spectator's experience of order may reverse the arrow of time, seemingly operating on the present from a point in the future; that is, earlier parts of a pattern have been arranged to fit with later parts.[60]

I believe that simultaneity, duration, causality, and order are not simply four items in a taxonomy of time, but are the results of four specific ways of *processing* data. Since the actual processing of data is not available to awareness, our experience of these aspects of time is better described as a diffuse *affect* responsive to the complexity of juxtaposition allowable under a particular method of associating data.[61]

THE GIRL AND HER TRUST

As an extended illustration of some of the above ideas concerning a narrative schema and its creation of different types of temporal experience through different ways of associating data, I wish to consider a

15-minute film that spectators easily recognize as a narrative – D.W. Griffith's *The Girl and Her Trust* (1912). I will concentrate on how a narrative schema works with local data on the screen to produce coherence on a large-scale.

The title of Griffith's film – functioning as an "abstract" – alludes to the fact that the film will actually be *two*, intertwined focused chains, or "stories": a romance involving an unmarried girl coupled with an adventure which tests her trustworthiness. The first shot of the film is an intertitle which begins the process of orientation: "Grace, the telegraph operator, is admired by all." The next shot shows a young woman – whom we now assume is Grace – busily reading near her telegraph key. Not only do we see that she is charming and graceful but we have been told that she has an inner beauty: an integrity worthy of complete trust. A would-be admirer enters the room but his clumsiness soon prompts Grace to send him scurrying. Next, the handsome station manager enters, but his aggressiveness in stealing a kiss causes Grace to order him to leave the room. After he has left, however, we see Grace's reaction change from being deeply offended to being secretly thrilled. She smiles and presses two fingers to her lips as if to reexperience that sudden kiss. Within the romance story, there has clearly been an initiating event which has aroused the heroine to form a goal which may become a match for the explicit goal of the handsome protagonist.

Grace's reverie is interrupted by a telegraph message. It reads, "National Bank sending $2000 on No. 7 for Simpson Construction Co." This is the initiating event for a new line of action – a crime story. Grace will be entrusted with money arriving on the next train. The telegraph message, however, *causes* the romance story to take a new turn. Grace allows the hero to return to her office to help plan for the arrival of the money. The advent of the crime story has allowed him to again approach within range of stealing a kiss. He takes out a revolver and bullets. Grace is nervous and afraid of the gun and shrinks back as he enthusiastically loads the gun very near her body (see fig. 2). With this gesture he has *regained* the authority and initiative he lost when Grace first banished him from the room. Correspondingly, she has now lost some of her brashness and control over the situation. They are coming closer to being a match for each other; that is, to have matching goals.

When the train arrives, we see something that no one else sees. Two tramps sneak off the train and hide. They plan to steal the money. This complicating action represents a goal hostile to Grace's obligation to protect the money. Grace, however, is unaware of the complicating action. The hero offers the revolver to her but she declines, "Danger? Nothing ever happens here." These words illustrate the ever-present activity of narration for the words are placed in a context which allows the spectator to appreciate the heroine's mistake. We immediately

21

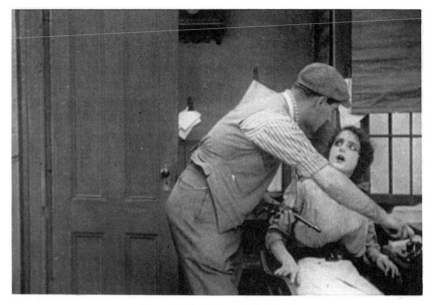

Figure 2 The Girl and Her Trust

reinterpret the words as saying to us, "Something dangerous (and interesting) will happen here!" The narration has demonstrated a power to know events by creating suspense (when will Grace realize the danger?), and has promised to repay our attention by exciting action. By operating from outside the diegetic world, the narration regulates our access to that world and thus produces effects based on knowledge not available to the characters.

The hero leaves the station on an errand and the train also leaves. Grace is alone. We have already seen the tramps watching the money and spying through a window at the hero. An intertitle announces "The tramps' opportunity." Why should the intertitle tell us something that is already obvious? The intertitle functions as an abstract for a new phase of the action and serves to explicitly mark the boundary between episodes. It aids the spectator in segmenting each of the two stories into abstract, orientation, initiating event, etc. The romance story is giving way again to the crime story and the spectator is being provided ample time to redirect his or her expectations. The overall narrative is being broken into component parts for the spectator and arranged into a hierarchy where general propositions about the events can be progressively modified and filled in by details. The crime story can now be elaborated.

We see the tramps spy on Grace through a window. The composition of this shot has been carefully contrived by the narration to show the tramps in the background peering through the window while Grace is in the foreground where her reactions are clearly visible and reveal that she has not yet seen the tramps. Since the spectator already knows about the presence of the tramps, new and valuable information in the scene will come only when Grace discovers them, and the spectator is perfectly placed to witness *that* event of recognition. Like the intertitle ("The tramps' opportunity"), this shot functions as an abstract since it reveals in a concise manner the elements and relations that will generate the succeeding action: a drama of seeing and being seen followed by a drama of breaking down (various) barriers separating the tramps from Grace. This shows that a narrative schema may be applied to actions on a small-scale: an action is named (e.g., "robbery"), put into context, initiated, responded to, opposed by a new action, and so forth, until the ebb and flow of action, goal, and reaction results in a temporary equilibrium allowing the next phase of the action to commence (with a new abstract, orientation, initiating event, and so forth).

The narration is planning a surprise. We expect the tramps to threaten Grace, but if our predictions always turned out to be correct, we would lose interest in the story – its focused chains would become too obvious and trivial. The tramps will indeed attempt to reach Grace and the money; but later the unexpected will occur when it will be she who breaks down barriers to reach them. But first, a drama of vision unfolds. Grace senses something behind her. She spins around, but the tramps have ducked down. She turns back, relieved. The tramps look again. She spins around again. They have ducked down. But they pop up again unexpectedly while Grace is still watching and are finally seen. Notice that this is not a plausible account of a robbery since there is no reason that the tramps shouldn't quickly sneak into the station or that they should risk looking through the window more than once. Instead of plausibility the narration has lingered on the "goal" stage of a narrative schema, creating a subjective reality by drawing out both the emotional impact on the heroine and the suspense felt by the spectator. Here Griffith's film goes beyond a simple narrative by dramatizing the heroine's interior reality. Griffith treats psychology itself as an embedded form of story and, moreover, a form of story that seems to dictate what is plausible.

A series of complicating actions occurs. The tramps rush to get into the station but Grace runs from her office to barricade the door. They break down the door but Grace runs back into her office and barricades that door. She sends a telegraph message for help. The tramps react by cutting the telegraph lines and return to batter her door. She repulses them with a bullet placed in the keyhole and detonated with the point of a pair of scissors. We are surprised by Grace's unusual solution to her problem which creates an effect on us something like the opposite of suspense; a character has been shown to have knowledge superior to the spectator. (Consider the change in effect if the narration had earlier presented the hero explaining to Grace that in an emergency she could use the keyhole as a gun barrel. These effects of narration will be considered in more detail in chapter 3.) Grace's ingenuity partially makes up for her failure to keep the revolver when it was offered to her by the hero. She is therefore not humiliated and will remain a match for the hero when that phase of the story resumes.

The tramps fail to capture Grace, and decide simply to take the locked strongbox and open it elsewhere without the key she possesses. This does not end Grace's ordeal, however, for it causes her to be tormented by a sense of duty. She decides that she must stop them. However, there is an obstacle: she discovers that she is now imprisoned in the office and so must break *out* to pursue the tramps. This effectively reverses the initial situation with the tramps breaking *in*. If the story were to end here, it would be construed as one about Grace's failure to respond (paralyzed and trapped in her office) or the failure to achieve a goal (she runs after the tramps but fails to catch them). She would still be a heroine for her valiant struggle and still be admired by all (and perhaps one person in particular). The difficulty would be that the chain of events of the crime story, focused through her psychological drama, would be incomplete with respect to expectations raised in the spectator that Grace's self-imposed devotion must be tested and renewed by events (does she actually deserve the admiration she receives?). Accordingly, the story does not end but begins a new phase as the narration searches for a resolution to close off all major questions and possible lines of action.

Grace rushes after the tramps who are attempting to escape on a railroad handcar. They beat her senseless but she clings to the handcar as it speeds down the tracks. An intertitle has already evaluated her conduct: "She risks her life for her trust." Meanwhile her telegraph message has resulted in a train being sent to provide aid, and the hero returns to the station just in time to leap aboard the train and direct it in pursuit of Grace and the tramps. The train eventually catches the handcar. Grace embraces the hero while the train engineer beats one of the tramps senseless. This task falls to the engineer because the hero belongs to the romance story and his aggressiveness (e.g., in stealing kisses) must now be moderated; a minor character can dispense the prosaic details of justice. The film ends as the engineer returns to the train while Grace and the hero jump onto the front of the locomotive above the cowcatcher (where their emotional reactions can be clearly seen by the spectator). There is no indication what has happened to the tramps; or rather, enough has happened to them to resolve the crime story and now the romance must be resolved.

The final shot of the film begins as a medium two-shot of Grace and the hero in earnest and happy conversation. He pulls a sandwich from his pocket and offers it to her. She happily takes a bite as the train is backing away from the camera into an extreme long shot. In the opening scene of the film, Grace had offered the hero a drink of soda pop which he had pretended to accept in order to bend near her and steal a kiss. Now, over the sandwich, *she* steals a kiss from *him*. A symmetry is completed in which the ending situation balances the opening.[62] They can dine together and indulge their appetites for he has proven his intentions were good and she has proven her worthiness as a recipient of those intentions. The locomotive suddenly sends out jets of white steam that swirl in front of the couple as the image fades to black. The archetypal extreme long shot which closes most classical films announces that we cannot see more details because the causal chain has played itself out.

In one sense the above action of the final two shots of the film, following the rescue and the beating of the tramps, seems trivial and redundant. In a deeper sense it allows the spectator time to formulate a response to the entire sequence of events and to appreciate that the sequence is in fact a powerfully focused chain of episodes which, like every narrative, reenacts "cultural beliefs about success."[63] The crime and romance stories have been *merged* in the epilogue in such a way that the heroine's place in an economic order (as trustee of capital) converges on her place in a social order (as an unmarried woman who must learn to trust in a man). The tramps exist as a catalyst to bring the man and woman together, to transform the woman as guardian of capital into property to be guarded. Grace herself has actually done nothing to delay the tramps in their flight or aid in their capture on the handcar. Her gesture has been one of pure devotion and sacrifice. Like many other Griffith heroines, she earns a man through noble self-sacrifice, strength of will, and patience, not through challenging the preconceptions of her society. As for the tramps, they are condemned for threatening the values and property of the middle and upper classes. To survive they will need property and wives. As Sergei Eisenstein recognized, Griffith perceived society *"only as a contrast between the haves and the have-nots"* and this contrast went *"no deeper than the image of an intricate race between two parallel lines"* of rich and poor.[64] Griffith's message and the schematic form of his narrative are essentially conservative and familiar even if some of his methods were innovative.

25

CAUSALITY AND SCHEMA

I would like to examine the notion of narrative causality in somewhat more detail and link it to the notion of a mental schema. Although *The Girl and Her Trust* presents events in chronological order and inventories certain actions (e.g., eating, spying, trusting, beating, and kissing), we do not perceive the film as a catalogue. The reason, of course, is that the film's events are principally defined through cause and effect (event B *because of* event A; scene Y *because of* scene X). The film's events are linked together by probability whereas elements of a heap or a catalogue are all equally likely with no single element necessary. Since episodes and narratives require a perceiver continually to assess and evaluate *probabilities* moment by moment, one might define narrative broadly as "an accepted technique for discussing the chances of life."[65]

Probability, however, comes in many degrees and types, and hence many sorts of causality may be appropriate in comprehending a narrative. Noël Carroll observes:

> Since most film narratives involve a series of actions, it may seem natural to think that causation is the major connective between scenes in movies. However, it is implausible to suggest that scenes follow each other in most film narratives via a chain of causal *entailments*. I would guess that most succeeding narrative scenes are causally underdetermined by what precedes them. Rather the connection is weaker than a causal one.[66]

Several questions arise: can events or scenes, which are themselves only moderately likely, be strung together to create another event or scene – say, a climax and resolution – which is obligatory? What kinds of judgments can be made about the *relative likelihood* of particular events appearing together?

Informally, one can imagine a spectator's causal evaluations as falling along a spectrum:[67]

1 Elements are merely consecutive ("and"); their order is arbitrary or optional.
2 Elements are chronological ("then"); order is governed only by duration.
3 Elements appear together conventionally; order is set by familiar social or generic practices.
4 An element (the "remote" cause) appears together with another element but only through the mediation of many other elements ("intervening" causes), the last of which is the immediate or "proximate" cause.
5 An element is necessary for the appearance of another (an "enabling" cause).

6 An element is sufficient for the appearance of another (a "direct" cause). If two or more elements are present, each of which is sufficient to cause a particular outcome, the effect is "overdetermined."

7 An element is both necessary and sufficient for the appearance of another (a "unique" cause).

L.B. Cebik imagines a complex but not atypical example of causality in narrative:

> If we let capital letters stand for events, objects, actions, and conditions, as appropriate, we might string together a perfectly understandable narrative in which A may cause B, B anticipate C, C accompany D, which may give E reason to go through F, G, and H as steps toward the achievement of I, where I forms the motive for J to do K, with the unintended consequence L, which marks the beginning of an M, an M that ends when N marks the shift to O, which along with P and Q comprises evidence for the occurrence of R, which causes S . . .[68]

Our experience of causality, then, depends upon our assessment of various probabilities. On a small scale, the connections among events may be quite weak and indirect even though on a large scale, an overall pattern may be evident. Recall that for Todorov "causality," or the logic of mere succession, was not enough to define a narrative: change must also emerge on a large scale in the form of a "transformation" among events. This global aspect of change in narrative is obscured when we describe causality as a *chain* of causes and effects. Although convenient, the chain metaphor focuses too much attention on local determinants, tends to make connections too strong, and remains uncomfortably close to the methodology of Behaviorism which posits a simple linear sequence of stimuli and responses. More promising, I believe, would be a psychological approach to narrative that would give equal weight to "top-down" frames of reference for grouping elements, that is, to principles and criteria that are not determined solely by local conditions but instead are responsive to larger contexts.

It is evident that in many cases our assessment of the "probabilities" draws upon broad *cultural* knowledge in judging which actions and transactions are *acceptable* as belonging together (and hence likely to occur together). Thus our comprehension of narrative causality – of what may follow what – may depend upon our general knowledge of social interactions; that is, the connections we are predisposed to call "causal." Roland Barthes argues that

> the logic to which the narrative refers is nothing other than a logic of the *already-read*: the stereotype (proceeding from a culture many centuries old) is the veritable ground of the narrative world, built

altogether on the traces which experience (much more bookish than practical) has left in the reader's memory and which constitutes it. Hence we can say that the perfect sequence [of actions], the one which affords the reader the strongest logical certainty, is the most "cultural" sequence, in which are immediately recognized a whole *summa* of readings and conversations. . . . Narrative logic, it must be admitted, is nothing other than the development of the Aristotelian *probable* (common opinion and not scientific truth); hence it is normal that, when an attempt is made to legalize this logic (in the form of esthetic constraints and values), it should still be an Aristotelian notion which the first classical theoreticians of narrative have advanced: that of *verisimilitude*.[69]

I wish to indicate briefly the great complexity of the "causes" at work even in a narrative as simple as *The Girl and Her Trust* and to illustrate that the "logic" involved is often based on what seems familiar and natural within a culture, within a way of life. Consider the variety of connections that we must imagine in justifying each of the following pairs of actions: the hero returns to the station from his errand *just as* an unscheduled train arrives; Grace is reading a book, *then* a suitor walks into the room; the suitor *offers* Grace a bottle of soda pop (intending to initiate a socially defined courtship ritual), *and then* offers a straw (a second act to solicit a response); stealing a kiss *causes* a man to be ordered out of the room; continued spying in a window *causes* two tramps to be seen; Simpson Construction Company's need for $2000 *causes* Grace to be beaten senseless and to kiss a man; white steam rises around Grace *while* she rides on the front of a locomotive. How does a spectator establish the proper context within which to judge the relative pertinence of such pairs of actions occurring together? Steam necessarily rises because it is a hot gas (and perhaps also because of the exuberance of the train engineer) and yet there are still other, more important reasons why it curls around the triumphant, virtuous, and passionate couple as the image fades to black. Establishing relevant contexts within which to evaluate causation is partly a matter of *segmentation*: how is something to be divided into parts that can be seen to interact? To anticipate my answer, I will state that an individual segments an event according to an explicit, or implicit, theory (or theories) of experience. A theory in this sense need not be as rigorous as a physics or a philosophy; all that is required is that a "fact" be given under a description and that we know how to produce descriptions. One of the important ways we produce descriptions is by utilizing schematic forms of knowledge.

In making a judgment about what properly goes with what, and in what context something can be seen in terms of something else, a perceiver is also implicitly making a choice about how elements should be selected and how they should be grouped on levels from the smallest to the largest scale of action. In understanding the world of the story, a perceiver may link two elements together to make a pair even if the two elements do *not* appear together on the screen, or in the plot. (Similarly, elements appearing together on the screen may not belong together. Thus a device like editing has a psychological dimension and cannot be defined in strictly material or formal terms.) Here is where a narrative schema becomes important. It helps direct our search for pertinent causes by proposing a segmentation applicable on many scales of action and then by "filling in" any connectives that are missing from the surface structure.[70] We discover and justify connections among narrative elements with respect to such schematic functions as goal, reaction, resolution, epilogue, and narration. Of course, a narrative schema does not provide all the answers: one still needs to weigh the evidence from the text as well as be acquainted with nonnarrative schemas and specific cultural knowledge (e.g., the routines of court-ship, and texts about courtship like the limerick of a woman riding on a tiger or the poem, "Roses are red"). One cannot use a schema as a search procedure without searching for and through some domain of knowledge.

In thinking about the types of causation which make up a narrative, one is led toward a deeper interpretation of a narrative "schema." Just as it is people who refer, not sentences, so it is people who judge plausibility, realism, and causal connection. What is familiar and real to an individual depends upon the regularities in that individual's environment which are judged to be important. Causes and effects fit together when they are part of an individual's plans and goals. Actions that occur become trapped within a cultural lexicon of human thoughts and deeds: accident, opportunity, hindrance, aspiration, decision, attempt, defeat, success, and so forth. A narrative schema, together with a host of related schemas,[71] encapsulates the interest we take in the world as humans. These schemas are a way of working through cultural assumptions and values. Thus "causes and effects" emerge, as it were, after the fact as explanatory labels for a sequence of actions viewed under a particular schematic description. (To have fallen in love, it was sufficient to. . . . In order to protect one's trust, it was necessary to. . . .) Our concept of narrative causation must be powerful enough to include these social and ethical factors so that when a statue acciden-tally falls and kills a man, we can also see that in another sense it was not an "accident" at all when the statue is later revealed to be that of a woman who was murdered by the man.[72] In this sense the epilogue of a narrative merely makes explicit the social judgment already contained within the causal chain; or, perhaps it would be better to say, the spectator makes a judgment about probabilities based upon life as experienced through the probabilities of his or her society.[73]

In *The Girl and Her Trust* two major causal chains involving crime and romance have been tightly wound together. Such a double causal structure is typical of the classical narrative film.[74] What is the relationship between such a pair of causal structures? Why not create interest only through a single focused chain of episodes?

One advantage of a double causal structure is that a narrative schema may actually operate more efficiently with two causal chains. Intertwining two stories provides the spectator with more ways to imagine causal connections and more opportunities for the overall story to advance. To clarify this idea consider an analogy with a character who has two motives to do something. Raymond Durgnat has argued that certain genres use "double motivation" (and even greater multiples of motivation) to portray the relationship between character goals and events. Double motives *prevent* the spectator from making a precise psychological analysis because one motive may be operating without the other, or if both must operate, the spectator does not know their relative contributions. This allows one motive to appeal to individuals who wouldn't respond to the other.[75] Perhaps more importantly, whatever a spectator *first believes* may be enough to drive the story forward. Just as essential plot details are usually repeated several times to promote clarity,[76] so a variety of motivations circulating in the text may be useful options in filling out, and making definite, causal sequences. If the text can suggest enough "intervening" and "enabling" causes (see above), a narrative schema will tend to generate a resolution which can be imagined as the closure of a "unique" cause implicit in the opening of the story. This allows the story to be made "unique" in many different ways to many spectators![77]

Grace's reaction as the hero brings a gun near her illustrates double causation at work. The composition which shows her reaction is carefully arranged and held as a tableau in the film (see fig. 2). Because of the preceding events, it is not really possible to say in what proportion her fear is caused by the gun and/or by the man's approach near her. Earlier when he approached and abruptly kissed her, she reacted with great anger; after he had left, however, she expressed an emotion of secret thrill. This ambivalence leaks into the film on many levels, providing several pathways along which the narrative can be seen to reach a definite resolution and epilogue. More importantly, if the spectator applies this notion of psychological ambivalence to the double causal structure of the story itself, the resolution of the film can be seen as a subtle transformation of Grace's initial situation. A second advantage of a double causal structure, then, is that it facilitates a more complex ending and epilogue than, say, the mere defeat of a threat. In the context of crime and romance, Grace may be seen as defending herself from thieves who seek to steal from her both money (the tramps) and kisses (the hero). Since the tramps provide a condition for the success of the hero (who also triumphs over another suitor), they can be seen as being totally unsuitable suitors who represent the ultimate reversal and perversity of courtship. (The threat of rape, though never made explicit in the film, is ever-present.) Thus the two causal lines allow complex metaphorical comparisons to form between, say, the goals of protecting hard-earned property, earning a mate, and being/becoming protected. Thus Grace's ambivalence (expressed well in fig. 2) functions as a "psychological" cause which finally unifies interior and exterior realities as she overcomes her initial fear(s) through both decisive action and submission. She is doubly rewarded at the end for her travail by a happy excitement caused by a job well done and a man well earned.

In summary, the double causal structure has two functions. It is *efficient* in producing an effect on a large number of spectators because the vagueness of multiple motivations grants individual spectators a limited freedom in singling out the local causes that bind a beginning, middle, and end. It is also *efficacious* in producing a desired effect because the expansive metaphors that are encouraged are aimed at matching a spectator's own goals and desires in watching and comprehending.

It is not enough, however, merely to juxtapose two motives and two causal chains, and hope for the best. The narration of the story must also *block* other possible combinations among goals and actions. When the tramps besiege Grace in her inner office, an intertitle explains, "The tramps want the key to the express box." The narration here seeks to *limit* the scope of metaphors based on property: we are assured that the tramps do not want to rape the woman nor attack her because of her economic class. Nonetheless, there is a sense in which such expansive metaphors cannot be entirely contained; they remain as symptoms of the underlying fears raised by the events of the narrative even if denied by an intertitle. Thus it would be better to think of narration not as a single process, but as several processes moving on different levels, proposing and abolishing contradictions with varying degrees of explicitness and success. These contradictions, anxieties, and vague metaphors are often important clues to our comprehension of a narrative and to our complicity in it. As we shall see in the next chapter, narration is able to create complex, even apparently "impossible," causal schemes which nevertheless exemplify the mapping of a powerful will and desire onto a world of objects. Narration, therefore, is not really on a par with the other elements of a narrative schema, but rather stands in for the operation of a still deeper schema that drives the story. Although the deeper schema may speak about a character and his or her goals, it must always be speaking to and for the multiple desires and fears of an author who must tell and a spectator who already knows.

2

STORY WORLD AND SCREEN

A PRELIMINARY DELINEATION OF NARRATIVE IN FILM

Narrative in film rests on our ability to create a three-dimensional world out of a two-dimensional wash of light and dark. A bare facticity of graphics on the screen – size, color, angle, line, shape, etc. – must be transformed into an array of solid objects; and a texture of noise must be transformed into speech, music, and the sounds made by solid objects. Light and sound in narrative film are thus experienced in two ways: virtually unshaped *on* a screen as well as apparently *moving within*, reflecting and issuing from, a world which contains solid objects making sounds. Every basic spatial and temporal relationship, such as position and duration, thus has a double interpretation. A green circle might be seen to the *left* of a square in the same plane, or alternatively, it might be seen to lie *behind* the square along a diagonal line to the left. In the latter interpretation, the circle may become a "sphere," the square a "box," and "size" and "color" will be adjusted according to our judgments about how distance and light are being represented in a given perspective system. Similarly, the green circle may appear for ten seconds on the screen but represent many hours of world time for the green sphere, especially if there is no other "action" by which to gauge duration. Rudolf Arnheim asserts:

> It is one of the most important formal qualities of film that every object that is reproduced appears simultaneously in two entirely different frames of reference, namely the two-dimensional and the three-dimensional, and that as one identical object it fulfills two different functions in the two contexts.[1]

The spectator, therefore, encounters at least two major frames of reference in film: the space and time of a *screen* as well as (a sample of) the space and time of a *story world*.[2] More than space and time, however, is at stake. Causality also has a double interpretation. Changes in light and sound patterns will be perceived in at least two ways: as motion across a screen and as movement among objects in a story world. Causality on a screen will involve patterns of a purely visual, phenomenal logic where, for example, one blob smashes into another but the resulting transformations in motion and color may not be analogous to the interactions of three-dimensional objects like billiard balls; the blobs may even "pass through" each other on the screen. Bizarre pictorial compositions and animation are clear examples of on-screen causality. In short, light and sound create two fundamental systems of space, time, and causal interaction: on a screen and within a story world. One of the tasks of narrative is to reconcile these systems.

It seems likely, in fact, that more than two frames of reference are active in our comprehension of film. It has even been argued that there is a stage of visual processing located halfway between two and three dimensional perception which produces a 2½ dimensional representation of space.[3] Clearly, major changes occur during the conversion from phenomenal appearances on the screen to functions in a story world. One of the essential tasks of a narrative theory is to specify the various stages through which we represent and comprehend a film as a narrative. On-screen patterns of light, sound, and motion do not denote and hence cannot be true or false; they are fully present and neither narrative nor fictive. Moreover, the time in which these patterns are present on the screen is determined initially by the film projector. By contrast, a story builds complex spatial and temporal contexts, makes references to things which are not present (and may not exist), and allows broad conclusions to be drawn about sequences of actions. Moreover, time in the world of the story may be quite different than the time of the projection of the film. For example, in *Letter from an Unknown Woman* (Ophuls, 1948) screen time is ninety minutes while the story covers three hours of an early morning during which a letter is read, and the letter, in turn, dramatizes events spanning fifteen years at the turn of the century in the world of Vienna.

Many concepts have been proposed to help describe how on-screen data is transformed through various spatial, temporal, and causal schemes culminating in a perceived story world. The various stages have been described with concepts like script, set decoration, technology, technique, performance, material, shot, form, style, plot, diegesis, code, narration, and referent. Since nonnarrative ways of organizing data may coexist with narrative, one might also recognize a conflict among discursive schemes, an "excess" within the story.[4] The processing of film data has an important effect on how a spectator feels about the conceptual structures which are ultimately constructed. Some of the metaphors offered by film theorists suggest that our comprehension of film proceeds only forward, one step at a time, and depends simply on local and immediate juxtapositions, but other metaphors are less

34

restrictive. Rudolf Arnheim speaks of picture postcards in an album while Noël Burch speaks of picture postcards suspended in a void, "radically autonomous."[5] Early in his career Eisenstein argued that shots are perceived not next to another in a horizontal or vertical chain, but on top of each other in collision.[6] Later he refined the idea to include layers of pictures "rushing towards the spectator," but not necessarily in a straight line. He proposed that film data might be perceived as arranged vertically in matrix form, exhibiting a multiplicity of criss-crossing relationships in an instant.[7] Finally, the psychologist Julian Hochberg mentions three types of perceptual analysis in film: simple summation, directional patterns, and cognitive maps.[8] With one exception, I will not explore these sorts of idea now, but rather will consider them in later chapters in the context of particular narrative theories.

It will be useful now, however, to separate the concept of "story world" into two parts: the diegetic and the nondiegetic. In talking about a "story," we often refer to certain events which surround a character, events which have already occurred, or might occur in a particular manner, in a certain sequence and time span, and so forth. We understand such events as occurring in a "world" governed by a particular set of laws. I will refer to that imagined world as the *diegesis*. The spectator presumes that the laws of such a world allow many events to occur (whether or not we see them), contains many objects and characters, contains other stories about other persons, and indeed permits events to be organized and perceived in nonnarrative ways. (Later I will argue that a documentary film also creates a diegetic world for its events.) The diegetic world extends beyond what is seen in a given shot and beyond even what is seen in the entire film, for we do not imagine that a character may only see and hear what we observe him or her seeing and hearing. The diegesis, then, is the implied spatial, temporal, and causal system of a character – a collection of sense data which is represented as being at least potentially accessible to a character.[9] A sound in a film, for example, is diegetic if the spectator judges that it has been, or could have been, heard by a character. However some on-screen elements (e.g., "mood" music) are *non*diegetic and addressed only to the spectator. These elements are *about* the diegetic world of a character and are meant to aid the spectator in organizing and interpreting that world and its events. Nondiegetic elements are not accessible to any of the characters. The spectator's organization of information into diegetic and nondiegetic story worlds is a critical step in the comprehension of a narrative and in understanding the relationship of story events to our everyday world.

Let us now attempt a preliminary delineation of narrative in film. This definition will aid us in examining narrative comprehension more precisely and will also provide a basis in chapter 4 for outlining five recent types of narrative theory, each of which stresses and interprets a different aspect of the narrative process.

Narrative is a way of comprehending space, time, and causality. Since in film there are at least two important frames of reference for understanding space, time, and causality, narrative in film is the principle by which data is converted from the frame of the *screen* into a *diegesis* – a world – that frames a particular *story*, or sequence of actions, in that world; equally, it is the principle by which data is converted from story onto screen. To facilitate analysis, narrative may be divided into a series of relationships. For example:

1 The relationship of diegesis and story may be analyzed with such narratological concepts as Todorov's "transformations," or a *narrative schema*. Which kinds of action sequences occurring in what kind of world will qualify as a narrative? For example, a narrative schema ("abstract," "orientation," "initiating event," etc.) describes how a reader collects a series of episodes into a focused causal chain (as opposed to a "heap," "catalogue," "unfocused chain," etc.).

  Causal chains are not just sequences of paired events, but also embody a desire for pairing events and the power to make pairs. Narrative causes ("remote," "intervening," "enabling," etc.) are thus principles of explanation which are derived from cultural knowledge as well as from physical laws. Narrative causality includes the human plans, goals, desires, and routines – realized in action sequences – which are encouraged, tolerated, or proscribed by a community.

2 The relationship of diegesis and screen may be analyzed with such concepts as script, set decoration, technology, technique, shot, form, style, material, and excess. The present chapter will demonstrate that these kinds of concept may be approached by measuring their effects on a spectator's judgments about the *ordering* of space, time, and causality on the screen and in the diegesis.

3 The relationship of diegesis and what is external to it – the nondiegetic – raises issues of *narration*: from what sort of "other world" has a diegesis been created, a character presented, events told? What has been concealed, or excluded? And, furthermore, how do we come to *believe* in a narrative diegesis and relate it to our own world; that is, what is the nature of *fictional and nonfictional* reference?

36

The previous chapter introduced some of the issues involved in analyzing diegesis and story (i.e., 1 above). In later chapters, I will deal with the problems of narration and fiction (3). But first we must examine the relationship of diegesis and screen, namely, how is data on the screen transformed into a story world? In order to answer this question, a distinction will be made between two types of perception operative in watching a film. These two types of perception produce different kinds of hypotheses about space, time, and causality. Distinguishing between them will allow us to examine closely how a spectator makes separate use of judgments about space, time, and causality, as well as how a spectator may integrate these judgments to produce an overall narrative rendering of experience.

TOP-DOWN PERCEPTION

The movement from screen to story world does not proceed along a smooth path and in only one direction. Many of our abilities are brought to bear simultaneously on a film, producing at least some conflict and uncertainty. As a first step toward unravelling some of these abilities and specifying the kinds of conflicts that arise, I will use a fundamental cognitive psychological distinction to divide perception into two kinds of process according to the "direction" in which they work. Some perceptual processes operate upon data on the screen in a direct, "bottom-up" manner by examining the data in very brief periods of time (utilizing little or no associated memory) and organizing it automatically into such features as edge, color, depth, motion, aural pitch, and so on. Bottom-up perception is serial and "data-driven," and produces only short-range effects. Other perceptual processes, however, are based on acquired knowledge and schemas, are not constrained by stimulus time, and work "top-down" on the data, using a spectator's expectations and goals as principles of organization. Top-down processes are indirect in the sense that they may reframe data in alternative ways independently of the stimulus conditions which govern the initial appearance of the data. Top-down processes must be flexible and general in order to be effective across a wide range of situations while allowing for (unpredictable) variations among specific cases. Top-down processes often treat data as an inductive sample to be projected and tested within a variety of parallel frames of reference while bottom-up processes are highly specialized and atomistic (e.g., detecting motion). Both kinds of process operate simultaneously on the data creating a variety of representations with varying degrees of compatibility.[10]

Because top-down processes are active in watching a film, a spectator's cognitive activity is not restricted to the particular moment being viewed in a film. Instead the spectator is able to move forward and backward through screen data in order to experiment with a variety of syntactical, semantic, and referential hypotheses; as Ian Jarvie notes, "We cannot *see* movies without *thinking* about them."[11] By experimenting with various methods for ordering data, the spectator creates spatial, temporal, and causal experiences which do not derive directly from screen time. Also critical in top-down processing are procedures which test the degree of "progress" which has been made toward solving a perceptual problem. Such procedures are active, for example, when we search for the "end" of a story. If we are unable to detect progress, we may begin to doubt the particular techniques we have been using, or even whether we have properly understood the goal. Because of the diversity of top-down and bottom-up processes which may be at work at a given moment in a text, perception as a whole is perhaps best thought of as a system which struggles to manage different and often conflicting interpretations of data.

In addition, the fact that comprehension may be divided into top-down and bottom-up kinds of activity helps explain some inconsistencies in the terminology employed by film writers. For example, some writers prefer to use the concept of "voice" in film as a means to identify the source of words that are actually heard by a spectator while other writers prefer to apply the concept more broadly in order to include a number of top-down factors that influence a spectator's perception. Bill Nichols argues for an expansive notion of "voice."

> [I]n the evolution of documentary [as a genre] the contestation among forms has centered on the question of "voice." By "voice" I mean something narrower than style: that which conveys to us a sense of a text's social point of view, of how it is speaking to us and how it is organizing the materials it is presenting to us. In this sense "voice" is not restricted to any one code or feature, such as dialogue or spoken commentary. Voice is perhaps akin to that intangible, moire-like pattern formed by the unique interaction of *all* a film's codes, and it applies to *all* modes of documentary.[12]

For Nichols, the concept of "voice" is not confined to words literally spoken, or written, nor confined to fictional narrative; instead, "voice" includes powerful, nonverbal patterns even in nonfiction (documentary) films. Accordingly, the "person" whose voice is "heard" in a text may be a much more complex (invisible and inaudible) entity than a voice-over narrator or someone being interviewed. Thus Nichols's approach is well-suited to an analysis of narration. As I will emphasize in this book, film narration cannot be limited to, say, an explicit commentary, or defined by literal, material, purely formal, stylistic, technical, technological, or "bottom-up" kinds of categories. Narration, and narrative, are preeminently top-down phenomena that require for their

38

analysis the use of wide-ranging, complex concepts like "point of view," or Nichols's "social point of view."

When we think of narrative as a general phenomenon that may appear in many physical forms (conversation, pictures, dance, music, etc.), we are thinking of it as a top-down cognitive effect. Wallace Martin may put it too strongly when he says that "narratives may be the source of the varied visual resources of the movies, rather than vice versa."[13] Nevertheless, much can be learned by concentrating on top-down processes in an attempt to isolate the psychological conditions that allow narrative to be understood in all media.

I wish to examine some of the top-down processes which seem to be relevant to our comprehension of narrative. I will begin by considering how our top-down search for a coherent causal system helps to organize screen data into diegetic and nondiegetic story worlds, each with a coherent temporal system. Later in the chapter, I will consider how judgments about screen space are related to judgments about story space and the causality of a story world. In general, we will discover that conflicts arise between top-down and bottom-up processing, between story and screen, and between the diegesis and what seems external to it. Hence we will find that the ongoing process of constructing and understanding a narrative is perhaps best seen as the moment by moment regulation of conflicts among competing spatial, temporal, and causal hypotheses. "Narrative" in film is therefore the overall process as well as the result of searching among hypotheses for an equilibrium, however precarious.

TEMPORAL AND SPATIAL ORDER

There is a sequence in *The Lady from Shanghai* (Welles, 1948) where three distinct actions are intercut through fifteen shots in such a way that it appears that when a woman presses a button, a door flies open allowing a dying man to drag himself into a room; when she presses the button again, a car is sent speeding down a road as a truck pulls up to a stop sign; and, when she presses the button a final time, the car is sent crashing into the back of the truck as the two men in the car react with horror at their helpless condition. The problem for the spectator of this film is how to interpret these events which can have no causal connection and yet are presented *as if* they were causally connected so that it seems that pushing a button brings a dying man into a room and creates a car accident.[14] In effect, we are being asked to accept a special fiction ("as if") within an already fictional mystery story.

In order to solve this causal problem the spectator must evaluate the temporal relationships posed by the sequence. Four important principles of causal reasoning are that a cause must precede an effect, an

39

effect cannot work backward in time to create a cause, certain patterns of *repetition* among events make a causal connection more likely (e.g., pushing a button three times . . .),[15] and a prior event which is temporally or spatially more proximate to the outcome than others is more likely to be a cause of the outcome.[16] Many different sorts of temporal situations, bearing on our judgments of causality, may be created through the juxtaposition of spatial fragments from different shots.[17] As Arnheim emphasized, "the fact that two sequences follow each other on the screen does not indicate in itself that they should be understood as following each other in time."[18] Thus before tackling the causal problem, we must briefly survey some of the possible temporal, and spatial, situations which may arise.

An extraordinary fact about the physical world is that virtually all phenomena can be explained in terms of interactions between parts *taken two at a time*. According to Marvin Minsky, "One could conceive of a universe in which whenever three stars formed an equilateral triangle, one of them would instantly disappear – but virtually no three-part interactions have ever been observed in the physical world."[19] I will assume that explanations of phenomena are constructed on this basis; specifically, that the spectator constructs temporal, spatial, and causal situations by assembling parts two at a time. Thus in figure 3, temporal situation AB_1 in the story is created by imagining a particular relationship between the durations of two on-screen spaces, A and B, resulting in such story relationships as temporal continuity, ellipsis, overlap, simultaneity, reversal, or distortion.

More specifically, these temporal relationships in the story may be described as follows:

B_1 represents the time of A as *continuing*[20] into B such that the story order AB_1 is presented as identical to the screen order AB.

B_2 represents the time of A as continuing into B but with an initial *ellipsis* so that the screen order is interpreted as having omitted something from the story (which must be restored by the spectator's imagination); that is, the true order is: A, X, B_2, where X is not represented on the screen. If the ellipsis is large, but later disappears when completed by new screen events, then B_2 is a flashforward.

B_3 represents the time of A as continuing into B but only after an initial *overlap* in which there has been a partial replay of time already experienced in A.

B_4 represents a complete overlap with the time of A so that story event B is understood to be *simultaneous* with story event A even

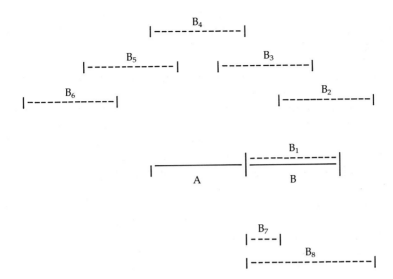

Figure 3 Story time
Graphic display of several varieties of story time created as a spectator relocates the on-screen time of spatial fragment B relative to the on-screen time of spatial fragment A resulting in a new and imaginary temporal order in the story, relationship AB_n. Some of the new relationships that may be created include temporal continuity, ellipsis, overlap, simultaneity, reversal, and distortion. The general principles illustrated here for time may also be applied to describe the ordering of space into such patterns as chains, gaps, reversals, and distortions (see text).

though B is seen to occur after A on the screen; that is, story time overrides the literal order on the screen.

B_5 represents an overlap with the time of A but with an initial brief jump back in time. This produces a fleeting but curious story time in which an effect (in A) has apparently been shown prior to its cause (in B). The spectator, in fact, is tempted to *mentally reverse* A and B_5 (creating a relation like A and B_3) in order to restore the forward arrow of time in which causes precede effects (i.e., prospective time). It is also possible that AB_5 may require the spectator to imagine an even earlier time (e.g., B_6) which is then taken as an explanation of A in the story – an implicit flashback – while B_5 continues to represent the "present time" of A. Using Noël Burch's terms, I will refer to the AB_5 type of story order as a *retrospective* or retroactive story time.[21] Our usual expectation is prospective time – A *and so* B. Less usual is retrospective time – A *because of* B.[22]

Here is an example of retrospective time: Shot A shows an object

41

from a certain position, but then shot B shows a person looking at the object from that previous position. In this way, we discover that the object we saw in A *had already been seen* by a character (and in fact, without knowing it at the time, we were seeing how that character saw the object). Thus with shot B we are forced to mentally readjust the order of events and reconceive shot A using the character as a new reference point, as a new condition for our seeing. We now conceive of the story event as composed of, first, a character who looks, followed by our view of what can be seen from that character's viewpoint. Part of shot B then comes to stand for either a literal, brief jump back in time, or else an approximation of what it would have looked like to have seen the character first looking. In any event, what is important is that the shots require the spectator to refigure the temporal scheme.[23]

B_6 represents a time prior to A – a *past* time, or flashback, which requires the spectator to reorder story events and imagine other events which have been omitted and not seen on the screen between B_6 and A.

B_7 and B_8 represent temporal *distortions*. The on-screen duration of B (with respect to A!) is radically altered in such a way that it is not immediately clear what relationship with A is appropriate. For example, the duration of B may be compressed or expanded by running the film at a new speed, showing it backwards, repeating B, showing alternative takes, omitting frames by step printing, using freeze frames, and so forth.[24] In these situations A and B do not seem commensurate and hence we cannot immediately decide what story order is appropriate. Also included in these categories is indeterminable time. For example, in Jean-Luc Godard's *Weekend* (1967) there is a shot (involving hippie-guerrillas) that is so carefully arranged that its time cannot be ascertained. In fact, the shot is a flashforward but it cannot be recognized as such until much later in the film when the event being depicted actually occurs! The shot is thus a retrospective, nonsubjective flashforward.[25]

The above scheme is a way of talking generally about principles of temporal ordering. However, it also applies to principles of *spatial ordering*. Although my discussion of the particular causal problem of the car crash in *The Lady from Shanghai* will center on time, it should be evident that, in general, space is just as relevant to the solution of causal problems. Therefore I wish to indicate briefly how the above scheme may be interpreted as an overview of some spatial principles of ordering. The scheme is not meant to be restrictive but merely to provide a way of comparing various narrative theories each of which will use specialized terms to examine space and time in still finer detail.

In order to demonstrate how figure 3 may be applied to space, I will for the moment make an artificial, but simplifying assumption about space. I will assume that space comprises only two sectors: a foreground and a background. The question then becomes, how may we recognize a *change* in space? How may a given space "connect to" and be related to another space to form a new ordered whole? For convenience I will also assume – as in the case of time – that the change is effected through the editing of shots even though the scheme applies to changes effected in other ways (e.g., through camera or character movement, sound, changes in lighting level). The result of these assumptions is that space may evolve in only three basic ways: a new background may appear with the old foreground; a new foreground may appear with the old background; or, both a new foreground and a new background may appear. In the first two cases, what is new is introduced in conjunction with what has already been seen (an old foreground, or else an old background). This means that spaces are being connected into a *chain*. In the third case (a new foreground and a new background) the relationship of the new space to the spaces which have already been seen is *open* and not yet defined; that is, there is a "gap" of some type between new and old space. Such a gap is indicated in figure 3 by the gap between fragment A and fragment B_2. On the other hand, fragments B_1, B_3, and B_4 represent a new space which either adjoins, overlaps, or repeats an old space so as to compose a *chain* of spaces.

There is a special case of the open space (A–B_2) which must be mentioned. When the new foreground is simply the old background and the new background is the old foreground, there has been no real change: foreground and background have simply been interchanged across the two shots. Space has been reversed, or mirrored between the shots. Fragments B_5 and B_6 are meant to represent this general class of *reverse angles* in film. A typical example is shot/reverse-shot editing which depicts a conversation between two characters by alternating shots taken over each character's shoulder.[26]

What can spatial "reversals" like B_5 and B_6 mean in terms of the story world being created by the spectator from a series of on-screen spaces? David Bordwell offers a proposal:

Shot/reverse-shot editing helps make narration covert by creating the sense that no important scenographic space remains unaccounted for. If shot two shows the important material outside shot one, there is no spatial point we can assign to the narration; the narration is always elsewhere, outside this shot but never visible in the next.[27]

In other words, when space is reversed we do not see a camera, sets, or technicians but only more diegetic space which seemingly is part of a consistent and unified group of spaces with no disturbing (causal) outside influences (e.g., by an "author"). The new and larger space being represented through a reversal is an imaginary space – a diegetic space of the characters that is seemingly like itself in every direction.

There are, of course, degrees and kinds of chains, gaps, and reversals of space; and our recognition of the kinds will depend on the nature of other conventions governing, say, camera placement (for example, whether spaces are oriented toward a 180 degree axis of action). Connecting screen spaces to a pattern of story space does not prohibit also using gaps (B_2 and B_6), or other distortions (cf. B_7 and B_8), to create a story space which is *not* the sum of spatial fragments on the screen.[28] Such a gap between screen and story space leads to degrees and kinds of "impossible" space; that is, *to space which can not be justified as existing wholly within the diegesis*. Impossible space leads to perceptual problems of a new kind that force the spectator to reconsider prior hypotheses about time and causality.

CAUSALITY AND METAPHOR

I will have more to say later about the narrative effects of spatial perception and the problem of "impossible" (nondiegetic) space, but for now I wish to return to the particular moment in *The Lady from Shanghai* in which it appears that a woman causes a car to crash into a truck by pressing a button. To work on this causal problem, the spectator must make a judgment about the temporal relationships of the three intercut actions. A number of factors point to some sort of continuity among the actions: no explicit motive is given for the woman's pressing of the button (hence we wonder what she is doing); she stares into space as if preoccupied by a thought (fear? determination?); it is clear from previous events that some sort of devious plan is being set in motion; the tempo of the editing increases to match the increasing speed of the diverse actions as if the actions form a group (a button is pressed, an indicator snaps on a display, a dying man quickly sits up, a car speeds along a road); and, most importantly, nondiegetic music which began with the first push of the button continues across all the spaces and rapidly builds to a loud and high-pitched climax coinciding, and merging, with the shrieking of automobile brakes and ending with the crash of glass (the final effect?). Furthermore, nothing about the representation of time in the scene rules out a causal link among the events: conjectured effects do not precede causes and the time of the causal interaction does not violate the presumed method of interaction. Pressing a button suggests the speed of light which is in accord with the

44

"instantaneous" transitions suggested by the editing, but *not* in accord with transitions, conspicuously avoided in the sequence, based on character movement, camera movement, or optical effects, since these latter transitions would consume a screen time requiring additional explanation within the story.

It is worth emphasizing again that what I am describing is the spectator's interpretive process (here involving time) which works top-down on the data. The impetus for creating a *story* time does not derive in any simple way from the running time of the film – screen time – but rather from top-down processes seeking a new order which will be sensitive to other constraints on the data, e.g. presumed causality and event duration. Even our judgment of an event as temporally continuus is *not* based on the *necessity* of its being physically complete on the screen. Perceptual illusions and constancies demonstrate that we may easily see what is not present, or fail to see what is present.[29] Physical continuity on the screen depends on the use of equipment (camera, printer, projector) while the *perception* of physical continuity on the screen is a matter of *bottom-up* processing (i.e., the operation of sensory mechanisms). The perception of *narrative* continuity, however, is a very different matter. Indeed, it turns out that the best perception of narrative continuity is often obtained by certain violations of physical continuity where part of an action is left out or sometimes briefly repeated.[30] Moreover, even blatant "mismatches" between shots will be overlooked by a spectator.[31] This demonstrates, again, that recognition of objects and actions in a setting through top-down processing takes precedence over involuntary, bottom-up processing, and certainly takes precedence over physical continuity on the screen.

There is no general set of necessary and sufficient conditions which determine how the results of bottom-up processing must be interpreted. The perception of continuous or discontinuous screen time may lead equally to judgments of either continuous or discontinuous story time. The fact of juxtaposition on the screen carries no necessary implication about temporal sequence or spatial relationship (cf. fig. 3), nor about causality (cf. temporal relationship AB$_5$ in fig. 3). Even a repetition of the *same shot* need not signify that the *same time* is again being represented. The reason is that more complex events may be represented than what only occurs in front of the camera and/or occurs only once.[32]

These ideas amount to saying that human comprehension does not proceed by progressively refining sensory data from lower to higher stages until a single thought is perfected and grasped by a singular Self. Rather, the human mind seems to be organized into modules that operate in parallel, are often too specialized to "communicate" with one another (or even to make use of "words"), and produce criss-crossing outputs which conflict as well as unify.[33] The Self in this view is not stable and unified, but instead is "diverse, capable of being all those it will at one time be, a group acting together."[34] Hume reached a similar conclusion from a much different perspective. He argued in 1739 that "what we call a *mind*, is nothing but a heap or collection of different perceptions." These perceptions, thoughts, and motives "succeed each other with an inconceivable rapidity, and are in a perpetual flux and movement." Hume could find no common feature, or continuing link, among the perceptions that could qualify as a unified Self; instead there are "the successive perceptions only."[35] In 1890 William James posited a "hierarchy" of selves to account for the felt presence in consciousness of an "ideal spectator," but he retained Hume's notions of multiplicity and conflict among the selves.[36] For Erving Goffman, "Self . . . is not an entity half-concealed behind events, but a changeable formula for managing oneself during them."[37] Marvin Minsky emphasizes that the Self also functions "to keep us from changing too rapidly."[38] Recently, similar conclusions about the "divided" self, or "split" subject, have been reached in certain film and literary theories inspired by post-structuralism, psychoanalysis, and ideological criticism.[39]

I believe that the diverse strategies used by an individual for managing perceptual and behavioral problems in general include the creation of hierarchies and an "ideal" position of spectatorship, and that such strategies have counterparts in an individual's comprehension of narrative texts and in an individual's construction of an efficient self in relation to a text. I will return to these notions in later chapters where they will be reflected in some basic concepts, such as "levels of narration."

What is certain about comprehension is that the perceiver must search, compare, test, discriminate, remember, and speculate within many realms and imagined contexts. Evidence on the screen cannot "speak for itself," for how can we know what is *implied* by the evidence and what limits may exist on a given (top-down) method of seeing? Switching to a new method of interpreting – i.e., a different top-down schema – may reveal that the data under the old method was actually inconsistent, fragmentary, mistaken, deceptive, or ambiguous. Switching methods again may recast the evidence a third time. This is particularly true for fictions which, as we shall see in chapter 7, exploit a qualified indeterminateness of signification (or, according to some radical theories, exploit the fundamental indeterminacy of signification). The necessary incompleteness of data under alternative interpretations highlights a critical fact: there is a *persistence* to top-down processing. A spectator is willing to fill in some data or ignore other data in order to maintain a particular temporal and spatial context – a master "frame" of reference or schema – for events and details. For example, we routinely ignore the break in time signalled by a change of camera angle in favor of maintaining an interpretation of temporal continuity in a story (relationship A–B$_1$ above), even if, say, the editing of a match on action is technically poor and requires us to fill in missing action or to overlook other details. Indeed, using a word like "technical" to characterize the editing betrays the decision we've already made to preserve story time. The relative persistence and autonomy of certain top-down narrative processes in our comprehension will be a recurrent theme of this book.

Returning to our analysis of *The Lady from Shanghai*, it must be said that the spectator does not finally believe that the woman has directly caused the violent actions. The spectator's perception of the distances among the spaces, coupled with culturally-acquired knowledge of how cars operate and of how rich people summon servants at the push of a button, suggests that there is no immediate causal connection among the events. Moreover, this conclusion is reinforced by a knowledge of genre – the story is a mystery, not science fiction – and by prior events in the story which intimate that each of the men in the car, though in different ways and unknown to each other, are her accomplices in some scheme, not enemies who must be killed. Still, she does seem to be standing contemplative and motionless at the very center of several violent actions and to be linked somehow to death. (Notice that our interpretation might be quite different if she were seen running up a flight of stairs or chatting with a friend during these events. In that case the causal problem might never have arisen.) The usual form of the mystery story has been turned upside down: the mystery here is why we should see these three events as mysterious when apparently there can be no mystery about them because we know their causes (including who shot the man who is dying in a nearby room). Ultimately, this specially created, but then rejected, fiction where a woman apparently causes men to die by pushing a button, must itself be seen as embedded within a larger fiction – a mystery story. The truth of the embedded fiction must be sought by looking for a fit with the questions posed by the plot and then, in a still larger sense, a fit with the presuppositions which may be held by a society about the concealed mystery of women, their danger to men, and their proper place.[40] That is, the woman character's desire is first analyzed through her different relationships with four men – what does she really want from them? – and then analyzed through the filter of what we are supposed to imagine generally that women must want. I do not wish to pursue this interpretation, but rather to extract from the analysis of this particular scene the following set of general proposals about narrative comprehension.

Interpretations of narrative depend in a crucial way upon the judgments we make about space, time, and causation as we work top-down on screen data. Identifying an event as a "story event" is a matter of deciding where actions begin, how they break off, and which actions belong together. We must judge not only the temporal status of special cross-cut actions but the time implied by the juxtaposition of *any* two shots including ensuring that time has not stopped or otherwise shifted *within* a shot. (Note, again, that the physical material of film – such as the break between shots – does not guarantee *a priori* a specific temporal relation nor guarantee a change in temporal relations.) We use hypotheses about time to search for causation and, reciprocally, we use hypotheses about causality to establish temporal order. Identifying what counts as an event involves searching for an "equilibrium" among possible "values" for space, time, and causation. Although other sorts of knowledge are clearly relevant, judgments about space, time, and causation are fundamental because they give us the means with which to see and hear: a framework within which to perceive. Even when the pushing of a button is meant to cause a car to crash (say, on an automobile test track), it is necessary to imagine the event within appropriate conditions of space and time. As George Wilson says, our task as spectators is ultimately "to work out how our perceptual comprehension of the relevant film world is related to our normal modes of ordering and understanding perception in everyday visual experience."[41]

In order to connect our understanding of film to our understanding of the ordinary world, we have to be sensitive to the specific techniques available in film for representing space, time, and causal relations. In watching a film, for example, we must respond to camera movements, matches on action, perspective relations, attached and cast shadows, optical transitions, screen direction, sound overlap, off-screen sound, voice-over and voice-under,[42] and an enormous number of other features of the medium. Although narrative may appear in any medium, the particular materials and techniques of a given medium partly determine when and how we apply our skills of spatial, temporal, and causal construction. In this sense, the break between shots does not usually "mean" anything; it is merely a catalyst for us to *proceed to generate hypotheses* using certain strategies. Many difficulties in narrative analysis and film theory have arisen through the failure to appreciate the difference between a "reference" – such as a denotation – and a "procedure" or instruction to be followed in discovering/assigning a reference.[43] The distinction between a reference that has been achieved and a procedure for referring is vital for any complete definition of narrative and will be addressed in chapters 3 and 4.

Thus, in summary, the spectator must find an interpretation of *The Lady from Shanghai* which assigns responsibility for the car crash to the woman but not on the basis of a button being pushed. The editing of the film is not dismissed as simply false, misleading, or accidental, but instead may be viewed as creating a second fiction in which a realization of the truth of the apparent causal connection is merely *deferred* to a later time. The contradiction whereby the woman both causes and does not cause the car crash may be represented by the spectator's grouping of on-screen elements into two simultaneous worlds: the diegetic and the nondiegetic. Nondiegetic references are not taken to be part of the character's world, and hence not subject to its laws, but instead are taken to be *about* that world and are addressed only to the spectator. In this way the film allows the spectator to begin to see one thing (a car crash) in terms of another (a woman), but not in a literal (diegetic) way. Just as a statue is said to emerge "out of" clay, the dying man and the car crash are to emerge metaphorically from a presumed feminine state of being: "She killed males *out of* desperation."[44] The metaphor ("out of") functions to describe the nature of the causation. This sequence in the film is particularly complex because neither the woman nor the spectator fully understands as yet the nature of her responsibility or its consequences.

Selecting something to be seen in terms of something else – that is, substituting one thing for another to highlight a shared quality – demonstrates the close connection between creating metaphors, and discovering causes.[45] To discover a "cause" in this sense is to recognize that the logic of grouping certain "events" together on the basis of a shared quality may point to an underlying, formative process. Such a formative process may act to transform that quality, thus drawing together still more events.[46] In representing the car crash, *The Lady from Shanghai* is at the very threshold of stating a "likeness," or shared bond, sufficient to support the conclusion that a woman, or Woman, is a source of deadly threat to males. This may be expressed in another way by saying that although we must conclude that time is merely chronological in the car crash sequence, the ordering of the event nonetheless seems to betray a larger principle or pattern beginning to emerge in which a threat to males arises from the *difference* between male and female. The paradoxical causality whereby a woman both causes and does not cause a car crash reflects a general principle of *The Lady from Shanghai* that a *dis*similarity between the sexes is the common link among a set of events. Indeed some writers have argued that narrative causality is essentially these larger principles of grouping (recall, for example, Todorov's notion of narrative reversals, or "transformations") which come to dominate a simple and irreversible kind of time like chronology. Roland Barthes asserts that

the mainspring of narrative is precisely the confusion of consecutiveness and consequence, what-comes-*after* being read in narrative as what-is-*caused-by*; in which case narrative would be a systematic application of the logical fallacy denounced by Scholasticism in the formula *post hoc, ergo propter hoc*.[47]

The car crash sequence of *The Lady from Shanghai* reveals chronological time in the very process of being transformed into narrative time.

It is clear that we will need the distinctions introduced in the previous chapter that were used to isolate types of time and types of causality. Also, in understanding the causal structure of a story and its associated metaphors a spectator may need to create further subdivisions of the broad categories of diegetic and nondiegetic in order to hold together data of different sorts until it is needed to produce through juxtaposition more complex and subtle descriptions of the references (and "causation") put into play by a story. In chapter 4, I will describe several more of these subdivisions utilizing the concept of "levels of narration" in order to make more precise the notion of related, yet distinct story "worlds," or "levels of reality."

IMPOSSIBLE STORY SPACE

In fashioning diegetic and nondiegetic worlds we are constantly required to keep track of the ways in which our perceptions are related to the perceptions of characters within the story.[48] The nature of a car crash will change according to whether we believe a woman is dreaming about a car crash, remembering one, or unaware that one is occurring. In the first two cases, the status we accord the crash – its spatial, temporal, and causal implications – derives from explicit relationships with the character; in the third case, the event is determined "negatively" as an independent occurrence, as unrelated to character perception.[49]

Our knowledge of the car crash is also affected if the woman is shown only to be *observing* it as a bystander. The reason is that our perception still coincides in some manner with that of the character; for example, we see the event at the same time as the woman. This fourth case falls between the first two and the third; the precise extent to which our perception coincides with the character has yet to be specified by the text. Nevertheless, the very existence of the character as she looks around her world and shares ideas with other characters testifies to our own perception of the diegetic world. Her act of perceiving seems to justify, and may even direct, the spectator's act of perceiving. Such a first-person account of space and time renders the "author" of the fiction invisible behind the character's experience. Like the apparent causation in *The Lady from Shanghai*, a first-person recounting of events is an illusion, but one which is bound up with the very conditions

50

which allow us to make sense of the fictional world. The creation of a "character" has enormous implications because a character is understood to perceive in ways that we might imagine ourselves imitating if we were in a similar situation.

There are, of course, many ways to show characters perceiving, and consequently many relationships we may have to their perceptions. "First-person" and "third-person" modes of perceiving may be visualized as acting at ninety degrees to one another. Actual cases, however, will place our involvement with a character at intermediate angles. For example, an eyeline match differs from a point-of-view shot according to the inferences a spectator may draw about the object that is seen. The former shows us what a character sees and when the character sees it; the latter shows us, in addition, the perspective of the character. Thus the point-of-view shot represents on screen an additional "subjective" feature. It is more *restricted* than the eyeline match because its representation of space and distance is tied much closer to the presumed place of the character. These sorts of (semi-subjective) effect must be taken into account as we construct the space and time of a story world.

The development of space through the perceptions of characters, like the impossible causality of *The Lady from Shanghai*, may create problems for the spectator that lead toward nonliteral interpretations of events. Fritz Lang's *Dr Mabuse, the Gambler* (Part One, 1922) opens on a close-up of photographs of men spread out in someone's hand as if they were playing cards. New photographs are selected as if from a "deck." In the second shot we see the man who was holding the "cards," Dr Mabuse, now shuffling them, though we do not see his eyes. There are no other "players" seated around the table. The third shot repeats the close-up framing of the first shot. One photograph is selected. In the fourth shot we again see Dr Mabuse as he holds the "card" up over his right shoulder, and finally we see his eyes as he looks up and stares into the right foreground (shot 4, fig. 4). The next shot presents a spatial problem. We see a man standing in another part of the room looking left (shot 5, fig. 5). Where is he? If he is responding to Mabuse, he would appear to be located in the room near where the camera was positioned in the previous shot. However in the next shot Mabuse turns to look back over his right shoulder (shot 6, fig. 6). Intertitle: "You've been taking cocaine again." Mabuse continues to stare. Then we see the man again but he is now looking right (shot 9, fig. 7). We did not see him turn to face in the opposite direction. (Has he now turned away from Mabuse?) Intertitle: "If you fire me, I'll kill myself." We are surprised both by the dialogue and the space: If he is responding to Mabuse, he is not near the camera where we first thought him to be (i.e., near the camera position of shot 4, fig. 4), but in the background off left. The following shots make clear that our first belief was in fact wrong. Initially neither man was looking at the other. The space seen in shots 5 and 9 (where the man is standing) must be relocated from the off-screen right foreground of shot 4 to the off-screen left background. It becomes clear that the man in shots 5 and 9 was avoiding Mabuse's gaze. Dominated by Mabuse, he responds instantly. Later in shot 12 he will enter obediently from behind Mabuse to take the photograph.

Shot 12 finally makes the organization of the space explicit. All of this strikes us as rather abrupt and confusing. If the man had been shown turning around, or Mabuse looking in the "proper" direction, we could have correctly understood the interior of the room. The space that we believed was created by the juxtaposition of shots 4 and 5 (figs 4 and 5) in the right foreground of shot 4 has been shown to be completely false. We did not in fact see it; we saw something else. At a thematic level, Mabuse is revealed to be at the very center of the event with the ability to create and destroy space through his powerful gaze (e.g., fig. 4). Moreover, we soon discover that Mabuse himself, as a master of disguises, will often be concealed. In this way we begin to see that appearances in the film may be misleading and real power concealed. We are perhaps reminded of the opening shot in which Mabuse – almost like the invisible maker of a fiction film – shuffles photographs of men as if he had an absolute power to control destiny or assume a new identity at will.

Lang has created these effects through editing and the use of angled glances. The space of the scene is developed through attention to various rules of continuity editing (e.g., the 180 degree axis of action, matches on movement, the 30 degree rule, etc.).[50] Lang has not used *mise-en-scène* or overlapping space to orient the spectator. We cannot, for example, decide from the background of shot 5 (fig. 5) where the man must be located with respect to Mabuse. Incredibly, not until shot 25 are we presented with an establishing shot of the room. Lang avoids techniques of the early cinema which would have presented the scene in a single shot as a distant tableau. Instead the spectator is initially placed "inside" the action. For this reason Noël Burch accords the film a special place in film history and praises its power to force the spectator to mentally create a continuous space and time out of a series of fragments and glances.[51] The spectator is induced to overlook what is literally on the screen – compositions which cut up the room coupled with frequent changes of angle – in order to imagine a coherent story event.

But Lang has achieved more than a mastery of the conventions of so-called invisible or transparent editing. His use of two contradictory spaces (figs 4–5 as opposed to figs 6–7) demonstrates that character glance has the power to generate a discontinuous, or impossible, space as well as to generate the illusion of an integrated space. At a global level, too, many events in the story will prove initially baffling or remain only partially comprehensible which spurs us to search for an underlying rationale, or better, an *underlying rationality*.[52] In the same way that a certain photograph, or image on the screen, offered to us by Lang is diegetically unassimilable (shot 5, fig. 5) so also are other playing-card photographs, and characters, apparently shuffled and discarded in the story world. The measured confusion we feel between screen and story may drive us toward an understanding of the demonic forms of causality which increasingly are associated with Mabuse and which, like those of *The Lady from Shanghai*, hold us in their grip.

Why should a glance have so much power to generate a narrative? The reason is that unlike, say, a shot of a character wiping his forehead or a shot of a vase on a table, a glance bristles with implications about space, time, and causality. A glance leaps across space: its direction orients us to something nearby and hence enables us to build spatial relationships within a scene. A glance implies temporal relationships as well: an object seen is interpreted to exist in a time continuous, or simultaneous, with the act of seeing.[53] Also, a glance may be linked directly to a character's intention, or to a forthcoming act by the character, or to a reaction (when the character is acted upon). A glance implies an interaction with an object. In fact, glances are so important to narrating a story world that the only glance that is generally avoided is a glance into the lens of the camera.[54] A look into the camera breaks the diegesis because it makes the conventional reverse shot or eyeline match impossible. (Such a match would reveal the camera itself; its absence would be just as revealing.) In a deeper sense, a character's glance is an important measure of the *acquisition of knowledge* by character and spectator. As we shall see in chapters 3 and 4, knowing, and thus being able to tell, is a fundamental property of narration. Psychoanalytic and feminist theories go even further: they tie the glance to fundamental human drives and to scenarios of unconscious desire; to forms of visual pleasure, anxiety, and fantasy (e.g., voyeurism and fetishism); and to the very constitution of a self and a gender distinct from an Other.[55]

The Lady from Shanghai illustrated that even impossible causation may affect our interpretation of diegetic events while *Dr Mabuse, the Gambler* illustrated that character glances may disrupt our perception of diegetic space. The impossible space created through Mabuse's false eyeline match (figs 4–5) has the effect of interrupting the flow of space around the spectator. In *Dr Mabuse* the frontality of early cinema is giving way to spatial articulations modeled on shot-reverse shot, creating more complex principles of spatial ordering as well as more complex forms of continuity and discontinuity. I want to turn now to screen space in order to consider how purely graphic patterns may also play a role in the spectator's experience of story space.

Figure 4 Dr Mabuse, the Gambler (shot 4)

Figure 5 Dr Mabuse, the Gambler (shot 5)

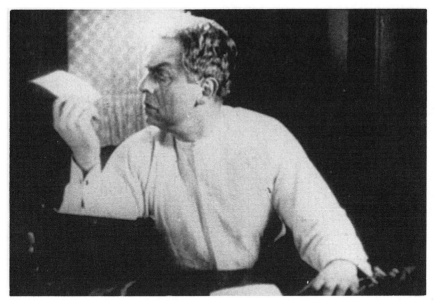

Figure 6 Dr Mabuse, the Gambler (shot 6)

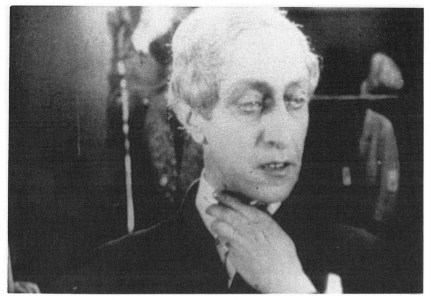

Figure 7 Dr Mabuse, the Gambler (shot 9)

SCREEN SPACE AND STYLISTIC METAPHORS

In Alfred Hitchcock's *The 39 Steps* (1935) a Scottish farmer and his young wife agree to allow the hero, Hannay, to spend the night with them. The wife discovers that Hannay is fleeing from the police who falsely believe that he is a murderer. She decides to help him. Her jealous husband, however, becomes suspicious of the way both of them are behaving toward each other. During supper he says that he must go outside to lock the barn. Once outside, however, he walks around the house to the kitchen window where we watch from behind him as he spies on his wife through the window. Next we see a medium close-up of his face from inside the house framed by the window bars (fig. 8) followed by his point-of-view from outside looking back through the window, again framed by window bars (fig. 9). This shot discloses the wife and Hannay leaning toward each other in earnest conversation. The point-of-view position is reinforced by our inability to hear what is being said because we are outside with the farmer. Next we see the husband's face framed by the window bars from the same camera position as before (cf. fig. 8). The scene then ends with a fade-out. We realize that the husband has been deceived by appearances for he believes that his wife has a sexual interest in Hannay and that they are secretly plotting to be together.

We discovered in *Dr Mabuse, the Gambler* that a shot could represent a fragment of story space as itself a collection of points, one of which could become the point *from which* the camera reveals the *next* fragment of story space. In this way a master space may be constructed by connecting spatial fragments from point to point in a transitive series from *within* the space of the story: if A is to the left of B and B is to the left of C then A is also to the left of C. In *The 39 Steps* the camera has actually taken the place of a character at a point in space in order to show us how the character sees (figs 8–9). The bars on the window and our distance from them in these two shots play a crucial role in our recognition that *the camera angle has changed by 180 degrees* between the two shots and that the camera has, in fact, assumed a point in space which has already been seen. By thus *following the angle* we are able to reorient ourselves to the story space and develop it in new directions. In recognizing the point-of-view structure we have converted a place *on* a flat screen (marked by one horizontal and one vertical line) into a place *in* the story world (two bars on a window). A continuity of story space is preserved between the two shots. But this is not all. I want to show that it is not a matter of indifference where the bars of the window appear on the screen to help us in marking story space.

Let's consider four basic possibilities for positioning the window bars in the point-of-view shot (fig. 9; see figs 10–13). One possibility would

Figure 8 The 39 Steps (shot 1)

Figure 9 The 39 Steps (shot 2)

be to show them exactly where they were in the previous shot of the husband's face looking in the window (fig. 8). Figure 10 shows this possibility using asterisks (* * *) to mark where the bars would be in the new shot. Through persistence of vision,[56] short-term memory, and the gestalt law of organization known as "proximity" (i.e., parts that are close together are grouped together and hence tend to be seen as one object, a whole) we would recognize an exact overlap with the previous shot. I will call this a "graphic match" between the two shots. It has an important disadvantage: it suggests that there has *not* been a 180 degree reversal of angle between the two shots. If the same window bars of the first shot are to be shown reversed 180 degrees in the second shot, then the vertical bar would switch from screen left to right while the horizontal bar would remain at the bottom of the screen. This *expectation* of what would result if the camera angle were reversed 180 degrees (i.e., if the story space were to be seen reversed) is shown in figures 10–13 as a solid line (＿＿＿). The graphic match thus works *against* our perception of spatial continuity in the story world by suggesting that there has been *no* change of angle and hence no point-of-view from the spatial position of the husband. We can, of course, still see the second shot as a point-of-view shot but we must rely on other cues and we must "overturn" the evidence of the immobile window bars (by, for example, believing that after reversing the angle 180 degrees, Hitchcock shifted the framing to show *different* window bars).

A second possibility for using the window bars in the point-of-view shot would be to show them reversed exactly as we would expect them to be if the camera had reversed 180 degrees (fig. 11). In this case the graphic configuration reinforces our spatial hypothesis and supports the spatial continuity of a character's point of view. I will call this a "spatial match" between the two shots.

A third possibility would be to show the window bars as if they were reflected along a diagonal line upwards to the right (fig. 12). This bizarre sort of movement does not accord with the normal way in which characters move through and view their world. On the other hand, there has been a clear change from the view presented in the first shot which is not inconsistent with a 180 degree reversal of angle: the vertical bar has in fact switched to the right side. Perhaps the horizontal upper bar, then, is simply a different part of the window. This graphic configuration is merely inconclusive. It neither encourages nor rules out spatial continuity in the story world. I will call this an "open match" between the two shots since graphic space and story space are represented as simply "decoupled" from one another.

A final possibility would be to show the bars as if they were merely reflected upwards (fig. 13). This is the choice that Hitchcock actually makes in the film (fig. 9). It is a decision *not* to show the same window

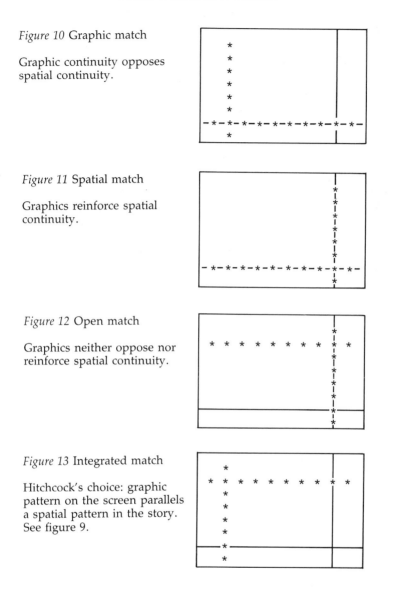

Figure 10 Graphic match

Graphic continuity opposes
spatial continuity.

Figure 11 Spatial match

Graphics reinforce spatial
continuity.

Figure 12 Open match

Graphics neither oppose nor
reinforce spatial continuity.

Figure 13 Integrated match

Hitchcock's choice: graphic
pattern on the screen parallels
a spatial pattern in the story.
See figure 9.

Figures 10–13 Story and screen matching
Four possible framings of an object seen through a window in *The 39 Steps*
representing the point-of-view of a character who is shown looking through
the window in the previous shot (see figure 8). Asterisks (* * *) represent
alternative locations for the position of the horizontal and vertical window
bars. Solid lines (_____) represent the position of the bars in the window *as
we would expect to see them if the camera angle were reversed 180 degrees from its
position in the previous shot.*

bars seen in the previous shot for at least one of the bars must be new. Hitchcock has given up a simple continuity (as in fig. 11) to obtain a most delicate effect. The new composition does not rule out spatial continuity since there has been a clear change in the graphic configuration between the two shots (the horizontal bar has shifted to the top). By keeping the vertical bar at the left, however, Hitchcock is able to *unify* a purely graphic pattern on the screen. It occurs in the following way: If the spectator perceives the old graphic configuration correctly reversed for the proper spatial continuity of the point-of-view shot *and* couples it with the new graphic configuration, the overall screen graphics of both shots form a closed inner frame within the frame of the shot. This unusual effect, I believe, results from exploiting two gestalt laws of organization: good continuation and closedness (closure). To put it another way, if one *anticipates* the 180 degree reversal of story space (by wondering what the husband will see if he looks in the window and how it will look to him), then one is rewarded by graphic continuation and closure *on the screen*. The graphics then attest to the pertinence of a question posed by the spectator of the narrative. The subtle power of this articulation is that screen space is allowed to close in on itself – apparently guaranteeing completeness in two dimensions – while story space reveals a maximum of information in three dimensions without breaking its essential continuity and completeness; that is, the two shots are linked through the shared space of the window pane while enabling us to see in two opposite directions in an instant.

In general, one can imagine other types of patterns besides an inner "rectangle" that may be fulfilled in a purely graphic way. Note especially that graphic patterns *may extend off-screen* (i.e., a spectator may imagine how a compositional pattern on screen may be continued off screen) and/or such patterns *may extend over several shots*. The important point is that the graphics of the screen complete a pattern in parallel with the completion of a coherent pattern in the story space. In such a situation, screen space neither directly opposes nor reinforces story space, nor is it neutral; instead, it complements story space. I will therefore call this an "integrated match" between the two shots. It is a moment in which our *top-down* processing of space – our expectation of what an invariant space in the story world should look like under a particular transformation – is smoothly integrated with our *bottom-up* perception of the new shapes on the screen.[57] The virtual space we anticipate in *The 39 Steps* is here amply confirmed whereas the virtual space of *Dr Mabuse, the Gambler* (figs 4–5) was overturned. Nevertheless, a spectator's conjectures about the space of *Dr Mabuse* are not wasted but rather, like the impossibilities of *The Lady from Shanghai*, are re-invested in a more powerful (nondiegetic) hypothesis *about* character and story world. The new hypothesis serves to organize and direct our search for entirely new sorts of data from the screen in succeeding shots.

The integrated match is also a moment when *stylistic metaphors* (i.e., metaphors joining style with story) become especially tempting for the spectator and critic. In the present case, for example, one might speculate that Hannay and the wife are "boxed in," *entrapped* by a husband's murderous jealousy; or that Hannay is being *doubly framed* for a murder he did not commit and a sexual liaison he does not intend; or that the camera's *double look* provides the spectator with greater knowledge than any of the characters but at the cost of making our perception congruent with the villain who places the man we sympathize with, Hannay, in great peril.[58] Moreover, Hitchcock later raises the stakes for there is a sense in which the false appearances turn out not to be false at all and the husband is right to be fearful (a reversal of what we had believed to be reversed): his wife is, in fact, trapped in a loveless marriage, he is inadequate as a husband, and Hannay is a "murderer" of women.[59] We will see in chapter 3 that these sorts of "problem" of perception, and especially the "reversals" of situation discussed in the previous chapter (e.g., Todorov's narrative "transformations"), are essential to any definition of narrative and narration. And we will see in chapters 4 and 5 that the point-of-view shot does not belong entirely to a character but rather is rendered logically possible for the character because of the simultaneous operation of more powerful, non-character narrations that are addressing the spectator by creating and manipulating "views."

One should not think that stylistic metaphors are merely a decorative use of language or a way of talking about what can be quickly verified by examining the screen. The story is not "objective" in this sense. These and other types of interpretive metaphor are being employed by a spectator in the process of comprehension. They provide a way of discovering and fashioning an appropriate story out of the material on the screen. They may be helpful or not helpful in focusing our thought; they may be consistent or inconsistent with other beliefs we hold about the story, or indeed with other beliefs we hold about the fundamental nature of film; but they cannot be right or wrong with respect to a story that is visible on the screen, for a story is created from the top down and is most certainly not visible.

Speaking broadly, then, we can say that screen and story may be related in four types of way. Graphics may exist simply (1) to reinforce the story, or (2) to complete a pattern analogous to a story pattern (as in figs 11 and 13, respectively). These are the ways commonly explored in the so-called classical Hollywood narrative which aims to create continuities between screen and story. By contrast, graphics may (3) be independent of story, or (4) actively oppose its coherence (figs 12 and 10, respectively). These are the ways associated with experimental cinema though they may also be systematically employed in certain narrative films.[60] Although the example from *The 39 Steps* emphasizes space, I believe that screen and story may be related in analogous types of way with respect to time and causality, and furthermore, that textures of sound may be integrated, or variously not integrated, with sounds heard in the story. It is thus only a first approximation to oppose "continuity" to "discontinuity," or even "spatial continuity" to "spatial discontinuity." What must also be kept in mind is the interplay between top-down and bottom-up processes as well as the effect of creating impossible space, impossible time, and/or impossible causality.

The four types of match reveal a basic tension in our comprehension of narrative in film. Our expectation that significant changes in camera angles will be correlated with changing events in the story world potentially conflicts with our actual perception of the two-dimensional plane of the screen which contains those light and dark shapes intended to represent the story world. In a similar way, temporal references in the story may conflict with our sense of the actual duration of the imagery appearing on the screen. Narrativity, or the narrative process, seeks to strike a balance between the demands of three-dimensional and two-dimensional space, between character time and spectator time. This suggests that narrative in general is a function which correlates imagined space-time with perceived space-time. Traces of such an activity may be found in the temporal anomalies and apparent causation of *The Lady from Shanghai*, the virtual space of *Dr Mabuse, the Gambler*, and the fitting together of story and screen in *The 39 Steps*. A narrative cannot avoid in some way telling the story of its own telling, just as the spectator cannot avoid retelling a story which exists less on the screen than in our predisposition to make sense, to apply what we already know from the top down.

3

NARRATION

KNOWING HOW

There are many ways to represent a particular event within a narrative schema. In *The Girl and Her Trust* Grace, clinging to a handcar, is pursued by the hero in a locomotive and finally rescued from the tramps. Griffith decides to represent this simple event through a subtle and intricate series of cross-cuts between the handcar and the locomotive. He could have chosen many other ways to represent the chase and rescue. What effect does Griffith's choice have on our comprehension of the story?

The chase comprises twenty-eight shots arranged into seven groups followed by two shots which end the film showing Grace united with the hero. In each group we see the handcar and the locomotive moving in the same direction on the *screen*: in the first group toward the left, in the second toward the right, then left again, and so on. In the *story* it is clear that the handcar and the locomotive move in only one direction; that is, they do not turn around, circle back, or take short cuts. The changes in direction exist only on the screen as an effect of the narration. The direction of the chase on screen and the number of shots in each group are as follows:

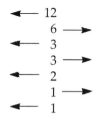

It is apparent that the number of shots in each group decreases proportionately resulting in more frequent changes of direction as the event approaches a climax and resolution. The amount of time each group is on the screen decreases according to the approximate ratio,

$16:16:4:4:4:1:1.$[1] Griffith is careful not to show the actual distance between the handcar and the locomotive until they are progressively brought together in four careful compositions in the final four shots.[2] This allows the rhythm of the editing, rather than the story locale, to direct the way in which we comprehend the chase. We are forced to constantly reassess the distances as we wonder how close the locomotive might be *now* and when Grace might be rescued.[3] Closure for the event is suggested visually by the fact that the camera frames the beginning and end of the chase from similar positions near the tracks and the chase ends in the same direction in which it began. Overall, the simple patterns created on the screen work in parallel with the simple actions and reactions of the participants in the chase to create a feeling of unity and inevitability.[4]

Part of the effect of this chase sequence on a spectator is due to the structure of expectations created by a narrative schema: the heroine's goal reaffirmed, new complicating action on a handcar, the hero's goal of rescuing Grace, an approaching collision of forces, and so forth. The chase sequence illustrates how a narrative schema in general works to create expectations which are clearly defined, validated at several points, directed toward a future outcome, and sharply exclusive (either Grace will protect her trust, be rescued, and fall in love, or else she will not); story time is rendered as a deadline to be met by the hero – stop the tramps before they escape and injure Grace.[5] However, the narrative schema does not account for the total impact on a spectator; part of the effect is due to the particular way in which the event is represented as a visual "spectacle." Christian Metz provides a hint about what is at stake in the Griffith film:

> When [alternating editing] first appeared in early films – and something of this still remains in films of our own time – it was a kind of phantasy of "all-seeingness," of being everywhere at once, having eyes in the back of your head, tending towards a massive condensation of two series of images.[6]

If the world consists of only three things – a girl, a boy, and forces of disruption (another suitor, the tramps) – and the teller of the story has the power to reveal their motives and to show us all three, each in its perfect time, then the teller has all the power in the world, but so also do we. The rhythm of alternation between the handcar and the locomotive forces time into a strict pattern at the same time that we are seemingly everywhere at once. I want to begin to address the ways in which a spectator acquires such power and is implicated in a "phantasy" of seeing where he or she can imagine seeing everything of importance. More generally, how is narrative comprehension affected by the particular way we imagine we are seeing events? How is it possible for us to possess the knowledge we come to possess in a narrative? The answer to these questions is given through the *narration* and so I turn to a closer examination of narration: the conditions under which it operates and its varieties.

Two fundamental concepts are required in order to analyze narration and evaluate competing theories of film narration. The first concept is that narration is concerned with *how* an event is presented, how it happens, rather than *what* is presented or what happens. A "how" question asks about the mechanism which has created a given state or situation and may also seek an "agent" or an agent's "purpose" in bringing about the situation. Although a "how" question may initially be answered in the story by presenting it in the mode of "what" (e.g., by identifying a particular character acting as an agent), such an answer is only provisional. The more important "how" question(s) will concern the very readability of the story and its characters: how is it possible for us to know what happens. By contrast, a "what" question merely asks that a situation or object (who, what, which one) be identified so that it may be referred to and talked about. Narrative – construed narrowly as *what* happens in the story – is then seen as the *object* or end result of some mechanism or process – narration.

We can carry this analysis one step deeper by associating "how" and "what" with two different ways of acting upon knowledge: "knowing how" and "knowing that."[7] It is important to realize that knowing *how* to do something is not reducible to knowing *that* something is the case. Knowing *that* something is round, or a whale, or a mammal, or erroneously called a fish is different than knowing *how* to follow a set of instructions or rules in accomplishing a result; such as, knowing how to apply criteria in determining whether a whale is a mammal, or knowing how to draw a picture of a whale. "Knowing how" involves the exercise of a skill in which something is achieved; it does not involve questions of truth or belief. Procedures may be more or less useful with respect to a purpose but not strictly true or false. (Knowing how to play the piano is neither true nor false.) Wittgenstein referred to such procedural knowledge as "knowing how to go on." Psychologically, "how" and "what" translate into two different types of knowledge: procedural knowledge and declarative (or postulated) knowledge. Of course, both are necessary for one cannot exercise a skill or method without exercising it on something with some result, while knowing *that* something is the case presupposes a procedure which has been exercised in knowing.[8] Applying this distinction to the study of narrative, we may say that narration addresses issues of procedure: *how* are we acquiring knowledge about what is happening in the story? To what degree are various procedures incompatible? Do conflicting interpretations of a text suggest conflicting procedures or points of view at work?

When specific narrative theories are examined in later chapters, we will discover that any complete model of narrative comprehension will need to incorporate both types of knowledge. The real issue will concern what knowledge to represent procedurally and what to represent declaratively, and how different the two formalisms should be that represent these types of knowledge.[9] In watching a film we acquire and exercise skills in managing experiences while at the same time we discover what happens through the exercising of those skills. The study of narration in film is the study of the skills and procedures we apply in order to know narrative events.

DISPARITIES OF KNOWLEDGE

The second fundamental concept that is needed to analyze narration is the notion of a *disparity* of knowledge. Narration comes into being when knowledge is unevenly distributed – when there is a disturbance or disruption in the field of knowledge. Informally, one can grasp the importance of disparity by imagining a universe in which all observers are perfect and all-knowing. In such a universe, there can be no possibility of narration since all information is equally available and already possessed in the same ways. Therefore I will posit that the most basic situation which gives rise to narration will be comprised of three elements: a *subject* in an *asymmetrical* relationship with an *object*. As we shall see, the perceiving "subject" may be a character, narrator, author, the spectator, or some other entity depending on the context that is being analyzed. The situation may be represented graphically as follows:

The vertical line acts as an "obstacle" which creates a disparity, or asymmetry, giving the "subject" a unique access to the "object."

For example, in *The 39 Steps* there is a literal obstacle, the window through which the husband is able to spy on his wife and Hannay, but without being able to hear what they are saying (see figs 8 and 9). This simple situation is used by Hitchcock to create a rather complex distribution of knowledge among the characters and the spectator which reverberates throughout the film creating various shades of truth and falsity. In *The Girl and Her Trust*, Griffith stretches out the action of the tramps surreptitiously watching Grace through a window into a mini-scene of being watched, growing suspicion, mistaken security, new apprehension, discovery, and fear.

It is no accident that flamboyant genres, such as melodramas and television soap operas, are filled with excessive forms of narration whereby characters spy upon, eavesdrop, and gossip about other characters, producing a chain of tellings and retellings based on various disparities. Each retelling manages to be slightly different from preceding ones by provoking differing reactions to the "same" event (outrage, sympathy, envy, puzzlement, scheming). Melodrama often seeks to exhaust a matrix of possible reactions to a single event by exploring differing points of view each of which reconstitutes the "event" in a new light because each is filtered through a different disparity. Comedy, too, often explores a variety of reactions to an event and often by the same person, the comedian.

I would like to offer a more detailed, concrete example of a disparity of knowledge at work in order to demonstrate how narration might be modulated through a spectrum of possibilities for the spectator of a filmed event. I will take as my "subject" character S who is spying around the corner of a building at two characters engaged in conversation, A and B. This entire event will then be represented as an "object" of perception for another subject – the spectator of the film. Just as the corner of the building functions as a barrier between S and A/B, so the motion picture screen functions as a barrier between the spectator and the diegetic world represented in the film. The situation may be depicted graphically as follows:

$$\text{Spectator} \; —— \; \Big|\!\!\xleftarrow{}_{\longrightarrow} \Big\{ \; S \; —— \; \Big|\!\!\xleftarrow{}_{\longrightarrow} A/B \; \Big\}$$

To simplify the discussion, I will make two further assumptions: First, the disparity of information (which is the condition for the narration) will be based only on what the spectator and the characters are able *to see* (not, for example, on what the spectator might hear, or might remember from previous scenes, or might expect because of genre conventions) and, second, the film's manipulation of this visual access to knowledge will be based only on a few variables associated with the *position of the camera*.

Figure 14 is an overhead view of character S looking around the corner of a building at characters A and B in conversation. How might this event be represented for the spectator? The illustration shows a number of alternative camera positions. The problem is to analyze how these camera positions function *to restrict* the spectator's access to visual information by creating different sorts of disparity. Notice that the illustration itself exhibits the principles of narration at work for we are

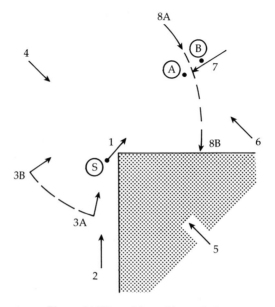

Figure 14 Disparities of knowledge
An overhead view of an event in which character S secretly watches characters
A and B from the corner of a building. Alternative camera set-ups suggest
different ways in which information about the event may be regulated and
distributed among the spectator and characters by creating disparities in a
subject's access to knowledge about an object. Dotted lines indicate camera
movement.

able to measure relative disparities among S, A/B, and the presumed
spectator of the film only because the illustration has been drawn from
an overhead angle which provides us, as readers of this book, a *different*
(visual) access to information than is available to either the presumed
spectator or the characters.

Camera position 1 is a near equivalent of S's view from the corner of
the building – a point-of-view shot. If the image were to be distorted
in some way (e.g., moving in and out of focus), we might as a first
hypothesis attribute the changes in screen space to the perception of
space *by* S (e.g., his tears, anger, or faintness at the sight of A and B).
If it turns out that S *has not yet arrived* at the corner of the building, or
can't bear to look, then the spectator's relationship to the shot with
respect to S's knowledge is entirely different from what was initially
believed. It would then not be judged a point-of-view shot. The *violation*
of this expectation by the film would, in turn, have to be separately
accounted for elsewhere in the epistemological field.

Camera position 2 does not show us A and B. Our knowledge of the
situation is *restricted* to what can be learned by watching S's reaction.

Camera position 3 begins like that of 2 but through camera movement ends by showing the spectator the precise relationship of S to A and B. This camera movement transforms screen duration into a story rhetoric of question and answer (what does S see?) followed by suspense (will A or B see S?). Although camera position 3B is not a point-of-view shot, it very nearly represents S's angle of view and distance to A and B, and hence our inferences about causality and action will develop in a context similar to that of S.[10] Note that other devices would measure out this knowledge of space and causality differently: an eyeline match would instantaneously frame the answer to the above questions while a somewhat broader use of juxtapositions, based on the competing intentions and goals of several characters, would yield the cross-cutting Griffith used in representing the chase in *The Girl and Her Trust*.

Camera position 4 will be referred to as the "best possible," or "perfect," view of the event since it simultaneously shows the spectator both S and A/B, each in a complete spatial and temporal context.[11] It is meant to show us everything of importance from the best possible angle. By contrast, position 5 is a perfect but "impossible" view.[12] It could be inside the building (if the walls become "transparent") or else underground (if the ground becomes "transparent") or suspended overhead. It is perfect, but "impossible" because it represents a position and view which no character in the diegetic world can possess.

Camera position 6 does not show us S. It is the inverse of position 2 and we must rely on the reactions of A and B to learn about the event. We do not yet know, for instance, if S is present. Position 7 is a shot of A over-the-shoulder of B. It is nearly the inverse of position 1. Whether S is seen in the background or is blocked by A's body, one of the questions posed by this articulation is whether B has noticed or will notice S, and how that will affect what is said to A.

Position 8 begins as a "best possible" view but only of A and B in conversation; it ends with the camera inexplicably moving away from this event in order to explore a wall of the building.[13] The spectator is thus faced with a sudden loss of information in favor of new information which may or may not be meaningful using S, A, and B as coordinates.

Filmmakers have employed all of the above ways of articulating disparities of knowledge, and many others, in order to elaborate significant patterns by which to develop and know an "object." A specific narrational device is only partially defined by technical criteria (e.g., the position of the camera); more important is an assessment of its relative "power to expand and contract perception." Narration is ultimately a way of making knowledge "intermittent"[14] and hence what is described in figure 14 is not a list of the elementary building blocks of visual narration but a set of possibilities for controlling time, for regulating our access to a fluctuating field of information. A point-of-view shot, for instance, or a camera position revealing the "best possible" view, must actually *transform knowledge* in a specified way for the spectator. The function of such camera set-ups cannot be determined strictly from the position of the camera but will also depend on broader (top-down) considerations which define knowledge and pertinence, including a narrative schema which defines characters who may have a sequence of views, and whose particular goals and actions may be *seen through their eyes* or *best seen* in a certain way (while other goals and actions will not be perfectly seen or known). A character's goal is seldom as simple as "looking toward" an object but more often includes a reason for looking, and the anticipated consequences of having seen. A spectator's assessment of these factors is a crucial part of what the spectator sees when he or she looks at a character. Thus in naming the camera set-ups of figure 14, I am only describing familiar or initial interpretations – conventions of seeing in film which may be revised or overturned in the proper circumstances when more is known about the events. To speak of a "convention" in this way is merely shorthand for the fact that a spectator must risk some hypothesis and *take on faith* that subsequent events will justify the interpretation; a "best possible" view, for example, must actually turn out to be such with respect to the narrative goals and actions of the characters, with respect to a sequence of events, with respect to the value system of the epilogue, and so forth. Even the point-of-view shot which appears to be formally precise because of its camera positioning is excessively fragile and depends on broad forms of knowledge to establish the pertinence of the camera positioning. The reason that certainty cannot be achieved through a limited empirical testing of the data on the screen (e.g., by locating the position of the camera) is that *any* spatial, temporal, and causal configuration *may denote any other* configuration, given the proper conditions. An apparent point-of-view shot, for example, may represent merely a view from very near a character's head, or represent what would have been seen if the character's eyes were open, or represent how a distant character imagines that he or she *might be seen* by another, or represent what might have been seen from that position if a character were not standing there.[15]

Let's alter slightly the event represented in figure 14 so as to highlight the temporal element of narration and include new types of information. Character S is now in a room with character A who is speaking on the telephone with character B. How might this event be represented for the spectator of the film? The most important obstacle that motivates the distribution of knowledge in this scene is the telephone. Therefore one method of presenting the event would be to intercut shots of A speaking on the phone with shots of B in a distant locale speaking on the phone. In this way we might come to know more than *any* of the three characters since A and B cannot *see* each other while we can see everyone's actions and hear everyone's words. This method is similar to the cross-cutting of *The Girl and Her Trust* during the chase sequence.

A second method would be to present shots of A and S, coupled with the voice of A talking on the phone. Suppose we do not actually hear what B is saying or see B; and perhaps his or her identity is withheld from us. In this situation our knowledge is restricted to what S, or perhaps an invisible witness in the room, might come to know about A's telephone conversation. Other factors in the scene would determine more exactly what knowledge we were able to acquire.

A third method would be to present close shots of A, coupled with the voice of B *as heard through* the telephone in A's hand. Here our knowledge is "subjective" in some measure because it is roughly congruent with *some* of the key information available to A to the exclusion of S who cannot hear what B is saying. (There are, of course, many *degrees* of character subjectivity: A's thoughts are not being represented, A's view of the telephone receiver is not shown, and so forth.) These three methods of presenting the event are entirely different and potentially *may make a difference* in how we understand the story. They may *not* make a difference, of course, if the filmmaker switches among them indifferently, or the story is not concerned with basic problems of knowledge and belief.

The example of the telephone conversation illustrates that narrative information acquired by the spectator cannot be evaluated in the abstract as to its quantity or relevance. Do we need to hear what B is saying, or do we learn more by watching A's behavior, or seeing S's reaction? What is the proper camera distance or angle to represent an object? In order to analyze the effects of narration, we first need to posit an epistemological boundary, or barrier (with respect to a narrative schema), then measure its changes, and then evaluate its interaction with the next boundary to appear. These boundaries, of course, need not correspond with material or onscreen divisions, such as the appearance of a new shot, decor, or camera movement. We cannot decide in advance the precise contours of a boundary nor can we state that only three boundaries are possible when only three characters are in the scene. For example, the following are some additional non-character sources of knowledge that could be part of the representing of the above event: a musical chord coupled with the expression on a character's face that "tells" us all we need to know; or, a "tell-tale" glance; or, a narrator's whispered commentary on what B must be saying on the telephone to A; or, a pattern of editing that shows A and B *but not* at the "best possible" or "perfect" time; or, especially unusual, a shot of A but matched with the sound of A's voice *as heard through the telephone by B* in a distant (unseen) locale.[16] Consider also the representation of

71

the following two telephone conversations in Jean-Luc Godard's *Sauve qui peut (la vie)* (*Every Man For Himself*, 1980):

1 We see and hear Denise speaking to Paul on the phone but the next shot does not show him talking on the phone, but instead speaking to someone else in a room (before, or after, Denise's phone call?). We cannot hear what is being said; we hear only nondiegetic music which is interrupted by Denise's voice continuing her phone conversation with Paul. We cut back to Denise still speaking on the phone, and then return to Paul who is now seen talking with Denise on the phone, continuing the same conversation. He is in the room where we previously saw him. The scene ends when Paul hands the phone to Yvette and asks her to finish the conversation with Denise for him. Yvette in her own voice converses with Denise but is saying what we imagine Paul might have said to Denise (or is she reciting for us what Paul actually did say to Denise to end the conversation?).
2 Paul gets up from a table in a restaurant to make a phone call. Cut to a very brief shot of Denise answering the phone and cut back to Paul already reseated at the table. We then hear Denise say, "Hello." Paul then talks about Denise with his companions in the restaurant.

The last several examples of unusual depictions of phone conversations illustrate that while a given narration may be familiar, or seem natural, or be consistent with previous scenes, it can, in fact, be only one of many ways of knowing an event, and only one of many ways an event may be told.

HIERARCHIES OF KNOWLEDGE

It should be clear from previous examples that the problem of describing narration becomes increasingly complex as one adds variables associated with character action, *mise-en-scène*, editing and dialogue, and considers their change *through time*. One must also expand the notion of a spectator's "knowledge" beyond immediate "seeing" to include various effects produced by the sound track, our *memory* of previous scenes, anticipated pleasure or anxiety, generic and cultural expectations, and so forth. Thus the knowledge we acquire need not coincide with "visual" forms of knowledge nor on-screen knowledge even in simple cases. For example, our ability to learn from a conversation between characters may not be attributable to the position occupied by the camera. We may seem to hear from a diegetic place distant from the camera (e.g., from a point closer to the conversation so that the words are more distinct) or from a place we never see which is evidence that *another* disparity, which is not visible, has been put into play allowing us a unique access to the object *different from* the nominal visual access.

Or, we may *not* hear what the visual position would allow. For example, in *The 39 Steps* the camera position of figure 8 from inside the house should allow us to hear the conversation between the wife and Hannay even though the husband cannot hear it. The sound track, however, is silent (without even music) because the disparity selected to be represented is that associated with the husband who is outside the house; in this case, *not* being able to hear helps us to define the actual disparity that underlies the representation of the event.

Theorists have proposed many sorts of schemes by which to analyze the fine details of disparities (i.e., epistemological boundaries) within texts. George Wilson proposes that narration be analyzed along three axes: the relative epistemic *distance* from our usual habits of perception and common-sense beliefs (including our knowledge of film conventions); the degree of epistemic *reliability* or justification for the inferences that we draw from the "visual manifolds" of film; and the epistemic *authority* or degree of alignment between audience knowledge and character knowledge (or other source of knowledge).[17] David Bordwell proposes that narration be analyzed along five axes: the *range* of knowledge (more or less restricted) presented to the spectator and its *depth* (more or less subjective); the degree of *self-consciousness* by which the narration addresses the audience (whether direct address or more covert); the degree of *communicativeness* shown by the narration, that is, how willingly it shares the information to which its degree of knowledge entitles it; and the *judgmental* attitudes shown by the narration (ranging from mockery to compassion).[18] My present purpose is not to appraise these sorts of scheme, but to establish the reasons why theorists identify "narration" as a special area of inquiry within a spectator's overall comprehension of narrative.

While the above categories of narration exploit an analogy with literal measurements ("distance," "depth," "alignment"), they are actually broader in scope and must be evaluated with entirely different procedures of inference, and within a very different time frame, than the split seconds of (bottom-up) spatial perception. In general, the spectator knows and anticipates much more than the information available on the screen at any point in a film. The spectator is subject to an array of (sometimes competing) clusters of knowledge and thus is in a very different epistemological "place" than the camera or the microphone.[19] This situation resembles the complexity attributed to perception by a modular description of mind (separate functions, often competing and unable to "communicate").[20] It is also consistent with the notion of an "unconscious" self which is deemed to be constructed and contradictory rather than unified: "I think where I am not and I am where I do not think."[21] In the next chapter we will discover that in order to analyze narration even more precisely, it will be necessary to distinguish several, potentially conflicting narrations which operate simultaneously on different "levels" of the discourse with varying degrees of explicitness, and are addressed to different disparities or contexts in which knowledge is being acquired (or rejected) by the spectator. First, however, we must examine disparity in greater detail.

Colin MacCabe has proposed that classical narratives are composed of a "hierarchy of discourses" which aim to place the spectator in a position of superior knowledge by using the camera to equate vision with truth.[22] A hierarchy permits the spectator to make judgments and to measure relative truth moment by moment. At the end of the story, for example, the spectator is finally able to solve all the enigmas of character and action because the structure of disparities responsible for managing the partial truths of the plot becomes known through the camera. Thus one function of a graded hierarchy is to conceal and delay the end of the story by presenting the events through "less knowledgeable" agencies (e.g., characters) at appropriate moments. Higher levels of the hierarchy are meant to be concealed from the spectator who is to witness partial truths developing into moral imperatives by seeing only the characters and the diegesis. By contrast, for MacCabe, "radical" narratives are constructed on the basis of unstable hierarchies in which the spectator alternately identifies with, and then is alienated or "separated" from, diegetic events. Some of the higher-level discourses may be made explicit early in a radical film. In this way the spectator is able to gain a critical "distance" from the hierarchy and its other "discourses," and so appreciate the "social and psychoanalytic" dimensions of being part of a community which uses specific discourses in thinking about the world.

The notion of a hierarchy is also a way of talking about the organization of a group of disparities whereby some perceivers are represented as acquiring more accurate knowledge about certain events relative to other perceivers. Ben Brewster has asserted that "changes of viewpoint" in a narrative "make possible hierarchies of relative knowledge for characters and spectators." He shows how early Griffith films create an "asymmetry of awareness" or "pyramid of knowledge."[23] Applying his notion to *The Girl and Her Trust*, we may say that in global terms the spectator is accorded a position of superior knowledge with the characters arranged in descending order as follows:

1 Spectator
2 Tramps (early events)
3 Grace
4 Tramps (later events)
5 Hero.[24]

Another way to measure relative knowledge is to evaluate whether the spectator knows more than ($>$), the same as ($=$), or less than ($<$) a particular character at a particular time. Although this is a crude measure for it says nothing about types or degrees of knowledge, it has the merit of suggesting broadly how the spectator is being asked to respond to a given narrative situation. Knowledge is linked to response as follows:

$S > C$ suspense
$S = C$ mystery
$S < C$ surprise

Alfred Hitchcock conceived his films in this way. Using the example of a bomb placed in a briefcase under a table, he explained how he could create feelings of suspense, mystery, or surprise in the audience. If the spectator knows about the bomb, but not the characters seated around the table, then the spectator will be in suspense and must anxiously await the bomb's discovery or explosion. If the spectator and a character both know that there is something mysterious about the briefcase but do not know its secret, then the spectator's curosity is aroused. Finally, if the spectator does not know about the bomb or the briefcase, then he or she is in for a shock. Hitchcock recognized that these effects can be intensified according to what we know about a character and our emotional involvement with him or her. He realized that there is a close relationship between a spectator's wish to know, and his or her wishful involvement with situations and persons in a film.[25]

One can compare the relative knowledge of subjects other than the spectator and a character in order to evaluate how the story is being disclosed moment by moment. For instance, a *narrator's* knowledge of an event may be greater than, the same as, or less than that of a particular character at a particular time. Such a comparison leads to additional typologies of narration besides introducing new complexities.[26] For example, in the next chapter we will see that some important narrators are only *implicit* in the text, that is, their "presence" must be inferred and constructed by the spectator. The knowledge possessed by an implicit narrator is thus difficult to compare with the knowledge of a character. Also, an implicit narrator who is not directly seen or heard, such as an implied author, raises a theoretical problem about narration: Is a narrator to be thought of as a real person, or instead as merely the personification of an abstract textual process? If it is decided that only an explicit narrator can be thought of as a real person, then defining what counts as "explicit" becomes crucial. (How explicit are the following narrations: fictional speech, an anonymous voice-over commentary, a written title containing sentences in the third-person, an eccentric camera angle?)

When one chooses to measure the spectator's knowledge by

comparing it with the knowledge of an implicit narrator, one can readily see that the notions of suspense, mystery, and surprise may be generalized and related more broadly to the manipulation of a spectator's expectations and to shifts in his or her attention. Thus narration in the widest sense may be defined as follows:

> Narration is the overall regulation and distribution of knowledge which determines *how* and when the spectator acquires knowledge, that is, how the spectator is able to know what he or she comes to know in a narrative. A typical description of the spectator's "position" of knowledge includes the invention of (sometimes tacit) speakers, presenters, listeners, and watchers who are in a (spatial and temporal) position to know, and to make use of one or more *disparities* of knowledge. Such "persons" are convenient fictions which serve to mark how the field of knowledge is being divided at a particular time.

It is evident that specific accounts of narration have many decisions to make. What is the status of "style"? In what ways do the stylistic devices of a given medium open up or constrain our abilities to acquire knowledge? What "abilities" of the spectator are to be included in deciding how the spectator is "able to know" something? How sensitive to context is seeing? Or, for that matter, hearing, prior knowledge, memory, anticipation, desire, gender, and social class? Moreover, knowledge cannot exist in a vacuum; it must be made "worthwhile" with respect to a use or purpose, otherwise it is not recognized. Thus in addressing how knowledge may be possessed, one must also address the desire to know, and the importance of knowing relative to a frame of action. I believe that the text, and its implicit "contexts," should be analyzed as a set of interacting "levels" or "strata" analogous to, but more complex than, the pyramid of character knowledge discussed above. The proliferation of disparities of knowledge creates a multiplicity of involvements for the spectator. The multiple disparities of narration break down the impression that a film narrative is a mere photographic record of a real environment.[27] Instead, references are generated which are only partially determined in contexts not yet fully known, leaving to the spectator the task of anticipating and constructing the various frames of reference that will be appropriate to an understanding of a world not yet seen.

NICK FURY AS AN EXAMPLE

So far I have examined narration in a rather artificial way either by describing the narration after the narrative has ended (a hierarchy of relative knowledge), or else by isolating a few moments of a narrative event (e.g., a glimpse from the corner of a building, figure 14; a phone conversation; a spectator's response of suspense, mystery, or surprise). I would now like to consider some dynamic properties of narration by looking at a short sequence in which narrative space, time, and causation are more extensively developed for a spectator. The sequence comprises the first sixteen panels of a comic book adventure featuring Nick Fury, Agent of SHIELD which could easily have been a storyboard for a film.[28] I will first simply trace *what* happens.

A man climbs up a fortress-like structure. In the moonlight we recognize him as Nick Fury. He climbs down into the fortress through a vent, cuts through a door, and discovers a robot guard. He throws a coin onto the floor, and when the robot bends down to pick it up, Nick swiftly knocks him unconscious with a kick to the head. Meanwhile another robot is rising up through a secret trapdoor in the floor behind Nick. Caught unawares, Nick is shot dead.

These events could be represented in many different ways and still be understood to refer to the same "focused chain" of actions as defined through a particular application of a narrative schema.[29] The "center" which gives the chain its focus is, of course, Nick Fury. When the panels are interpreted in this manner (as opposed to other, nonnarrative interpretations), a host of elements are understood as merely *parts* of larger, directed movements. Although all the elements in the panels are significant, the elements are not all equally significant. For example, in panels 3 and 4, the pipe on the roof, Nick's rope and blue uniform, and his action of climbing into the vent are seen as merely initial conditions and initiating actions toward larger goals. Moreover, there is no reason to doubt that the character in the shadows in panel 4 is the same one we saw in 3; or that panel 8 continues the action of 7. These are the sorts of effect produced by a narrative schema which works to generate a focused, causal chain as opposed to, for example, a *catalogue* of Nick's arm movements which would organize the panels in a quite different way. However, rather than examining what the narrative schema has accomplished, I want to concentrate on *how* the spectator is being asked to use the narrative schema to build up a scene through partitioning and embedding a series of actions on various scales of space, time, and causality. How has the spectator been encouraged and constrained moment by moment in achieving a large-scale structure with which to represent the 16 panels as a single narrative event?

Consider the "camera" positions through which the spectator builds the experiences of Nick Fury. In panel 1 we are so close to the action that paradoxically we cannot decide what the action is: is someone climbing a wall, or pulling on two handles, or hanging helplessly? Though it would seem to be almost a point-of-view shot (because of the position of the hands), we have no idea who the person is or what

Figure 15 Nick Fury (panels 1–4)

Figure 16 Nick Fury (panels 5–8)

Figure 17 Nick Fury (panels 9–12)

Figure 18 Nick Fury (panels 13–16)

he or she looks like or even if this is what the person is looking at. Normal schema order – orientation followed by initiating event – is violated, resulting in a delay in recognizing the situation. Panel 2 begins to answer some of these questions while posing new ones, but its framing goes to the opposite extreme: radically external to the event from an improbable overhead position; that is, from a place no character is likely to occupy – a god's eye view (cf. panels 1 and 2 with set-ups 1 and 5 in figure 14). These extremes seem to promise the spectator that a storyteller is in command of a vast range of information from the intimate to the grand, and that all important information will be provided. Yet these somewhat arbitrary extremes of framing also seem to be a warning that the story will be marked by sudden turns of events and even *deceptive* storytelling.[30] The spectator should anticipate the pleasure of *being surprised*; the question is how and when.

Panels 3–9 establish new, temporary limits on what can be known by putting the spectator back inside diegetic space and time as encountered by Nick Fury. The representation of space and time in this segment of the story is loosely restricted to what Nick knows and when he knows it (i.e., in narratological terms events are *focalized*[31] through Nick), and his central role is confirmed by another near point-of-view shot (panel 9). This pattern, however, is being established only to be suddenly broken.

Panel 10 represents a break in the narration. For the first time we do not see Nick. Where is he? Is it important that we don't see him, or is it merely an "objective" view of the robot bending down? Will we return to Nick, and if so, how? The lack of background detail and the uncertainty of where the coin lands in the previous panel leaves the spatial orientation of panel 10 indefinite and fuzzy so that whatever we first believe about the space seems sufficient to comprehend the event.[32] In the next panel, however, Nick seems to come from out of nowhere to deliver a knockout blow to the robot. Nick is now *ahead* of events, and too fast for us. He has, in fact, emerged from out of the *foreground* of panel 10, from the very *position* of the camera! We did not see that the robot had turned around (between panels 9 and 10, as it were) in order to bend down toward the coin.[33] Our perception of the robot bending down became a blind spot to be exploited by the next panel. In this case our view of the robot cannot have been an objective view, but must have been still another point-of-view shot which is abruptly terminated in panel 11 by Nick's knockout blow to the robot. The spectator's perception of the event has been carefully embedded in the perceiving of the event by a character, and then apparently relaxed, but only to be explosively reasserted.

Panel 13 represents another break in the narration, but one more serious in relation to the story. A second robot is suddenly revealed pointing a weapon. Where is this robot? What is happening? More importantly, where is Nick? Again, clues are suppressed by the lack of background detail.[34] The final panels show Nick being surprised from behind and killed. Thus within the story Nick has been shown to know more than the first robot but less than the second. These disparities of knowledge may be diagrammed as follows:

$$\text{2nd Robot} > \text{Nick} > \text{1st Robot}$$

or:

2nd Robot $\longrightarrow \left|\begin{array}{c}\longleftarrow\\\longrightarrow\end{array}\right.\left\{\begin{array}{c}\text{Nick} \longrightarrow \left|\begin{array}{c}\longleftarrow\\\longrightarrow\end{array}\right. \text{1st Robot}\end{array}\right\}$

It is evident that *choices are being made* for the spectator by presenting the events in one way rather than another. After all, the second robot could have been shown earlier hiding under the floor which would have altered our relationship to Nick and his actions even though it would not have altered the outcome. (The spectator would feel suspense; Nick would seem less invincible.) Broadly speaking, the spectator's knowledge has been presented as equal to Nick's – producing "mystery" – in panels 1–12 and greater than Nick's – producing "suspense" – in panels 13–16. These responses, however, have been punctuated by moments of insufficient knowledge and surprise in panels 1, 11, and 13. Thus what initially appears as a smooth string of events is actually composed of a rapid oscillation in the balance of knowledge. Roland Barthes suggests that classical narration in literature "alternates the personal and the impersonal very rapidly . . . so as to produce . . . a proprietary consciousness which retains the mastery of what it states without participating in it.[35] In order to describe the effects associated with such an oscillation, one must specify a *reference point*. Thus when the first robot bends down in panel 10, the spectator feels suspense *with respect to* the robot (i.e., we know more than it does) but mystery or surprise *with respect to* Nick. The ambiguity of our response with respect to Nick is then forcefully resolved in the next panel as Nick is shown capable of taking us by surprise. We did not know as much about him as we thought; or rather, he has demonstrated what we had hoped such a hero could do. The chain of events in the first 9 panels, encouraging us to use Nick as a reference point rather than an unknown robot, has been validated.

Curiously, there is a moment in the story which reveals an almost pure movement of narration – where knowledge is being shifted and realigned but nothing else is happening. Consider the space of panel 12 which seems to halt the story. We see Nick's shadow falling gracefully across a door as he stands offscreen, pensive, dreamy, unmoving. This is the sort of transitional moment that Barthes calls a "catalyst."

He argues that it is of great importance in a narrative because it acts to maintain contact with the spectator. A catalyst addresses the spectator's interest and attention by enhancing, accelerating, or (here) slowing down an event but without altering its course.[36] It encourages a spectator to remain attentive by relating fascinating but minor incidents, or by providing additional description and detail (perhaps even offering a spectacle). It sums up, anticipates, and promises further significant events. (By contrast, a "nucleus" for Barthes is an action which determines or constitutes a causal sequence; adding or deleting a nucleus would alter the course of events.) Panel 12 seems to hint that there is something important on the other side of the door. Also, Nick's shadow on the door captures our attention by asking us to pause and admire the beauty of the composition, the harmony of angle and color, the mastery and brilliance of the artist who has drawn it. But equally important for the narration is the fact that the door and the shadow are an elaborate decoy! We are looking in exactly the wrong direction. The door and the shadow are *not* significant in the way that the previous panels have been; what is important is a new robot rising up through the floor tiles behind Nick – a robot who is not seen because we are busy admiring a shadow. We have been misled by a view of the action.[37] The shadow must now be reinterpreted, perhaps reclassified as some type of "symbol" that prefigures an epilogue brought on by Nick's untimely death and the end of the causal sequence. Again we must pause and wonder what Nick has really meant to us.

Nick's shadow illustrates two crucial facts about narration that we've already encountered. First, narration involves *concealing* information as much as revealing it. Secondly, the function of narration – what it conceals and reveals – cannot be fully determined in advance by bottom-up processing, or by comparing it against formal criteria (e.g., shot or camera position). Despite initial appearances, the view of the shadow on the door is neither the best view of the action nor the view of the second robot (cf. panel 12 with 14) nor the view of an "invisible witness" at the scene nor even Nick's view (why should he, or a witness, pause to marvel at a shadow?). Narration is determined by a flow of knowledge, not by surface features of a text. Moreover, a flow of knowledge means that some knowledge is excluded and not shown. One of the tasks of a narrative theorist is to provide a set of terms and categories with which to uncover the distribution of knowledge in a text and define the logic which moves our thinking through a series of phases. I have used these panels to demonstrate that the logic of recognizing, for example, a detail within its setting (panels 1 and 2), or an exterior space adjoining an interior one (panels 7 and 8), or sudden changes in our inferences about story time (cf. panels 5 and 6 with 10 and 11, and with 12 and 13) is no less special and exact than a point-of-view articulation (panels 8 and 9). As figure 14 demonstrates, each moment of the story has the potential of opening new ways for the spectator to acquire knowledge and solve perceptual problems. A theory of narration must define this ongoing potential for meaning and specify the effects of what is actualized.

Although Nick is apparently dead in panel 16, we cannot accept this pause in the action as a resolution for the story as a whole. The narration has presented Nick throughout as strong, acrobatic, resourceful, courageous, and pensive while the second robot seems to be merely a vicious coward. Nick has come to an inappropriate end; a more complete explanation must be offered. When the story continues (after a full-page advertisement), a narrative schema again dictates the rhythm: the spectator is reoriented, exposition is given, a new initiating event occurs, and so on. Previous events are transformed and reversed. We learn that the "Nick Fury" who penetrated the fortress was, in fact, only a robot; the real Nick Fury was disguised as the robot who emerged through the floor and was forced to shoot "himself." Even more surprising is the fact that someone else was in the room waiting to kill Nick and, fooled by the robot, also shot and killed "Nick Fury." This other person was not seen by us, the robot guard, or by either of the two Nick Furys. He or she must certainly be powerful, cunning, and dangerous. The only clue to this person's identity is a tiny disk left behind with a scorpion engraved on it . . .

As the story continues, our former knowledge is entirely recast. We knew much less than we imagined and will need to know much more. The first sixteen panels, however, are not rendered irrelevant by the new events nor were our initial interpretations simply a mistake; rather, the first sixteen panels embodied a phase of our thinking about the story. By rationalizing step by step its method for knowing a story world, narration confronts a spectator in the most profound and subtle way with a representation of what that world is or might be, what it might become, and how other, similar worlds might be found.

FORGETTING AND REVISING

As a spectator engages the procedures which yield a story world, something extraordinary occurs: his or her memory of the actual images, words, and sounds *is erased* by the acts of comprehension that they require.[38] Comprehension proceeds by cancelling and discarding data actually present, by revising and remaking what is given. A new representation is created which is not a copy of the original stimuli nor an imperfect memory of it. In comprehending a narrative, the spectator routinely sees what is not present and overlooks what is present.[39] For example, the viewer of *Nick Fury* probably does not notice that the floor tiles of panels 9, 12, and 14 have disappeared in panel 16; or that the shoulder strap of the second robot mysteriously changes shoulders in panels 14, 15, and 16; or that color schemes change drastically from panel to panel.[40] In *The Girl and Her Trust* a truly startling range of "mismatches" that are plainly visible are seldom noticed even by experienced viewers.[41] Recall also the "impossible" causation of *The Lady from Shanghai*, the virtual space of *Dr Mabuse, the Gambler*, and the integrated match of *The 39 Steps*. All these effects rely upon, or else counter the conventions of, a so-called "transparency" or "invisibility" of classical texts. Defining "transparency" in film, however, has proven no easier than defining it in semantics (where it is entangled with questions of synonymy and modal logic). Transparency may be achieved for a spectator even when continuity conventions (e.g., "invisible" editing) are violated, or may not be achieved when continuity conventions are adopted.[42] This demonstrates once more that such effects cannot be explained simply by formal and technical criteria but require a theory of top-down processing in human perception.

Many explanations have been offered for transparency effects ranging from the purely perceptual (based on the fact that visual illusions and constancies are part of everyday perception) to the psychical (e.g., deferred revision, repression, and hallucination) and the ideological (e.g., "false consciousness"). In some theories transparency and invisibility become faintly sinister because they are believed to promote a dangerous illusionism which, in turn, may be complicitous with custom, ordinary language, narrative, and/or art. Certain anti-narrative devices, e.g. reflexivity, irony, paradox, contradiction, novelty, or alienation, may be prescribed to provide a critical and intellectual distance ("opacity") that frees the viewer from delusion.

Alan Williams addresses the issue of transparency by arguing that when we watch a narrative film we are actually watching four films: a celluloid strip of material; a projected image with recorded sound; a coherent event in three-dimensional space; and finally a story we remember (i.e., the film we think we have seen).[43] There are perceptual "gaps" between each of these four films in which certain facts are concealed and "forgotten" about one film in order to perceive another. For example, the perception of movement in the projected image depends on not seeing the individual frames on the celluloid strip which do not move (or do not move in the same way). By contrast, if some of these same facts separating the films were emphasized, the spectator could not so easily substitute one "film" for another with the result, presumably, that a new critical distance as well as new kinds of reference would be possible. Although the notion that watching a film entails watching several films is one that is open to interpretion, it is a natural consequence of a theory of mind based on modularity and levels of structure.[44]

Using Williams's four films, narration could be defined quite broadly by simply saying that narration is the process that operates to transform one "film" into the next. Nevertheless, we seldom define narration in such a sweeping way, preferring instead to limit it to processes operating near the "remembered film." The reason is that we seem to resist the idea that a film projector could be conceived of as a "narrator" who transforms celluloid into moving images. We resist personifying a machine in this way perhaps because a narrative schema emphasizes goals and characters, and we naturally expect that such goals and characters have been produced for us by other, albeit concealed, agents with similar goals and human-like qualities. However, we are less successful in resisting the urge to personify the camera as an "eye" perhaps because the camera seems to act from within the diegesis in proximity to the goals of characters.[45] Therefore, in general, an important issue for a narrative theory will concern how narration should be connected to an explicit human activity and which metaphors should be selected to pose the connection. For example, one may choose to say simply that a screenwriter "communicates," or a director "intends," or a community value is "expressed" in narrating. Still another possibility explored by some narrative theories is the rather startling belief that the spectator is the narrator. In this approach to narration, the spectator both identifies with, and misrecognizes, only himself or herself in the perceiving of the "remembered film." Such concepts as "narrator," "character," and "implied author" (and perhaps even "camera") are then merely *convenient labels* used by the spectator in marking epistemological boundaries, or disparities, within an ensemble of knowledge; or rather, the labels become convenient in responding to narrative.

In order better to understand the commitments of specific narrative theories to human activities, we must investigate such terms as author, narrator, voice, viewing, camera, character, narratee, and invisible witness. The next chapter will demonstrate how narrative theories seek to explain narration by breaking it into constituent parts. We shall see that for some theories, the parts will merely open new gaps and indeterminacies, open new kinds of "films" within the film. These kinds of gap will reaffirm a tension and conflict internal to texts (and to perceiving, and perceivers). The resulting conflicts can never be totally resolved but at best can only be concealed anew by an arbitrary "end" to the story, and in the widest sense, by an arbitrary end to language and perception.

4

LEVELS OF NARRATION

EIGHT LEVELS

Perception must occur within boundaries and limits: perception *of* what *under* which conditions? It is not enough to simply locate film comprehension under the general conditions imposed by the projection of a strip of celluloid containing photographic transparencies and recorded sound. More and finer distinctions about perceptual "contexts" will be required in order to understand how our understanding of narrative proceeds. The basic organization of events into a narrative pattern is directed by a narrative schema. However, as the focus of inquiry shifts from "what happens" to the "how and when" of our knowing what happens, a deeper narrational schema will be found setting the conditions for, and directing, the operation of a narrative schema. These conditions may change from moment to moment. Colin MacCabe's "hierarchy of discourses," Ben Brewster's "hierarchies of relative knowledge," and Alan Williams's "four films" can all be interpreted as attempts to define suitable contexts, or *levels*, within which specific mental operations will be successful in organizing aural and visual data into a narrative pattern of events. Levels of a text are postulated in order to explain how data is systematically recast by the spectator from one perceptual context to another. What is remembered and what is forgotten by a spectator is systematic, not accidental. Generally the spectator engages the text in multiple ways, assuming a variety of roles for different contexts at different times. In order to delineate the various roles that specify how information may be acquired and shaped into a narrative pattern, we will need a new vocabulary.

Susan Lanser, drawing on the work of many theorists, has proposed a hierarchy of roles, or levels, which describe typical ways that a reader participates in a literary text. An actual text may be described according to how it shifts among these levels to build a hierarchy (or other configuration) of relative knowledge. In figure 19, I have expanded Lanser's basic levels from six to eight and represented them as positions on a

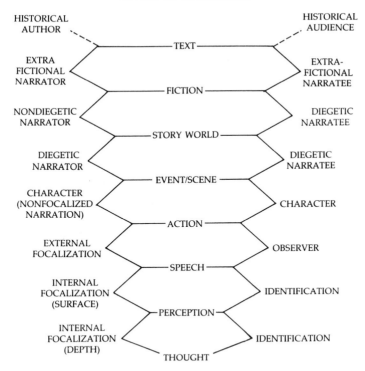

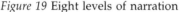

Figure 19 Eight levels of narration
A text is composed of a hierarchical series of levels of narration, each defining
an epistemological context within which to describe data. A particular text
may define any number of levels to any degree of precision along a continuum
from the internal dynamics of a character to a representation of the historical
conditions governing the manufacture of the artifact itself.

continuum rather than as sharply exclusive alternatives.[1] I will now
examine these levels in relation to film comprehension.

I will define a "text" as a certain *collection of descriptions of an artifact*
where the artifact must be one that materializes a symbol system, and
the descriptions that are offered of it must be sanctioned by a society.[2]
Thus a "text" is more than the material of an artifact and more than
the symbols materialized; a text is always subject to change according
to a social consensus about the nature of the symbols that have been
materialized.

The concept of a "historical author" of a text has a similar complexity:
part psychological, part social. As for the psychological, Roland Barthes
observes, "The one *who speaks* (in the narrative) is not the one *who writes*
(in real life) and the one *who writes* is not the one *who is*."[3] An author,
however, exists not only as a biographical person, or persons, who has
created a text, but also as a cultural *legend* created by texts (i.e., under

one or more descriptions).[4] Being an author is performing for/in a social group. For example, Alfred Hitchcock as an individual is defined by the events of his life, traits of his personality, the labor he expended in making films, his view of himself, and the shaping influences of his time. He is one of the text's first critics. With respect to the "historical audience," however, he is also a character, or legend of the time. The audience knows Hitchcock on the basis of popular beliefs about him and by virtue of sharing with him certain kinds of knowledge about society. Hitchcock's public persona (which he alertly helped to author) is composed of his famous profile, a bit of theme music, television monologues, interviews, publicity, cameo appearances in his films, and so on. As a result his name has become a *brand name* guaranteeing a certain kind of experience: "Alfred Hitchcock's" *Vertigo* promises suspense, obsession, deceit, ambivalence, mordant wit, violence, and sexual malaise. We bring this "Hitchcock" with us to the theater because we are members of his community and use his name in describing certain artifacts. In this sense, "Hitchcock" is not only the one "who writes" for an audience, but also the one "who is written by" his audience.

A text emerges, then, from a historical situation that presupposes a social consensus about artifacts and biographical authors. All texts have such a *non*fictional dimension: films are made with materials and labor, marketed, and have measurable social and psychological effects; costs are incurred. However, films may also exist as interpreted fictionally, and may even explicitly address the problem of interpreting a world fictionally. Thus there must exist a transitional level that mediates between nonfiction and fiction. In order to avoid contradiction and paradox, then, statements *about* an embedded fiction cannot be made from within the fiction itself, but rather must emerge from a context more abstract than that to which they refer.[5] Hence an *extra*-fictional level in the text is required in order to talk about objects *as* fictional on a "lower" level of the text. Fiction arises out of nonfiction. The truth or falsity of a fictional reference is, of course, another matter. The reason that nonfictional descriptions are "prior" to fictional descriptions in this way is that fictional descriptions do not yet refer, or refer only partially, and one must begin interpreting somewhere; that is, one must begin with at least a reference to the possibility of referring fictionally. (Chapter 7 will consider in more detail the distinction between nonfiction and fiction.)

Consider the extra-fictional narrator in the precredit sequence of *The Wrong Man* (1956). A distant figure is strongly backlit, casting a gigantic shadow into the foreground of what appears to be a vast empty soundstage. The person's features cannot be distinguished. We hear:

This is Alfred Hitchcock speaking. In the past, I have given you many kinds of suspense pictures. But this time I would like you to see a different one. The difference lies in the fact that this is a true story, every word of it. And yet, it contains elements that are stranger than all the fiction that has gone into many of the thrillers that I've made before.

The third sentence with its ambiguous use of "different one" (a new kind of suspense picture, or a new kind of picture?) together with the last sentence[6] manage to intimate that truth is only another kind of "suspense" and will be fully as entertaining as the fiction films the audience has come to expect from Hitchcock's work. And indeed the explicit pronouncements about a simple truth do not prevent what follows from incorporating both fictional and narrative patterns.[7] But this is not to say that the precredit speech is merely a deception; rather, its function is to begin to put into place an *ordered* sequence of perspectives within which to interpret the "truth" of the story. After all, the audience is well aware that "every word" of the story cannot be *equally* true as claimed; that is, true to the same degree and in the same way. The film has clearly been made after the fact, with actors and dialogue; it includes picture and music as well as word; events are witnessed without the witness being seen, and so forth. The film depends on us accepting these sorts of stipulations; it does not attempt to hide them, but merely to organize them. Because of the necessity of imposing an organization on our interpretive activities, "Hitchcock" – although existing in the film considered as a text – must stand "outside" the film considered as a fiction in talking about what is to follow; that is, Hitchcock's voice and image here are extra-fictional.[8] Thus at least two films are working on us at this moment: a historical artifact of a man who talked on a soundstage, and a (purported) nonfictional discourse in which a man is talking about what will later be talked about and shown. These "two films" are the first two levels of figure 19: the historical and the extra-fictional.

The extra-fictional voice need not be as "personalized" and explicit as the dim figure who speaks in the precredit sequence of *The Wrong Man*. Either the actual speaker may become more prominent and intrusive, and be given psychological traits, or else he or she may become less identifiable,[9] even (as we will shortly discover) invisible and inaudible. Both the location and time of the speaking act may also be made relatively explicit or implicit. What defines the extra-fictional is its relationship to the other levels: how we imagine visual and/or aural data to be functioning with respect to other conceivable groupings of visual and/or aural data. Thus within each of the levels of narration displayed in figure 19, there exist many fine gradations which may be

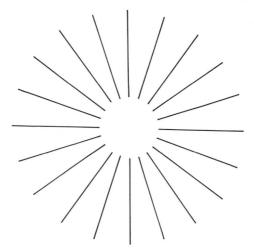

Figure 20 An implicit circle
An implicit circle composed of what is missing from a series of straight lines.
Narration, too, may be implicit, composed of what is missing from a pattern
of explicit narrations.

exploited by a given text in presenting a variety of contexts for its
information.

It is essential to realize that a narration may be *implicit* in a text. I
will risk a visual analogy in order to clarify the important concept of
implicitness. In figure 20, a series of straight lines have been used to
create an implicit, or virtual circle.[10] The circumference of the circle
is nonphysically existent. The circle emerges as a pattern of what has
been omitted, or is missing, in the actual configuration of lines. One
can imagine, of course, a more complex series of lines, perhaps criss-
crossing, that would render the implicit circle less certain or open to
other interpretations. My claim is that narration may be implicit in a
similar way. In order to recognize such a narration, one will need to
be sensitive to the explicit narrations, especially to what has been omitted, or is missing, in the direct regulation of knowledge in a text.[11]

I would like to analyze a particular implicit narration by focusing on
one that is quite powerful and the topic of much general study by
narrative theorists – an implicit extra-fictional narration that theorists
often personify as "the implied author." The opening scene of *The
Wrong Man* ends by following a character, Manny Balestrero (Henry
Fonda), as he leaves a nightclub. We first see two policemen who
happen to be walking by the front of the club (fig. 21; shot 1). Then
each of the next two shots, because of a meticulous blocking of the
action combined with exact compositions and cutting, *make it appear*

visually that Manny (entering frame left through a door) is overtaken by the police and is walking with a policeman on each side (figs 22–4; shots 2A, 2B, 3). We know that this is only a visual illusion – that is, an effect produced by the timing and unique angles of view – for we can also clearly see that both of the policemen walk past Manny on his left and not on both sides of him. Nevertheless, in both shots it does appear as though Manny is wedged between the policemen and has been trapped. There is an unmistakable sense in which Manny, who has committed no crime, has been seized by the police as their man. We neither see nor hear any obvious narrator describe the significance of this event. We have, however, literally seen how circumstances may create a false impression; how Manny may become a wrong man. Fortunately, the mistaken impression is seemingly ours alone and has caused no harm. This "perception of a misperception" (if we have even noticed it!) exists *only under a particular description* of the text; that is, only within a certain inscribed context can we recognize the event in this way. (We must, for example, be especially sensitive to the space and time created on the screen by cinematic devices and to relationships with the space and time of the story world.[12]) I will refer to this particular context as an implicit extra-fictional narration, or as the "voice" of an "implied author." A very powerful narration is at work here; one which virtually defines the limits of what can be seen and heard by us in the film but without defining the conditions of its own existence; one, moreover, which is able to predict events and anticipate the moral of the story prior to the epilogue. Indeed variations on this composition which places Manny between two threatening figures will appear throughout the film. Furthermore, the implied authorial narration *reminds* us about the police in the next scene when we hear distant sirens while Manny reads a newspaper. The sirens mean nothing to Manny and there is no indication that he notices them at all. The spectator, however, is already being positioned to know more than Manny and to fear for him. Just as "Manny" himself may be interpreted from an abstract, non-character context, so the explicit "Hitchcock" that we saw and heard in the precredit sequence may be *reinterpreted* as merely a kind of character playing a role in a still more abstract film, framed by yet another "Hitchcock" who is *not* seen and heard, namely, the implied author of *The Wrong Man*. The implied author, in turn, is framed by – but not reducible to – the historical "Hitchcock" who, unlike the other two Hitchcocks (one implied by an extra-fictional context, and one explicit in an extra-fictional role), expressed general distaste for the film, except for its aesthetic juxtaposition of fear and irony.[13]

Figure 21 The Wrong Man (shot 1)

Figure 22 The Wrong Man (shot 2A)

Figure 23 The Wrong Man (shot 2B)

Figure 24 The Wrong Man (shot 3)

AN IMPLIED AUTHOR AND A CHAMELEON TEXT

We have already encounted the subtle but powerful effects of an implied author in analyzing films other than *The Wrong Man*: In chapter 2 we found an implicit (extra-fictional) pattern of impossible causation in *The Lady from Shanghai*, virtual space in *Dr Mabuse, the Gambler*, and an integration of graphic and story patterns in *The 39 Steps*. I will not attempt to adjudicate among the various definitions and types of "implied author" that have been proposed by theorists.[14] It will be useful, however, to examine one formulation of the concept. My purpose will be to illustrate that concepts in narrative theories are closely aligned with more general theories directed at the ontology and epistemology of film.

Christian Metz describes the implied author in the following way:

> The impression that *someone is speaking* [in a narrative] is bound not to the empirical presence of a definite, known, or knowable speaker but to the listener's spontaneous perception of the linguistic nature of the object . . . The spectator [of a narrative film] perceives images which have obviously been selected (they could have been other images) and arranged (their order could have been different). In a sense, he is leafing through an album of predetermined pictures, and it is not he who is turning the pages but some "master of ceremonies," some "grand image-maker" who (before being recognized as the author, if it is an *auteur* film, or, if not, in the absence of an author) is first and foremost *the film itself as a linguistic object* . . . or more precisely a sort of "potential linguistic focus" situated somewhere behind the film, and representing the basis that makes the film possible.[15]

Metz is striving to isolate an aspect of our narrative comprehension which is not reducible to what a biographical author says he or she intended to accomplish with a film. For Metz, the implied author is merely an anthropomorphic and shorthand way of designating a rather diffuse but fundamental set of operations which we sense as underlying what *we* do in making sense and in making patterns. Metz believes that these operations are amenable to linguistic analyses in accordance with his view of the nature of film as a kind of linguistic (and social) object. He mentions two fundamental operations – selection and arrangement – though others may be imagined, such as duration (the amount of time that something consumes), exclusion, and emphasis. These are subtle effects because if they were made *explicit* in the film, one would simply be forced to analyze another process of *implicit* selection and arrangement to account for the creation of a context in which something *else* could be made explicit. No matter how "objective" and final the narration seems, it could be the result of any one of many implicit narrations that might be imagined one level higher. Hence there will always be a measure of *uncertainty* about what is being depicted.[16] Although a film may explicitly dramatize what goes on "behind" the scenes – such as the setting up of the lights and camera – such a drama itself is really only another scene, and the dramatizing or construction of *that* scene is *not* shown explicitly. Clearly, with the concept of implied authorial narration one is at the very boundary of the text, at the very limit of what might still be justified as being *in* the text as opposed to being in a world, or in an intertext, which frames the text.

The point I wish to make is that for Metz, one must analyze the implicit selection and arrangement of film narration by using linguistic concepts, such as paradigm and syntagm, because linguistics is conceived as the master epistemological framework for describing human knowledge. One may reject some or all of Metz's linguistic assumptions and still hold on to the concept of an implied author, but only by creating a new set of terms and concepts which themselves imply a view of the fundamental nature of film and how it may be known.

I wish to return to the two shots in *The Wrong Man* which seem to show Manny walking between two policemen (figs 21–4). Although I have described these shots as being part of an implied authorial narration, they may be described in a very different way as follows: "Manny emerges from the nightclub, saying 'Goodnight John' " to the doorman, and walks toward the subway while two policemen stroll by the front of the club and cars are heard passing in the street." One could imagine this sort of description being offered by a casual bystander who happened to be near the club when Manny emerged. It is just as accurate as the first description, but its context, or epistemological boundary, is different: it is justified by the diegesis, by the world of the characters as we understand *that* world by apparently being *in* it as a bystander might be in it. That is to say, the accuracy of this new description is being judged against a new epistemological background. I will refer jointly to the new description and its background as an implicit diegetic narration, or implied "diegetic narrator." (I will discuss *non*diegetic narration later.) How can a narrator be both "implied" and "diegetic"; that is, be invisible and yet within the story world? This situation is the pictorial equivalent of a subjunctive conditional: "If a bystander *had been* present, he or she *would have seen* Manny emerge from the club . . . and *would have heard* . . . ." Though a bystander was not present, we presume such a person could have been (and might have been dramatized by the text), and if so, would have been subject to the same physical laws and conditions which govern Manny. There is nothing illegitimate about posing a hypothesis or making a stipulation about the "facts" so long as the frame of reference for arranging the data (here, the diegesis) is not confused with the data itself; this is why it is important to keep in mind the assumptions under which data is being interpreted – assumptions which I have referred to as different "levels" of the narration. The same two shots of Manny and the policemen can be differently described, and function differently in our comprehension, because in the case of implied authorial narration our frame of reference is the entire (nonfictional) text while in the case of implied diegetic narration our frame of reference is the (fictional) story world.

The differing descriptions of these two shots of *The Wrong Man* ascribed to an implied author and to an implied diegetic narrator illustrate a crucial principle of narration:

> In general, several levels of narration will be operating simultaneously with varying degrees of explicitness and compatibility; that is, the spectator may describe the text in several different ways, all of which may be accurate, each within a particular context and for a particular purpose.

Thus one may say that the opening of *The Wrong Man* is a product of the implied author, but in doing so, one is merely offering a specific kind of generalization which has specific limits. The implied author is at work, but not exclusively, for at a finer grain (another segmentation or analytical breakdown) other boundaries on our knowledge are temporarily in effect. In analyzing narration, one must ask what degree of precision will be necessary in order to answer a given question about a spectator's state of knowledge.

The simultaneity of narrations can also explain how the music heard by the spectator in the first scene of *The Wrong Man* may be interpreted in three very different ways without necessarily producing confusion or contradiction.[17] The scene opens with an exterior shot of the nightclub and then moves inside. However the music heard from outside the club is just as loud as what we hear inside. The lack of "sound perspective" strongly suggests that the music is initially extra-fictional. The music accompanies the credit sequence whose titles are superimposed over the interior of the nightclub. The credits are extra-fictional: "Warner Bros. Pictures Presents . . . Henry Fonda . . . Vera Miles . . . in Alfred Hitchcock's . . . 'THE WRONG MAN'. . . ." By being associated with the credits, the music becomes extra-fictional. While the credits are being shown, however, we see a series of dissolves within the nightclub which indicate that we are also seeing *excerpts* from an *entire evening* of dancing at the club. That is, the music that we hear is also being presented as *typical* of an evening of dancing at the club. Such music is *non*diegetic because it can only be heard by us; patrons of the club are hearing specific music at specific times, not a sample of the music that was played during the evening. By keeping the dissolves of the title superimpositions separate from the dissolves which condense story time within the club, two levels of narration are defined – the extra-fictional and the nondiegetic – allowing the music to shift from one to the other, or be in both places at once. However, as the evening wears on and the density of people in the club decreases, the orchestration of the music decreases and a band in the background becomes visible. When the credits finish we continue to hear the "same" musical number but now it is revealed that it is *diegetic* music being played by the band, one of whose members is Manny. When the band stops playing, the music ceases. Evidently the single musical number which we have heard could not have been played for an entire evening; instead, approximately 1¾ minutes of screen music is used to present the (extra-fictional) credits, represent typical (nondiegetic) music for an evening at the club, and be the actual, final (diegetic) song played by the band that evening. The "same" music functions very differently depending upon the context, precisely because several distinct contexts are made to fit. Thus the music may sound the "same" to us throughout and yet be heard in three different ways. Our (bottom-up) perception of the musical sounds emanating from the screen has been smoothly integrated with our (top-down) hypotheses about the relationships of music to a story world.[18]

The integration of screen data with events from a particular story through the use of music is also manifested through our natural use of the preposition "in" when describing these musical events. The music is "in" the club in many ways. It accompanies the credits which are seen "in" the club, but equally we may imagine that it is: typical music for the club, typical music for a jazz band of 1953, typical music for this band, music heard by a typical patron or someone in particular, as well as the last song played that night of January 14. The text is open and receptive to a number of interpretations; yet, at the same time, the verbal description we apply is seemingly quite definite about what it means to be "in" the club at the beginning of the film. The "camera," too, appears to be both in the club with the patrons and yet not quite in the club when showing the title credits. In fact, we are forced to conclude that the preposition "in" is flexible and adaptable and, like "implicit" narration, may be found to have many uses. This illustrates how a number of interpretations by different spectators may be accommodated by this preposition *without* suggesting that there is necessarily more than one interpretation or that a spectator must search for another one. I believe that this use of the music, and this use of the preposition describing the music, is in miniature form what is meant by the "excessive obviousness" of classical film narrative: the text sustains a reading which is generally compatible with whatever we *first* believe and does not usually demand a unique or counterintuitive explication. Normally, the classical narrative does not give the appearance of ambiguity, nor does it encourage multiple interpretations, but rather, like the chameleon, it is adaptable, resilient and accommodating.[19] It will try to be what the spectator believes it to be.

There are limits, of course, to the amount of textual material that can be absorbed into a chameleon effect. For example, the relationships among the resolution, epilogue, and the other elements of a narrative schema need not be peaceful, and may be dramatized to a greater or lesser degree. David Bordwell observes that in *The Wrong Man* an *uncaused* resolution (based on a prayer and a "miracle") is joined with *two* epilogues (the first unhappy but caused; the second happy but uncaused). According to Bordwell, these aberrations leave the spectator "not only dispirited but dissatisfied."[20] This is true, however, only within the context of the large-scale structure of the film, for the ending of the film need not greatly affect our understanding of particular episodes and causal sequences, or the implications of those sequences. Moreover, the beginning of the film, which stages the presence of Hitchcock and his declarations about a factual film, predicts that there will be friction among the levels of narration. Endings are not supposed to be "neat" in the genre of the documentary. Furthermore, the implied authorial narration, which in the opening scene dramatized the perception of a misperception (Manny apparently being "arrested" by two policemen), prepares the spectator for unsettling, and uncaused, effects. Two apparently arbitrary camera views were allowed to affect our beliefs about Manny's world, even though at that time our beliefs were unwarranted. The implication was that a misperception could arise in quite an arbitrary and unpredictable way. Thus a kind of fatalism mixed with punishment might be at work in the text and detected in Hitchcock's other films. (For example, in typical fashion the psychological trauma is ultimately focused on a woman – in this case Manny's wife.) By "remembering" the documentary genre and Hitchcock's other films, we open a gap in the text of *The Wrong Man*: descriptions of the power that is apparently applied in the telling (through authorial narration) now conflict with descriptions that make the story cohere in the fashion of a narrative schema. That is, a fatalistic attitude appears in spite of (or perhaps, because of) opposition from other aspects of the story-telling that strive for "consistency" among the narrations. Here, "consistency" is earned through the temporal presuppositons of a narrative schema that encapsulates our belief that certain kinds of causality rule our world, and may be found in the basic unity of initiating event, resolution, and epilogue. The ending of Hitchcock's film can be of little comfort when our happiness is shown to be as arbitrarily obtained as our unhappiness.

I want to mention a final type of narration that appears in the opening of *The Wrong Man* and that bears upon our judgments of consistency and inconsistency in the film. While we listen to the music "in" the club, but before the credits begin, a title appears on the screen that represents a new sort of narration:

> The early morning hours of January the fourteenth, nineteen hundred and fifty-three, a day in the life of Christopher Emanuel Balestrero that he will never forget . . .

In terms of a narrative *schema*, this title combined with the picture we see functions to *orient* us with respect to the present state of affairs in the story world. The title is *about* the story world and hence derives from what I will call an unmarked *non*diegetic narration, or implied "nondiegetic narrator." The narrative could have oriented us by presenting the same information in another way; for example, by allowing us to overhear a conversation at one of the tables in the club. The information would be the same, but its method of presentation (as diegetic narration) would be different. A character's knowledge is limited in a way in which the words of the title are not and hence we could not ascribe the same authority and reliability to the words of a character as we can to the superimposed title. When the title assures us that something decisive will happen to Manny, we must pay serious attention to whatever may happen.[21] In a sense, we might say that the narration is not "implied" at all because the title card itself is explicitly present, even though we do not know the precise identity of the person "speaking." Implicit and explicit are a matter of degree and judgment, but that does not mean they are vague or indistinct since one may be as precise in describing the narration as the occasion demands; the important task is to measure differences from one narration to the next.[22]

One may choose to believe that this explanatory title ("a day . . . he will never forget") is actually a continuation of the same voice we heard earlier ("This is Alfred Hitchcock speaking"); that is, we may believe that the title speaks *about* the fiction from a nonfictional standpoint, not just *about* the story world from within the fiction. If so, one must at least concede that the "voice" is less personalized when rendered in a written, third-person form, and that both a fade and a dissolve have intervened between the two "voices" making the place and time of the second utterance less definite: is "Hitchcock" still standing on the empty soundstage? Does he speak, write, or silently think these words of the explanatory title? (As we shall see in chapter 7, a lack of specificity is a mark of the fictional.) There is no answer to these questions in the film; more importantly, any answer we may give is uninformative beyond the fact that there are differences (i.e., if it is still "Hitchcock," he has at least become more distant as the story world gains in prominence). Our uncertainty about the "voice" of the title is confined to a relatively narrow range and has no important effect on our global interpretation of the film. We may believe whatever we wish about the speaker of this title card so long as our beliefs take their place in a hierarchy with respect to the other narrations. Narration, too, may exhibit a chameleon effect. (However, as we shall see in chapters 6 and 7, a film may exploit uncertainties of narration and fuzzy boundaries to create startling and far-reaching effects.) A text is under no obligation to make use of a level of narration, much less make good use of it. Establishing exact categories for the narrations is usually less important than recognizing pertinent relationships and gradations among the narrations. By continuing to experiment and to search for possible configurations for the various levels, a spectator becomes sensitive to the changing boundaries of sense data which the text wishes to impose. Ultimately it is the spectator's task to judge when there is enough difference to make a difference in the role he or she must play in making sense of the text.

FOCALIZATION

The first four levels in the hierarchy of narrations that we have discussed make use of narrators. The last four levels recognize that characters also provide us information about the story world, but in ways quite different from narrators. A character who acts, speaks, observes, or has thoughts is not strictly telling or presenting anything to us for the reason that spectators, or readers, are not characters in that world. Characters may "tell" the story to us in a broad sense, but only through "living in" their world and speaking to other characters. Indeed, one might almost say that these conditions, or restrictions, define what we mean by the concept of a "character."

There are, however, several different ways in which characters may "live in" their world. One way we learn about characters is through their actions and speech in much the same way that characters learn from each other. In this special context, our knowledge is limited to what is explicitly enacted by the characters, what they do and say. In this limited context, a character is essentially an *agent* who is defined by actions.[23] For example, a plot synopsis of *The Wrong Man* – explaining who the story is about and *what* happens – is a way of thinking about character agency in this way: "Frightening account of what happens to a man and his wife when he is wrongly accused of being the man who has performed a series of hold-ups."[24] In chapter 1, I argued that narrative may be conceived as "a series of episodes collected as a *focused* causal chain." In this definition the notion of a focus, "continuing center," or protagonist, is inextricably bound up with the very notion of cause and effect: character and action define, as well as limit, each other's logical development. The spectator has an intrinsic interest in characters as agents since comprehending a narrative event requires at least recognizing how agents interact with one another in a *causal* framework, rather than, for instance, interacting as storytellers or dreamers. Characters, of course, may become storytellers or dreamers by recounting events to someone. These events may even be dramatized visually for the spectator as in a character flashback or dream sequence. In both these cases, however, the character has a new and *different* function in the text at another level, no longer as an actor who defines, and is defined by, a causal chain, but as a diegetic narrator (i.e., a narrator limited by the laws of the story world) who is now recounting a story within the story: he or she as an actor in a past event becomes the *object* of his or her narration in the present. Levels may multiply but there still exists a primary character-agent defined by actions and events. I will refer to this primary level of actions as a neutral, or nonfocalized, narration (or depiction) of character. Introducing the narratological concept of *focalization* is meant to remind us that a character's role in a narrative may change from being an actual, or potential, *focus* of a causal chain to being the *source* of our knowledge of a causal chain: the character may become either a (higher level) narrator or a (lower level) focalizer. How does a "focalizer" differ from a "narrator"?

Identifying a character as an agent within a causal scheme is already to implicitly raise the issue of that character's *awareness* of events in his or her world. An agent is a subject with a presumed, but as yet unspecified, set of personality traits, or subjectivity. A narrative text, however, is under no obligation to provide information about an agent's awareness beyond the tentative inferences we may draw from causal events. To the degree that specific information is provided, however, one may speak of focalization through (by) a character, either internally or externally. For Henry James, such a character was a "reflector." The term is apt since it replaces the notion of "communication" with the notion of "private thought" – a reflection *on* something – that nevertheless manages to sum up and clarify a surrounding situation and so also become a reflection *of* something. Focalization (reflection) involves a character neither speaking (narrating, reporting, communicating) nor acting (focusing, focused by), but rather actually *experiencing* something through seeing or hearing it.[25] Focalization also extends to more complex experiencing of objects: thinking, remembering, interpreting, wondering, fearing, believing, desiring, understanding, feeling guilt. Such verbs of consciousness are marked in language by the fact that an indirect object is not appropriate: we can say "Manny sees the police," but not "Manny sees the police to John." By contrast, verbs of communication (e.g., say, claim, shout, advise, reply, promise, ask, read, sing, confess) may take indirect objects designating a recipient of the communication: "Manny said goodnight *to* John." When consciousness is represented in pictures rather than in words, the indirect object which is inappropriate becomes the observer who is ineffective: a diegetic observer at the scene would be limited to external cues and could not know the character's experience. For example, if John sees that Manny looks toward the police, he may *infer* that Manny sees the police; nevertheless this inference may be false or incomplete (Manny looks but sees something else; or he sees the police but does not take special notice of them; or sees them and thinks about mowing his lawn, etc.). In general, inferences that John might make about Manny's thoughts are only speculative.

The auditory equivalent of the distinction between "looking" and "seeing" is "listening" and "hearing." The first term of each of these pairs has an *inter*subjective quality to it (i.e., a person's behavior may suggest when he or she is looking or listening), and hence is appropriate in a communicative context (where such a fact could be reported by a narrator), or for nonfocalized description, while the second term of each pair is more closely aligned to a private (internally or externally focalized) experience or thought which is not open to inspection in the same way (and hence can be reported only by a focalizer).[26] In the case of complex experiences of character consciousness, a diegetic observer, or narrator, would be wholly inadequate to the task. For example, if Manny's memories were to motivate a flashback sequence in the film, a diegetic observer would see only that Manny was staring vacantly into space. The spectator of the film, however, might well see and hear Manny's conscious memories (initiated perhaps by a dissolve), but only by identifying them uniquely as Manny's, that is, as inaccessible to a diegetic observer – experienced by Manny but not narrated literally by him to us or to a bystander. In *internal* focalization, story world and screen are meant to collapse into each other, forming a perfect identity in the name of a character: "Here is exactly what Manny sees: these shapes and colors are in his head," or "Here are his thoughts." The spectator's task is to identify the story world with the mental understanding of a specific character. (Hence in figure 19 the spectator's role in internal focalization is one of "identification."[27]) Of course, in the broadest sense Manny and his memories are created for us by higher-level narrations (e.g., the extra-fictional narrator); but even so, one cannot simply equate focalization with narration since incomplete or inaccurate character perception is attributed first to the character, not to a narrator. Focalization displays character perception as a consequence of the events of the character's world even if other (nondiegetic) worlds are also affected. That is, focalization represents the *fact* of character perception, even if we may discover later that the character misperceived and even if our misperception about the character turns out to have other consequences in our ongoing experience of the story. Although the levels of narration are arranged as a series of dependencies, like the folds of an accordion, that does not mean that each level, within its prescribed context, does not have a unique function to perform in representing a complex epistemological field.

Private experiences of a character may be rendered externally or irternally. External focalization represents a measure of character awareness but from outside the character. It is semi-subjective in the manner of an eyeline match: we see *what* Manny looks at, *when* he looks, but *not from* his unique spatial position; we must *infer* that we have seen what he has seen and how he has seen it. An eyeline match, however, is only one device which acts to externally focalize narrative through character. Three of the first five shots following the credit sequence of *The Wrong Man* as well as the next twenty-seven shots isolate Manny and his activities through a variety of techniques. For example, the camera moves to follow Manny's movements and also to anticipate his movements. The camera *waits* on a subway platform as a train stops and Manny gets off; later the image is black as the camera waits in a darkened bedroom for him to arrive and turn on the lights. The camera also follows his attention as he looks at four separate pages of a newspaper with varying expressions on his face. We see each of the pages and are invited to imagine Manny's thoughts: what significance do these specific pages have for him and what are the connections among them? (The connections will become clearer as the narrative progresses.) The scene ends on a close-up of him. The first thirty-two shots of the film clearly establish Manny as a center of attention, and we learn much about him even though he has said nothing about himself and there is virtually no dialogue ("Hi ya Manny. How's the family?"). Overall the narrative of these shots has been externally focalized through Manny.[28]

Internal focalization is more fully private and subjective than external focalization. No character can witness these experiences in another character. Internal focalization ranges from simple perception (e.g., the point-of-view shot), to impressions (e.g., the out-of-focus point-of-view shot depicting a character who is drunk, dizzy, or drugged), to "deeper thoughts" (e.g., dreams, hallucinations, and memories).[29] One of many examples of internal focalization in *The Wrong Man* occurs when Manny is placed alone in a prison cell. We see twenty-one shots of Manny looking at objects and walking nervously about the cell (external focalization). These shots are interrupted by another scene so we do not know exactly how long Manny's intense feelings build up within him; or rather, we are invited to imagine whatever amount of time we believe necessary for such feelings to become excruciating. Finally, we see Manny, horrified and ashamed, clench his hands, lean against a wall, and *close* his eyes. The camera then begins a sequence of jerky, swaying movements that increase in speed and spiral around Manny's head and the wall but without moving closer to him. The shot ends with a crescendo of discordant music and a long fade-out. The bizarre camera framings are meant to represent Manny's deep (nonverbal?) internalization of his circumstances.

Focalization through a character depends upon other, higher levels of narration that, for example, define and ground the character who is to have an experience.[30] These other narrations are always superimposed in a film; occasionally several may be relatively explicit, and may even be in conflict with one another. This situation may produce unusual representations of character subjectivity. For example, in Ingmar Bergman's *Wild Strawberries* (1957) a character holds up a mirror to reflect the face of another character. This shot, however, is actually the result of at least six different levels of narration operating simultaneously, but not always in harmony.[31] We understand this particular mirror shot in relation to a historical author, "Ingmar Bergman," who is (1) presenting a story in which a character in the story, Isak Borg, becomes a diegetic narrator who is (2) recounting in voice-over a story he has written about an automobile trip he took one day. We hear Borg narrating the story about himself but we never see him speaking. Instead we see Borg (3) riding in the automobile and conversing with various people he meets during the fateful automobile trip; that is, another Borg is now acting, and being acted upon, in the diegesis as simply a (nonfocalized and externally focalized) character. While riding in the car, however, we also see him fall asleep and hear the "previous" Borg explain in voice-over: "I dozed off, but was haunted by vivid and humiliating dreams." The sleeping Borg (4) imagines seeing himself at his present age of 78 in a new locale. This "new" 78-year-old Borg then (5) witnesses various events of his boyhood (many of which he could not actually have seen when he was a boy). We see him as a witness within his own dream and we also see the past events he watches/remembers/infers; that is, we see two degrees of internal focalization. The people he sees within his dream are shown at the age they were when Borg was a boy. One of these persons, a 20-year-old woman named Sara, however, suddenly confronts the 78-year-old Borg within his dream as he is observing past events. In confronting him, she has assumed a new role since the Sara that Borg remembers as a 20-year-old could not, of course, have had a conversation with the person Borg would become fifty-eight years later. In fact, in an earlier dream/memory he had tried to speak with her but had discovered that he was apparently invisible and inaudible. Nevertheless, in this particular dream/memory of Borg she suddenly speaks to him and holds up a mirror that (6) reflects his face as a 78-year-old man taking an automobile trip: "Have you looked in the mirror, Isak? Then I'll show you what you look like." We see the reflection of Borg in the mirror, first over his shoulder, and then later, the reflection alone. It seems to be an external focalization. Isak Borg has become an object for himself, but which "Isak Borg" is being thus framed and reflected, for what purpose, and who is really presenting it? Sara's "impossible" words may be understood figuratively: by allowing him to view himself simultaneously from multiple "distances," Borg is being prodded to consider the kind of person he has become.

The narrational structure of the shot may be represented as a sequence of six frames within frames as follows:

$$[\, [\, [\, [\, [\, [\, \ldots \text{ mirror reflection } \ldots \,] \,] \,] \,] \,] \,]$$

The power of the shot derives in part from its sudden knotting together of distinct narrations to create contradiction and paradox. The distinct time frames in which Isak Borg functions as a voice-over narrator, actor, and focalizer are collapsed by the mirror reflection into a paradoxical time in which the notion of "Isak Borg" has an unexpected complexity. One might even include "Ingmar Bergman" within the tangle of narrations by noticing that his initials are the same as those of "Isak Borg" and that his surname can nearly be shortened to "Borg." The subtle intricacy of this moment depends upon the creation of various levels within the narration that are posited as logically distinct, followed by a transgression of the boundaries.[32]

Levels of the narration may be structured to create unusual effects because they mark differing epistemological domains which may be complementary or opposed. Moreover, there are three distinct types of narration. In a strict sense, a narrator offers statements *about*; an actor/ agent acts *on* or is acted upon; and a focalizer has an experience *of*. More precisely, narration, action, and focalization are three alternative modes of describing how knowledge may be stated, or obtained. Since all three modes may be used to describe the same character or object, what distinguishes them is the differing presuppositions imposed on the spectator, or reader, as a condition of acquiring knowledge. Further, there is evidence that this tripartite division is connected to universal features of human language.[33] At the very least, these three types of "agency" are convenient fictions which serve to mark how a field of knowledge is being divided at a particular time (see fig. 25).[34] Note that, in general, since several narrations may be operating simultaneously, a shot in a film may be subject to different interpretations with respect to each of these three possibilities for perception. Also, the terminology will shift depending upon the selection of a reference point. For exam-

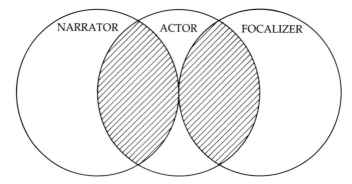

Figure 25 The three types of agency
Narration in general is the overall regulation and distribution of knowledge which determines when and how a reader acquires knowledge from a text. It is composed of three related activities associated with three nominal agents: the narrator, actor, and focalizer. These agents are convenient fictions which serve to mark how the field of knowledge is being divided at a particular time. Some theorists would add a fourth overlapping circle to the left of "narrator" to create, in effect, two types of narrator: on the far left, a "pure showing" by an unobtrusive "presenter" which intersects with a circle which would be confined to "verbal recounting." The new contrast would be between narrators who show (present) and those who tell (speak and write); or perhaps the contrast would be between narrators who use pictures and those who use words.

ple, if a character in a film is watching a television show, all the music from the television will be diegetic with respect to that character even if some of the music is nondiegetic with respect to characters who exist only on the show. Therefore, in interpreting narration it will be crucial for the analyst to specify the arrangement of levels and the (top-down) course of reading that is in effect.

Although there is a firm distinction among narration, (nonfocalized) action, and (external and internal) focalization, it is often convenient in analyzing narrative to use the terms "narration" and "narrator" in a general sense to refer to all three types of agency in order to concentrate on the overall regulation and distribution of knowledge throughout a text that determines how and when a reader acquires knowledge. I will usually use "narration" and "narrator" in a broad way, relying upon context to indicate when they are to be understood in a narrow way (i.e., as opposed to both acting and focalizing).

Focalization is an attempt to represent "consciousness of."[35] In treating it as part of the above tripartite division of activities, I have defined focalization (in figs 19 and 25) in a way significantly different from other writers.[36] For instance, Mieke Bal allows unidentified and undramatized *narrators* as well as characters to focalize events.[37] However, allowing experiences to appear without a definition of an "experiencer" – that is, experiences not attributed to a particular individual but rendered in the "third person" – risks dissipating the distinction between narration and focalization. How are we to know the difference among narrators who remember, imagine, or directly experience a scene? And how would these situations differ from an invisible narrator who merely presented a scene by "setting the stage" and arranging the action for us to witness? Or who merely reported a scene without mentioning any of the experiences which led to the report? Moreover, what is to be gained by allowing impersonal, "personal" experiences in the text? Of course, if a narrator is given a body and a personality, then he or she may focalize events, but only because he or she has thereby become a "character" of sorts. Seymour Chatman argues that a narrator cannot focalize at all because a narrator is outside the story, in a different time and place, and thus can only report, not see and hear events unfold.[38] The very act of reporting implies that the narrator already knows more than a reader, or knows it sooner, and hence is on a different level of the hierarchies of relative knowledge. (However, Chatman goes even further and concludes that focalization is not a distinct or viable category with which to analyze narration.)

I have also defined "nonfocalization" in a new way. Gérard Genette, for instance, treats it as a global aspect of narration related to the "omniscience" of a narrator. He argues that a narrator's power to know more than any character or reader may be demonstrated by entering many characters' minds resulting in a net zero focalization, or non-focalization, for the text as a whole.[39] Nonfocalization in Genette's sense might better be called "multifocalization." Even so, it is not a necessary component of omniscience nor is it useful in examining local effects of character action and awareness.

COMMUNICATION

Susan Lanser incorporates three additional concepts in her version of figure 19 which I have not used: status, contact, and stance. The reason is that Lanser interprets the levels of narration as a *communication* between a "sender" (on the left side of the illustration) and a "receiver of a message" (on the right). Her three concepts describe the sender's relationships, respectively, to his or her "speech act," to the receiver, and to the message. The goal of the entire system is "maximal author-ity" and "maximal reception."[40] I have avoided these three concepts in an attempt to remain neutral between a communication theory and various other theories which seek to explicate in quite different ways the goals and processes which drive narration. I do not wish to debate here the merits and demerits of a communication approach to an analysis of the comprehension of narrative texts. I do believe, however, that communication theories have substantial limitations. The following are typical statements in support of a communication model:

> Just as there is, within the narrative, a large exchange function (enacted by giver and recipient), similarly, in homological fashion, the narrative, viewed as object, is the basis of a communication: there is a giver of narrative and a recipient of narrative. In linguistic communication, *I* and *you* are presupposed by each other; similarly, a narrative cannot take place without a narrator and a listener (or reader).[41]
>
> (Roland Barthes, 1966)

> Every narrative . . . is a *mélange* of four basic components: speaker, speech event, agents, and narrated event. As such it is structurally equivalent to instances of daily discourse in which someone reports something.[42]
>
> (Dudley Andrew, 1984)

> A narrative is a communication; hence, it presupposes two parties, a sender and a receiver.[43]
>
> (Seymour Chatman, 1978)

Barthes begins with the fact that characters communicate with each other and then decides that narrative must be the most general communication of all. Chatman begins with narrative as a communication and then discovers perceivers who must be in communication. Both arguments seem to reduce the processes, effects, and uses of narrative to a single purpose so that perceiving has a single goal; as Barthes suggests, "listening" becomes the same as "reading." James Kinneavy flatly states that "all uses" of language depend upon an encoder, a signal, a decoder, and the reality to which the message refers. This four-part structure, he asserts, is so basic that it simply "speaks for itself"![44] Apparently, everything that solicits meaning is to be imagined as a speech, a hypothetical speech, or a message transmitted from somewhere.

Other theorists have been much more skeptical about communication models:

> Writing is not the communication of a message which starts from the author and proceeds to the reader; it is specifically the voice of reading itself: *in the text, only the reader speaks.*[45]
>
> (Roland Barthes, 1970)

[W]e have come to take for granted that we explain textual details

108

by adducing narrators and explain narrators by adducing qualities of real people. . . . [However, much of] literature is interesting and compelling precisely because it does something other than illustrate the personality of a narrator. For the moment I want to suggest that this strategy of naturalization and anthropomorphism should be recognized not as an analytical perspective on fiction, but as part of the fiction-making process. That is to say, making narrators is not an analytical operation that lies outside the domain of fiction but very much a continuation of fiction-making: dealing with details by imagining a narrator; telling a story about a narrator and his/her response so as to make sense of them.[46]

(Jonathan Culler, 1984)

No trait we could assign to an implied author of a film could not more simply be ascribed to the narration itself: it sometimes suppresses information, it often restricts our knowledge, it generates curiosity, it creates a tone, and so on. To give every film a narrator or implied author is to indulge in an anthropomorphic fiction. . . . I suggest . . . that narration is better understood as the organization of a set of cues for the construction of a story. This presupposes a perceiver, but not any sender, of a message. This scheme allows for the possibility that the *narrational process may sometimes mimic the communication situation more or less fully*. A text's narration may emit cues that suggest a narrator, or a "narratee," or it may not. . . . [T]here is no point in positing communication as the fundamental process of all narration, only to grant that most films "efface" or "conceal" this process. Far better, I think, to give the narrational process the power to signal under certain circumstances that the spectator should construct a narrator. When this occurs, we must recall that this narrator is the product of specific organizational principles, historical factors, and viewers' mental sets. Contrary to what the communication model implies, this sort of narrator does not create the narration; the narration, appealing to historical norms of viewing, creates the narrator. . . . [W]e need not build the narrator in on the ground floor of our theory. No purpose is served by assigning every film to a *deus absconditis*.[47]

(David Bordwell, 1985)

It is not merely in the contexts of literature and film that communication models seem inadequate; they have also been attacked on general linguistic and philosophical grounds.[48] Nevertheless, escaping the "anthropomorphic fiction" embodied in the word "narrator" is not easy. Bordwell still speaks of narration in vaguely animate terms as an "organization" that has the power to "suppress," "restrict," "generate," "emit cues," "signal," "mimic," and "create." It may well be that "narrator" is a metaphor, but if so, one that permeates our thinking about the world, and is in need of explanation on that basis. "Narrator" and related terms are well-established in critical practice as well as in ordinary language. Are such metaphors an accident of speaking, a mere convenience, a delusion we should learn to live without, or something more fundamental dealing with our embodiment in a world? How do these ways of speaking address our intuitive sense of the appropriateness of speaking in this way? Perhaps these metaphors are evidence of a displacement of the human ego onto the world, or else of an overriding faith in *ordinary causality* and in our presumed roles as *actors* able to make order in the world.[49] Personifying narration would seem to have a real function in our lives even if narration is not a personality made real nor a communication made public.[50]

According to Wallace Martin, most theorists of narrative attempt to find a position somewhere between accepting or rejecting the communication model.[51] He suggests three intermediate positions, which I interpret as follows:

1 Narrative texts contain special and private spaces for a reader's personal involvement with the story beyond what may be communicated.
2 Narrative is a cooperative enterprise whereby both reader and writer contribute [equally?] by virtue of being members of particular historical commmunities that share cultural values and literary conventions. Although the reader and writer share the responsibility for producing sense, they may perform different functions.
3 Narrative is the product not of readers, writers, and conventions, but of an act of reading. Readers and writers possess identical skills of comprehension. A writer is merely the first reader. The central problem therefore is to describe consciousness and investigate the various skills of comprehension: what conditions make a reading possible?

It would seem that these intermediate positions might overlap with one another and even be compatible with certain communication theories.[52] This reminds us that there are many functions for perceivers to perform in using and exchanging narrative, and many ways for perception to relate to purpose. If a text is sometimes a "communication," it is almost certainly operating in other ways as well.

TEXT UNDER A DESCRIPTION

In Wallace Martin's third option above, the act of reading is seen as an act of problem-solving by the reader. According to Robert de Beaugrande, problem-solving means that:

> The elements of knowledge are considered already present in the mind, and the task is to decide how to connect them together to suit a plan and a topic . . . . The task of communicating is then not to *fill* other people's minds with content, but to instruct them *how* to *limit* and *select among* the content they already have in their minds.[53]

When the narrative object is narrowed to the acts of comprehension by which it is known, then I believe it is possible to conceive of an "author" as merely another reader with no *a priori* message to deliver. Narration becomes the labor through which a reader generates any warranted description of sensory data – any admissible way of segmenting which yields perceptual boundaries, the collection of which becomes "the text." "Narrator," "actor," and "focalizer" are then merely convenient labels which allow the reader to fashion his or her own redescription, or transformation, of one perception of the "here-and-now" context into a new perception of it. All three types of agent are *in* the text according to a differential hierarchy. The complexity of the preposition "in" and its relationship to embedding and being embedded (recall our discussion of the credit music being heard "in" the club) points to a dynamic and basic quality of narration: the transformation of one epistemological context into another, a movement from (embedded) level to (embedding) level. As an illustration of this way of avoiding a communication model, and as a summary of the levels of narration discussed above in connection with *The Wrong Man*, consider the following verbal (re)descriptions of the film:

1 *Historical author*: "But I did fancy the opening of the picture because of my own fear of the police."[54]
2 *Implied author*: "Manny is overtaken by two policemen who seem to walk on either side of him *as if* to take him into custody, but in fact they do not walk on either side of him and do not (yet) take him into custody."
3 *Extra-fictional narrator*: "This is Alfred Hitchcock speaking."
4 *Nondiegetic narrator*: Title card: "The early morning hours of January the fourteenth, nineteen hundred and fifty-three, a day in the life of Christopher Emanuel Balestrero that he will never forget. . . ."
5 *(Implied) diegetic narrator*: "If a bystander *had been* present, he or she *would have seen* Manny emerge from the club . . . and *would have heard.* . . ."

111

6 *Nonfocalized narration* (*character as agent*): "Frightening account of what happens to a man and his wife when he is wrongly accused of being the man who has performed a series of hold-ups."[55]

7 *External focalization*: Eyeline match: "Manny *looks at* x."

8 *Internal focalization* (*surface*): Point-of-view shot: "I [Manny][now] *see* x [there][from where I stand]."

9 *Internal focalization* (*depth*): "I [Manny] remember . . . wish . . . fear . . . x."

My claim is that "narration" exists whenever we *transform* data from one to another of the above forms.[56] Whether we are an "author" or a "reader" is no longer pertinent: the central activity of narration is the redescription of data under epistemological constraint. The subtle ways in which we apply and use prepositions are often a clue to the constraints in effect for a given description.[57] For example, an interpretive statement may be justified by saying that we are looking "over," "at," "with," "through," or "into" a character (according to whether we adopt a nondiegetic, diegetic, nonfocalized, externally focalized or internally focalized frame of reference). The use of these sorts of preposition does not signify an attitude toward the character, but merely declares the set of assumptions by which we imagine a given relationship to the character and to his or her world, and by which we justify an interpretive statement. One may also imagine degrees by which we see "into" a character (how far? how deeply?), degrees by which we see "through" a character (how completely? how clearly?), and degrees of involvement associated with the other prepositions.

By conceiving narration as a type of verbal (and imagistic?) description offered by a spectator, one is, in effect, analyzing *interpretive* statements. One is mapping a course of thought, the use of language, rather than discovering the absolute properties of an object or discovering "cues" that are "in" an object – the text objectified. Interpretation thus construed exhibits something of the nature of an explanatory "theory." Interpretation in this sense includes the "filling in" of certain data (from the top down) which seems to be "missing" at some moment in the text as well as the construction of macro-propositions which are *about* the text though not strictly *in* it, or denoting it. Structures that are achieved in cognition cannot be reduced to a list of phenomenal forms or cues. We demonstrate our knowledge of narration, of "how to go on," by interpreting, by going on.

The notion of levels, I believe, provides a way of escaping a simple structuralism as well as a strict empiricism, because comprehension is not made to depend upon a few basic surface units, or "cues," which may be endlessly combined in strings through addition and subtraction. Some aspects of narrative *can* profitably be analyzed in this way, but the notion of levels brings with it the relationships of embedding and hierarchy, which, in turn, provide mechanisms for a fundamentally different kind of contribution to human cognition than laws of addition and subtraction, or the rules of branching networks. A higher level, acting like an exemplar or guiding procedure, may constrain, but does not determine, the organization of data rising from below, or arriving from other sources. Thus "levels" are a way of talking about flexibility, complexity, and efficiency in modeling a situation – how different processes interact and how data is discarded, compared, and integrated.[58] In this sense, a set of levels may be thought of as a "vertical" partitioning of data that operates simultaneously with a "horizontal" segmentation across a specified range of knowledge. Moreover, since a lower level depends upon the working assumptions of *all* of the levels above it, each step down the hierarchy increases the number of assumptions that must be made and narrows the range of knowledge available to the spectator. Thus the hierarchy of levels may be seen as a set of probabilities that predicts the likelihood of hypotheses. For example, unless there is evidence to the contrary, an image is more likely to be interpreted as "objective" (i.e., nonfocalized) than "subjective" (externally or internally focalized) because fewer assumptions are necessary.

A hierarchy of levels also helps to explain what Richard Gerrig calls "anomalous suspense" (a person may continue to feel suspense while reading a story even though he or she has read the story many times) and "anomalous replotting" (a person may wish for a different outcome even though he or she knows the plot).[59] Since these responses may occur in reading either nonfiction (e.g., history or biography) or fiction, the explanation must lie partly in the dual nature of narrative: the *declarative* knowledge of narrative (given through a narrative schema) depends upon an awareness of the *contingency* of cause and effect chains – that is, depends upon a person's ongoing assessment of the probabilities which govern the grouping of events – while the *procedural* knowledge of narrative (given through narration) is stratified into *levels*, allowing a person to respond to the contingency of cause and effect chains in multiple ways. Thus a reader's participation in narrative is not limited to the binary choice of whether to know, or not to know, but may assume more complex nuances within a range of epistemological contexts each of which, in turn, defines a limited form of contingency.

One should not think that analyzing narration as a series of levels implies that the narrations must be consistent or assembled into a single hierarchy (see fig. 26).[60] For example, Tzvetan Todorov asserts that narrations may interact in three fundamental ways through linking, alternating, or embedding and thus may be seen rhetorically as repetitive, progressive, antithetical, complementary, parallel, nested, and so forth.[61] Presumably, levels may also be overlapping, deceptive,

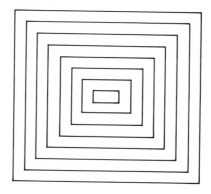

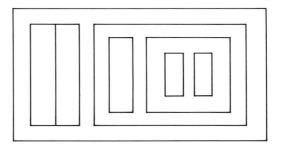

Figure 26a & b Simple and complex configurations of narration
Figure 26a is a box diagram showing a hierarchical arrangement of the eight levels of narration of figure 19. Figure 26b is a box diagram showing one of many possible nonhierarchical arrangements of the levels of narration in a text. Each level is shown as a box. A level is represented as being subordinate to another level by being enclosed within a box.

contradictory, ambiguous, implicit, and uncertain. The next three chapters will examine some arrangements of narrations from simple to complex in particular films.

A COMPREHENSIVE DESCRIPTION OF NARRATIVE

I am now in a position to summarize three concepts of narrative theory that have traditionally been viewed as fundamental: point of view, omniscience, and narrative. These characterizations will be basic enough to allow competing narrative theories to develop and elaborate the concepts in different ways. Formulating general definitions will also allow us to compare a variety of narrative theories and evaluate the particular decisions each theory must make about methodology.

Narrative *point of view* is the relationship between *any pair* of levels of narration, not necessarily adjacent. The relationship between a pair of levels may be analyzed in various ways.[62] Even so, point of view is only a partial description of the movement of narration through a text. For example, although the choice of a particular point of view is frequently analyzed in terms of the information which is thereby suppressed, other effects – such as the overall management and delay of enigmas, the arrangement of action sequences, and soliciting the reader's, or spectator's, interest – are more global in nature and are best analyzed when narration is considered as an interlocking system of many levels.

Narrative *omniscience* refers to any one of the higher levels of narration. The level may be relatively explicit (e.g., intrusive commentary) or implicit (e.g., implied authorial evaluation). The highest level of narration – that which frames all the other levels but which cannot itself disclose its own framing – is simply everything the reader, or spectator, comes to know about the structure of the text and provides a reference point from which to measure any other level. Omniscience does not mean that the reader finally knows all, or that there is an author/ narrator who knows all, but merely refers to the reader's toleration of a boundary or *limit* to what finally can be known *in* the text.[63] This boundary, in a more or less arbitrary manner, usually attempts to dissipate the desire to know more. Just as a narrative schema attempts to shape causality on both large and small scales to achieve a closure effect, so narration typically seeks a measure of completeness, an "omniscience effect." For example, to narrate the "end" of a story one must do more than merely stop: an appropriate ending normally requires a point of overview from which the previous knowledge that has been gained by the reader is shown to have been acquired through a comprehensive power to know. Of course, even the most explicit assertion that a power to know *is* comprehensive is still not an explicit assertion of its own power to know.

I conclude by offering a characterization of film narrative which draws upon topics discussed in this and previous chapters.

Film *narrative* is a way of understanding data under the illusion of *occurrence*; that is, it is a way of perceiving by a spectator which organizes data as if it were witnessed unfolding in a temporal, spatial, and causal frame. In understanding a film narrative, a spectator employs top-down and bottom-up cognitive processes to transform data on the *screen* into a *diegesis* – a world – that contains a particular *story*, or sequence of events.

"Story" data takes two forms: declarative knowledge ("what"

happens) and procedural knowledge ("how" it is witnessed and known).

1 Declarative knowledge is generated by a *narrative schema* ("abstract," "orientation," "initiating event," etc.) which yields a series of episodes collected as a focused causal chain (as opposed to a "heap," "catalogue," "unfocused chain," etc.). An experience of time emerges as data is processed and associated, that is, as the spectator *reorders* fragments on the screen (creating such story relationships as temporal continuity, ellipsis, overlap, etc.). Different experiences of time ("description," "duration," "causal implication," "order") are produced according to the complexity of juxtaposition allowed by the particular method (heap, catalogue, episode, etc.) being used to associate data. These temporal experiences related to the story may reinforce, oppose, or be variously integrated with screen time.

An experience of space, too, emerges as data is processed and associated, creating such story relationships as spatial chains, gaps, and reversals that in turn may reinforce, oppose, or be variously integrated with the two-dimensional space of the screen.

Focused causal chains are not just sequences of paired story events in time and space, but embody a desire for pairing events and the power to make pairs. Narrative causes ("remote," "intervening," "enabling," etc.) are thus principles of explanation, or criteria for grouping elements, which are derived from cultural knowledge as well as from physical laws: the human plans, goals, desires, and routines – realized in action sequences – which are encouraged, tolerated, or proscribed by a community.

2 Procedural knowledge is generated by a *narration* (or narrational schema) which yields a series of levels, or epistemological boundaries ("disparities"), associated with such nominal agents as narrators, actors, and focalizers. Acts of witnessing by these agents (similar to the spectator's acts of perceiving) function as explicit frames of reference for declarative knowledge. Several levels may operate simultaneously with varying degrees of compatibility and explicitness producing multiple descriptions of the data.

Procedural knowledge is limited to specific epistemological domains but the domains may be connected to one another. For instance, an event may appear to the spectator as if it were being directly witnessed ("scene"), or alternatively the event may appear in the second degree as merely referred to, or "mentioned," by a witness ("summary").[64] This is a simple illustration of the recursive nature of narration: a given level – describing how an object is being perceived – may itself be dramatized and become an object of perception, that is, become declarative and known through another (higher-level) procedure, one step more distant, which merely "mentions" the object. Hence a common structure for narration is hierarchical where one subject–object pair (describable in a temporal, spatial, and causal frame of reference) becomes the embedded object of another (more powerful) subject in a higher frame of reference. Levels may be linked, alternated, or embedded, and may assume a variety of rhetorical functions.

As a medium, film is a distinctive collection of techniques for representing time, space, and causality on the screen. Normally these techniques (e.g., sound and picture editing, camera movement, and *mise-en-scène*) should be understood not as conveying a "meaning" in themselves, but as "instructions" relating to procedures and rules used by a spectator in constructing a set of interrelationships. Such procedures are neither true nor false, but are measured only by their success or failure with respect to some goal.

By contrast, the declarative knowledge being produced by a spectator is true or false about the story world and may also be converted into propositions which the spectator believes to be true or false about his or her own, ordinary world. The operation of this latter type of reference, and its relationship to story and screen, is governed by a theory of *fiction* (see chapter 7).

The concepts in these general definitions must be supplemented, interpreted, and refashioned in accordance with the aims of particular narrative theories. Take, for example, my claim that narrative is a way of understanding data under the "illusion of occurrence." One way to interpret "illusion of occurrence" would be to seize upon the word "illusion" and argue that the perceptual illusions presented on the screen (e.g., of three-dimensional depth and motion) are the basis for cognitive *delusions* in which a spectator mistakes narrative patterns for the real world, or else imagines himself or herself within the story world. In this interpretation, narrative would be seen as attempting to psychologically baffle or transport the perceiver.

Another way of interpreting "illusion of occurrence" would be to emphasize the word "occurrence," embracing Arthur Danto's formulation of narrative as

an account in which the *general* knowledge of what *kind* of thing must have happened [under a known general law] is replaced by the *specific* knowledge of what *specific* thing, of the required kind, *in fact* occurred.[65]

117

Narrative in Danto's view is the end result of substituting concrete instances into laws covering causal interactions. Danto's formulation explains why one cannot argue with the logic of a fictional narrative by simply asserting that a given event "didn't happen." The reason is that a narrative explanation of data *begins* with a representation of space and time, begins with "what happened" as a premise for its instantiation of general laws. One can disagree with the general law which seems to be at work, or with its application, but not with "what happened," for that is a category mistake. Danto's concern – narratives constructed by historians – is thus doubly constrained: specific events occurring in the real world must be collected and then subsumed under one or more master narratives of greater generality.

Not all theories make the kinds of distinction I have used above in my general definition of narrative. Nevertheless I believe that my distinctions will be useful in evaluating how a concept is functioning within a particular theory. I also believe that many basic concepts (e.g., realism, time, editing, the camera, space, causality, voice, text) should be broken up into components and redefined according to their top-down and bottom-up aspects as well as their declarative and procedural aspects. The result will be a new complexity for some familiar concepts, but a better fit with the powers of narrative.

FIVE TYPES OF NARRATIVE THEORY

Narrative is enormously complicated even when we set aside its exchange value as a manufactured object in a community and concentrate on its use value as a psychological object for a perceiver. Many theories of narrative may be constructed by beginning at different points, highlighting different aspects of the phenomenon, and ignoring others. Roughly speaking, I believe that one can mark out five recent types of narrative theory using the above general definition of narrative as a frame of reference.[66] The five types of theory differ in the relative weight they assign to various aspects of narrative and especially in how they draw the line between declarative and procedural knowledge and the importance they assign to sensory knowledge. Without denying the sophistication and subtlety of individual theories, I will refer to the types broadly as being distinguished by an emphasis on plot, style, communication, reception, or the human drives.

One type of theory concentrates on the developmental logic of that "series of events" which is collected into a focused causal chain. This aspect of narrative organization may be termed the "plot." Vladimir Propp broke it down into a set of minimal actions each of which was further classified as a particular "function," conceived as "an act of a character, defined from the point of view of its significance for the

118

course of the action." Propp insisted that the study of *what* is done in a narrative should precede "questions of who does it and how it is done."[67] An important result of research based on this type of narrative theory emphasizing plot was that different actions in diverse stories could be shown to perform *similarly*, that is, to have the same "function" in producing the coherence of the events. For example, Propp argues that identical functions underlie each of the following events producing a powerful similarity among them in spite of the fact that they come from different stories.

1 A tsar gives an eagle to a hero. The eagle carries the hero away to another kingdom.
2 An old man gives Sucenko a horse. The horse carries Sucenko away to another kingdom.
3 A sorcerer gives Ivan a little boat. The boat takes Ivan to another kingdom.
4 A princess gives Ivan a ring. Young men appearing from out of the ring carry Ivan away into another kingdom.[68]

In a classic study, Propp found that in a hundred Russian folktales, there were only thirty-one functions and that while some of them could be omitted in particular stories, they almost always occurred in the same order in all the stories. The idea of a fixed set of functions in an unvarying order helps to explain some of the underlying similarities that may be perceived among certain groups of stories. In this way, "plot" becomes a theoretical and abstract concept capable of explaining a range of data, including the data of stories not yet invented.[69] Plot theories of narrative, though, have little to say about procedural knowledge and narration. Only a few of Propp's functions touch on the issue of the regulation and distribution of knowledge in a text; hence, his method will be inadequate for analyzing plots that depend on complex enigmas, psychological attitudes, or subtle shifts in perception and awareness.[70] At best, plot theories are confined to the aspect of narrative that I have called nonfocalized narration.

A second type of theory concentrates on style, on how the devices and techniques which are *specific*, or intrinsic, to a given medium operate to convert a "plot" into a "story." Style in film is conceived as a relatively autonomous system comprised of a set of uniquely cinematic techniques. However, defining the differences between plot and story, and the interactions between them that betray style at work, is a most delicate task. According to David Bordwell's definition, plot is at one remove from what is visibly and audibly present in the film before us; it includes certain inferences about narrative events as well as certain nondiegetic material bearing upon those events. Story is at a further remove from plot; it is a mental reconstruction of some of the events of narrative which are not witnessed by the spectator, though it also includes what is explicitly presented. For example, explicit events presented out of order in the plot are reordered by the spectator and supplemented by inferred events in constructing the story. However, Bordwell says that in some cases (a particular shot, or scene) the differences between plot and story vanish.[71] This raises a question: what is the appropriate temporal scale with which to measure plot and how does the spectator know what is appropriate? For instance, are both shots of an eyeline match part of the plot, or only the shot on the screen? Clearly, the notion of plot here is much more intricate and powerful than envisioned by the first type of theory discussed above. Plot has become more than a simple analysis of character action; it is now part of a larger cognitive process *intermediate* between the phenomenal text (which includes aspects of "style") and the "story" as mentally completed by the spectator (with all of its many implications). The concept of plot now carries great weight and has become a fulcrum for the explanation of narrative comprehension in terms of a "style." Indeed when this stylistic account of narrative is itself viewed as an Aristotelian narrative with a beginning in phenomenal form, a middle in plot, and an end in story, one may glimpse the true importance of "plot" as that "middle term" which separates style from story – preserving the integrity of each – while explaining the transformation of first into last.[72]

A second crucial problem for a narrative theory emphasizing style is to draw a firm distinction between the aesthetic and the nonaesthetic (the "practical") so that the effects of "style" – the particular use of materials and techniques that are deemed unique to a given art medium – may be better isolated. Kristin Thompson, building upon the work of the Russian formalists, asserts the importance of "art" as follows:

> The nature of practical perception means that our faculties become dulled by the repetitive and habitual activities inherent in much of daily life. Thus art, by renewing our perceptions and thoughts, may be said to act as a sort of mental exercise, parallel to the way sports is an exercise for the body.[73]

Thompson approves Victor Shklovsky's pronouncement that the "purpose of art is to impart the *sensation* of things as they are perceived, and not as they are *known*."[74] Art is a ceaseless and never-ending struggle to "defamiliarize" the familiar.[75] Thus it may be that Russian formalism, as one stylistic theory of narrative, has no need for a theory of interpretation separate from a theory of the sensation of things as they are perceived. The emphasis on sensation here recalls Bertrand Russell's "knowledge by acquaintance" from which he derives all other knowledge (e.g., "knowledge by description," or "knowing that").[76]

Russell argues that "knowledge by acquaintance" includes an acquaintance with all the sense-data of things and with oneself (memory, introspection) as well as with certain *universals* (e.g., qualities like redness, spatial and temporal relations, and logical universals like resemblance). Russell also argues that the notion of knowledge by acquaintance is fully compatible with ontologies based upon materialism, idealism, or dualism; that is, a strong form of empiricism is not a necessary consequence of this type of knowledge. It would seem that something akin to knowledge by acquaintance is the epistemology underlying Russian formalism and its varieties. Consistent with the idea that acquaintance is *logically prior* to all other forms of knowledge and reasoning, Thompson, along with David Bordwell, is able to forcefully argue that the goal of narrative criticism is not to uncover meanings or connotations, or to produce interpretations, but to analyze the actual patterns of the specific and concrete devices in each art medium that engage our perception of narrative.[77] This bold attempt to rethink the role of interpretation, and our interaction with the knowledge produced by narrative, will no doubt attract considerable comment.

A third type of theory treats narrative itself as a general, transcendent sort of medium – as a discourse or speech act – which is superimposed upon specific media like film and literature. This approach concentrates on how the techniques of "narration" (e.g., knowing how to do things with words or pictures) function as a general means of "communication," much like ordinary language and rhetoric, in altering and conveying a pre-existent story (setting, character, action, theme) for a spectator or reader. Narration in this sense is not confined to, or derived from, "aesthetic" discourse, but rather is powerfully connected to human goals and the exchange of information. As discussed earlier, works by Susan Lanser, Seymour Chatman, Mary Louise Pratt, and Wolfgang Iser illustrate the approach.[78]

The most recent approaches to narrative comprehension continue to focus on "narration," and "knowing how," but have shifted the attention from authors and narrators toward the reader – toward the reception of narrative and its immediacy for a reader.[79] What are the conditions which make possible a reading? How is sense made by the reader? In what ways does a reader imagine and construct authors and narrators? "Our easiest approach to a definition of any aspect of fiction," says E.M. Forster, "is always by considering the sort of demand it makes on the reader." In the reception approach, discovering "messages" from an author becomes less important than studying the psychology of a reader and how he or she is engaged by/in a text. For example, suspense, mystery, and surprise might be defined according to a reader's response to what he or she knows relative to what a particular character knows; or, a genre might be defined according to a reader's hesitation between two competing interpretations.[80] Reception theories may also define a reader's "horizon of expectation" in historical or sociological terms. These theories mark a return to the perceptual processes that were important to the Russian formalists even though they never developed a detailed theory of perception.[81] Nevertheless, reception theories differ strikingly from style and communication theories across a range of basic philosophical beliefs concerning the nature of meaning.[82]

A reception theory may make use of linguistic methods without thereby being committed to the assumptions underlying a communication theory. Recall that for Metz the spectator's perception of film *imagery* was a "spontaneous perception" of a "potential linguistic focus."[83] This notion may be developed in several different ways by a reception theory. For example, language may be connected to a theory of "inner speech" activated in a film spectator (conceived as either preconscious speech or conscious pre-speech);[84] or, it may be connected to a theory of the ordinary ways we create and exchange verbal reports about visual experiences. One need not posit an author, or delivery man, against which to measure the discovery of subvocal or vocal meanings. David Alan Black has created from these kinds of ideas virtually a new area of film study which he calls a theory of "synopsis." He argues that particular films are understood as narratives, and function within political settings, according to certain highly condensed verbal summaries we make of them.

> [R]ather than saying that a film shows us something . . . we have reason to want to say – however circuitous it may sound – that the viewing of the film has authorized us to *say*, to relate, that we have seen something: in fact, that we have seen something said, related.[85]

Black's novel theory and terms are meant to describe at the same moment both the reception of film narrative through what can be said of it, and the possibilities of its comprehension within languages already established and spoken in society.

A fifth type of narrative theory is related to reception theories, but asserts that the cognitive abilities of a reader used in producing various types of knowledge do not exhaust what is at work in responding to a narrative. There are forces "driving" cognition itself. Prominent among the class of so-called drive theories is psychoanalysis. It begins with the assumption that the instinctual drives are defined as *mental representations* of stimuli originating within the organism; that is, it is assumed that the human body creates representations not just of the external world but also of various internal, physiological states.[86] Internal and external representations jostle and intermix, and are not always clearly distinguishable or conscious: what is seen in the external world, especially, may have an origin from within – may be dictated by desire or fear. The study of human *memory* thus becomes critical because in storing and interconnecting information, it may erase such traits as the "source" of the information when assigning it a new meaning within a mental structure. Since "consciousness" is a relatively high-level form of awareness with severe capacity limitations (similar to the restrictions on short-term memory), it cannot be a full measure of what we know or why we act.

Like other types of theory applied to narrative texts, psychoanalysis may seize upon one or another aspect of the narrative phenomenon. It may, for instance, interpret the "plot" as a set of symptoms or distorted symbols analogous to a patient's dream; or, more fundamentally, it may challenge the very idea that a "story" underlies a plot. Jonathan Culler argues, for example, that studying the formal relations between story and plot neglects the insights offered through Freudian mechanisms, like deferred action. (Deferred action involves experiences and memories that are revised at a later date, acquiring new meanings to fit new circumstances or a later stage of psychic development.[87]) The operation of such Freudian mechanisms makes it "difficult to establish a bedrock of events which then get reordered by narrative; for narrative ordering may be what constitutes key events as events."[88] Furthermore, unconscious desires and fantasies, may construct a "plot" by concealing and repressing other plots. These ideas hint that the "narration" we imagine in a narrative may be interpreted in terms of a "primary process" of human thought governed by the pleasure principle (and anxiety) and not just as an aspect of the preconscious–conscious system governed by the reality principle and rationality, i.e., a "secondary process" perfectly generating an underlying, coherent "story."[89] Narration in this deeper psychoanalytic sense engages a reader in bringing forth unconscious (infantile) wishes and conflicts as well as provoking the reader *to react to* what is brought forth, or merely threatened (or possibly threatened!) to be brought forth, in his or her interactions with the text. A psychoanalytic approach stresses that the spectator's conscious understanding of a text is inseparable from his or her often unconscious memories and feelings. Under psychoanalysis the narrative object becomes fully as dense, complex, and contradictory as the human mind.

One of the difficulties a drive theory encounters in explaining narrative is that there is little agreement on which psychic mechanisms are pertinent, how they function, how they may be represented, and when they may appear in a text. Furthermore, unconscious drives, or "instincts," are contradictory by definition because they spring from unresolved tensions which must be repressed – desires that have been driven out of conscious experience (under the influence of the "reality principle"). Contradiction in its many guises is crucial to a psychoanalytic theory of narrative for it testifies to the actions of the unconscious. Thus the critic must search for the structure of narrative in unlikely places (or at several strata of human thought). The critic must boldly read against the grain, searching for the *non*literal, the counterintuitive, and for what is *not* said and *not* shown (i.e., repressed, forgotten, distorted, or disowned).[90] The critic looks for what is incompatible in the text (i.e., for evidence of conflict and anxiety) and hence he or she must strive to disunify what appears to be complete. This remains true even if the human drives are rendered as explicit themes in the form of *declarative* knowledge (e.g., films about psychoanalysis like *Freud*, *Spellbound*, and *Secrets of a Soul*) because the drives will continue to operate as (contradictory) *procedural* principles for the generation of the textual material. Psychoanalysis thus acknowledges a limit to what can be made explicit and coherent in a text as well as a limit to the types of knowledge humans can acquire about the psyche. At the center of the psychoanalytic method is a search for what is invisible and implicit and what may never be known. Such material of the irrational provides few landmarks for the analyst. Nevertheless I believe that cognitive psychology, like other reception theories, needs a drive theory. I also believe that psychoanalysis needs a more complete theory of the secondary process. Whether cognitive psychology and psychoanalysis need each other, however, is still another question.

Our perception of events in a story occurs within a variety of epistemological boundaries set by the levels of a narration which we initially believe are "in" a text that is "out there," rather than also in our own perceptions and imaginings. A narrative theory, too, initially classifies human experiences by setting boundaries on our thinking about objects that exist "out there." It specifies what will count as a narrative; what psychological effects may be produced by it; the possible uses, social value, and aesthetics of narrative; and how a history of narrative should be written. As such, however, a given theory is responding to some of our deepest beliefs about human beings and the nature of society, and reveals not only a narrative artifact, but also how we are thinking about the working of the human mind.

5

SUBJECTIVITY

LEVELS IN *HANGOVER SQUARE*

As we watch a film, the camera seems to reach out toward us, eliciting hypotheses about space and time, answering our thoughts at the same moment that a world is given shape on a screen. Paradoxically, the camera seems to be both a pretext for our speculations about an event and the already completed, material record of what must be experienced. The camera through its framings seems to become the very embodiment of narration, of "knowing how to go on . . ." about a world it already knows. In this sense, every theory of film narrative will make claims about the nature of the camera and its functioning. Roughly, its functioning will be described as being either "subjective" or "objective." In this chapter I will examine various claims about subjective uses of the camera; the next chapter will consider objectivity.

A camera's subjectivity becomes important when a narrative theory seeks to explain how a spectator may be put in contact with an author who is a subject, as well as with a world of characters and narrators who are also "subjects." I want to begin to address how a camera may be thought "subjective" by first looking closely at the levels of narration in the opening shots of John Brahm's *Hangover Square* (1944) (see figs 27–46). I will then consider particular issues bearing on subjectivity, and how these issues have been formulated in distinctive ways by particular narrative theories.

Overall, the opening shots of *Hangover Square* take us steadily "downward" through the levels of narration from powerful, extra-fictional narrations to nondiegetic and diegetic narrations, and finally to characters and internal focalization through a specific character. The 20th Century Fox logo and such opening credits as "Directed by John Brahm" point toward a historical author (figs 27, 29) while the title "in Hangover Square" which follows the names of three actors and appears in special lettering points in two directions: "up" toward a historical context where property rights are defined for the artifact with this name

125

Figure 27 Hangover Square

Figure 28 Hangover Square

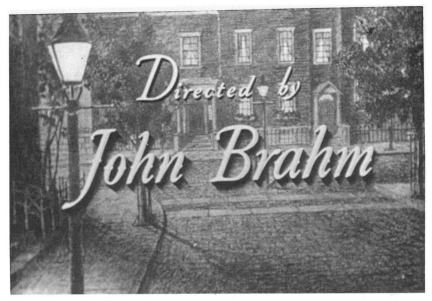

Figure 29 Hangover Square

Figure 30 Hangover Square

Figure 31 Hangover Square (shot 1A)

Figure 32 Hangover Square (shot 1B)

Figure 33 Hangover Square (shot 1C)

Figure 34 Hangover Square (shot 1D)

Figure 35 Hangover Square (shot 1E)

Figure 36 Hangover Square (shot 1F)

Figure 37 Hangover Square (shot 1G)

Figure 38 Hangover Square (shot 2A)

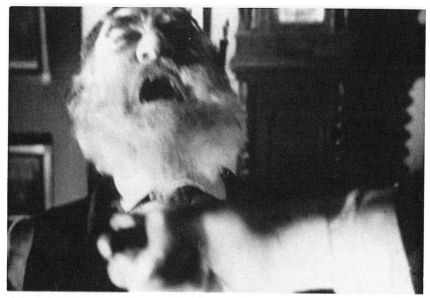

Figure 39 Hangover Square (shot 2B)

Figure 40 Hangover Square (shot 2C)

Figure 41 Hangover Square (shot 2D)

Figure 42 Hangover Square (shot 3)

Figure 43 Hangover Square (shot 4)

Figure 44 Hangover Square (shot 5A)

Figure 45 Hangover Square (shot 5B)

Figure 46 Hangover Square (shot 6)

(the word "in" implies an "outside") and down toward an embedded (fictional) story where the same name functions as an *abstract* for the narrative schema to be constructed (fig. 28). These opening titles are extra-fictional.

The tenth and final opening title (fig. 30) resembles the written, explanatory preface of *The Wrong Man* discussed in the previous chapter. It is a combination of extra-fictional and nondiegetic narrations which tells us *about* the story which is to follow:

> This is the story of George Harvey Bone who resided at number 12, Hangover Square, London, S.W. in the early part of the Twentieth Century. The British Catalogue of Music lists him as a Distinguished Composer – – –

These two sentences are a strange mixture of the exact ("number 12 . . . S.W.") and the indefinite ("in the early part of the Twentieth Century"), soliciting both an extra-fictional interpretation and a fictional, nondiegetic interpretation, respectively. The sentences mark a transition from nonfiction to fiction. They appear nonfictional when one focuses on the overprecision of the description. The relative insignificance of what is described only heightens the sense that the concrete details that are being evoked have come from a real world. Further, the details are themselves said to be detailed in an "authoritative" source (the British Catalogue of Music).[1]

On the other hand, the indefinite time stated in the written title is more typical of fictional reference (as if to say, "One day early in the twentieth century . . .").[2] The text seemingly offers facts while beginning the fiction. The second sentence does not end with a period. Instead, it is marked by unusual punctuation (three dashes) and seems to suggest that the statement in the British Catalogue is incomplete or wrong in a significant way; perhaps calling George Harvey Bone "distinguished" needs to be qualified. Additionally, the spectator may wonder why the story of a man's life is named for a street. Like Hitchcock's opening pronouncement in *The Wrong Man* that facts are thrilling, the narration here carefully preserves suspense by announcing a "story," citing an authority, intimating that these words are not as specific as they appear, and then inviting the spectator to participate in a search for more complete references, including a (moral) pertinence for us in another part of the twentieth century. The words themselves on the title card are suggestive, but indefinite about *their* authority ("This is the story . . . "). As our analysis of the following shots will make clear, although the search may be based on fact, it will be dominated by cognitive processes that are characteristic of a narrative reasoning that makes use of fictional references. The ten opening titles thus begin to put into place an ordered sequence of perspectives within

which to interpret the "truth" of the story. By citing the British Catalogue, the narration conceals the extent of its knowledge while allowing
the story to proceed through a series of less knowledgeable sources of
information.

The story continues with a fade-in to a close-up of fire spurting from
the end of a barrel organ followed by an iris-out and dolly-back to show
an organ grinder turning the crank (fig. 31; shot 1A). The opening
image is no accident; both fire and the melody of the organ grinder's
music will be important motifs throughout the story, helping to generate a large-scale pattern among local causes. The camera continues its
bold, assertive framing of the action by *craning up and away* from the
organ grinder, finding and following a lamplighter while gliding above
the street (fig. 32; shot 1B), and reaching the next street lamp *before* it
can be lit (fig. 33; shot 1C). When the lamp is lit the camera is *already*
on the same level as a second-floor window of an Antiques store in the
near background (fig. 34; shot 1D) and is ideally positioned to see into
the window. The camera dollies forward to the window where we see
the back of a man who is turned toward the frightened face of an old
man (fig. 35; shot 1E). The camera then moves impossibly *through* the
glass window and up behind the shoulder of the unknown man (fig.
36; shot 1F). From the title that functioned as an explanatory preface to
this point the narration is best described as nondiegetic. Even though
the narration is no longer describing the story in words (as in the
written title, fig. 30) and though the drawings behind the titles have
become moving photographs (suggesting a new causal and epistemological situation), the camera has continued to both anticipate the action
and provide perfect views of it (e.g., from above the street). These
views are impossible for characters in the diegesis to possess.[3] In its
foreknowledge of diegetic events as well as through its independence
from diegetic physical constraints, the camera acknowledges the diegetic world but is not (at this time) submitting to it.

The spectator may wonder when the camera will submit to diegetic
constraints; that is, restrict its framing in such a way as to blend in with
such elements as the decor, costumes, lighting, and the music of the
street organ in order to strengthen the dominant epistemological context
– a London street during one night in the early part of the twentieth
century. The old man, trying to defend himself, is throwing objects at
his attacker. Diegetic sound in the form of noise being made by the
two men as they struggle mixes with the music and slowly becomes
more prominent. The camera moves forward past the shoulder of the
attacker to confront the old man who now looks directly into the camera
and throws an object which momentarily blacks out the image (fig. 37;
shot 1G). With this brief movement past the man's shoulder, the camera
has abandoned the possibilities of nonfocalization or external

focalization in favor of an internal focalization through the eyes of the attacker – a point-of-view shot (hereafter abbreviated as "POV shot"). The blacked-out image minimizes the on-screen cues for a new shot and allows a cut (probably for technical reasons) to a new shot while *maintaining* the narrative continuity of an internal focalization (figs 37–8; shots 1G–2A). The camera continues to advance on the old man (fig. 38; shot 2A) who is stabbed (fig. 39; shot 2B) and drops from sight. The camera then moves upward as the killer's hand grasps a kerosene lamp (fig. 40; shot 2C) and rapidly tilts down to follow the lamp being hurled onto the old man's body lying on the stairs (fig. 41; shot 2D). The camera's move upward and tilt down represent the still unseen gaze of the killer. The total effect has been that of a smooth progression from the framing of fire at the end of a barrel organ to the internal view of a killer setting fire to his victim.

We finally see the face of the killer as flames leap upward (fig. 42; shot 3). The unusual, or eccentric, angle from below (cf. fig. 42 with figs 31–41) places the killer's head within a corner of the ceiling. The distorted, artificial perspective of the diagonal lines encourages the spectator to experiment with stylistic metaphors, to charge space itself with the demonic force of a personality. Such a description of the composition, especially if it is connected to other moments in the text, is evidence of another, simultaneous narration at work – an implied nondiegetic, or else implied extra-fictional, narration. The explicit narration also is subtly changing our access to narrative information. The face of the killer has been revealed (but not his emotions or motivation) and the next shot is an eyeline match (or possibly a POV shot) showing the stairs engulfed in flames (fig. 43; shot 4). The narration is withdrawing slightly from the killer so that his experiences, though still central, may be externally focalized allowing the spectator to learn more about his intentions and the causal underpinning of these events.

The final shots of the scene take us back outside the antiques store where the organ grinder sees the fire (fig. 44; shot 5A) and runs to the store window drawing a crowd and a policeman (fig. 45; shot 5B). The policeman then runs to sound the alarm and the scene ends on a fade-out as he is ringing a fire alarm (fig. 46; shot 6). These final two shots outside the store mark the end of a narrative unit, but not the end of the narrative. We have returned to our starting point in the street with the organ grinder, but not quite. Shot 5 *crosses* the 180 degree axis of action established by shot 1 (cf. fig. 44 with fig. 32) thus marking a slight departure from the beginning space and qualifing the geographical closure by promising to open new space: though we have returned to our starting point, the mystery of a burning building and a murder must now be resolved. Shot 6 just prior to the fade-out is left as a kind of narrative excess to be carried forward into the following scenes.

Although we look into the store from the outside (shot 5B), we possess more knowledge than any of these characters and will soon know a great deal more, for we will soon discover that the killer is the composer George Harvey Bone.

If one were to represent graphically the changes in narration through the ten titles and first six shots of *Hangover Square*, the result would be something like an inverted pyramid: a smooth v-shaped curve beginning with the extra-fictional logo of 20th Century Fox and progressing steadily "down" through other layers of the narration, becoming more and more restrictive until reaching an internal focalization through George Harvey Bone at the bottom tip of the "v." The narration then withdraws from him, moving back "upward," until it reaches an external view of the burning Antiques store. This view is a general view (i.e., diegetic narration) of a crowd of people who are distinguishable only for being onlookers, one of whom is a policeman who exists only to perform the action of sounding a fire alarm. The narration at this point has become diegetic and/or *non*focalized; it merely reports an event and is indifferent to the way in which any single individual might have seen it.

> 20th Century Fox
> (historical author)
>
> a fire alarm is sounded
> (nonfocalization)
>
> George Bone's perceptions
> (internal focalization)

The narration, however, has not returned to the type of narration that began the film, but rather has left us anchored in diegetic space and time, ready for the next scene to extend our understanding of these events. After establishing its power and credibility (e.g., through the perfect but impossible views of the moving camera in shot 1A–F, figs 31–6), the narration may operate in less explicit ways (e.g., through the eccentric angle of shot 3, fig. 42). Overall our knowledge has been distributed in a precise, hierarchical manner and in such a way as to make clear that the method of distribution will continue to yield information. Our knowledge has been balanced between external and internal views, and arranged in a formal symmetry (v-shaped and nearly closed) that both reveals and conceals information. Disorder in the story world has yielded to carefully controlled spectacle. The change from one narration to the next has been almost imperceptible (like slowly deflating and then inflating a balloon) even if large-scale changes are easy to see (e.g., from expansive written titles to a highly restricted

POV shot). The narration is economical, continuous, unified, productive, and by the end of the sequence, self-effacing: in a word, "classical." Most importantly, we are prepared to accept further explorations of these same types of restrictions on our knowledge, especially a continuing (and deeper) display of the psychology of George Harvey Bone. In the next scene, for example, moving distortions overlaid on a POV shot will represent not only George's disturbed perception but the blinking of his eyes!

SEPARATION OF MATERIAL AND STRUCTURE

The classical arrangement of the opening narrations in *Hangover Square* functions as a prototype for the film to develop and play against. In particular, it allows the musical track to indulge in a variety of excesses in characterizing the mind of a mad composer. The waltz music of the street organ is heard not only during the murder inside the Antiques store, but also later as a *non*diegetic accompaniment to the action and, remarkably, as part of George's climactic piano concerto. His psychosis, activated by "discordant sounds," is triggered when he plays and hears the organ grinder's waltz which he has unconsciously written into his composition, leading him to set fire to the concert hall and perish in the flames madly playing at his piano. In fact, his concerto turns out to contain most of the film's significant musical motifs and to also recall George's murder of an enticing but scheming nightclub singer and the burning of her body. Music, murder, art, madness, sexuality, discordant sound, genius, mood, and fire are being compressed by the sound track into a dense tangle. As Claudia Gorbman observes:

> The viewer starts to notice music from all sources . . . interpenetrating in the most disturbing manner. Concurrently with the progressive blending of musical types and levels of narration, the distinction between George and his murderous alter ego begins to break down. . . . In narrative cinema, music actively crosses narrational boundaries – between the objective and subjective, the diegetic and nondiegetic and metadiegetic – and *Hangover Square* foregrounds this liberty of the musical score to a hallucinatory degree.[4]

The visual narrative of *Hangover Square* provides a background against which the music may be "parsed" in a variety of ways and may interact with many textual elements from moment to moment. The music itself does not prescribe a "meaning" nor does it necessarily mark the boundaries of the narration, even though at times it expresses the madness of a particular character. The ebb and flow of the music and the simultaneity of various narrations again illustrates a fundamental principle of the analysis of narrative: narrative and narration are critically dependent upon top-down cognitive processes and are not determined by the formal boundaries of the material on screen, the "techniques" for displaying material, phenomenal categories that describe material, nor bottom-up cognitive processes. This concept is so important that I will refer to it as the principle of the "separation of material and structure." As we shall see, "structure" will be variously interpreted by different narrative theories. In empiricist accounts, structure resides in patterns in the material text (and the question then becomes what should count as being "in" the text); in rationalist accounts, structure is mental (and the question becomes what should count as being mental beyond "immediate consciousness").

Material and structure are not identical: it is a fact that different materials may achieve the same structure (synonymy) and that different structures may be achieved by the same material (ambiguity); or, when spread out in time, the same structure may reoccur in different materials (repetition), or the reoccurrence of the same material may nonetheless elicit different structures (multiplicity). The basic idea is that a pattern is more than a listing of its elements: some powerful rule or (top-down) process must bridge the separation in order to draw various elements into relationships. One of the problems for a narrative theory, then, is to explain how a spectator decides how much and what kind of knowledge will form a (structured) unit at a given time. In what ways may on-screen data be partitioned and reformed? What role do bottom-up processes play in overcoming separation? These questions are ways of asking how much separation between material and structure will be posited by a narrative theory.

The principle of separation applies not just to music, but to *any* sound or picture element, or technique (e.g., camera "angle" or "match" cutting). Consider the POV shot. On the model of shot 1 of *Hangover Square* (figs 31–7), one could easily imagine a POV shot comprising only a portion of a single shot. For example, the camera could begin with framings and movements which provide the spectator with a privileged access to *non*diegetic knowledge (e.g., anticipating events through perfect but impossible views), then the camera could move steadily closer and into the mind of a particular character, adopting the character's perception, and finally back out again to allow the character to move in front of the camera so that we might objectively see his or her facial reactions. Only a portion of this shot would be subjective. On the other hand, the transition between shots 1 and 2 of *Hangover Square* (figs 37–8), which makes use of a match on action across a momentarily black image, demonstrates that a POV shot actually could be comprised of a sequence of shots and still maintain the strict temporal and spatial continuity of a narrative internally focalized through a single character.

141

Therefore the presence of the POV shot as a narrative structure cannot be determined mechanically by measuring such material divisions as shots.[5] Even in a wider context, the relationship between narration and the editing of shots is not fixed but must be discovered. Although the spectator often relies on editing to highlight, say, the performances of actors which, in turn, help in establishing pertinent narrative units and boundaries (e.g., ending a scene at the proper time, cutaways, perfect views, reaction and detail shots), there is no *necessary* relationship between editing and narrative structure.

A key question for a narrative theory is how to describe the causal connection between the structure of a text and materials, or techniques; that is, in a film text, the connection between the spectator's formulation of structure and the physical camera (or the microphone), or else their technical "representatives" on the screen (e.g., angle and aural pitch). I want to begin to examine some of the ways in which this question has been addressed by different theories of film narrative and to show that narrative theories are based on assumptions about the appropriate connection of structure and material. I will begin by focusing on how depictions of character subjectivity in film narrative may be related to the spectator's perception of the material on screen.

WHAT MAKES FILM SUBJECTIVE?: A CASE STUDY OF *LADY IN THE LAKE*

Sooner or later most writers on cinema mention Robert Montgomery's *Lady in the Lake* (1946). It is one of the few classics whose fame rests on its convincing "failure." Writers, however, are sharply divided over the reasons for the failure and the conclusions to be drawn about the nature of narrative in film. For most of its 103 minutes, the film appears to be an elaborate POV shot from the private eye of detective Phillip Marlowe (played by Robert Montgomery). Characters look directly into the camera when speaking to Marlowe. At various times we see Marlowe's arms and feet at the edges of the frame; we see his shadow, smoke from his cigarette, his image in mirrors; we see extreme close-ups of a telephone receiver as he talks, lips approaching for a kiss, an on-rushing fist approaching for a knockout blow. The camera sways as Marlowe walks, shakes when he is slapped, loses focus when liquor is splashed in his eyes, and blacks out when his eyes close for a kiss and when he's knocked out.

There are six notable exceptions to Marlowe's pervasive POV: the opening and closing titles, and four scenes of Marlowe at a desk in his office speaking directly into the camera. These office scenes appear to take place shortly after a murder case has been solved. As Marlowe explains in the office scene which follows the opening titles:

Right now you're reading in your newspapers and hearing over your radios about a murder. They call it "The Case of the Lady in the Lake." It's a good title. It fits. What you've read and what you've heard is one thing. The real thing is something else. There's only one guy who knows that. I know it.

Marlowe announces his power and authority to tell the story and teases us with the strange, but appropriate, name of the case. He even tells us how he will tell the story:

You'll see it just as I saw it. You'll meet the people. You'll find the clues. And maybe you'll solve it quick. And maybe you won't. You think you will, eh? OK [points finger at camera]. You're smart. But let me give you a tip. You've got to watch them. You've got to watch them all the time. Because things happen when you least expect them.

Although Marlowe acts as a diegetic narrator (telling his own story), there are hints that other, implicit narrations are at work; or alternatively, one might say, other epistemological descriptions offered by a spectator will apply. For example, the opening titles present important clues and motifs; the unpolished phrasing and choice of words in Marlowe's speech at his desk links the film as a historical artifact to the genre of hard-boiled detective fiction; and his speech has an introductory quality to it reminiscent of Hitchcock's opening monologue in *The Wrong Man*.

Writers concerned with this film, however, have not pursued the implicit narrations, nor the explicit narration by Marlowe. One reason for this neglect is the final scene of the film which occurs with Marlowe at his desk. The case has been solved and Marlowe is explaining a few loose ends when into the room walks the female character who for most of the film has been Marlowe's adversary and a prime murder suspect. They declare their love and announce that they are going away together to make a new life. The film ends on a passionate kiss. The effect of this ending is to suddenly merge Marlowe's role as a diegetic narrator into Marlowe's role as a character. The time and place of Marlowe's telling apparently collapses into the continuing action of the story; personalized narration becomes simply *non*focalized narration. Closure is achieved for the two causal lines of the story that involve crime and romance.[6] The overall flashback structure of the film is dissolved and forgotten as the telling of the story seemingly disappears without a trace into the character of Phillip Marlowe who has solved the case, won the woman, and has no further point of view to offer. This makes it seem as if the rest of the film is subjective and present, that the POV shot is its only device, and that all other aspects of the story (decor, the end of a scene, ellipses) must be related to the surface perception of the character Marlowe who speaks from his office until finally his own story catches up with him and his narrating is no longer needed. It is not surprising, then, that critics take the POV shot as a synecdoche for the film's narrative and a test for how spectators relate generally to the experience of the medium of film where someone apparently has the power both to narrate and to share experiences with the spectator. *Lady in the Lake* is therefore useful as an extreme film because it has a way of bringing forth basic premises in a critical method. These premises and their bearing on narrative comprehension will be my main interest in discussing critical reactions to the film.

Julio Moreno rejects the use of the POV shot as a depiction of Marlowe's experiences in *Lady in the Lake*, asserting that "in cinema it is not possible to speak, in the strict sense, of a *narrator*. The film does not narrate, but rather it places the spectator directly without intermediaries, *in the presence* of the facts narrated."[7] For Moreno, cinema is too real to represent a fictional subjectivity because the spectator's eye is *equivalent* to the camera's *objective* lens. He stresses that the "nature" and "essence" of cinema is photography. The search for a "first-person visual" narration cannot succeed because photography can capture only the external world, not private experience. Even if we may sometimes think in images, photography cannot capture those pictures. Moreno contrasts the "purely visual" qualities of cinema to the "verbal" nature of literary narrative and concludes that the POV shot is at best merely "imitating . . . a *form* of literary narration." In attempting to recreate a verbal "I see x," the POV shot is not being true to the nature of cinema. Words on a page, however, can capture verbal thought and thus literature is the proper medium for first-person narration. Predictably, Moreno is suspicious of the use of spoken words in film, and nostalgic for the silent cinema which was purely visual, though he does not oppose certain visual metaphors expressive of character nor what I have earlier classified as an "external focalization" of narrative through a particular character – for example, through the use of eyeline matches – since these devices do not threaten the inherent objectivity of the external views provided by photography.[8]

Moreno's argument is reminiscent of aspects of André Bazin's theory of cinema. According to Bazin the film image acquires a fundamental objectivity because of its causal history: the spectator knows that an object which was once in front of the camera has left its imprint on film automatically through the action of light waves on a chemical emulsion. Moreover, the recording process occurs with no significant intervention by a human agent. Bazin disliked *Lady in the Lake*, German Expressionism, and Eisenstein's montage effects because the techniques employed seemed designed only to manipulate the natural recording process in favor of contriving abstract meanings and promoting an author's evaluation of reality. Bazin wanted the spectator to be an "invisible witness" whose freedom to see and interpret the image would be limited only by external conditions imposed on the camera by a concrete situation, even though the situation might be fictional.[9]

Bazin's ideas have been central to many debates in film theory. I cannot here survey the range of arguments that have been raised against Bazin and that, by extension, could also be raised against Moreno. One important line of criticism, however, has been that Bazin places too much faith in the techniques and institutions of cinema; that the spectator encounters facts only under a description and through a practice, not directly through a quality of "presence" on the screen; that cinema constructs a world rather than captures a pre-existent one; that what is comprehended as "real" in film is not exhausted by what is *visible* and *audible*.[10]

If cinema is too real to support a narrated subjectivity for Moreno, it is not real enough for Joseph Brinton. The spectator's eye, he says, is always *superior* to the camera's lens:

> Just as the dramatic perceptions of everyday life lie beyond the optical scope of the eye, striking cinematic effects depend on what the spectator apprehends outside the scope of the camera. . . . The relationship of human vision to the camera is a variable one, determined not by the eye itself, but by the human mind behind its retina . . . . Realistic utilization of a movie camera, whether "subjective" or "objective," does not rely on the physical science of photography, but on the psychological science of human perception.[11]

Again *Lady in the Lake* is held to be a failure, but now because it was not sufficiently subjective, rather than because it was false to the objective nature of photography. Brinton itemizes some of the "distinct superiorities" of the eye over the camera (greater mobility, efficiency, angle of view, resolution of depth, etc.) and argues further that representing true subjectivity depends upon exploiting a spectator's shifts of attention and memory through a *blend* of subjective and objective techniques. The cinema will need to adjust all of its resources to the psychology of the spectator; or, to put it another way, *all* film techniques have a subjective use, not just the familiar "subjective" devices like the POV shot. The aim is to show *how* a character thinks, not just *what* a character thinks about or sees. According to Brinton, this involves a spectator's entire process of thinking and hence a wide range of techniques will be required with no technique necessarily excluded.[12]

One premise of Brinton's approach is that it is people who make narratives and meanings, not sentences or cinematic shots. While

145

Moreno believes it is vital to draw a line between literature and film (and others in the same spirit have drawn lines between theater and film, painting and film, music and film, etc.), Brinton suggests that narrative is not defined by specific material forms, or stimuli emanating from such forms, but rather is defined through a person's predisposition to make narrative and meaning using whatever is at hand. Brinton is thus suggesting a cognitive-psychological approach where narrative is a mode of reasoning and is not visible in the way that a photograph or a material object is. Still, Moreno does not go so far as to adopt Bazin's distrust of editing and, though Moreno emphasizes the nature of different media, materials and techniques, he would agree with Brinton that editing might be a useful tool to represent character subjectivity.[13] Thus there seems to be an area of overlap between the two positions that would permit new approaches to utilize features of both in seeking to explain subjectivity in film.

A SYNTHESIS: TELLING/SHOWING/SUMMARY/SCENE

André Gaudreault draws on a widely used distinction in narrative theory to propose that there are two master types of film narration. Whereas verbal narrative uses only "telling" and theatrical narrative uses only "showing," film has a special nature which allows it to utilize both telling and showing, or what Gaudreault calls "narration" and "monstration." This raises the possibility that much of Brinton's theory may be combined with Moreno's theory. Telling involves a "narrator" who places the events of the narrative in the *past*, or creates some other non-present temporal modality, such as the conditional. (Recall Phillip Marlowe at his desk telling the audience, "You'll see it just as I saw it.") The film narrator works *only through editing*. By contrast, showing involves a "monstrator" who places the events of the narrative directly in front of the spectator in *present* time. The monstrator works only during the process of shooting the film. The monstrator delegates power to the camera to occupy the place of the spectator at the scene of the action which is to be recorded. Gaudreault says that the monstrator's actual "speech act" occurs only during projection of the film at which time the monstrator creates an illusion of presence for the spectator by *quoting* what was recorded in the past, but without acknowledging that it is a quotation. It is clear that the success of Gaudreault's theory will depend upon further careful elaborations on the troublesome issue of time in film, on the unresolved relationship of speech and language to pictures, and on the nature of *covert* monstration.[14]

Gaudreault's notion of monstration seems to have been devised in order to embrace ideas like those of Bazin and Moreno. Monstration allows one to imagine a narrative "scene" as simply an event happening in front of a camera rather than as something *already* invented and narrated (i.e., as already told). Monstration exists only in the present tense. The result for Gaudreault is that one of the two components of the film experience (showing) may be imagined by us to have existed independently of the camera and, moreover, we may witness it again by searching for its causal traces in the film image. On the other hand, Gaudreault's notion of "telling" seeks to account for the other great tradition in film theory associated with Sergei Eisenstein (and Brinton) which emphasizes the film's active engagement with a spectator's processes of thought and emotion, traditionally associated with editing, producing a sort of mental realism. Thus the nature of editing for Gaudreault would seem to reduce to an intricate *ellipsis*: a breaking apart and omission, a "summary" of a pre-existent scene, or scenes, which acts to color something old or construct something new. Gaudreault insists that the opposition between telling and showing is exactly the opposition between editing and shooting a film. The resultant theory is a unique hybrid of ideas which achieves breadth and empirical precision at the cost of a certain rigidity which, if it doesn't violate the principle of the separation of material (and technique) from structure, at least reduces the distance between material and its function to an uneasy minimum. This leads to a number of questions about Gaudreault's scheme. What exactly does the camera record: an actor, or a character who is already fictional, or both? Does monstration include set design, composing the image, anticipatory camera movements, performance, and sound? Is off-screen space simply what is not being shown at present, or is it space which has been withheld in the telling of the event? Does the sound of a door opening off-screen tell us, or show us, the door?[15] And finally, does telling include slow motion, the 180 degree axis of action, and editing which has been "displaced" into the *mise-en-scène* (as in work by Sergei Eisenstein, Miklós Jancsó, and Jean-Luc Godard)? These problems are perhaps not insurmountable. Relaxing the definitions of telling and showing would allow more flexibility in describing related effects on a spectator, but would also tend to slide Gaudreault's theory back toward an acknowledgement of the two great traditions of Eisenstein and Bazin (Brinton and Moreno) without specifying their interrelationship.[16]

Gaudreault's linking of showing to "scene"[17] hints at another, closely related opposition which is variously defined and employed in theories of narrative: scene versus summary. Classical film narrative, like the traditional novel, appears to alternate between scene and summary. David Bordwell remarks, "By the early 1930s, montage sequences became so common that we can say that the classical Hollywood film consisted of only two types of decoupage units: *scenes* and *summaries*."[18] The basic idea behind this dichotomy is that the spectator must presume that a narrator (usually nondiegetic) is explicitly at work "telling" the story when the story appears in some abbreviated form (e.g., a synopsis of the action, or a rearrangement of story events by the plot) but need not imagine such a narrator when space, time, and causality are rendered in some standard form – a "scene" – that appears to respect an action's duration, plausibility, and definiteness (mere "showing"). In this sense, a "scene" may be taken as a zero-degree line for measuring how space, time, and causality may be manipulated in a narrative until their construction becomes "obvious" or pertinent in a summary, or telling. For Gaudreault there is a strict alignment among scene, monstration, cinematography, presence, and present time which is opposed, point for point, to a second alignment among summary, narration, editing, absence, and non-present (all other) time. Writers such as Bazin and Eisenstein, however, attain greater flexibility in their theories than Gaudreault by introducing additional concepts to widen the "separation" between material and structure.[19] For example, several varieties of scene and summary may be defined, or else scene and summary may become points on a spectrum along with other forms of dramatic presentation. Using concepts for the most part quite different from one another, Genette finds a total of four dramatic forms, Chatman and Wollen find five, Metz eight (the "Grande Syntagmatique"), Bordwell nine, and Burch fifteen.[20] The reason that the forms of a scene begin to multiply is that a "scene" cannot simply be identified with the presence of "dialogue" but must include other variables chosen by a theorist that relate, for example, to the "quantity" and "plausibility" of information, the absence of "overt" narration, and/or the treatment of "time."

In order to map the kinds of dramatic form, one must compare the duration of a segment of narration to that of the story event it represents. When the imagined duration of a story event is approximately "equal" to the time of its telling/reading, according to criteria selected by the theorist, the result is a "scene." Genette argues that measuring duration in literature, however, is a tricky operation because the actual reading time depends on the individual who is reading. But he suggests that in the case of some arts, such as music and film, there may be an objective way to determine the speed of reading.[21] Bordwell develops this idea by asserting that in film *all* aspects of time, including duration, are "strictly governed" by the projector. "Just as we cannot choose to skip around in a film or go back and rewatch a portion, so we cannot control how long the narration takes to unfold. This is of capital importance for filmic construction and comprehension." Bordwell continues: "Since screen duration is ingredient to the very medium of cinema, all film techniques – mise-en-scène, cinematography, editing, and sound – contribute to its creation."[22] For Bordwell the importance of projection time is that it makes "narration" dependent on the nature of the medium (it is projected in real time). The medium, in turn, includes the unique qualities of a film's techniques and *stylistic system*. In effect, Bordwell shifts the objectivity that Bazin and Moreno found in the film image, and that Gaudreault found in the shooting time of monstration, to the mechanism of projection. His purpose, however, is to give a weight and priority to style, to the concrete materials of the medium. By linking style to the fundamental time of projection, style becomes a basic ingredient of cinema – one of the ways in which the medium controls narration and the spectator's perception of plot and story. Style, thus separated from the profilmic, is free to exist in certain situations only for itself as a purely artistic and arbitrary manifestation of the film medium as a medium. Style becomes "palpable," working on us just as relentlessly as the projector.[23] Furthermore, style becomes worthy of study in its own right; as we have seen, this view spawns a class of narrative theories distinct from reception theories, even though style need not be entirely decoupled from other textual and historical factors.

Genette's temporal distinction between film and literature, when combined with Bordwell's emphasis on the importance of medium-specificity for narrative, may divide these media too much. The *conventional* nature of the equality between narrating time and story time in literature, stressed by Genette, may be just as valid for film.[24] What one sees in the split-seconds of cinema's screen time may depend on one's skills in looking, purposes, background knowledge, attention, and accidental circumstances. Our ability to process data top-down should not be confused with the mandatory nature of bottom-up processing. The intercut chase sequence in *The Girl and Her Trust*,[25] for example, and the chameleon-like time of the credit music of *The Wrong Man* demonstrate that there are occasions in which the spectator has great freedom to adjust and fill out a temporal sequence. (Recall that even though the classical, chameleon narrative presents a range of correct choices, it will congratulate the spectator for his or her particular selection by intimating that that selection is uniquely correct.) Projection time may set certain limits and thresholds but the extent to which it determines or "strictly governs" narrative comprehension is an open question. This is especially true when one considers the powerful effects of a spectator's memory and the organization of his or her conceptual system. In another context, Bordwell says of space: "By using conventional schemata to produce and test hypotheses about a string of shots, the viewer often knows each shot's salient spatial information *before* it appears."[26] In some measure this idea should apply to time as well: the spectator should be able to anticipate, rethink, or construct time in ways quite apart from the time of projection.

SUBJECTIVITY IN NARRATIVE THEORIES

The somewhat modest conclusion to be drawn from the above range of arguments is that although one may begin with what seems to be a straightforward way of describing events in a story as occurring in either a scene or summary format, one is soon led into more fundamental issues concerning the nature of cinema, how we watch it, the relationship of the eye and "I" to the camera and editing, the role of the film projector, qualities of the medium, problems of narration (e.g., telling and showing), and what constitutes realism. In other words, the narratological terms used in describing film are built upon more basic assumptions about the nature of cinema, what cinema does best, and what it ought to do. Since these narrative terms and descriptions may also be used to chronicle changes among a group of narratives and establish period classifications, they may be employed to write a *history* of narrative cinema and a history of its value in society. (For example, Gaudreault claims that films in the period 1895–1910 were exclusively constructed on the principles of monstration.[27]) The starting point for a narrative theory may be humble and even obvious but the path soon enters a thicket where hard decisions must be made about large expanses of territory.

Again, we see that narrative theories are not neutral but derive from more fundamental beliefs including implicit theories of perception, the importance of vision in knowing the world, how that world may be seen, and what it should look like when we understand it (cf. "I *see* what you mean"). As a narrative theory moves deeper into the human mind to explain our ability "to see," it begins to draw on one or more general theories of consciousness and the human drives. Thus it should not be surprising that the narrative of *Lady in the Lake* may come to embody such processes as dream, fetishism, anxiety, perversion, and universal myths. In calling attention to reception and style-based theories of narrative above, I have hardly begun to sketch the range of theories that may be applied to explain the subjectivity of *Lady in the Lake*. It will be worthwhile to consider some additional judgments about the film and their relationships to narrative theories.

A drive theory: narrative as driven by dreams and instincts

Robert Eberwein claims that *Lady in the Lake* is

> possibly the most sustained equivalent in film of a *genuine* dream.
> . . . What Montgomery did, in trying to present the equivalent of
> a literary first person point of view was – I believe unwittingly –
> to duplicate the conditions of a dream. But not OUR dream, surely.
> The perspective of viewing which the audience is presented is,

thus, in its consistent use of a method (although at times inconsistent), actually *less* cinematic, less like our ordinary experience of film. . . . In effect, the film denies its fictive significance as a film by restricting itself to the subjective camera. It offers the equivalent not of a first person narrative, but of one written in the *second* person. It is as if we were being told for the duration of a novel: "Then you watched the woman enter the building"; "you drove faster and faster until the car crashed against the post"; "you shot at the man with your revolver," etc. Unbearable. It breaks down the barrier between art and life.[28]

Like Moreno (who says film cannot have a literary narrator) and Gaudreault (who says film does have a literary narrator but one who must compete with a monstrator), Eberwein builds his idea of narrative on the *differences in material* between film and literature, and ultimately, on the differences between art and life. He decides that, both as a "logical necessity" and as an "artistic consideration," a dream sequence in film requires a combination of subjective and objective shots to maintain the integrity of art as opposed to life.[29] *Lady in the Lake* is too pure and too intense.

Eberwein develops his particular notion of dreamwork by drawing on the psychoanalytic theory of Jacques Lacan.[30] Stuart Marshall also uses Lacan in explaining the "failure" of *Lady in the Lake*, but argues that Montgomery's attempt to create a "total" identification between the spectator and Phillip Marlowe is in actuality not an important part of the film.[31] Marshall finds such psychic mechanisms as scopophilia, fetishism, and the Oedipal drama – which refer back to the original trauma of the recognition of sexual difference – much more significant than dreamwork in assessing the subjectivity of *Lady in the Lake*. Furthermore, he argues that the film works on the spectator in an entirely unexpected and surprising way by actually being the narrative of a *heroine* – with the unlikely name of Adrienne Fromsett – who is radically transformed through the socialization of *her* drives – not those of the hero – and through *her* submission to the Law of the Father. The result for the heroine is a new name (by marriage), and for the spectator a rather complex and *contradictory* working through of a male castration anxiety.[32] For Marshall, subjectivity cannot be isolated in a single character or a single experience but must be defined through conflict and opposed experiences. If male subjectivity is at stake in the film, it is not because Phillip Marlowe is a male, but because the processes at work narrating the story enact a typically male psychic drama for the spectator.

One may think of a drive theory as probing an extreme of a spectator's psychological labor. Drive theories like those of Eberwein and Marshall attempt to explain what allows our thought to be coherent. Since narrative is one form of coherence, it is natural that psychoanalysis itself in its theory and practice makes explicit use of narrative fictions, such as the "primal scene" and "family romance," in describing how thinking progresses from the instinct-determined autism of the infant to the socially adaptive and veridical thinking of the adult.[33] These foundational scenarios may then be compared to more prosaic narratives. One problem that remains is how to describe the impact on an individual psyche of other forces, such as the social and political; or, in a more limited sense, how to describe the impact of the actual materials and style put forward by a textual object. Without some conception of external influences and material effects, a drive theory (or a reception theory for that matter) moves toward solipsism.

Narrative as a manifestation of plots

William Luhr approaches *Lady in the Lake* by comparing the *plot* devices used in four versions of the story – in the novel, two drafts of the screenplay, and in the film. He analyzes references to "female impersonation" in the plot of the film and finds that the action of the film "establishes a rigidly oppositional, partially sado-masochistic structure of sexual interactions."[34] Though his method is based on a study of action and plot, not on psychoanalysis, he reaches a conclusion similar to that of Marshall: the central character is actually Adrienne Fromsett, not Phillip Marlowe. The story is about her "duty" to help "her man." By the end of the film this duty has been made clear. "Nothing else, not her career, not any other aspect of her personal life, is important. She has learned her place."[35] Like the lesson of Griffith's *The Girl and Her Trust*, a girl must find her man and trust in him. For Marshall, however, the effects of the theme of "impersonation" found by Luhr would extend far beyond the actions of an enigmatic character and instead reach toward the dynamic and shifting emotions which make up the personality of the spectator. In the context of psychoanalysis, the very ideas of "Fromsett" and "Marlowe" are already impersonations – constructions standing in for the shaping of a spectator's sense of self.

It is clear that different approaches to narrative may reach conclusions that are compatible. In the present case, one could imagine Marshall's psychoanalytic method being applied to an analysis of plot (e.g., searching for Freudian "symbols" in *Lady in the Lake*) or Eberwein's method being applied to style (e.g., drawing parallels with dream processes[36]). An analyst might also seek to expose the psychopathology of character, or to produce a psycho-biography of a historical author or other communicant,[37] including the recipient. Additionally, psychoanalysis could be applied to an analysis of the *narration* of a text, to its procedural principles, as if the text itself were on the analyst's couch generating a discourse implicating the spectator in processes of transference and counter-transference.[38]

Luhr also examines *Lady in the Lake* in relation to its historical authors (Raymond Chandler, Steve Fisher, Robert Montgomery), studio economics, and genre. He notes, for example, that the genre of film noir permits, and even encourages, unusual stylistic experiments like bizarre POV shots. He thus opens the film toward biographical, economic, and historical factors – toward the social substance which underlies the exchange value of narrative as a manufactured object. His discussion of the "intentions" of the authors could be further developed into a communication theory (of the use value) of narrative; that is, the film could be seen as conveying messages, or as embodying an *a priori* personal (or studio) vision of the world, which it is the task of the reader to decode and recover from the impersonality of the material object.

Narrative as a manifestation of history

It is not uncommon for a theory to make some connections between the psychological labor of recognizing narrative – its use value – and the social, economic, and institutional base which regulates how capital, resources, and physical labor bring forth narrative as a material object with a purpose and exchange value. Again, this touches on an area that is not my main concern in this book. Nevertheless, it might be instructive to examine one set of premises which connect narrative to society and history.

Dana Polan, following Pierre Macherey, holds that "narrative is an imaginary solution to a problem posed . . . by its social moment."[39] Polan traces in American films of the 1940s the social problems of war, postwar communism, consumerism, and the changing roles of women. He discovers that

> a dominant power and a disturbing paranoia interweave and find each to be a parodic mirror image of the other. Power here is the power of a narrative system especially – the power that narrative structure specifically possesses to write an image of life as coherent, teleological, univocal; narrative, then as a power to convert contingency into human meaning. Paranoia here will first be the fear of narrative, and the particular social representations it works to uphold, against all that threatens the unity of its logical framework. Against the horror of all that escapes its seemingly overwhelming force, narrative takes on a number of possible strategic forms.[40]

153

For Polan, the structure of narrative thinking is also the power to justify social values by creating an order (and a destiny) for them. By contrast, paranoia is the fear of narrative power. This fear may itself be represented in a text by elements which seek to escape or work against narrative unity – elements which are "excessive."[41] The belief is that power and fear "mirror" each other in narrative texts in the same way that dominant and subversive social values contest one another in a historical situation. For Polan, *Lady in the Lake* is not the triumph of a personalized vision but the mark of a loss of control, an inability to escape a point of view. The sustained POV shot in the film dramatizes a descent into paranoia, aggression, doubt, sadism, and masochism which intermittently attacks the power of narrative to make conventional sense of the social issues of the 1940s.[42]

In spite of worthwhile efforts like that of Polan and Bill Nichols, and the more conservative approach of Will Wright,[43] the sense of history produced through most narrative theories is often tentative and self-serving. It is no easy task to match a powerful psychological theory of narrative to a theory of the balance between stability and change in a social and political setting. If history is somehow "expressed" by narrative, one will still need to know the detailed psychological (and biological) conditions which make expression possible.

There is a danger that a narrative theory might imagine history in its own image or attempt to explain it away by simply absorbing it. For example, J.P. Telotte, like Eberwein, finds dream at work in *Lady in the Lake*, but then argues that in moving away from the normal world, dream establishes contact with an archetypal realm which is part of a *social* self – a sense of community that denies all egocentric perspectives and holds itself strangely open to history. In a typical passage Telotte argues that the pervasive POV shot functions to make Phillip Marlowe "lost" for much of the narrative and thus he becomes the object of the spectator's search for a *social* identity.

> Our narrative placement in Marlowe's perspective and the paradoxical incarnation that results – simultaneously an absence and a presence – point up the fundamental purpose of such dream-like experiences. They involve us in a search for ourselves, for some mysterious element of the psyche that might render us *complete* by enabling us to find *our own correct place in the world*. In *Lady in the Lake*, we especially look into those stares directed at the camera by the other characters in the narrative and find in this "gimmick" a tentative rendering present of a normally absent portion of the self, a human complicity affirmed in spite of the usual sense of spectator absence that film typically affirms. Through this mechanism, then, the film points up a basic function of the detective story: it engages

us in a dream of individual *and cultural completion*, forcing us to recognize how much we are indeed the stuff that dreams are made of.[44]

Telotte's argument celebrates *paradox* by embracing several senses of "presence" and "absence" (simultaneously present!) to suggest the impossible union of personal and social (the word "completion" appears often in his essay); but since he mentions nonpsychological determinants only in psychological terms, he never quite reaches the actual social and historical dimension of human experience. Instead he shuttles between the concrete and the incredible using his own brand of dream reading to imagine a spectator in history. He claims, for example, that the ambiguous references to "them" – as in "You've got to watch them" – in Marlowe's introductory speech (more fully quoted above) refer to *dream images* which will erupt suddenly from within our own psyches during the film to reveal ourselves in our own dream. Telotte admits that these private and reflexive dream images cannot appear in the film and must remain "unframed," but the film can nonetheless refer to them indirectly by using Marlowe's introductory speech to frame a story (an "imaginal trip") which then frames *door images* which literally frame characters who enter or exit in a search for social and cultural completion; presumably this is meant to suggest that the spectator must be ever alert to what can *not* be framed and to his or her own search for social (and metaphorical?) completion.[45]

Telotte discovers that *Lady in the Lake* contains forty-five different door shots and proceeds to interpret them in a variety of metaphorical ways, apparently looking for what cannot be explicitly framed – that is, history. Telotte's argument connects stylistic metaphors into chains that embrace each metaphor's negative (e.g., framed but not framed). For example, he says that no truth comes "neat," but like a door always "opens onto," and leads into, another enigmatic area. He then connects doors to windows, archways, and mirrors, and then to characters who erect disguises as "barriers" for anyone who seeks to "enter their realm." Ultimately these characters, he declares, are victims of their own *mise-en-abyme*,[46] becoming "disconcertingly unfixed and unpredictable, much like the figures of dreams." Characters are caught up in a chain of actions: framing, framed, reframed, unframed, and unhinged.[47]

For Telotte (and drive theories in general) what the camera actually frames is merely the beginning of what must be framed by the spectator in comprehending the film. Clearly we are a long way from the simple camera of Julio Moreno. One can, however, go still further.

Holistic theories of narrative

Telotte's myth of human "completion" and oneness – an end to a *mise-en-abyme* – is fully realized in Vivian Sobchack's application of phenomenology to the experience of film. For her, *Lady in the Lake* is an illustration of a more fundamental, astonishing fact: film itself has a "body" which is quite literal, and not at all metaphorical, and its bodily functions may be compared directly with human ones. She describes the "failure" of *Lady in the Lake* in the following way:

> Although the *function* of both Marlowe's body and the film's body is the *same* (i.e., to focus attention within a visible intentional horizon and express that perception as a viewed view), the *bodily means* by which that function is achieved are *visibly different* – and dependent upon the different material nature of the respective bodies. . . . That is, the human lived-body does not attend to the world and realize its intentional projects of attention in the same visible manner as does the film's lived-body. . . . *Lady in the Lake* also problematizes another aspect of the failure of the film's body to disguise itself as human. . . . [A]s the film's lived-body emphasizes its perception as grounded in a human body, it becomes a slave to that body, afraid to leave it for fear it will lose its already tenuous hold on its disguise. Thus, *Lady in the Lake* becomes peculiarly claustrophobic to watch. Its perceptive and expressive behavior is *curtailed* and *constrained* by bodily existence rather than *enabled* by it. Marlowe, and we as spectators, are literally grounded in bodily existence, and perceptually and expressively live the body through none of the other modalities of experience it should enable: dreaming, imagining images, projecting situations, temporarily assuming an other's situation as a subject.[48]

For Sobchack, what is "visible," even in cinema, is only contingent and not fundamental. In a somewhat complementary way, Bruce Kawin believes that cameras, projectors, and films literally have a "mind."[49] Thus the starting point for these writers is that the film possesses a body and a mind. In a sense, we have moved full circle from empiricist accounts which seek to minimize the separation between the material and structure of a text by giving great weight to the differences between the arts and distinctive styles, to rationalist accounts which widen the separation by positing unobservable processes driving consciousness (reaching a maximum with psychoanalysis), and now back to holistic accounts like those of Telotte, Sobchack, and Kawin which again virtually abolish separation, but by concentrating on a phenomenology of appearances that refuses to distinguish between subjective and objective, mind and material.[50] In the holistic accounts, thinking about

156

material operates to fully animate it. Such accounts are monisms and are an extreme version of a reception approach to narrative; the ones just mentioned take consciousness (intention, attention, memory, dream, expression . . .) to be the unifying principle of all phenomena, whatever their material forms. It is an open question, however, whether consciousness is whole or modular, whether it is the central reality of existence, and in what ways it is identical to other existents.[51]

HOW MANY CAMERAS ARE IN A FILM?

It should be clear that one cannot arrive at an explanation for the perceived "failure" of *Lady in the Lake* without specifying the narrative and perceptual theory to be used in analyzing the film. Therefore I will be content with a narrow and limited conclusion. If one takes *Hangover Square* with its large number of explicit and rapidly shifting levels of narration as a reference point, then *Lady in the Lake* will appear strange and constricted. The comparison suggests that if the purpose of Montgomery's film is to create an identity between spectator and character, the primary reliance on a single device of internal focalization – the point-of-view shot – actually *limits* what the spectator can easily know about the character. Though a POV shot may appear simple and straight-forward in comparison with "objective" narration, it actually requires the spectator to hold together a greater number of assumptions – corresponding to the descriptive assumptions of *all* of the levels of narration above it – and hence is more restrictive than higher-level narrations. For example, the specific *angle* of view on an object is normally irrelevant to our comprehension of the object in space – any one of several angles would suffice in a nonfocalized narration. However, in a POV shot the specific angle of view is importantly tied to the attention and awareness of a specific character and thus the angle must be captured and held in working memory by the spectator. Or, to put it another way, the spectator's recognition of a character's awareness depends crucially on a *counterpoint* of character awareness with a *non*-psychological narration, such as a nonfocalized or even externally focalized narration.[52] The sustained use of a single type of narration reduces the range of information available since the spectator must attempt to continuously infer relevant contexts while holding surface details in place – details normally discarded in creating a narrative when contexts are objectively narrated.[53]

The above argument can be restated in psychoanalytic terms. For Freud, "personality" depends for its definition on an Other, or perhaps Others. There is no absolute Self in this view, but only a series of relationships that have been experienced with others – a series of relative contexts that have taught a sense of "self." Levels of narration in this view, then, become a mechanism for providing the spectator with the possibility of multiple, fluid identifications with a character by providing additional contexts (Others) against which to know the character. Moreover, since levels of narration need not be compatible, the possibility arises that contradictory desires/anxieties may be represented for the spectator through overlaps, juxtapositions, and breaks in the narration. With a multiplicity of levels, the text may work through complex forms of Otherness: archaic stages of development, paradoxical feelings, disguise, ambivalence, bisexuality, and masochism.[54] Therefore, in a psychoanalytic explanation, complexity of narration facilitates story and character complexity; simplicity obstructs it.

What can be said, then, about the relationship between the spectator and the "subjective camera"? I believe that the concept of a camera can be defined only within a particular theory of narrative or nonnarrative comprehension in film.[55] A theorist uses concepts like "camera" and "screen" in order to describe a spectator's degree of "separation" from the material of film (as a condition for his or her "comprehension" of the experience of film). Further, the idea of levels of narration hints that Gaudreault's two kinds of camera – one which narrates and one which monstrates – may not be enough within a given narrative theory. Perhaps there is a different kind of camera for each level of narration! The historical, profilmic camera (which usually rests on a tripod) is not quite the same camera which we reconstruct under the pressure of organizing data narratively in our effort, say, to imagine an organ grinder in *Hangover Square* as he discovers a fire in an antiques store, or Phillip Marlowe's ability to have a point of view on a lady.

We perhaps may go still further, and wonder what other constructs of the spectator undergo subtle changes in function from one level of narration to the next. For example, when the frame of reference is one of the higher levels of narration, it may be appropriate to conceive of "character" more in terms of the qualities we imagine for "real persons." Comprehending characters *in relation to* real persons is not a naive way to understand narrative, just as it is not inappropriate to comprehend steam rising in a film in relation to our experience of the physical laws of the world. What is inappropriate is confusing a character with a real person, or failing to recognize the diversity of levels and functions in a narrative text when the task is to understand not what, but how, we understand.[56]

To return to the notion of a camera, there would seem to be two basic choices: one could simply say that the camera as such is relatively unimportant (recall Brinton's comment that "striking cinematic effects depend on what the spectator apprehends *outside the scope* of the camera"[57]); or, alternatively, one could broaden the notion of camera to include its immediate "context" which would include the (top-down) skills and knowledge brought to the film by the spectator. Christian Metz asserts:

> When I say that "I see" the film, I mean thereby a unique mixture of two contrary currents: the film is what I receive, and it is also what I release, since it does not pre-exist my entering the auditorium and I only need close my eyes to suppress it. Releasing it, I am the projector, receiving it, I am the screen; in both these figures together, I am the camera, which points and yet which records.[58]

In defining a broader (top-down) context for a "camera," one would need to recognize at least three variables (each of which could take a range of values): person (or nominal agent), time, and place. That is, the "camera" would be defined according to how pictures and sounds condense at a given moment into a single hypothesis that stands for an event occurring in a time and place for a given person, such as an author, narrator, character, or spectator. For example, in comprehending a particular moment in *Hangover Square* we may say to ourselves, "*here* is George Harvey Bone's reaction to a prior event at the same moment that he is being told about it"; or, "since George already knows about the event, *here* is his public reaction"; or, "George's public reaction *here* alters my beliefs about the prior event." There are, of course, many ways of being "here," many situations, many kinds of observers and agents, and many ways to view temporal and spatial order and duration. This means that the spectator typically will be engaged in a myriad of ongoing and changing relationships with the text, each of which will be marked as intelligible from one moment to the next by his or her sense of a "camera" that marks for someone a time and a place: present, past, or hypothetical; here and now, but moving to there and then. The goal is finally to be able to say, "now I know," or "now I know how to go on."[59] In this way, the meaning of "camera" may abruptly shift as the occasion demands, much as the meaning of "I" or "now" or "here" shifts on the occasion of its use. The "camera" is both an effect of the text and a trace of the process of our reading.

Whether a narrative theory has one camera or many, the concept of a camera cannot be used merely to separate what is "out there" from what is "inside" the spectator unless the concept is rendered trivial, and a battery of new terms is created with psychological overtones to describe the spectator's experiences. Thus to say that "the camera never lies" in taking shots is to miss the point, for how can "the camera" be separated from the rhetoric of its shots, from the many ways in which it is itself taken by an audience? Though theorists may agree that the

159

POV shot is "subjective," there is little agreement on how it is subjective. The reason is that "shot," "photograph," "image," and "picture" are not equivalent terms even though they are all related to a camera. A narrative theory will need to specify how such terms are to be used in explaining the spectator's engagement with a representation of experience that is one or more times removed – experience which is surely "present" to the spectator in the theater, if only to a degree. In short, the narrative theorist in fashioning his or her terms must deal not just with the reality of stories, but with how stories are made real by the spectator.

6

OBJECTIVITY AND UNCERTAINTY

FROM SUBJECTIVITY TO INTERSUBJECTIVITY

Focalization of narrative through a character, whether explicit as in a point-of-view shot or implicit as in certain "expressive" uses of technique, is dependent upon the possibility of its opposite: a refusal to focalize. In this chapter, I wish to examine the conditions which govern our perception of images and sounds when we imagine that we experience them *independently* of a character, even if we imagine that a character might also have had, or will have, similar experiences. What we see is diegetically intersubjective, or "objective," in the sense that it is reported independently by a narrator, or else appears seemingly without any mediation as a "fact" of some kind. In this way, objectivity becomes a pertinent opposite to the forms of subjectivity examined in the previous chapter.

I also wish to examine how conditions in a film may be varied to produce different sorts of objectivity. My goal is ultimately to confront the issues that arise when objectivity and subjectivity interact in a narrative film by being alternated, overlapped, or otherwise mixed, producing complex descriptions of space, time, and causality. How do such juxtapositions affect the spectator, and moreover, what happens when the spectator is unable to decide on the status of an image or sound – when narration is multiple, inconsistent, or indeterminate? All of these situations, at least on a small scale, produce effects quite different from the normal process of embedding that promises to place various narrations in a strict hierarchy from historical and implied authors to internal focalizations through characters. That is, objectivity as classically conceived is dependent on a firmly delineated hierarchy of the levels of narration. (The notion of levels was introduced in chapter 4 as a way of making precise distinctions among the epistemological contexts that may be used by a spectator in making judgments about objectivity and subjectivity.) Although we must make choices and try out hypotheses in order to interpret a text, there is no requirement that certainty be achieved. A given theory of narrative, therefore, must include concepts that are capable of describing complex mixtures of objectivity and subjectivity.

Let's begin by considering one way that an objective narration might be created, step by step, in opposition to a subjective narration. I will take character S as my subject and begin with character S's point-of-view of object O, rendered in two shots: (S, O). The first step of the transformation will be to reverse the shots so that the object appears, followed by a shot of the character who is looking (from the same position from which we saw the object in the previous shot): (O, S). In this way, our perception of temporal *order* has been subtly affected: by reversing the usual "arrow" of implication, one has opened the potential for other kinds of temporal sequences and relationships. Next, another shot might be inserted between O and S (say, cutaway X_1) so as to *delay* showing the character who is looking at object O. Finally, the film might *never* show the character who is looking at O even though it is still the character's point-of-view. These steps may be summarized as follows:

S, O	point-of-view (POV) shot
O, S	discovered (retrospective) POV
O, X_1, S	discovered and delayed POV
O, X_1, . . . X_n, S	discovered and delayed POV
O . . . [S]	discovered and open POV[1]

This sequence represents a movement from what is *explicit* to what is *implicit* about character S's perceiving of O. (The square brackets indicate implicit knowledge.) We do not doubt that character S looked at O, but in the discovered and open version of the POV shot, for example, we will never know exactly how character S's face looked when he looked at O; that is, our procedural knowledge concerning O has been reduced because the representation of character S has been made implicit, i.e. "[S]."[2] Note especially that what is at issue in this sequence of transformations is our procedural knowledge of O, *not* our procedural knowledge of S. I am not examining the issue of how we come to know about S (as an object), only how we come to know about O as an object.

Now let's imagine a second set of cues, operating in parallel with those cues pushing the sequence toward implicit knowledge, that instead take the representation step by step from what is *definite* about the character who sees O to what is *indefinite* about the seeing of O. In this situation we move from a feeling of confidence that it is character S, and no other, who sees O, to uncertainty about which character, or characters – if any – see O. Schematically, the two movements are as follows:

explicit   definite
| |
implicit   indefinite

Combinations of these two movements produce gradations in our beliefs:

1. we see that S sees O (first four versions above of the POV shot – explicit and definite POVs);
2. we infer that S sees O (implicit and definite POV, e.g., last version above – discovered and open POV);
3. we see that someone sees O (explicit and indefinite POV);
4. we infer that someone sees O (implicit and indefinite POV).

The movement from explicit to implicit measures the inferences that we must make in determining a reference to a type of thing in the diegetic world while the movement from definite to indefinite measures the specificity of the reference that is made. The more "implicit" a representation becomes, the more it relies upon inferential chains and a prior knowledge of the spectator to make it emerge. The more "indefinite" a representation becomes, the more uncertain it is *which one* of the relevant class of things is being referred to. What interests me for present purposes is the extreme case above (4): implicit *and* indefinite reference. An example would be a discovered and open POV shot where we begin to wonder *which* character actually has seen the object. Suppose further that we begin to sense that this question cannot be answered. Here we are not far from imagining that the object *might* have been seen by *any*one, or has been seen by *no* one as yet. In this case, our view of the object has become idealized: simply *a* view that is unattributed – an "objective" view – rather than *the* view of a unique person – someone whose identity is definite, *the* character. Of course, we will be surprised if it is later revealed that all of the shots actually were the views of a particular character. Surprises, however, cannot be avoided: a spectator cannot make sense without risking hypotheses, and these hypotheses may need to be revised or discarded.

Accordingly, the sequence of POV shots discussed above may be extended as follows:

O . . . [S]   discovered and open (implicit and definite) POV (i.e., 2 above)

O . . . ?   explicit and indefinite POV (3 above) (here the notation "?" stands for a shot which does not identify which character sees O, e.g., a shot of the legs of the character who is watching)

O . . . [?]	implicit and indefinite POV (4 above) (i.e., we presume that some character is seeing O)
O . . .	POV?
O	non-POV ("objective" view)

As a view is made increasingly indefinite, "responsibility" for its accuracy is dispersed until we reach the non-POV shot which offers knowledge about an object without relying on a character. A theorist may interpret such a diffuse, intersubjective view in one of two ways: as simply a fact which cannot be challenged; or else as a suspicious statement or view (by *some*one unknown) for which no explicit context has been provided, nor any evidence supplied, that would permit the truth to be evaluated. In the former interpretation, the object is only itself (an ontological datum); in the latter interpretation, the object is only a conclusion with some of its (epistemological) premises missing. Applying this rather harsh dichotomy to narrative theories results in two classes of theories: one class adopts the former interpretation and trusts third-person narration to be potentially the most accurate about objects while another class of theories adopts the latter interpretation and trusts first-person narration to be potentially the most accurate. In order to untangle the assumptions being made by these two classes of theories about the nature of "third-person" and "first-person," it will be useful to analyze a concrete example of objective narration.

THE HISTORICAL PRESENT OF INVISIBLE OBSERVATION

I now wish to try to formulate one specific type of implicit and indefinite reference that is not a POV shot in order to bring out some of the variables at work in "objective" reference. Recall my discussion in chapter 4 of two shots from the opening of Hitchcock's *The Wrong Man* (figs 22–4). I described these shots within two very different frames of reference: first, within the film considered as a nonfictional text (producing an implied authorial narration), and, secondly, within the film's fictional story world (producing an implied diegetic narration). Under the first description, the spectator sees Manny Balestrero (Henry Fonda), emerging from a nightclub, being overtaken by two policemen who walk up behind him and *appear* to walk with him, one on each side, as if to arrest him. The spectator clearly sees, however, that this impression is only an illusion created by two particular camera angles, since both of the policemen actually pass Manny on his left and take no interest in him. Still, this moment which dramatizes how a misperception might arise will have repercussions later as Manny in fact becomes a "wrong man," accused of a crime he did not commit. This is a powerful and "objective" description of the film for it addresses

164

knowledge not possessed by any character in the story world and predicts (indeed knows!) the epilogue of the narrative.

As important as implied authorial narration is to our comprehension of the text, I wish to concentrate here on the second description of these same shots which produces a less powerful, objective narration: an implied diegetic narration. Within the limited context of the film's fictional story world, then, the shots might be described more modestly as follows:

> Manny emerges from the nightclub, saying "Goodnight John" to the doorman, and walks toward the subway while two policemen stroll by the front of the club and cars are heard passing in the street.

In chapter 4, I argued that one could imagine this sort of description being offered by a casual bystander who happened to be near the club when Manny emerged (and who, naturally, would have been subject to the same physical laws and conditions governing Manny). Since a bystander was not present, however, and not dramatized by the film, the above description must be modified as follows: "If a bystander *had been* present, he or she *would have seen* Manny emerge from the club . . . and *would have heard*. . . ." The description is now in the subjunctive conditional mood. It represents a hypothesis, contrary to fact, that we are making about our perception of the world of the characters as we understand *that* world by apparently being *in* it; that is, we are perceiving the world of the characters through projecting and imagining a situation in the diegesis whereby declarative knowledge of the relevant kind could be obtained and a description produced.[3] In effect, we are merely testing and ratifying what we think we know by saying that we expect Manny's world to behave in certain ways and to possess certain properties. This film's world *as itself an object* must be independent of certain angles of view, even if it is dependent on certain others (e.g. an "implied author's" view). Analytically, then, one may think about this contrary-to-fact hypothesis in several ways. It may be said to represent the spectator's procedural knowledge of the event in any of the following ways:

1 a stipulation about possible facts in the diegesis;
2 the perception of a bystander who could have been created to perceive the event had the author chosen to do so;
3 the perception of a patron of the nightclub who was created by the author and who could have been present, but was not;
4 a view that was seen by no one but might have been seen by *some*one (cf. the implicit and indefinite POV shot discussed above); or,
5 one or more observers at the scene who are "invisible."

All of these ways of describing our knowledge of the event make use of counterfactual conditionals. A counterfactual may be accepted as true despite its false antecedent; for example, the statement, "If I had dropped a pear out of the window yesterday instead of eating it for lunch, it would have fallen at an acceleration of 32 feet per second per second," is true. (In fact, it is true even though I have only imagined it as an example in an argument.) Philosophically, these sorts of statement require a special analysis that goes well beyond immediate data; general sets of covering laws and discursive contexts must be weighed and reviewed.[4] Psychologically, this is precisely the sort of analysis best suited to top-down perceptual mechanisms which must be able to handle an enormous number of specific cases that have not yet, and may never, occur. To return to the example from *The Wrong Man*, I believe that we cannot rid ourselves of such hypotheticals unless we interpret a diegetic event within a different epistemological context (and even then certain conditions may be presupposed). Consider how the following descriptions avoid counterfactuals by invoking other epistemological contexts:

1 "Manny took the subway home after work" (a synopsis: non-focalized narration).
2 "Henry Fonda, under the direction of Alfred Hitchcock, emerges from the nightclub . . . " (text as historical record).
3 "The early morning hours of January the fourteenth, nineteen hundred and fifty-three, a day in the life of Christopher Emanuel Balestrero that he will never forget . . ." (nondiegetic narration as presented in an opening title).
4 "It was now early morning and Manny was leaving the club after he had played in the band all night. Two policemen suddenly come up behind him as he walks slowly toward the subway station, thinking of nothing in particular. Every step brings them nearer to Manny"[5] (narration in the epic preterite and historical present tenses).

Only the final description seems equivalent to the implied diegetic narration that we have been discussing. But notice in this new description (4) that the anomaly engendered by the counterfactual of an assumed diegetic narration – positing, say, an "invisible" observer who is witnessing Manny's emergence from the club – has been replaced by an equally anomalous verb tense, the "historical present" or "past present."[6] Such a description of time paradoxically combines a past tense or past progressive with a present deictic ("It *was now* early morning"; "Manny *was* [*now*] leaving") and uses the past perfect ("he *had played*") to indicate an earlier event. In this way the past tense comes to indicate the diegetic present, and the past perfect tense the diegetic past. The entire tense system is thus shifted forward in time so that a past event (Manny's walk) is made to appear in the present ("come up," "walks," "thinking," "brings") while its narration comes impossibly from the future and is premised on knowledge gained *after* the event occurred.[7] The past is being narrated with knowledge from the present, but when the past becomes the present ("was now"), there seems to be no diegetic place or role remaining for the narrator except as invisible, timeless oracle. Left undefined (indefinite) is the time and place of the telling, as well as the specifics of the knowledge base being exploited by that unknown person(s)/narrator(s)/historian(s). Built into such narration is an evaluation of the past from a perspective much later in time. Thus there arises a fundamental and ongoing tension between presenting a past scene as it is – or, as if it were – occurring *now* and presenting its "significance," its important aspects, in light of future events which have already occurred: an event's beginning in the "present" must be made congruent with its ending *as already known* by the narrator.[8]

The essential nature of implied diegetic narration – including interpretive statements about the diegesis offered by a spectator who has adopted the diegetic world as a frame of reference – is captured equally by the historical present tense or by an implied counterfactual. One cannot escape the internal tension in a text between present and future times because some minimal principle of selection and organization must be – must have been – at work. Therefore to the degree that the reader or spectator is able to even more clearly sense in a narrative description what must/will have happened, he or she becomes aware of an implicit *authorial* narration that overtakes the implicit diegetic narration: "was now" is mixed with warning signals to become a "rhetoric of anticipatory caution," to borrow Meir Sternberg's phrase.[9] (For example, camera angles make it appear that the police surround Manny as if to arrest him.) When we use this new information – these more explicit anticipatory signs – as a basis for guesses about the future of the event, then we are attempting to characterize a still more powerful (authorial) narration; attempting, that is, to impose our will on the future of the event being represented, rather than being confined to imagining how it is being lived now by a character. As a result we have moved beyond the historical present of diegetic narration to posit an extra-fictional, authorial narration.

The historical present tense has been a topic of debate among those who theorize verbal narrative. It closely resembles the "objective," third-person narration of historians since historical accounts routinely offer a fact or an event under a description which could not have been known to be true at the time nor have been witnessed by an observer at the time. (Hence, the explanatory power of such an account.) For example, "The Thirty Years' War began in 1618" could not have been known to be true in 1618. Arthur Danto maintains that narrative structures are not just at the center of historical inquiry, but in fact "penetrate our [everyday] consciousness of events in ways parallel to those in which . . . theories penetrate observations in science."[10] On the other hand, Käte Hamburger and others argue that this way of creating the time of certain "facts" is what actually defines a text *as fiction*, not fact.[11] The consequence is that for Hamburger, first-person narration can*not* be "fictional" because of its uncomplicated tense. Without attempting to adjudicate this dispute, I will only remark that Hamburger's claim, in assuming that first-person narration is more likely to be comprehended as free of error and prejudice, seems in danger of confusing narrative with fiction by concentrating on one simple feature they share – a certain organization of temporality – instead of isolating the differing cognitive goals of each. My own approach in analyzing narration is to emphasize the complexity of such temporality whether stated in a "third-person" or "first-person" mode. The fictional or nonfictional status of a given narration is a separate issue.[12]

SIMULTANEOUS TIME SCHEMES

The existence of the historical present tense suggests that there may be other complicated time systems at work in narrative. Consider some examples of how character thought could be represented:

1 I know Manny must have been thinking about his evening when he left the club (explicit, first-person narration that summarizes/interprets the speech/thought of a character).
2 Manny seemed to be thinking, "It sure has been a long night!" (implicit, first-person external focalization of narrative through Manny).
3 Manny thought about his evening and the subway (unattributed report of an internal focalization).
4 Manny thought, "It sure has been a long night! I wonder if the train will be on time?" (direct discourse, i.e. quoted, interior monologue).
5 Manny felt that it had been a long night and he hoped that his subway train would be on schedule (indirect discourse). [Notice the shift from first to third-person, the back-shift of tenses, a mild use of summary in a propositional format, and the tag clauses – "Manny felt that," "he hoped that."]
6 Sure he was tired but a man like him worked long hard nights and now his train better be on time (free indirect discourse).

In the free indirect version above (6) of internal focalization through Manny, portions of Manny's actual thoughts (4) ("sure," "long," "train," "be on time") have been mixed with a narrator's interpretation of those thoughts in such a way that the reader *cannot separate the two* nor evaluate the accuracy of the interpretation (cf. the minor change from "night" to "nights" with the major change from indicative mood – "I wonder . . . " – to imperative mood – "[it] better be on time"). The reader knows only that there exists a mixture of internally focalized and narrated descriptions. The narrator's interpretation, of course, may be more perceptive about Manny's thought than is Manny himself. Notice that something similar to the historical present tense ("was now") has reappeared in the free indirect ("was tired . . . now"). Notice also that, with the exception of the direct quotation of Manny's interior mono-logue (4), the appearance of a verb of consciousness in a sentence need *not* imply that Manny is thinking in just those words and no others. Similarly, if Manny's experiences were to be internally focalized *through images* in a film, it does not necessarily follow that the images seen by the spectator must be taken as literal representations of Manny's mental images (or even direct translations of his thoughts as expressed in words). There are many ways of rendering character thought in litera-ture and film without purporting to (nearly) reproduce that thought.[13]

It seems clear that in comprehending narrative scenes, a perceiver is able to make use of complex time schemes whether he or she is initially confronted by sentences or by pictures, by subjective or by objective representations. The often-stated belief that film images are always in the "present tense" fails to take into account top-down perceptual processing and is inexact even in the simple case of comprehending a scene. As I argued in chapter 1, our experience of time in a text emerges when data is processed and associated. Different experiences of time are related to the complexities of juxtaposition allowed by different methods of associating data (e.g., through a heap, catalogue, episode, etc.). The lines between "scene" and "summary," and "first-person" and "third-person" narration, are not easily drawn even in sentences, much less in pictures.[14] Distinctions based on grammatical surface features like pronouns neglect top-down processing, and at best furnish only rough approximations for the spatial, temporal, and causal net-works that define our procedural knowledge of an event. How pictures acquire a narrative significance cannot be reduced to how surface features and techniques are delineated, or marked by bottom-up per-ceptual processing, but instead must be analyzed in terms of the top-down cognitive processes which drive us to offer descriptions and apply (macro)propositions to what is seen and heard and read. One need not worry about whether a shot, or something else in a film, can be equated with a "word," for this equation and similar ones are never reached: neither a shot nor a word is determinative in an analysis of either a film or a sentence.

Complex narrations like the historical present may be analyzed in several ways. I have chosen to collect narrations into broad categories, such as the categories of diegetic narration and internal focalization (see chapter 4). These categories could be further subdivided according to degrees of implicitness and indefiniteness, and their effects on what is given as explicit and definite. An implicit "negative," for example, acts to completely overturn what is explicit, resulting in irony. Certainly other criteria will also be relevant. One could expand this approach even further by deciding to analyze a complex temporal narration in terms of two or more major types of narration which would then be viewed as *operating simultaneously*. This may well produce incompatibilities which the perceiver must strive to understand and resolve. For example, what is called a "scene" (in the historical present tense) might be a kind of reconciliation between an implicit authorial narration and an indefinite diegetic narration where each balances the other. This kind of analysis begins to approach narration not just as a structure but as a process, and also recognizes that a point may be reached where two narrations cease to be perceived as simply a mixture of separate features but instead become a blend with entirely new properties able to generate entirely new effects.[15] (As an analogy, consider that table salt is a blend of a poisonous gas, chlorine, and a corrosive metal, sodium, that reacts explosively with water.) It is important to keep in mind that a complex narration, such as the historical present, is neither ambiguous nor vague, but merely composite and open in a specific way. We are not being asked to *choose* between two possible narrations, nor are we bewildered by the sentences or pictures which actually appear. The historical present is merely indeterminate – implicit and indefinite – about one aspect of its temporal organization, but is no more confusing than the appearance of indefinite articles in general, such as references to "*a* tree in *some*one's backyard."

Complex narrations pose crucial problems for narrative theories. A communication theory of film narrative, for example, must try to locate the communicant of an implicit and indefinite narration, such as implied diegetic narration. That is, when the temporal complexity of a shot is at issue, how is one to interpret the "invisible observer" who creates the present while acting from the future? Is the "invisible observer" a stand-in for an author or narrator (who created the artifact in the "past"), or a stand-in for a narratee (who is prophetic)? Are shots in a film the result of mental images thrown outward by certain entities in an effort to communicate? Is the "invisibility" of an implied diegetic narrator to be thought of as someone's "intention" to communicate "covertly" (i.e., to disguise the communication)?[16] These questions are not meant to be a critique of communication theories, but merely

170

illustrative of the questions which will arise and an indication of the grounds of the debate.

Narrative theories based on "reception" – the responsive activities of the reader or spectator – do not have the above kinds of problem. The invisible observer is merely a shorthand description for a counterfactual conditional statement expressing the spectator's knowledge of an event (e.g., "If I had been there, then this is what I would have seen"). Reception theories must, however, describe invisible observation in more detail if the concept is to have explanatory power. Reception theories must also be careful to avoid a blatant anthropomorphism[17] and especially to avoid a claim that invisible observation is the foundation for a general theory of film, or for a theory of editing in narrative cinema.[18]

Consider, for example, the following list of the major components of one common type of invisible observation. The list is an attempt to make explicit the assumptions which taken together underlie our comprehension of a scene when that comprehension is stated in terms of one type of "invisible observer."[19]

1 Invisibility. The observer has no causal interaction with the events which are witnessed and thus cannot, for example, control the entrances and exits of characters. The observer is an eavesdropper who is unheard as well as unseen.

2 Ubiquity. The observer has the ability to move instantaneously throughout scenic space[20] and to remember what has been seen and heard, but not to move forward or backward in time.

3 Alertness. The observer is attentive to events so as to be able to avoid obstructions and assume the "best" or "perfect" angle on the action at all times (as in camera position 4 of fig. 14). This implies appropriate shifts in distance.

4 Neutrality. The observer assumes a "standard," often straight-on angle to the action. By contrast, an "eccentric" or awkward angle (for example, fig. 42) would be interpreted simply as a failure of ubiquity (see 2 above); or as an emotional reaction, emphasis, or evaluative judgment on the action (i.e., as the appearance of a more powerful and intrusive narration).

5 Impersonality. The unique personality traits as well as the gender, age, race, class, etc. of the observer are muted – made indefinite – so that what is displayed is strictly a perceptual experience and, in principle, intersubjective, i.e. regulated by general norms of seeing. This rules out looking into the minds of characters or perceiving data which is impossible for characters to experience, such as nondiegetic music or privileged views (as in the impossible camera movement, figs 31–6). Perceptions are represented as if they were capable of

171

being detached from an actual observer and transferred elsewhere without loss.

6 Passivity. Observation is governed by the limits of immediate diegetic space and time; that is, no views from impossible positions (as in camera position 5 of fig. 14), or views which depend on anticipating the action (foreknowledge), or views which independently search for information.

The above blend of features in invisible observation hints at the variety of narrations that are possible in a text. Note that it also shows the inadequacy of simple labels traditionally used to describe narration, e.g. "objective," "omniscient," or "scenic." Simple labels can be useful, but they should not substitute for a close analysis.

The invisible observer has been rendered "visible" here, but only within an analytical frame of reference that defines a spectator's comprehension in such terms as the diegetic and the nondiegetic. What is being analyzed is not simply a technique, or a device or a style, but the elements that define a mode of comprehension. As a convention of reading, invisible observation asks the spectator to accept (or impose) a restriction on the amount and type of knowledge available from the text at a given moment. A convenient way to describe this particular restriction on knowledge is to imagine an "observer" with specific qualities. However, it should not be forgotten that what is being described is a limitation on the spectator's access to information and on his or her ability to manipulate symbols. There is a danger that it will be understood in too literal a way and that the text will be seen as anthropomorphous.[21]

The question of restrictions on knowledge is at the very center of narration (see chapter 3). For the spectator to attain knowledge from a narrative at least some of these restrictions must be overcome. The text must, to a greater or lesser degree, inscribe – make explicit and definite – its own spatial, temporal, and causal coordinates for at least *some* of its levels of narration. This enables the spectator to judge how knowledge may be acquired by a "person": an author, narrator, character, or observer, and ultimately the spectator himself or herself. The possibility of knowing the truth about the/a world, however, necessarily raises the possibility of misunderstanding, misperceiving, and lying about that world.[22] We may not be certain that a restriction has been overcome. Hence our fascination with such complex and explicit "first-person" films as *Citizen Kane*, *Letter from an Unknown Woman*, and *Sans Soleil*. I turn in this chapter and the next to these three films and their unique structures of objectivity and subjectivity.

FLASHBACK

In an empty room a sudden gust of wind blows through an open window and turns back the pages of a calendar; the story then moves into the past.[23] Such a flashback is "objective" in the sense that it has not been inaugurated by a character. A change in the ordering of events is made explicit but is not attributed to a character's thought. The past is simply made present. Nevertheless it might have made no difference if the past had been evoked by a character who was remembering it from the "present" because what we see in a subjective flashback is often stubbornly independent of the character's recollection. This is perhaps to be expected given the fact that internal focalization through a character is located near the bottom of the hierarchy of narrations and must be embedded within various non-character narrations (see chapter 4). Therefore we will need to probe carefully the degrees by which objective and subjective narrations may be combined in a single representation.

Orson Welles's *Citizen Kane* (1941) presents five characters who reminisce about the central character, Charles Foster Kane, whose death we witness at the beginning of the film. The structure of the film – investigation through reminiscence – is so strongly marked that Bruce Kawin, on the basis of admittedly inconclusive evidence, can speculate that Kane's death at the beginning of the film actually may not have been seen by the spectator in the present, but may already have been placed in the past, interpreted through the memory of some unknown person.[24] In any case, it is true that our principal knowledge of Kane throughout the film is linked to the descriptions of first-person narrators who knew Kane in diverse ways. This has led critics into disputes concerning the accuracy of the various portrayals of Kane by the narrating characters. Walter Thatcher's reminiscence, for example, has been judged objective by one critic, and subjective and biased by another.[25] Both arguments, however, miss the point. Thatcher's flashback is much more complex than the dichotomy, objective versus subjective; instead, his flashback involves multiple and competing levels of narration that vary in their degrees of explicitness and definiteness. Thatcher's flashback represents at least an implied author's view of the reporter Thompson's view of Thatcher's view of Kane. (Thompson is reading Thatcher's memoirs.) Other views also appear within the same, nominal flashback, such as those of Kane and his mother. This complexity produces an extraordinary result: Kane is represented in a favorable and sympathetic light in spite of the fact that the sequence is ostensibly narrated by Thatcher who was Kane's enemy. Recent studies of the sequence have begun to uncover evidence of an inconsistent, ambiguous, and shifting narration that may, in fact, embody the answer to the

173

enigma of Charles Foster Kane: he was an inconsistent, ambiguous, and finally unknowable man.[26]

Examining *Citizen Kane* as a whole, one can pick out not just subtle, but spectacular shifts in the narration that are not unlike those analyzed in *Hangover Square* in the previous chapter. There are departures from the "best view" of an event (e.g., within the "newsreel" sequence, figs 47, 48); impossible camera movements (e.g., three camera movements involving the side and rooftop of the El Rancho Cabaret including moving "through" the glass of a skylight); impossible and omniscient camera movements (which reveal at the end of the film a secret no character is able to discover); and eccentric views (e.g., Jed Leland's memory of an event he did not witness in Susan Alexander's apartment that is rendered in six shots, four of which are reflections in a mirror). In addition, there is an odd present-time (past-time?) reverie of the dying Kane in the opening scene: five consecutive shots reveal snow falling inside his room and across his face. For only a portion of one of these shots do we see that the snow is artificial and falling within a small transparent globe held in Kane's hand. But is this the same snow that is falling in the other shots? The barrier separating an "outside" of something from its "inside" is thus shown to be problematic; or rather, it is represented as a barrier that will be penetrated freely in the film in exploring psychological mysteries and making the past present.

In an ordinary narrative film we may know quite well what a character is thinking about, and we may even see the distant object that is the subject of thought. Still, this does not guarantee that a shot of the distant object is meant to represent the actual contents of the character's thought. For example, a character glancing over his shoulder in a significant direction, or staring straight ahead fixedly as he travels to confront someone, need not imply that the object of attention, when finally shown, must be a representation of a (present or past) mental image. A simple example: a character stares angrily at a building; cut to a new character inside the building; then the first character walks into the room. Although the second shot is clearly tied to the first character's plans and goals, it is also "objective" in another sense; as such, it could be merely an "external focalization" of narrative through the first character. ("X stares angrily at a building; at that moment, inside the building, Y. . . . ")

Here is a slightly more complicated example: in *Point Blank* (Boorman, 1967), we see shots of the Lee Marvin character searching for his unfaithful lover and hear the powerful, staccato beat of his footsteps. These images are intercut with shots of the woman in her present surroundings – which are unknown to Marvin – *while the sound of his footsteps* continues over images of her. (In the first shot of her, we see her eyes spring open as if she has heard his footsteps.) Later we see

Figure 47 Citizen Kane

Figure 48 Citizen Kane

Lee Marvin and hear the footsteps even though he is *no longer* walking, but waiting and spying on her. Hence this representation seems to have crossed the line from external focalization into a type of internal focalization (obsession, premonition).[27]

The examples above illustrate that when we see what we believe a character to be thinking about, we may only be seeing the object of his or her thought as it exists independently in the world even if an obsessive desire for the object continues to be represented. Similarly, when a character remembers the past, we may only be seeing the past as it might have been represented earlier in the story when the character was then living it as the "present." There are still further, distinct possibilities for the flashback:

1 we see an actual, present memory image of the character (reliving the experience); or,
2 we see what the character remembers has been remembered on other occasions (a mental image formed from repeated retellings of the past); or,
3 we see a summary of the character's present *words* as they are being written, thought, read, or spoken, silently or aloud in a monologue or dialogue; or,
4 we see "objective" glimpses of the events upon which the recollection is based but mixed with the character's desires and fears (cf. free indirect written discourse and the example from *Point Blank*).

These possibilities raise again the sorts of issue that we considered in discussing how Manny's thoughts on leaving the nightclub could be represented in direct, indirect, or free indirect discourse, or in other ways. This is no coincidence since a flashback may be taken as merely a special instance of the historical present tense where a *character* makes the past present for the spectator by providing narration from a (diegetic) "future." Needless to say, the character in the future is functioning differently in the narration than when he or she is seen captured in the past. One cannot analyze narration in a text without clearly distinguishing the relevant levels of narration that may explicitly overlap as well as the levels that may be presupposed by a representation. It should also be clear that in general representing narrative events in pictures makes them no more explicit, detailed, consistent, objective, certain, present, or precise than representing them in words.

Given a character flashback in a film, then, which of the above interpretations of the sequence is correct? The answer is that it seldom matters! There often is no need for a text to be definite, or for us to decide. (Try to determine the status of Lee Marvin's footsteps: are they literal or metaphorical? Do they qualify as an aural flashback? If so, whose?) Recall that the "chameleon" text, which I have associated with classical storytelling, usually adapts to whatever the spectator *first* believes about the story. The greater the latitude allowed for the spectator, the greater the number of spectators who may participate. Of course, representations that are less explicit and definite create dangers as well as opportunities for story telling. I would like to examine two films – one in the next section and one at the end of the next chapter – that exploit the intricacies of flashback narration to make a great many possibilities count. These films will show some of the ways in which our narrative comprehension of objective and subjective, past and present, may be profoundly challenged and, in some cases, rendered inadequate.

MULTIPLICITY IN *LETTER FROM AN UNKNOWN WOMAN*

Lisa's voice-over narration and the film's imagery

Max Ophuls's *Letter from an Unknown Woman* (1948) was the first film Joan Fontaine produced through her independent production company, Rampart. It was a romance adapted from a Stefan Zweig novella and designed for an audience of women. Joan Fontaine plays the tragic heroine whose continuous, confessional voice-over dominates the action. In spite of the fact that it is a classic "woman's film" focused almost entirely on a woman, I believe that it is marked by a relentlessly masculine attitude. The masculinity, however, emerges only when one examines the subtleties and contradictions of the film's narration. An important component of any narration concerns what has been excluded from the story – what has *not* been selected, given a duration, organized, and emphasized in the telling. In *Letter from an Unknown Woman*, a hidden and powerful masculine discourse can be traced through a series of omissions and incomplete structures. By closely examining the film's narration, I will demonstrate how a text may exploit what is missing and undecidable about a narration in order to raise fundamental issues about character and spectator perception. In this case the issues specifically concern gender, the developing sexuality of an adolescent girl, and how a world may be made and encountered through one's body. It will also be discovered that different conceptions of narrative, and narration, underlie some of the sharply different interpretations of the film offered by critics.

The film opens one night in Vienna at the turn of the century with a handsome, dissolute concert pianist, Stefan Brand (Louis Jourdan), preparing to flee from a duel that has been arranged for dawn. His mute manservant, John, hands him a letter. He begins reading and we hear the voice of Lisa Berndle (Joan Fontaine) speaking the words of the letter:

177

By the time you read this letter, I may be dead. I have so much to tell you and perhaps very little time. Will I ever send it? I don't know. . . . If this reaches you, you will know how I became yours when you didn't know who I was or even that I existed.

Stefan does not know who has written the letter or what relationship he might have had with the woman. As Lisa continues to speak, we move into the past and see her as a 15-year-old adolescent schoolgirl who becomes infatuated with her new neighbor, Stefan, and the music she hears him play. Lisa's secret love for him grows into an obsession and even though her family moves away from Vienna, she admits that "Quite consciously, I began to prepare myself for you." She becomes a young woman of eighteen, returns to Vienna, and is finally able to contrive a meeting with Stefan. They spend a passionate night together, then are separated; Lisa gives birth to their son, Stefan Jr, and nine years later marries a wealthy, high-ranking military officer, Johann, who adopts her son, knowing the father's identity.

By chance several years later Lisa meets Stefan again. He does not recognize her but believes they may have met in the past. She goes to his apartment at night but still he does not remember her. Devastated, she leaves the apartment to roam the streets. Within days her son dies of typhus. We then see her the day after her son's death writing the letter to Stefan shortly before her own death from typhus. We realize that Johann, who had followed Lisa to Stefan's apartment, is the person who has challenged Stefan to a duel.

Four times during Lisa's voice-over in the film, we return to the present to see Stefan reading the letter. When he reaches the final page, a note informs him that the writer had died before finishing it. Stefan is finally able to remember Lisa and we see his memory images which are fragments from previous scenes narrated by Lisa. When John writes Lisa's name on a piece of paper, Stefan learns that John had not forgotten her.

The carriage arrives to take Stefan to the duel. He decides to accept certain death. Stefan climbs into the carriage after seeing a final image of the 15–year old Lisa and hearing her voice, "Oh, if only you could have recognized what was always yours, could have found what was never lost."[28] The film ends with the departure of the carriage which parallels the beginning of the film with Stefan's arrival in the carriage.

Unlike the flashback structures of *Lady in the Lake* or *Citizen Kane*, the representation of memory in *Letter from an Unknown Woman* raises immediate and unsettling problems. I would like to summarize some of these problems by listing various ways in which one might interpret Lisa's voice-over narration, specifically, the relationship of her words to the accompanying images.

1 The voice-over is independent of the images. The images of the flashback are "objective," showing us what really happened.

2 The voice-over is merely illustrative. It is an "objective," present translation of words previously written on a page; i.e., it draws on a film convention which allows the free substitution of words for images, and images for words.

3 The voice-over is past and subjective, and the images we see are determined/directed by Lisa.

   (a) The images are equivalent to *words* in Lisa's mind (or to her "thoughts") *while* she was writing, i.e., image and voice-over are both past tense. Thus Lisa may on occasion speak to Stefan independently of the words in the letter but he could only guess at these words (see below 4(a)(i)). (Remember: Lisa is dead and we see her writing the letter only briefly.)[29]

      (i) The images represent how Lisa *imagines* the future. We are seeing only what she *believes will happen* when her letter is delivered. Does she desire Stefan's death as the final proof of his love?

   (b) The images are equivalent to her mental *images* while writing the words, i.e., her visual memories.

   (c) The images are equivalent to her unconscious (i.e., deep internal focalization). Her mental images reveal desires and fears which she refuses to recognize in herself. Do her images conflict with her words?[30]

4 The voice-over is present and subjective, and the images we see are determined/directed by Stefan.[31]

   (a) The images are equivalent to *words* in Stefan's mind (or to his "thoughts") *while* he is reading/interpreting her letter, i.e., image and voice-over are both present tense.

      (i) The images represent how Stefan *imagines* her voice as he reads. (But remember: initially she, and her voice, are "unknown" to him so that he could not consciously hear her voice in his head.)

   (b) The images are equivalent to his mental *images* while reading the words, i.e., he is slowly remembering and visualizing past scenes as he reads.

   (c) The images are equivalent to his unconscious, to what he will come to remember (i.e., deep internal focalization).

5 The voice-over is mutually subjective. It is a remembering by both Lisa and Stefan, past and present woven together; e.g., Lisa starts a sentence and Stefan finishes it.[32]

Though initially plausible, each of these possible relations between voice-over and image leads to contradictory and insoluble problems.

Even if the viewer were to split apart voice-over and image by imagining them arising in different temporal contexts, or were to assume that one of them might be objective while the other is subjective, difficulties will remain. In order to account for the complexity of the film, I believe that additional sonic and visual elements will need to be separated from one another and that elements excluded from the narration will need to be considered. Furthermore, since the viewer comes to believe that the film is accurately reporting events, the possibility arises that *non*-character narrations are interacting with, or supplementing, narrations attributed to Lisa and Stefan.

It is a fact that Lisa's letter delays Stefan's escape and in some measure causes his death. Therefore what judgment of Lisa is the viewer expected to make? The answer to this question will depend in part upon the viewer's assessment of Lisa's intentions which, in turn, will depend upon *which* Lisa is being represented at a given moment (i.e., the 15-year-old, the 18-year-old, or the dying Lisa), *how deeply and accurately* the film enters her consciousness, and *how often* there are fluctuations in the degree to which events are rendered objectively, or subjectively. Critics are greatly divided on these questions. One reason for the lack of consensus is that Ophuls creates a measure of uncertainty about Lisa's motives while clearly dramatizing the intensity of what she feels. She is an unknown woman in more than one sense. Karel Reisz observes:

> [Ophuls's] approach to character is oblique, under-emphatic, hint-ing at emotions rather than portraying them directly. Lisa's story is recounted with great tenderness and revealing detail, but the real source of her passion somehow never emerges: it is too superficially motivated and remains, at last, unassessed.[33]

To illustrate the interpretive difficulties that result from Ophuls's approach to telling the story, I will pick six possibilities – from extreme to relatively moderate – for the rendering of events through Lisa's subjectivity. I will correlate these degrees of subjectivity with the kinds of judgment we might make of Lisa.

1 The film plunges very deeply into Lisa's consciousness. She is an obsessed, hysterical romantic; she lives a fantasy existence where the perfect love can be perfect only in heaven.[34] Some of the events we see may be part of a hallucination by Lisa or the product of a delirium associated with typhus.
2 Lisa is overcome with her hopes and dreams. She forces Stefan to share those dreams. By writing the letter, she makes her memories become his, and he goes to his death.[35]
3 Lisa unintentionally draws Stefan to his death.[36]

4 Lisa is a victim of her own personal feelings as well as the selfishness of Stefan.[37]
5 Lisa is a tragic heroine caught "between what she conceives of as a biologically rooted duty and her spiritual wish to be free" within a rigid, patriarchal society.[38]
6 Lisa and Stefan are innocent victims of a malicious fate. The film portrays their world in an objective way.[39]

Tony Pipolo adopts an extreme, subjective position. He claims that Ophuls fully evokes Lisa's consciousness by

> linking the various postures, movements, and framing gestures of the camera with the various moods of restlessness, contemplation, anticipation, and dejection of Lisa, the unknown woman. . . . [Ophuls] invests a silent image, a slight camera movement, an unusual camera angle with heightened emotional power that instantaneously conveys exhilaration, joy, despondency. Such a close correspondence between the camera's attitudes and the character's emotional and psychological states can be found throughout the film.

Pipolo concludes:

> As a result, [Ophuls] has achieved much more than an approximation between camera view and character consciousness, for at such moments as those described, the camera almost attains an actual consciousness itself. In effect, . . . the correspondences between character and camera "behavior" amount to this: the camera is personified to the degree that it acts in unison with, and often as a substitute for, the character consciousness which controls it.[40]

Moreover, for Pipolo it is not just the camera which embodies Lisa's consciousness, but also the *mise-en-scène*, shot composition, editing, and sound.[41] Pipolo is able to reach these conclusions because he has a holistic theory of narrative (see chapter 5).

George Wilson promotes a more moderate view of the film's narration. He permits *non*-character narrations to coexist with Lisa's voice-over so that the viewer is able to clearly see what Lisa cannot see, namely, that she has an imperfect understanding of herself. These non-character narrations allow Lisa to be "viewed throughout with tact, sympathy, and serious affection." Indeed for Wilson the film is able to promote the idea that certain mysteries cannot be penetrated or understood and hence that Lisa cannot be judged.[42]

Lisa's exclusion by the film's narration

I would like to look closely at a few sequences in the film that draw the attention of most commentators and a few sequences that no one notices. My aim will be to untangle some of the complexities of the narration as well as to demonstrate some of the assumptions about narrative that underlie diverse interpretations of the film.

Early in the film there is a scene in which the 15–year old Lisa steals into Stefan's apartment in order to walk through his rooms and touch his belongings. In one room she discovers his piano. With her back to the camera, she slowly walks toward a sofa. The camera moves smoothly to center not Lisa, but the piano in the background about thirty feet from Lisa. There is now a cut to Lisa on the far side of the piano walking slowly around it to touch the keyboard (figs 49, 50). What is startling about this cut is that no spectator ever notices the flagrant disregard of space: Lisa has leaped over the sofa and the piano to travel thirty feet across the room. This powerful effect of forgetting is the result of comprehending the narrative.[43] For the first second of shot 2 (twenty-eight frames), we do not see Lisa. (I will assume that we disregard her shadow on the wall which places her just off-screen!) One second of screen time, however, is apparently enough to make the actual time that must have elapsed in crossing the room vanish; in its place is something less easy to measure – *our anticipation of her anticipation*. Our anticipation is an imaginary time attributable to Lisa's desire for Stefan through his piano. Fixated on the piano, she advances toward it, and the spectator completes the action; or rather, the spectator constructs a virtual time in which the action is realized.

On a fairly basic level, then, we see that one of the ways that narration may create a virtual reality is by leaving something out, leaving something behind; in this case, the time of walking across the room. The film's narration creates Lisa as a narrator/character who is creating a fantasy that will exact a price: she and her illegitimate son will die of typhus. However, the film also represents Lisa and her punishment more subtly and in ways that continue to draw upon what is missing and excluded from the story. Here is where a masculine discourse addressed to the spectator will make itself known in the film.

Shortly after touching the piano, Lisa is discovered by John and flees from the apartment. She rushes onto a staircase and is shocked to discover her mother secretly kissing a man – an act not unrelated to Lisa's own secret longing for Stefan. Nevertheless, for Lisa it is an *illicit* view – one of many views she must deny having in the film. In fact, the film's narration will consistently work to dispossess Lisa of a viewpoint and take away her power to see, leaving only, as it were, blind desire.[44]

Figure 49 Letter from an Unknown Woman (shot 1)

Figure 50 Letter from an Unknown Woman (shot 2)

Another example of the film's exclusion of Lisa occurs when the 15-year-old Lisa spies on Stefan late one night as he brings a woman home to his apartment. We watch from behind Lisa as she stands in the shadows on the staircase above Stefan's entrance hall. Holding Lisa on the right, the camera displays her illicit view and follows Stefan as he leads an unknown woman into his apartment.[45] Later in the film from the identical camera position we watch as Stefan late one night brings the 18-year-old Lisa home to his apartment for the first time and the camera again follows him as he leads her into his apartment, the unknown woman-to-be. It is evident that Lisa has become that other woman she saw as an adolescent. The spectator witnesses this transformation from a viewpoint on the staircase associated with a now *absent* character – the 15-year-old Lisa. The 18-year-old Lisa can no longer be a witness because she has become Stefan's object, an object of his sight and touch.

George Wilson argues that the repetition of the camera position on the staircase is meant to show that the 18–year old Lisa *lacks* self-awareness. He finds it significant that in the first staircase shot Ophuls chose not to represent Stefan and the other woman through a point-of-view shot attributed to the adolescent Lisa because such a shot would not afford the sharpest comparison between the two epistemological fields.[46] Tony Pipolo, however, argues for another interpretation of such repetition in the film since he believes that "Lisa's and the camera's consciousness are, for the most part, one and the same." Thus, he claims, repetition "perfectly manifests the behavior of [Lisa's] *fixated* consciousness."[47] In particular, the repeated camera position on the staircase is an "involuntary projection" of the 18-year-old Lisa, and the camera movement which follows her as she is being led into Stefan's apartment is the 18–year old Lisa's "invisible but vibrant consciousness re-viewing a memory [of what she experienced on the staircase when she was 15 years old]."[48]

It seems to me that the film oscillates between portraying Lisa as a distant, unacknowledged subject who is denied a legitimate position of view and portraying her as overpowered by an intimacy wholly defined by the male subject, Stefan. Lisa is thus depicted as an object of both fear and desire, as someone to be kept at a distance and brought close. Her subjugation – or, "sacrifice" as some would say – begins with an early scene in which the 15-year-old Lisa is in the courtyard listening rapturously to Stefan's music. She has not yet seen Stefan, only heard his music. The spectator, however, sees more than the adolescent Lisa. Seven shots of Stefan at the piano are intercut with eight shots of Lisa conversing with a girlfriend in the courtyard.[49] In the following diagram I have arranged the seven shots of Stefan in sequence with the largest

184

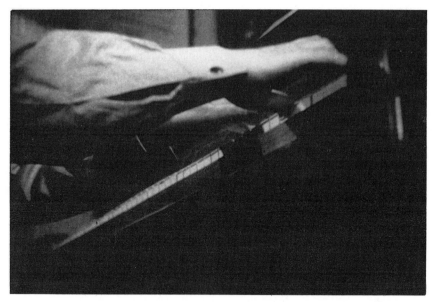

Figure 51 Letter from an Unknown Woman (set-up 1*)

scale shot (two extreme long shots) at the top and the smallest scale (two close-ups) at the bottom.

One notices immediately that when the seven intercuts of Stefan are placed together they form a familiar pattern by which space is developed in classical narrative: a detail shot (set-up 1) followed by an establishing shot, and then progressively closer shots until a "climax" is reached (in this case a repetition of the initial close-up, set-up 1*; fig. 51) followed by a gradual expansion of the scale to close the sequence.[50]

XLS:		2				2
LS:			3	3		3
CU:	1				1*	

Set-ups
1 – high angle close-up of hands at keyboard
1* – low angle close-up of hands at keyboard (fig. 51)
2 – extreme long shot of Stefan at piano
3 – long shot of Stefan at piano

Thus if Lisa's voice-over is truly in control of every aspect of the film, then it would seem that her consciousness is organized in classical Hollywood fashion to promote continuity and clarity; or alternatively, that a non-character narration has organized the space surrounding Stefan's piano in order that *Lisa's* relationship to Stefan might be experienced in a particular way *by us*.

185

The courtyard scene excludes Lisa in a remarkable way. She is not present to have any of these views of Stefan; she can only imagine them from the courtyard, or remember having imagined them while writing the letter just before dying. Yet Stefan's hands are being emphasized in relation to the absent Lisa. The first shot of the fifteen-shot courtyard scene shows Stefan's hands at the keyboard (set-up 1). It is marked by an introductory and closing dissolve which leaves the space of the hands initially undefined and relatively "free-floating." The two dissolves are not directly related to the voice-over narration nor to a break in time since the music being played is not interrupted between shots 1 and 2; rather, the dissolves allow the hands to become a detail shot for *two* spaces: the interior room where Stefan is playing the piano and the courtyard where Lisa is gently swinging on a swing. Further, as we shall see, the hands will become part of a complex and intricate causal pattern that will extend beyond these two spaces and beyond the playing of a piece of music on a particular day. Although this causal pattern will not draw our attention through paradox or "impossibility" as in *The Lady from Shanghai* where a woman apparently causes a car to crash by pressing a button (see chapter 2), it will nevertheless reverberate across the film as part of an emerging, nondiegetic metaphor linking Stefan's hands to Lisa's femininity: to desire, memory, loss, rejection, danger, and death.[51]

The second shot of the courtyard scene begins by revealing a second-floor window in extreme long shot from which we hear the music; the camera then moves down and back to further establish the space of the courtyard and reveal Lisa on the swing as seen through a V-shaped fork of a tree.[52] This second shot thus explicitly defines two distinct spaces separated by a barrier (the second-floor window) but joined through the sound of Stefan's music and the image of his hands at the piano. The barrier creates a disparity of awareness between Lisa and Stefan that is exploited by the narration to merge Lisa's aural point-of-view with Stefan's hands.

The five shots of Stefan at the piano (set-ups 2 and 3) continue to show us his hands reflected in the raised lid of the grand piano. The climactic shot of the hands (set-up 1*) occurs between two long shots of Stefan at the piano (set-up 3); these three shots appear together in a concentrated burst, embedded in the courtyard scene. There has been, however, one significant change in the shot of the hands for the climax (set-up 1*): we now see them from below rather than from above (fig. 51). The time being marked here is not simply that of obsessive recurrence, or of Lisa's obsession with Stefan from the courtyard below, but also is ordered and developmental on a larger scale, and as we shall see, still incomplete.

Beyond plot: the complex temporality of hyperdiegetic narration

Just before Stefan brings Lisa home to his apartment (where we watch from the staircase as discussed earlier), he plays the piano for her in an empty dance hall. She kneels down at his right side and looks up adoringly at him, and also looks at his hands as he plays. There are three shots of this situation: two high angle, medium long shots of Stefan in profile with Lisa kneeling in the distance (fig. 52), and between these shots a high-angle, medium close-up of Lisa's face with Stefan's hands in the foreground (fig. 53). What is striking about this articulation of space is that Lisa has again been denied a view. She has finally managed to place herself at/into his hands, but we see only these three reverse angles of her; there is no point-of-view shot from Lisa's position.

Incredibly, however, we are mistaken! We have in fact been given Lisa's POV shot. The object of her view kneeling in the dance hall is almost identical to the climatic, low angle close-up of Stefan's hands in the courtyard scene (fig. 51; set-up 1*). In effect, the earlier shot predicts what will occur 151 shots later in the film; or, to put it differently, the earlier shot is not completed until twenty scenes later. Placing these two shots together creates Lisa's POV (fig. 53 with fig. 51). This articulation is a *delayed* or suspended POV structure.[53] In a sense it is an elaborate "decontraction" of a POV shot which opens a vast "middle" between a beginning in the courtyard and an end in the dance hall, and thus invites the spectator to experience a narrative fantasy from part (hands) to whole.[54]

Lisa's delayed POV shot is the result on a large scale of the same principle that was used when I extracted seven shots of Stefan at the piano from the courtyard scene and grouped them in a new way in order to analyze the underlying logic of the film's narration. If one were to insist that the events of the film be interpreted only through Lisa's consciousness, then one would have to say that the low angle shot of Stefan's hands in the courtyard scene (fig. 51) already represents a complex imbrication of (1) the 15-year-old Lisa's projection of a wish from the courtyard, (2) the older, dying Lisa's anticipation of its later fulfillment in the dance hall when she was eighteen as well as (3) the older Lisa's pain in writing/remembering how her hopes finally came to be dispersed (like the POV shot) and lost.

At the end of the film we again see the medium close-up of Lisa's face as she kneels at Stefan's hands (fig. 53). It appears as the last of seven shots constituting Stefan's memory, and final acceptance, of Lisa. The background music for his flashback is a combination of the waltz music he played for Lisa in the dance hall (fig. 53) and the Franz Liszt music he played while the adolescent Lisa listened in the courtyard (fig. 51). Thus the repetition of the two musical pieces together with

Figure 52 Letter from an Unknown Woman (shot 1)

Figure 53 Letter from an Unknown Woman (shot 2)

the shot of her kneeling at the piano summon to mind that earlier shot from the courtyard scene (fig. 51) which defined her wish to be near his hands. At the end of the film, then, Lisa's delayed POV expands to include Stefan. Though strictly she is no longer an unknown woman, she is still absent for now she exists only in *his* memory; her POV remains fragmented. The repetition of the medium close-up of Lisa's face at the piano in Stefan's flashback thus suggests a fourth temporal context relevant to our interpretation of the courtyard scene: (4) the dying Lisa's *desire to narrate her story* in order to make herself known and present to Stefan, and become loved by him. Like other authors, Lisa seeks to present a story objectively even though in telling the story there is no way to avoid speaking the desire that underlies the pairing of events (no matter how delayed) into narrated, causal sequences. Although her letter ends in mid-sentence ("If only . . . "), it can now be completed by Stefan – and his love affirmed through his decision to die – because the events that he is interpreting narratively through the "historical present" of Lisa's letter already embody what must/will have happened. In this way, the courtyard scene as narrated by Lisa – especially the images of Stefan's hands – contains a future tense.

From the preceding analysis it would seem that at least four time schemes are relevant simultaneously in the courtyard scene and that no simple ascription of objectivity, or of a character's subjectivity, will fully account for the spectator's response to the images accompanying Lisa's voice-over narration. I believe that a number of narrations are operating simultaneously in the film; that is, several contexts are relevant to the interpretation of a given image, not merely the context afforded by the immediate time of the characters nor the time of the *plot*. In particular, I would like to suggest that the narration which produces Lisa's delayed POV shot (fig. 53 with fig. 51) as well as other measurements of large-scale change (e.g., the two identical camera positions on the staircase) is a special case of implied authorial narration. I will call it *hyperdiegetic* narration. Jacques Aumont has noticed another example of such narration in the opening scene of *The 39 Steps*. He argues that if the spectator were to imagine shot 14 out of sequence and then *juxtapose* it with shot 22, he or she would see the true relationship between two men as well as appreciate the future importance of this relationship to the events of the story. The narration needs to introduce the men through an early encounter, but also needs to conceal important aspects about their relationship. Hence the shots are separated in the opening scene and their significance attenuated by other actions. Aumont remarks that since the juxtaposition of shots 14 and 22 is "diegetically unactualized" in the plot, the true significance of the event is "unreadable to the spectator." Even though the narrative significance here is not derivable "from a simple seeing," the articulation nevertheless "is effected in a directly symbolic" and purely visual way.[55]

The hyperdiegetic, then, stands for the barest trace of another scene, of a scene to be remembered at another time, of a past and future scene in the film (a hybrid scene), or of a scene that is evaded and remains absent. I have urged that what is deferred and finally denied in *Letter from an Unknown Woman* is a position for its heroine, Lisa. I believe that if the spectator wishes to understand the film's complexity as a "woman's film" within a historical context of patriarchy, one will need to give up simple answers to the problems posed by its surface narrations, and instead search for opposing, masculine discourses interwoven with feminine discourses.

Tania Modleski argues that women spectators are attracted to *Letter from an Unknown Woman* because it portrays a tragic situation for women: "Lisa's is the classic dilemma of what psychoanalysis calls the hysterical woman, caught between two equally alienating alternatives: either identifying with the man or being an object of his desire."[56] Later in her argument she reverses her contention: "Closer analysis, however, reveals that Stefan is the hysteric . . . whereas Lisa adopts an altogether different relationship to time and desire which points beyond this deadly antinomy."[57] Modleski concludes by claiming that films like *Letter from an Unknown Woman* actually appeal quite generally to men because they provide

> a vicarious, hysterical, experience of femininity which can be more definitively laid to rest for having been "worked through." . . . And it may be that one of the appeals of such a film for women is precisely its tendency to feminize the man, to complicate and destabilize his identity.[58]

For Modleski *Letter from an Unknown Woman* is still a "woman's film," even though it is also a story of and for the male. Modleski is able to respond to the subtle conflicts among the film's narrations which are speaking differently to men and women because she believes that narrative is ultimately driven by contradictory and unconscious psychic states, by human instincts and dreams, involuntary memory, loss and nostalgia. For her, the master plot is the one specified by Freud where contradictions and reversals are both fundamental and fundamentally different for men and women.[59]

Robin Wood offers another response to the ambivalence elicited by the film.

> The fascination of certain films depends on our (often uncomfortable) awareness of the suppressed, ghostly presence of an alternative film saying almost precisely the opposite, lurking just beneath

the surface. . . . [T]he more times one sees [*Letter from an Unknown Woman*], the more one has the sense – it is a mark of its greatness – of the possibility of a film *against* Lisa: it would require only a shift of emphasis for this other film to emerge. It is not simply that Ophuls makes it possible for us to blame Lisa for destroying her eminently civilized marriage to a kind (if unpassionate) man, and the familial security he has given her and her son; it is also *almost* possible to blame Lisa, and her refusal to compromise, for Stefan's ruin.[60]

Modleski's psychoanalytic method and Wood's notion of an alternative plot are ways of interpreting those multiple narrations in the film that create a feeling of uncertainty and anxiety in the spectator. I believe that such approaches also point toward a reconceptualization of that other subjectivity in film – the author – the source, ironically, of a film's objectivity. It may be that the fractured collection of narrations we encounter in a text – including what has been excluded (or, in psycho-analytic terminology, repressed or censored) by a narration – is all that we can ever know about that underlying authorial omniscience that has generated a world of characters. The splitting into many voices is the voice. Paradoxically, the more exactly we describe the narration, the more fragmented it becomes and the less certain is the voice of an author. What we normally construct in the reading as an "author," therefore, is only a convenient summing-up – male or female, or some-how beyond gender – merely a shorthand for a multiplicity that satisfies our urge to name and make final in order to achieve the objective.

7

FICTION

FICTION AS PARTIALLY DETERMINED REFERENCE

Narrative and fiction are quite different things even if they often appear together in public. Narrative involves such processes as creating a scene of action, defining a temporal progression, and dramatizing an observer of events. Narrative is a particular way of assembling and under-standing information that is best contrasted to a *non*narrative way of assembling information. Nonnarratives may be found in classifications, inventories, indexes, diagrams, dictionaries, recipes, medical state-ments, conference papers, job descriptions, legal contracts, and in many other places.

By contrast, "fiction," and its opposite "nonfiction," involve a quite different question, namely, how can the data that has been organized into a narrative, or nonnarrative, pattern be connected, matched, or fitted to the world and to our projects in the world? How do we find pertinent relationships between data and world? The assumption here is that our ability to *understand* a narrative, or nonnarrative, is distinct from our *beliefs* as to its truth, appropriateness, plausibility, rightness, or realism. In *understanding*, we make connections and construct pat-terns by using references; in *believing*, we make connections to the world, to a "referent" in the world, by using constructed patterns. We may understand a narrative, or for that matter, a sentence, without believing in it just as an argument may be valid (i.e., the relations among the premises may be logically correct) without the conclusion being true.[1] This division between understanding and belief – between comprehending that a pattern is narrative as opposed to judging its accuracy or relevance in a world – directly raises the problem of how a text may be taken as true, if at all, in one or another interpretation and how it may have consequences for our conception of the ordinary world. A study of the fictional aspect of narrative is concerned with how we are able to learn from/through narrative, with how we come to believe in a narrative "truth" and find a value in it. In believing, we do more than believe that we comprehend; we discover a connection to our world.

A reader may interpret a text fictionally or nonfictionally, or in both ways.[2] The analyst's task is to define what the reader is doing – what sorts of mental calculation are being made – when a portion of a text is responded to in one way rather than another. Ultimately both ways of responding (if successful) connect to the world; both are "real" in the sense that they have the power to teach us something about the world. Additionally, both fiction and nonfiction may utilize either literal or figurative representations. (For example, both a fictional character and Winston Churchill may be depicted metaphorically as a bulldog.) Thus neither truth-claims nor rhetoric can be taken as features that distinguish between fiction and nonfiction.[3] Rather, my argument will be that the *method or procedure* for making decisions about assigning reference is different in each case even if the results are the same (i.e., knowledge about some condition in the world).

The problem of how a fiction is able to procure belief is seldom discussed in the field of film studies; when it is discussed, it tends to be lost within a crazy quilt of related issues involving realism, film technology, rhetoric, documentary genres, ideology, the spectator's hallucination/fascination with film, and whether style is invisible or contrived.[4] Philosophers, however, have sharpened the issues while proposing many theories of what constitutes a fictional relationship with the world. My present purpose is not to survey alternative theories in detail but merely to illustrate the claim that narrative and fiction are distinct areas of inquiry, and to offer one theory of fiction that is consistent with my approach to narrative.

It is clear that we are influenced by, and learn from, fictional statements even though they are literally false. According to John Searle:

> Fiction is much more sophisticated than lying. To someone who did not understand the separate conventions of fiction, it would seem that fiction is merely lying. What distinguishes fiction from lies is the existence of a separate set of conventions which enables the author to go through the motions of making statements which he knows to be not true even though he has no intention to deceive.[5]

The problem, then, is to describe the "conventions" that allow an author to pretend with no intention to deceive, and a reader to learn without relying upon the pretense. An individual does not mistake a fiction for the real world; fiction is neither an "illusion" nor a "false belief." Rather, fiction seems to require that an individual connect text and world in a special way, that is, through a different type of logic than is used with, say, a verifiable proposition, inductive statement, or axiom. Experiment, evidence, and stipulation are not relevant to establishing the truths (or falsities) of fiction. What sort of procedure, then, is relevant; that is, how does fictional reference refer?

According to Hartley Slater, fictional terms denote real things, though not determinate ones. The real thing denoted is not indeterminate in the sense that it is some curious "vague" object in a "possible" world; rather it is indeterminate in the sense that it is not yet fully specified, i.e. not controlled entirely by features of the fictional terms.[6] For example, if "a is a *picture of* b" is taken as a fictional relationship between "a" and "b," then it would be understood on the model of "g is an *outfit for* a gentleman" which is not an assertion that there is some nameable, actually or not actually existing gentleman the outfit was designed for (or that it was designed for every gentleman), but, instead, as *leaving open* which gentleman (or gentlemen) would suit it.[7] A fiction does not determine exactly which object or objects it represents, and this openness is what distinguishes fictional reference from other sorts of reference. An element of choice is built into the text requiring the perceiver to search and exercise discrimination in assigning a reference to the fiction and in applying it to a more familiar world.

Consider as an analogy the equation, $x + y - 1 = 0$. Although this equation specifies a rigid interdependence among its terms, it does not determine a *unique* solution as does the equation, $x - 1 = 0$. The first equation is only "partially determined" or "incompletely determinate" and requires another function for its full solution, or several functions if additional variables are introduced.[8] By analogy, to interpret a symbol fictionally is to operate in a precarious, intermediate zone between sets of possible references (open functions) and a specific reference (a given "solution" or "referent"). Interpreting a symbol fictionally requires that one qualify the immediacy of the symbol itself: its material presence must not imply an immediate reference, nor a simple reference to something atomic, nor indeed any reference at all, much less one that is true or false in our familiar world. Further information and calculation is required. It is perhaps not surprising, then, that prior to the approximate age of seven children assume stories to be *either* "real" or mere nonsense. Not until after this age do children firmly expect stories to be something "made up," that is, something new and more complex: neither "real" in any ordinary way nor mere nonsense.[9] Considered as a cognitive activity, fiction is a complex way of comprehending the world in which one is first required to hold open sets of variables while searching for a reasonable fit between language and lived experience, between sets of symbols and acts of the body. In appreciating a fiction, one cannot judge it piecemeal; nor can it be collapsed into a kind of comprehension whereby if it makes sense, it must be real.

How does a perceiver search for a reasonable fit between fictional language and the world? Complex predicates in a text (e.g., "Sherlock Holmes lives on Baker Street, plays the violin, and becomes irritable when his rational powers seem inadequate to a task.") are first evaluated within a *structure of knowledge* (e.g., sets of schemas) already possessed by the perceiver. These complex predicates may effect changes in a schema through altering its organization, or altering the methods of its regulation and retrieval.[10] Fiction has a major impact on the processes of sorting and matching which operate within a perceiver's memory. For example, if our concept of a chair were suddenly to change after visiting an exhibition of contemporary art, then what was formerly true of chairs (or of "rationality" prior to a redescription under the label "Sherlock Holmes") may now be false, and we may come to see chairs (or solutions to problems) where we saw none before.[11]

L.B. Cebik argues that "The sentences of fiction . . . do not imply general truths in the sense of being evidence for them. Rather, they imply general truths in the sense of *presupposing* them."[12] That is to say, fiction moves backward to presupposition, prior belief, and knowledge rather than forward to derivation and confirmation. According to Cebik, in claiming to understand certain sentences of fiction, one is committed to the acceptance *as true* of another set of sentences outside of the text (that state the general truth which is presupposed).[13] I believe that in order to understand how fiction works on us, it is necessary to understand how the mind works with knowledge. As we saw in chapters 1 and 2, knowledge is not distributed in a random fashion in a person's mind; rather, it is organized according to its means of retrieval. Most importantly, it is *represented*, i.e. encoded in particular forms which are quite different from visual or auditory stimuli.[14] I believe that Cebik's notions of implied general truths and prior beliefs can be analyzed in terms of schemas. In short, what is "presupposed" is contained in schemas and other forms of organized knowledge.

The measure of indeterminateness built into a fictional text, then, acts *to delay* and expand the kinds of searching and restructuring of prior knowledge undertaken by a perceiver. In Freudian terms, incomplete textual reference could be said to function as a "disguise" necessary for slipping such fantasies as castration, the primal scene, family romance, and seduction, past the censor into conscious thought (albeit in distorted form) in much the same way that the unconscious circulates "unacceptable" desires through dream and daydream by altering their form, or "recognizes" those desires when they appear in altered form, such as in a joke that is heard.[15] The "presuppositions" which are exposed through fictional reference are interpreted by psychoanalysis as the very "preconditions" of thought itself – the preconditions that underlie, or "drive," the schemas and other mental structures studied by cognitive psychology. Thus indefinite reference does not mean that we can't have specific and intense emotional reactions to fiction; quite the contrary, indefinite reference may facilitate such reactions.[16]

Let me summarize by offering a general characterization of fiction that takes into account a perceiver's structure of knowledge, or "presuppositions."

> A "fiction" is neither simply false nor obviously true but initially is merely indeterminate and nonspecific. The challenge of fiction is to discover what it is about. Fictional reference is judged on a case by case basis and is ultimately decided through the filter of a perceiver's already existing (and perhaps now reorganized) structure of knowledge, or presuppositions. In fiction we must try out descriptions ("x is a y") until a good one is found for present purposes. By contrast, in nonfiction no initial redescription is necessary since we assume as a starting point for our interpretation that the reference is determinate, particular, and unique ("this *is* x: it exists as such"). In nonfiction, our purpose is to accumulate evidence to confirm a thesis or topic whereas in fiction our purpose is to discover how the text refers to what we already know. In fiction, there is always the possibility that a new referent or description which better fits the text and our presuppositions will be discovered, thus altering its application and truth value. Hence one of the values of fiction resides in its ability to explore the assumptions underlying our presuppositions and to suggest how they could be altered by us to fit, recognize, or create, new situations in the world that we deem important. In short, fiction is *partially determined reference* which is initially neither true nor false; its usefulness must be found and demonstrated.

This characterization stresses that fiction is a particular mental *process* of assigning reference. However, one should not forget that the word "fiction" may also be applied to the object that stimulates that cognitive process, or the object that is created through that process. In this respect, the word "fiction," like the word "narrative," may be ambiguous – designating a process and/or a product of the process.

PSYCHOLOGICALLY REAL THEORIES OF FICTION

In trying to formulate a psychologically real notion of fiction, I am trying to avoid both a theory of symbolic processes that would posit reference to the world as automatic and a matter of empirical verification, as well as a theory which would deny that the real world can serve in any way as a measure of reference. In the latter, idealist theory, meaning and reference are exclusively mental: to every *list* of properties, even if contradictory, there corresponds an "object," existent or not.

This has two undesirable consequences: first, that fictions, and everything else, are always true by virtue of existing mentally, and second, that far too many objects of reference are created since every thought of every person creates something new and unique. Reference to a specific world that is intersubjective disappears within the infinities of private meanings.

On the other hand, the problem with an empiricist theory of language is that it is far too narrow because every statement is said to contain a built-in existential assertion to one, and only one, world. Thus the statement, "The present king of France is bald," asserts, first, that there exists a present king of France and, second, that the predicate, "is bald," applies to him. The statement is false if either the existential condition fails or the predication does not correspond to actuality. In the case of fiction this leads to the result that *all* statements in the fiction are strictly false and merely elaborate lies since reference can only be to existents capable of being tested for their attributes (there is no present king of France to undergo testing).[17]

Both empiricist and idealist theories have difficulty analyzing "mixed" fictions which contain some words or sentences that are apparently not fictional, or not fictional in all the same ways.[18] For instance, a reference to "London" in a Sherlock Holmes story would seem to have a different status than a reference to Holmes. By contrast, in a "realist" account, if one allows a fiction to be described by a logic containing more than two values (i.e., more than "true" and "false"), then one will be able to assess *probabilities*: what is impossible, likely, indeterminate, or even, known to be *false* about the fiction. The "realist" theory I have sketched above anticipates that partially determined (fictional) predicates may be graded according to their fit with language, knowledge, and lived experience, and that fictional predicates must eventually operate on, or with, specific, intersubjective references.[19]

The basic failure of the empiricist account is that it is people who refer, not sentences or pictures.[20] Meanings and regularities are not *in* sentences, but rather are *in* human design and use. To understand the nature of reference, one must study the rules, habits, and conventions of a community of individuals. In my view, fiction involves a reference to a world whose shape is determined by a community. Thus there may be many worlds but not an infinity of them. I am trying to avoid extreme positions. Belief in only one world – *the* world – suggests that a single, absolute world may be fixed by a perceiver's innocent eye; belief in an infinity of worlds leads toward solipsism or radical relativism; belief in no world or an indeterminable world (i.e., a fundamental indeterminacy) suggests nihilism or radical skepticism. The methods of cognitive science address one aspect of a study of community rules by focusing on real psychological constraints on the processing of

knowledge. Thus despite the fact that fiction often deals in exotic subjects, a theory of fiction should be built upon a careful examination of
our ordinary ways of thinking and our everyday abilities.

FICTIONAL PICTURES

As an illustration of the above principles, consider a photograph of an
object in a fiction film; that is, a photograph interpreted fictionally in a
film. We normally think of a photograph as having recorded the actual
presence of an object in accordance with certain physical laws involving
chemistry and optics.[21] The object photographed seems to testify to its
own existence. Nevertheless, when the photograph is construed as a
fictional entity, it becomes a picture of a *nonspecific* object. Our interpretation is not constrained by the particularity of detail in the photograph,
but acts to hold reference open while building complex predicates about
what the photograph pictures.[22] In effect, we begin to construct mini-
theories about what we believe about the "world" of that object. What
we see literally in the photograph is then merely an "actor" or a "prop"
as a stand-in for something else which has yet to be fully defined and
made real. A fiction is not about an actor, but about a character; not
about a prop, but about a character's possession. Therefore a person
recorded by a photograph acquires, when seen fictionally, a new dimension as a label within a complex, developing predicate, i.e. within a
nexus of labels that define some of our presuppositions about persons.
A real person – an actor – who has been photographed is thus transformed into a nominal entity – a placeholder – when interpreted fictionally.

There is no contradiction here. A person in a photograph can be
simultaneously both specific and (fictionally) nonspecific in the same way
that a photograph of a tiger in a dictionary can be both a specific tiger
and many tigers; that is, some tigers not photographed will still qualify
as proper referents of the photograph even though they may have, say,
different numbers of stripes. Nonspecific photographs thus also acquire
a *future* tense; tigers not yet born may become proper referents.[23] Of
course, a photograph in a dictionary is not finally taken to be fictional
because the language accompanying the photograph is overwhelmingly
denotative and acts to limit and confine the range of possible referents
to a specific class.[24] By contrast, a fiction continues to open up references
by freely cutting across many classes as linked and coordinate terms
are themselves shown to be open.[25]

Just as a photograph may be interpreted fictionally, so also may a
word, even one which seems concrete and real. Consider the sentence,
"I'm looking for a tiger." The phrase "a tiger" is ambiguous on a simple
level for we can continue by saying either "and when I find it . . . "

(i.e., when I find "the" tiger), or else "and when I find one . . ." (or even, "and when I find a tame one . . . ").[26] I am suggesting basically that fiction asks us to respond in the latter way to statements, namely, to conduct a search on the basis of being offered a partially determined object, signalled by an indefinite article ("an" x). One might object that a photograph of a tiger seems to say, "here is *the* tiger." However I believe that a fiction asks us not to connect a shot to the actual animal in front of the camera but rather to move forward and backward within the overall sequence of shots and to wait before deciding significance. We are asked to judge the shot as follows: "This sequence of pictures includes *a* tiger; here is *that* tiger (the tiger)." Reference does not immediately jump outside of the shot to a specific tiger but is deferred and moves among the shots themselves (the tiger's relation to a character; the character's relation to an action; the action's relation to . . .). Thus, although we may see "the" tiger, in a larger context it remains "a" tiger until its significance is further defined. In my view, comprehending a fiction requires a complex reassignment of what seems concrete ("the" x) into what is only partially determined ("an" x, or "a certain sort of" x). "Truth" is deferred in order to be judged within a variety of (new) nonstandard contexts. Fictive meaning is typically judged not on the basis of a sentence or a proposition, but on the basis of a discourse, a network of sentences or propositions. Fiction thus operates not between the narrow poles of nonreference and unique reference, but rather between indeterminate or multiple (cross-) reference and unique reference.[27] The truth or falsity of fictive, or indeed nonfictive, reference is a separate issue and concerns reference in the narrow sense of "a referent" that exists uniquely in, or fails to exist in, the world. Fictive reference generally concerns the systematic mapping and exploration of a discourse through indefinite articles (as well as indefinite pronouns) which eventually may, or may not, point toward a unique referent. Fictive reference is well-illustrated by literary formulas which cue us to interpret fictionally by attaching an indefinite marker to time itself; for example, "Once upon *a* time . . ."; "Once upon *a* midnight dreary . . ." (Edgar Allan Poe's "The Raven"); "*One* day . . ."; "*A* long time ago in *a* galaxy far, far away . . ." (*Star Wars*, Lucas, 1977); "Vienna *About* 1900" (*Letter from an Unknown Woman*).[28]

Jean-Luc Godard's *Band of Outsiders* (1964) illustrates the demands placed on a spectator by fictional reference. Early in the film we hear the roaring of a tiger (or a similar sound).[29] Is there a tiger just off screen? Is a character imagining a tiger? Is the sound an aural flashforward to *the* tiger which will be in the story? or does the sound combine only with the music to form a metaphor suggesting a mood of violence and instability, or dehumanization? Interpreting the sound fictionally means that we cannot trust the "particularity" of the sound since which detail, or details, of the sound are relevant will depend on defining an appropriate context; or rather, interpreting fictionally means that we cannot decide in advance what will count as a "detail." In spite of these warnings, when the/a tiger suddenly appears in a later scene we are shocked because of the improbable circumstances which lead to its appearance in a parking lot and because we do not expect a tiger to appear in a gangster film. (If the film were about a circus, we would watch and listen for "the" tigers.) The actual appearance of the tiger forces us to reevaluate previous events. For example, what seemed initially to be insignificant – a character searching for meat in a refrigerator – is now elevated to causal significance when the meat is given to the tiger. The result is that we expect the tiger to appear again as part of the story, but we are wrong: it never appears again and was, in fact, only *a* tiger – peripheral and ephemeral. In the context of the story, it has been converted back into a metaphor. This illustrates the way in which *Band of Outsiders* as a whole sets up a complex struggle between definite and indefinite reference. The spectator must hesitate and weigh multiple possibilities and wrestle with the ways in which Godard encourages, defeats, and stretches genre expectations by employing, for example, documentary techniques to treat fictional events. Godard's fiction forces us to see that photography, like language, is not unequivocal reference but may be qualified by an indefinite article.

In summary, when a film is experienced fictionally, reference is not to the *profilmic* event in which a set is decorated and an actor given direction, but rather to a *postfilmic* event in which patterns are discovered through active perceiving that affects the overall structure of our knowledge. Although the profilmic set design has a (complex) causal relationship to the postfilmic experience of a fictively construed set design, the two should not be confused because different clusters of concepts and theories are relevant to explaining each. The profilmic may be a sufficient cause for some aspects of comprehending the postfilmic but the latter is not merely a reworking of the former. Truth-values for a fiction are projected (top-down) through schemas and presuppositions and cannot be arrived at by a shortcut through causal history. The material nature of the text and its history may be relevant to, but cannot determine, reference.[30] More important are the methods of evaluating and arranging data used by a perceiver in seeking to fit the text with a world already known, i.e. with other data in memory.

One further problem should be mentioned: if fiction may be useful to us, how do we know when to read fictively? Initially we may rely on cues and conventions in the text and interactions with our memory; ultimately, we rely on the "success" achieved in redescribing the text as a social object. Normally a fiction film includes cues which announce its "artifice." (These cues must be read nonfictionally! One must begin somewhere.) Sets, costumes, composition, music, dramatic dialogue, and other aspects, may signal their role in a scheme of nonliteral and nonspecific reference. The simplest case is the representation of something nonexistent, such as a griffin, which signals its fictional status by an obvious *dissimilarity* to real things – by being judged a *poor* picture of either an eagle or a lion – but perhaps a good and true picture of certain yet-to-be-determined cultural presuppositions about eagle–lion qualities and their application to human problems.[31] There are also conventions and genres, such as the romantic melodrama, and the marketing of particular texts, which may prompt a spectator to begin interpreting fictively. In addition, certain types of film *editing* may suggest that the space and time of a sequence of photographs is denotatively nonspecific in spite of the apparent concreteness of the individual photographs.[32] This suggests that there are many formal and structural aspects of a film that may encourage us to interpret fictively.

In the previous chapter, I considered how the film *Letter from an Unknown Woman* functions as fiction in just these sorts of way while placing women spectators in a definite relationship to a patriarchy. In the next two sections, I will analyze the film *Sans Soleil* which strongly challenges the very line between fiction and nonfiction by deploying incompatible and ambiguous cues to guide interpretation. The result, not surprisingly, is a dense and mystifying experience for many viewers. It becomes all the more baffling when a viewer realizes that the cues and conventions being relied upon are treated as mere devices which may themselves be authentic or counterfeit, adopted or refused. This directly raises the question of how a text – whether fiction or nonfiction – may have a referent and be true. *Sans Soleil* will bring us full circle: in attempting to show how narrative fiction may acquire a referent, we will suddenly discover that the referent of narrative nonfiction may not be certain. What will be illustrated is that film and its modes of reference operate finally within a social setting and are governed by consensus. In exploring a psychology of "narrative" and of "fiction," one is at the same time exploring the social dimension of signification which creates the pertinence of such a category as fiction, establishes its opposite, designs standard types of reference, specifies when reference is not to be taken as specific, and trains our faculties in the proper manipulations. Hence, in dramatizing the power of pictures and language to reorganize knowledge, a text like *Sans Soleil* declares the suspicion that what is newly organized may be true but only in one world.

NONFICTIONAL PICTURES

I would like to consider more closely the boundary between fiction and nonfiction as well as some other boundaries that have been important in this book: narrative and nonnarrative, story world and screen, subjective and objective. As in previous chapters, I will approach these general issues by examining how various responses are being elicited from a spectator. Thus I will be using concepts that relate to the cognitive skills and psychological constraints that make comprehension possible; such concepts as top-down and bottom-up perception, procedural and declarative knowledge, and levels of narration. The notion of multiple levels in a text, for example, provides a useful way of describing complex temporal experiences like the "historical present." As we shall see, certain nonfiction films attempt to explain the significance of a past event by seemingly reproducing the past, by making the past present for us.

Chris Marker's *Sans Soleil* (*Sunless*, 1982) has the appearance of a nonfiction film. It is not an instructional film, news report, commercial, or political advertisement, but rather a species of nonfiction known as "documentary." What is a "documentary"? Arthur Danto states that of all the materials available to a historian, "Something is truly . . . a document only if caused by the events it records."[33] A document testifies to something because it has been produced by the thing itself. Similarly, the images and sounds of a film documentary are said to have a relationship so close to reality that they become proof of, or at least evidence for, the events that were in front of the camera and microphone at a past time. Though seldom stated, these ideas are commonly extended to describe the activities of the spectator of a film documentary who is supposed to be convinced that a set of causal principles similar to those governing the events on the screen are responsible for placing those events on the screen in a given order. That is, the spectator assumes in a documentary that there is a close (causal) connection between the logic of the events depicted and the logic of depicting. Or, to put it another way, the world on the screen has left its trace on film because it is closely connected to our ordinary world and to our familiar ways of depicting.

But what will count as a "close connection" and what really is a "cause"? In answering this question, I will set aside nonfiction films which are constructed using only nonnarrative principles (e.g., a film of the planet Mars made through a telescope to illustrate a scientific paper). Instead I will concentrate on the many documentary films that make use of narrative principles at least to some degree.[34] I have argued in chapter 1 that causality in narrative is defined through a narrative *schema* which arranges our knowledge under many different types of description, or function (abstract, orientation, initiating event, etc.). As demonstrated by our discussion of *The Girl and Her Trust*, narrative causality cannot be limited to a single type of description like physical causality (e.g., steam rises; or, light strikes a photographic emulsion), nor limited to a single type of implication (e.g., necessary and sufficient conditions), but must include more expansive, cultural forms of knowledge (e.g., the routines of courtship; beliefs about property, unmarried women, and trust) as well as including judgments about the *relative probability* of events, and the effects of multiple (unconscious, conflicting) character motives.

Our knowledge of narrative causality, then, arises from interrelationships among the kinds of description within a narrative schema. Furthermore, as our discussion of *The Lady from Shanghai* illustrated, the spectator's ongoing construction of metaphors is a crucial part of discovering and posing causal connections among (like) descriptions that, in turn, liken events to one another, bringing them together. Finding connections using metaphor and language is preeminently a social act. Thus we may conclude that narrative "causes" come in many varieties, strengths, and sizes. In comprehending "reality," this means that a given event is actually the effect of a great many kinds of cause, only some of which, if any, will become *signs* of the event.[35] A documentary is not just the record of some physical cause, but also testifies to one or more top-down (narrative) procedures that link events. Therefore the causal principles that are pertinent in a given documentary are never obvious.

Stephen Heath argues that every film is an effect of the historical and social conditions of its activity of representing.

> What needs particularly to be emphasized here is that history in cinema is nowhere other than in representation, the terms of representing proposed, precisely the *historical present* of any film; no film is not a document of itself and of its actual situation in respect of the cinematic institution and of the complex of social institutions of representation.[36]

Despite the notion of a "documentary record," then, history is not captured intact in a documentary film by some privileged physical connection to the world, but instead is the result of more expansive causal principles that include a spectator's present experiences and expectations within a community. In effect, Heath begins with the irreducible complexity of time embodied in an "objective" image – what I analyzed in the previous chapter as the "historical present" tense – and enlarges that notion of time to include the present conventions, social situations, and conflicts which call forth and enable a telling of the past through the use of a particular narrative "tense."

Thus, as others have argued, the distinction between nonfiction and fiction is not based on truth versus falsity, nor on some process of copying/imitating as opposed to creating/fabricating, nor on the relative degree of manipulation of some pre-existent reality.[37] Instead, I believe that the distinction is based on the social conventions and categories that specify causality for a community. More exactly, I believe that comprehending nonfictionally is dependent upon the conventions that enable us to reason about causality which, in turn, governs our understanding of the *specificity* of the references being made to the world of a given community.

I would like to indicate briefly how a prominent type of documentary – call it a "classical" documentary – organizes its narration so as to focus the spectator's attention on the specificity of events.[38] This will allow a more precise description of the unusual aspects of *Sans Soleil* and open new issues about narrative comprehension. My description will be based on the eight levels of narration introduced in chapter 4 (see fig. 19, p. 87).

A classical documentary seeks to present an event as nonfocalized and/or externally focalized; that is, to present only its public, or intersubjective, aspects. Characters are observed acting and speaking, or providing summaries of an event as "witnesses" or participants. Internal focalization through a character is not permitted since a mental experience is not intersubjective. This rules out such devices as dream sequences, subjective flashbacks, and even point-of-view shots.[39] A character may, however, *narrate* images of the past in voice-over. Since a character in this situation is exercising a measure of control over the images of the past, he or she is no longer merely an actor within a nonfocalized and/or externally focalized sequence of events; instead, the character has assumed a more powerful role in a higher level of narration which allows him or her to talk *about* events *as* those events are presented from another time. Nevertheless, the classical documentary seeks to minimize character voice-over as well as to minimize other, similar narrations that intervene between nonfocalized narration and the historical situation of the filming; that is, to minimize diegetic, nondiegetic, and extra-fictional narrations.[40]

The reason is that in answering the spectator's question – "Is this narration competent and credible in reporting specific events?" – a nonfiction text relies upon an entirely different notion of *authority* than does fiction. In nonfiction, we begin our interpretation at the *"higher"* levels of narration and work downward toward the nonfocalized: We begin with a belief in a historically "real" situation and a mechanism of production – such as camera and microphone technology – and then attempt to infer the direct, and relatively unmediated, consequences of the conjunction of that situation and that production, namely, what could be known through nonfocalization. Indeed, a powerful and anonymous third-person voice-over (sometimes referred to as a "voice of God" commentary) may appear in the film to assure us (usually implicitly) of the potency of the technology and its ability to know. Another variant is the first-person, "collective" voice: "we the people." Both narrations create a pure form of the "historical present" tense. By contrast, fiction asks us to begin at the *"lower"* levels of narration with the mere presence of a picture or word; the direction of inference is reversed as we attempt to construct a plausible set of higher mediations with which to justify the depicted events.[41] Thus the status of what we see in a fiction is initially tentative and contingent (i.e., a *non*specific picture) and its definition will depend upon our faith in an implied author that must be created by us; whereas in nonfiction we begin with an explicit mechanism of production and then attempt to build a faith in the accuracy of the results.

Classical nonfiction presents the historical through the nonfocalized by minimizing the presence of intervening levels, such as diegetic narration. These intervening levels are kept implicit, or else are consistent with other levels, well-motivated, and unobtrusive. In this way, classical documentary seeks to limit the range of interpretations that will be judged to be "correct." By contrast, a fiction seeks to expand the levels of narration in order to provide greater definition for its pictures and words as well as to suggest appropriate methods for converting a fictional world into one that is ordinary. (One can comprehend, say, *Star Wars*, without believing that its world is ordinary, and yet making it ordinary is what gives it a truth value.) Furthermore, classical fiction – the "chameleon" text – seeks to create a multiplicity of interpretations in order to accommodate what a spectator first believes to be "correct." Both classical fiction and classical nonfiction attempt to discover meanings that lie "behind" (beyond, below) events; they merely start in different places and one expands, while the other contracts, the levels of narration.

Because the classical documentary aspires to map the historical situation of the making of a film into a nonfocalized rendering of events, it is sometimes said to differ from a fiction film by its immediate power to persuade, convince, command allegiance, and solicit action from the spectator concerning a social and historical reality.[42] According to C.G. Prado: "The difference between [fact and fiction] lies not in the contrast between referential and nonreferential language or narrative but in types of responses to narratives, in the differences among answers to the question 'What should I do?'"[43] In the classical documentary, we are being addressed as members of a community. Stated in terms of the narrative schema presented in chapter 1, the "goal," or response to an initiating event, is usually given as social rather than personal.

While it is true that many classical documentaries ask us to take action with respect to a social problem or political issue, I believe that the basic analytical issue is to identify the *conventions* that tell us that we're supposed to react as members of a community to an "objective" social problem that is capable of rational solution.

Some of the conventions of classical documentary as indicated above are the following:

1 a rejection of internal focalization;
2 a minimizing of the number of levels of narration that intervene between the historical and the nonfocalized and/or externally focalized;
3 a rendering of intervening levels as consistent and unobtrusive; and,
4 the creation of an anonymous narration to assert (usually implicitly) a power to know through access to a privileged method or technology.

How is the spectator able to judge the presence or absence of these sorts of convention of narration? The answer to this question lies in still more localized conventions. For example, Herb Lightman advises the documentary filmmaker to avoid using reflectors in outdoor scenes since "the rather harsh quality of natural sunlight . . . has a realistic feeling to it that is desirable in documentary." Lighting for indoor scenes, he says, should duplicate existing light sources so that the added light is not noticable to the spectator. Lightman also says that the camera should be hidden in crowd scenes to prevent persons from looking into the lens, and that movement of the camera should "never" be unmotivated (cf. camera position 8A–B in fig. 14, chapter 3); instead, camera movement should be used only to follow the action or, rarely, to move along a static subject.[44] These sorts of prescription are aimed at reducing the perceptibility of the levels of narration operating between the historical and the nonfocalized. Lightman summarizes: "By keeping himself inconspicuous, by holding his action to a simple pattern, and by avoiding obvious 'arty' touches, the director can produce a true documentary feeling on the screen."[45] Lightman is well aware that a "true feeling" is not necessarily the "truth." Truth and falsity cut across both a fictional and nonfictional comprehension of narration.

Additional prescriptions for the documentary filmmaker can be found in the theories of André Bazin who advocates, for example, long takes, deep focus in on-screen space, "lateral depth of field" in the activation of off-screen space, a relatively unstructured *mise-en-scène*, "found" stories, camera movements that cannot keep up with the action, and camera positions that are limited by the diegetic conditions governing the events that are being represented (e.g., figs 47, 48).[46] For David Alan Black, Bazin's theory is an example of a "deductive realism" that emphasizes phenomenal reality as opposed to an "inductive realism" that begins by positing the integrity of a fictional diegesis through deferring to a spectator's usual beliefs about a world.[47] Rather than exploring the details of such Bazinian theories, the localized conventions they sanction, and their fit with the large-scale narrational structures of the classical documentary, I will turn toward *Sans Soleil* and the challenge it poses to traditional nonfiction narrative.

POST-MODERNISM AND DOCUMENTARY IN *SANS SOLEIL*

As a first approximation, one might say that *Sans Soleil* appears to be a travelogue where a number of exotic places are visited (while traveling by airplane, boat, train, bus, subway, and department store escalator) and impressions of different cultures are registered in an ethnographic manner. Here are the major places we see:

Japan
    Hokkaido (second largest island of Japan)
    Honshu (largest island of Japan)
        Tokyo
        Nara
        Narita International airport
Iceland
    Heimaey
Africa
    Guinea-Bissau
        Bijagos Islands
    Cape Verde Islands
Ile-de-France (the "Island of France" is a region of France including
    Paris)
Holland (we see a bird sanctuary)
Okinawa (largest of the Ryukyu Islands)
    Itoman
San Francisco
Island of Sal (a small island in the Atlantic)

The list itself already suggests some themes of the film: island nations, isolation, concentration of culture, cities, non-Western societies, and the contrast between industrial nations and their former colonies. Stories and anecdotes that relate to these themes emerge from each place and are strung together through the overall story of a voyage. In effect, this principle of grouping stories amounts to a *catalogue* of stories embedded within the narration of a voyage.[48]

The voyage in the film covers approximately sixteen years, from 1965 to 1981. It is, however, more than a journey from a place of departure to a final destination. Indeed the film begins in the midst of a journey from Hokkaido to Honshu, which stirs memories of a visit to Africa. We see excerpts from the African trip during a visit to Tokyo and only much later in the film will we see Hokkaido (when memories of it have been summoned by an event in Tokyo). The various locales in the film are visited and revisited several times; and then brought back again apparently through association and memory. Only a few of the many visits we see in the film are precisely located within the sixteen-year period of traveling. Thus the geographical patterns traced in *Sans Soleil* are quite intricate and may be mapped in many different ways. In addition, the identity of the person who is making the trip, and the manner in which impressions are being registered, becomes progressively less certain. To make matters still more complex, the film undertakes to document the general problems of documenting a place and culture as well as to speculate about the interpretive problems being posed for a spectator by its own images and sounds.

One could at this point mount an argument that *Sans Soleil* is better classified as an instance of post-modernism rather than travelogue. One could begin with a list of traits associated with a post-modern aesthetics:[49]

1 lists of things and permutations, rather than a series of events in causal interaction which derive from an origin and move step by step toward a conclusion;
2 middles without explicit beginnings or ends;
3 inconclusiveness, indeterminacy;
4 surface, randomness, and possibility;
5 diversity and plurality without hierarchy;
6 fragmentation, dissonance, admixture, layering;
7 incongruity, rather than unity or purity;
8 multiple media, eclecticism, pastiche, intertextuality;
9 pop culture, stereotypes, cult of the everyday;
10 quotation, distance;
11 detachment, self-consciousness.

It is possible to match many, perhaps all, of these general traits with effects produced in *Sans Soleil*. For instance, early in the film the traveler admits that "now only banality still interests me." Accordingly, he proceeds to investigate ordinary life in a society as experienced through popular imagination and mass media. The ordinary, however, is broken up in unexpected ways and rendered fragmentary.[50] Sudden freeze frames, television images, still photographs, and flashcuts forward or backward in time are juxtaposed with hallucinatory long takes of repetitive action and imagery altered by a video synthesizer. The spectator is assailed by a multiplicity of techniques that interrupt and disconnect time, that give space and causality an unstable existence, and that seemingly reduce our experience of time to the mere duration of imagery on the screen. The simple presence of things seems to have triumphed over causality.

But perhaps this interpretation goes too far. The film purports to be the history of a journey in which a traveler recounts the history of various places. If it is a history, then we must ask how a nonfictional narrative can survive in an environment that does not clearly delineate a "before" and an "after" sufficient to establish a causal principle which would enable image and sound to become documentary evidence. That is, how do radical shifts in *time* from one moment to the next in *Sans Soleil*, coupled with the invocation of multiple temporal contexts, affect the traditional documentary conceit that the time of a profilmic event can be mapped one to one onto a screen to produce an ordered history of events for the spectator? We will discover that *Sans Soleil* challenges the premises of the classical documentary and installs a new set of principles to anchor image and sound.

Consider the precredit sequence of *Sans Soleil*. The sequence functions both as a prologue to the story of the voyage and as a preview of how the story will be told. It consists of the following shots:

1 Fade-in written title:
> "Because I know that time is always time. And place
> is always and only place . . . "
> > T.S. Eliot – Ash-Wednesday

Fade-out.
2 Black image.
> VOICE-OVER BY A WOMAN:
> The first image he told me about was of three
> children on a road in Iceland in 1965.
3 Cut to: three young girls walking away while looking into a hand-held camera as it pans left to follow them.
4 Cut to: black image.
> VOICE-OVER (cont'd):
> He said that for him it was the image of happiness
> and also that he had tried several times to link it to
> other images.
5 Cut to: an American warplane being lowered from a flight deck into the interior of an aircraft carrier.
> VOICE-OVER (cont'd):
> But it never worked. He wrote me:
6 Cut to: black image.
> VOICE-OVER (cont'd):
> "One day I'll have to put it all alone at the beginning

of a film with a long piece of black leader. If they
don't see happiness in the picture, at least they'll see
the black."

7 Cut to: opening titles, followed by a scene on a boat traveling from
Hokkaido to Honshu.

Although the presence of a cameraman is clearly evident in the hand-
held shot (shot 3), we will never see him nor learn his identity. Instead
an unknown woman who is never seen will read letters from him
throughout the film, occasionally summarizing his words:

He described to me . . .
He contrasted . . .
He told me the story of . . .
He saw . . .
He remembered . . .
He imagined . . .
He was pleased that . . .
He didn't like to dwell on . . .
He had tried several times to . . .
Every time he came back from Africa . . .
Everything interested him . . .

She will also *make comments* on his letters: "He liked the fragility of those
moments suspended in time – those memories whose only function is
to leave behind nothing but memories."[51] What is striking about this
procedure is that it is not always possible to distinguish the actual
reading of a letter from a summary or commentary. We do not know,
for instance, who is responsible for the final words of the film: "Will
there be a last letter?" Nor are times and places specified for either the
writing or the reading of the letters. Is it the man's or the woman's
thoughts that we hear? How interpretive are the words meant to be?
Whose images do we see? In this way *Sans Soleil* raises some of the
same problems of voice-over and image found in *Letter from an Unknown
Woman*. Both of these films establish a fundamental ambiguity between
subjective and objective.

The narration is indeterminate in still other ways. The woman often
reminds us that she is reading, not seeing the images that we see (hence
her knowledge is limited):

One day he writes to me . . .
He writes me . . .
He used to write me . . .
He wrote me . . .
He said that . . .
He spoke to me of . . .

The first image he told me about was . . .
Later he told me . . .
He claimed that . . .

Moreover, the cameraman is writing about his *memory* of places and his *memory* of making a film (hence his knowledge, too, is limited):

> I remember that month of January in Tokyo, or rather I remember
>   the images I filmed of the month of January in Tokyo.
> Did I write you that there are . . . ?
> I think of a world where . . .
> I am writing you all this from another world, a world of appear-
>   ances.

He also frequently *quotes* other authors and texts. Thus the images we see are explicitly filtered and qualified by a number of "intervening" and supplementary memories that are only partially defined. The proliferation of these sorts of indeterminate narrations – intervening between the historical and the externally focalized – work against the aims of the classical documentary. Because the voices in the film – one heard directly and others heard second and third-hand – are rendered nonspecific (i.e., only partially determined) in the above sorts of ways, the words we hear become *fictionalized*. The spectator is confronted by the paradox of a fictional commentary, or commentator, alongside nonfictional images that are precise and rich in detail. This raises doubts about the overall causal situation, and hence about the genesis and logic of the images.

The problem of specificity becomes all the more acute in light of the obvious manipulation of sound and image. The hand-held camera, color shift, lack of ambient sound, and the look into the lens in the third shot juxtaposed with black leader and a confessional narration clearly announce that a self-conscious rhetoric will be at the center of the film. The question then is: of what, or which, mental or physical events do the images offer proof?

Matters are not clarified when we consider the status of the black images in the precredit sequence. Are we to understand the blackness as simply the absence of an image, a non-image that allows us to hear something? Or is the blackness instead an image that is somehow unable to show? An image that negates? A missing image? An exclusion? A forgetting? A void? A silence? All of these possibilities, and others, will be raised in various ways throughout *Sans Soleil* in an effort to explore the limits of understanding an image as a document. In the prologue, for example, the black image seems to provide the viewer with an opportunity to imagine his or her own image of "happiness." But, at the same time, the black image seems to be exploiting one of the connotations of the color of blackness as the *opposite* of happiness (i.e., a despair, darkness, sunlessness) and is thereby anticipating the *failure* of the viewer to find a suitable image. Even the presumed antithesis of happiness (shot 5) seems unable to bring happiness to mind. The prologue leaves the viewer with the idea of happiness, but without offering its documentary embodiment; instead, the viewer is allowed merely to perceive ("at least they'll see the black."). What is perceived, however, is perilously close to "nothing" and thus should alert the viewer to the fact that the film as a whole will be questioning some of the presuppositions of traditional nonfiction film, such as, the supposed primacy of the image in finding truth and proving reality. As the words we hear assume a fictive (nonspecific) aspect, the details we see become less specific, less tied to an immediate situation, and more tied to the voices in the film, more the pretext for a wide-ranging examination of preconceived ideas. Thus one of the projects of *Sans Soleil* will be to demonstrate the inadequacy of the epigraph (shot 1): time and place will be shown to be neither concrete nor absolute, nor even visible in certain ways.

During the prologue, the cameraman states that one day he will juxtapose the image of the three children with black leader at the beginning of a film (shot 6). Is that future film, then, the one we are now watching? Later in *Sans Soleil*, the cameraman returns to a discussion of the shot of the three children. He now says that filming them was his first act toward making "an imaginary film." The shot of the children is not repeated as he speaks; instead we see a series of paths in a bird sanctuary in Holland. Do these paths recall for the cameraman that road in Iceland with the children, or are the paths merely an emblem for travel and search? ("Now why this cut in time, this connection of memories?"[52]) He explains in detail the story of his "imaginary film." It involves a time traveler from the future of our planet, the year 4001. The time traveler has lost the power of forgetting so that he carries with him always the unhappiness that has been in the past. The traveler revisits sites of unhappiness in our time and finds them just as unbearable as in his memory. He takes solace only in listening to a song cycle by Moussorgski called *Sans Soleil* (*Sunless*). This music is still played in the fortieth century though its meaning has been forgotten. We never see the time traveler nor learn his name, but we do hear the music and we see a series of images of the places he is apparently visiting. We cannot recognize all these images, but some of them strongly resemble places we've seen earlier in the film and others may be near places seen earlier. As we watch these places appear again, there emerges an unmistakable sense that the cameraman himself has become the imaginary time traveler; that is, we come to believe that in telling the story the cameraman is attempting to represent his own feelings of dislocation while traveling. Or perhaps we might say that "Chris Marker" in documenting his travels has come to experience his present in terms of how he *imagines* it may be experienced in the future; that is, he seeks to recognize in his own activity of perceiving how his memory will in the future rework these events into a *history*, a causality appropriate to a future moment. In formal terms, we have already analyzed the occurrence of such a time in narrative: the historical present tense. The unknown "time traveler" is simply a device – a way of embodying the presence of a future in events being interpreted narratively in the present. I believe that in this sequence Marker is attempting to capture the fantastic time of making a narrative out of the everyday, and the wonder of finding a possible future already within the present.

The cameraman concludes by saying, "Of course I'll never make that film." This statement raises new questions about the film *Sans Soleil* which does, of course, begin with the image of the three children. Are we to think that he changed his mind yet again, and did make the imaginary film – the one we are now seeing – or did he only make one similar to it? The cameraman's statement also raises questions about the shots we have just been watching which purport to be *excerpts* from the imaginary film, or at least to be *samples* of what such a film might contain. What have we really seen? It is as if one were to bestow a certain concreteness onto hypothetical imagery, but only to say later that the gift itself was merely hypothetical. We are left wondering about the status of those views of the time traveler, some of which seem to be actual *point-of-view* shots: what has been their future?

Incredibly, the cameraman continues to talk about his imaginary film: "I've even given it a title, indeed the title of those Moussorgski songs – *Sunless*." Is *Sans Soleil*, then, after all, the real embodiment of the imaginary film? Or rather, in what measure is it to be thought imaginary and tentative, and not a document?

The voice-over for this segment about the "imaginary film" now ends but we continue to hear the Moussorgski music as we see a final six shots which are still-lifes.[53] The first shot lasts about fourteen seconds, and the others about three seconds each. The lack of commentary functions here as the aural equivalent of the black images in the prologue: there are no verb tenses to impose a time, measure duration, or order subtle movements in the images. The problem confronting the spectator is how to imagine the time of these final images that are offered as the final word on the imaginary film.

The locale of the six shots is not recognizable from previous shots in the film. We first see a path leading through a tunnel of trees. The wind is blowing and suddenly the light on the trees darkens noticeably as if the sun has gone behind a cloud (shot 1). Next we see a large foreground tree and lawn (shot 2). Then we see a small interior room with a writing desk and a bright window with trees visible outside (shot 3) followed by a corner of a room with a bed covered by a white bedspread and a bright, oval mirror on the wall (shot 4). Next we see a circular, reflecting pond in the foreground with a tunnel of trees framing a bright white house in the distance (shot 5). Finally we see a close view of part of a circular piece of marble on which rain is falling. The rain has made the marble reflective (shot 6). The sequence allows the viewer to judge these shots as a series of variations on lightness, reflectivity, and circularity. But who has seen, or else who is seeing and imagining, these places, this representation of solitude, of sunlessness (cf. shot 1), of writing itself (cf. shot 3)? Is it the time traveler, the cameraman, the woman narrator, "Chris Marker," or some other person from another time and place in the film? The viewer may wonder, for example, whether the time traveler is attempting to recapture the lost meaning of the music, or whether "Chris Marker" is offering the shots as pictures that could inspire the music – a way of remembering another Moussorgski composition, *Pictures from an Exhibition*. I would suggest that the memory that is in the process of being formed for us through these six shots is expressible only through a complex imbrication of a great many possibilities and as such rivals the complexity achieved by Proust in *A la recherche du temps perdu*. A multiplicity of spatial and temporal coordinates seems to apply. What is being represented in these shots, and elsewhere in the film, is the pertinence of multiple times and the effort of memory.[54]

Later, near the end of *Sans Soleil*, the cameraman is stirred by an event he witnesses in Japan: the Dondo-yaki, a Shinto blessing of objects that have been part of a celebration but are now debris. The blessing acknowledges a right of immortality for the objects before they are consumed by fire. This event prompts the cameraman to return to a discussion of the image of the three children. On this occasion we see the entire shot, not just the truncated version shown in the prologue. It is as if every frame of the shot has now become precious and must be acknowledged. The shot is presented in the context of footage showing what happened to that place in Iceland five years later in 1970: a volcano erupted and fiery lava obliterated the town where the three girls presumably lived. Does the image of the children now remind the cameraman that it is *too late* to reconstruct, or remember, the happiness that must have been in the image when it was filmed in 1965? Does the shot now stand for a *belated*, or lost memory – a memory that should have been recognized as it was being formed in 1965 but instead is recognized only after an act of destruction? He states, "it was as if the entire year '65 had just been covered with ashes." Paradoxically, we might say that the cameraman, in seeing the image again, *was now unhappy*. The appearance of the historical present tense in this formulation ("was now" unhappy), and the copresence of the antithesis of happiness, suggests the dynamism of memory that is being experienced by the cameraman and represented for the viewer. Memory is functioning independently of the desire to remember and the desire to remember happiness. The cameraman flees from his memory, but only to find another poignant memory. Early in the film we had seen a ceremony for a lost cat in Tokyo. Now he gives us the prayer: "Cat, wherever you are, peace be with you."

I think that we can now appreciate that the image of the three children – the "first image he told me about" as well as the first image we see in the film (shot 3) – is not the start of a journey, but rather, like many other images in the film, was discovered as a complex memory, and acquired its purpose, *while* he was traveling, or *while* he was assembling images of traveling. Nor is this image the final image that brings order and purpose to his journey. It is merely one image sharply etched with emotion – the result not of traveling from one place to the next, but of having been in a number of places at once, and of having remembered in different contexts. Representations from/of the past accumulate and conflict, and what perishes is the notion of a unique time and place.

I would like to suggest that the film *Sans Soleil* is a cautionary tale. The cameraman is aware that in remembering images he has filmed, he may be too late in recognizing their significance and emotional value. He wishes to compensate by filming images that are "too early." Thus in filming and writing letters, "only banality" and the "ordinary" will interest him. The resulting mood in many sequences of the film might be termed one of "premature nostalgia." Further, the use of complex tenses in *Sans Soleil* (historical present, belated past, premature nostalgia) is meant to raise questions about the power of film to document absolutely only one, past time rather than to simultaneously document present and future times as well. If true, the anomalous time schemes normally created within both narrative and fiction, and associated with a hierarchy of levels of narration, will have a legitimate role to play within "documentary" filmmaking. More broadly, the insistent use of complex tenses is a way of breaking away from conventional forms of temporal articulation.

If modernism makes problematic the links among things, and raises the issue of causality, one might say that the post-modernism of *Sans Soleil* never reaches the issue; instead, time is seemingly *pre*causal or *post*causal – prior, or subsequent, to a formal periodization of events. Unusual evocations of time, as in *Sans Soleil*, permanently suspend the parts that might otherwise form a causal unity of beginnings, middles, and ends in favor of surveying a field of possibilities: a multiplicity of partially realized narratives and nonnarratives competing equally.

A BRIEF CONCLUSION

Sans Soleil is balanced on the edge between fiction and nonfiction. There are a number of intensely subjective sequences within *Sans Soleil* (e.g., the bird sanctuary in Holland, the boat trip from Hokkaido, a "description of a dream" in the subterranean tunnels of Tokyo and on a train) as well as scenes about the problems of depicting the imaginary (e.g., a partial reconstruction of Hitchcock's *Vertigo* (1958)). These sequences are coupled with a measure of indeterminateness about person, time, and place so that both voice and the resultant dream are fictionalized. Nevertheless, there are other elements in the film that are highly specific and unique (e.g., the hand-held camera which seems to respond directly to the diegetic world, the savage death of a giraffe, visits to prominent landmarks). The blending of nonspecific and specific forces the viewer to interpret events both fictionally and nonfictionally.

Sans Soleil is also balanced precariously between narrative and non-narrative. Stories and anecdotes collected during a journey are arranged in a dramatic way to suggest the changing attitude of the traveler toward memory and history (e.g., his recognition of the significance of the children in Iceland, his discovery of various kinds of thirst). On the other hand, the appearance of complex time schemes – beyond "before" and "after," shall we say – is part of a post-modernist aesthetic which halts the careful ordering of a cause and effect chain in favor of pursuing multiple, perhaps infinite, sets of affinities among groups of objects. The result is neither catalogue, concordance, nor index, but rather something like a "hyperindex" of stories where one can begin with any "entry," or item in a story, and discover not only references to particulars of the story but also references to additional "entries" that collect related sets of particulars from other stories. A "hyperindex" does not terminate with one or several particulars, but continues to disperse outward onto a network of other entries and cross-references offering an indefinite number of routes by which to trace the knowledge base.[55] The relatively open, associational logic of such an arrangement of data produces an experience of time quite different from local, unidirectional cause and effect. Hence *Sans Soleil* becomes the experience not of a world with one time, but of a world of worlds in multiple times.

The simultaneity of fiction and nonfiction, narrative and non-narrative, permits *Sans Soleil* to explore some of the general forms of intelligibility available in our society. It also allows us a valuable perspective on narrative that is neither too distant nor too close to discern major features. If I were forced to use a single word to characterize a narrative organization of data, that word would be "causality." Creating time and place in a narrative is not as important as constructing a possible logic for the events that occur. Or, rather, time and place seem to be a prerequisite for our reasoning about causality and hence exist on a different level of generality than cause and effect.

If I were allowed a second word as a qualification to my description of narrative, it would be "efficacy." I believe that narrative comprehension is a way of recognizing the "causal efficacy" of an object. In understanding a story, we are imagining and tracing out several, or many, of the possibilities for the being of an object. In everyday life we make choices in light of the way, or ways, we believe the world may become. Narrative is one powerful framework that poses the connection of objects in time. It allows us to make cause and effect pairs, to connect pairs with other pairs, to construct a linked set of events. One of the purposes of a narrative is to demonstrate how certain effects that are desired may be achieved, how desire is linked to possibilities for being, how events may proceed. In this way, narrative operates to draw the future into the present.

Reasoning about cause and effect is inherent in our language and in the social consensus that produces language. Causality is not simply "out there," but a way of thinking, acting, and desiring. Consider, for example, a dictionary. Arthur Danto argues that "the dictionary encapsulates a kind of encyclopedia, in that it is part of the very meaning of certain terms in it that certain explanations are true; and we internalize a body of causal laws as we acquire our language."[56] We may need, however, to expand the notion of "language" and "dictionary" in analyzing the causality of films. Certainly we hear an enormous number of words in *Sans Soleil* making and remaking causality through language. But these words also interact with a multitude of images and sounds. The images offered in the film are no less an embodiment of a desired, or feared, possible causality. It might be better, then, to expand the notion of language so that vast dictionaries composed only of pictures and pictorial sequences may be included within that library that makes possible our awareness of things, and our awareness of the causal efficacy of things. Narrative could then be seen as a psychological process that responds to our desire to know how a world, and we ourselves, may become within one or several languages.

NOTES

1 NARRATIVE SCHEMA

1 C.G. Prado argues that narrative may be found at the very threshold of perception where consciousness itself begins. *Making Believe: Philosophical Reflections on Fiction* (Westport, Conn.: Greenwood Press, 1984), pp. 15, 115–38, 150–3. On narrative as a fundamental mode of thought see, e.g., *Narrative Psychology: The Storied Nature of Human Conduct*, ed. by Theodore R. Sarbin (New York: Praeger, 1986); Brian Wicker, *The Story-Shaped World: Fiction and Metaphysics: Some Variations on a Theme* (London: Athlone Press, 1975).

2 See, e.g., James Boyd White, *Heracles' Bow: Essays on the Rhetoric and Poetics of the Law* (Madison: University of Wisconsin Press, 1985), chap. 8, "Telling Stories in the Law and in Ordinary Life," pp. 168–91; Dennis Kurzon, "How Lawyers Tell Their Tales: Narrative Aspects of a Lawyer's Brief," *Poetics*, vol. 14, no. 6 (Dec. 1985), pp. 467–81.

3 See, e.g., Lionel Gossman, "History and Literature" and Louis O. Mink, "Narrative Form as a Cognitive Instrument" in *The Writing of History: Literary Form and Historical Understanding*, ed. by Robert H. Canary and Henry Kozicki (Madison: University of Wisconsin Press, 1978), pp. 3–39, 129–49 as well as several essays by Hayden White: "The Historical Text as Literary Artifact," *ibid.*, pp. 41–62; "The Narrativization of Real Events," *Critical Inquiry*, vol. 7, no. 4 (Summer 1981), pp. 793–8; "The Historical Text as Literary Artifact" and "The Fictions of Factual Representation" in *Tropics of Discourse: Essays in Cultural Criticism* (Baltimore: Johns Hopkins University Press, 1978), pp. 81–100, 121–34; and "The Value of Narrativity in the Representation of Reality" in *The Content of the Form: Narrative Discourse and Historical Representation* (Baltimore: Johns Hopkins University Press, 1987), pp. 1–25.

4 See, e.g., the special issue of *Poetics* on "Narrative Analysis: An Interdisciplinary Dialogue," vol. 15, nos. 1/2 (April 1986) and Wallace Martin, *Recent Theories of Narrative* (Ithaca, N.Y.: Cornell University Press, 1986), esp. pp. 71–8. For Martin, "Any explanation that unfolds in time, with surprises during its progress and knowledge only through hindsight, is just a story, no matter how factual. What histories and biographies share with novels and romances is temporal organization." (p. 187) I will attempt to elucidate the consequences of such "temporal organization" in every chapter of this book.

5 Cf. Mary Louise Pratt, *Toward a Speech Act Theory of Literary Discourse* (Bloomington: Indiana University Press, 1977) p. 72.

6 On the definition of "game," see Ludwig Wittgenstein, *Philosophical Investigations* trans. by G.E.M. Anscombe (New York: Macmillan Publishing Co., 3rd edn 1958), paras 66–75.

7 Tzvetan Todorov, "The Two Principles of Narrative," *Diacritics*, vol. 1, no. 1 (Fall 1971), p. 39 (the two principles are causality and transformation); Barbara Leondar, "Hatching Plots: Genesis of Storymaking" in *The Arts and Cognition*, ed. by David Perkins and Barbara Leondar (Baltimore: Johns Hopkins University Press, 1977), p. 176. See also Todorov's "Categories of the Literary Narrative," trans. by Ann Goodman, *Film Reader* 2 (Evanston, Ill.: Northwestern University Press, 1977), esp. pp. 21–8; *The Poetics of Prose*, trans. by Richard Howard (Ithaca, N.Y.: Cornell University Press, 1977); *Introduction to Poetics*, trans. by Richard Howard (Minneapolis: University of Minnesota Press, 1981), esp. pp. 41–58.

8 See, e.g., Seymour Chatman, *Story and Discourse: Narrative Structure in Fiction and Film* (Ithaca, N.Y.: Cornell University Press, 1978), pp. 31–2, 267. A.J. Greimas and J. Courtès make the distinction between "being" and "doing" a centerpiece of their theory, deriving from it such dualities as narrative versus narration, objective discourse versus subjective discourse, horizontal meaning versus vertical meaning, and cognitive positions versus cognitive events. "The Cognitive Dimension of Narrative Discourse," *New Literary History*, vol. 7, no. 3 (Spring 1976), pp. 433, 436–7, 440.

Ray Jackendoff claims that the conceptual structure of English verbs of predication, possession, and spatial position is actually tripartite where each class of verbs may be subdivided into ones which designate a state ("be"), a change in state ("go"), or the persistence of a state ("stay"). See *Consciousness and the Computational Mind* (Cambridge, Mass.: MIT Press, 1987), pp. 152–8. Suzanne Fleischman employs a four-part distinction among predicates – states, activities, accomplishments, and achievements. Activities are general and open-ended ("sing," "build," "drive a car") while accomplishments and achievements have natural endpoints. Accomplishments ("sing a song," "build a house," "recover from illness") possess inherent duration while achievements ("recognize someone," "find or lose something," "be born or die") are punctual and instantaneous. See *Tense and Narrativity: From Medieval Performance to Modern Fiction* (Austin: University of Texas Press, 1990), pp. 20–1.

9 Todorov's notions of inversion and recognition closely resemble two of Aristotle's three crucial parts of a tragic plot – reversal of the situation and recognition; see *Poetics*, chap. 11 (the third part of a tragedy is pathos, or the scene of suffering). Peter Brooks has argued that Todorov's narrative "transformation" through five stages may also be understood as the re-animation of an initial narrative metaphor: "We start with an inactive, 'collapsed' metaphor and work through to a reactivated, transactive one, a metaphor with its difference restored through metonymic process." *Reading for the Plot: Design and Intention in Narrative* (New York: Alfred A. Knopf, 1984), p. 27; cf. p. 29.

10 See, e.g., *Spatial Form in Narrative*, ed. by Jeffrey R. Smitten and Ann Daghistany (Ithaca, N.Y.: Cornell University Press, 1981); E.M. Forster, *Aspects of the Novel* (New York: Harcourt, Brace & Co., 1927), chap. 8, "Pattern and Rhythm," pp. 213–42. Cf. Northrop Frye, *Fables of Identity: Studies in Poetic Mythology* (New York: Harcourt, Brace & World, 1963), pp. 13–15, 21, 23.

11 Christian Metz, *Film Language: A Semiotics of the Cinema*, trans. by Michael

Taylor (New York: Oxford University Press, 1974), chap. 2, "Notes Toward a Phenomenology of the Narrative," p. 24.

12 This example and the one following ("Roses are red"), but not the analyses of them, are taken from Shlomith Rimmon-Kenan, *Narrative Fiction: Contemporary Poetics* (New York: Methuen, 1983), p. 1. Gerald Prince also uses the following example ("Roses are red"), but with a different analysis, in *Narratology: The Form and Functioning of Narrative* (New York: Mouton, 1982), pp. 1–2, and in "Aspects of a Grammar of Narrative," *Poetics Today*, vol. 1, no. 3 (1980), p. 49.

13 On the limerick's theme of a woman being away from her family, compare a similar fate suffered by the boy who runs away in the American folktale, "The Gingerbread Boy."

14 Rick Altman, *The American Film Musical* (Bloomington: Indiana University Press, 1987), pp. 16–27. See also Altman, "Dickens, Griffith, and Film Theory Today," *The South Atlantic Quarterly*, vol. 88, no. 2 (Spring 1989), pp. 321–59.

15 I will make a distinction between the "center" of a catalogue and the "focus" of a causal chain. I will also distinguish focus from types of "focalization." Other discriminations will include types of time, types of causality, "double" character motivation, a "double" causal structure, and metaphors of similarity and dissimilarity.

16 The concept of a narrative "transformation" has been understood in many ways. Gerald Prince, for example, uses a set of rewrite rules to analyze narrative in strict conformity with a transformational-generative grammar. *A Grammar of Stories: An Introduction* (The Hague: Mouton, 1973). Transformations have also been described in terms of an extended predicate calculus (e.g., Todorov) and in more expansive ways as intertextual, historical phenomena (e.g., the study of myth and the evolution of a genre). See also Jean Piaget's definition of transformation in *Structuralism*, trans. by Chaninah Maschler (New York: Harper & Row, 1970), pp. 5, 20, 36, 52.

17 On Vladimir Propp, see discussion in chapter 4.

18 A.J. Greimas and François Rastier, "The Interaction of Semiotic Constraints," *Yale French Studies* 41 (1968), pp. 86–105; Edward Branigan, *Point of View in the Cinema: A Theory of Narration and Subjectivity in Classical Film* (New York and Berlin: Mouton, 1984), pp. 160–2 and n. 26. See generally, Algirdas Julien Greimas, *On Meaning: Selected Writings in Semiotic Theory*, trans. by Paul J. Perron and Frank H. Collins (Minneapolis: University of Minnesota Press, 1981); Claude Bremond, "The Logic of Narrative Possibilities," *New Literary History*, vol. 11, no. 4 (Spring 1980), pp. 387–411; and three articles in *Diacritics*, vol. 7, no. 1 (Spring 1977), pp. 2–40, including an article on Claude Bremond and Greimas's "Elements of a Narrative Grammar." For a detailed application of Greimas's method, see Garrett Stewart, "Singer Sung: Voice as Avowal in Streisand's *Yentl*," *Mosaic*, vol. 18, no. 4 (Fall 1985), pp. 135–58.

19 See, e.g., George Lakoff, *Women, Fire, and Dangerous Things: What Categories Reveal about the Mind* (Chicago: University of Chicago Press, 1987) and Marvin Minsky, *The Society of Mind* (New York: Simon & Schuster, 1986). For an attempt to apply the linguistics of Ferdinand de Saussure to film and prose, see Steven Cohan and Linda M. Shires, *Telling Stories: A Theoretical Analysis of Narrative Fiction* (New York: Routledge, 1988), esp. chaps 1 and 2, pp. 1–51.

20 Martin, *Recent Theories of Narrative*, p. 90.

21 For an excellent survey of the issues and methods of cognitive science and

NOTES TO CHAPTER 1

a discussion of psychological reality as a goal for film study, see David Bordwell's "A Case for Cognitivism" in a special issue of *Iris* 9 devoted to "Cinema and Cognitive Psychology," vol. 5, no. 2 (Spring 1989), pp. 11–40.

22 Stephen Heath, "Film and System: Terms of Analysis," Part I, *Screen*, vol. 16, no. 1 (Spring 1975), pp. 48–9 (Heath's emphases); cf. p. 10. See also Part II in *Screen*, vol. 16, no. 2 (Summer 1975), pp. 91–2, 98, 110, and *"Touch of Evil*, the Long Version – a Note" in *Screen*, vol. 17, no. 1 (Spring 1976), pp. 115–17.

For a critique of Heath's definition of narrative and an angry response to contemporary film analysis, see Noël Carroll, *Mystifying Movies: Fads & Fallacies in Contemporary Film Theory* (New York: Columbia University Press, 1988), pp. 160–70. Carroll proposes a model of narrative with six basic types of scene, all based on a rhetoric of question and answer coupled with three basic ways of directing a spectator's attention; see pp. 170–81, 199–208. Carroll outlines his approach in "Toward a Theory of Film Editing," *Millennium Film Journal*, no. 3 (Winter/Spring 1979), pp. 79–99. On question and answer, see also Roland Barthes' definition of a "hermeneutic code" in *S/Z*, trans. by Richard Miller (New York: Hill & Wang, 1974), sects 32, 37, 89. A formal treatment of plot in terms of "problem and solution" may be found in Thomas G. Pavel, *The Poetics of Plot: The Case of English Renaissance Drama* (Minneapolis: University of Minnesota Press, 1985). Such prototypical patterns of argumentation as question and answer, problem and solution, attribute and listing, and contrasting alternatives apply also to the organization of expository, nonnarrative texts. See, e.g., Joseph E. Grimes, *The Thread of Discourse* (The Hague: Mouton, 1975) and Bonnie J.F. Meyer, *The Organization of Prose and its Effects on Memory* (Amsterdam: North-Holland, 1975).

23 Heath, "Film and System," p. 49 (his emphasis).

24 See Raymond Bellour's "Segmenting/Analyzing" and "The Obvious and the Code" in *Narrative, Apparatus, Ideology: A Film Theory Reader*, ed. by Philip Rosen (New York: Columbia University Press, 1986), pp. 66–101. Even the most extreme, "modernist" narrative must submit to *some* demands if it is to be a "narrative"; cf. Roy Armes, "Robbe-Grillet, Ricardou and *Last Year At Marienbad*," *Quarterly Review of Film Studies*, vol. 5, no. 1 (Winter 1980), pp. 14–15. Armes contends that *Marienbad* (Resnais, 1962) qualifies as a narrative only by virtue of certain large-scale patterns, not on the basis of action and scene.

25 Chatman, *Story and Discourse*, p. 31 (his emphasis).

26 Metz, *Film Language*, p. 28. On discourse as a sequence of predicative statements, see pp. 20, 25–6. Metz italicizes the entire sentence but I have dropped the emphasis except in two places.

27 Prince, *Narratology*, p. 68; cf. pp. 61, 77.

28 On intellectual cinema, see Sergei Eisenstein, "The Dramaturgy of Film Form (The Dialectical Approach to Film Form)," p. 180, "The Fourth Dimension in Cinema," pp. 193–4, and Richard Taylor's "Introduction," pp. 16–21 in *S.M. Eisenstein: Selected Works*, vol. I: Writings, 1922–34, trans. by Richard Taylor (Bloomington: Indiana University Press, 1988). See also the discussion of documentary film in chapter 7 below.

29 The first pair of sentences (1a and 1b) is analyzed by E.M. Forster, *Aspects of the Novel*, p. 130. The second pair is analyzed by Prince, *Narratology*, pp. 61, 63; see also pp. 64, 66; and cf. the methods and analysis of chap. 3, "Narrative Grammar," pp. 79–102, with chap. 5, "Narrativity," pp. 145–61.

Note that for Prince, causality is *not* an essential feature of narrative: although the queen does die because of "grief" (1b), Shirley's "life of crime" (2b) does not result from her being "good." In an earlier work Prince uses a different set of criteria in defining the minimal narrative; *A Grammar of Stories*, p. 31. See also Rimmon-Kenan, *Narrative Fiction*, pp. 17–19; Chatman, *Story and Discourse*, pp. 30–1, 45–8; and Todorov, *Introduction*, pp. 41–46. Gérard Genette argues that all of the following are minimal narratives: "the king died," 'Pierre has come," "I walk." See *Narrative Discourse Revisited*, trans. by Jane E. Lewin (Ithaca, N.Y.: Cornell University Press, 1988), pp. 18–20. Perhaps one might introduce a distinction between minimal narrative and minimal story; see Prince, *A Dictionary of Narratology* (Lincoln: University of Nebraska Press, 1987), p. 53.

30 See Julian E. Hochberg, *Perception* (Englewood Cliffs, N.J.: Prentice-Hall, 2nd edn 1978), chap. 4, "Perceiving Objects as Structures of Sensations," pp. 48–104.

31 Kendall L. Walton, "What is Abstract About the Art of Music?," *The Journal of Aesthetics and Art Criticism*, vol. 46, no. 3 (Spring 1988), p. 357 (Walton's capitalization). Although Walton's project does not involve a consideration of narrative, his example illustrates how generalized the notion of it can become.

32 William C. Dowling, *Jameson, Althusser, Marx: An Introduction to "The Political Unconscious"* (Ithaca, N.Y.: Cornell University Press, 1984), p. 96. Dowling likens narrative to the Kantian concepts of space and time. Dowling's claim is not that "we make up stories about the world to understand it, but the much more radical claim that the world comes to us in the shape of stories" (p. 95; cf. p. 115). Also, his view of the nature of "fiction" is so broad as to simply deny that there is any special problem with fictional reference (pp. 122–4); but see chapter 7 below.

33 Dan Lloyd, *Simple Minds* (Cambridge, Mass.: MIT Press, 1989), pp. 209–37. On concepts in narratology, see Prince, *A Dictionary of Narratology*. For a recent assessment of the field, see two special issues of *Poetics Today* on "Narratology Revisited," vol. 11, nos 2 and 4 (Summer and Winter 1990). On cognitive science and narratology, see especially Jackson G. Barry, "Narratology's Centrifugal Force: A Literary Perspective on the Extensions of Narrative Theory," *ibid.*, no. 2, pp. 295–307.

34 See, e.g., James C. Mancuso, "The Acquisition and Use of Narrative Grammar Structure" in *Narrative Psychology*, ed. by Sarbin, p. 94. See generally *Categorical Perception: The Groundwork of Cognition*, ed. by Stevan Harnad (New York: Cambridge University Press, 1987), esp. chaps 9, 16, and 19, "Perceptual Categories in Vision and Audition," "Categorization Processes and Categorical Perception," and "Category Induction and Representation." There is a crucial connection between naming behavior and nonlinguistic social behavior. See Lakoff, *Women, Fire, and Dangerous Things*, pp. 31–54, 199–201, 260–303.

35 Jean Matter Mandler, *Stories, Scripts, and Scenes: Aspects of Schema Theory* (Hillsdale, N.J.: Lawrence Erlbaum Associates, 1984), p. ix; see also pp. 19–21, 56–7, 85, 101. In this important book on the nature of a narrative schema, Mandler distinguishes schematic mental structures in general from categorical, matrix, and serial structures and discusses the psychological reality of such implicit or tacit knowledge; pp. 1–36. See also Mandler, "On the Psychological Reality of Story Structure," *Discourse Processes*, vol. 10, no. 1 (Jan.–March 1987), pp. 1–29.

On the development of the notion of schema as an explanatory concept in psychology, see Howard Gardner, *The Mind's New Science: A History of the Cognitive Revolution* (New York: Basic Books, expanded edn 1987), pp. 58–9, 114–16, 118, 124–8, 130, 163, 165–7, 317, 383. See also Deborah Tannen, "What's in a Frame? Surface Evidence for Underlying Expectations" in *New Directions in Discourse Processing*, ed. by Roy O. Freedle (Norwood, N.J.: Ablex, 1979), pp. 137–44; Reid Hastie, "Schematic Principles in Human Memory" in *Social Cognition: The Ontario Symposium*, vol. I, ed. by E. Tory Higgins, C. Peter Herman, and Mark P. Zanna (Hillsdale, N.J.: Lawrence Erlbaum Associates, 1981), pp. 40–3.

36 On a schema for narrative, see generally Thomas H. Carr, "Perceiving Visual Language" in *Handbook of Perception and Human Performance*, vol. II, "Cognitive Processes and Performance", ed. by Kenneth R. Boff, Lloyd Kaufman, and James P. Thomas (New York: John Wiley & Sons, 1986), sect. 6.2, "Narrative Organization," pp. 29-57 and 29-58; Teun A. van Dijk and Walter Kintsch, *Strategies of Discourse Comprehension* (New York: Academic Press, 1983), chap. 2.9, "Schematic Superstructures," sect. 2.9.1, "Story Grammars and the Narrative Schema," pp. 55–9, and see generally chap. 10.2, "A Framework for a Process Model," pp. 346–51. A good introduction to the issues may be found in Gordon H. Bower and Randolph K. Cirilo, "Cognitive Psychology and Text Processing" in *Handbook of Discourse Analysis*, vol. 1: *Disciplines of Discourse*, ed. by Teun A. van Dijk (New York: Academic Press, 1985), pp. 71–105; see also Elisabeth Gulich and Uta M. Quasthoff, "Narrative Analysis" in vol. 2: *Dimensions of Discourse*, pp. 169–97, and Csaba Pleh, "On Formal- and Content-Based Models of Story Memory" in *Literary Discourse: Aspects of Cognitive and Social Psychological Approaches*, ed. by Laszlo Halasz (New York: Walter de Gruyter, 1987), pp. 100–12.

37 See Nancy L. Stein, "The Comprehension and Appreciation of Stories: A Developmental Analysis" in *The Arts, Cognition, and Basic Skills*, ed. by Stanley S. Madeja (St Louis: Cemrel, 1978), pp. 231–49; David Bordwell, *Narration in the Fiction Film* (Madison: University of Wisconsin Press, 1985), chap. 3, "The Viewer's Activity," esp. sect. on "Narrative Comprehension," pp. 33–40.

38 See Teun A. van Dijk and Walter Kintsch, *Strategies of Discourse Comprehension* (New York: Academic Press, 1983), p. 348.

39 Minsky, *Society of Mind*, p. 114; Branigan, *Point of View*, p. 179.

40 Cf. George Lakoff and Mark Johnson, *Metaphors We Live By* (Chicago: University of Chicago Press, 1980), chap. 24, "Truth," pp. 159–84.

41 The perceiver's ability to "fill in" data missing in the text has prompted literary theorists to examine the types of gaps that may be created in a text (e.g., diffused, focused, flaunted, suppressed, temporary, permanent). See, e.g., Meir Sternberg, *Expositional Modes and Temporal Ordering in Fiction* (Baltimore: Johns Hopkins University Press, 1978) and Wolfgang Iser, *The Act of Reading: A Theory of Aesthetic Response* (Baltimore: Johns Hopkins University Press, 1978).

42 Cf. Bordwell, *Narration*, p. 120. See generally Arthur C. Graesser and Leslie F. Clark, *Structures and Procedures of Implicit Knowledge* (Norwood, N.J.: Ablex Publishing, 1985), pp. 39–43, and chap. 5, "Constructing Structures During Narrative Prose Comprehension," pp. 189–244; Prince, *Narratology*, chap. 4, "Reading Narrative," esp. sect. "Legibility," pp. 132–43.

43 Virginia Brooks, "Film, Perception and Cognitive Psychology," *Millennium*

Film Journal, nos 14/15 (Fall/Winter 1984–5), p. 116. See esp. Julian Hochberg, "Representation of Motion and Space in Video and Cinematic Displays" in *Handbook of Perception and Human Performance*, vol. I, "Sensory Processes and Perception", ed. by Kenneth R. Boff, Lloyd Kaufman, and James P. Thomas (New York: John Wiley & Sons, 1986), pp. 22–47 and pp. 22–48 ("the schematic events that the viewer has in mind and can bring to the moving picture are, in normal usage, at least as important as the stimulus information. . .''); cf. pp. 22–51, and pp. 22–57 through pp. 22–60. Hochberg also discusses the evidence for mental structures based on experiments involving the "mental rotation" of objects, pp. 22–48; and see Jackendoff, *Consciousness and the Computational Mind*, pp. 179–85, and Norman N. Holland, "Film Response from Eye to I: The Kuleshov Experiment," *The South Atlantic Quarterly*, vol. 88, no. 2 (Spring 1989), pp. 415–42.

44 An intermediate case between conventional narrative and a narrative generated from nonsense data is the so-called "natural narrative," or nature narrative, which tells the story of a sequence of physical events. For example: "A sudden gust of wind snaps a tree branch which falls into a pond creating a ripple that upsets the reflection of a passing cloud. . . ." Cf. Walt Disney's *The Old Mill* (1935). The term "natural narrative," however, is usually applied to personal-experience anecdotes related in ordinary conversation. See note 48 below.

45 See, e.g., Howard Gardner, "From Melvin to Melville: On the Relevance to Aesthetics of Recent Research on Story Comprehension" in *The Arts, Cognition, and Basic Skills*, ed. by Stanley S. Madeja (St Louis: Cemrel, 1978), pp. 250–6.

46 See Edward Branigan, " 'Here is a Picture of No Revolver!': The Negation of Images, and Methods for Analyzing the Structure of Pictorial Statements," *Wide Angle* vol. 8, nos. 3/4 (1986), pp. 8–17, and John R. Anderson, *Language, Memory, and Thought* (Hillsdale, N.J.: Lawrence Erlbaum Associates, 1976), pp. 10–13.

47 According to Metz, "It is not because the cinema is language that it can tell such fine stories, but rather it has become language because it has told such fine stories." *Film Language*, p. 47.

48 See Pratt, *Toward a Speech Act Theory*, chap. 2, "Natural Narrative," pp. 38–78; William Labov, *The Social Stratification of English in New York City* (Washington, D.C.: Center for Applied Linguistics, 1966) and *Language in the Inner City* (University Park: University of Pennsylvania Press, 1972). For a summary of how Labov's method has been applied to spoken and written narrative, see Michael J. Toolan, *Narrative: A Critical Linguistic Introduction* (New York: Routledge, 1988), chap. 5, "Narrative as socially situated: the sociolinguistic approach," and chap. 6, "Children's narratives," pp. 146–225.

49 James Paul Gee and François Grosjean, "Empirical Evidence for Narrative Structure," *Cognitive Science*, vol. 8, no. 1 (Jan.–Mar. 1984), pp. 59–85. Cf. Jackendoff, *Consciousness and the Computational Mind*, p. 69, and Branigan, "Here is a Picture," pp. 11–14.

50 Cf. Mandler's discussion of the debate in the field of psychology concerning "advance organizers" that are supposed to provide information to a perceiver about how to order the information given in a text; *Stories, Scripts, and Scenes*, pp. 112–13.

51 In addition to sources cited in other notes of this chapter, see, e.g., Beth Haslett, "A Developmental Analysis of Children's Narratives" and Sally Planalp, "Scripts, Story Grammars, and Causal Schemas" in *Contemporary*

Issues in Language and Discourse Processes, ed. by Donald G. Ellis and William A. Donohue (Hillsdale, N.J.: Lawrence Erlbaum Associates, 1986), pp. 87–125; Brian Sutton-Smith, "Children's Fiction Making" in *Narrative Psychology,* ed. by Sarbin, pp. 67–90; Nancy L. Stein and Christine G. Glenn, "Children's Concept of Time: The Development of a Story Schema" in *The Developmental Psychology of Time,* ed. by William J. Friedman (New York: Academic Press, 1982), pp. 255–82; and Barbara Leondar's "Hatching Plots: Genesis of Storymaking," pp. 172–91.

In surveying this literature, it seems remarkable that no one has undertaken to discover what special problems of narrative comprehension may be posed to a child by filmed narratives. For example, when and how do children understand an eyeline match, screen direction, cross-cutting, an unusual angle, off-screen space, or nondiegetic sound?

52 Arthur Applebee has attempted to extend Lev Vygotsky's theory of a child's general development of concepts to the issue of a child's acquisition of narrative. In summarizing Applebee I have changed the names of some of his stages and modified some of his definitions in order to draw more exact boundaries. Arthur Applebee, *The Child's Concept of Story: Ages Two to Seventeen* (Chicago: University of Chicago Press, 1978), chap. 4, "Narrative Form," pp. 55–72 and 166–7; L.S. Vygotsky, *Thought and Language,* trans. by Alex Kozulin (Cambridge, Mass.: MIT Press, rev. edn 1986).

At the beginning of this chapter, I offered a (nonnarrative!) list of nonnarrative ways of organizing data. The principles at work in narrative perception (e.g., centering and chaining), however, have counterparts in general systems of human categorization. Cf. Lakoff, *Women, Fire, and Dangerous Things,* pp. 92–6, 102–4.

53 Cf. Noël Burch, *Theory of Film Practice,* trans. by Helen R. Lane (Princeton, N.J.: Princeton University Press, 1981), chap. 7, "Chance and Its Functions," pp. 105–21. What at first appears as chance may, of course, be shown to have an underlying pattern when a relevant context is found.

54 Consider:

> Fuzzy Wuzzy was a bear
> Fuzzy Wuzzy had no hair
> Fuzzy Wuzzy wasn't fuzzy
> Was he?

This verse catalogues certain phonemes to highlight a syntactic ambiguity ("Was he?") and a semantic paradox: was Fuzzy properly named? Was Wuzzy really a bear?

55 Notice that as one changes the "center," the list changes. If the catalogue were centered on "recipients of action X," then the list would be simply "N, O, and P." Many of the classic cartoons of Chuck Jones, Tex Avery, and Friz Freleng are constructed as simple inventories of "complicating actions" that arise in failing to achieve a goal: A tries R; A tries S; A tries T which yields the catalogue, R, S, T, with A as the "center" (e.g., Tweety Pie and Sylvester; Road Runner).

As another example of a catalogue, consider the following "story" told by a girl 2½ to 3 years old:

> The cat went on the cakies.
> The cat went on the car.
> The cookie was in my nose.
> The cookie went on the fireman's hat.

The fireman's hat went on the bucket.
The cookie went on the carousel.
The cookie went on the puzzle.
The cookie went on the doggie.

Brian Sutton-Smith refers to this type of story as a "theme and variation" structure and argues that for children melody comes before meaning ("Children's Fiction Making", pp. 73–6). Cf. the notion of "parametric" narration in David Bordwell, *Narration*, chap. 12, pp. 274–310 and Kristin Thompson, *Breaking the Glass Armor: Neoformalist Film Analysis* (Princeton, N.J.: Princeton University Press, 1988), Part 6, pp. 245–352. See generally, Smitten and Daghistany, *Spatial Form in Narrative*.

On the use of catalogue structures by avant-garde filmmakers and the relationship to narrative structures, see James Peterson, "The Artful Mathematicians of the Avant-Garde," *Wide Angle*, vol. 7, no. 3 (1985), pp. 14–23, and "Bruce Conner and the Compilation Narrative," *Wide Angle*, vol. 8, nos. 3/4 (1986), pp. 53–62.

56 The fact that an episode allows better recall than a heap or a catalogue derives from its relationship to a schematic organization; cf. Mandler, *Stories, Scripts, and Scenes*, pp. 15, 52. Cf. also heap, catalogue, and episode both with David Bordwell and Kristin Thompson's notions of abstract, categorical, and associational nonnarrative form in *Film Art: An Introduction* (New York: McGraw-Hill, 3rd edn 1990), chap. 4, "Nonnarrative Formal Systems," pp. 89–124, and with Nelson Goodman's story, study, and symphony in *Of Mind and Other Matters* (Cambridge, Mass.: Harvard University Press, 1984), chap. 4, sect. 1, "Twisted Tales," pp. 109–22.

The following "story" told by a boy 3½ years old begins as a heap and moves toward an episode:

> A girl and a boy, and a mother and maybe a daddy. And then a piggy. And then a horse. And maybe a cow. And a chair. And food. And a car. Maybe a painting. Maybe a baby. Maybe a mountain stone, somebody threw a stone on a bear, and the bear's head broke right off. A big stone, this big [holds out arms]. And they didn't have glue either. They had to buy some at the store. You can't buy some in the morning. Tomorrow morning they're gonna buy some. Glue his head on. And the baby bear will look at a book.
>
> (Applebee, *The Child's Concept of Story*, pp. 58–9.)

57 On closure, see note 62 below.

58 In claiming that "description" portrays elements arranged in a simultaneity, one is not claiming that description itself takes no time, nor that dynamic entities – such as, events, actions, and motions – are incapable of being described. On the nature of description, see, e.g., Seymour Chatman, "What Is Description in the Cinema?," *Cinema Journal*, vol. 23, no. 4 (Summer 1984), p. 4 ("The chief structural property of description is its atemporality"); Gérard Genette, "Boundaries of Narrative," trans. by Ann Levonas, *New Literary History*, vol. 8, no. 1 (Autumn 1976), p. 7 ("[D]escription, because it lingers over objects and beings considered in their simultaneity and because it envisages the actions themselves as scenes, seems to suspend the flow of time and to contribute to spreading out the narrative in space."). See also Philippe Hamon, "Rhetorical Status of the Descriptive," *Yale French Studies* 61 (1981), pp. 1–26; Chatman, *Coming to Terms: The Rhetoric of Narrative in Fiction and Film* (Ithaca, N.Y.: Cornell University Press, 1990), chap. 3,

pp. 38–55. Cf. Bordwell's notion of a "spatializing narration" in *Narration*, pp. 317–21.

59 Chatman divides causal sequences into only two, rather than four types: the narrative of revelation and the narrative of resolution. *Story and Discourse*, p. 48.

60 The next chapter will discuss some principles of temporal ordering (see, e.g., fig. 3). In chapters 4 and 6, I will discuss three narrations which create an experience of time for the spectator that is more powerful than simple duration: implied authorial narration, historical present narration, and hyperdiegetic narration. These narrations seem to affect the present by coming from a future time; that is, the spectator recognizes a pattern in the present by conjecturing about elements not yet present that will bring the pattern into existence: what future will justify (has already justified) the present?

Gerald Prince refers to anomalous time schemes as the "orientation" of narrative. He quotes Gérard Genette:

These *retrograde* definitions are precisely what we call the arbitrariness of narrative: not at all a lack of determination but the determination of means by ends . . . of causes by effects. It is this paradoxical logic of fiction which requires one to define any element, any unit of narrative by its functional character, that is to say among other things by its correlation with another unit, and to account for the first (in the order of narrative time) by the second, and so on – whence it results that the last is the one which governs all others and is governed by nothing: this is the essential locus of arbitrariness, at least in the immanence of narrative itself, for it is then easy to find for it all the psychological, historical, or esthetic determinants that we want.

(*Narratology*, p. 157; see also pp. 27–9, 149–50, 155–8.)

61 Cf. Jackendoff's discussion of "meaningful" versus "meaningless" as a particular affect deriving from the registration or lack of registration among certain levels of the description of data in short-term memory (*Consciousness and the Computational Mind*, p. 306). On the fact that we cannot be conscious of our own processing of data, see pp. 46, 277, 304, 319.

Time is not just periodicity but *hierarchical* periodicity. Cf. Jackendoff, *Consciousness and the Computational Mind*, pp. 253–4. Figure 3 in chapter 2 displays a less complex notion of temporal ordering since it analyzes temporal relationships in terms of the possible juxtapositions of only a pair of consecutive spatial fragments. However, by organizing a larger number of fragments according to, say, principles which create a catalogue or an episode, new global and hierarchical structures of time will appear. In general, this means that several time schemes will be appropriate simultaneously when we read.

62 The reason that "symmetry," or rhyme, may provide a sign of closure is that one of the properties of symmetry is that it portrays a relationship of *equivalence* which is fully reversible. When X and Y are symmetrical, X is equivalent in some respect to Y, and Y is equivalent in the same degree to X. Each mirrors the other. In the context of time, an equivalence between X and Y presupposes that there is no further change. If time has thus been halted, so too has cause and effect. In symmetry and equivalence, then, one comes full circle, returning to a version of the initial situation. In terms of narrative this may mean that there are no further necessary effects and that an "end" has been reached which is a unique transformation of the initial

state which itself had no necessary cause. A narrative ends when its cause and effect chains are judged to be totally delineated and can no longer continue nor be seen as other than uniquely determined by an initial state. This does not mean, of course, that an end must always be signalled by an explicit symmetry, or that a symmetry actually resolves in a deep sense the enigmas raised by the cause and effect chains. It means only that an explicit or implicit symmetry is a way of intimating that certain changes are complete.

See David Bordwell, "Classical Hollywood Cinema: Narrational Principles and Procedures" in *Narrative, Apparatus, Ideology: A Film Theory Reader*, ed. by Philip Rosen (New York: Columbia University Press, 1986), pp. 21–2, adapted from *Narration*, p. 159 ("Perhaps instead of 'closure' it would be better to speak of a 'closure effect,' or even, if the strain of resolved and unresolved issues seems strong, of 'pseudo-closure.' "). See also Bordwell, "Happily Ever After, Part II," *The Velvet Light Trap* 19 (1982), pp. 2–7, and Frank Kermode, "Sensing Endings," *Nineteenth-Century Fiction*, vol. 33, no. 1 (June 1978; special issue on "Narrative Endings"), pp. 144–58.

63 Sutton-Smith, "Children's Fiction Making," p. 82. Sutton-Smith argues that stories told by children may be classified into four types based on the ways in which characters resolve conflicts: no response to conflict (paralysis), failure, nullification, and transformation; pp. 83–8.

64 Sergei Eisenstein, "Dickens, Griffith, and the Film Today" in *Film Form: Essays in Film Theory*, trans. by Jay Leyda (New York: Harcourt, Brace & World, 1949), pp. 234–5 (Eisenstein's emphasis).

65 I have changed the context of the quotation. The author is considering the nature of fiction, not narrative or causation. D. W. Harding, "Psychological Processes in the Reading of Fiction," *The British Journal of Aesthetics*, vol. 2, no. 2 (April 1962), p. 139. The importance of making judgments about probability in the comprehension of both narrative and fiction makes studies like that of Gilberte Pieraut-Le Bonniec especially pertinent; *The Development of Modal Reasoning: Genesis of Necessity and Possibility Notions* (New York: Academic Press, 1980). On fiction, see chapter 7.

66 Carroll, *Mystifying Movies*, p. 172 (Carroll's emphasis).

67 Legal theory provides some useful classifications of causation because, like narrative, it must make a judgment based on community beliefs about certain combinations of human act and physical law. See, e.g., Henry Campbell Black, *Black's Law Dictionary* (St Paul, Minn.: West Publishing, 5th edn, 1979), "cause" and "cause of action."

68 L.B. Cebik, *Fictional Narrative and Truth: An Epistemic Analysis* (New York: University Press of America, 1984), p. 160 (Cebik's ellipsis points).

69 Roland Barthes, *The Semiotic Challenge*, trans. by Richard Howard (New York: Hill & Wang, 1988), "The Sequences of Actions," p. 144 (Barthes's emphases); see also p. 147, and "Semantics of the Object," pp. 179–90. For Barthes, the "proairetic" code is an amalgam of actions, consequences, gestures and behaviour which become sequences (e.g., stroll, murder, rendezvous) when and because they are given a name in the process of interpreting a text. The proairetic code is a cause and effect chain whose logic is that of the probable, of practical experience, of psychology, of culture, of history, of what is familiar: the "already-done," "already-written," or "already-seen." *S/Z*, sects 36, 56, and 86. See also Barthes, *The Semiotic Challenge*, "Textual Analysis of a Tale by Edgar Allan Poe," pp. 261–93.

70 Mandler, *Stories, Scripts, and Scenes*, p. 26. Jackendoff claims that human

comprehension makes use of "preference rule systems" which involve a weighing of evidence rather than a strict testing for necessary and sufficient conditions; pp. 143–8. See also an experiment by Keith Stenning and Lynn Michell in which a story was presented to a child exclusively in sequences of pictures. The child's grasp of types of causal connections in the story was then measured through the use of conjunctions and adverbials when the child was required to retell the story in words and answer questions about it. "Learning How to Tell a Good Story: The Development of Content and Language in Children's Telling of One Tale," *Discourse Processes*, vol. 8, no. 3 (July–Sept. 1985), pp. 261–79.

Filling in blanks as well as creating blanks by taking elements out of sequence are both related to the discovery of elements that are "missing" within an implicit paradigm. In this chapter, I am limiting myself to a narrative schema; in chapter 6, I will consider the film *Letter from an Unknown Woman* in relation to other paradigms related to human emotions and to the social regulation of emotions.

71 Some forms of cultural knowledge (concerning, for example, going to the movies, attending a birthday party, buying groceries, making dinner, taking a trip, eating at a restaurant, visiting a doctor's office) may be organized as sets of schemas though not necessarily as a narrative schema. See Roger C. Schank and Robert P. Abelson, *Scripts, Plans, Goals and Understanding* (Hillsdale, N.J.: Lawrence Erlbaum Associates, 1977).

72 Martin, *Recent Theories of Narrative*, pp. 127–9. Similarly, as we will see in the next chapter, a car accident in *The Lady from Shanghai* is not an accident considering the nature of a woman (Woman) and the circumstances of her marriage.

73 See, e.g., Victor Turner, "Social Dramas and Stories about Them," *Critical Inquiry*, vol. 7, no. 1 (Autumn 1980), pp. 141–68. This special issue of the journal has been published as a book, *On Narrative*, ed. by W.J.T. Mitchell (Chicago: University of Chicago Press, 1981).

74 See Bordwell, "Classical Hollywood Cinema," p. 19; *Narration in the Fiction Film*, chap. 9, "Classical Narration: The Hollywood Example," pp. 156–204. On the nature of classical narrative in film, see David Bordwell, Janet Staiger, and Kristin Thompson, *The Classical Hollywood Cinema: Film Style & Mode of Production to 1960* (New York: Columbia University Press, 1985), esp. Parts I and III, pp. 1–84, 155–240.

Hiroshima mon amour (Resnais, 1960) both solicits and defies attempts to link its romance plot to the dropping of the atomic bomb on Hiroshima. A triple causal structure which is employed to undermine a certain tradition of storytelling is analyzed by Manthia Diawara in "Oral Literature and African Film: Narratology in *Wend Kuuni*," *Presence Africaine* 142 (1987), pp. 43–5.

75 Raymond Durgnat, *The Strange Case of Alfred Hitchcock, or The Plain Man's Hitchcock* (Cambridge, Mass.: MIT Press, 1974), pp. 150–1 (on *The Lady Vanishes*). Alain Robbe-Grillet goes even further with the idea of double character motivation:

> Everything is contaminated. . . . From all mistresses-turned-nuns to all detective-gangsters, by way of all tormented criminals, all pure-souled prostitutes, all the just men constrained by conscience to injustice, all the sadists driven by love, all the madmen pursued by logic, a good "character" in a novel must above all be *double*. The plot will be "human" in

proportion to its *ambiguity*. Finally the whole book will be true in proportion to its contradictions.

> ("Nature, Humanism, Tragedy" in *For A New Novel: Essays on Fiction*, trans. by Richard Howard (New York: Grove, 1965), p. 62, Robbe-Grillet's emphases.)

76 It should be no surprise that narrative is redundant. Natural language seeks to ensure comprehension by being 60–70 per cent redundant. See Branigan, *Point of View*, pp. 31–4.

77 I will argue in chapter 4 that making a story appear "unique" to spectators who are actually interpreting it in many different ways is a characteristic of a classical, or "chameleon," narrative.

2 STORY WORLD AND SCREEN

1 Rudolf Arnheim, *Film as Art* (Berkeley: University of California Press, 1957; first published in 1933), p. 59; see also pp. 12, 24–29.

2 H.G. Barrow and J.M. Tenenbaum demonstrate the importance of a two-dimensional perception of space to our normal perception of depth. A two-dimensional stage of perception would seem even more important to film which begins on a flat screen. See "Computational Approaches to Vision" in *Handbook of Perception and Human Performance*, vol. II, "Cognitive Processes and Performance," ed. by Kenneth R. Boff, Lloyd Kaufman, and James P. Thomas (New York: John Wiley & Sons, 1986), p. 38-19, and pp. 38-27 through 38-34.

On the distinction between screen and story world see, e.g., Alexander Sesonske, "Cinema Space" in *Explorations in Phenomenology*, ed. by David Carr and Edward S. Casey (The Hague: Martinus Nijhoff, 1973), pp. 399–409; Haig Khatchadourian, "Space and Time in Film," *The British Journal of Aesthetics*, vol. 27, no. 2 (Spring 1987), pp. 169–77.

3 David Marr, *Vision: A Computational Investigation into the Human Representation and Processing of Visual Information* (San Francisco: W. H. Freeman, 1982). According to Julian Hochberg, there is "some evidence that, at least in still pictures, perception of space is not all or none"; "Representation of Motion and Space in Video and Cinematic Displays" in *Handbook of Perception and Human Performance*, vol. I, "Sensory Processes and Perception," ed. by Kenneth R. Boff, Lloyd Kaufman, and James P. Thomas (New York: John Wiley & Sons, 1986), p. 22-8; cf. p. 22-30. Cf. also Arnheim, *Film as Art*, p. 12 ("The effect of film is neither absolutely two-dimensional nor absolutely three-dimensional, but something between"). I will argue in this and later chapters that "time," too, has a variety of intermediate forms and therefore that "narration" must be analyzed as a series of *levels*.

4 Kristin Thompson argues that "A film depends on materiality for its existence; out of image and sound it creates its structures, but it can never make all the physical elements of the film part of its set of smooth perceptual cues. . . . [E]xcess arises from the conflict between the *materiality* of a film and the unifying structures within it." For other views of "excess" and its relation to film and narrative, see the discussion of the work of Stephen Heath in the previous chapter and Dana Polan in chapter 5. Kristin Thompson, "The Concept of Cinematic Excess" in *Narrative, Apparatus, Ideology: A Film Theory Reader*, ed. by Philip Rosen (New York: Columbia University Press, 1986), pp. 131–2 (Thompson's emphasis); see also pp. 133–5. The

concept of excess is sometimes paired with its opposite, a lack or lacuna, especially in psychoanalytic theories of narrative.

5 Noël Burch, "Carl Theodor Dreyer: The Major Phase" in *Cinema: A Critical Dictionary – The Major Film-Makers*, vol. 1, ed. by Richard Roud (New York: The Viking Press, 1980), pp. 298–9; Arnheim, *Film as Art*, pp. 26–8. For Arnheim it is the spectator of a film who is turning the pages of a picture album of postcards whereas for Metz it is the implied author. When one isolates the activity or process suggested by the metaphor (i.e., "turning" the pages), rather than the structures which are being mapped (i.e., picture postcards), the nature of the inquiry shifts from problems of declarative knowledge toward problems of procedural knowledge and "narration." On Metz's use of the metaphor, see text accompanying note 15 in chapter 4. On procedural knowledge and narration, see chapter 3.

6 Sergei Eisenstein, "A Dialectic Approach to Film Form" in *Film Form: Essays in Film Theory*, trans. by Jay Leyda (New York: Harcourt, Brace & World, 1949), pp. 49, 54–7. Hugo Münsterberg apparently conceived of shots as more benignly superimposed on one another than Eisenstein's collision of shots. *The Film: A Psychological Study: The Silent Photoplay in 1916* (New York: Dover, 1970; first published in 1916), pp. 44–6, 79. See also the discussion of temporal articulation accompanying figure 3.

7 Sergei Eisenstein, *The Film Sense*, trans. by Jay Leyda (New York: Harcourt, Brace & World, 1947), pp. 74–81, 201–3. I have been somewhat free in interpreting Eisenstein's notions of vertical and polyphonic montage.

8 Julian Hochberg, "Representation of Motion and Space in Video and Cinematic Displays," p. 22-58.

9 See Edward Branigan, "Diegesis and Authorship in Film," *Iris* 7, vol. 4, no. 2 (Fall 1986), pp. 37–54.

10 The existence of bottom-up and top-down processes significantly alters the traditional distinction between perception and cognition. Ray Jackendoff, *Consciousness and the Computational Mind* (Cambridge, Mass.: MIT Press, 1987), pp. 271–2. On the distinction between the two processes, see Howard Gardner, *The Mind's New Science: A History of the Cognitive Revolution* (New York: Basic Books, expanded edn 1987), pp. 96–7. See also Barnard J. Baars, *The Cognitive Revolution in Psychology* (New York: Guilford, 1986) and George Mandler, *Cognitive Psychology: An Essay in Cognitive Science* (Hillsdale, N.J.: Lawrence Erlbaum Associates, 1985). For an account of film perception describing some of these processes, see Julian Hochberg, "Representation of Motion and Space in Video and Cinematic Displays," pp. 22-1 through 22-64 and Virginia Brooks, "Film, Perception and Cognitive Psychology," *Millennium Film Journal*, nos. 14/15 (Fall/Winter 1984–5), pp. 105–26. See generally David Bordwell's "A Case for Cognitivism" in a special issue of *Iris* 9 devoted to "Cinema and Cognitive Psychology," vol. 5, no. 2 (Spring 1989), pp. 11–40.

It is not immediately clear whether the distinction between bottom-up and top-down processes is coextensive with the distinction between what is on the "screen" – what perhaps may be an expression of the medium itself – and what is in the "story" – what perhaps may be translated into other media. Even a basic percept like motion is not free of top-down effects. Hochberg argues that there are multiple mechanisms in human motion perception, each with quite different characteristics, which produce multiple modes of movement experiences. What appear as simple experiences of movement turn out to be based on elaborate and sometimes startling partitionings of stimuli. Further, Hochberg claims that many of the rules of film editing reduce to the problem of preventing unintentional apparent movements. See pp. 22–6 through 22–8, 22–35, and 22–38; cf. Arnheim, *Film as Art*, pp. 99–102. Indeed one may construct a general theory of film by starting with the problem of movement and slowly expanding it through its intersections with various bottom-up and top-down processes. For a unified theory of gesture, dance, camera movement, editing, development of plot, changes in point of view, and emotional effects on a spectator, see Marcia Butzel, *Motion as Narration: Theory and Practice of Cinematic Choreography* (forthcoming, University of Illinois Press).

One may extend the notions of "top-down" and "bottom-up" processing to cover two different approaches to research and theoretical activity. See, e.g., Zenon W. Pylyshyn, "Metaphorical Imprecision and the 'Top-Down' Research Strategy" in *Metaphor and Thought*, ed. by Andrew Ortony (New York: Cambridge University Press, 1979), pp. 420–36.

11 Ian Jarvie, *Philosophy of the Film: Epistemology, Ontology, Aesthetics* (New York: Routledge & Kegan Paul, 1987), p. 130 (Jarvie's emphases).

12 Bill Nichols, "The Voice of Documentary" in *Movies and Methods: An Anthology*, vol. 2, ed. by Bill Nichols (Berkeley: University of California Press, 1985), pp. 260–1 (my emphases). Cf. John Belton's claim, quoted in chap. 5 n. 50 below. See also Charles Wolfe, "Voice-Over in the 'Classical' Documentary Film" (Santa Barbara: University of California, unpublished paper, 1991). I will discuss documentary film and its relationship to narrative in more detail in chapter 7.

Seymour Chatman proposes a definition of voice that is less expansive than the one offered by Bill Nichols. Chatman confines "voice" to instances of "telling," that is, to narration composed of non-iconic (unmotivated, arbitrary) signs as opposed to "showing" which utilizes iconic signs (i.e., signs based on a form of resemblance between signifier and signified). However, Chatman also argues that not every use of words constitutes a "telling" and, further, that some nonverbal signs count as "telling." For Chatman, a certain hand gesture may count as a "telling" but not a scene which contains only dialogue. See *Coming to Terms: The Rhetoric of Narrative in Fiction and Film* (Ithaca, N.Y.: Cornell University Press, 1990), pp. 111–14, 118–19, 145. "Focalization" is another example of a concept that like "voice" has become greatly confused by the attempt to model it too simply on a human activity, in this case "seeing." Difficult questions soon arise concerning who is seeing, and how literal the seeing must be. I will discuss focalization in more detail in chapter 4.

13 Wallace Martin, *Recent Theories of Narrative* (Ithaca, N.Y.: Cornell University Press, 1986), p. 144.

14 My discussion of this scene in *The Lady from Shanghai* is based on George M. Wilson's suggestive comments in *Narration in Light: Studies in Cinematic Point of View* (Baltimore: Johns Hopkins University Press, 1986), pp. 1–4, 10, 202–4. There are, however, many inaccuracies in Wilson's description of the shots and story events, including the number of shots and their order.

15 More precisely, this principle of causal reasoning that focuses on patterns of repetition among events is composed of John Stuart Mill's five methods of inductive inference.

16 See Merry Bullock, Rochel Gelman, and Renee Baillargeon, "The Development of Causal Reasoning" in *The Developmental Psychology of Time*, ed. by William J. Friedman (New York: Academic Press, 1982), pp. 210–15. In

order to apply these principles of causal reasoning to film, a perceiver must also know how objects may be represented through the materials of film as well as how spatial and temporal relations among objects might be represented through film techniques. Such questions (how can editing be used?) quickly open up to include historical questions (how has editing been used?).

Welles's "impossible" causation in *The Lady from Shanghai* is achieved by bringing elements that are normally noncausal into proximity. Filmmakers like Bresson, Dreyer, Godard, Ozu, and Straub and Huillet achieve similar effects by *separating* an actual cause from its effect thereby muting connections and making (conventional) causality a problem.

The power of proximity to affect our judgments of causality extends to language as well. Consider the following sentences:

1 Haydn taught counterpoint to Beethoven.
2 Haydn taught Beethoven counterpoint.

The first sentence is somewhat "weaker" than the second because it allows the inference that Beethoven may have been inattentive to his lessons. It is weaker because the words "taught" and "Beethoven" are not as proximate as in the second sentence. There are many other examples of this principle of proximity, e.g. "John is not happy" vs "John is unhappy," "She caused him to die" vs "She killed him" (the first sentence of each pair is weaker than the second). See George Lakoff and Mark Johnson, *Metaphors We Live By* (Chicago: University of Chicago Press, 1980), "Closeness Is Strength of Effect," pp. 128–32.

17 For simplicity I will consider the creation of temporal situations only through the editing of a film. Other techniques may be employed to change a temporal situation within a single shot. Note that in isolating temporal order, I am holding temporal "duration" constant (i.e., all lines are drawn the same length unless our inferences about order are affected by an unknown or distorted duration as in B_7 and B_8). Similarly, when the principles of figure 3 are applied to the ordering of space, the "depth" of the space is held constant. Order and duration may be separated because they have a distinct psychological basis analogous to the orientation (i.e., directionality) and extent of a space. See my "Sound and Epistemology in Film," *The Journal of Aesthetics and Art Criticism*, vol. 47, no. 4 (Fall 1989), esp. sect. "Two Perceptions of Time and Two Types of Perception," pp. 315–17. I discuss duration in more detail in chapter 5, section entitled "A Synthesis."

A great number of analytical schemes have been proposed by which to analyze time. Some of the important ones which bear on my discussion in the text are as follows: Ralph Stephenson and Jean R. Debrix, *The Cinema as Art* (Baltimore: Penguin Books, 2nd edn 1976; 1st edn 1965), chaps 4 and 5, "Time in the Cinema: Physical, Psychological, Dramatic" and "Space-Time in the Cinema," pp. 103–56; Christian Metz, "Problems of Denotation in the Fiction Film" in *Film Language: A Semiotics of the Cinema*, trans. by Michael Taylor (New York: Oxford University Press, 1974; originally published in French, 1968), pp. 125–7, 130–2; Noël Burch, *Theory of Film Practice*, trans. by Helen R. Lane (Princeton, N.J.: Princeton University Press, 1981; originally published in French, 1969), chap. 1, "Spatial and Temporal Articulations," pp. 3–16; Gérard Genette, *Narrative Discourse: An Essay in Method*, trans. by Jane E. Lewin (Ithaca, N.Y.: Cornell University Press, 1980; originally published in French, 1972), chaps 1–3, "Order," "Duration," and "Frequency," pp. 33–160; Peter Wollen, "Introduction to *Citizen Kane*," *Film Reader* 1 (1975), pp. 9–15; Meir Sternberg, *Expositional Modes and Temporal*

Ordering in Fiction (Baltimore: Johns Hopkins University Press, 1978); Alexander Sesonske, "Time and Tense in Cinema," *The Journal of Aesthetics and Art Criticism*, vol. 38, no. 4 (Summer 1980), pp. 419–26; David Bordwell, *Narration in the Fiction Film* (Madison: University of Wisconsin Press, 1985), chap. 6, "Narration and Time," pp. 74–98.

18 Arnheim, *Film as Art*, p. 24.

19 Marvin Minsky, *The Society of Mind* (New York: Simon & Schuster, 1986), p. 329; cf. pp. 78, 149, 249.

20 The experience of "continuity" may not be the most basic way of comprehending time. Continuity is apparently built upon still more basic skills acquired in infancy. See James C. Mancuso, "The Acquisition and Use of Narrative Grammar Structure" in *Narrative Psychology: The Storied Nature of Human Conduct*, ed. by Theodore R. Sarbin (New York: Praeger, 1986), pp. 100–1; W.V. Quine, *Quiddities: An Intermittently Philosophical Dictionary* (Cambridge, Mass.: Harvard University Press, 1987), "Things," pp. 204–6.

21 Burch, *Theory of Film Practice*, pp. 12–14, 78–9. According to Prado, "Retrospective consideration is rather like reading the solution to a mystery story and having otherwise unconnected events cohere as a special sequence that explains what happened." For Prado, retrospective attention is fundamental to narrative, imagination, and to thought itself; C.G. Prado, *Making Believe: Philosophical Reflections on Fiction* (Westport, Conn.: Greenwood Press, 1984), pp. 125–6, 129, 136, 143.

22 Cf. Deborah Schiffrin, "Multiple Constraints on Discourse Options: A Quantitative Analysis of Causal Sequences," *Discourse Processes*, vol. 8, no. 3 (July–Sept. 1985), pp. 281–303. Cf. also the general problem of "inversions" in stories told by children; Nancy L. Stein and Christine G. Glenn, "Children's Concept of Time: The Development of a Story Schema" in *The Developmental Psychology of Time*, ed. by William J. Friedman (New York: Academic Press, 1982), pp. 261–9, 271–2, 278–9.

23 Retrospective attention by a spectator, in its widest sense, extends to revisions and reorderings of our hypotheses about space and causality as well as time. Consider three shots: X, A, and B. Shot X is a detail shot of an object. Shot A appears to be merely another angle on the object, but when linked to an establishing shot, B, turns out to be that object at a later time in an entirely new setting. We now reappraise A and see it in a new context with B rather than with X. Action in B may preclude us from moving B backwards in time (prior to A). Nevertheless we readjust our conception of space and causality so that we may conclude that the object *had been transported* to the new space of B (at a time earlier than the time in which we saw B) permitting us to see the object in A. Shot A now registers the effect of an *unseen* cause and is within a space like space B but a moment earlier.

   Note that initially we need not believe shot A to be ambiguous or puzzling; our reappraisal comes with shot B. Moreover, our first belief is not an "error" in any simple way, for A is what might have been seen after X. The anomaly of shot A may be linked in more complicated ways to the narrative process. See the following discussion of "impossible" causation in *The Lady from Shanghai* and "virtual" space in *Dr Mabuse, the Gambler*. Cf. also the distinction between an error and hyothesis theory of reading in Edward Branigan, "The Spectator and Film Space – Two Theories," *Screen*, vol. 22, no. 1 (1981), pp. 55–78.

24 In figure 3, I am treating Genette's concept of temporal "frequency" – how

often an event occurs on the screen as compared with how often it occurs in the story – as a special case of temporal "order." Thus the screen sequence, "a-x^1-b-c-x^2," would be analyzed by saying that "x^2" occurs after "c" on the screen but maps into the same position in the story as did "x^1" which occurred between "a" and "b" on the screen. Note also that some effects of duration (e.g., rhythm) do not normally affect story order and hence are not included in figure 3.

25 The retrospective flashforward is so anomalous that it cannot initially be interpreted by a spectator; that is, it functions at a residual, unconscious level from which the spectator can project no temporal hypotheses. Cf. the discussion of "hyperdiegetic" narration in chapter 6. The parallel, but more common, temporal anomaly is the "retrospective flashback." For example, after an event is shown, we see a character "awaken" from a memory; we then understand the event (retrospectively) as a subjective flashback.

26 Fragment B$_5$ in figure 3 would include over-the-shoulder shots because in such shots space is not exactly reversed, but instead includes some overlap between the two spaces. If the camera were turned on its axis exactly 180 degrees before the next shot, leaving neither an overlap nor a gap between the two spaces, the result would be a true reversal. It would be represented in figure 3 by a new line, like B$_1$, joining A but extending backwards. A true reversal is rare in classical narrative space perhaps because it may be difficult for a spectator to determine whether the new space is immediately adjacent to the old space or whether there is a *gap* between the spaces which is *not* visible (cf. A and B$_6$). This suggests that in classical narrative the most common articulation for space is a partial overlap (i.e., B$_5$ and B$_3$).

27 David Bordwell, Janet Staiger, and Kristin Thompson, *The Classical Hollywood Cinema: Film Style & Mode of Production to 1960* (New York: Columbia University Press, 1985), chap. 5, "Space in the Classical Film," p. 59. Another way to think about the importance of a spatial reversal is to realize that it establishes an anchor line that allows us to move through nearby spaces by calculating new angles and distances and thereby build a cognitive map of the spaces.

Jean-Pierre Oudart locates the unique nature of spatial reversals, which he says involve a "suturing" of space, on the level of the human unconscious as described by Freud. Bordwell argues that Oudart's process of suturing, however, belongs in the preconscious. Still open is the possibility that similar processes operate on both levels. See ibid., p. 421 n. 48 and Bordwell, *Narration in the Fiction Film*, esp. chap. 7, "Narration and Space," sect. "Ideal Positionality: Shot/reverse Shot," pp. 110–13. See generally Kaja Silverman, *The Subject of Semiotics* (New York: Oxford University Press, 1983), chap. 5, "Suture," pp. 194–236.

Who, or what process, gives space and its ordering a *unity* in perception? For Oudart the apparent independence of space, highlighted in a reversal, must have as its counterpart the illusory identity of an experiencing ego – an absent Other. In one type of narrative theory, the Other may be interpreted as an "author" or "narrator." In another type of theory, the Other may be a misrecognition of the spectator himself or herself. Thus there is no reason to exclude subjective shots from the process of suturing, as does Oudart, if one accepts that spaces generated by a character are simply embedded within, and ultimately dependent upon, a non-character epistemological system. An interesting question is whether there are "temporal" sutures analogous to spatial sutures.

28 Drawing on an analogy with Cubism, Noël Burch asserts that in certain scenes Eisenstein, Dreyer, and other filmmakers manage "to create a very unusual sort of cinematic space: It exists only in terms of the totality of shots included in the sequence; we no longer have any sense of a surrounding space endowed with independent existence from which a sequence of shots has somehow been excerpted." Burch, *Theory of Film Practice*, p. 39 (footnote omitted).

29 What is remembered and what is overlooked in comprehending a film is not, however, a matter of chance. In chapter 1, I examined one of the major top-down mechanisms which guides perception – a narrative schema.

30 See, e.g., Karel Reisz and Gavin Millar, *The Technique of Film Editing* (New York: Hastings House, 2nd enlarged edn 1968), pp. 227–32; Edward Dmytryk, *On Film Editing: An Introduction to the Art of Film Construction* (Boston: Focal Press, 1984), pp. 27–33. See also David Bordwell and Kristin Thompson, *Film Art: An Introduction* (New York: McGraw-Hill, 3rd edn 1990), p. 226 (the narrative causality of the "cheat cut" overrides physical continuity).

In this connection one should also recall that one second of continuous action on the screen is in fact normally produced by flashing each of twenty-four still photographs two or three times for a spectator. These photographs, of course, represent only certain fragments of the original action recorded by the camera. The missing action is not noticed by a spectator even though it can *never* appear on the screen because it was not photographed. On the perception of motion in film see, e.g., Joseph and Barbara Anderson, "Motion Perception in Motion Pictures," and Bill Nichols and Susan J. Lederman, "Flicker and Motion in Film" in *The Cinematic Apparatus*, ed. by Teresa de Lauretis and Stephen Heath (New York: St Martin's Press, 1980), pp. 76–105.

31 I discuss shots that are mismatched but overlooked by a spectator in note 41 of chapter 3 (*The Girl and Her Trust*), note 5 of chapter 5 (*Lady in the Lake*), and note 43 of chapter 6 (*Letter from an Unknown Woman*).

32 The representation of complex temporal events suggests that the notion of "the camera" as a unique entity existing in a single time will need to be reexamined and made more sensitive to the complexity of the spectator's ongoing judgments. See chapter 5.

33 See, e.g., Jackendoff, *Consciousness and the Computational Mind* (Cambridge, Mass.: MIT Press, 1987); Andy Clark, *Microcognition: Philosophy, Cognitive Science, and Parallel Distributed Processing* (Cambridge, Mass.: MIT Press, 1989); Jerry Fodor, *The Modularity of Mind* (Cambridge, Mass.: Bradford Books/MIT Press, 1983); Howard Gardner, *Frames of Mind: The Theory of Multiple Intelligences* (New York: Basic Books, 1983); Minsky, *Society of Mind*; Margaret S. Livingstone, "Art, Illusion and the Visual System," *Scientific American*, vol. 258, no. 1 (Jan. 1988), pp. 78–85. See also note 10 above.

34 This description is taken from an analysis of literary character by Hélène Cixous, "The Character of 'Character,'" *New Literary History*, vol. 5, no. 2 (Winter 1974), p. 387.

35 David Hume, *A Treatise of Human Nature*, ed. by L.A. Selby-Bigge (London: Oxford University Press, 1951), Book I, Part IV, sects II and VI, pp. 207, 252, 253 (Hume's emphasis).

36 William James, *The Principles of Psychology*, vol. I (Cambridge, Mass.: Harvard University Press, 1981), chap. 10, "The Consciousness of Self," pp. 279–379.

37 Erving Goffman, *Frame Analysis: An Essay on the Organization of Experience*

(Cambridge, Mass.: Harvard University Press, 1974), p. 573; and see pp. 575–6.

38 Minsky, *Society of Mind*, p. 42 (emphasis omitted); cf. pp. 50–1.

39 See, e.g., Robert Stam, Robert Burgoyne, and Sandy Flitterman-Lewis, *New Vocabularies in Film Semiotics: Structuralism, Post-Structuralism and Beyond* (New York: Routledge, 1992).

40 See generally E. Ann Kaplan, *Women and Film: Both Sides of the Camera* (New York: Routledge, 1983), chap. 4, "The struggle for control over the female discourse and female sexuality in Welles's *The Lady from Shanghai* (1946)," pp. 60–72.

41 Wilson, *Narration in Light*, p. 2.

42 The concept of voice-under refers to speech that is synchronized to the lips of a person but which also accompanies other images and spaces. Its importance lies in the fact that a place for the speaker is explicitly represented while in "voice-over" the speech is nonsynchronous with an image of the speaker (perhaps indicating character thought or memory) or no image of the speaker is presented (creating an abstract space of speaking). These techniques have implications for the "levels of reality" we imagine in the story world, that is, levels of the narration. See chapter 4.

43 I will return to the relationship between narrative comprehension and the specific techniques and materials of the film medium in chapter 3 in the context of a distinction between procedure and substance, between "knowing how" to do something and "knowing that" something is the case.

44 See Lakoff and Johnson, *Metaphors We Live By*, chap. 14, "Causation: Partly Emergent and Partly Metaphorical," pp. 73–5.

45 See Lakoff and Johnson, *Metaphors We Live By*, pp. 69–76; Prado, *Making Believe*, p. 130.

46 See Arthur C. Danto, *Narration and Knowledge* (including the integral text of *Analytical Philosophy of History*) (New York: Columbia University Press, 1985), pp. 242–3, 251. The views of both Hume and Kant on causation are compatible with the approach I have taken in the text. For Hume, causation was a habit of mind resulting from a perceiver's experiences of the regular and constant (but non-necessary) conjunction of two events. This is compatible with Lakoff and Johnson's analysis of causation in terms of common metaphors. For Kant, causality was an a priori principle of understanding that makes possible the existence of propositions which are synthetic rather than analytic (i.e., propositions judged through experience and observation not reason or stipulation). Under this view metaphor would become a fundamental (innate) top-down process of mind. See also the discussion of causality in chapter 1 above.

47 Roland Barthes, "Introduction to the Structural Analysis of Narratives" in *Image – Music – Text*, trans. by Stephen Heath (New York: Hill & Wang, 1977), p. 94. I have slightly altered Heath's translation.

48 Cf. Wilson, *Narration in Light*, p. 2.

49 This argument does not depend on using character as a reference point. One could begin with "independent" events and then say that when they are not independent, they are defined "negatively" as related to a character's perception of them. The important point is that there is a relationship between our perception of characters who perceive and our perception of that world that includes characters. I will make this relationship more precise by using the concept of levels of narration in chapter 4. In chapters 5 and 6, I will consider subjectivity and objectivity in detail.

50 For a description of the major rules of continuity editing, see Bordwell and Thompson, *Film Art*, pp. 206–43. The recognition of spatial and temporal continuity also depends on the use of certain other techniques relating to lighting, prop management, camera movement and lenses, sound (e.g., sound overlap, dialogue hooks, synchronous sound), etc. Continuity is also affected by top-down processes involving our knowledge of the world and our expectations of narrative coherence; see text accompanying note 30 above.

51 In addition, Burch argues that continuity editing allows the use of facial close-ups without disrupting the scene and hence promotes a character density and credibility typical of the novel. See Noël Burch, "Fritz Lang: German Period" in *Cinema: A Critical Dictionary – The Major Film-Makers*, vol. 2, ed. by Richard Roud (New York: The Viking Press, 1980), pp. 584–88; "Notes on Fritz Lang's First Mabuse," *Cine-Tracts* 13, vol. 4, no. 1 (Spring 1981), pp. 1–13 plus eight unnumbered pages of stills. For Burch's approach to the traits of early cinema and their relationship to other historical modes of organizing film space and time, see "Primitivism and the Avant-Gardes: A Dialectical Approach" in *Narrative, Apparatus, Ideology*, ed. by Philip Rosen, pp. 483–506.

52 I owe this observation to Lea Jacobs and Garrett Stewart. See also Burch, "Notes," paragraphs numbered 10, 13, 23, 27, and 38.

53 Since the spectator is apparently looking at objects at the same time as a character, there is a tendency to describe the objects and events of a film as existing in a "present tense" for the spectator. This is highly misleading if one seeks to analyze how the experience of narrative has been created and what mental computations allow us to imagine the presence of the present. See, e.g., Edward Branigan, " 'Here is a Picture of No Revolver!': The Negation of Images, and Methods for Analyzing the Structure of Pictorial Statements," *Wide Angle*, vol. 8, nos. 3/4 (1986), pp. 10–11. See also the discussion of the "historical present" tense in chapter 6.

54 Figure 8 illustrates how camera angle and character glance typically do not meet. The camera angle is straight-on but the character's eyes are angled 30 degrees off right while his head is angled 30 degrees off left. Centering the character at the vanishing point of these two "diagonals" while using only horizontals and verticals elsewhere in the composition serves to visually emphasize the way in which this space (as well as the next space; see fig. 9) is constituted and given significance through a particular and intense *awareness* by the character.

Dr Mabuse's hypnotic powers will be such that he will be allowed to look into the camera which is to say that he will be represented as being able to disengage himself from normal, diegetic space. Shot 4 (fig. 4) illustrates this power as does shot 35 in which he stares wildly up over the camera (imagining the top of the telephone pole of shots 34 and 36?). See Burch, "Notes," especially paragraphs numbered 20 and 21.

55 See, e.g., Charles F. Altman, "Psychoanalysis and Cinema: The Imaginary Discourse," *Quarterly Review of Film Studies*, vol. 2, no. 3 (Aug. 1977), pp. 257–72; D.N. Rodowick, "The Difficulty of Difference," *Wide Angle*, vol. 5, no. 1 (1982), pp. 4–15; Christian Metz, *The Imaginary Signifier: Psychoanalysis and the Cinema*, trans. by Celia Britton, Annwyl Williams, Ben Brewster, and Alfred Guzzetti (Bloomington: Indiana University Press, 1982); *Feminism and Film Theory*, ed. by Constance Penley (New York: Routledge, 1988).

56 Although "persistence of vision" is no longer accepted as an explanation of motion on the screen, it is relevant to the perception of other qualities, like

color and shape, which are affected by positive and negative after-images produced by changes on the screen.

57 I believe that the role played by top-down processes in the "integrated match" demonstrates why a gestalt form is believed to represent knowledge which is more than the sum of the "parts" of the form. What "emerges" in a gestalt form is the product of two different mental strategies – top-down and bottom-up – working to organize and manipulate data.

Notice that the integrated match (fig. 13) achieves the graphic perception of a frame within the frame in a fundamentally different manner than if, say, by persistence of vision or short-term memory, the old pattern is merely superimposed on the new one (which would be possible with the "open match" of fig. 12). In the latter case, bottom-up processing from the previous shot simply meets bottom-up processing from the new shot. There is no integration of top-down and bottom-up hypotheses and no (graphic) incentive to build a story space. I will call this simple combining of bottom-up effects "graphic expressionism" since it functions much like Expressionist decor where a graphic configuration is essentially unhooked from the dynamic perception of space through editing.

Hitchcock could have achieved the simpler effect of graphic expressionism by merely pulling his camera back slightly to show a fully enclosed window pane with four bars in the point-of-view shot (fig. 9) instead of showing us two shots with two bars in each. Needless to say, Hitchcock does use graphic expressionism in his films and such instances are a favorite site for the interpretive activity of critics. See, e.g., an interpretion by William Rothman in note 59 below.

One might conjecture that through integrated matches it is possible to *learn* to recognize conventional story-screen articulations like the point-of-view shot because such articulations can be reached either from the top-down through an understanding of story action or from the bottom-up through an understanding of graphics that have been recognized as familiar objects (decor).

58 Nick Browne argues that the ambiguity of the scene is created by superimposing two ways of perceiving. His description of a shot sequence earlier in the scene could apply equally to our perception of the (doubled) frame within the frame of figures 8–9, 13.

> The narrator gives us a viewpoint on the action . . . which, until the husband appeared, was only virtual, and which originally we could not have sustained, but are now implicated in. We are put in the position, different from any of the characters, of appreciating this ambiguity of interpretation by recognizing that the husband's suspicion, though founded on a misperception, is not entirely without foundation. As long as the husband occupies the frame, our innocent view is suspended, replaced by one that sees the couple as guilty. The [husband's] passing out of the frame, while confirming that what we have seen was his view, does not restore our initial innocence.
>
> (*The Rhetoric of Filmic Narration* (Ann Arbor, Mich.: UMI Research Press, 1976), chap. 2, "Representation and Story: Significance in *The 39 Steps*," p. 31 (including stills and dialogue for twenty-seven shots).)

59 An example of Hannay's punishment of women is the story he tells Pamela on their "wedding" night. In general, Hitchcock's integration of story space with graphics (e.g., in the point-of-view shot of figs 8–9) encourages the

creation of stylistic metaphors and brings onto the screen characteristic themes of passion, desire, dread, guilt, and death, producing the ambivalence – the "pleasurable anxiety" – typical of the suspense genre.

Hitchcock's use of expressionist *mise-en-scène* also encourages the spectator to search for stylistic metaphors. For example, Hannay, and the husband and wife, are later framed *through the bars* of a chair. This unusual camera position moves William Rothman to summon the author of such a style:

> With this signature shot, the author steps forward and declares the imprisonment of these people. John [the husband] is imprisoned in his anguished, vengeful nature. Margaret [the wife] is imprisoned in her marriage and can only dream of freedom (how can she leave her husband when his anguish is too terrible for him to bear alone and when she holds herself responsible for him?). And Hannay is no more free to save Margaret than she is to release John from his curse.

Rothman's use of an imprisonment/freedom metaphor radiates outward into his descriptions and elaborate summaries of the action as well as infuses his speculations and pronouncements about character thought ("locked in the spirit of revenge"; "one cannot escape the condition of being human"; "closes out her dream of freedom"; "resent those terms and rebel," etc.). *Hitchcock – The Murderous Gaze* (Cambridge, Mass.: Harvard University Press, 1982), pp. 134–41. Nick Browne constructs a stylistic metaphor by linking the bars to certain effects of the lighting, "Representation and Story," pp. 38–9 ("the darkening prospect of liberty"). On expressionism, see note 57 above.

60 On the relationship of graphics to experimental cinema see, e.g., Maureen Turim, "The Place of Visual Illusions" in *The Cinematic Apparatus*, ed. by Teresa de Lauretis and Stephen Heath, pp. 143–50 and "Symmetry/Asymmetry and Visual Fascination," *Wide Angle*, vol. 4, no. 3 (1980), pp. 38–47. Jean-Luc Godard and Yasujiro Ozu are narrative filmmakers who at times use the screen in complex opposition to the story. On Godard see, e.g., Bordwell, *Narration in the Fiction Film*, chap. 13, pp. 311–34. On Ozu see, e.g., Edward Branigan, "The Space of *Equinox Flower*" in *Close Viewings: An Anthology of New Film Criticism*, ed. by Peter Lehman (Tallahassee: Florida State University Press, 1990), pp. 73–108; and David Bordwell, *Ozu and the Poetics of Cinema* (Princeton, N.J.: Princeton University Press, 1988).

3 NARRATION

1 Griffith could have created an accelerated montage by systematically varying any of a number of parameters. The screen durations of the twenty-eight shots does not reveal a simple pattern. Similarly, although a variety of angles is employed, resulting in movement along diagonal lines, the only simple pattern seems to be based on whether the movement is toward screen left or right. Movement which is almost directly toward or away from the camera, I have considered as neutral since Griffith uses it as a way of crossing the 180 degree axis of action, that is, as a transition between groups of shots.

I have not counted the first shot after Grace rushes from the interior of the station as part of the chase sequence even though she confronts the tramps at the handcar. I have considered the next shot as the beginning of the chase because, rather than be left safely behind, she takes the decisive action of jumping onto the handcar and refusing to leave without the strong-box. Grace's action has thus escalated the confrontation. Moreover, this shot ends with a near match on action as the tramps react by putting the handcar into motion in spite of Grace.

Screen duration for the seven groups was based on a projection speed of sixteen frames per second and derived from a frame count of a 16mm print of the film. The actual times in seconds were as follows: 67.1, 65.0, 16.7, 18.8, 18.8, 4.2, and 5.2. In computing the duration of the last shot of the sequence, I have used only that portion of the shot which shows the tramps jump off the handcar followed by Grace jumping off the handcar.

2 The chase sequence ends with the following four shots: the handcar and the locomotive are both in the same shot but at different times; the handcar is shown but with only the smoke of the locomotive behind it; the handcar and the locomotive appear together; the locomotive is now so close that the tramps abandon the handcar.

3 The time of the chase is left largely to our imagination: do the cross-cuts signify continuous time, simultaneous time, or something in between? Cf. temporal situations B_1, B_2, B_3, and B_4 in figure 3 of chapter 2 which depicts several varieties of story time relationships AB_n. The rhythmic aspects of the film are heightened by the fact that there are only nine intertitles in the film and none in the final thirty-three shots.

4 The patterns on the screen in this chase scene are primarily rhythmic and directional. They act in parallel, rather than duplicating or opposing, the rhythm and direction of the story event; both screen and story patterns are completed at the same time. Cf. figures 10–13 in chapter 2 which show possible relations between two-dimensional screen and three-dimensional story spaces in representing an event in *The 39 Steps*. Joyce E. Jesionowski, however, argues that the scene does use graphic matches in an important way, and has a graphic resolution and climax; *Thinking in Pictures: Dramatic Structure in D.W. Griffith's Biograph Films* (Berkeley: University of California Press, 1987), pp. 47–52, 138, 177–8 (includes some stills from the chase sequence).

5 See David Bordwell, *Narration in the Fiction Film* (Madison: University of Wisconsin Press, 1985), pp. 157–8, 164–5. Bordwell emphasizes story "dead-lines" and character "appointments" as ways for a narrative schema to map diegetic time onto screen time.

6 Christian Metz, *The Imaginary Signifier: Psychoanalysis and the Cinema*, trans. by Celia Britton, Annwyl Williams, Ben Brewster, and Alfred Guzzetti (Bloomington: Indiana University Press, 1982), p. 299 n. 9. Hugo Münster-berg argued in 1916 that film is unique among the arts in its ability to create a feeling of "omnipresence." He discusses some examples in which a certain notion of time as succession is abolished so that the spectator feels as if he or she is in several places at once and a single action "irradiates in all directions." *The Film: A Psychological Study: The Silent Photoplay in 1916* (New York: Dover, 1970), p. 45.

7 See Gilbert Ryle, "Knowing How and Knowing That," *Proceedings of the Aristotelian Society* 46 (1945–6), pp. 1–16, and *The Concept of Mind* (London: Hutchinson, 1949), pp. 25–61. See also Alvin I. Goldman, *Epistemology and Cognition* (Cambridge, Mass.: Harvard University Press, 1986), pp. 369–73.

8 Ryle, "Knowing How and Knowing That," pp. 4–5, 11–12, 15–16. Ryle asserts that "knowing . . . a rule [of inference] is not a case of knowing an extra fact or truth; it is knowing *how* to move from acknowledging some

facts to acknowledging others" (p. 7; my emphasis). In a larger sense, comprehension itself is a matter of "knowing how" since one may comprehend a sentence without believing it. On procedural knowledge and declarative knowledge, see generally John R. Anderson, *Language, Memory, and Thought* (Hillsdale, N.J.: Lawrence Erlbaum Associates, 1976), chap. 3, "Models of Procedural Knowledge," pp. 78–113; Paul A. Kolers and Henry L. Roediger, "Procedures of Mind," *Journal of Verbal Learning and Verbal Behavior*, vol. 23, no. 4 (Aug. 1984), pp. 425–49. Cf. Ludwig Wittgenstein, *Philosophical Investigations*, trans. by G.E.M. Anscombe (New York: Macmillan, 3rd edn 1958), sects 151 and 179, pp. 59–60, 72–3.

9 For example, one might take the elements of a narrative schema as essentially representing declarative knowledge; or, alternatively, one might define the elements of the schema as procedural by using rewrite rules on the model of a transformational-generative grammar, or some other processing algorithm, resulting in a "story grammar." Both approaches to narrative are common. Cf. generally Anderson, *Language, Memory, and Thought*, p. 78, with Sally Planalp, "Scripts, Story Grammars, and Causal Schemas" in *Contemporary Issues in Language and Discourse Processes*, ed. by Donald G. Ellis and William A. Donohue (Hillsdale, N.J.: Lawrence Erlbaum Associates, 1986), p. 120; and see Howard Gardner, *The Mind's New Science: A History of the Cognitive Revolution* (New York: Basic Books, expanded edn. 1987), pp. 161–2, and Terry Winograd, "Frame Representations and the Declarative/Procedural Controversy" in *Representation and Understanding: Studies in Cognitive Science*, ed. by Daniel G. Bobrow and Allan Collins (New York: Academic Press, 1975), pp. 185–210.

10 In chapter 6 I will analyze a camera position like that of 3B from *Letter from an Unknown Woman* where a character, Lisa, secretly watches from a staircase as Stefan brings a woman to his apartment.

11 The usual form of a "split-screen" technique shows S in one panel and A/ B in another and represents simultaneity but does not show the direct spatial relationship between the characters. It is thus intermediate between a "best possible" view (which represents simultaneity and the continuity of space between the characters) and an eyeline match (which usually represents neither simultaneity nor direct spatial continuity). A flashback might represent direct spatial continuity without simultaneity.

12 On "impossible" camera framings see Edward Branigan, *Point of View in the Cinema: A Theory of Narration and Subjectivity in Classical Film* (New York and Berlin: Mouton, 1984), pp. 62, 158–9, 197.

13 The camera movement from position 8A to 8B in figure 14 is an example of "unmotivated" framing and is derived from examples in Antonioni's *Red Desert* (1964) and *The Passenger* (1975). On unmotivated camera movement see Branigan, *Point of View*, pp. 45–6.

14 E.M. Forster speaks of expanding and contracting perception, and "intermittent" knowledge in *Aspects of the Novel* (New York: Harcourt, Brace & Co., 1927), p. 123.

15 There are many ways to destabilize this convention. See Branigan, *Point of View*, chap. 5, "The Point-of-view Shot," pp. 103–21, and also pp. 17–19, 73–5, 96–7, 172–4, 182–4. There may even be point-of-view shots in which we never see the watcher because it is invisible in some sense; p. 120 n. 13.

16 A variety of ways of representing telephone conversations that are crucial to the kind of story being told may be found in *Trouble in Paradise* (Lubitsch, 1932), *The Man Who Knew Too Much* (Hitchcock, 1934), *You Only Live Once*

(Lang, 1937), *His Girl Friday* (Hawks, 1940), *Pillow Talk* (Gordon, 1959), *The Misfits* (Huston, 1961), *The Rain People* (Coppola, 1969), *The Mirror* (Tarkovsky, 1975), *All the President's Men* (Pakula, 1976), *Stalker* (Tarkovsky, 1979), and *When Harry Met Sally. . .* (Reiner, 1989).

17 George M. Wilson, *Narration in Light: Studies in Cinematic Point of View* (Baltimore: Johns Hopkins University Press, 1986), pp. 4–5. See also my review of this book in *Sub-Stance* 56, vol. 17, no. 2 (1988), pp. 118–21.

18 Bordwell, *Narration in the Fiction Film*, pp. 57–61.

19 Branigan, *Point of View*, pp. 96, 179.

20 See, e.g., Jerry Fodor, *The Modularity of Mind* (Cambridge, Mass.: Bradford Books/MIT Press, 1983); Marvin Minsky, *The Society of Mind* (New York: Simon & Schuster, 1986); and my discussion of modularity in chapter 2.

21 Colin MacCabe paraphrasing Jacques Lacan in "Realism and the Cinema: Notes on some Brechtian Theses," *Screen*, vol. 15, no. 2 (Summer 1974), pp. 17–18. MacCabe draws on two Lacanian formulations: "I think where I am not, therefore I am where I think not" and "I am not, wherever I am the plaything of my thought; I think of what I am wherever I don't think I am thinking." "The Insistence of the Letter in the Unconscious," *Yale French Studies* 36/37 (1966), p. 136.

22 See MacCabe, "Realism and the Cinema," pp. 7–27; "The Politics of Separation," *Screen*, vol. 16, no. 4 (Winter 1975–6), pp. 46–57; "*Days of Hope* – a Response to Colin McArthur," *Screen*, vol. 17, no. 1 (Spring 1976), pp. 98–101; "Theory and Film: Principles of Realism and Pleasure," *Screen*, vol. 17, no. 3 (Autumn 1976), pp. 7–27; and "The Discursive and the Ideological in Film: Notes on the Conditions of Political Intervention," *Screen*, vol. 19, no. 4 (Winter 1978–9), pp. 29–43. The first and fourth essays are reprinted in MacCabe's *Tracking the Signifier: Theoretical Essays: Film, Linguistics, Literature* (Minneapolis: University of Minnesota Press, 1985).

23 Ben Brewster, "A Scene at the 'Movies,' " *Screen*, vol. 23, no. 2 (July/Aug. 1982), pp. 7, 9, 12.

24 Grace's boyfriend is at the bottom of the pyramid of knowledge because events of the romance and crime stories mostly catch him unawares: he does not know that Grace was secretly thrilled by his kiss nor does he know about the danger posed by the tramps.

25 See François Truffaut, *Hitchcock* (New York: Simon & Schuster, rev. edn 1984), pp. 72–3, 109, 243–4. See also Paul Comisky and Jennings Bryant, "Factors Involved in Generating Suspense," *Human Communication Research*, vol. 9, no. 1 (Fall 1982), pp. 49–58, and two articles by Noel Carroll, "Toward a Theory of Film Suspense," *Persistence of Vision*, 1 (Summer 1984), pp. 65–89, and "Toward a Theory of Point-of-View-Editing: Communication, Emotion and the Movies," *Poetics Today* (forthcoming).

For another approach, see Mieke Bal, *Narratology: Introduction to the Theory of Narrative*, trans. by Christine van Boheemen (Toronto: University of Toronto, 1985), pp. 114–15. Bal, A.J. Greimas, and J. Courtès analyze character knowledge using a logical square that relates "true," "false," "secret," and "delusion." Cf. Bal, pp. 34–6 with Greimas and Courtès, "The Cognitive Dimension of Narrative Discourse," *New Literary History*, vol. 7, no. 3 (Spring 1976), p. 440.

The following films illustrate a range of possibilities for creating suspense, mystery, or surprise using a bomb as a narrative device: *Sabotage* (Hitchcock, 1936), *The Wages of Fear* (Clouzot, 1953), *Touch of Evil* (Welles, 1958), *Juggernaut* (Lester, 1974), *Sorcerer* (Friedkin, 1977), *Outrageous Fortune* (Hiller, 1987), and *The Untouchables* (De Palma, 1987).

On a spectator's wishful involvement in a film, Christian Metz remarks: "I shall say that behind any fiction there is a second fiction: the diegetic events are fictional, that is the first; but everyone pretends to believe that they are true, and that is the second; there is even a third: the general refusal to admit that somewhere in oneself one believes they are genuinely true." Metz, *The Imaginary Signifier*, p. 72. Cf. chapter 7 below on the notion of fiction and see chapters 4, 5, and 6 on psychoanalytic theories of narrative. See also Peter Wollen, "The Hermeneutic Code" in *Readings and Writings: Semiotic Counter-Strategies* (London: Verso, 1982), pp. 40–8.

26 See, e.g., Gérard Genette, *Narrative Discourse: An Essay in Method*, trans. by Jane E. Lewin (Ithaca, N.Y.: Cornell University Press, 1980), pp. 188–94.

27 Cf. Brewster, "A Scene at the 'Movies,'" p. 14.

28 The story is entitled "Who is Scorpio?" and appears in *Nick Fury, Agent of S.H.I.E.L.D.*, vol. 1, no. 1 (Marvel Comics, June 1968). The writer and illustrator is Jim Steranko. Though Nick Fury had appeared in numerous earlier comics, this issue was the first to be devoted entirely to him. Lenny Lipton reproduces these sixteen panels as an example of a good storyboard in *Independent Filmmaking* (San Francisco: Straight Arrow Books, rev. edn 1973), pp. 378–9. The extraordinary sophistication of recent comic art is well illustrated by the *Watchmen* series (1986), the new versions of *Batman*, and in many issues of *Swamp Thing* (all from DC Comics).

29 Recall that the concept of a "narrative schema" is meant to be a concise explanation of certain remarkable facts about narrative comprehension while a "focused chain" is shorthand for a type of causal organization. See chapter 1.

30 I am here ignoring the first page of the story which is a full page drawing of the fortress showing a figure on the wall seen impossibly from the waves of a raging ocean. The title of the story appears on the fortress walls and other credits and publication data are given.

The representation of space introduces a metaphor of power and conflict. The extreme framing of panel 2 highlights a sharply receding linear perspective to create a fortress of monumental dimensions. But panel 3 shows that Nick is equally imposing: his hand reaching into the foreground is shown as three times the size of his head. A narrative schema is already at work.

31 On focalization, see chapter 4, p. 100 ff.

32 Creating a "fuzzy" space has many uses and is analogous to the creation of "fuzzy" concepts and "fuzzy" causation; cf. the discussion of "double motivation" in chapter 1.

33 An alternate interpretation would be that it was not necessary for the robot to turn around to pick up the coin and that Nick came up from behind the robot (even though Nick is not seen in panel 10), then jumped in front of the robot to knock it down. Notice that in either interpretation the uniform size and spacing of the comic panels does not indicate a uniform passage of story time. As in the case with film, time cannot be determined mechanically but must be made to fit with other judgments about space and causality consistent with a narrative schema.

34 The spectator may not notice the lack of background detail because previous panels also exhibit a suppression of spatial information (e.g., panels 1, 5, 6, 10, and 11) and the suppression is connected in various ways to the causal chain (e.g., low light conditions in the story space, explanatory close-up, etc.) and thus is made to seem merely descriptive.

35 Roland Barthes, "To Write: An Intransitive Verb?" in *The Structuralist Contro-versy: The Languages of Criticism and the Sciences of Man*, ed. by Richard Macksey and Eugenio Donato (Baltimore: Johns Hopkins University Press, 1972), p. 140.

36 Roland Barthes, "An Introduction to the Structural Analysis of Narrative," trans. by Lionel Duisit in *New Literary History*, vol. 6, no. 2 (Winter 1975), pp. 247–9. Two other translations of this important article may be found in Barthes's *Image – Music – Text*, trans. by Stephen Heath (New York: Hill & Wang, 1977), pp. 79–124, and Barthes's *The Semiotic Challenge*, trans. by Richard Howard (New York: Hill & Wang, 1988), pp. 95–135. In addition to a catalyst addressing the spectator's interest by providing detail, Barthes finds that overly precise descriptions and/or apparently trivial data may function to create an impression of reality. See "The Realistic Effect," trans. by Gerald Mead, *Film Reader* 3 (1978), pp. 131–5; another translation appears as "The Reality Effect" in Barthes's *The Rustle of Language*, trans. by Richard Howard (New York: Hill & Wang, 1986), pp. 141–8.

Since a catalyst literally is a chemical that is not consumed in a reaction, Barthes may have chosen the term in order to suggest that some aspects of a text (narration, realism, fascination) are of a different order than narrative cause and effect, and hence are not subject to the irreversible time of the plot. Barthes's catalyses are opposed to cardinal functions, or nuclei, and are analogous to the Russian formalists' notion of "free" motifs as opposed to "bound" motifs.

37 Cf. the misleading view provided in panel 12 with the view of a wall provided by set-up 8B, figure 14.

38 Alan Larson Williams, *Max Ophuls and the Cinema of Desire: Style and Spectacle in Four Films, 1948–1955* (New York: Arno Press, 1980), p. 41.

39 In some contexts it is important to distinguish between seeing something which is not present (transparency) and not seeing what is present (invisi-bility). However, usually I will not draw this distinction and instead will use both concepts to refer to either situation.

40 The reader typically does not notice, for example, that in panels 14, 15, and 16, the robot changes color from yellow and magenta to totally blue, and back again while Nick changes from deep blue to red and black, and then back. Nick's shadow and the door change colors in panels 12 and 14. Also background color is used freely in panels 5, 10, 11, 13, and 15.

41 The most remarkable instance in *The Girl and Her Trust* where the spectator perceives "continuity" in spite of what is present on the screen is when an event which happens only once in the story is actually shown in its entirety happening *twice* in two consecutive shots. After the tramps have been dis-covered by Grace, we see them rise up from the window that they have been spying through and rush away. First they are seen leaving in the background as Grace is shown terrified in the foreground; next, the entire action is replayed in medium shot from outside Grace's office. Incredibly, the tramps exit in different directions in the two shots! A much earlier film by Edwin Porter – *The Life of an American Fireman* (1903) – is more famous for its use of such a temporal duplication. The Griffith film demonstrates the extent to which such an "anomaly" may persist into later films and still not be noticed by an audience.

There are many other continuity violations which are overlooked in *The Girl and Her Trust* involving mismatched action (when the hero offers Grace a sandwich), direction (in the distant telegraph office), and *mise-en-scène* (a tramp is in the "wrong" corner of a window spying on the hero; the strongbox "suddenly" appears on the front of the locomotive between Grace and the hero). The film also includes flawless matches on action and careful uses of an axis of action.

In chapter 6 I will examine a specific instance in which a spectator produces a continuous action in spite of what is literally discontinuous on the screen; see discussion of figures 49, 50 from *Letter from an Unknown Woman*.

42 Art films of the 1960s showed that invisible editing was no guarantee of invisibility. See above, p. 45.

43 Williams, *Max Ophuls*, pp. 17–24, 35–6. Although Williams focuses on only "two films," I think that a fair reading of his essay points to at least four films. One could, of course, further subdivide these four films or extend them in either direction; that is, extend them backward in time toward an optical printer film, an edited film, a profilmic film (principal photography), a scripted film, etc., as well as forward in time toward the writing of a review, a meeting with a friend who has a different opinion of the film, the recognition of a place or situation from the film, etc.

44 On modularity and levels of structure in human cognition, see generally Ray Jackendoff, *Consciousness and the Computational Mind* (Cambridge, Mass.: MIT Press, 1987). See also note 33 in chapter 2 above.

45 Do we personify the microphone or the tape recorder or the loudspeaker in the theater as an "ear"? How is listening to a diegetic world fundamentally different from seeing a diegetic world? I examine these issues in "Sound and Epistemology in Film," *The Journal of Aesthetics and Art Criticism*, vol. 47, no. 4 (Fall 1989), pp. 311–24.

4 LEVELS OF NARRATION

1 I have added the bottom two levels and have renamed several of Lanser's levels consistent with my terminology; for example, Lanser's "public" and "private" narrators become "nondiegetic" and "diegetic" narrators. I have also made other changes, most notably reversing Lanser's levels of "focalizer" and "character" consistent with my revised definition of "focalization." See Susan Sniader Lanser, *The Narrative Act: Point of View in Prose Fiction* (Princeton, N.J.: Princeton University Press, 1981), chap. 3, "From Person to Persona: The Textual Voice," esp. pp. 131–48.

2 My definition of a text is meant to rule out, for example, such objects as trees and tables, as well as a book being used to patch a hole in the roof.

3 Roland Barthes, "An Introduction to the Structural Analysis of Narrative," trans. by Lionel Duisit, *New Literary History*, vol. 6, no. 2 (Winter 1975), p. 261 (Barthes's emphases).

4 On the "biographical legend," see David Bordwell, *Ozu and the Poetics of Cinema* (Princeton, N.J.: Princeton University Press, 1988), "A Filmmaker's Legend," pp. 5–7, and *The Films of Carl-Theodor Dreyer* (Berkeley: University of California Press, 1981), "An Author and His Legend," pp. 9–24. On authorship generally, see *Theories of Authorship: A Reader*, ed. by John Caughie (London: Routledge & Kegan Paul, 1981) and Stephen Crofts, "Authorship and Hollywood," *Wide Angle*, vol. 5, no. 3 (1983), pp. 16–22.

5 See my discussion of the paradoxical statement, "I am lying" in *Point of View in the Cinema: A Theory of Narration and Subjectivity in Classical Film* (New York and Berlin: Mouton, 1984), pp. 2–5, 172–3, 182–4. The analysis of

narration into "levels," each with a nominal subject, is one way of talking about how a text as a whole may represent a "splitting of the subject."

6 Recall that a narrative schema organizes causal patterns in order to make important, and make relevant, our already existing interests and activities. Hitchcock promises such an organization and solicits our attention. Hitchcock's opening statement is based upon pressing together two familiar metaphors: fact is stranger than fiction (but otherwise is like it), and life is (like) a story. His opening, "And yet . . . ", inaugurates the complex interplay between the probable and the improbable, nonfiction and fiction, nonnarrative and narrative that is held together by the metaphors.

7 See Marshall Deutelbaum, "Finding the Right Man in *The Wrong Man*," in *A Hitchcock Reader*, ed. by Marshall Deutelbaum and Leland Poague (Ames: Iowa State University Press, 1986), pp. 207–18.

8 Initially the distant figure walks toward the camera but then stops, plants his feet squarely, and begins to speak. The figure has not really come any closer to us nor can we see him any better. Why has he moved at all? By moving he has demonstrated that he is *facing us directly* and has emphasized that we are being specially addressed as extra-fictional spectators. By pointing his gigantic shadow into the camera, he has drawn attention to himself and demonstrated that his role will be active. Characters in the story, however, will not look directly into the camera and speak to us in this way (addressing us as "you"). Certainly there are conventions involved here, but more importantly the conventions are being used to draw epistemological boundary lines within this particular text. Also, the shot permits us to indulge in *stylistic metaphors*, if we wish, by, for example, relating the size of Hitchcock's shadow to an otherworldly power to create; or, by relating the shadow to a presumed, and prior, "first cause" of the story who is dimly seen as a figure that breaks the light and has the power to "shed light" on (enlighten, illuminate) matters.

9 After the end title of *The Wrong Man* a final title appears:

> We are grateful to Mr. Sherman Billingsley for his gracious cooperation in permitting scenes of this picture to be photographed at the Stork Club in New York City.

This title amounts to a final assertion by an extra-fictional narration that what we have seen is true by virtue of being filmed on location. The Hitchcock "I" is now hidden behind a "we."

10 Figure 20 is taken from Ray Jackendoff, *Consciousness and the Computational Mind* (Cambridge, Mass.: MIT Press, 1987), p. 169. Jackendoff uses the figure in discussing David Marr's theory of vision.

11 In chapter 6, I will analyze in detail how an implicit narration is created from elements that are missing from the explicit narrations of *Letter from an Unknown Woman*. Also relevant to the concept of implicitness is the general issue of the separation of material and structure which is discussed in chapter 5.

12 In chapter 2, I examined the relation of screen and story space in the context of another sort of "perception of a misperception" that concerned a husband spying on his wife in Hitchcock's *The 39 Steps*.

13 Hitchcock qualified his dislike for *The Wrong Man* by saying, "But I did fancy the opening of the picture because of my own fear of the police. I also liked the part where the real culprit is discovered just as [Henry] Fonda is praying. Yes, I liked that ironic coincidence." François Truffaut, *Hitchcock* (New York: Simon & Schuster, rev. edn 1984), p. 243.

14 For various definitions of the implied author, see, e.g., Wayne C. Booth, *The Rhetoric of Fiction* (Chicago: University of Chicago Press, 1961), pp. 67–77; Shlomith Rimmon-Kenan, *Narrative Fiction: Contemporary Poetics* (New York: Methuen, 1983), pp. 86–9, 101–4; Seymour Chatman, *Story and Discourse: Narrative Structure in Fiction and Film* (Ithaca, N.Y.: Cornell University Press, 1978), pp. 147–51, and *Coming to Terms: The Rhetoric of Narrative in Fiction and Film* (Ithaca, N.Y.: Cornell University Press, 1990), chaps 5 and 6, "In Defense of the Implied Author" and "The Implied Author at Work," pp. 74–108; Marjet Berendsen, "The Teller and the Observer: Narration and Focalization in Narrative Texts," *Style*, vol. 18, no. 2 (Spring 1984), pp. 146–8; Sarah Kozloff, *Invisible Storytellers: Voice-Over Narration in American Fiction Film* (Berkeley: University of California Press, 1988), pp. 80–1, 109, 117–26; Edward Branigan, "Diegesis and Authorship in Film," *Iris* 7, vol. 4, no. 2 (Fall 1986), pp. 52–3. Gérard Genette has argued that the concept of an implied author serves no purpose; *Narrative Discourse Revisited*, trans. by Jane E. Lewin (Ithaca, N.Y.: Cornell University Press, 1988), pp. 135–50.

15 Christian Metz, *Film Language: A Semiotics of the Cinema*, trans. by Michael Taylor (New York: Oxford University Press, 1974), chap. 2, "Notes Toward a Phenomenology of the Narrative," pp. 20–1 (Metz's emphases except for the final phrase; footnote omitted). See also Metz, "The Impersonal Enunciation, or the Site of Film (In the margin of recent works on enunciation in cinema)," *New Literary History*, vol. 22, no. 3 (Summer 1991), pp. 747–72.

16 See Branigan, *Point of View*, pp. 172–3, 182–4. For more on objectivity and uncertainty, see chapter 6 below.

17 Some speech-act theories of fiction allow several narrations to exist simultaneously by recognizing that a text is composed of "layers" whereby an author "delegates" responsibility for making assertions to "substitute" speakers who contest with one another in an environment of "simultaneous" utterances. See Marie-Laure Ryan, "Fiction as a Logical, Ontological, and Illocutionary Issue," *Style*, vol. 18, no. 2 (Spring 1984), esp. pp. 135–8.

18 On the integration of bottom-up and top-down perceptual processes through the opening music of *The Wrong Man*, compare the discussion of the "integrated spatial match" in *The 39 Steps* in chapter 2, and the discussion of the creation of an inverted pyramid of narrations in the opening of *Hangover Square* in chapter 5.

   The key issue in the credit sequence of *The Wrong Man* concerns types of narration, and contexts of perception, not, as Deutelbaum believes, the "temporal vagueness" of the music – which is not vague – nor the "legibility" of the shots which are perfectly clear ("Finding the Right Man in *The Wrong Man*," pp. 214–15). In general, the spectator is *revising* hypotheses and searching for a fit, not making "mistakes" or being "misled." The analyst's choice of a theory of reading (by hypothesis, or by error) leads to larger theoretical issues. See Edward Branigan, "The Spectator and Film Space – Two Theories," *Screen*, vol. 22, no. 1 (1981), pp. 55–78.

19 Compare the notion of a chameleon text with the discussion of "double causal motivation" in chapter 1. My use of the notion of a chameleon text differs from that of Robert Stam and Ella Shohat; see "*Zelig* and Contemporary Theory: Meditation on the Chameleon Text," *Enclitic* 17/18, vol. 9, nos. 1–2 (1987), pp. 185–6.

20 David Bordwell, "Happily Ever After, Part II," *The Velvet Light Trap* 19 (1982), p. 5. See generally Roger Seamon, "The Story of the Moral: The Function

of Thematizing in Literary Criticism," *The Journal of Aesthetics and Art Criticism*, vol. 47, no. 3 (Summer 1989), pp. 229–36.

21 The concept of nondiegetic narration also explains why we know what happens in the story world *after* this particular story is finished and as a "new" story in that world is beginning. Just prior to the end title of *The Wrong Man*, the following title appears:

> Two years later, Rose Balestrero walked out of the sanitarium – completely cured.
>
> Today she lives happily in Florida with Manny and the two boys . . and what happened seems like a nightmare to them – but it did happen . . .

Because of its nondiegetic position, the narration may pronounce Rose Balestrero "completely cured" and summarize character beliefs today ("seems like a nightmare to them"). Since the new story is beginning "today," it cannot yet be narrated and so the nondiegetic narrator must fall silent.

22 What will count as "explicit" rather than "implicit," or indeed as "nonexistent," haunts theories of narrative and cannot be defined without reference to the theory as a whole. Rimmon-Kenan's six "degrees of perceptibility" of the narrator illustrate some of the issues; see *Narrative Fiction*, pp. 52, 88–9, 96–100, 108. Cf. Gérard Genette's notion of the "pseudo-diegetic" in *Narrative Discourse: An Essay in Method*, trans. by Jane E. Lewin (Ithaca, N.Y.: Cornell University Press, 1980), pp. 236–7. The pseudo-diegetic is analyzed by David Alan Black in "Genette and Film: Narrative Level in the Fiction Cinema," *Wide Angle*, vol. 8, nos. 3/4 (1986), pp. 19–26.

Is it possible for a story to have *no* narrator, or is the narration merely covert? This question leads to a theory's basic grounding in rationalism or empiricism. Cf. Rimmon-Kenan, *Narrative Fiction*, pp. 88 n. 4 and 96 n. 9 with Branigan, *Point of View*, pp. 168–71. See also Dorrit Cohn, "Signposts of Fictionality: A Narratological Perspective," *Poetics Today*, vol. 11, no. 4 (Winter 1990), pp. 794–8; and p. 109 above. Chapter 6 will address the issue of explicit versus implicit in the context of "objective" narrations.

23 Stephen Heath distinquishes five modes of characterization in film: agent, character, person, image, and figure. "Film and System: Terms of Analysis," Part II, *Screen*, vol. 16, no. 2 (Summer 1975), pp. 102–7.

24 *Movies On TV: 1982–1983 Edition*, ed. by Stephen H. Scheuer (New York: Bantam, 9th rev. edn 1981), p. 741. A character's speech on thought is nonfocalized when it is rendered in a highly abbreviated form. For example, in the sentence, "Manny decided to take the train home," no details are provided about how the decision was reached; the decision is merely reported as an action. For Genette, such speech or thought is *narratized* (narrated, narrativized). See *Narrative Discourse*, pp. 170–1. Cf. the examples discussed on pp. 168–9 above.

25 See Edward Branigan, "Point of View in the Fiction Film," *Wide Angle*, vol. 8, nos. 3/4 (1986), pp. 6–7.

26 Some narrative theorists refer to the distinction between representing an experience as intersubjective versus representing it as private as an opposition between "voice" – literally, whose words do we hear? – and "point of view."

27 I am not using the concept of "identification" in its full psychological sense of "identification with." Making the levels of narration more precise is not yet a theory of a spectator's fascination with character and story.

28 Hitchcock has discussed the techniques he used to portray events through

the viewpoint of Manny. Hitchcock's memory of some of the scenes is not entirely accurate but nonetheless is revealing about external focalization:

> The whole approach is subjective. For instance, they've slipped on a pair of handcuffs to link him [Manny] to another prisoner. During the journey between the station house and the prison, there are different men guarding him, but *since he's ashamed*, he keeps his head down, staring at his shoes, so we never show the guards. From time to time one of the handcuffs is opened, and we see a different wrist. In the same way, during the whole trip, we only show the guards' feet, their lower legs, the floor, and the bottom parts of the doors.
>
> (Truffaut, *Hitchcock*, p. 239, my emphasis.)

For another example of external focalization, see p. 78 above, figs 15 and 16, panels 3–8 of *Nick Fury*.

29 On the various ways in which events may be externally and internally focalized through character, and on the conventions of subjectivity in film, see Branigan, *Point of View*, chaps 4–6.

30 Stephen Heath, for example, asserts that

> Point of view . . . depends on an overlaying of first and third person modes. There is no radical dichotomy between subjective point-of-view shots and objective non-point-of-view shots; the latter mode is the continual basis over which the former can run in its particular organization of space, its disposition of the images.
>
> ("Narrative Space" in *Questions of Cinema* (New York: Macmillan, 1981), p. 48. See also pp. 51, 54.)

31 *Wild Strawberries* creates its effects by defining, and then subverting, a single hierarchy of narrations. However, as suggested by figure 26, narrations may be arranged in more complex ways. Depictions of memory that are more complex and radical than *Wild Strawberries* may be found in *Life is a Dream* (Ruiz, 1986), *Distant Voices, Still Lives* (Davies, 1988), and *Sans Soleil* (Marker, 1983). I will discuss the latter film in chapter 7.

32 For Genette, the sudden transgression of a boundary between two levels of the narration would be a metalepsis and is related to paralepsis and paralipsis (i.e., exceeding, or else withholding, information called for by the logic of a given focalization). In general, such a transgression is called an "alteration" or "infraction." See *Narrative Discourse*, pp. 234–7, 194–8. The permeability of narrational boundaries has been addressed by theorists in a variety of ways. David Bordwell speaks of the "degree" of communicativeness of a narration *with respect to* a given "range" and "depth" of knowledge. Didier Coste defines the "informative performance" of a "voice" based on a relationship between "cognitive competence" and "informative competence." Finally, William F. Edmiston analyzes Genette's paralipsis as a "hyper-restriction"; that is, a narration that falsely represents itself as too restrictive to convey certain important information. Presumably, the opposite case would be termed a *hypo*-restriction which would be applied to the situation where a nominal restriction is briefly *exceeded* (thus providing more information than is allowed by the given restriction). The terms proposed by Bordwell, Coste, and Edmiston give the analyst a way of comparing the source of information that is named in the text with the actual inferences that the reader is able to make.

The general problem being addressed by these terminologies concerns issues of the segmentation and large-scale form of narration, local changes in narration (e.g., intrusions, transitions), and the ways in which a given narration may be emphasized, defied, or concealed. In deciding whether to analyze a segment as the momentary transgression of a single narration (e.g., a hyper- or hypo-restriction), or instead as the alternation of two distinct narrations, the analyst will need to weigh such factors as the suddenness, duration, relevance, and saliency of a change in the information against the scope of the analysis. Note also that similar issues arise in assessing the function of a "character" in a narrative: a character may know "too little" or "too much" (e.g., by speaking more than he or she knows – dramatic irony – or by being in the perfect place at the perfect time). As Genette notes, "Narrative always says less than it knows, but it often makes known more than it says" (p. 198). Compare the issues discussed on p. 170 above; compare also the notion of a "hyperdiegetic" narration on p. 189 above. See generally Bordwell, *Narration in the Fiction Film* (Madison: University of Wisconsin Press, 1985), pp. 57–61; Coste, *Narrative as Communication* (Minneapolis: University of Minnesota Press, 1989), pp. 178–9; Edmiston, "Focalization and the First-Person Narrator: A Revision of the Theory," *Poetics Today*, vol. 10, no. 4 (Winter 1989), p. 741.

33 In a study of fifty-three languages representing fourteen different language stocks from all the major parts of the world, Ake Viberg found that all the verbs of perception of the five senses (sight, hearing, touch, taste, smell) could be classified according to whether they indicated an activity of a subject, an experience of a subject, or the subject itself as an object to be perceived. The following is an example of these three possibilities for verbs of sight:

1 Peter *looked at* the birds.
2 Peter *saw* the birds.
3 Peter *looked* happy (cf.: Peter is *good-looking*).

An example for verbs of hearing:
1 Peter *listened to* the birds.
2 Peter *heard* the birds.
3 Peter *sounded* happy.

A number of important syntactic, morphological, and semantic characteristics common to all fifty-three languages can be explained using this approach. "The Verbs of Perception: A Typological Study" in *Explanations for Language Universals*, ed. by Brian Butterworth, Bernard Comrie, and Osten Dahl (New York: Mouton, 1984), pp. 123–62. Compare also the two, or perhaps three or four, types of verbs that state narrative predications discussed in chapter 1 above (e.g., the modes "to be," "to go," "to stay").

Reformulating this tripartite division of the verbs of perception in order to match the types of perceiving and knowing characteristic of *narration* would result in three sorts of subject (i.e., a subject in one of three possible narrative roles): actor, focalizer, and narrator, respectively. The reason that I treat the third case above (i.e., where a subject becomes an object to be perceived by another, unidentified subject) as analogous to narration involving a narrator, rather than narration involving an actor/agent or a focalizer, is that I interpret sentences like 3 as containing an implicit and undefined perceiver who becomes, in effect, the justification for our interpretation of the sentence as a statement *about* what could be seen (or heard), a perceptual judgment that has been rendered *about* something that has been objectified for someone (and for us). Thus:

3 Peter *looked* happy [to *someone* who looked at, or saw, or could have

looked at, or could have seen, him and consequently would have been in a position to make the judgment about him and "narrate" it for us].

Positing someone as an implicit "narrator" who reports an event, then, is shorthand for saying that we are seeing what is, or could be, *seen to be*. The context for the "seeing" (which need not be literal) is not defined, leaving merely the judgment. For more discussion of "objective" narration, see chapter 6.

34 Cf. Mieke Bal, "The Narrating and the Focalizing: A Theory of the Agents in Narrative," *Style*, vol. 17, no. 2 (Spring 1983), pp. 243–5. I have reversed the positions that Bal assigns to actors and focalizers because I have restricted focalization to characters.

35 Focalization is not defined by the binary contrasts of either recounting versus enacting nor telling versus showing. See Bordwell, *Narration in the Fiction Film*, pp. 77–80; and chaps 1 and 2 on mimetic and diegetic theories of narration. Focalization is also not defined by speaking versus seeing. See William Nelles, "Getting Focalization into Focus," *Poetics Today*, vol. 11, no. 2 (Summer 1990), pp. 366–8. George M. Wilson shows the logical absurdities which result when a film image is deemed to be literally spoken by a narrator as a "speech-act" or "visualized" as a mental image. *Narration in Light: Studies in Cinematic Point of View* (Baltimore: Johns Hopkins University Press, 1986), chap. 7, "On Narrators and Narration in Film," pp. 126–44. Furthermore, the above contrasts are singularly misleading about many other aspects of the narrative process.

36 See, e.g., Genette, *Narrative Discourse*, pp. 188–94; Mieke Bal, *Narratology: Introduction to the Theory of Narrative*, trans. by Christine van Boheemen (Toronto: University of Toronto Press, 1985), pp. 100–26; Rimmon-Kenan, *Narrative Fiction*, pp. 71–85; Lanser, *The Narrative Act*, pp. 37–8, 141–8, 212–14; Berendsen, "The Teller and the Observer," pp. 140–58; Edmiston, "Focalization and the First-Person Narrator," pp. 729–44; Nelles, "Getting Focalization into Focus," pp. 365–82; Steven Cohan and Linda M. Shires, *Telling Stories: A Theoretical Analysis of Narrative Fiction* (New York: Routledge, 1988), pp. 94–104.

37 Bal, *Narratology*, pp. 100–18.

38 Seymour Chatman, "Characters and Narrators: Filter, Center, Slant, and Interest-Focus," *Poetics Today*, vol. 7, no. 2 (1986), esp. pp. 193–7. For an illustration of these concepts, see Chatman, "Who Is the Best Narrator? The Case of *The Third Man*," *Style*, vol. 23, no. 2 (Summer 1989), pp. 183–96.

39 Genette, *Narrative Discourse*, pp. 188–94. Genette's "external focalization" also differs from my use of the concept. For Genette, it refers to a nonpsychological ("behaviorist") rendering of character from an external position. This seems to be what I have referred to as "nonfocalization." Genette also distinguishes among fixed, variable, and multiple focalization. However these categories exist only at a global level of the text and result from particular patterns of change in internal focalization.

40 Lanser, *The Narrative Act*, cf. p. 96 with p. 85. In Lanser's version of figure 19, the diagonal line above each sender on the left is labelled "status"; the diagonal line below each sender becomes a dotted line and is called "stance"; and a new horizontal dotted line is drawn between each sender and receiver, and called "contact." Status describes the speaker's right to communicate: the authority, competence, and credibility which the communicator is conventionally and personally allowed by a linguistic community. Stance describes the speaker's ideological and psychological attitudes toward the

message he or she is uttering. Contact describes the speaker's physical and psychological relationship to the audience. Lanser, *The Narrative Act*, pp. 64–77, 84–97, 145, 223–5.

41 Barthes, "An Introduction to the Structural Analysis of Narrative," p. 260 (Barthes's emphases).

42 Dudley Andrew, *Concepts in Film Theory* (New York: Oxford University Press, 1984), p. 81; but cf. pp. 44, 48, 92, 138, 167–71.

43 Chatman, *Story and Discourse*, p. 28. Chatman also says, "Narratives are communications, thus easily envisaged as the movement of arrows from left to right, from author to audience" (p. 31; and see his diagram of narrative structure on p. 267).

44 James L. Kinneavy, *A Theory of Discourse: The Aims of Discourse* (New York: W.W. Norton & Co., 1971), p. 19. Other formulations of a communication theory may be found in Didier Coste's *Narrative as Communication*; Roman Jakobson, "Linguistics and Poetics" in *The Structuralists: From Marx to Lévi-Strauss*, ed. by Richard and Fernande de George (Garden City, N.Y.: Doubleday, 1972), esp. pp. 89–97; and Umberto Eco, *A Theory of Semiotics* (Bloomington: Indiana University Press, 1976), pp. 32–47, 139–42.

45 Roland Barthes, *S/Z*, trans. by Richard Miller (New York: Hill & Wang, 1974), p. 151 (Barthes's emphasis); see also pp. 10–11, 41–2. Barthes transforms the notion of "voice" into a "code" that "de-originates" the utterance (p. 21). See generally Barthes, "The Death of the Author" in *Image – Music – Text*, trans. by Stephen Heath (New York: Hill & Wang, 1977), pp. 142–8; *The Pleasure of the Text*, trans. by Richard Miller (New York: Hill & Wang, 1975); "To Write: An Intransitive Verb?" in *The Structuralist Controversy: The Languages of Criticism and the Sciences of Man*, ed. by Richard Macksey and Eugenio Donato (Baltimore: Johns Hopkins University Press, 1972), pp. 134–45.

46 Jonathan Culler, "Problems in the Theory of Fiction," *Diacritics*, vol. 14, no. 1 (Spring 1984), pp. 5–6.

47 Bordwell, *Narration in the Fiction Film*, p. 62 (Bordwell's emphasis). See also n. 22 above.

48 See, e.g., Noam Chomsky, *Reflections on Language* (New York: Pantheon, 1975), p. 69 ("Communication is only one function of language, and by no means an essential one."); Michael J. Reddy, "The Conduit Metaphor – A Case of Frame Conflict in Our Language about Language" in *Metaphor and Thought*, ed. by Andrew Ortony (New York: Cambridge University Press, 1979), pp. 284–324; William Frawley, *Text and Epistemology* (Norwood, N.J.: Ablex, 1987); Ann Banfield, *Unspeakable Sentences: Narration and Representation in the Language of Fiction* (London: Routledge & Kegan Paul, 1982). Alain Robbe-Grillet argues that communication metaphors and anthropomorphisms encourage a false metaphysics; "Nature, Humanism, Tragedy" in *For A New Novel: Essays on Fiction*, trans. by Richard Howard (New York: Grove, 1965), pp. 49–75. But see Mark Johnson, *The Body in the Mind: The Bodily Basis of Meaning, Imagination, and Reason* (Chicago: University of Chicago Press, 1987).

49 Cf. Friedrich Nietzsche, *Beyond Good and Evil: Prelude to a Philosophy of the Future*, trans. by Walter Kaufmann (New York: Vintage, 1966), sects 16 and 17.

50 I will readdress the question of using anthropomorphic metaphors to describe narration when we consider the holistic theories of Telotte, Sobchack, and Kawin in chapter 5 and the concept of an invisible observer

in chapter 6. Cf. George Lakoff and Mark Johnson's general discussion of "orientational metaphors" and the "canonical person" in *Metaphors We Live By* (Chicago: University of Chicago Press, 1980), pp. 14–21, 41–5, 132–8, 160–2, and see David Bordwell, *Making Meaning: Inference and Rhetoric in the Interpretation of Cinema* (Cambridge, Mass.: Harvard University, 1989), chap. 7, "Two Basic Schemata," sect. "Making Films Personal," pp. 151–68. For detailed arguments about the communication metaphor as applied to film narrative, see, e.g., Branigan, *Point of View*, pp. 8–9, 14, 39–40, 59, 194–5; Seymour Chatman's review of this book in *Film Quarterly*, vol. 40, no. 1 (Fall 1986), pp. 45–6; my reply to the review and his response in *Film Quarterly*, vol. 41, no. 1 (Fall 1987), pp. 63–5; Sarah Kozloff's review of Bordwell's *Narration in the Fiction Film* in *Film Quarterly*, vol. 40, no. 1 (Fall 1986), pp. 43–5; Chatman's review of this book in *Wide Angle*, vol. 8, nos. 3/4 (1986), pp. 139–41; and Bordwell's reply (unpublished).

51 See Wallace Martin, *Recent Theories of Narrative* (Ithaca, N.Y.: Cornell University Press, 1986), p. 156. On the search for an intermediate position, see also Robert Burgoyne, "The Cinematic Narrator: The Logic and Pragmatics of Impersonal Narration," *Journal of Film and Video*, vol. 42, no. 1 (Spring 1990), pp. 3–16.

52 Shlomith Rimmon-Kenan adopts Chatman's communication model for narrative but excludes the implied author and the implied reader from the communication situation even though she stresses that these two constructs remain essential to an analysis of a reader's comprehension of narrative fiction. In addition, she includes the narrator and the narratee as constitutive, not just optional, elements in the communication situation; *Narrative Fiction*, pp. 2–4, 86–9. Chatman has responded with some changes to his model; *Coming to Terms*, p. 218 n. 29.

53 Robert de Beaugrande, *Text, Discourse, and Process: Toward a Multidisciplinary Science of Texts* (Norwood, N.J.: Ablex, 1980), p. 125 (Beaugrande's emphases except for the word "how"); cf. his list of ten universals of language and twenty-one cognitive skills in processing texts, pp. 125–6, 278–9.

54 See note 13 above.

55 Scheuer (ed.) *Movies On TV*, p. 741.

56 On the theoretical status of verbal descriptions of pictorial data, see especially David Alan Black, *Narrative Film and the Synoptic Tendency* (Ph.D. diss.: New York University, 1988).

57 In arguing against Genette's theory of focalization, Mieke Bal notes that "the nonchalant use of a preposition is enough to overturn a theory," "The Narrating and the Focalizing," p. 241. In my arguments I have tried to be sensitive to the nuances of such prepositions as over, at, with, through, into, in, and about. In chapters 6 and 7, I will explore the nuances of definite and indefinite articles in relation to narrative.

58 Cf. Marie-Laure Ryan, "Stacks, Frames and Boundaries, or Narrative as Computer Language," *Poetics Today*, vol. 11, no. 4 (Winter 1990), pp. 873–99. As an example of how differing levels of representation operate in perception, consider that our perception of a visual object, say, on a motion picture screen is initially dependent on our *angle* of view while higher-level recognition of the "same" object (e.g., our memory of it) is *not* dependent on *that* point of view and, moreover, may be translated into other, nonvisual epistemological schemes (and thus may be stored and retrieved in quite different formats under different "views"). Of course, we have no awareness at all of some levels and processes of perception; for example, we lose all

awareness of an image in its initially inverted, curvilinear, and tiny state within the retina. I believe that the above sorts of considerations also govern higher-level cognitive processes like narrative comprehension when it, too, is seen as multi-layered. Cf. the discussion of some remarkable facts about narrative comprehension on pp. 14–15.

59 Richard J. Gerrig, "Reexperiencing Fiction and Non-Fiction," *The Journal of Aesthetics and Art Criticism*, vol. 47, no. 3 (Summer 1989), pp. 277–80.

60 Figure 26b is based on box diagrams showing the relationships of various narrations in Maturin's *Melmoth the Wanderer* and Longus's *Daphnis and Chloe*; Joseph Kestner, "Secondary Illusion: The Novel and the Spatial Arts" in Jeffrey R. Smitten and Ann Daghistany (eds), *Spatial Form in Narrative* (Ithaca, N.Y.: Cornell University Press, 1981), pp. 111, 115. Marvin Minsky contrasts a hierarchy with a "heterarchy" that is organized as a series of cross-connected rings and loops. *The Society of Mind* (New York: Simon & Schuster, 1986), p. 35.

61 Tzvetan Todorov, "Categories of the Literary Narrative," trans. by Ann Goodman, *Film Reader* 2 (1977), cf. p. 29 with p. 21; *Introduction to Poetics*, trans. by Richard Howard (Minneapolis: University of Minnesota Press, 1981), pp. 52–3.

62 The concept of "point of view" is misleading in that it suggests that there is a single principle (a "point") that accounts for the unity of a perceptual judgment (a "view"), rather than a series of relationships spanning a range of mental activities. For example, Seymour Chatman argues that "point of view" should be analyzed in terms of four variables: centrality (the relative importance of an entity to the cause–effect chain); filter (the represention of a perception, a "consciousness of"); slant (the representation of an attitude); and finally, the reader's interest-focus. See Chatman, "Characters and Narrators," and *Coming to Terms*, chap. 9, "A New Point of View on 'Point of View,'" pp. 139–60.

In the case of film, Jacques Aumont also finds four aspects to point of view: the point from which a gaze originates, i.e., the position of the camera; the spatial perspective in which an event is represented, i.e., the particular way in which an illusion of depth is created on the screen; the "narrative" point of view which is, in turn, comprised of three additional places from which a gaze originates – from the character, auteur, and spectator; and finally, the mental attitude (e.g., an intellectual, moral, or political attitude) that conveys the narrator's judgment on the event. Aumont believes that the history of narrative cinema (as well as perhaps the history of film theory) is one of the discovery and fixing of "the rules of correspondence" among these four aspects of point of view. "The Point of View," trans. by Arthur Denner, *Quarterly Review of Film and Video*, vol. 11, no. 2 (1989), pp. 2–3.

63 Branigan, *Point of View*, pp. 40–2, 46, 48–9, 68 n. 18, 120 n. 22, 171–3, 182.

64 For further discussion of "scene" and "summary," see chapter 5.

65 Arthur C. Danto, *Narration and Knowledge* (including the integral text of *Analytical Philosophy of History*) (New York: Columbia University Press, 1985), p. 238 (Danto's emphases except for the word "specific").

66 I have recast Wallace Martin's description of four varieties of narrative theory along somewhat different lines using different terms. I add a new, fifth major type and relate his fourth type of theory to topics discussed in his chapter 7 rather than to his choice which is chapter 6; see *Recent Theories of Narrative*, pp. 107–11. Dudley Andrew proposes eight types of narrative theories in *Concepts in Film Theory*, pp. 81–8.

67 Vladimir Propp, *Morphology of the Folktale*, trans. by Laurence Scott, rev. and ed. by Louis A. Wagner (Austin: University of Texas Press, 2nd edn 1968), pp. 20 and 21 (emphases omitted from both quotes).

68 Propp, *Morphology of the Folktale*, pp. 19–20.

69 In film studies, Propp's approach has been applied in especially novel and provocative ways to define three types of plot in the Western genre, Frederick Wiseman's documentary films, the Japanese "Sword Film," and an underlying plot for the films of Yasujiro Ozu. See Will Wright, *Six Guns and Society: A Structural Study of the Western* (Berkeley: University of California Press, 1975), pp. 40–9, 64–9, 99–113; Bill Nichols, *Ideology and the Image: Social Representation in the Cinema and Other Media* (Bloomington: Indiana University Press, 1981), pp. 212–16; David Desser, *The Samurai Films of Akira Kurosawa* (Ann Arbor, Mich.: UMI Research Press, 1983), pp. 48–51; and David Bordwell, *Ozu and the Poetics of Cinema*, pp. 56–64.

On Propp's theory and its relatives, see David Bordwell, "ApProppriations and ImProprieties: Problems in the Morphology of Film Narrative," *Cinema Journal*, vol. 27, no. 3 (Spring 1988), pp. 5–20; and Wallace Martin, *Recent Theories of Narrative*, pp. 88–98. For a recent application to film narrative, see Richard Abel, "*Notorious*: Perversion par Excellence" in *A Hitchcock Reader*, ed. by Marshall Deutelbaum and Leland Poague (Ames: Iowa State University Press, 1986), pp. 162–69.

For extensions of Propp's method into other areas of study, see Claude Lévi-Strauss, *Structural Anthropology*, trans. by Claire Jacobson and Brooke Grundfest Schoepf (Garden City, N.Y.: Doubleday, 1967) and Claude Bremond, "The Logic of Narrative Possibilities," *New Literary History*, vol. 11, no. 3 (Spring 1980), pp. 387–411. See generally, Jonathan Culler, *Structuralist Poetics: Structuralism, Linguistics and the Study of Literature* (Ithaca, N.Y.: Cornell University Press, 1975).

70 Five of Propp's thirty-one functions touch on the manipulation of character knowledge: reconnaissance (4), delivery of information (5), deception by villain (6), recognition of hero (27), and exposure of villain (28). These five, however, seem even less important when Propp lists all 151 elements of the wondertale. Propp, *Morphology of the Folktale*, Appendix I, pp. 119–27 (elements 37, 41, 43, 143, 145).

71 On the distinction between plot and story, cf. Bordwell, *Narration in the Fiction Film*, pp. 50–7, 77–88, 77 n. 6, with Bordwell and Kristin Thompson, *Film Art: An Introduction* (New York: McGraw-Hill, 3rd edn 1990), pp. 55–8, 85–6. For an examination of how the definition of plot responds to the underlying assumptions of a narrative theory, see Ruth Ronen, "Paradigm Shift in Plot Models: An Outline of the History of Narratology," *Poetics Today*, vol. 11, no. 4 (Winter 1990), pp. 817–42.

72 On the general function of a "middle term" in explaining change within a three-term narrative sequence, see Danto, *Narration and Knowledge*, pp. 233–56. Danto argues that the logic of narrative is *identical* to the logic of *any* causal explanation (e.g., he says, an account of the movement of billiard balls) and is also closely related to a deductive argument. For Danto, narrative constitutes a fundamental form of knowledge and is the basis for all historical explanation. His ideas would seem to be in accord with Bordwell and Thompson's general definition of narrative which is powerful enough to describe both a novel and the motions of a planet orbiting the sun. Bordwell and Thompson define narrative as "a chain of events in cause-effect relationship occurring in time and space." *Film Art*, p. 55 (emphasis

omitted). One should not believe, however, that such a theory of narrative is necessarily empiricist, or depends on a positivist theory of language. See Danto, *Narration and Knowledge*, chaps 3–6.

This footnote would not be complete without placing Danto's book between Edward W. Said's *Beginnings: Intention and Method* (New York: Basic Books, 1975) and Frank Kermode's *The Sense of an Ending: Studies in the Theory of Fiction* (New York: Oxford University Press, 1967). Despite their selective emphases, it seems to me that each of these three books reasserts, at least as a first approximation, the essential unity and closure that we expect from a "narrative."

73 Kristin Thompson, *Breaking the Glass Armor: Neoformalist Film Analysis* (Princeton, N.J.: Princeton University Press, 1988), chap. 1, "Neoformalist Film Analysis: One Approach, Many Methods," p. 9; see also pp. 21, 27, 32, 36, 43. Basic assumptions of Russian Formalism are described by Thompson in *Eisenstein's Ivan the Terrible: A Neoformalist Analysis* (Princeton, N.J.: Princeton University Press, 1981), esp. chap. 1, pp. 8–60; on narrative, pp. 37–46. See also Herbert Eagle's introductory essay in *Russian Formalist Film Theory*, ed. by Herbert Eagle (Ann Arbor, Mich.: University of Michigan Press, 1981), pp. 1–54, and Peter Steiner, *Russian Formalism: A Metapoetics* (Ithaca, N.Y.: Cornell University Press, 1984).

74 Thompson, *Breaking the Glass Armor*, p. 10 (my emphases); cf. p. 7.

75 Russian formalism may have no need for a theory of fiction (and belief) separate from a theory of narrative because of its emphasis on the dulling and repolishing of human perception that is posited as distinct from a specific language or communication faculty (which would involve reference and knowing).

76 Bertrand Russell, *The Problems of Philosophy* (London: Oxford University Press, 1972), pp. 43–59, 108–9; *Mysticism and Logic and other Essays* (London: George Allen & Unwin, 1949), chap. 10, "Knowledge by Acquaintance and Knowledge by Description," pp. 209–32.

77 Thompson, *Breaking the Glass Armor*, pp. 12–15, 21. See David Bordwell, *Making Meaning*. Noël Carroll introduces four distinctions which appear to address epistemological issues: "knowing that," "believing that," "seeing that," and "seeing how." The distinctions, however, are drawn in such a manner that problems of knowledge, interpretation, and narration are reduced to aspects of *style* and to a perceiver's acquaintance with the sensuous surface of film. See Carroll, "Buster Keaton, *The General*, and Visible Intelligibility" in *Close Viewings: An Anthology of New Film Criticism*, ed. by Peter Lehman (Tallahassee: Florida State University Press, 1990), pp. 132–3.

78 In setting up a communication theory of narrative, Lanser and Chatman attempt to incorporate the work of the Russian formalists who developed what I have termed a style-based theory of narrative while Pratt and Iser attack the formalists. See, e.g., Lanser, *The Narrative Act*, p. 32 n. 27; Chatman, *Story and Discourse*, pp. 15–22; Mary Louise Pratt, *Toward a Speech Act Theory of Literary Discourse* (Bloomington: Indiana University Press, 1977), pp. 67–78; Wolfgang Iser, "Narrative Strategies as a Means of Communication" in *Interpretation of Narrative*, ed. by Mario J. Valdes and Owen J. Miller (Toronto: University of Toronto Press, 1978), pp. 102–7.

79 See, e.g., Martin, *Recent Theories of Narrative*, chap. 7, "From Writer to Reader: Communication and Interpretation," pp. 152–72; Horst Ruthrof, *The Reader's Construction of Narrative* (London: Routledge & Kegan Paul, 1981); and especially Janet Staiger, *Interpreting Films: Studies in the Historical Recep-*

tion of American Cinema (Princeton, N.J.: Princeton University Press, 1972). For brief overviews of some of the issues, see Sarah Ruth Kozloff, "Narrative Theory and Television," and Robert C. Allen, "Reader-Oriented Criticism and Television" in *Channels of Discourse: Television and Contemporary Criticism*, ed. by Robert C. Allen (Chapel Hill: University of North Carolina, 1987), pp. 42–112.

    Since I have formulated the basic issues and concepts of film narrative against the backdrop of the cognitive abilities of a reader, my general approach in this book would fit into this fourth class of theories emphasizing the reception of narrative.

80 E.M. Forster, *Aspects of the Novel* (New York: Harcourt, Brace & Co., 1927), p. 158. On suspense, mystery, and surprise, see chapter 3 above; on a genre defined by the duration of a reader's uncertainty, see Tzvetan Todorov, *The Fantastic: A Structural Approach to a Literary Genre*, trans. by Richard Howard (Ithaca, N.Y.: Cornell University Press, 1975), p. 25.

81 An exception is the Russian formalist Boris Eikhenbaum who developed a perceptual theory based on "inner speech." See note 84 below.

82 See, e.g., Richard Shusterman, "Interpretation, Intention, and Truth," *The Journal of Aesthetics and Art Criticism*, vol. 46, no. 3 (Spring 1988), pp. 399–411. More polemical is Bill Nichols, "Form Wars: The Political Unconscious of Formalist Theory," *The South Atlantic Quarterly*, vol. 88, no. 2 (Spring 1989), pp. 487–515.

83 Metz, *Film Language*, p. 21; more fully quoted in the text above at note 15.

84 See, e.g., Paul Willemen, "Cinematic Discourse: The Problem of Inner Speech," *Screen*, vol. 22, no. 3 (1981), pp. 63–93; Sergei Eisenstein, *The Film Sense*, trans. by Jay Leyda (New York: Harcourt, Brace & World, 1947), esp. part I, "Word and Image," pp. 1–65. See also Nelson Goodman, *Of Mind and Other Matters* (Cambridge, Mass.: Harvard University Press, 1984), chap. 1, sects 5 and 6, "Can Thoughts Be Quoted?" and "On Thoughts Without Words," pp. 19–28; Nelson Goodman and Catherine Z. Elgin, *Reconceptions in Philosophy and Other Arts and Sciences* (Indianapolis: Hackett, 1988), chap. 5, "Sights Unseen," pp. 83–92.

85 David Alan Black, *Narrative Film and the Synoptic Tendency*, p. 142 (Black's emphasis).

86 See F. Xavier Plaus, "Freudian Drive Theory and Epistemology," in *The Psychology of Knowing*, ed. by Joseph R. Royce and William W. Rozeboom (New York: Gordon & Breach, 1972), pp. 413, 420, 424.

87 In deferred action, or deferred revision, sensory material stored in memory is subject always to being recalled, repressed, or drastically reinterpreted in light of new circumstances including the maturation of the organism. Through deferred action, original stimuli stored in memory may produce entirely new feelings not experienced originally (guilt, anxiety, pleasure). Effects of the "present" may not be determined, much less known, until later. The temporality of the human psyche is thus much more complex than the temporality of initial stimuli. See J. Laplanche and J.-B. Pontalis, *The Language of Psycho-Analysis*, trans. by Donald Nicholson-Smith (New York: W. W. Norton & Co., 1973), "Censorship," "Deferred Action," "Phantasy," and "Secondary Revision," pp. 65–6, 111–14, 314–19, and 412.

88 Culler, "Problems in the Theory of Fiction," p. 3. See also Culler, "Fabula and Sjuzhet in the Analysis of Narrative: Some American Discussions," *Poetics Today*, vol. 1, no. 3 (1980), pp. 27–37; Peter Brooks, *Reading for the Plot: Design and Intention in Narrative* (New York: Alfred A. Knopf, 1984),

chaps 1, 4, 10; and Eric S. Rabkin, "Spatial Form and Plot" in Smitten and Daghistany, *Spatial Form in Narrative*, pp. 83, 90.

89 By contrast, Kristin Thompson argues that the unconscious level of mental processes is largely an unnecessary construct for criticism. "For the neo-formalist critic, conscious processes are usually the most important ones, since it is here that the artwork can challenge most strongly our habitual ways of perceiving and thinking and can make us aware of our habitual ways of coping with the world. In a sense, for the neoformalist, the aim of original art is to put any or all of our thought processes onto this conscious level." Thompson also discusses the specific failings of psychoanalytic criticism; *Breaking the Glass Armor*, pp. 27–8.

90 See E. Ann Kaplan's "Introduction: From Plato's Cave to Freud's Screen" in *Psychoanalysis & Cinema*, ed. by E. Ann Kaplan (New York: Routledge, 1990), pp. 1–23. For an example of reading against the grain, see Stuart Marshall's discovery of three contradictory views of female sexuality at work in the representation of the character Adrienne Fromsett in *Lady in the Lake*, quoted in note 32 in chapter 5 below.

Recall in the context of a counterintuitive reading, the discussion of Alan Williams's "four films," the spectator's systematic "forgetting," and the dyad "transparency–invisibility" in chapter 3. The fact that some things have slipped from consciousness explains the attraction of such concepts as "suture" and "excess" for psychoanalytic criticism. On suture, see note 27 in chapter 2 above; on excess, see note 4 in chapter 2 above. Marshall draws on suture to explain the "failure" of *Lady in the Lake*; "*Lady in the Lake*: Identification and the Drives," *Film Form*, vol. 1, no. 2 (Autumn 1977), pp. 38, 42.

5 SUBJECTIVITY

1 See Roland Barthes, "The Realistic Effect," trans. by Gerald Mead, *Film Reader* 3 (1978), pp. 131–5. Two other translations appear as "The Reality Effect" in Barthes's *The Rustle of Language*, trans. by Richard Howard (New York: Hill & Wang, 1986), pp. 141–8, and in *French Literary Theory Today: A Reader*, ed. by Tzvetan Todorov, trans. by R. Carter (Cambridge: Cambridge University Press, 1982), pp. 11–17. See also Barthes, *S/Z*, trans. by Richard Miller (New York: Hill & Wang, 1974), sects 13, 22, 44, 77, and lexias 55, 107, 134, 436, 545. As we shall see in chapter 7, documentary films will go much further than fiction films in focusing a spectator's attention on the authoritative sources and causal mechanisms which supposedly link a text to the world.

2 On indefinite time, and on the general importance of indefinite reference to fictional interpretation, see chapter 7.

3 On perfect but impossible camera framing, see camera position 5 in figure 14, chapter 3. Also relevant in describing parts of shot 1 in *Hangover Square* is the concept of "unmotivated" camera movement; see camera positions 8A-B in figure 14.

4 Claudia Gorbman, *Unheard Melodies: Narrative Film Music* (Bloomington: Indiana University Press, 1987), pp. 152, 158. There are minor inaccuracies in Gorbman's shot breakdown for the opening sequence of *Hangover Square*. David Bordwell discusses the reappearance of the credit music of *Hangover Square* in George's concerto as well as more general issues about music and narration in *The Classical Hollywood Cinema: Film Style & Mode of Production*

to 1960 (New York: Columbia University Press, 1985), "Music as Destiny," pp. 33–5, 72. Cf. the discussion in chapter 4 above of how the opening credit music in *The Wrong Man* crosses narrational boundaries.

5 For example, most spectators never notice that in *Lady in the Lake*, to be discussed below, there are at least five matches on action within an ostensibly continuous POV shot. One of the reasons that a match on action does so little damage to narrative is that in a single stroke it reinforces the prevailing continuity of a causal sequence – a motion – in a unique space and time already defined by a narrative schema.

For another illustration of the separation of the narrative structure of the POV shot from its material or technical manifestation, see my discussion of *The Quiller Memorandum* in *Point of View in the Cinema: A Theory of Narration and Subjectivity in Classical Film* (New York and Berlin: Mouton, 1984), p. 113; see also note 15 in chapter 3 above.

6 The double causal structure of crime and romance discussed in chapter 1 in connection with *The Girl and Her Trust* is particularly evident in *Lady in the Lake*.

7 Julio L. Moreno, "Subjective Cinema: And the Problem of Film in the First Person," *The Quarterly of Film, Radio and Television*, vol. 7 (1952–3), p. 354 (Moreno's emphases); see also p. 344.

8 Moreno, "Subjective Cinema," p. 349 (Moreno's emphasis); see also pp. 342, 357–8. On Moreno's preference for the purely visual, see pp. 346–9.

9 See André Bazin, "Theater and Cinema – Part One," trans. by Hugh Gray in *What Is Cinema?*, vol. I (Berkeley: University of California Press, 1967), p. 92; and see chaps "Theater and Cinema – Part Two," "The Ontology of the Photographic Image," "The Evolution of the Language of Cinema," and "The Virtues and Limitations of Montage." See generally, Branigan, *Point of View*, Appendix, "Orthodox Theories of Narration," sect. 3, "André Bazin: Point of View as a Real Condition of Vision," pp. 198–212.

10 For a recent assessment of Bazin's theory, see Philip Rosen's "History of Image, Image of History: Subject and Ontology in Bazin" in a special issue of *Wide Angle* devoted to Bazin, vol. 9, no. 4 (1987), pp. 7–34.

11 Joseph P. Brinton, "Subjective Camera or Subjective Audience?," *Hollywood Quarterly*, vol. 2, no. 4 (July 1947), pp. 361–2. Brinton decides that *Lady in the Lake* fails because of the superiority of the human eye over the camera while John McCarten decides that it fails because of the inferiority of the human eye:

> One major trouble with [*Lady in the Lake*] . . . is its brushing aside of the facts of optometry. Substituting for the human eye, the camera constantly fails to realize the limitations of that organ, and it etches into sharp focus all kinds of scenes that the eye could never see that clearly.
>
> (*The New Yorker*, vol. 22, no. 51 (Feb. 1, 1947), p. 64.)

12 Brinton, "Subjective Camera," p. 365; see also pp. 360–3. Cf. the blend of subjective and objective narration in *Nick Fury*, chapter 3 above. Brinton remarks that "Scenes in the classic *Cabinet of Dr Caligari* [Wiene, 1919] and *Last Will of Dr Mabuse* [Lang, 1933], for example, express a subjective point of view in virtually every aspect of their production except the camera, and this inconsistency perhaps accounts for the difficulty with which spectators follow their narratives" (p. 365).

13 Moreno, "Subjective Cinema," pp. 351–2; Brinton, "Subjective Camera," pp. 362–3.

14 André Gaudreault, "Narration and Monstration in the Cinema," *The Journal of Film and Video*, vol. 39, no. 2 (Spring 1987), pp. 31–3, and n. 12. Cf. figure 25 in chapter 4, p. 106. Gaudreault's assertion that the monstrator does not acknowledge the fact of "quotation," raises the general issue of the "perceptibility" of narration; see, e.g., note 22 in chapter 4 above.

For Gaudreault the concept of quotation seems to involve *extracting* something from a context and presenting it anew (p. 33); but this seems closer to the activities of editing and telling than to showing. The relationship of language and cinema has been one of the intractable problems of contemporary film theory.

One may also wonder exactly what in film is "in present time" for Gaudreault. Is it a photograph, a shot, the experience of an image, spoken language, a performance by an actor, a fiction, a narrative enacted, or a narrative interrupted – a *tableau vivant*? I suggest that the film image is perhaps merely atemporal, or "open," and that time is not a *property* at all but a function of the descriptive method being employed by the spectator to sequence and juxtapose elements.

15 The theoretical status of what is "off-screen" at any given moment is a concrete test of how a theory conceives the general problem of *presence and absence* which, in turn, is at the center of any explanation of representational, or symbolic, activity. When can it be said that something is no longer present, not there, at an end, no longer causally effective? Is the answer: when we no longer see or hear it? Or, when we no longer believe it to be present? Or, when we no longer have sufficient justification to believe it to be present? (Note that still other answers are possible.)

A similar issue is raised in narrative theories which attempt to distinguish plot from story: when does something off-screen pass from the plot into the story? After the present shot is over? How much and what kind of arranging, selecting, emphasizing, or tampering with story events will count as "plot?" These are not easy questions to decide. Clearly, if "plot" is to be a central term in a theory and not trivial, then it will depend on a battery of other concepts (e.g., "scene") to define its scope. Again, one cannot avoid the problem of relating, on the one hand, a spectator's perception of structure to, on the other hand, a camera and the effects of material. On plot versus story, see the discussion of style-based theories of narrative in chapter 4.

16 Charles Derry, like Gaudreault, conceives film narrative as a product of "literary or verbal" narration that is operating simultaneously with a "visual" narration. Derry, however, leaves open the possibility that there may be still other sorts of narrations, and also relaxes the connection between literary narration and "telling," and between visual narration and "showing." He argues, for instance, that synchronous dialogue is shown to us, not told. "Towards a Categorization of Film Narrative," *Film Reader* 2 (1977), esp. pp. 114–17. Seymour Chatman makes use of the concepts of telling and showing in *Story and Discourse: Narrative Structure in Fiction and Film* (Ithaca, N.Y.: Cornell University Press, 1978), pp. 31–4.

On the problems surrounding the distinction between telling and showing, see, e.g., Branigan, *Point of View*, Appendix, sect. 1, "Orthodox Literary Theories of Point of View and a Fatal Distinction: Telling versus Showing," pp. 190–6; David Bordwell, *Narration in the Fiction Film* (Madison: University of Wisconsin Press, 1985), esp. pp. 77–80, and chaps 1 and 2 on mimetic and diegetic theories of narration. For a defense of the distinction, see Seymour Chatman, *Coming to Terms: The Rhetoric of Narrative in Fiction and*

Film (Ithaca, N.Y.: Cornell University Press, 1990), chaps 7 and 8, "The Literary Narrator" and "The Cinematic Narrator," pp. 109–38.

17 Gaudreault, "Narration and Monstration," p. 31. Cf. Gérard Genette's method of linking showing and scene in *Narrative Discourse: An Essay in Method*, trans. by Jane E. Lewin (Ithaca, N.Y.: Cornell University Press, 1980), p. 166.

18 Bordwell, *Narration in the Fiction Film*, p. 188 (his emphases); and see pp. 158, 162. On the alternation of scene and summary in the traditional novel, see, e.g., Percy Lubbock, *The Craft of Fiction* (New York: Charles Scribner's Sons, 1921), pp. 64–73, 93–109, 267–70.

19 The theories of Bazin and Eisenstein do not rest on particular techniques. Bazin's realism is not necessarily the long take in deep focus; Eisenstein's montage is not necessarily editing. See, e.g., Bazin, "A Pure Masterpiece: *The River*" in *Jean Renoir*, trans. by W.W. Halsey and William H. Simon (New York: Dell Publishing, 1973), pp. 104–19; Vladimir Nizhny, *Lessons with Eisenstein*, trans. by Ivor Montagu and Jay Leyda (London: George Allen & Unwin, 1962), chap. 4, "Mise-en-Shot," pp. 93–139.

20 Genette, *Narrative Discourse*, pp. 86–95; Chatman, *Story and Discourse*, pp. 67–78; Peter Wollen, "Introduction to *Citizen Kane*," *Film Reader* 1 (1975), pp. 9–15; Christian Metz, "Problems of Denotation in the Fiction Film" in *Film Language: A Semiotics of the Cinema*, trans. by Michael Taylor (New York: Oxford University Press, 1974), pp. 108–46; Bordwell, *Narration in the Fiction Film*, pp. 80–8; Noel Burch, *Theory of Film Practice*, trans. by Helen R. Lane (Princeton, N.J.: Princeton University Press, 1981), chap. 1, "Spatial and Temporal Articulations," pp. 3–16. Burch's definition of temporal articulation in film combines certain aspects of temporal duration with order and frequency. Other writers prefer to separate these aspects of time. I discuss order and frequency in conjunction with figure 3 in chapter 2.

Note that the duration of time has its analogue in the *depth*, or extent, of space. The word "long," for example, may be used to describe either time or space. For an overview of the problems associated with relating depth cues on the screen to the depth of a master story space, see Bordwell, *Narration in the Fiction Film*, chap. 7, "Narration and Space," pp. 99–146.

I have used the opposition between scene and summary in my general definition of "narrative" in chapter 4. The above theories of time may be seen as offering particular elaborations of that opposition. Cf. also the notion of a summary with the "abstract" of a narrative schema (chapter 1) and with a "nonfocalized" level of narration (chapter 4). This illustrates that the problem of scene and summary must be solved within a theory of both declarative knowledge (i.e., story in a limited sense) and procedural knowledge (i.e., narration). The subtle interrelationships between types of knowledge and types of temporal representation may be posed in concrete terms by asking whether, or when, character narration qualifies as scene or summary.

21 Genette, *Narrative Discourse*, pp. 86–7 (his emphasis); see also pp. 94–5.

22 Bordwell, *Narration in the Fiction Film*, pp. 80–1; see also pp. 74–6. Cf. Lubomír Doležel's use of Russian formalism, "A Scheme of Narrative Time" in *Semiotics of Art: Prague School Contributions*, ed. by Ladislav Matejka and Irwin R. Titunik (Cambridge, Mass.: MIT Press, 1976), pp. 209–17.

Bordwell's notion that time and narration in film are "strictly governed" by aspects of the medium has its counterpart in literary theory despite Genette's claim. According to Shlomith Rimmon-Kenan:

The disposition of elements in the [literary] text, conventionally called text-time, is bound to be one-directional and irreversible, because language prescribes a linear figuration of signs and *hence* a linear presentation of information about things. We read letter after letter, word after word, sentence after sentence, chapter after chapter, and so on. . . . Text-time is thus inescapably linear, and therefore cannot correspond to the multilinearity of "real" story-time.

I have omitted a footnote in which Rimmon-Kenan offers some exceptions and qualifications to her claims about "text-time." What is implied by the exceptions, however, may be enough to swallow her doctrine. Perhaps we may "look at" word after word in a text in the way that a film projector apparently forces us to look at image after image, but it is far from clear that we "comprehend" the written text (or the film) in such a linear fashion. As Roman Jakobson notes: "The primacy of successivity in language has sometimes been misinterpreted as linearity. . . . [I]t is the linearity dogma which prompts its adherents . . . to overlook the hierarchical arrangement of any syntactic construction." I believe that many narrative theories also fail adequately to take into account hierarchies and dependencies with the result that their objects are rendered "too flat." Roman Jakobson, "Visual and Auditory Signs" in *Selected Writings*, vol. 2: Word and Language (The Hague: Mouton, 1971), p. 336. Shlomith Rimmon-Kenan, *Narrative Fiction: Contemporary Poetics* (New York: Methuen, 1983), p. 45 (my emphasis); see also pp. 119–20.

 The issue of linearity also raises questions about the normative status of "chronology" in narrative theories; see Meir Sternberg, "Telling in Time (I): Chronology and Narrative Theory," *Poetics Today*, vol. 11, no. 4 (Winter 1990), pp. 901–48.

23 See, e.g., Bordwell, *Narration in the Fiction Film*, pp. 49–53, 280, and chap. 12, "Parametric Narration," pp. 274–310. He states, "Film style may be organized and emphasized to a degree that makes it at least equal in importance to [plot] patterns" (p. 275). See also Kristin Thompson, *Breaking the Glass Armor: Neoformalist Film Analysis* (Princeton, N.J.: Princeton University Press, 1988), Part 6, "The Perceptual Challenges of Parametric Form," pp. 245–352.

24 Indeed one can locate within Genette's own comments a basis for extending the conventional nature of the dramatic forms of duration in literature to music and film. Genette compares the "canonical forms of tempo" in the novel with the "canonical movements" in music (andante, allegro, presto, etc.) (cf. pp. 86–7 – quoted in the text above – with pp. 94–5). Thus he seems to imply that absolute speed may no longer be the decisive criterion by which to measure effects of duration in music and film but rather relative speed becomes the criterion; that is, speed relative to particular speeds in each medium that have become conventional for certain forms of dramatic duration. The speed of the film projector, then, would be relevant to the quality of motion on the screen but would not strictly determine the experience of duration in the story world, or in film generally.

25 See note 3 in chapter 3 above.

26 Bordwell, *Narration in the Fiction Film*, p. 112 (his emphasis).

27 Gaudreault, "Narration and Monstration," p. 35 n. 19.

28 Robert T. Eberwein, "The Filmic Dream and Point of View," *Literature/ Film Quarterly*, vol. 8, no. 3 (1980), pp. 198–9 (Eberwein's emphases and capitalization).

29 Eberwein, "The Filmic Dream," pp. 199, 202.
30 Eberwein, "The Filmic Dream," pp. 200–1. Eberwein surveys psychoanalytic and physiological theories of dream and then sets forth his own theory in *Film & The Dream Screen: A Sleep and a Forgetting* (Princeton, N.J.: Princeton University Press, 1984). He asserts that

> Our relationship to the physical screen in the theater as we watch any film owes much to our experience as nurtured infants and to our earliest dreams. . . . The actual screen in the theater functions as a psychic prosthesis of our dream screen, a structure constituted by the mother's breast, or a surrogate for it, and by our own ego.
>
> (p. 192.)

For an extensive bibliography on film narrative as dream, see his book, pp. 221–37, and a special issue on "Dream & Film," *Dreamworks*, vol. 1, no. 1 (Spring 1980), pp. 88–93.
31 Stuart Marshall, "*Lady in the Lake*: Identification and the Drives," *Film Form*, vol. 1, no. 2 (Autumn 1977), pp. 39–43. Drawing on psychoanalytic theories of narrative, Noël Burch argues that because camera movements are made obtrusive and actors look into the lens, the spectator's primary and secondary identification with *Lady in the Lake* is fatally disrupted. Burch, *Life to those Shadows*, trans. and ed. by Ben Brewster (Berkeley: University of California Press, 1990), pp. 250–2, 254.
32 Marshall, "*Lady in the Lake*," pp. 44–9. According to Marshall, *Lady in the Lake* maintains the anxiety of the castration threat by promoting three different (and contradictory) views of female sexuality using a single character:

> The suggestion that Adrienne [the heroine] is somehow involved in the murder of Lavery [a man] redefines her sexuality as problematic. It suggests the definition of her desire as Oedipally male (desiring the death of the father) and hence as phallic, *or* for the destruction of the object of her desire (as castrating woman), *or* as a contradictory complicity in the Oedipal male child's [i.e., Phillip Marlowe's] hostile identification with the father in her desire to sustain the child as phallus (according to the symbolic equation) and so hold him in the Imaginary [a maternal] relation to her always short of the castration complex.
>
> (p. 49; my emphases.)

See generally, Dennis Turner, "Film Noir and the Apparatus of the Fetish: Introduction to 'Flickerings of Black and White,'" *Structuralist Review*, vol. 2, no. 3 (Spring 1984), pp. 34–43.
33 My statement of the descriptive aim of psychoanalysis derives from Plaus's quotation of Gill and Klein's formulation; F. Xavier Plaus, "Freudian Drive Theory and Epistemology" in *The Psychology of Knowing*, ed. by Joseph R. Royce and William W. Rozeboom (New York: Gordon & Breach, 1972), p. 413.
34 William Luhr, "Raymond Chandler and 'The Lady in the Lake,'" *Wide Angle*, vol. 6, no. 1 (1984), p. 30. The film is based on Chandler's 1943 novel which perhaps accounts for the fact that many writers incorrectly give the title of the film as "*The* Lady in the Lake."
35 Luhr, "Raymond Chandler," p. 33; see also p. 32.
36 On dream processes, see the concepts of condensation, displacement, representability, and secondary elaboration in J. Laplanche and J.-B. Pontalis,

The Language of Psycho-Analysis, trans. by Donald Nicholson-Smith (New York: W. W. Norton & Co., 1973), pp. 82–3, 121–4, 389–90, 412.

37 Both meanings of "communicant" seem relevant to me in discussing a communication theory of narrative: a person who communicates and a person who receives/shares in a communion.

38 On the processes of transference and counter-transference, see Laplanche and Pontalis, *The Language of Psycho-Analysis*, pp. 455–62, 92–3. For a succinct statement of how psychoanalysis might intersect a reception theory of narrative, see Ien Ang's commentary on Janice Radway's *Reading the Romance: Women, Patriarchy and Popular Literature*, "Feminist Desire and Female Pleasure," *Camera Obscura* 16 (Jan. 1988), pp. 178–91. Psychoanalysis, like other theories of narrative (based on plot, style, communication, or reception), has a social exchange value: on the relationship of history and psychoanalysis within select films, see part 3 of *Psychoanalysis & Cinema*, ed. by E. Ann Kaplan (New York: Routledge, 1990), pp. 110–80.

39 Dana Polan, *Power and Paranoia: History, Narrative, and the American Cinema, 1940–1950* (New York: Columbia University Press, 1986), pp. 12, 38–9; see also pp. 18–19, 32–3, 52, 56, 98–9.

40 Polan, *Power and Paranoia*, p. 12.

41 Polan, *Power and Paranoia*, pp. 105–7, 202, 209, 214–18. In the same spirit, Ien Ang contends ("Feminist Desire," p. 187):

> In [Janice] Radway's account [of romance novels], fantasy is too easily equated with the unreal, with the world of illusions, that is, false ideas about how life "really" is. . . . If, however, we were to take fantasy seriously as a reality in itself, as a necessary dimension of our psychical reality, we could conceptualize the world of fantasy as the place of excess, where the unimaginable can be imagined. Fiction could then be seen as the social materialization and elaboration of fantasies, and thus, in the words of Allison Light, "as the explorations and productions of desires which may be in excess of the socially possible or acceptable."

On excess, see note 4 in chapter 2 above. On fiction, see chapter 7.

42 See Polan, *Power and Paranoia*, pp. 209, 211–12, 224. Cf. pp. 193–6 where Polan analyzes the use of the POV shot in *Dark Passage*. Although Polan associates *Lady in the Lake* only with sadism, his example of film masochism would apply equally to the camera in *Lady in the Lake* which comes under regular assault.

43 Bill Nichols seeks to create a narrative theory by integrating theories of perception, style, psychoanalysis, and society in *Ideology and the Image: Social Representation in the Cinema and Other Media* (Bloomington: Indiana University Press, 1981); see, e.g., pp. 73–80. Will Wright, by combining Vladimir Propp's analysis of narrative with Claude Lévi-Strauss's analysis of myth, is able to match three types of plots in the Western genre with the social actions and beliefs characteristic of three types of economic institution: a market economy, planned economy, and corporate economy (p. 187). *Six Guns and Society: A Structural Study of the Western* (Berkeley: University of California Press, 1975), esp. chaps 2, 4, and 8.

44 J.P. Telotte, "The Detective as Dreamer: The Case of *The Lady in the Lake*," *The Journal of Popular Film and Television*, vol. 12, no. 1 (Spring 1984), p. 13 (my emphases); on the cultural dimension of dreaming, see also pp. 6, 8, 11, 12, 15.

45 Telotte, "The Detective as Dreamer," p. 9.

46 Roughly, the French phrase *mise-en-abyme* refers to the situation where an object is placed into an endless sequence of relationships with itself; for example, an object that is reflected in mirrors within mirrors indefinitely.

47 The argument of Telotte that I have outlined in the text may be found principally on pp. 8–12 of "The Detective as Dreamer." According to Telotte, Marlowe escapes the rigid frames by becoming a "chameleon" who undergoes an almost "protean shapeshifting." Significantly, Telotte's own shift from inanimate (door and frame) metaphors to an animate (chameleon) metaphor, signals the importance that he attaches to *a protagonist's reaction and change* within that mode of comprehension that I have identified as a narrative schema. If *Lady in the Lake* is a dream – either private or communal – it is one organized by Telotte in a most traditional and ahistorical manner.

48 Vivian Sobchack, *The Address of the Eye: A Phenomenology of Film Experience* (forthcoming, Princeton University Press; Sobchack's emphases).

49 See Bruce Kawin, *Mindscreen: Bergman, Godard, and First-Person Film* (Princeton, N.J.: Princeton University Press, 1978), pp. 8, 44, 190, and my discussion of this book in *Point of View*, Appendix, "Orthodox Theories of Narration," sect. 5, "From Literature to Film: Narration as Consciousness," pp. 216–21. As illustrated by Telotte's argument, a film's "frame" may also be personified. Elaborate examples may be found in Charles Affron, *Cinema and Sentiment* (Chicago: University of Chicago Press, 1982), chap. 2, "Thresholds of Feeling," pp. 24–52.

50 See generally my discussion of empiricist versus rationalist theories of narration in *Point of View*, pp. 168–71. For another statement of a holistic approach to film, consider the following:

> In the cinema, there is always present, in the positioning of the camera and the microphone(s), a consciousness that sees and (in the sound film) hears and that coexists with what is seen or heard. Even in the silent cinema, someone is always speaking and something is always spoken. In the sound cinema, we always see and hear events *through* images and sounds of them. The cinema remains the phenomenological art par excellence, wedding, if indeed not collapsing, consciousness with the world.
> (John Belton, "Technology and Aesthetics of Film Sound" in *Film Sound: Theory and Practice*, ed. by Elisabeth Weis and John Belton (New York: Columbia University Press, 1985), p. 71; Belton's emphasis.)

51 The tenor of my arguments in this book favours a modular organization of mental activity. For criticism of holistic theories of mind, see, e.g., Marvin Minsky, *The Society of Mind* (New York: Simon & Schuster, 1986).

52 See, e.g., Lubbock, *The Craft of Fiction*, pp. 85–90, 161–71; Branigan, *Point of View*, pp. 92, 120 n. 22.

53 Even if one considers only the explicit forms of narration in *Lady in the Lake*, one may wonder whether the sound track matches the internal focalization of the visual track. Marlowe's *voice* in the film (though no other sound) is recorded in a muffled way during the POV shots but recorded naturally for his direct speeches to the audience. The distortion of Marlowe's voice is designed to simulate the imperfect way an individual hears his or her own voice. If Marlowe were to offer an account of his experiences to us on this basis, it would amount to something like the following: "I saw her five feet away and she said . . . and then I heard myself reply. . . ." However, there are profound differences between sound and image which affect how we perceive and understand them. A muffled sound may not be the analogue

of an angle of view. Of the many false statements about sound offered by theorists, perhaps the most misleading is to say that sound and image have an equal status in film. See Edward Branigan, "Sound and Epistemology in Film" *The Journal of Aesthetics and Art Criticism*, vol. 47, no. 4 (Fall 1989), pp. 311–24.

54 See Gaylyn Studlar, "Masochism and the Perverse Pleasures of the Cinema," *Quarterly Review of Film Studies*, vol. 9, no. 4 (Fall 1984), pp. 267–82.

55 See generally Edward Branigan, "What Is a Camera?" in *Cinema Histories, Cinema Practices*, ed. by Patricia Mellencamp and Philip Rosen (Frederick, Md.: University Publications of America, 1984), pp. 87–107, and Bordwell, *Narration in the Fiction Film*, p. 119.

56 The concept of character is an important aspect of narrative that has not been treated in this book. See, e.g., Oswald Ducrot and Tzvetan Todorov, *Encyclopedic Dictionary of the Sciences of Language*, trans. by Catherine Porter (Baltimore: Johns Hopkins University Press, 1979), "Character," pp. 221–6; Wallace Martin, *Recent Theories of Narrative* (Ithaca, N.Y.: Cornell University Press, 1986), pp. 116–22; Uri Margolin, "Individuals in Narrative Worlds: An Ontological Perspective," *Poetics Today*, vol. 11, no. 4 (Winter 1990), pp. 843–71; Stephen Heath, "Film and System: Terms of Analysis," Part II, *Screen*, vol. 16, no. 2 (Summer 1975), pp. 102–7, and *Questions of Cinema* (New York: Macmillan, 1981), chap. 8, "Body, Voice," pp. 176–93; Richard Dyer, *Stars* (London: British Film Institute, 1979), esp. Part 3, "Stars as Signs," pp. 99–181; Robert Burgoyne, "The Interaction of Text and Semantic Deep Structure in the Production of Filmic Characters," *Iris*, vol. 4, no. 2 (1986), pp. 69–79; Rimmon-Kenan, *Narrative Fiction*, chap. 3, pp. 29–42; James Naremore, *Acting in the Cinema* (Berkeley: University of California Press, 1988); and a special issue of *New Literary History*, vol. 5, no. 2 (Winter 1974).

57 More fully quoted above at note 11 (my emphasis). Cf. also Chatman, *Coming to Terms*, p. 212 n. 10 (" 'Camera,' here and throughout, is synecdochic for the whole cinematic apparatus.").

58 Christian Metz, "The Imaginary Signifier" in *The Imaginary Signifier: Psychoanalysis and the Cinema*, trans. by Celia Britton, Annwyl Williams, Ben Brewster, and Alfred Guzzetti (Bloomington: Indiania University Press, 1982), p. 51.

59 On Ludwig Wittgenstein's notion of "knowing how to go on," see *Philosophical Investigations*, trans. by G.E.M. Anscombe (New York: Macmillan, 3rd edn 1958), sects 151 and 179, pp. 59–60, 72–3. I make use of this notion in defining narration as "knowing how" in chapter 3.

6 OBJECTIVITY AND UNCERTAINTY

1 The terminology I am using to describe discovered, delayed, and open variants of the POV shot derives from Edward Branigan, *Point of View in the Cinema: A Theory of Narration and Subjectivity in Classical Film* (New York and Berlin: Mouton, 1984), chap. 5, "The Point-of-view Shot," pp. 111, 113–14; and cf. p. 120 n. 13. This chapter, based on a 1975 article, has been reprinted with minor corrections in *Movies and Methods: An Anthology*, vol. II, ed. by Bill Nichols (Berkeley and Los Angeles: University of California Press, 1985), pp. 681, 683–4; and cf. p. 689 n. 13.

2 A shot of S in a POV structure (S, O) prior to a shot of what is seen by S performs at least the introductory function that a tag clause does for what

is spoken directly by a character in literary discourse: *"He said, '. . .'. "* Removing some of the special punctuation (e.g., quotation marks, dash lines, or paragraphing) as well as the tag clauses from a written dialogue produces a series of *free* direct speeches which require the reader to make additional inferences – because the tag clause narrations are now implicit – but does not alter the specificity of the speakers or their words any more than removing most of the shots of Marlowe in *Lady in the Lake* makes the spectator doubt who he is or whether he is the subject who sees.

Note that *non*verbal perceptions of a character may be represented in literary discourse in ways analogous to representing verbal thoughts: "From his peripheral vision, Manny saw the policemen coming closer, their shiny buttons pointing at him like eyes in the dark." The first six words introduce the character's visual perception and derive from a more powerful narration than the representing of the perception itself in words.

3 The very words used by Percy Lubbock in describing Flaubert's scenic narration in *Madame Bovary* betray the essential subjunctive conditional mood demanded by such (diegetic) narration:

> Sometimes he [Flaubert] seems to be describing what he has seen himself, places and people he has known, conversations he may have overheard; I do not mean that he is literally retailing [i.e., telling and retelling] an experience of his own, but that he writes *as though* he were. His description, in that case, touches only such matters as you or I *might have* perceived for ourselves, if we *had happened* to be on the spot at the moment. His object is to place the scene before us, so that we may take it in like a picture gradually unrolled or a drama enacted.
>
> (*The Craft of Fiction* (New York: Charles Scribner's Sons, 1921), p. 65, my emphases.)

As we will discover in chapter 7, various forms of implied diegetic narration are prominent in classical documentary films in order to suggest an invisible observation of "objective facts." Cf. Bill Nichols, "The Voice of Documentary" in *Movies and Methods*, vol. II, (1985), p. 262 (". . . moments of 'pure observation' capture the social presentation of self we too would have witnessed had we actually been there to see for ourselves"); "History, Myth, and Narrative in Documentary," *Film Quarterly*, vol. 41, no. 1 (Fall 1987), p. 11 ("what we see is what we would have seen had we been there").

4 See Nelson Goodman, *Fact, Fiction, and Forecast* (Cambridge, Mass.: Harvard University Press, 4th edn. 1983); A.J. Ayer, *Probability and Evidence* (New York: Macmillan, 1972), "The Problem of Conditionals," pp. 111–39. See generally Edward Branigan, *Point of View* pp. 229–30 n. 136.

5 I have modeled the description of these shots from *The Wrong Man* (in 4) on Wallace Martin's analysis of the opening sentence of Ernest Hemingway's story, "The Short Happy Life of Francis Macomber": "It was now lunch time and they were all sitting under the double green fly of the dining tent pretending that nothing had happened." *Recent Theories of Narrative* (Ithaca, N.Y.: Cornell University Press, 1986), pp. 136–7.

6 Käte Hamburger makes a distinction between the epic preterite and the historical present "tenses" even though as forms of narration they produce the same effect. The epic preterite combines a past tense or past progressive with an explicit or implicit present deictic; the historical present combines an explicit or implicit past deictic with a present tense or present progressive. Strictly speaking, neither one is a tense. I will use "historical present" to refer to both forms.

7 The paradox of the historical present tense may be extended to the representation of space in a film. André Bazin likens film to the Egyptian practice of embalming the dead and to the preservation of the bodies of insects intact in pieces of amber. In a similar fashion, Roland Barthes concludes that a photograph shows "that-has-been," eliciting from the spectator: "I also will-have-been (will die)." This notion of a past space preserved and threatening our future, co-exists with an impression that space in film is ever-present, filled with motion, capable of being summoned again and again to happen in our present. The result is that, phenomenologically, our experience of space in film appears shifted forward in time compressing "there" with "here." André Bazin, "The Ontology of the Photographic Image" in *What Is Cinema?*, vol. I, trans. by Hugh Gray (Berkeley: University of California Press, 1967), pp. 9–16. Roland Barthes, *Camera Lucida: Reflections on Photography*, trans. by Richard Howard (New York: Hill & Wang, 1981), pp. 31–2, 85–100. See also Garrett Stewart, "Photo-gravure: Death, Photography, and Film Narrative," *Wide Angle*, vol. 9, no. 1 (1987), pp. 11–31.

8 Peter Brooks describes the historical present tense as follows: "If the past is to be read as present, it is a curious present that we know to be past in relation to a future we know to be already in place, already in wait for us to reach it." It is my belief that what we "already must know" in order to interpret time as the historical present can be analyzed in terms of a narrative schema and of a hierarchy of levels of narration. Peter Brooks, *Reading for the Plot: Design and Intention in Narrative* (New York: Alfred A. Knopf, 1984), p. 23; cf. p. 34.

The voice-over narration of *Sans Soleil* – discussed in more detail in the next chapter – occasionally makes explicit the complex time of viewing film images as (historically) present. Consider the various tense shifts in the following excerpt (my emphases):

> My personal problem was more specific: how to film the ladies of Bissau? Apparently, the magical function of the eye was working against me there. It was in the market places of Bissau and Cape Verde that I could stare at them again with equality. [We see a particular woman reacting to the camera.] I *see* her. She *saw* me. She knows that I see her. She drops me her glance, but just at an angle where it is still possible to act as though it was not addressed to me – and at the end, the real glance, straight forward, that lasted a twenty-fourth of a second, the length of a film frame.

The concept of a historical present tense is one way of interpreting the "illusion of occurrence" under which a perceiver understands narrative data. See my general definition of narrative in chapter 4. One way in which film semiotics has addressed the question of the historical present is by utilizing Emile Benveniste's linguistic distinction between *histoire* and *discours*. See, e.g., Christian Metz, "Story/Discourse (A Note on Two Kinds of Voyeurism)" in *The Imaginary Signifier: Psychoanalysis and the Cinema*, trans. by Celia Britton, Annwyl Williams, Ben Brewster, and Alfred Guzzetti (Bloomington: Indiana University Press, 1982), pp. 91–8.

9 Meir Sternberg, *Expositional Modes and Temporal Ordering in Fiction* (Baltimore: Johns Hopkins University Press, 1978), chap. 5, pp. 129–58.

10 Arthur C. Danto, *Narration and Knowledge* (including the integral text of *Analytical Philosophy of History*; New York: Columbia University Press, 1985), p. xii; see esp. chaps 8 and 15, "Narrative Sentences" and "Narration and

Knowledge," pp. 143–81, 342–63. My example of a historical fact is from p. xii; cf. pp. 345–7.

11 See Käte Hamburger, *The Logic of Literature*, trans. by Marilynn J. Rose (Bloomington: Indiana University Press, 2nd rev. edn 1973; first published in 1957), pp. 55–134. On the historical present tense, the "narrative imperfect" tense, and the uses of the perfective/imperfective contrast in narrative verbs, see esp. Suzanne Fleischman, *Tense and Narrativity: From Medieval Performance to Modern Fiction* (Austin: University of Texas Press, 1990).

12 It is true that my account of fiction in chapter 7 and of objective narration in the present chapter emphasizes indefinite reference as a feature shared by both fiction and narrative. Also, aspects of both fiction and narration may be analyzed with counterfactual conditionals. Moreover, establishing the "facts" in a nonfiction film seems to be related to certain "objective" narrations that attempt to establish the "facts" in a "story" world. Nevertheless, fiction and narrative as two ongoing cognitive processes should be kept distinct.

Narration involves many variables other than its degree of indefiniteness (e.g., its degree of explicitness or implicitness; its regulation of character knowledge; its creation of space; its judgmental tone). There are also many temporal schemes and levels of narration other than the complex time of the historical present of (implicit and indefinite) diegetic narration (which is only one form of "objectivity"). Some of these other types of narration (e.g., a credit sequence, first-person voice-over, character dialogue, point-of-view shot) refer in more straightforward ways, or at least in different ways, than implied diegetic narration, and they play a vital role in our comprehension of stories.

Fiction, for its part, includes problems not associated with narration. In general, fiction addresses a more global issue: how is the perceiver able to connect a given pattern of data to the world; how is he or she to discover a specific link between narrative data and some other semantic field of experience outside of the artifact, i.e. outside our immediate perception of the artifact.

13 On various types of complex internal focalization in film, see, e.g., Maureen Turim, *Flashbacks in Film: Memory & History* (New York: Routledge, 1989); Jeffrey S. Rush, " 'Lyric Oneness': The Free Syntactical Indirect and the Boundary Between Narrative and Narration," *Wide Angle*, vol. 8, nos. 3/4 (1986), pp. 27–33; David Alan Black, "Genette and Film: Narrative Level in the Fiction Cinema," ibid., pp. 19–26; Branigan, *Point of View*, chap. 6, "Character Reflection and Projection," pp. 122–42.

14 Note that summary and scene may be rendered by either first-person or third-person narration. Although Bruce Kawin develops an ingenious typology of film narrations based on the grammatical distinctions between first-person, second-person, and third-person pronouns, the many refinements that he is forced to add to the typology demonstrate that his linguistic categories become metaphorical when applied rigorously to film. "An Outline of Film Voices," *Film Quarterly*, vol. 38, no. 2 (Winter 1984–5), pp. 38–46. Perhaps sentences and pictures should be analyzed as special cases of a more fundamental paradigm.

15 According to Wallace Martin, Ann Banfield's analysis of free indirect discourse shows that in it

consciousness and the self are . . . cut loose from 'I,' and we as readers are allowed to experience something we cannot otherwise experience in this world: subjectivity freed from its connection with our own bodies and voices. The emergence of fiction in the seventeenth century, Banfield implies, may be connected to new ways of conceiving the self.

(Martin, Recent Theories of Narrative, p. 141.)

Cf. Banfield, Unspeakable Sentences: Narration and Representation in the Language of Fiction (London: Routledge & Kegan Paul, 1982). The freeing of a subjectivity from its physical connections would seem to be a routine effect of narrative film and goes far towards explaining why narrative film established an early dominance over competing forms of filmmaking.

16 Ann Banfield argues that free indirect discourse cannot be derived from direct discourse and that its unique grammatical features prohibit its being used as a "communicative" act.

17 I have discussed anthropomorphism in the contexts of a narrative schema, Metz's conception of an implied author, and Bordwell's critique of communication models of narrative. See pp. 16, 92 and 109 above. Cf. the holistic theories of Telotte, Sobchack, and Kawin discussed in the previous chapter.

18 See David Bordwell, Narration in the Fiction Film (Madison: University of Wisconsin Press, 1985), pp. 9–12, 66, 161–2, passim; Branigan, Point of View, pp. 122, 136, 158, 197, 203, 208–9. Bordwell argues that the invisible observer is an effect created by the overall construction of some films and that even when present it depends on the operation of still more powerful narrations which, for example, arrange the mise-en-scène for optimal viewing by the spectator.

19 My description of one of the conventions of invisible observation is taken from my essay, "Diegesis and Authorship in Film," Iris 7, vol. 4, no. 2 (1986), n. 16. Cf. the qualities associated with a "degree zero narratee" in literary discourse; Susan Sniader Lanser, The Narrative Act: Point of View in Prose Fiction (Princeton, N.J.: Princeton University Press, 1981), pp. 180–2. Cf. also the implicit "canonical person" which is the basis for many everyday metaphors; George Lakoff and Mark Johnson, Metaphors We Live By (Chicago: University of Chicago Press, 1980), p. 132, passim.

Documentary films also create types of invisible observer. See note 3 above and Dai Vaughn, "The Space Between Shots" in Movies and Methods, vol. II, ed. by Bill Nichols, p. 710. Vaughn quite rightly dismisses the idea that invisible observers provide a definition of the "objectivity" of documentary film. I do not believe, however, that this means that such a convention of narration could not exist within a matrix of other narrations operating within a particular documentary film.

20 When we characterize our experience of a scene in terms of a feeling of moving instantaneously through space, we mean that the time of the representing of the scene is not the represented time of the scene itself. In order to talk about the time of the representing of the scene – the time of the "instantaneous" cuts – in relation to an ongoing scenic time, one is forced into such aberrant locutions as positing a camera "movement" that occurs "between the shots." This illustrates that we normally think of a scene by assigning what is explicit to the "present," leaving undefined both the past (which includes the time when the film was made) and the future (which includes the time when the significance of the scene will be known). Both of these times, however, past and future, already exist in the present of the narrative and exert an influence on our interpretation; cf. the historical present tense. Complex time means that the concept of film editing will be complex; cf. note 54 below.

21 The spectator may have a stake in deferring an emotional response by displacing his or her desires, participation, and complicity in the events of the text onto a hypothetical observer – a fantasmatic Other. This is made possible because the spectator is seemingly both present at the scene and absent from it. Such "invisible observation" may point toward basic properties of the cinematic apparatus and its engagement with a spectator. For psychoanalysis, presence and absence is exactly the sort of contradiction which exists in the "unconscious" region of thought; indeed, contradictory states existing side by side constitute the unconscious.

Some psychoanalytic elaborations of invisible observation in film may be found in the following: Alan Williams, "Is Sound Recording Like a Language?," *Yale French Studies* 60 (1980), esp. pp. 55–61; Mary Ann Doane, "The Voice in the Cinema: The Articulation of Body and Space," ibid., esp. pp. 33–7; Daniel Dayan (with Brian Henderson), "The Tutor Code of Classical Cinema," *Film Quarterly*, vol. 28, no. 1 (Fall 1974), pp. 22–31; Metz, "The Imaginary Signifier" and "Story/Discourse (A Note on Two Kinds of Voyeurism)" in *The Imaginary Signifier*, e.g, sect. 3, "Identification, Mirror," pp. 42–57.

22 Martin, *Recent Theories of Narrative*, p. 142; Branigan, *Point of View*, pp. 171–3, 180–4.

23 Douglas Sirk's *Written on the Wind* (1956) opens with this sort of objective flashback except that a character has fainted in the room prior to the flashback and the past begins with that character looking at the same calendar in a different locale. Thus the film suggests continuities in character and action but without revealing motivations or causation. The problem for the spectator is to discover the relevant continuities.

24 Bruce Kawin, *Mindscreen: Bergman, Godard, and First-Person Film* (Princeton, N.J.: Princeton University Press, 1978), p. 29.

25 Seymour Chatman, "Narration and Point of View in Fiction and the Cinema," *Poetica*, 1 (1974), pp. 43–4 (objective); Kawin, *Mindscreen*, pp. 30, 33–4, 42, 44 (subjective).

26 Leonard Leff, "Reading *Kane*," *Film Quarterly*, vol. 39, no. 1 (Fall 1985), pp. 10–20; Frank P. Tomasulo, "Narrate *and* Describe? Point of View and Narrative Voice in *Citizen Kane*'s Thatcher Sequence," *Wide Angle*, vol. 8, nos. 3/4 (1986), pp. 45–52.

27 The separation of the sound of Lee Marvin's footsteps from his movements may also be interpreted in a more powerful, non-psychological way as part of a rhetoric of "anticipatory caution": unknown to us and to Marvin, he is not really in control of his actions, but instead is being driven forward on a secret quest by the ambitions of another character. Since the ending of the story is being kept as a surprise, our interpretation of Marvin's walking is more likely to be affected by his name in the film – Walker – than by the idea that he is merely an instrument and his awareness is irrelevant. This example from *Point Blank* illustrates how the technical features of film ebb and flow in importance, and may work at cross-purposes under the pressure of narrative comprehension. That is, the "same" material may be organized in many ways by top-down processing, and yet be reorganized at a later time to be perceived anew.

28 The status of these words is not clear. Except for the introductory exclamation, "Oh," we heard Lisa utter these same words a few moments earlier in the film at the conclusion of her letter. However, the line is now spoken differently by her, in a deeper whisper. Are the words, then, to be attributed

somehow to Stefan, or to Lisa at an unspecified, later time (after she stops writing)? As we shall see, this is merely one example of a more general, perplexing uncertainty in the film about what is "objective."

29 For Robert Chamblee the "emphasis" of the film is on Lisa's consciousness and "what is represented is represented largely in terms of the way Lisa describes it. . . . [W]hat we know of Stefan is mediated by Lisa" (p. 160). Chamblee argues that it is conventional for the spectator of a film to hear a letter "read by the writer rather than by the person receiving the letter." Moreover, the words that the spectator hears were spoken "at the time the letter was written" (p. 163 n. 6; Chamblee's underlining). See "Max Ophuls' Viennese Trilogy: Communications Styles and Structures" (Ph.D. diss.: New York University, 1981), pp. 160, 162–4, 169, 191.

30 See George M. Wilson, *Narration in Light: Studies in Cinematic Point of View* (Baltimore: Johns Hopkins University Press, 1986), p. 123 (the film's "theatricality defines [Lisa's] unconscious self-dramatization"). See also note 59 below.

31 Kaja Silverman asserts that "Lisa's narration is obedient to Stephan's [sic] desires, to his ear" and that "her voice is his mental construction." She concludes, "In the same way, what we see is what he imagines." "Dis-Embodying the Female Voice" in *Re-Vision: Essays in Feminist Film Criticism*, ed. by Mary Ann Doane, Patricia Mellencamp, and Linda Williams (The American Film Institute Monograph Series vol. 3, Frederick, Md.: University Publications of America, 1984), p. 136. See also Silverman's *The Acoustic Mirror: The Female Voice in Psychoanalysis and Cinema* (Bloomington: Indiana University Press, 1988), p. 58 (Lisa's "voice exists only in and through Stefan's consciousness.").

32 Britta Sjogren opposes the views of both Silverman and Modleski, and argues that Lisa's letter triggers an "interior bi-logue" between Lisa and Stefan:

> He "listens" . . . to what is written; we understand this as spectators to be his imagining of the source of the words, as his fantasm, and also, simultaneously, as her voice-off speaking directly to him. Thus, it is both his voice and her voice. . . . Stefan does not speak, he receives the voice, desires it, and in this sense, "speaks" with it as it "inhabits" his image.

Sjogren also argues that the shot of Lisa writing her letter belongs neither to the letter nor to Stefan with the result that "Lisa's voice, here, seems equally the voice *as Stefan imagines it in reading* and that *of her writing, imagining him reading*." "Sustaining Difference: The Female Voice-Off in *Letter from an Unknown Woman*" (Los Angeles: University of California, unpublished paper, 1990), pp. 4–5, 7 (Sjogren's emphases; footnote omitted).

33 Karel Reisz, "Ophuls and *La Ronde*," *Sequence* (Jan. 1952), p. 34.

34 See Michael Walker, "Ophuls in Hollywood," *Movie* nos. 29/30 (Summer 1982), p. 48 ("It's as if, in order to fulfil her fantasy, Lisa wishes Stefan to die, too."); V.F. Perkins, "*Letter from an Unknown Woman*," *Movie* nos. 29/30 (Summer 1982), p. 71 (Lisa's letter "is pointless except as an invitation to suicide, persuading Stefan to let death prove what life could not.").

35 See Alan Larson Williams, *Max Ophuls and the Cinema of Desire: Style and Spectacle in Four Films, 1948–1955* (New York: Arno Press, 1980), pp. 47–55, 58; p. 159 (Lisa "seduces" Stefan "into thinking he seduces her").

36 Douglas McVay believes that Stefan's "guilt-ridden desire to make atonement" causes him to view the duel with Johann as the "perfect means of

quixotically suicidal expiation." *"Letter from an Unknown Woman,"* Focus on Film 35 (April 1980), p. 28.

37 See Claudia Gorbman, *Unheard Melodies: Narrative Film Music* (Bloomington: Indiana University Press, 1987), p. 151 (Lisa "is 'tricked' by a decadent womanizer"); Barry Salt, *Film Style and Technology: History and Analysis* (London: Starword, 1983), chap. 19, "Stylistic Analysis of the Films of Max Ophuls," p. 370 (the tragedy is the result of Lisa's "perversity" and Stefan's "shallowness"); Roger Greenspun, "Corrections: Roger Greenspun on *Letter from an Unknown Woman,"* Film Comment, vol. 11, no. 1 (Jan.–Feb. 1975), p. 91 ("The duel her letter forces upon him is no more than just recompense for a lifetime of seducing other men's wives.").

38 Molly Haskell, *From Reverence to Rape: The Treatment of Women in the Movies* (Chicago: University of Chicago Press, 2nd edn 1987), p. 186 (Ophuls "captures the inner movement of the soul in its rare, solitary passage to tragedy and grace.").

39 See Norman Hale, *"Letter from an Unknown Woman*: The Dance of Time and Space," Cinemonkey, vol. 5, no. 16 (Winter 1979), p. 14 (Lisa and Stefan are "hostage to events contrived by a mysterious agent of fate. No one is to blame."). For Hale, the depictions of Lisa's subjectivity are essentially objective renderings of her world and fate. For example, her memory of Stefan bringing her home to his apartment is shown to us through "the omniscient eye" that is located above her on the staircase. Hale goes even further by arguing that subjective "memory" becomes the one objective "value" within the "futility and emptiness" of Ophuls's world: "To be able to remember is to escape the tyranny of time" (p. 14).

40 Tony Pipolo, "The Aptness of Terminology: Point of View, Consciousness and *Letter from an Unknown Woman,"* Film Reader 4 (1979), pp. 169, 172. But cf. Lucy Fischer's interpretation of the close correspondence between Lisa and some of the camera movements in the film: "The tracking shot is so omnipresent, so tied to her (in its anthropomorphic fluctuations), that we almost feel it her companion – a dream lover that stands in Stefan's place." *Shot/Countershot: Film Tradition and Women's Cinema* (Princeton, N.J.: Princeton University Press, 1989), p. 101; cf. p. 107.

41 Pipolo, "The Aptness of Terminology," p. 171.

42 Wilson, *Narration in Light*, pp. 104, 106, 108, 120–1, 124. According to Wilson, "If the central personages are hopelessly blind in different ways to one another, the film, through its construction and its style, continuously affirms the possibility of a wider and more accurate perception of the human affairs that it portrays. Again and again, the film establishes a larger viewpoint which its characters do not attain" (p. 105).

Similarly, Robin Wood argues that "Ophuls's camera-work achieves a perfect balance – in terms of the spectator's involvement – between sympathy and detachment" by maintaining a "pervasive tension between subjective narrative and objective presentation." *Personal Views: Explorations in Film* (London: Gordon Fraser, 1976), pp. 126–7.

Wilson believes that the representation of Lisa's subjectivity resides primarily in her spoken *words* not in her thoughts or mental images. Since he also believes that the shots of a film must always reveal "far more information" that what is being said (because showing exceeds telling?), he concludes that there must exist a narration which acts *independently* of Lisa and Stefan (pp. 105–6). These claims plainly illustrate the close relations among film theory, narratology, and criticism.

43 Chapter 2 (see p. 45) emphasized that because of the crucial importance of top-down cognitive processes, physical continuity (ordering) on the screen is neither a necessary nor a sufficient condition for a spectator's perception of spatial, temporal, or causal continuity in the narrative. The scene described in the text has continuous nondiegetic music but no voice-over. Another significant cheat cut occurs later when Stefan first notices the 18-year-old Lisa as she waits in the snow near his apartment. He begins walking toward her. A match on action covers a large gap in space when we see Lisa in the background from over his shoulder as he draws near her.

44 Stephen Heath asserts that *Letter from an Unknown Woman* is about the problem of seeing and knowing, and the relationship of women to looking and being looked at; "The Question Oshima" in *Ophuls*, ed. by Paul Willemen (London: British Film Institute, 1978), p. 77, and "Postscript," pp. 85–7. See also Paul Willemen, "The Ophuls Text: A Thesis," ibid., pp. 71–2. E. Ann Kaplan argues that "men do not simply look: their gaze carries with it the power of action and of possession which is lacking in the female gaze. Women receive and return a gaze, but cannot act upon it." *Women and Film: Both Sides of the Camera* (New York: Routledge, 1983), p. 31. See generally Linda Williams, "When the Woman Looks" in *Re-Vision*, pp. 83–99. Lisa not only must deny having seen certain sights, but also deny having heard certain sounds: she eavesdrops on Stefan's music from the courtyard during the day and from the hall at night by opening a transom above his door.

45 The camera position on the staircase articulates knowledge in a way similar to camera position 3B in figure 14, p. 68.

46 Wilson, *Narration in Light*, pp. 103–4.

47 Pipolo, "The Aptness of Terminology," p. 173 (my emphasis); p. 178.

Inez Hedges apparently argues for an interpretation that is a compromise between Wilson and Pipolo. She claims that in the second staircase shot

> the perspective of the third-person camera narrator and the character are fused as the spectator realizes that Lisa's alter ego also watches from that position, triumphing in her success. Yet, although able on the one hand to identify with Lisa's happiness, the spectator also identifies with the third-person narrator and knows that she is no different from the others, as far as [Stefan] is concerned.
>
> (*Breaking the Frame: Film Language and the Experience of Limits* (Bloomington: Indiana University Press, 1991), p. 73 (fn. omitted).)

48 Pipolo, "The Aptness of Terminology," p. 175; cf. pp. 174, 176. Critics have also interpreted repetition in the film generically as tied to certain psychic states (e.g., romantic melodrama and conversion hysteria) and thematically as a sort of powerful, abstract narration which mimics the working of "destiny," or "fate." On the latter, see, e.g., Wood, *Personal Views*, pp. 130–2; on the former, see, e.g., Walker, "Ophuls in Hollywood"; Haskell, *Reverence to Rape*; Williams, *Max Ophuls*; and Tania Modleski, "Time and Desire in the Woman's Film," *Cinema Journal*, vol. 23, no. 3 (Spring 1984), esp. pp. 20–3. Stanley Cavell argues that the film belongs to a particular genre that dramatizes gender asymmetry in terms of women having a different relationship than men to skepticism and doubt (in the philosophical sense). "Psychoanalysis and Cinema: The Melodrama of the Unknown Woman" in *Images in Our Souls: Cavell, Psychoanalysis, and Cinema*, ed. by Joseph H. Smith and William Kerrigan (Baltimore: Johns Hopkins University Press, 1987), pp. 29–31, 34–6, 40.

Virginia Wright Wexman finds a connection between stylistic repetitions and the political situation of Max Ophuls; "The Transfiguration of History: Ophuls, Vienna, and *Letter from an Unknown Woman*" in *Letter from an Unknown Woman*, ed. by Virginia Wright Wexman with Karen Hollinger (New Brunswick, N.J.: Rutgers University Press, 1986), pp. 11–12, 14. This book includes the continuity script as well as essays on the film and a bibliography.

49 The seven shots of Stefan at the piano were shot by Ophuls during postproduction and added to the film apparently over his objection. There were other instances of studio interference with the film resulting in several much-discussed, and admired, shots (e.g., the shots of Stefan in the audience at the opera; see note 50 below). Ophuls did, however, direct all of the shots of the film and thus had the opportunity to attempt to integrate the various materials. Even so, it should be remembered that analyzing the interactions of spectator and text cannot be reduced to analyzing the explicit "intentions" of Ophuls or other persons involved in the production. See generally Lutz Bacher's extraordinarily detailed account of the production of the film, "Max Ophuls's Universal-International Films: The Impact of Production Circumstances on a Visual Style" (Detroit, Mich.: Ph.D. diss.: Wayne State University, 1984). On the shots of Stefan at the piano, see pp. 428, 651.

50 Placing a detail shot first in a sequence marks its importance in advance; usually, however, in classical narrative a detail shot is placed later in a sequence after a context has been gradually developed that defines the significance of the detail. Hence, the more usual sequence opens with an establishing shot.

There is one extraordinary sequence in the film, however, in which Ophuls does not unequivocally locate a character in space. When Stefan notices the older Lisa at the opera ten years after their last meeting, he senses that he may know her. However, his position in the theater, and consequently the significance of his glances, is not clearly specified with respect to Lisa. We hear her say in voice-over: "Suddenly in that one moment everything was in danger, everything I thought was safe. Somewhere out there were your eyes and I knew I couldn't escape them."

51 The link between Lisa's growing awareness of her sexuality and Stefan's hands is also made explicit in the dialogue. Lisa's girlfriend complains to Lisa, but with animated delight, about a boy that the girlfriend knows: "I'm going to have to do something about him if he doesn't keep his hands to himself. The things he does and right out in the street." Lisa then looks up at Stefan's window and we cut to a long shot of Stefan at the piano (set-up 3), then to a low angle close-up of Stefan's hands (fig. 51; set-up 1*), then back to him at the piano (repeat of set-up 3) before returning to Lisa in the courtyard.

52 A question arises: are these camera movements that self-consciously frame and reframe the adolescent Lisa on the swing through a V-shaped fork of a tree to be attributed only to the older Lisa's self-consciousness in writing the letter, or are they evidence of other narrations at work in the film?

53 Strictly speaking, placing the low angle close-up of Stefan's hands as he plays the piano in the courtyard scene (fig. 51; set-up 1*) together with the high-angle medium close-up of Lisa's face as she watches Stefan playing the piano in the dance hall scene (fig. 53) does not create the type of discovered and delayed POV structure discussed earlier in this chapter ($O, X_1, \ldots X_n, S$). The reason is that the second shot here portrays a different space and

Lisa is three years older. However, the articulation does not go so far as to become a discovered and open POV (O . . . [S]) since we have no doubt that two of the three "Lisas" (the 15–year-old, the 18-year-old, and the dying Lisa) are involved in closely related actions in each of the two shots. Hence I will refer to this type of juxtaposition as a hyperdiegetic, discovered, and delayed POV.

Another way to describe this anomalous POV shot in *Letter from an Unknown Woman* is as a hypothetical point-of-view of the 15-year-old Lisa that is actualized three years later by Lisa in a similar situation, though the spectator does not see the actualization. Thus what the spectator first sees and what can only be imagined by the character is later transformed into what the character sees and what can only be imagined by the spectator. Note that this description of Lisa's delayed POV as a hypothetical POV is not equivalent to the description of it that I offered above as a hyperdiegetic POV. The second description is primarily restricted to a diegetic frame of reference while the first takes into account some nondiegetic factors.

Fred Camper contends, "On several occasions during the film, Ophuls takes the camera to a place which would make a fine point-of-view shot, except that there is no one there watching the action." "Distance and Style: The Visual Rhetoric of Max Ophuls: *Letter from an Unknown Woman*," *Monogram* 5 (1974), p. 24. On the variants of the delayed point-of-view shot, see Branigan, *Point of View*, pp. 112–14. I am indebted to Stephen Heath for calling to my attention in 1977 this example of a delayed POV.

54 On "decontraction" generally, see Geoffrey H. Hartman, "The Voice of the Shuttle: Language from the Point of View of Literature" in *Beyond Formalism: Literary Essays 1958–1970* (New Haven: Yale University Press, 1970), pp. 343–4. With the notion of decontraction, and related concepts like the hyperdiegetic, one glimpses a definition of film *editing* that does not simply rely on local, surface juxtapositions but rather utilizes top-down and procedural aspects of our comprehension to address a spectator's ability to recognize new sequences by taking elements out of sequence (creating, and subject to, complex time schemes). Cf. note 20 above.

55 Jacques Aumont, "The Point of View," trans. by Arthur Denner, *Quarterly Review of Film and Video*, vol. 11, no. 2 (1989), pp. 15–16. Aumont's numbering of the shots in the opening of *The 39 Steps* is inaccurate. The hyperdiegetic narration of shots 14 and 22 in my analysis corresponds to shots 23 and 31 in Aumont's scheme.

I have selected the name hyperdiegetic in part to suggest cognitive affinities with the operation of a hypertext data base. Note that the hyperdiegetic in which dispersed images are reconvened is a figure of narration and is not a "connotation." Compare the notion of "hyper-restriction" in note 32 in chapter 4 above. Garrett Stewart has raised with me the possible theoretical connections between the hyperdiegetic and Saussure's work on the anagram, along with related work by Derrida, Riffaterre, and others. See generally Stewart's *Reading Voices: Literature and the Phonotext* (Berkeley: University of California Press, 1990).

56 Modleski, "Time and Desire," p. 20.

57 Modleski, "Time and Desire," p. 24; see also p. 29.

58 Modleski, "Time and Desire," p. 25.

59 See the discussion in chapters 4 and 5 of a type of narrative theory that is premised on a theory of the human drives. On the relationship of Oedipal logic and narrative, see, e.g., Teresa de Lauretis, *Alice Doesn't: Feminism,*

Semiotics, Cinema (Bloomington: Indiana University Press, 1984), chap. 5, "Desire in Narrative," pp. 103–57; Teresa de Lauretis, *Technologies of Gender: Essays on Theory, Film, and Fiction* (Bloomington: Indiana University Press, 1987), chap. 7, "Strategies of Coherence: Narrative Cinema, Feminist Poetics, and Yvonne Rainer," pp. 107–26; Mary Ann Doane, *The Desire to Desire: The Woman's Film of the 1940s* (Bloomington: Indiana University Press, 1987), chap. 1, "The Desire to Desire," pp. 1–37; Laura Mulvey, *Visual and Other Pleasures* (Bloomington: Indiana University Press, 1989), chaps 14 and 15; and a special issue devoted to the female spectator, *Camera Obscura*, nos 20–1 (1990). See generally Susan Winnett, "Coming Unstrung: Women, Men, Narrative, and Principles of Pleasure," *PMLA*, vol. 105, no. 3 (May 1990), pp. 505–18; Roland Barthes, *The Pleasure of the Text*, trans. by Richard Miller (New York: Hill & Wang, 1975), pp. 10, 47.

Lucy Fischer applies De Lauretis's interpretation of Oedipal logic to *Letter from an Unknown Woman*:

> At the moment of Stefan's comprehension of the *dual* nature of his attraction to women (lover as mother/mother as lover), he faces a *duel* (a challenge of phallic swords) with an elderly opponent worthy of his infantile hostility and fear [i.e., his Father].
>
> (Fischer, *Shot/Counter Shot*, p. 106, (Fischer's emphases.) See also pp. 104–5, 107, 110.)

Two ingenious accounts of the psychosocial dimensions of *Letter from an Unknown Woman* begin with the premise that Lisa's Other is her (dead) father and, in general, the Father(s) of patriarchy (e.g., her stepfather, and her husband Johann). See Howard Davis, "Form and the Function of the Father: An Alternative Analysis of Max Ophuls' *Letter from an Unknown Woman*" (Los Angeles: University of California, Master of Arts thesis, 1983), and "The Unconscious Subject in *Letter from an Unknown Woman*" (Los Angeles: University of California, unpublished paper, 1984); Donna S. Cunningham, "Dear Dad: A Daughter's Discourse in *Letter from an Unknown Woman*" (Los Angeles: University of Southern California, unpublished paper, 1989).

60 Wood, *Personal Views*, pp. 129–30 (Wood's emphases). In a perceptive close analysis of the importance of style to narrative comprehension in the two Linz scenes, V.F. Perkins, *"Letter from an Unknown Woman,"* shows how Ophuls carefully balances Lisa's destructiveness with her nobility. Compare the following assertions:

> Lisa's devotion here [to Stefan] is every bit as murderous as her husband's.
>
> (p. 71)
>
> Lisa never sees, never approaches the insight, that her predicament is related to the definitions and constraints that her society imposes on womanhood. Instead she rationalises her servitude and naturalises her passivity through her submission to Fate.
>
> (p. 72)

Cf. pp. 65–6 on servitude and "alienated" labor in Lisa's society.

7   FICTION

1 On the distinction between understanding and belief, see, e.g., Michael Dummett, "Frege: Sense and Reference" in *Philosophy Through Its Past*, ed. by Ted Honderich (New York: Penguin, 1984), p. 447. For related distinc-

tions, see Nelson Goodman and Catherine Z. Elgin, *Reconceptions in Philo-sophy and Other Arts and Sciences* (Indianapolis: Hackett, 1988), chap. 10, pp. 153–66. Goodman and Elgin argue that much broader notions of truth, certainty, and knowledge (namely, rightness, adoption, and understanding) are necessary if one is to evaluate how verbal and nonverbal symbols create worlds in all the fields of cognition.

2 For example, a text may be interpreted fictionally on a small scale but nonfictionally at a larger scale. This situation occurs in the sciences when "thought" experiments are proposed or counterfactual conditionals are used to state physical laws. In the legal system, "fictions" are used to implement judicial policies and to acknowledge social truths, a social consensus. See, e.g., the concepts of "fiction of law," "legal fiction," and "constructive" in Henry Campbell Black, *Black's Law Dictionary* (St. Paul, Minn.: West Publish-ing, 5th edn 1979). (A fiction of law is an "assumption or supposition of law that something which is or may be false is true, or that a state of facts exists which has never really taken place.") The legal system is also careful to protect certain commonly recognized fictions, such as political satire, precisely because they may be "true." Moreover, something which is liter-ally, and even figuratively, *false* and which causes great harm may neverthe-less escape a defamation suit because of social policy (e.g., under the First Amendment).

3 According to D.W. Harding, "The ends achieved by fiction and drama are not fundamentally different from those of a great deal of gossip and everyday [nonfictional] narrative." "Psychological Processes in the Reading of Fic-tion," *The British Journal of Aesthetics*, vol. 2, no. 2 (April 1962), p. 138.

4 See, e.g., *Realism and the Cinema: A Reader*, ed. by Christopher Williams (London: Routledge & Kegan Paul, 1980); Colin MacCabe, *Tracking the Signi-fier: Theoretical Essays: Film, Linguistics, Literature* (Minneapolis: University of Minnesota Press, 1985), esp. pp. 59–69, 140–9. An exception is Christian Metz who explicitly considers the problem of fiction and belief in "The Imaginary Signifier" in *The Imaginary Signifier: Psychoanalysis and the Cinema*, trans. by Celia Britton, Annwyl Williams, Ben Brewster, and Alfred Guzzetti (Bloomington: Indiana University Press, 1982), pp. 42–5, 56–7, 61–3, 66–8, 71–3.

5 John R. Searle, "The Logical Status of Fictional Discourse," *New Literary History*, vol. 6, no. 2 (Winter 1975), p. 326. See also Richard Rorty, "Is There a Problem about Fictional Discourse?" in *Consequences of Pragmatism (Essays: 1972–1980)* (Minneapolis: University of Minnesota Press, 1982), esp. sect. 6, pp. 127–32.

6 Hartley Slater, "Fictions," *The British Journal of Aesthetics*, vol. 27, no. 2 (Spring 1987), p. 146. On "indeterminate" objects, cf. Terence Parsons, "A Meinongian Analysis of Fictional Objects," *Grazer Philosophische Studien*, 1 (1974), p. 80.

7 Slater, "Fictions," p. 148. Slater's example of searching for a gentleman to suit the clothes suggests Nelson Goodman's notion of "exemplification" as well as Goodman's criterion of *rightness of fit* which is developed as a stan-dard of acceptability more general than truth or falsity (which is reserved for statements in a written or verbal language). Goodman's expansion of the notion of truth is significant in light of his strict view of fiction which treats "is a picture of" as a non-relational predicate, i.e. as an "x-picture" rather than a "picture of x." Goodman is also concerned to indicate that the standards for judging the acceptability of a representation will vary

depending on both the type of reference (e.g., denotation, exemplification, expression) and the qualities of the notational system (e.g., disjointness, differentiation, compliance). Even so, fiction has a special relation to exemplification. See Nelson Goodman, *Ways of Worldmaking* (Indianapolis: Hackett, 1978), chap. 7, "On Rightness of Rendering," pp. 109–40; *Languages of Art: An Approach to a Theory of Symbols* (Indianapolis: Hackett, 2nd edn 1976), chap. 1, sect. 5; chap. 2, sect. 4, p. 66 (fictive representation reduces to exemplification of a special kind); chap. 4; *Of Mind and Other Matters* (Cambridge, Mass.: Harvard University Press, 1984), pp. 123–30 (five theses about fiction and three types of realism); Catherine Z. Elgin, *With Reference to Reference* (Indianapolis: Hackett, 1983), pp. 43–54.

Slater's "outfit" for a gentleman reminds us that the notion of a "fit" is itself metaphorical and, moreover, according to Paul Kay, is one of two conflicting "folk theories of reference." See "Linguistic Competence and Folk Theories of Language: Two English Hedges" in *Proceedings of the Ninth Annual Meeting of the Berkeley Linguistics Society* (Berkeley: Berkeley Linguistics Society, 1983), pp. 128–37. (The second folk theory of reference relies on a special group of people to stipulate authoritative definitions.) My justification for the use of the metaphor of a "fit" in a theory of fiction is presented in the text; see also note 19 below.

8 The example in the text has been taken from another context, though perhaps one not unrelated to the problem of fictional reference. See Mario Bunge, *Causality and Modern Science* (New York: Dover Publications, 3rd rev. edn 1979), p. 8.

9 Arthur N. Applebee, *The Child's Concept of Story: Ages Two to Seventeen* (Chicago: University of Chicago Press, 1978), pp. 38–47, 52. Fiction as I present it relies upon rather complex cognitive operations and hence it is not surprising that the recognition of fiction is a late achievement for children. I know of no work on the developmental psychology of "fiction" or "make-believe." It seems obvious, however, that more than so-called "basic-level categorization" will be required. On basic-level categories, see George Lakoff, *Women, Fire, and Dangerous Things: What Categories Reveal about the Mind* (Chicago: University of Chicago Press, 1987), pp. 31–54, 199–201, 265–71, 296–7.

10 A noteworthy theory of the psychology and structure of knowledge is presented in Marvin Minsky's *The Society of Mind* (New York: Simon & Schuster, 1986). On the notion of a fictional character as a complex predicate that a real person might also bear see Gilbert Ryle, "Imaginary Objects," *Proceedings of the Aristotelian Society*, Supplementary vol. 12 (1933), pp. 18–43.

11 See Albert W. Hayward's review of L.B. Cebik's *Fictional Narrative and Truth: An Epistemic Analysis* (New York: University Press of America, 1984) in *The Journal of Aesthetics and Art Criticism*, vol. 45, no. 2 (Winter 1986), p. 208. Cf. also Minsky, *The Society of Mind*, pp. 119–20.

12 Cebik, *Fictional Narrative and Truth*, p. 123 (my emphasis). Cebik's use of "presuppositions" in the analysis of fictional discourse derives from P.F. Strawson, "On Referring," *Mind*, vol. 59, no. 235 (July 1950), pp. 320–44.

13 Cebik, *Fictional Narrative and Truth*, pp. 116, 123–4, 136–42. Cebik is responding to certain philosophical problems that arise when referring and nonreferring expressions are mixed in the same sentence. For example, a reference to Winston Churchill and London appearing in a fiction; or, an explicit generalization offered by a fictional character or narrator, e.g. the temperature at which water freezes, or the statement that war is hell.

14 See, e.g., *Readings in Knowledge Representation*, ed. by Ronald J. Brachman and Hector J. Levesque (Los Altos, Ca.: Morgan Kaufmann, 1985); *Knowledge and Representation*, ed. by Beatrice de Gelder (London: Routledge & Kegan Paul, 1982).

15 It might also be possible in a psychoanalytic approach to model the indeterminateness and delay characteristic of fiction on the psychic mechanism of "deferred action." On deferred action, see note 87 in chapter 4 above. For an unusual explanation of fiction that depends on combining psychoanalysis with narratology, see Michael Riffaterre, *Fictional Truth* (Baltimore: Johns Hopkins University Press, 1990), chap. 4, "The Unconscious of Fiction," pp. 84–111. For one approach to the difference between fiction and nonfiction from a psychoanalytic standpoint, see William Guynn, *A Cinema of Nonfiction* (London and Toronto: Associated University Presses, 1990), chap. 5, "The Nonfiction Film and Its Spectator," pp. 215–31.

16 Cf. Jerrold Levinson, "The Place of Real Emotion in Response to Fictions," *The Journal of Aesthetics and Art Criticism*, vol. 48, no. 1 (Winter 1990), pp. 79–80; Jerry R. Hobbs, *Literature and Cognition* (Stanford, Ca.: Center for the Study of Language and Information, 1990), chap. 2, "Imagining, Fiction, and Narrative," pp. 33–40; and the Ien Ang quotation in note 41, chapter 5 above. In addition, the redescription of a fictional object from one level of narration to the next may produce a variety of emotional responses to the object; see the discussion of "anomalous suspense" and "anomalous replotting" on p. 113 above.

17 In an empiricist account of language a fictional statement may be true only if it is taken as an indirect reference to sets of (false) sentences. For example, talk about Sherlock Holmes can be true only if made outside a story context and about sentences in the Holmes stories written by Sir Arthur Conan Doyle. See C.G. Prado, *Making Believe: Philosophical Reflections on Fiction* (Westport, Conn.: Greenwood Press, 1984), pp. 12–14, 95–8. The empiricist account descends from Bertrand Russell's "theory of descriptions." See his *Logic and Knowledge: Essays, 1901–1950*, ed. by Robert Charles Marsh (New York: Macmillan, 1956). An idealist account based on the work of Alexis Meinong may be found in Terence Parsons, *Nonexistent Objects* (New Haven, Conn.: Yale University Press, 1980). For a related account based on modal semantics (possible worlds) and a good bibliography, see Thomas G. Pavel's *Fictional Worlds* (Cambridge, Mass.: Harvard University Press, 1986).

A major view of fiction which I do not discuss is derived from the works of J.L. Austin and John R. Searle on speech act theory. See, e.g., Pratt and Searle, *Toward a Speech Act Theory of Literary Discourse* (Bloomington: Indiana University Press, 1977). For criticism see Cebik, *Fictional Narrative and Truth*; Pavel, *Fictional Worlds*; Prado, *Making Believe*; and Rorty, *Consequences of Pragmatism*. For more criticism, see Joseph Margolis, *Art and Philosophy: Conceptual Issues in Aesthetics* (Brighton, England: Harvester, 1980), pp. 235–51; and Jonathan Culler, "Problems in the Theory of Fiction," *Diacritics*, vol. 14, no. 1 (Spring 1984), pp. 2–11. For support see Steven Mandelker, "Searle on Fictional Discourse: A Defense Against Wolterstorff, Pavel and Rorty," *The British Journal of Aesthetics*, vol. 27, no. 2 (Spring 1987), pp. 156–68.

18 On the problem of "mixed" fictions, see note 13 above.

19 For an example of a cognitive theory which seeks a middle course between empiricism and idealism, see George Lakoff's "experiential realism" in *Women, Fire, and Dangerous Things*, pp. 260–303. Notice that the word "see"

is interpreted differently in these theories. "I see" may mean either "I am looking" (cf. empiricism) or "I understand" (cf. idealism). Accordingly, how we describe film "viewing" will depend on our notion of "fictional seeing" and ultimately on our theory of film, since a particular theory will make interrelated claims about the nature of fiction, narrative, film, and perception. Lakoff's description of our common sense, folk theory of "seeing" (pp. 125–30) seems to have much in common with certain film theories.

Gregory Currie searches for a middle course between empiricism and idealism by combining a theory of communication and intention based on the ideas of Paul Grice with the notion that the reader of fiction adopts a special attitude of "make-believe," *The Nature of Fiction* (New York: Cambridge University Press, 1990), pp. 1–51. On the nature of pictorial fictions, see Currie, pp. 35–42, 92–8. I discuss some of the problems of communication theories in chapter 4 above.

20 Strawson, "On Referring," pp. 324–9, 331.

21 It is well to keep in mind that when we look at a photograph we must take on faith that it is a photograph; we must assume that a very great number of procedures were correctly followed from framing and exposure through developing and printing. Recently it has become possible to use special graphics computers to shift elements from one photograph to another and to create new elements and relationships without leaving a detectable trace. See Michael W. Miller, "Creativity Furor: High-Tech Alteration of Sights and Sounds Divides the Arts World," *The Wall Street Journal*, vol. 117, no. 45 (Sept. 1, 1987), pp. 1, 19.

Note that by thinking of both artworks and scientific laws as counterfactual conditionals, one preserves the notion that knowledge is not ready-made but relative to tacit conditions, hypotheses, and theories. How a photograph functions symbolically in an artwork or a scientific essay, then, is not determined by its being a photograph. On counterfactuals, see p. 268 above.

22 I will not consider the problem of how a spectator is able to construct "statements" out of visual materials nor how such "statements" and their truth values may change with time.

23 My suggestion that photographs may have a future tense should be contrasted with André Bazin's argument that photographs, like mummies, preserve the dead and Roland Barthes' view that photographs elicit a premonition of death. André Bazin, "The Ontology of the Photographic Image" in *What is Cinema?* vol. I, trans. by Hugh Gray (Berkeley: University of California Press, 1967), pp. 9–16; Roland Barthes, *Camera Lucida: Reflections on Photography* trans. by Richard Howard (New York: Hill & Wang, 1981), pp. 31–2, 85–100.

24 The phrase "possible referents" here is shorthand for saying that the decision about whether an object fits with the given criteria is to be made on a case by case basis, not that there exist "possible objects" hovering between existence and nonexistence.

The phrase "a specific class" suggests that the photograph of a tiger in a dictionary becomes nonfictional when interpreted as a representation of a *specific kind* of animal. The tiger pictured in the dictionary, of course, may actually be a house cat that has been painted and photographed close up, or merely a piece of painted cardboard, so long as we understand that what is being specified is a kind of animal. This suggests that the dictionary example may be stretched to explain how we understand some films as

282

nonfictional even though they contain fictional devices. Consider the following argument by Hayden White:

> Thus, for example, the depiction, in Richard Attenborough's film *Gandhi* [1982], of the anonymous South African railway conductor who pushed the young Gandhi from the train, is not a misrepresentation insofar as the actor playing the role may not have possessed the physical features of the actual agent of that act. The veracity of the scene depends on the depiction of *a* person whose historical significance derived from the *kind* of act he performed at a particular time and place, which act was a function of an identifiable type of role-playing under the kinds of social conditions prevailing at a general, but specifically historical, time and place. And the same is true of the depiction of Gandhi himself in the film. Demands for a verisimilitude in film that is impossible in any medium of representation, including that of written history, stem from the confusion of historical individuals with the kinds of "characterization" of them required for discursive purposes, whether in verbal or in visual media.
>
> (Hayden White, "Historiography and Historiophoty," *The American Historical Review*, vol. 93, no. 5 (Dec. 1988), pp. 1198–9, White's emphases.)

Note, again, that nonfiction and fiction are a matter of the procedures by which we read and depend on the specificity of *discourse and reference*; they are not determined by the specifically visual and auditory (bottom-up) features of a text. Also, a reference may be specific without being true. Thus a nonfictional text that is false does not thereby become a fiction.

25 Is it possible for a fiction film to incorporate photographs which are nonfictional and/or quite specific (e.g., when a character handles a photograph within the story or the film uses freeze frames)? See Garrett Stewart, "Photogravure: Death, Photography, and Film Narrative," *Wide Angle*, vol. 9, no. 1 (1987), pp. 11–31.

26 Cf. F.R. Palmer, *Semantics: A New Outline* (London: Cambridge University Press, 1976), pp. 108–9.

27 Note that an indefinite article does not make the object it modifies indefinite; it merely leaves unanswered the question "which one, or ones," of the relevant class of objects is being specified. A reference that is indefinite, or nonspecific, should not be confused with a reference that is vague, cryptic, unarticulated, implicit, or ambiguous; nor should it be confused with a reference to the inexpressible or ineffable.

Note especially that making a reference indefinite is *not* the same as making a reference *general*. An example of a general reference would be a reference to "the average consumer," or to the behavior of "an ideal gas." Another example of a general reference would be a universal statement like "*all* tigers are mortal," or "tigers *usually* fear the unknown." A narrative interpreted fictionally includes many explicit and implicit generalizations (for example, in the epilogue), but these are accomplished through a sequence of indefinite (i.e., fictional), singular affirmations rather than through a sequence of particular (i.e., nonfictional), singular affirmations. This illustrates again that fiction cannot be distinguished from nonfiction on the basis of its inability to make general truth claims about a condition in the world. Fiction and nonfiction are different because they involve different cognitive procedures, different methods of constructing and construing statements about a world, not because of what results from the procedures.

In this chapter I've associated the logic of one type of use of definite and indefinite articles with the creation of fictional reference. However, a statement may be made indefinite without the use of an indefinite article and, conversely, an indefinite article may be used in ways other than to make a statement indefinite. As just noted, definite and indefinite articles may be used to state a generalization in a fictional or nonfictional context. (Definite and indefinite articles then become equivalent: *"The* tiger is a mammal," *"A* tiger is a mammal," "All tigers are mammals," "Tigers are mammals.") In addition, articles may have a deictic function: "Move *the* vase to *the* table." I mention this possibility because it is often assumed that the "camera" must always have a deictic function, that is, must always specify a determinate piece of the world by "pointing" and "recording." However I believe that the camera is not confined to this function and therefore film is neither *essentially* deictic nor is its comprehension measured only with respect to the existence of a (nonfictional) object that was once in front of the/a "camera."

28 In the opening title of *Star Wars* – "A long time ago in a galaxy far, far away" – notice how the indefinite article "a" considered simply as a vowel sound spreads (poetically) through the entire phrase ("ago," "a galaxy," "away") and how the indefiniteness of time ("A long time") is extended to space ("far, far away"). If the fiction is also to be a narrative, however, the indefiniteness of time (. . . *a* time) must be balanced by a distinctness (*once* upon a . . .) that is capable of singling out the events of a unique cause–effect chain.

29 The tiger can be heard roaring after Odile, Franz, and Arthur – shown together for the first time in their car – decide to stop in order to talk. Later the roaring is heard accompanied by jazz music as Odile runs along a wall. The roaring is similar to the harsh sounds of traffic noise in the film and especially to the sound of the protagonists' car.

30 My definition of "interpreting fictively" seems to leave out the evidence that could be supplied by social and historical contexts. Walter Benjamin, for example, argues that a work of art has an "aura" that is the result of its unique form of existence and its unique place in a history and tradition. In effect, the notion of an aura is a broader conception of the "causal arrow" linking profilmic and postfilmic. Benjamin argues (sects 2 and 3) that the mechanical reproduction of art destroys the specificity of an art object. My analysis of "fiction" as nonspecific reference is not meant to bear directly on the various claims made by Benjamin. My analysis conflicts with Benjamin's claims only if one collapses such distinctions as narrative and fiction, art work and the working of art, ontology and epistemology, exchange value and use value. "The Work of Art in the Age of Mechanical Reproduction" in *Illuminations*, trans. by Harry Zohn (New York: Schocken, 1968), pp. 217–51.

31 See Slater, "Fictions," p. 148.

32 Two types of editing within Christian Metz's eight-part "grande syntagmatique" would seem especially suited to promote nonspecific reference. First, the "bracket syntagma" offers "typical samples" of an order of reality, or a sample that typifies a recurring event. (For example: a series of shots of destruction, bombings, and grief to illustrate the idea of "disasters of war.") Second, the "episodic sequence" offers a "symbolic summary," or condensation, of the successive stages of a much longer progression such that "each image stands for more than itself," rather than merely presenting an unskipped moment of the progression. (For example: in *Citizen Kane* (Welles,

1941) a series of brief scenes at a breakfast table spanning nine years that depict the gradual deterioration of a marriage.) Both types of editing are nonspecific at a denotative level. See "Problems of Denotation in the Fiction Film" in *Film Language: A Semiotics of the Cinema*, trans. by Michael Taylor (New York: Oxford University Press, 1974), pp. 125–7, 130–2. Cf. Gérard Genette's notion of the "iterative" and "pseudo-iterative" in *Narrative Discourse: An Essay in Method*, trans. by Jane E. Lewin (Ithaca, N.Y.: Cornell University Press, 1980), pp. 116–17, 121–2; and see Marsha Kinder, "The Subversive Potential of the Pseudo-Iterative," *Film Quarterly*, vol. 43, no. 2 (Winter 1989–90), pp. 3–16.

33 Arthur C. Danto, *Narration and Knowledge* (including the integral text of *Analytical Philosophy of History*; New York: Columbia University Press, 1985), p. 347.

34 William Guynn asserts that "Narrative is never absent in documentary films, even if its presence is more or less marked." *A Cinema of Nonfiction* (London and Toronto: Associated University Presses, 1990), p. 154.

35 Even the weaker claim that a film selects only *some* causal principles in order to present a mere *sample* of reality cannot support a theory of documentary film. Nelson Goodman has demonstrated that the significance of a sample – for instance, a tailor's cloth sample – is not determined simply by its causal history, or causal future, but by an act of (present) perceiving that makes of it a symbolic exemplification. *Languages of Art: An Approach to a Theory of Symbols* (Indianapolis: Hackett, 2nd edn 1976), chap. 2, pp. 45–95.

36 Stephen Heath, *Questions of Cinema* (New York: Macmillan, 1981), pp. 237–8. Although Heath is not discussing the "historical present" tense, I have emphasized these words in his quote in order to suggest a connection between the representation of history and certain complex tense systems in narrative representation.

37 See, e.g., Carl Plantinga, "The Mirror Framed: A Case For Expression in Documentary," *Wide Angle*, vol. 13, no. 2 (April 1991), pp. 40–53; "Defining Documentary: Fiction, Non-Fiction, and Projected Worlds," *Persistence of Vision* 5 (Spring 1987), pp. 44–54; Michael Renov, "Re-thinking Documentary: Toward a Taxonomy of Mediation," *Wide Angle*, vol. 8, nos. 3/4 (1986), pp. 71–7.

38 I am using the word "classical" in the sense of "typical," not in the sense of "exemplary"; that is, I am not attempting to describe films in the documentary canon but rather to describe routine and standard practices used in such nonfiction films as industrial, educational, and nature documentaries.

39 Dai Vaughn analyzes two documentary films and shows how the traditional notion of a documentary is subverted by the use of such subjective devices as the point-of-view shot, ambiguous voice-over, and hypothetical imagery (e.g., what could, or might actually, have been seen through a battlefield periscope). "Arms and the Absent," *Sight and Sound*, vol. 48, no. 3 (Summer 1979), pp. 182–7. The films analyzed are Franju's *Hôtel des Invalides*, 1952, and Cowell's *The Tribe that Hides from Man*, 1970.

40 Christian Metz argues that a film's fiction effect is increased by the presence of dream sequences, voice-off commentary, and films within the film. All of these devices may be found in *Sans Soleil*. Metz, "The Imaginary Signifier" in *The Imaginary Signifier*, pp. 73–4.

41 Cf. Susan Sniader Lanser, *The Narrative Act: Point of View in Prose Fiction* (Princeton, N.J.: Princeton University Press, 1981), p. 146 n. 39.

42 On the argumentative form of narrative (e.g., Eisenstein's "intellectual cinema"), see chapter 1.

43 Prado, *Making Believe*, p. 134.

44 Herb A. Lightman, "The Technique of the Documentary Film," *American Cinematographer*, vol. 26, no. 11 (Nov. 1945), pp. 378, 402.

45 Lightman, "The Technique of the Documentary Film," p. 378.

46 See the discussion of the ideas of Moreno, Bazin, and Gaudreault in chapter 5. Many of Bazin's prescriptions for the documentary filmmaker must be derived from his analyses of fictional narratives. On restricted camera positions in documentary film, see, e.g., André Bazin, "Cinema and Exploration" in *What is Cinema?*, pp. 154–63. In this essay, Bazin is intrigued by the extreme case in which an event being documented can not be shown at all because of the conditions governing the filming; thus the event exists for the spectator only through its absence on film. As we shall see, Chris Marker's *Sans Soleil* will push signs of absence even further within a documentary format.

On documentary conventions, see generally Bill Nichols, "The Voice of Documentary" in *Movies and Methods: An Anthology*, vol. II, ed. by Bill Nichols (Berkeley: University of California Press, 1985), pp. 258–73, as well as essays in the same volume by Thomas Waugh, David MacDougall, and Dai Vaughn. See also Nichols, "History, Myth, and Narrative in Documentary," *Film Quarterly*, vol. 41, no. 1 (Fall 1987), pp. 9–20, and Jeffrey Youdelman, "Narration, Invention, & History: A Documentary Dilemma," *Cineaste*, vol. 12, no. 2 (1982), pp. 8–15.

Note that the convention of a "relatively unstructured" *mise-en-scène* rules out dramatic reenactments for a documentary film but does not rule out a painstaking search for the "perfect situation" that can be filmed in order to advance an argument. Various documentary conventions are used in the false newsreel sequence of *Citizen Kane* (figs 47, 48, p. 175) as well as in the false documentaries *The Battle of Algiers* (Pontecorvo, 1966), *David Holzman's Diary* (McBride, 1967), *Zelig* (Allen, 1983), and *This Is Spinal Tap* (Reiner, 1984).

47 David Alan Black, "Cinematic Realism and the Phonographic Analogy," *Cinema Journal*, vol. 26, no. 2 (Winter 1987), pp. 40–2.

48 For Gérard Genette, this principle of grouping stories in *Sans Soleil* would be a "geographical syllepsis"; *Narrative Discourse*, p. 85 n. 119; and see pp. 40, 29, 27. The relationship of a "catalogue" structure, and its "focus," to narrative structure was examined in chapter 1. Catalogue structures combine with indeterminate narration in *Sans Soleil* to attenuate the focus of cause–effect chains and weaken our sense that a sequence of events is being presented to us as nonfocalized and/or externally focalized. By simultaneously attacking both the organization of narrative (focus organized causally) and the goal of nonfiction (history focalized), *Sans Soleil* undermines the classic form of a documentary which acts to fuse narrative and nonfiction.

49 See, e.g., Jim Collins, *Uncommon Cultures: Popular Culture and Post-Modernism* (New York: Routledge, 1989). For an informal introduction to post-modernism, see *Utne Reader* 34 (July/Aug. 1989), pp. 50–76.

50 For example, the dream sequence on the train is multiply ambiguous. It may represent the thoughts of sleeping passengers; or, represent what the cameraman imagines about these people; or, represent how extraordinary images from Japanese television may nonetheless be found in ordinary life and become evidence of a collective dream. Indeed, what is found on the

train may be evidence of a collective nightmare: on the boat trip from Hokkaido, while many of the passengers are asleep, the cameraman discovers "small fragments of [a past or future] war enshrined in everyday life."

51 An end title of the film states, "Sandor Krasna's letters were read by Alexandra Stewart." Sandor Krasna, however, is an imaginary person; hence, in reading the letters Stewart has assumed a fictional role. Extracts from her narration may be found in Chris Marker's "Sunless," *Semiotext(e)*, vol. 4, no. 3 (1984), pp. 33–40.

Allan Casebier connects *Sans Soleil* to an ancient Japanese literary form in which diary writing was presented through a special kind of narration by a woman (*Utanikki*). See "A Deconstructive Documentary," *Journal of Film and Video*, vol. 40, no. 1 (Winter 1988), p. 36. In addition, the film is a perfect example of what James Clifford calls "ethnographic surrealism"; see "On Ethnographic Surrealism," *Comparative Studies in Society and History*, vol. 23, no. 4 (Oct. 1981), pp. 539–64.

On *Sans Soleil* generally, see Michael Walsh, "Around the World, Across All Frontiers: *Sans Soleil* as *Depays*," *CineAction!* 18 (Fall 1989), pp. 29–36; Janine Marchessault, "*Sans Soleil*," *CineAction!* 5 (Spring 1986), pp. 2–6; Yvette Biro, "In the Spiral of Time," *Millennium Film Journal* nos. 14/15 (Fall/ Winter 1984–5), pp. 173–7; Terrence Rafferty, "Marker Changes Trains," *Sight and Sound*, vol. 53, no. 4 (Autumn 1984), pp. 284–8; Nataša Ďurovičová, "Letter to an Unknown Woman: Reading Markers in *Sans Soleil*" (Los Angeles: University of California, unpublished paper 1989); and Michael Renov, "Documentary/Technology/Immediacy: Strategies of Resistance" (Los Angeles: University of Southern California, unpublished paper 1986). For some useful reviews of the film, see Steven Simmons, "Man Without a Country," *The Movies* (Nov. 1983); J. Hoberman, "Dis Orient, Dat Occident," *The Village Voice* (Nov. 1, 1983); and Vincent Canby, "Film: 'Sans Soleil,' Views of People," *The New York Times* (Oct. 26, 1983).

52 Near the end of *Sans Soleil* the cameraman will refer to memory itself as a "path."

53 The cameraman's statement that he has decided to give his imaginary film the name "Sunless" marks the end of the spoken commentary in this segment of *Sans Soleil*. It occurs during the first half of the first shot of the final six shots of the segment. The stark Moussorgski music features a rhythmic, two-part sound similar to a heartbeat that is coordinated with the duration of each of the final six shots. In the sixth shot, the heartbeat is suspended after we hear the first part of its beat. A similar two-part sound is heard with the end titles of the film and it, too, is suspended when we reach the final title.

54 A quite different way of representing a multiplicity of times was analyzed on pp. 104ff. in *Wild Strawberries*.

55 I have derived the notion of a "hyperindex" from the operation of "hypertext" computer software.

56 Danto, *Narration and Knowledge*, p. 348.

WORKS CITED

Abel, Richard. "*Notorious*: Perversion par Excellence." In *A Hitchcock Reader*, ed. by Marshall Deutelbaum and Leland Poague. Ames: Iowa State University Press, 1986.

Affron, Charles. *Cinema and Sentiment*. Chicago, Ill.: University of Chicago Press, 1982.

Allen, Robert C. "Reader-Oriented Criticism and Television." In *Channels of Discourse: Television and Contemporary Criticism*, ed. by Robert C. Allen. Chapel Hill: University of North Carolina Press, 1987.

Altman, Rick [Charles F.]. "Psychoanalysis and Cinema: The Imaginary Discourse." *Quarterly Review of Film Studies* 2 (August 1977): 257–72.

—— *The American Film Musical*. Bloomington: Indiana University Press, 1987.

—— "Dickens, Griffith, and Film Theory Today." *South Atlantic Quarterly* 88 (Spring 1989): 321–59.

Anderson, John R. *Language, Memory, and Thought*. Hillsdale, N.J.: Erlbaum, 1976.

Anderson, Joseph and Barbara. "Motion Perception in Motion Pictures." In *The Cinematic Apparatus*, ed. by Teresa de Lauretis and Stephen Heath. New York: St Martin's Press, 1980.

Andrew, Dudley. *Concepts in Film Theory*. New York: Oxford University Press, 1984.

Ang, Ien. "Feminist Desire and Female Pleasure." Commentary on Janice Radway's *Reading the Romance: Women, Patriarchy and Popular Literature*. *Camera Obscura* 16 (January 1988): 178–91.

Applebee, Arthur N. *The Child's Concept of Story: Ages Two to Seventeen*. Chicago, Ill.: University of Chicago Press, 1978.

Armes, Roy. "Robbe-Grillet, Ricardou and *Last Year At Marienbad*." *Quarterly Review of Film Studies* 5 (Winter 1980): 1–17.

Arnheim, Rudolf. *Film as Art*. Berkeley: University of California Press, 1957.

Aumont, Jacques. "The Point of View," trans. by Arthur Denner. *Quarterly Review of Film and Video* 11 (1989): 1–22.

Ayer, A.J. *Probability and Evidence*. New York: Macmillan, 1972.

Baars, Barnard J. *The Cognitive Revolution in Psychology*. New York: Guilford, 1986.

Bacher, Lutz. "Max Ophuls's Universal-International Films: The Impact of Production Circumstances on a Visual Style." Ph.D. dissertation. Detroit, Mich.: Wayne State University Press, 1984.

Bal, Mieke. "The Narrating and the Focalizing: A Theory of the Agents in Narrative." *Style* 17 (Spring 1983): 234–69.

_____ *Narratology: Introduction to the Theory of Narrative*, trans. by Christine van Boheemen. Toronto: University of Toronto Press, 1985.

Banfield, Ann. *Unspeakable Sentences: Narration and Representation in the Language of Fiction*. London: Routledge & Kegan Paul, 1982.

Barrow, H.G. and J.M. Tenenbaum. "Computational Approaches to Vision." In *Handbook of Perception and Human Performance* 2: *Cognitive Processes and Performance*, ed. by Kenneth R. Boff, Lloyd Kaufman, and James P. Thomas. New York: John Wiley & Sons, 1986.

Barry, Jackson G. "Narratology's Centrifugal Force: A Literary Perspective on the Extensions of Narrative Theory." *Poetics Today* 11 (Summer 1990): 295–307.

Barthes, Roland. "To Write: An Intransitive Verb?" In *The Structuralist Controversy: The Languages of Criticism and the Sciences of Man*, ed. by Richard Macksey and Eugenio Donato. Baltimore, Md.: Johns Hopkins University Press, 1972.

_____ *S/Z*, trans. by Richard Miller. New York: Hill & Wang, 1974.

_____ *The Pleasure of the Text*, trans. by Richard Miller. New York: Hill & Wang, 1975.

_____ "An Introduction to the Structural Analysis of Narrative," trans. by Lionel Duisit. *New Literary History* 6 (Winter 1975): 237–72.

_____ "Introduction to the Structural Analysis of Narratives." In *Image–Music–Text*, trans. by Stephen Heath. New York: Hill & Wang, 1977.

_____ "The Death of the Author." In *Image–Music–Text*, trans. by Stephen Heath. New York: Hill & Wang, 1977.

_____ "The Realistic Effect," trans. by Gerald Mead. *Film Reader* 3 (1978): 131–5.

_____ *Camera Lucida: Reflections on Photography*, trans. by Richard Howard. New York: Hill & Wang, 1981.

_____ "The Reality Effect." In *French Literary Theory Today: A Reader*, ed. by Tzvetan Todorov, trans. by R. Carter. Cambridge: Cambridge University Press, 1982.

_____ "The Reality Effect." In *The Rustle of Language*, trans. by Richard Howard. New York: Hill & Wang, 1986.

_____ "Introduction to the Structural Analysis of Narratives." In *The Semiotic Challenge*, trans. by Richard Howard. New York: Hill & Wang, 1988.

_____ "Semantics of the Object." In *The Semiotic Challenge*, trans. by Richard Howard. New York: Hill & Wang, 1988.

_____ "Textual Analysis of a Tale by Edgar Allan Poe." In *The Semiotic Challenge*, trans. by Richard Howard. New York: Hill & Wang, 1988.

_____ "The Sequences of Actions." In *The Semiotic Challenge*, trans. by Richard Howard. New York: Hill & Wang, 1988.

Bazin, André. "Cinema and Exploration." In *What is Cinema?* 1, trans. by Hugh Gray. Berkeley and Los Angeles: University of California Press, 1967.

_____ "Theater and Cinema – Part One." In *What is Cinema?* 1, trans. by Hugh Gray. Berkeley and Los Angeles: University of California Press, 1967.

_____ "Theater and Cinema – Part Two." In *What is Cinema?* 1, trans. by Hugh Gray. Berkeley and Los Angeles: University of California Press, 1967.

_____ "The Evolution of the Language of Cinema." In *What is Cinema?* 1, trans. by Hugh Gray. Berkeley and Los Angeles: University of California Press, 1967.

_____ "The Ontology of the Photographic Image." In *What is Cinema?* 1, trans. by Hugh Gray. Berkeley and Los Angeles: University of California Press, 1967.

_____ "The Virtues and Limitations of Montage." In *What is Cinema?* 1, trans.

by Hugh Gray. Berkeley and Los Angeles: University of California Press, 1967.

―――― "A Pure Masterpiece: *The River*." In *Jean Renoir*, trans. by W.W. Halsey and William H. Simon. New York: Dell, 1973.

Bellour, Raymond. "Segmenting/Analyzing." In *Narrative, Apparatus, Ideology: A Film Theory Reader*, ed. by Philip Rosen. New York: Columbia University Press, 1986.

―――― "The Obvious and the Code." In *Narrative, Apparatus, Ideology: A Film Theory Reader*, ed. by Philip Rosen. New York: Columbia University Press, 1986.

Belton, John. "Technology and Aesthetics of Film Sound." In *Film Sound: Theory and Practice*, ed. by Elisabeth Weis and John Belton. New York: Columbia University Press, 1985.

Benjamin, Walter. "The Work of Art in the Age of Mechanical Reproduction." In *Illuminations*, trans. by Harry Zohn. New York: Schocken, 1968.

Berendsen, Marjet. "The Teller and the Observer: Narration and Focalization in Narrative Texts." *Style* 18 (Spring 1984): 140–58.

Biro, Yvette. "In the Spiral of Time." *Millennium Film Journal* (Fall/Winter 1984–5): 173–7.

Black, David Alan. "Genette and Film: Narrative Level in the Fiction Cinema." *Wide Angle* 8 (1986): 19–26.

―――― "Cinematic Realism and the Phonographic Analogy." *Cinema Journal* 26 (Winter 1987): 39–50.

―――― "Narrative Film and the Synoptic Tendency." Ph.D. dissertation. New York University, 1988.

Black, Henry Campbell. *Black's Law Dictionary*. St Paul: West, 5th ed., 1979.

Boff, Kenneth R., Lloyd Kaufman, and James P. Thomas, eds. "Cognitive Processes and Performance." In *Handbook of Perception and Human Performance* 1. New York: John Wiley & Sons, 1986.

―――― "Representation of Motion and Space in Video and Cinematic Displays." In *Handbook of Perception and Human Performance* 1. New York: John Wiley & Sons, 1986.

Booth, Wayne C. *The Rhetoric of Fiction*. Chicago, Ill.: University of Chicago Press, 1961.

Bordwell, David. *The Films of Carl-Theodor Dreyer*. Berkeley: University of California Press, 1981.

―――― "Happily Ever After, Part 2." *Velvet Light Trap* 19 (1982): 2–7.

―――― *Narration in the Fiction Film*. Madison: University of Wisconsin Press, 1985.

―――― "Classical Hollywood Cinema: Narrational Principles and Procedures." In *Narrative, Apparatus, Ideology: A Film Theory Reader*, ed. by Philip Rosen. New York: Columbia University Press, 1986.

―――― *Ozu and the Poetics of Cinema*. Princeton, N.J.: Princeton University Press, 1988.

―――― "ApProppriations and ImProprieties: Problems in the Morphology of Film Narrative." *Cinema Journal* 27 (Spring 1988): 5–20.

―――― *Making Meaning: Inference and Rhetoric in the Interpretation of Cinema*. Cambridge, Mass.: Harvard University Press, 1989.

―――― "A Case for Cognitivism." *Iris* 9 (Spring 1989): 11–40.

―――― Reply to Seymour Chatman's review of Bordwell's *Narration in the Fiction Film*. Unpublished.

Bordwell, David and Kristin Thompson. *Film Art: An Introduction.* New York: McGraw-Hill, 3rd ed., 1990.

Bordwell, David, Janet Staiger, and Kristin Thompson. *The Classical Hollywood Cinema: Film Style & Mode of Production to 1960.* New York: Columbia University Press, 1985.

Bower, Gordon H. and Randolph K. Cirilo. "Cognitive Psychology and Text Processing." In *Handbook of Discourse Analysis* 1: *Disciplines of Discourse*, ed. by Teun A. van Dijk. New York: Academic Press, 1985.

Brachman, Ronald J. and Hector J. Levesque, eds. *Readings in Knowledge Representation.* Los Altos, Calif.: Morgan Kaufmann, 1985.

Branigan, Edward. "The Spectator and Film Space – Two Theories." *Screen* 22 (1981): 55–78.

_____ *Point of View in the Cinema: A Theory of Narration and Subjectivity in Classical Film.* New York and Berlin: Mouton, 1984.

_____ "What Is a Camera?" In *Cinema Histories, Cinema Practices*, ed. by Patricia Mellencamp and Philip Rosen. Frederick, Md.: University Publications of America, 1984.

_____ "The Point-of-View Shot." In *Movies and Methods: An Anthology* 2, ed. by Bill Nichols. Berkeley and Los Angeles: University of California Press, 1985.

_____ "Diegesis and Authorship in Film." *Iris* 7 (Fall 1986): 37–54.

_____ " 'Here is a Picture of No Revolver!': The Negation of Images, and Methods for Analyzing the Structure of Pictorial Statements." *Wide Angle* 8 (1986): 8–17.

_____ "Point of View in the Fiction Film." *Wide Angle* 8 (1986): 4–7.

_____ "Controversy and Correspondence: Narration Issues." Reply to Seymour Chatman. In *Film Quarterly* 41 (Fall 1987): 63.

_____ Review of George M. Wilson's *Narration in Light: Studies in Cinematic Point of View.* In *SubStance* 56 (1988): 118–21.

_____ "Sound and Epistemology in Film." *Journal of Aesthetics and Art Criticism* 47 (Fall 1989): 311–24.

_____ "The Space of *Equinox Flower*." In *Close Viewings: An Anthology of New Film Criticism*, ed. by Peter Lehman. Tallahassee: Florida State University Press, 1990.

Bremond, Claude. "The Logic of Narrative Possibilities." *New Literary History* 11 (Spring 1980): 387–411.

Brewster, Ben. "A Scene at the 'Movies.' " *Screen* 23 (July/August 1982): 4–15.

Brinton, Joseph P. "Subjective Camera or Subjective Audience?" *Hollywood Quarterly* 2 (July 1947): 359–65.

Brooks, Peter. *Reading for the Plot: Design and Intention in Narrative.* New York: Knopf, 1984.

Brooks, Virginia. "Film, Perception and Cognitive Psychology." *Millennium Film Journal* (Fall/Winter 1984–5): 105–26.

Browne, Nick. *The Rhetoric of Filmic Narration.* Ann Arbor, Mich.: UMI Research Press, 1976.

Bullock, Merry, Rochel Gelman, and Renée Baillargeon. "The Development of Causal Reasoning." In *The Developmental Psychology of Time*, ed. by William J. Friedman. New York: Academic Press, 1982.

Bunge, Mario. *Causality and Modern Science.* New York: Dover Publications, 3rd ed., 1979.

Burch, Noël. "Carl Theodor Dreyer: The Major Phase." In *Cinema: A Critical Dictionary – The Major Film-Makers* 1, ed. by Richard Roud. New York: Viking Press, 1980.

_____ "Fritz Lang: German Period." In *Cinema: A Critical Dictionary – The Major Film-Makers* 2, ed. by Richard Roud. New York: Viking Press, 1980.

_____ *Theory of Film Practice*, trans. by Helen R. Lane. Princeton, N.J.: Princeton University Press, 1981.

_____ "Notes on Fritz Lang's First Mabuse." *Cine-Tracts* 13, 4 (Spring 1981): 1–13 plus 8 unnumbered pages of stills.

_____ "Primitivism and the Avant-Gardes: A Dialectical Approach." In *Narrative, Apparatus, Ideology: A Film Theory Reader*, ed. by Philip Rosen. New York: Columbia University Press, 1986.

_____ *Life to those Shadows*, trans. and ed. by Ben Brewster. Berkeley: University of California Press, 1990.

Burgoyne, Robert. "The Interaction of Text and Semantic Deep Structure in the Production of Filmic Characters." *Iris* 4 (1986): 69–79.

_____ "The Cinematic Narrator: The Logic and Pragmatics of Impersonal Narration." *Journal of Film and Video* 42 (Spring 1990): 3–16.

Burgoyne, Robert, Sandy Flitterman-Lewis, and Robert Stam. *New Vocabularies in Film Semiotics: Structuralism, Post-Structuralism and Beyond*. London: Routledge, 1992.

Butzel, Marcia. *Motion as Narration: Theory and Practice of Cinematic Choreography*. University of Illinois Press, forthcoming.

Camper, Fred. "Distance and Style: The Visual Rhetoric of Max Ophuls: *Letter from an Unknown Woman*." *Monogram* 5 (1974): 21–4.

Canby, Vincent. "Film: 'Sans Soleil,' Views of People." *New York Times*. October 26, 1983.

Carr, Thomas H. "Perceiving Visual Language." In *Handbook of Perception and Human Performance* 2, "Cognitive Processes and Performance," ed. by Kenneth R. Boff, Lloyd Kaufman, and James P. Thomas. New York: John Wiley & Sons, 1986.

Carroll, Noël. "Toward a Theory of Film Editing." *Millennium Film Journal* (Winter/Spring 1979): 79–99.

_____ "Toward a Theory of Film Suspense." *Persistence of Vision* (Summer 1984): 65–89.

_____ *Mystifying Movies: Fads and Fallacies in Contemporary Film Theory*. New York: Columbia University Press, 1988.

_____ "Buster Keaton, *The General*, and Visible Intelligibility." In *Close Viewings: An Anthology of New Film Criticism*, ed. by Peter Lehman. Tallahassee: Florida State University Press, 1990.

_____ "Toward a Theory of Point-of-View-Editing: Communication, Emotion and the Movies." *Poetics Today* (forthcoming).

Casebier, Allan. "A Deconstructive Documentary." In *Journal of Film and Video* 40 (Winter 1988): 34–9.

Caughie. John, ed. *Theories of Authorship: A Reader*. London: Routledge & Kegan Paul, 1981.

Cavell, Stanley. "Psychoanalysis and Cinema: The Melodrama of the Unknown Woman." In *Images in Our Souls: Cavell, Psychoanalysis, and Cinema*, ed. by Joseph H. Smith and William Kerrigan. Baltimore, Md.: Johns Hopkins University Press, 1987.

Cebik, L.B. *Fictional Narrative and Truth: An Epistemic Analysis*. New York: University Press of America, 1984.

Chamblee, Robert. "Max Ophuls' Viennese Trilogy: Communications Styles and Structures" [sic]. Ph.D. dissertation, New York University, 1981.

Chatman, Seymour. "Narration and Point of View in Fiction and the Cinema." *Poetica* 1 (1974).

―――― *Story and Discourse: Narrative Structure in Fiction and Film*. Ithaca, N.Y.: Cornell University Press, 1978.

―――― "What Is Description in the Cinema?" *Cinema Journal* 23 (Summer 1984): 4–11.

―――― "Characters and Narrators: Filter, Center, Slant, and Interest-Focus." *Poetics Today* 7 (1986): 189–204.

―――― Review of David Bordwell's *Narration in the Fiction Film*. In *Wide Angle* 8 (1986): 139–41.

―――― Review of Edward Branigan's *Point of View in the Cinema: A Theory of Narration and Subjectivity in Classical Film*. In *Film Quarterly* 40 (Fall 1986): 45–6.

―――― "Controversy and Correspondence: Narration Issues." Reply to Edward Branigan in *Film Quarterly* 41 (Fall 1987): 63–5.

―――― "Who Is the Best Narrator? The Case of *The Third Man*." *Style* 23 (Summer 1989): 183–96.

―――― *Coming to Terms: The Rhetoric of Narrative in Fiction and Film*. Ithaca, N.Y.: Cornell University Press, 1990.

Chomsky, Noam. *Reflections on Language*. New York: Pantheon, 1975.

Cixous, Hélène. "The Character of 'Character.'" *New Literary History* 5 (Winter 1974): 383–402.

Clark, Andy. *Microcognition: Philosophy, Cognitive Science, and Parallel Distributed Processing*. Cambridge, Mass.: MIT Press, 1989.

Clifford, James. "On Ethnographic Surrealism." *Comparative Studies in Society and History* 23 (October 1981): 539–64.

Cohan, Steven and Linda M. Shires. *Telling Stories: A Theoretical Analysis of Narrative Fiction*. New York: Routledge, 1988.

Cohn, Dorrit. "Signposts of Fictionality: A Narratological Perspective." *Poetics Today* 11 (Winter 1990): 775–804.

Collins, Jim. *Uncommon Cultures: Popular Culture and Post-Modernism*. New York: Routledge, 1989.

Comisky, Paul and Jennings Bryant. "Factors Involved in Generating Suspense." *Human Communication Research* 9 (Fall 1982): 49–58.

Coste, Didier. *Narrative as Communication*. Minneapolis: University of Minnesota Press, 1989.

Critical Inquiry 7 (Autumn 1980). Special issue on "On Narrative."

Crofts, Stephen. "Authorship and Hollywood." *Wide Angle* 5 (1983): 16–22.

Culler, Jonathan. *Structuralist Poetics: Structuralism, Linguistics and the Study of Literature*. Ithaca, N.Y.: Cornell University Press, 1975.

―――― "Fabula and Sjuzhet in the Analysis of Narrative: Some American Discussions." *Poetics Today* 1 (1980): 27–37.

―――― "Problems in the Theory of Fiction." *Diacritics* 14 (Spring 1984): 2–11.

Cunningham, Donna S. "Dear Dad: A Daughter's Discourse in *Letter from an Unknown Woman*." Unpublished paper. Los Angeles: University of Southern California, 1989.

Currie, Gregory. *The Nature of Fiction*. New York: Cambridge University Press, 1990.

Danto, Arthur C. *Narration and Knowledge*. Including the integral text of *Analytical Philosophy of History*. New York: Columbia University Press, 1985.

Davis, Howard. "Form and the Function of the Father: An Alternative Analysis of Max Ophuls' *Letter from an Unknown Woman*." MA dissertation. Los Angeles: University of California, 1983.

―――― "The Unconscious Subject in *Letter from an Unknown Woman.*" Unpublished paper. Los Angeles: University of California, 1984.

Dayan, Daniel with Brian Henderson. "The Tutor Code of Classical Cinema." *Film Quarterly* 28 (Fall 1974): 22–31.

de Beaugrande, Robert. *Text, Discourse, and Process: Toward a Multidisciplinary Science of Texts.* Norwood, N.J.: Ablex, 1980.

de Lauretis, Teresa. *Alice Doesn't: Feminism, Semiotics, Cinema.* Bloomington: Indiana University Press, 1984.

―――― *Technologies of Gender: Essays on Theory, Film, and Fiction.* Bloomington: Indiana University Press, 1987.

Derry, Charles. "Towards a Categorization of Film Narrative." *Film Reader* 2 (1977): 111–22.

Desser, David. *The Samurai Films of Akira Kurosawa.* Ann Arbor, Mich.: UMI Research Press, 1983.

Deutelbaum, Marshall. "Finding the Right Man in *The Wrong Man.*" In *A Hitchcock Reader*, ed. by Marshall Deutelbaum and Leland Poague. Ames: Iowa State University Press, 1986.

Diacritics 7 (Spring 1977). Issue on Bremond and Greimas.

Diawara, Manthia. "Oral Literature and African Film: Narratology in Wend Kuuni." *Presence Africaine* 142 (1987): 36–49.

Dmytryk, Edward. *On Film Editing: An Introduction to the Art of Film Construction.* Boston, Mass.: Focal Press, 1984.

Doane, Mary Ann. *The Desire to Desire: The Woman's Film of the 1940s.* Bloomington: Indiana University Press, 1987.

―――― "The Voice in the Cinema: The Articulation of Body and Space." *Yale French Studies* 60 (1980): 33–50.

Doležel, Lubomír. "A Scheme of Narrative Time." In *Semiotics of Art: Prague School Contributions*, ed. by Ladislav Matejka and Irwin R. Titunik. Cambridge, Mass.: MIT Press, 1976.

Dowling, William C. *Jameson, Althusser, Marx: An Introduction to "The Political Unconscious."* Ithaca, N.Y.: Cornell University Press, 1984.

Dreamworks 1 (Spring 1980). Special issue on "Dream and Film."

Ducrot, Oswald and Tzvetan Todorov. *Encyclopedic Dictionary of the Sciences of Language*, trans. by Catherine Porter. Baltimore, Md.: Johns Hopkins University Press, 1979.

Dummett, Michael. "Frege: Sense and Reference." In *Philosophy Through Its Past*, ed. by Ted Honderich. New York: Penguin, 1984.

Durgnat, Raymond. *The Strange Case of Alfred Hitchcock, or The Plain Man's Hitchcock.* Cambridge, Mass.: MIT Press, 1974.

Ďurovičová, Nataša. "Letter to an Unknown Woman: Reading Markers in *Sans Soleil.*" Unpublished paper. Los Angeles: University of California, 1989.

Dyer, Richard. *Stars.* London: British Film Institute, 1979.

Eagle, Herbert, ed. *Russian Formalist Film Theory.* Ann Arbor: University of Michigan Press, 1981.

Eberwein, Robert T. *Film and The Dream Screen: A Sleep and a Forgetting.* Princeton, N.J.: Princeton University Press, 1984.

―――― "The Filmic Dream and Point of View." *Literature/Film Quarterly* 8 (1980): 197–203.

Eco, Umberto. *A Theory of Semiotics.* Bloomington: Indiana University Press, 1976.

Edmiston, William F. "Focalization and the First-Person Narrator: A Revision of the Theory." *Poetics Today* 10 (Winter 1989): 729–44.

Eisenstein, Sergei. *The Film Sense*, trans. by Jay Leyda. New York: Harcourt, Brace & World, 1947.

———— "A Dialectic Approach to Film Form." In *Film Form: Essays in Film Theory*, trans. by Jay Leyda. New York: Harcourt, Brace & World, 1949.

———— "Dickens, Griffith, and the Film Today." In *Film Form: Essays in Film Theory*, trans. by Jay Leyda. New York: Harcourt, Brace & World, 1949.

———— "The Fourth Dimension in Cinema." In *S.M. Eisenstein: Selected Works 1, Writings 1922–34*, trans. by Richard Taylor. Bloomington: Indiana University Press, 1988.

———— "The Dramaturgy of Film Form (The Dialectical Approach to Film Form)." In *S.M. Eisenstein: Selected Works 1, Writings 1922–34*, trans. by Richard Taylor. Bloomington: Indiana University Press, 1988.

Elgin, Catherine Z. *With Reference to Reference*. Indianapolis, Ind.: Hackett, 1983.

Fischer, Lucy. *Shot/Countershot: Film Tradition and Women's Cinema*. Princeton, N.J.: Princeton University Press, 1989.

Fleischman, Suzanne. *Tense and Narrativity: From Medieval Performance to Modern Fiction*. Austin: University of Texas Press, 1990.

Fodor, Jerry. *The Modularity of Mind*. Cambridge, Mass.: Bradford Books/MIT Press, 1983.

Forster, E.M. *Aspects of the Novel*. New York: Harcourt, Brace, 1927.

Frawley, William. *Text and Epistemology*. Norwood, N.J.: Ablex, 1987.

Frye, Northrop. *Fables of Identity: Studies in Poetic Mythology*. New York: Harcourt, Brace & World, 1963.

Gardner, Howard. "From Melvin to Melville: On the Relevance to Aesthetics of Recent Research on Story Comprehension." In *The Arts, Cognition, and Basic Skills*, ed. by Stanley S. Madeja. St Louis, Mo.: Cemrel, 1978.

———— *Frames of Mind: The Theory of Multiple Intelligences*. New York: Basic Books, 1983.

———— *The Mind's New Science: A History of the Cognitive Revolution*. New York: Basic Books, expanded ed., 1987.

Gaudreault, André. "Narration and Monstration in the Cinema." *Journal of Film and Video* 39 (Spring 1987): 29–36.

Gee, James Paul and François Grosjean. "Empirical Evidence for Narrative Structure." *Cognitive Science* 8 (January–March 1984): 59–85.

Genette, Gérard. "Boundaries of Narrative," trans. by Ann Levonas. *New Literary History* 8 (Autumn 1976): 1–13.

———— *Narrative Discourse: An Essay in Method*, trans. by Jane E. Lewin. Ithaca, N.Y.: Cornell University Press, 1980.

———— *Narrative Discourse Revisited*, trans. by Jane E. Lewin. Ithaca, N.Y.: Cornell University Press, 1988.

Gerrig, Richard J. "Reexperiencing Fiction and Non-Fiction." *Journal of Aesthetics and Art Criticism* 47 (Summer 1989): 277–80.

Goffman, Erving. *Frame Analysis: An Essay on the Organization of Experience*. Cambridge, Mass.: Harvard University Press, 1974.

Goldman, Alvin I. *Epistemology and Cognition*. Cambridge, Mass.: Harvard University Press, 1986.

Goodman, Nelson. *Languages of Art: An Approach to a Theory of Symbols*. Indianapolis, Ind.: Hackett, 2nd ed., 1976.

———— *Ways of Worldmaking*. Indianapolis, Ind.: Hackett, 1978.

———— *Fact, Fiction, and Forecast*. Cambridge, Mass.: Harvard University Press, 4th ed., 1983.

WORKS CITED

—— *Of Mind and Other Matters*. Cambridge, Mass.: Harvard University Press, 1984.

Goodman, Nelson and Catherine Z. Elgin. *Reconceptions in Philosophy and Other Arts and Sciences*. Indianapolis, Ind.: Hackett, 1988.

Gorbman, Claudia. *Unheard Melodies: Narrative Film Music*. Bloomington: Indiana University Press, 1987.

Gossman, Lionel. "History and Literature." In *The Writing of History: Literary Form and Historical Understanding*, ed. by Robert H. Canary and Henry Kozicki. Madison: University of Wisconsin Press, 1978.

Graesser, Arthur C. and Leslie F. Clark. *Structures and Procedures of Implicit Knowledge*. Norwood, N.J.: Ablex, 1985.

Greenspun, Roger. "Corrections: Roger Greenspun on *Letter from an Unknown Woman*." *Film Comment* 11 (January–February 1975): 89–92.

Greimas, Algirdas Julien. *On Meaning: Selected Writings in Semiotic Theory*, trans. by Paul J. Perron and Frank H. Collins. Minneapolis: University of Minnesota Press, 1981.

Greimas, Algirdas Julien and François Rastier. "The Interaction of Semiotic Constraints." *Yale French Studies* 41 (1968): 86–105.

Greimas, Algirdas Julien and Joseph Courtès. "The Cognitive Dimension of Narrative Discourse." *New Literary History* 7 (Spring 1976): 433–47.

—— "The Cognitive Dimension of Narrative Discourse." Reprinted in special issue on "Greimassian Semiotics" in *New Literary History* 20 (Spring 1989): 563–79.

Grimes, Joseph E. *The Thread of Discourse*. The Hague: Mouton, 1975.

Gulich, Elisabeth and Uta M. Quasthoff. "Narrative Analysis." In *Handbook of Discourse Analysis 2: Dimensions of Discourse*, ed. by Teun A. van Dijk. New York: Academic Press, 1985.

Guynn, William. *A Cinema of Nonfiction*. London and Toronto: Associated University Presses, 1990.

Hale, Norman. "*Letter from an Unknown Woman*: The Dance of Time and Space." *Cinemonkey* 5 (Winter 1979): 11–14.

Hamburger, Käte. *The Logic of Literature*, trans. by Marilynn J. Rose. Bloomington: Indiana University Press, 2nd rev. ed., 1973.

Hamon, Philippe. "Rhetorical Status of the Descriptive." *Yale French Studies* 61 (1981): 1–26.

Harding, D. W. "Psychological Processes in the Reading of Fiction." *British Journal of Aesthetics* 2 (April 1962): 133–47.

Harnad, Stevan, ed. *Categorical Perception: The Groundwork of Cognition*. New York: Cambridge University Press, 1987.

Hartman, Geoffrey H. "The Voice of the Shuttle: Language from the Point of View of Literature." In *Beyond Formalism: Literary Essays 1958–1970*. New Haven, Conn.: Yale University Press, 1970.

Haskell, Molly. *From Reverence to Rape: The Treatment of Women in the Movies*. Chicago, Ill.: University of Chicago Press, 2nd ed., 1987.

Haslett, Beth. "A Developmental Analysis of Children's Narratives." In *Contemporary Issues in Language and Discourse Processes*, ed. by Donald G. Ellis and William A. Donohue. Hillsdale, N.J.: Erlbaum, 1986.

Hastie, Reid. "Schematic Principles in Human Memory." In *Social Cognition: The Ontario Symposium* 1, ed. by E. Tory Higgins, C. Peter Herman, and Mark P. Zanna. Hillsdale, N.J.: Erlbaum, 1981.

Hayward, Albert W. Review of L.B. Cebik's *Fictional Narrative and Truth: An*

Epistemic Analysis. In *Journal of Aesthetics and Art Criticism* 45 (Winter 1986): 205–9.

Heath, Stephen. "Film and System: Terms of Analysis 1." *Screen* 16 (Spring 1975): 7–77.

———. "Film and System: Terms of Analysis 2." *Screen* 16 (Summer 1975): 91–113.

———. "*Touch of Evil*, the Long Version – a Note." *Screen* 17 (Spring 1976): 115–17.

———. "Postscript." In *Ophuls*, ed. by Paul Willemen. London: British Film Institute, 1978.

———. "The Question Oshima." In *Ophuls*, ed. by Paul Willemen. London: British Film Institute, 1978.

———. "Body, Voice." In *Questions of Cinema*. New York: Macmillan, 1981.

———. "Contexts." In *Questions of Cinema*. New York: Macmillan, 1981.

———. "Narrative Space." In *Questions of Cinema*. New York: Macmillan, 1981.

———. "The Question Oshima." In *Questions of Cinema*. New York: Macmillan, 1981.

Hedges, Inez. *Breaking the Frame: Film Language and the Experience of Limits*. Bloomington: Indiana University Press, 1991.

Hobbs, Jerry R. *Literature and Cognition*. Stanford, Calif.: Center for the Study of Language and Information, 1990.

Hoberman, J. "Dis Orient, Dat Occident." *Village Voice*. November 1, 1983.

Hochberg, Julian E. *Perception*. Englewood Cliffs, N.J.: Prentice-Hall, 2nd ed., 1978.

———. "Representation of Motion and Space in Video and Cinematic Displays." In *Handbook of Perception and Human Performance* 1, ed. by Kenneth R. Boff, Lloyd Kaufman, and James P. Thomas. New York: John Wiley & Sons, 1986.

Holland, Norman N. "Film Response from Eye to I: The Kuleshov Experiment." *South Atlantic Quarterly* 88 (Spring 1989): 415–42.

Hume, David. *A Treatise of Human Nature* 1, ed. by L.A. Selby-Bigge. London: Oxford University Press, 1951.

Iser, Wolfgang. *The Act of Reading: A Theory of Aesthetic Response*. Baltimore, Md.: Johns Hopkins University Press, 1978.

———. "Narrative Strategies as a Means of Communication." In *Interpretation of Narrative*, ed. by Mario J. Valdes and Owen J. Miller. Toronto: University of Toronto Press, 1978.

Jackendoff, Ray. *Consciousness and the Computational Mind*. Cambridge, Mass.: MIT Press, 1987.

Jakobson, Roman. "Visual and Auditory Signs." In *Selected Writings* 2. The Hague: Mouton, 1971.

———. "Linguistics and Poetics." In *The Structuralists: From Marx to Lévi-Strauss*, ed. by Richard and Fernande de George. Garden City, N.Y.: Doubleday, 1972.

James, William. *The Principles of Psychology* 1. Cambridge, Mass.: Harvard University Press, 1981.

Jarvie, Ian. *Philosophy of the Film: Epistemology, Ontology, Aesthetics*. New York: Routledge & Kegan Paul, 1987.

Jesionowski, Joyce E. *Thinking in Pictures: Dramatic Structure in D.W. Griffith's Biograph Films*. Berkeley: University of California Press, 1987.

Johnson, Mark. *The Body in the Mind: The Bodily Basis of Meaning, Imagination, and Reason*. Chicago, Ill.: University of Chicago Press, 1987.

Kaplan, E. Ann. *Women and Film: Both Sides of the Camera*. New York: Methuen, 1983.

———— "Introduction: From Plato's Cave to Freud's Screen." In *Psychoanalysis & Cinema*, New York: Routledge, 1990.

Kaplan, E. Ann, ed. *Psychoanalysis & Cinema*. New York: Routledge, 1990.

Kaufmann, Morgan. *Knowledge and Representation*, ed. by Beatrice de Gelder. London: Routledge & Kegan Paul, 1982.

Kawin, Bruce. *Mindscreen: Bergman, Godard, and First-Person Film*. Princeton, N.J.: Princeton University Press, 1978.

———— "An Outline of Film Voices." *Film Quarterly* 38 (Winter 1984–5): 38–46.

Kay, Paul. "Linguistic Competence and Folk Theories of Language: Two English Hedges." In *Proceedings of the Ninth Annual Meeting of the Berkeley Linguistics Society*. Berkeley, Calif.: Berkeley Linguistics Society, 1983.

Kermode, Frank. *The Sense of an Ending: Studies in the Theory of Fiction*. New York: Oxford University Press, 1967.

———— "Sensing Endings." *Nineteenth-Century Fiction* 33. (June 1978): 144–58.

Kestner, Joseph. "Secondary Illusion: The Novel and the Spatial Arts." In *Spatial Form in Narrative*, ed. by Jeffrey R. Smitten and Ann Daghistany. Ithaca, N.Y.: Cornell University Press, 1981.

Khatchadourian, Haig. "Space and Time in Film." *British Journal of Aesthetics* 27 (Spring 1987): 169–77.

Kinder, Marsha. "The Subversive Potential of the Pseudo-Iterative." *Film Quarterly* 43 (Winter 1989–90): 3–16.

Kinneavy, James L. *A Theory of Discourse: The Aims of Discourse*. New York: W.W. Norton, 1971.

Kolers, Paul A. and Henry L. Roediger. "Procedures of Mind." *Journal of Verbal Learning and Verbal Behavior* 23 (August 1984): 425–49.

Kozloff, Sarah Ruth. Review of David Bordwell's *Narration in the Fiction Film*. In *Film Quarterly* 40 (Fall 1986): 43–5.

———— "Narrative Theory and Television." In *Channels of Discourse: Television and Contemporary Criticism*, ed. by Robert C. Allen. Chapel Hill: University of North Carolina Press, 1987.

———— *Invisible Storytellers: Voice-Over Narration in American Fiction Film*. Berkeley: University of California Press, 1988.

Kurzon, Dennis. "How Lawyers Tell Their Tales: Narrative Aspects of a Lawyer's Brief." *Poetics* 14 (December 1985): 467–81.

Labov, William. *The Social Stratification of English in New York City*. Washington, D.C.: Center for Applied Linguistics, 1966.

———— *Language in the Inner City*. University Park: University of Pennsylvania Press, 1972.

Lacan, Jacques. "The Insistence of the Letter in the Unconscious." *Yale French Studies* 36/37 (1966): 112–47.

Lakoff, George. *Women, Fire, and Dangerous Things: What Categories Reveal about the Mind*. Chicago, Ill.: University of Chicago Press, 1987.

Lakoff, George and Mark Johnson. *Metaphors We Live By*. Chicago, Ill.: University of Chicago Press, 1980.

Lanser, Susan Sniader. *The Narrative Act: Point of View in Prose Fiction*. Princeton, N.J.: Princeton University Press, 1981.

Laplanche, J. and J.B. Pontalis. *The Language of Psycho-Analysis*, trans. by Donald Nicholson-Smith. New York: W.W. Norton, 1973.

Leff, Leonard. "Reading Kane." *Film Quarterly* 39 (Fall 1985): 10–20.

Leondar, Barbara. "Hatching Plots: Genesis of Storymaking." In *The Arts and*

Cognition, ed. by David Perkins and Barbara Leondar. Baltimore, Md.: Johns Hopkins University Press, 1977.

Lévi-Strauss, Claude. *Structural Anthropology*, trans. by Claire Jacobson and Brooke Grundfest Schoepf. Garden City, N.Y.: Doubleday, 1967.

Levinson, Jerrold. "The Place of Real Emotion in Response to Fictions." *Journal of Aesthetics and Art Criticism* 48 (Winter 1990): 79–80.

Lightman, Herb A. "The Technique Of The Documentary Film." *American Cinematographer* 26 (November 1945): 371, 378, 402.

Lipton, Lenny. *Independent Filmmaking*. San Francisco, Calif.: Straight Arrow Books, rev. ed., 1973.

Livingstone, Margaret S. "Art, Illusion and the Visual System." *Scientific American* 258 (January 1988): 78–85.

Lloyd, Dan. *Simple Minds*. Cambridge, Mass.: MIT Press, 1989.

Lubbock, Percy. *The Craft of Fiction*. New York: Charles Scribner & Sons, 1921.

Luhr, William. "Raymond Chandler and 'The Lady in the Lake.' " *Wide Angle* 6 (1984): 28–33.

MacCabe, Colin. "Realism and the Cinema: Notes on some Brechtian Theses." *Screen* 15 (Summer 1974): 7–27.

―――― "The Politics of Separation." *Screen* 16 (Winter 1975–6): 46–57.

―――― "*Days of Hope* – a Response to Colin McArthur." *Screen* 17 (Spring 1976): 98–101.

―――― "Theory and Film: Principles of Realism and Pleasure." *Screen* 17 (Autumn 1976): 7–27.

―――― "The Discursive and the Ideological in Film: Notes on the Conditions of Political Intervention." *Screen* 19 (Winter 1978–9): 29–43.

―――― *Tracking the Signifier: Theoretical Essays: Film, Linguistics, Literature*. Minneapolis: University of Minnesota Press, 1985.

McCarten, John. Review of *Lady in the Lake*. *The New Yorker*. February 1, 1947.

MacDougall, David. "Beyond Observational Cinema." In *Movies and Methods: An Anthology* 2, ed. by Bill Nichols. Berkeley: University of California Press, 1985.

Macksey, Richard and Eugenio Donato, eds. "To Write: An Intransitive Verb?" In *The Structuralist Controversy: The Languages of Criticism and the Sciences of Man*. Baltimore, Md.: Johns Hopkins University Press, 1972: 134–45.

McVay, Douglas. "Letter from an Unknown Woman." *Focus on Film* 35 (April 1980): 28–30.

Mancuso, James C. "The Acquisition and Use of Narrative Grammar Structure." In *Narrative Psychology: The Storied Nature of Human Conduct*, ed. by Theodore R. Sarbin. New York: Praeger, 1986.

Mandelker, Steven. "Searle on Fictional Discourse: A Defense Against Wolterstorff, Pavel and Rorty." *British Journal of Aesthetics* 27 (Spring 1987): 156–68.

Mandler, George. *Cognitive Psychology: An Essay in Cognitive Science*. Hillsdale, N.J.: Erlbaum, 1985.

Mandler, Jean Matter. *Stories, Scripts, and Scenes: Aspects of Schema Theory*. Hillsdale, N.J.: Erlbaum, 1984

―――― "On the Psychological Reality of Story Structure." *Discourse Processes* 10 (January–March 1987): 1–29.

Marchessault, Janine. "*Sans Soleil*." *CineAction!* 5 (Spring 1986): 2–6.

Margolin, Uri. "Individuals in Narrative Worlds: An Ontological Perspective." *Poetics Today* 11 (Winter 1990): 843–71.

Margolis, Joseph. *Art and Philosophy: Conceptual Issues in Aesthetics*. Brighton, Sussex: Harvester, 1980.

Marker, Chris. *"Sunless." Semiotext(e)* 4 (1984): 33–40.

Marr, David. *Vision: A Computational Investigation into the Human Representation and Processing of Visual Information*. San Francisco, Calif.: W.H. Freeman, 1982.

Marshall, Stuart. *"Lady in the Lake*: Identification and the Drives." *Film Form* 1 (Autumn 1977): 34–50.

Martin, Wallace. *Recent Theories of Narrative*. Ithaca, N.Y.: Cornell University Press, 1986.

Metz, Christian. *Film Language: A Semiotics of the Cinema*, trans. by Michael Taylor. New York: Oxford University Press, 1974.

‗‗‗ *The Imaginary Signifier: Psychoanalysis and the Cinema*, trans. by Celia Britton, Annwyl Williams, Ben Brewster and Alfred Guzzetti. Bloomington: Indiana University Press, 1982.

‗‗‗ "The Impersonal Enunciation, or the Site of Film (In the margin of recent works on enunciation in cinema)." *New Literary History* 22 (Summer 1991): 747–72.

Meyer, Bonnie J.F. *The Organization of Prose and its Effects on Memory*. Amsterdam: North-Holland, 1975.

Miller, Michael W. "Creativity Furor: High-Tech Alteration of Sights and Sounds Divides the Arts World." *Wall Street Journal* 117. September 1, 1987.

Mink, Louis O. "Narrative Form as a Cognitive Instrument." In *The Writing of History: Literary Form and Historical Understanding*, ed. by Robert H. Canary and Henry Kozicki. Madison: University of Wisconsin Press, 1978.

Minsky, Marvin. *The Society of Mind*. New York: Simon & Schuster, 1986.

Mitchell, W.J.T., ed. *On Narrative*. Chicago, Ill.: University of Chicago Press, 1981.

Modleski, Tania. "Time and Desire in the Woman's Film." *Cinema Journal* 23 (Spring 1984): 19–30.

Moreno, Julio L. "Subjective Cinema: And the Problem of Film in the First Person." *Quarterly of Film, Radio and Television* 7 (1952–3): 341–58.

Mulvey, Laura. *Visual and Other Pleasures*. Bloomington: Indiana University Press, 1989.

Münsterberg, Hugo. *The Film: A Psychological Study: The Silent Photoplay in 1916*. New York: Dover, 1970.

Naremore, James. *Acting in the Cinema*. Berkeley: University of California Press, 1988.

Nelles, William. "Getting Focalization into Focus." *Poetics Today* 11 (Summer 1990): 365–82.

New Literary History 6, 11 (Winter 1975 and Spring 1980). Special issues on "On Narrative and Narratives."

Nichols, Bill. *Ideology and the Image: Social Representation in the Cinema and Other Media*. Bloomington: Indiana University Press, 1981.

‗‗‗ "The Voice of Documentary." In *Movies and Methods: An Anthology* 2, ed. by Bill Nichols. Berkeley: University of California Press, 1985.

‗‗‗ "History, Myth, and Narrative in Documentary." *Film Quarterly* 41 (Fall 1987): 9–20.

‗‗‗ "Form Wars: The Political Unconscious of Formalist Theory." *South Atlantic Quarterly* 88 (Spring 1989): 487–515.

Nichols, Bill and Susan J. Lederman. "Flicker and Motion in Film." In *The Cinematic Apparatus*, ed. by Teresa de Lauretis and Stephen Heath. New York: St Martin's Press, 1980.

Nietzsche, Friedrich. *Beyond Good and Evil: Prelude to a Philosophy of the Future*, trans. by Walter Kaufmann. New York: Vintage, 1966.

300

Nizhny, Vladimir. *Lessons with Eisenstein*, trans. by Ivor Montagu and Jay Leyda. London: George Allen & Unwin, 1962.

Palmer, F.R. *Semantics: A New Outline*. London: Cambridge University Press, 1976.

Parsons, Terence. "A Meinongian Analysis of Fictional Objects." In *Grazer Philosophische Studien* 1 (1974).

_____ *Nonexistent Objects*. New Haven, Conn.: Yale University Press, 1980.

Pavel, Thomas G. *The Poetics of Plot: The Case of English Renaissance Drama*. Minneapolis: University of Minnesota Press, 1985.

_____ *Fictional Worlds*. Cambridge, Mass.: Harvard University Press, 1986.

Penley, Constance, ed. *Feminism and Film Theory*. New York: Routledge, 1988.

Perkins, V.F. "*Letter from an Unknown Woman*." *Movie* (Summer 1982): 61–72.

Peterson, James. "The Artful Mathematicians of the Avant-Garde." *Wide Angle* 7 (1985): 14–23.

_____ "Bruce Conner and the Compilation Narrative." *Wide Angle* 8 (1986): 53–62.

Piaget Jean. *Structuralism*, trans. by Chaninah Maschler. New York: Harper & Row, 1970.

Pieraut-Le Bonniec, Gilberte. *The Development of Modal Reasoning: Genesis of Necessity and Possibility Notions*. New York: Academic Press, 1980.

Pipolo, Tony. "The Aptness of Terminology: Point of View, Consciousness and *Letter from an Unknown Woman*." *Film Reader* 4 (1979): 166–79.

Planalp, Sally. "Scripts, Story Grammars, and Causal Schemas." In *Contemporary Issues in Language and Discourse Processes*, ed. by Donald G. Ellis and William A. Donohue. Hillsdale, N.J.: Erlbaum, 1986.

Plantinga, Carl. "Defining Documentary: Fiction, Non-Fiction, and Projected Worlds." *Persistence of Vision* 5 (Spring 1987): 44–54.

_____ "The Mirror Framed: A Case For Expression in Documentary." *Wide Angle* 13 (April 1991): 40–53.

Plaus, F. Xavier. "Freudian Drive Theory and Epistemology." In *The Psychology of Knowing*, ed. by Joseph R. Royce and William W. Rozeboom. New York: Gordon & Breach, 1972.

Pleh, Csaba. "On Formal- and Content-Based Models of Story Memory." In *Literary Discourse: Aspects of Cognitive and Social Psychological Approaches*, ed. by Laszlo Halasz. New York: Walter de Gruyter, 1987.

Poetics 15 (April 1986). Special issue on "Narrative Analysis: An Interdisciplinary Dialogue."

Poetics Today 11, 12 (Summer and Winter 1990, Fall 1991). Special issues on "Narratology Revisited."

Polan, Dana. *Power and Paranoia: History, Narrative, and the American Cinema. 1940–1950*. New York: Columbia University Press, 1986.

Prado, C.G. *Making Believe: Philosophical Reflections on Fiction*. Westport, Conn.: Greenwood Press, 1984.

Pratt, Mary Louise. *Toward a Speech Act Theory of Literary Discourse*. Bloomington: Indiana University Press, 1977.

Prince, Gerald. *A Grammar of Stories: An Introduction*. The Hague: Mouton, 1973.

_____ "Aspects of a Grammar of Narrative." *Poetics Today* 1 (1980): 49–63.

_____ *Narratology: The Form and Functioning of Narrative*. New York: Mouton, 1982.

_____ *A Dictionary of Narratology*. Lincoln: University of Nebraska Press, 1987.

Propp, Vladimir. *Morphology of the Folktale*, trans. by Laurence Scott, rev. and ed. by Louis A. Wagner. Austin: University of Texas Press, 2nd ed., 1968.

Pylyshyn, Zenon W. "Metaphorical Imprecision and the 'Top-Down' Research Strategy." In *Metaphor and Thought*, ed. by Andrew Ortony. New York: Cambridge University Press, 1979.

Quine, W.V. *Quiddities: An Intermittently Philosophical Dictionary*. Cambridge, Mass.: Harvard University Press, 1987.

Rabkin, Eric S. "Spatial Form and Plot." In *Spatial Form in Narrative*, ed. by Jeffrey R. Smitten and Ann Daghistany. Ithaca, N.Y.: Cornell University Press, 1981.

Rafferty, Terrence. "Marker Changes Trains." *Sight and Sound* 53 (Autumn 1984): 284–8.

Reddy, Michael J. "The Conduit Metaphor – A Case of Frame Conflict in Our Language about Language." In *Metaphor and Thought*, ed. by Andrew Ortony. New York: Cambridge University Press, 1979.

Reisz, Karel. "Ophuls and *La Ronde*." *Sequence* (January 1952): 33–5.

Reisz, Karel and Gavin Millar. *The Technique of Film Editing*. New York: Hastings House, 2nd ed., 1968.

Renov, Michael. "Documentary/Technology/Immediacy: Strategies of Resistance." Unpublished paper. Los Angeles: University of Southern California, 1986.

———— "Re-thinking Documentary: Toward a Taxonomy of Mediation." *Wide Angle* 8 (1986): 71–7.

Riffaterre, Michael. *Fictional Truth*. Baltimore, Md.: Johns Hopkins University Press, 1990.

Rimmon-Kenan, Shlomith. *Narrative Fiction: Contemporary Poetics*. New York: Methuen, 1983.

Robbe-Grillet, Alain. "Nature, Humanism, Tragedy." In *For A New Novel: Essays on Fiction*, trans. by Richard Howard. New York: Grove, 1965.

Rodowick, D.N., "The Difficulty of Difference." *Wide Angle* 5 (1982): 4–15.

Ronen, Ruth. "Paradigm Shift in Plot Models: An Outline of the History of Narratology." *Poetics Today* 11 (Winter 1990): 817–42.

Rorty, Richard. "Is There a Problem about Fictional Discourse?" In *Consequences of Pragmatism. Essays: 1972–1980*. Minneapolis: University of Minnesota Press, 1982.

Rosen, Philip. "History of Image, Image of History: Subject and Ontology in Bazin." *Wide Angle* 9 (1987): 7–34.

Rothman, William. *Hitchcock – The Murderous Gaze*. Cambridge, Mass.: Harvard University Press, 1982.

Rush, Jeffrey S. " 'Lyric Oneness': The Free Syntactical Indirect and the Boundary Between Narrative and Narration." *Wide Angle* 8 (1986): 27–33.

Russell, Bertrand. *Mysticism and Logic and other Essays*. London: George Allen & Unwin, 1949.

———— *Logic and Knowledge. Essays, 1901–1950*, ed. by Robert Charles Marsh. New York: Macmillan, 1956.

———— *The Problems of Philosophy*. London: Oxford University Press, 1972.

Ruthrof, Horst. *The Reader's Construction of Narrative*. London: Routledge & Kegan Paul, 1981.

Ryan, Marie-Laure. "Fiction as a Logical, Ontological, and Illocutionary Issue." *Style* 18 (Spring 1984): 121–39.

———— "Stacks, Frames and Boundaries, or Narrative as Computer Language." *Poetics Today* 11 (Winter 1990): 873–99.

Ryle, Gilbert. "Imaginary Objects." In *Proceedings of the Aristotelian Society*. Supplementary 12 (1933): 18–43.

———— "Knowing How and Knowing That." In *Proceedings of the Aristotelian Society* 46 (1945–6): 1–16.

———— *The Concept of Mind*. London: Hutchinson, 1949.

Said, Edward W. *Beginnings: Intention and Method*. New York: Basic Books, 1975.

Salt, Barry. *Film Style and Technology: History and Analysis*. London: Starword, 1983.

Sarbin, Theodore R., ed. *Narrative Psychology: The Storied Nature of Human Conduct*. New York: Praeger, 1986.

Schank, Roger C. and Robert P. Abelson. *Scripts, Plans, Goals and Understanding*. Hillsdale, N.J.: Erlbaum, 1977.

Scheuer, Stephen H., ed. *Movies On TV: 1982–1983 Edition*. New York: Bantam, 9th rev. ed., 1981.

Schiffrin, Deborah. "Multiple Constraints on Discourse Options: A Quantitative Analysis of Causal Sequences." *Discourse Processes* 8 (July–September 1985): 281–303.

Seamon, Roger. "The Story of the Moral: The Function of Thematizing in Literary Criticism." *Journal of Aesthetics and Art Criticism* 47 (Summer 1989): 229–36.

Searle, John R. "The Logical Status of Fictional Discourse." *New Literary History* 6 (Winter 1975): 319–32.

Sesonske, Alexander. "Cinema Space." In *Explorations in Phenomenology*, ed. by David Carr and Edward S. Casey. The Hague: Martinus Nijhoff, 1973.

———— "Time and Tense in Cinema." *Journal of Aesthetics and Art Criticism* 38 (Summer 1980): 419–26.

Shusterman, Richard. "Interpretation, Intention, and Truth." *Journal of Aesthetics and Art Criticism* 46 (Spring 1988): 399–411.

Silverman, Kaja. *The Subject of Semiotics*. New York: Oxford University Press, 1983.

———— "Dis-Embodying the Female Voice." In *Re-Vision: Essays in Feminist Film Criticism*, ed. by Mary Ann Doane, Patricia Mellencamp and Linda Williams [The American Film Institute Monograph Series 3]. Frederick, Md.: University Publications of America, 1984.

———— *The Acoustic Mirror: The Female Voice in Psychoanalysis and Cinema*. Bloomington: Indiana University Press, 1988.

Simmons, Steven. "Man Without a Country." *The Movies* (November 1983).

Sjogren, Britta, "Sustaining Difference: The Female Voice-Off in *Letter from an Unknown Woman*." Unpublished paper. Los Angeles: University of California, 1990.

Slater, Hartley. "Fictions." *British Journal of Aesthetics* 27 (Spring 1987): 145–55.

Sobchack, Vivian. *The Address of the Eye: A Phenomenology of Film Experience*. Princeton, N.J.: Princeton University Press, forthcoming.

Staiger, Janet. *Interpreting Films: Studies in the Historical Reception of American Cinema*. Princeton, N.J.: Princeton University Press, 1992.

Stam, Robert and Ella Shohat. "*Zelig* and Contemporary Theory: Meditation on the Chameleon Text." *Enclitic* 17/18 (1987): 176–93.

Stein, Nancy L. "The Comprehension and Appreciation of Stories: A Developmental Analysis." In *The Arts, Cognition, and Basic Skills*, ed. by Stanley S. Madeja. St Louis, Mo.: Cemrel, 1978.

Stein, Nancy L. and Christine G. Glenn. "Children's Concept of Time: The Development of a Story Schema." In *The Developmental Psychology of Time*, ed. by William J. Friedman. New York: Academic Press, 1982.

Steiner, Peter. *Russian Formalism: A Metapoetics*. Ithaca, N.Y.: Cornell University Press, 1984.

Stenning, Keith and Lynn Michell. "Learning How to Tell a Good Story: The Development of Content and Language in Children's Telling of One Tale." *Discourse Processes* 8 (July–September 1985): 261–79.

Stephenson, Ralph and Jean R. Debrix. *The Cinema as Art*. Baltimore, Md.: Penguin, 2nd ed., 1976.

Steranko, Jim. "Who is Scorpio?." In *Nick Fury, Agent of S.H.I.E.L.D.* 1. Marvel Comics, June 1968.

Sternberg, Meir. *Expositional Modes and Temporal Ordering in Fiction*. Baltimore, Md.: Johns Hopkins University Press, 1978.

—————— "Telling in Time (I): Chronology and Narrative Theory." *Poetics Today* 11 (Winter 1990): 901–48.

Stewart, Garrett. "Singer Sung: Voice as Avowal in Streisand's *Yentl*." *Mosaic* 18 (Fall 1985): 135–58.

—————— "Photo-gravure: Death, Photography, and Film Narrative." *Wide Angle* 9 (1987): 11–31.

—————— *Reading Voices: Literature and the Phonotext*. Berkeley: University of California Press, 1990.

Strawson, P.F. "On Referring." *Mind* 59 (July 1950): 320–44.

Studlar, Gaylyn. "Masochism and the Perverse Pleasures of the Cinema." *Quarterly Review of Film Studies* 9 (Fall 1984): 267–82.

Sutton-Smith, Brian. "Children's Fiction Making." In *Narrative Psychology: The Storied Nature of Human Conduct*, ed. by Theodore R. Sarbin. New York: Praeger, 1986.

Tannen, Deborah. "What's in a Frame? Surface Evidence for Underlying Expectations." In *New Directions in Discourse Processing*, ed. by Roy O. Freedle. Norwood, N.J.: Ablex, 1979.

Taylor, Richard. "Introduction." In *S.M. Eisenstein: Selected Works 1. Writings 1922–34*, trans. by Richard Taylor. Bloomington: Indiana University Press, 1988.

Telotte, J.P. "The Detective as Dreamer: The Case of *The Lady in the Lake*." *Journal of Popular Film and Television* 12 (Spring 1984): 4–15.

Thompson, Kristin. *Eisenstein's Ivan the Terrible: A Neoformalist Analysis*. Princeton, N.J.: Princeton University Press, 1981.

—————— "The Concept of Cinematic Excess." In *Narrative, Apparatus, Ideology: A Film Theory Reader*, ed. by Philip Rosen. New York: Columbia University Press, 1986.

—————— *Breaking the Glass Armor: Neoformalist Film Analysis*. Princeton, N.J.: Princeton University Press, 1988.

Todorov, Tzvetan. "The Two Principles of Narrative." *Diacritics* 1 (Fall 1971): 37–44.

—————— *The Fantastic: A Structural Approach to a Literary Genre*, trans. by Richard Howard. Ithaca, N.Y.: Cornell University Press, 1975.

—————— *The Poetics of Prose*, trans. by Richard Howard. Ithaca, N.Y.: Cornell University Press, 1977.

—————— "Categories of the Literary Narrative," trans. by Ann Goodman. *Film Reader* 2 (1977): 19–37.

—————— *Introduction to Poetics*, trans. by Richard Howard. Minneapolis: University of Minnesota Press, 1981.

Todorov, Tzvetan, ed. *French Literary Theory Today: A Reader*, trans. by R. Carter. Cambridge: Cambridge University Press, 1982.

Tomasulo, Frank P. "Narrate and Describe? Point of View and Narrative Voice in *Citizen Kane*'s Thatcher Sequence." *Wide Angle* 8 (1986): 45–52.

Toolan, Michael J. *Narrative: A Critical Linguistic Introduction.* New York: Routledge, 1988.

Truffaut, François. *Hitchcock.* New York: Simon & Schuster, rev. ed., 1984.

Turim, Maureen. "The Place of Visual Illusions." In *The Cinematic Apparatus,* ed. by Teresa de Lauretis and Stephen Heath. New York: St Martin's Press, 1980.

—— "Symmetry/Asymmetry and Visual Fascination." *Wide Angle* 4 (1980): 38–47.

—— *Flashbacks in Film: Memory and History.* New York: Routledge, 1989.

Turner, Dennis. "Film Noir and the Apparatus of the Fetish: Introduction to 'Flickerings of Black and White.' " *Structuralist Review* 2 (Spring 1984): 34–43.

Turner, Victor. "Social Dramas and Stories about Them." *Critical Inquiry* 7 (Autumn 1980): 141–68.

Utne Reader 34 (July/August 1989): 50–76. Special section on "Postmodernism and beyond . . . ."

van Dijk, Teun A. and Walter Kintsch. *Strategies of Discourse Comprehension.* New York: Academic Press, 1983.

Vaughn [Vaughan], Dai. "Arms and the Absent." *Sight and Sound* 48 (Summer 1979): 182–7.

—— "The Space Between Shots." In *Movies and Methods: An Anthology* 2, ed. by Bill Nichols. Berkeley: University of California Press, 1985.

Viberg, Ake. "The Verbs of Perception: A Typological Study. . . . " In *Explanations for Language Universals,* ed. by Brian Butterworth, Bernard Comrie, and Osten Dahl. New York: Mouton, 1984.

Vygotsky, L.S. *Thought and Language,* trans. by Alex Kozulin. Cambridge, Mass.: MIT Press, rev. ed., 1986.

Walker, Michael. "Ophuls in Hollywood." *Movie* (Summer 1982): 39–48.

Walsh, Michael. "Around the World, Across All Frontiers: *Sans Soleil* as *Depays.*" *CineAction!* (Fall 1989): 29–36.

Walton, Kendall L. "What is Abstract About the Art of Music?" *Journal of Aesthetics and Art Criticism* 46 (Spring 1988): 351–64.

Waugh, Thomas. "Beyond *Verité*: Emile de Antonio and the New Documentary of the Seventies." In *Movies and Methods: An Anthology* 2, ed. by Bill Nichols. Berkeley: University of California Press, 1985.

Wexman, Virginia Wright. "The Transfiguration of History: Ophuls, Vienna, and *Letter from an Unknown Woman.*" In *Letter from an Unknown Woman,* ed. by Virginia Wright Wexman with Karen Hollinger. New Brunswick, N.J.: Rutgers University Press, 1986.

White, Hayden. "The Fictions of Factual Representation." In *Tropics of Discourse: Essays in Cultural Criticism.* Baltimore, Md.: Johns Hopkins University Press, 1978.

—— "The Historical Text as Literary Artifact." In *The Writing of History: Literary Form and Historical Understanding,* ed. by Robert H. Canary and Henry Kozicki. Madison: University of Wisconsin Press, 1978.

—— "The Narrativization of Real Events." *Critical Inquiry* 7 (Summer 1981): 793–8.

—— "The Value of Narrativity in the Representation of Reality." In *The Content of the Form: Narrative Discourse and Historical Representation.* Baltimore, Md.: Johns Hopkins University Press, 1987.

———— "Historiography and Historiophoty." *American Historical Review* 93 (December 1988): 1193–9.

White, James Boyd. *Heracles' Bow: Essays on the Rhetoric and Poetics of the Law*. Madison: University of Wisconsin Press, 1985.

Wicker, Brian. *The Story-Shaped World: Fiction and Metaphysics: Some Variations on a Theme*. London: Athlone Press, 1975.

Wide Angle 8 (1986). Special issue on "Narrative/Non-Narrative."

Willemen, Paul. "The Ophuls Text: A Thesis." In *Ophuls*, ed. by Paul Willemen. London: British Film Institute, 1978.

———— "Cinematic Discourse: The Problem of Inner Speech." *Screen* 22 (1981): 63–93.

Williams, Alan [Larson]. "Is Sound Recording Like a Language?" *Yale French Studies* 60 (1980): 55–61.

———— *Max Ophuls and the Cinema of Desire: Style and Spectacle in Four Films, 1948–1955*. New York: Arno Press, 1980.

Williams, Christopher, ed. *Realism and the Cinema: A Reader*. London: Routledge & Kegan Paul, 1980.

Williams, Linda. "When the Woman Looks." In *Re-Vision: Essays in Feminist Film Criticism*, ed. by Mary Ann Doane, Patricia Mellencamp, and Linda Williams [The American Film Institute Monograph Series 3]. Frederick, Md.: University Publications of America, 1984.

Wilson, George M. *Narration in Light: Studies in Cinematic Point of View*. Baltimore, Md.: Johns Hopkins University Press, 1986.

Winnett, Susan. "Coming Unstrung: Women, Men, Narrative, and Principles of Pleasure." *PMLA* 105 (May 1990): 505–18.

Winograd, Terry. "Frame Representations and the Declarative/Procedural Controversy." In *Representation and Understanding: Studies in Cognitive Science*, ed. by Daniel G. Bobrow and Allan Collins. New York: Academic Press, 1975.

Wittgenstein, Ludwig. *Philosophical Investigations*, trans. by G.E.M. Anscombe. New York: Macmillan, 3rd ed., 1958.

Wolfe, Charles. "Voice-over in the Classical Documentary Film." Unpublished paper. Santa Barbara: University of California, 1991.

Wollen, Peter. "Introduction to *Citizen Kane*." *Film Reader* 1 (1975): 9–15.

———— "The Hermeneutic Code." In *Readings and Writings: Semiotic Counter-Strategies*. London: Verso, 1982.

Wood, Robin. *Personal Views: Explorations in Film*. London: Gordon Fraser, 1976.

Wright, Will. *Six Guns and Society: A Structural Study of the Western*. Berkeley: University of California Press, 1975.

Youdelman, Jeffrey. "Narration, Invention, and History: A Documentary Dilemma." *Cineaste* 12 (1982): 8–15.

INDEX

316

and story world xi, 36, 56, ch. 3 nn. 4, 5; and stylistic metaphors 61; in *The 39 Steps* 55, 56–62; time on 97, 149, ch. 3, nn. 1, 33; and types of story matching 58–60, 61–2; *see also* continuity; story

Seamon, Roger ch. 4 n. 20

Searle, John 193, ch. 7 nn. 5, 17

Secrets of a Soul (Pabst, 1926) 124

self-consciousness 73, 211, ch. 6 n. 52

separation of material and structure 70, 71, 83, 112, 146, 147, 148, 156, 158; definition 141–2; and implicitness ch. 4 n. 11; and point-of-view shot ch. 5 n. 5; story and plot ch. 5 n. 15; story and screen 29, 40, 45, 46; *see also* time, double interpretation of

Sesonske, Alexander ch. 2 nn. 2, 17

Shires, Linda M. ch. 1 n. 19, ch. 4 n. 36

Shklovsky, Victor 120

Shohat, Ella ch. 4 n. 19

shot/reverse-shot *see* reverse angle

shot scales, inverted pyramid of 185; not used 52, ch. 6 n. 50

showing 122, 146–9, 150, 151, 158; contrasted with telling 146, fig. 25 p. 106, ch. 2 n. 12, ch. 5 n. 16, ch. 6 n. 42; definition 146–7, ch. 2 n. 12

Shusterman, Richard ch. 4 n. 82

Silverman, Kaja ch. 2 n. 27, ch. 6 nn. 31, 32

Simmons, Steven ch. 7 n. 51

Simon, William H. ch. 5 n. 19

simultaneity *see* description; narration, levels of

Sirk, Douglas ch. 6 n. 23

Sjogren, Britta ch. 6 n. 32

slant ch. 4 n. 62

Slater, Hartley 194, ch. 7 nn. 6, 7, 31

Smith, Joseph H. ch. 6 n. 48

Smitten, Jeffrey R. ch. 1 nn. 10, 55, ch. 4 nn. 60, 88

Sobchack, Vivian 156, ch. 4 n. 50, ch. 5 n. 48, ch. 6 n. 17

Sorcerer (Friedkin, 1977) ch. 3 n. 25

space: chain of 43, 56; continuity 56, 58, 60; depth and duration ch. 5 n. 20; in *Dr. Mabuse* 51–5; double interpretation of 33–4, 62; and

historical present tense ch. 6 n. 7; impossible 44, 52, 55, 62; shot/reverse-shot 43–4; in *The 39 Steps* 56–62; top-down component of 118; types in story 42–4; virtual 60, 62, 84; *see also* camera position; match; shot scales

spectator: first belief of 30, 51, 80, 97–8, 176, 205, ch. 2 n. 23; invisible ch. 6 n. 21; *see also* chameleon text; schema, narrative; subject

speech: holistic speech ch. 5 n. 50; inner speech 122; speech act 107, 121, 146, ch. 4 nn. 17, 35, ch. 7 n. 17; synoptic speech 122; *see also* discourse; voice

Spellbound (Hitchcock, 1945) 124

Staiger, Janet ch. 1 n. 74, ch. 2 n. 27, ch. 4 n. 79

Stalker (Tarkovsky, 1979) ch. 3 n. 16

Stam, Robert ch. 2 n. 39, ch. 4 n. 19

stance ch. 4 n. 40

Star Wars (Lucas, 1977) 199, 205, ch. 7 n. 28

status ch. 4 n. 40

Stein, Nancy L. ch. 1 nn. 36, 51, ch. 2 n. 22

Steiner, Peter ch. 4 n. 73

Stenning, Keith ch. 1 n. 70

Stephenson, Ralph ch. 2 n. 17

Steranko, Jim ch. 3 n. 28

Sternberg, Meir 167, ch. 1 n. 41, ch. 2 n. 17, ch. 5 n. 22, ch. 6 n. 9

Stewart, Garrett ch. 1 n. 18, ch. 2 n. 52, ch. 6 nn. 7, 55, ch. 7 n. 25

story and screen xi, ch. 2 n. 10, ch. 3 n. 5, ch. 6 n. 43; in *Dr. Mabuse* 51–2; in *The Girl and Her Trust* 63–4; in *The 39 Steps* 56–62, ch. 3 nn. 3, 4; *see also* match

story world xi, 33–4, 36, 200; definition 119, 120; diegetic and nondiegetic 35; distinguished from plot 119–20, ch. 5 n. 15; and psychoanalysis 123; and stylistic metaphors 61, 138, 155; and types of screen matching 58–60, 61–2; *see also* screen; diegesis

Straub, Jean-Marie ch. 2 n. 16

Strawson, P.F. ch. 7 nn. 12, 20

Studlar, Gaylyn ch. 5 n. 54

style: definition 119, 120; and fiction

Working with
Americans

Working with Americans

How to build profitable business relationships

Allyson Stewart-Allen and Lanie Denslow

Prentice
Hall
BUSINESS

---

an imprint of **Pearson Education**

London • New York • Toronto • Sydney • Tokyo • Singapore • Hong Kong • Cape Town

New Delhi • Madrid • Paris • Amsterdam • Munich • Milan • Stockholm

PEARSON EDUCATION LIMITED

Edinburgh Gate
Harlow CM20 2JE
Tel: +44 (0)1279 623623
Fax: +44 (0)1279 431059
www.pearsoned.co.uk

First published in Great Britain in 2002

The right of Allyson Stewart-Allen and Lanie Denslow to be identified as Authors of this Work has been asserted by them in accordance with the Copyright, Designs and Patents Act 1988.

ISBN-10: 0-273-65626-0
ISBN-13: 978-0-273-65626-5

British Library Cataloguing in Publication Data
A CIP catalogue record for this book can be obtained from the British Library

10 9 8 7 6 5 4

Designed by Claire Brodmann Book Designs, Lichfield, Staffs
Illustrated by M Nadler
Typeset by Land & Unwin (Data Sciences) Ltd, Bugbrooke
Printed and bound in Great Britain by Bell & Bain Ltd, Glasgow

The Publishers' policy is to use paper manufactured from sustainable forests.

Contents

Foreword

With shelves in bookstores heaving with volumes on how to do business with almost every nationality, it seems odd that the denizens of one of the world's largest markets have been overlooked. That is, until now.

As an American expat living in Britain since 1993, now working as the Vice President of Group External Affairs at Shell International, I feel this book is required reading for everyone who has, or would like to have, American business partners, employees or colleagues. These valuable insights facilitate understanding and save precious time and frustration in working with the "cut to the chase" approach of most Americans in business.

As American-style capitalism becomes the norm in even the most remote parts of the world, business men and women will gain an insider's view of the what, why and how of the American business psyche. You will learn that things often are exactly as they seem and that Americans usually do say exactly what they mean.

As an American myself, I wish that this book had been available when I first embarked on my expatriate career; my life – and the lives of those with whom I've worked – would have been made much easier with the knowledge of what makes Americans tick.

Every American should think about giving this book to overseas colleagues, and every company to its managers to make them even more effective in their US business pursuits.

Mary Jo Jacobi

Acknowledgements

From Allyson Stewart-Allen

To list all those who encouraged me to write this guide for better understanding of Americans at work would be like giving an endless Oscar acceptance speech. Special thanks *are* due to Graham and Grace Allen, who have been, and always are, supportive, loving and insightful and without whose encouragement I'd be lost. I also owe a great debt to my parents, who taught me the value "hard work gets results", as well as how to use commas correctly, appreciate the value of good writing, and communication.

I certainly owe significant thanks to each of my European clients and colleagues (you know who you are!) who regularly engaged me in conversation about American foreign policy, business and cultural values which was instrumental in allowing me to crystallize my thoughts for this exposé.

Others who have inspired and helped me include Mary Jo Jacobi, Dr Peter Drucker, Philip Kotler, Ernest Beck, the business programme producers at Sky News and CNN London among many, many others.

From Lanie Denslow

That this book exists is testimony to the support, encouragement, advice and good humour of my family and friends. Colleagues, friends and clients generously shared their experiences and provided introductions to people they knew. Strangers around the world responded and became friends. To each of them I owe a debt of thanks.

My special appreciation and endless thanks go to those who read, commented and reread the manuscript as it developed. The final product reflects their thoughtful comments.

My hope is that this book is useful, that it helps people build bridges to share their work, their experiences and lead them to the rich special friendships I've discovered working across cultures.

From both authors

Our publishers – Richard Stagg, Rachael Stock, Rachel Russell – are due special thanks for believing in us and this project, and helping us see what a wonderful, real intellectual property we have thanks to their leadership and navigation. Their graciousness and encouragement at every step were invaluable! Our editing team kept us moving with tact and humour too.

We also owe a debt to all the many people who have touched our lives, informed our work, shared our journey – we say **Thank You!**

Allyson (allyson@workingwithamericans.com)
Lanie (lanie@workingwithamericans.com)

Introduction

You might wonder why we decided to write this book about Americans in business, when it seems so many legal and accounting firms, and culture gurus have already covered this topic before? Isn't working with Americans just like working within any other culture, just with a different accent? In simple terms, no. We couldn't find a book or reference guide specifically on this topic – so we decided to write one ourselves.

And why us, you may ask? Because, as well as both being Americans, we have, between us, over 40 years' experience living and working in Europe. Allyson Stewart-Allen (*allyson@workingwithamericans.com*) lives in London, and makes her living advising European and US companies wanting to cross the Atlantic with their products and services. Lanie Denslow (*lanie@workingwithamericans.com*) lives in Los Angeles and spends a significant part of each year working in London and Paris. Her work advising individuals and institutions in the US and Europe has shown differences in business cultures do exist and understanding these differences helps build profits.

Over the years we've been developing the ideas contained in this book with our non-American clients and network of experts. We've learned there hasn't been anything compiled that focuses on helping you interpret the *business* culture of the connected, global, hyperspeed American business world. There must be something about the American culture (or the water) that produces seven of the top ten most respected companies in the world,[1] and we hope in the course of this book you discover for yourself what that magic might be.

According to Felix Rohytan, "today approximately four and a half million Americans work for European companies. About the same number of Europeans are employed by American companies."[2] Viewed from our

[1] *Financial Times* survey, *World's Most Respected Companies*, 17 December 2001
[2] Felix G. Rohytan, "US and Europe Can do Business", *Wall Street Journal*, 11 July 2001: A22

perspective, this provides millions of possibilities for conflicts and confusion, humour misunderstood and opportunities missed. It is no longer sufficient to just "get on with it", to do business as usual and take your chances. "Too bad if they don't get it. We'll sell our titanium eyelashes elsewhere." But then you find that "elsewhere" has its own culture too.

When working in American fast paced, complex business environments, you probably wish "it could be easier" and wonder when your American colleagues will behave in a "reasonable" fashion. This book is meant to help you understand that the definition of "reasonable" varies by culture, to understand what drives American business behaviours, to learn what is typical, and thereby reduce potential levels of stress when you encounter business values and decisions which feel very different from those that would be the norm in your home business culture.

As Americans and authors, we know it is impossible to describe the complete diversity of the US business culture within these covers. This is *not* an absolute guide. There are no "one-size-fits-all" explanations as people and situations will be different – influenced by family, upbringing, education and personal experience. But we hope we've gone some way towards demystifying the American approach to business, and at the same time by helping you better understand Americans, they'll in turn better understand your business culture too.

We'd like to invite you to send us your stories about your best and worst moments when working with Americans, and your questions so you can be an even more effective internationalist, to *www.workingwithamericans.com*.

Culture is business too

Culture is comprised of the behaviours that are prized – within a society, a company, and even a family. We learn these behaviours by experience and example. The lessons and the rules become so deeply embedded within us that our actions are automatic, leading culture to be called the "software of the mind".[3] We know what's right and wrong, how to make a friend, share information, where to stand during a conversation, and even what time to expect lunch. All these matters, big and small, are dictated by our culture.

Culture doesn't only guide our personal lives. According to the political economist Max Weber, culture is critical to business, to our economic development. He said "If we learn anything from the history of economic development it is that culture makes almost all the difference."[4] The noted author Michael Porter states that "Economic culture is defined as the beliefs, attitudes, and values that bear on the economic activities of individuals, organizations, and other institutions." Simply, it is how we do business.

"All cultures have wisdom"[5] but cultures vary between companies and countries and when these differences collide with each other, problems can arise. As our global economy expands and creates connections that are extensive, the possibilities for collisions increase.

Our focus in this book is the American culture as it reveals itself in a business environment. Culture in this context is about individual behaviours or patterns of behaviour. No one description fits all Americans. They are complex, independent, proactive and proud. They can be fun loving and optimistic, or stern and anxious. The variations can often be linked to age or location. Our goal is to help you understand what makes us "tick" so you can steer clear of misunderstandings and capitalize on your business opportunities.

Read on to learn how this shared cultural background influences American business behaviour today, and gain some practical tips for smoothing the way.

---

[3] G. Hofstede, *Cultures and Organizations*, McGraw-Hill, 1997: 4
[4] L. Harrison and S. Huntington, *Culture Matters*, Basic Books, 2000: 2
[5] J. Hammond and J. Morrison, *The Stuff Americans Are Made Of*, Macmillan, 1996: 271

part

1

background

1:

the tea party and the great frontier

INTRODUCTION

Back to the beginning. Where are you from? Today there are 281,421,906 people in the USA[1] and most of them can trace their family origins to another country. With the exception of American Indians, Hawaiians, Pacific Islanders and Alaskan natives, we are a nation of immigrants.

The attitudes and spirit, the hope and energy that propelled the first people to come, and that continue to entice people even now, are the foundations of the America we see today. A few words and phrases capture the essence of the country's spirit: Equality. Independence. Curiosity. Change is Good. New is Better. Hard work. Opportunity. In our lives, personal and professional, these words shape actions.

WHAT YOU'LL LEARN

➡ The attitudes, not just the results of the actions of the country's founders are in evidence today.

➡ America, the Land of Opportunity, is also the Land of Variety. The origins of the population can be traced to all parts of the globe.

➡ Although the country can be considered young, with little history, it does have a history – one that influences the actions of its people today.

➡ There's no harm in trying. Americans embrace the idea that change can be a good thing and, even if things don't work out as you might wish, you can always have another go.

[1] US Census Bureau Quick Facts, http://quickfacts.census.gov/qfd/states/36000.html, printed 15/9/01

America for

Situation

Overheard in the corporate halls of Britain Plc: "It's big, but so what, everyone speaks English, there's that 'special relationship' with the UK, so it's part hot and part cold, but how complicated can the market be?" The answer is – very complicated. With a rebellious history, a population representing the nations of the world, and an emphasis on independence, the American market can be segmented by age, sex, income, education, reading habits, even to blocks within zip codes! Complicated, segmented but still tied together by history and attitude.

Explanation

It's a New World

The USA is often referred to as the "New World" and by contrast Europe stands as the "Old World". The label "New World" is interpreted as a destination for a fresh start, an untouched place, one ready to accept everyone, a world that can be shaped in new ways, an implied promise. A place where you can realize your vision.

Although there are many today who would suggest that this time has past, that opportunities are limited, the actions of millions of others argue against this perspective. The continuing flow of immigrants suggests otherwise. (See Chapter 5 for a more detailed look at this

many remains the Land of Opportunity

topic.) While Americans may complain about reduced opportunities, people from other places have a different view. America for many remains the Land of Opportunity.

Who were they?

We think first of the settlers, the Pilgrims from the United Kingdom. America was, after all, a British colony. However, the founders represented a broader spectrum of Europeans: French, Irish, German and Spanish. Slavery brought people from Africa and the construction of the railroads drew workers from Asia. Although the majority of immigrants were Western Europeans, we count over 40 different countries as the original home of members of the US population.[2]

As people still do today, when they come to a new country, the early arrivals tended to settle in specific areas, with others from their country and culture. This created cities with concentrations of people from specific places, influencing the culture in each city. For example, Chicago drew people from Poland, Boston the Irish; New York is known for Italians and Puerto Ricans, and San Francisco for its Chinese community. The pattern continues today with Texas home to many from Mexico, Cubans living in Florida and California drawing from many countries in the Americas as well as being home to large

[2] Infoplease.com "Immigrants to the US by Country of Origin", http://www.infoplease.com/ipa/A0201398.html, printed 17/11/01

Korean, Chinese and Vietnamese groups. You can analyze almost any US city and identify representatives of many nationalities, early arrivals and newcomers alike.

In some US cities architecture tells the story of their inhabitants' origins. The churches and buildings of Europe are reflected in the architecture of East Coast cities such as New York and Boston. Spain and Mexico are the inspiration for the West's distinctive missions and haciendas, and Louisiana shows the influence of France in the colours of its buildings and the famous ironwork balconies found in New Orleans. When an American visits London for the first time, the city looks familiar: "It's Boston!" or "It's New York!" they say, seldom stopping to acknowledge which city was first.

To understand what brought people to the US it is useful to look beyond their place of origin and consider their motivations and attitudes. One point of view is that the people who founded the US were explorers, adventurers, independent thinkers and risk takers. They risked everything, whatever they had, to start anew.

But, before we deify these people, it is worth noting that some were probably opportunists, thieves and misfits with nothing to lose, nothing to risk, by making the journey. They were revolutionaries focused on change, ready to use violence to achieve their ends. A management consultant has suggested that "they were the ones who, for whatever reason, couldn't fit in – some of them would be 'the best' and some would be 'the worst' (of their societies)".

However you view them, it is reasonable to hypothesize that there was a common tie. They were all willing to take a risk, to act upon their belief that changing their circumstances and their environment would bring about a better life for themselves and their families.

The US, the former colony, still has strong ties to the United Kingdom. It is often said we are "two countries separated by a common language".[3] Traditions, history and more than 200 years of experience tie the two countries together. Today American Presidents acknowledge the connections by saying we have "a special relationship" between the two countries.

But not so widely recognized is that another country, one that has a somewhat tumultuous relationship with the US, played a critical role in US history. That country is France which provided both financial aid and philosophical support, during the American Revolution.

Today when the news is filled with stories of French farmers attacking McDonald's it is hard to recall that early support. Overall the links to both countries remain strong not only from history and habit, but now through economics and institutions. The UK and France rank among the top ten US trading partners and all three are connected through treaties and membership in a multitude of institutions, including the United Nations, the WTO and NATO.

Independent and still young

The creation of the British Parliament in 1215 is often marked as the beginning of democratic traditions.[4] In 1776, 461 years later, the Declaration of Independence was signed creating the United States which has come to be known as the Home of Democracy.

The country, the United States of America, with scarcely more than two centuries of history, *is* still young. Its present configuration – a total of 50 states and the District of Columbia – was completed with the addition of Hawaii in 1959, only some 40 odd years ago.

Contrast this with the longevity of England and France – two countries that can trace their culture to Roman times. As distinct

---

[3] Attributed to George Bernard Shaw
[4] Dean Foster, *The Global Etiquette Guide to Europe* (John Wiley & Sons, 2000): 12

nations, their histories date back to the eleventh and ninth centuries respectively, more than 1,000 years ago.

A Los Angeles based advertising executive, originally from the UK, likens the US to a teenager. He says the country has all the qualities of a young person: boundless optimism, vast energy, confidence, certainty that their opinions are correct, a sense of invincibility. The United States, which based on his description could be called a precocious youngster, thinks of itself as mature and wise, the leader of the free world.

The rebels and their tea party

Ask people what they remember about American history and many will tell you, it started with the Tea Party. They may not remember exactly where this happened, or the exact sequence of events, but they generally recall the idea of citizens throwing tea into the harbour as an act of rebellion against financial injustice.

Today one may argue that this was an act of urban protest no different than those targeted against globalization. But for American children learning the history of their country, this story is about freedom fighters, brave men, standing up for their rights.

Lost in history is the fact that this specific act was a protest against "taxation without representation", only one element of a larger revolution seeking freedom and rights for each individual. Considered broadly, the American Revolution was a rebellion against traditional thinking and behaviour, against the formality and rigidity of existing society and institutions.

The new nation was created to be a land of freedom and opportunity for all, to give concrete form to the ideal that "all men are created equal". Not only were people to be equal, they were to be free (with freedom defined broadly): to speak, to travel, to assemble, to bear arms, to be considered innocent until proven guilty. These philosophical concepts were codified in the Bill of Rights, further defined in the Constitution and have been the subject of debate, interpretation and legislation for the past 225 years.

History has been portrayed in many ways in many movies. For a clear statement of the idea of freedom of speech and responsibility, listen to Michael Douglas's speech towards the end of *The American President*. It is a light-hearted movie while at the same time giving this powerful explanation of American democracy.

The American view of history

Americans tend to see their history as triumphant. We tamed a wilderness and created a dynamic, free society with endless opportunities. We are a "melting pot" with arms open to receive the newcomer.

Unfortunately, such a view tends to overlook the treatment of the Native Americans, the problems of slavery and of prejudice today. Americans fought a civil war (1860 to 1865) to end slavery. Slavery created the "separate but equal" relationship between whites and blacks, majority and minority. Although blacks were freed, they were still segregated in schools, in housing, in the marketplace. This division existed until the 1960s with the emergence of the Civil Rights movement. Then the battles that filled the nation were more often fought with words than with guns, with people marching in the

In America basic and business can

streets to press their demands. The goal was not to eliminate slavery but to end the concept of "separate but equal", to bring full equality to all minorities as well as the descendants of the freed slaves.

But that was only part of the story of the decade. It was a time of great social unrest, of change, of slogans like "power to the people", "make love not war". America again rebelled against tradition and the existing definitions of roles for people and institutions.

According to David Brooks in his book *Bobos in Paradise*, "the experiences and authors of the 60s influenced the thinking of today's business leaders".[5] Some of today's advertising slogans echo those days and capture the attitudes that continue now – phrases like "Revolution not Evolution" and the famous Nike slogan "Just Do It". We can hear the 1960s echo in people's conversation when work is explained as "doing something you love, something meaningful", not just "earning a living".

When Americans shift their focus and think of history in terms of the world rather than their nation, they generally regard themselves as the guardians of the free world. Keepers of the flame of democracy.

[5] David Brooks, *Bobos in Paradise* (Simon & Schuster, 2000)

attitudes about work be traced back to the country's founders

The contributions of the Americans in World War I and World War II are widely documented and celebrated, in books, films, songs and stories. We were the saviours, the "good guys". We've attempted to forget Vietnam and the way it divided the country and seldom discuss recent conflicts including the Gulf War and the war in Afghanistan.

Economically, the US sees itself as the leader, the superpower, although in the aftermath of 11 September 2001, Americans are being forced to recognize that this positive view of themselves is not shared by the entire world.

Business

In America basic attitudes about work and business can be traced back to the country's founders. As a beginning, everyone came here for a change, a "fresh start" – embracing the idea that change has the potential to be good and that if matters didn't work out as you wished at first, you could try again. In today's society, a fresh start and change may mean a new job, a new city, a new marketing campaign, a new product, a company that you create.

An unspoken but critical element in the acceptance of this experimentation with new beginnings is the view that a failed attempt is merely a learning experience. If you try and something doesn't succeed as hoped, too bad, but "no harm done" and you should "put it behind you" as you "get on with it" (moving to the next idea). Failure, disappointment should not stop your efforts. Every school age child knows the saying: "If at first you don't succeed, try, try again."

Listen to the comments of two professional women from France when asked what surprised them about life in the United States: "Changing careers is okay. It's OK to fail and try again. Americans are so open, willing to experiment. It's okay to try something new even in your 40s. You can start a company or go back to school. People will help you and support you. If it doesn't work out that's fine too. No one thinks less of you. In fact, they will encourage you and help you to try again."

We often hear the expression "Protestant work ethic" to describe the American approach to work, the idea that work is important and one must be serious, focused, and above all, hard working. But Protestantism may have had a far wider impact, one that affects the entire world. According to Max Weber in the book *Culture Matters,* "Protestantism promoted the rise of modern capitalism by defining and sanctioning an ethic of everyday behaviour that was conducive to economic success."[6] The idea that your success showed that you were leading a good life created an environment where it was acceptable, you could be proud of being a success in business. It was no longer your inherited title or wealth that marked your success – it was your own achievements resulting from your efforts.

[6] Max Weber, "Culture Makes Almost All the Difference", *Culture Matters*, edited by Lawrence E. Harrison and Samuel P. Huntington (Basic Books, 2000): 11

So if you combine these concepts – change can be good, experimentation is approved of, hard work is valued, and achievement and success depend on individual effort and can be displayed – then you have the basis for the strong entrepreneurial attitudes that are fundamental to the US economy.

Is everyone alike and equal?

American society is varied and complex with such issues as age, education, income (yours, your family's), values, experience and location (rural, urban, suburban) influencing attitudes, employment and lifestyle.

Marketing companies study, dissect and discuss the American population looking for clues to values and resulting behaviours. Probably best known are the divisions by age: Baby Boomers, Generation X and Generation Y. Less well known is the concept of lifestyle clusters that segment the population into groups such as New eco-topia, Old money flats, Kids & Cul-de-sacs and more.[7] Each has its specific outlook but there are still values shared throughout the society.

Among those basic values is a generally shared view of America as a "classless" society where all are created equal. This is not entirely true. For example in the East and the South, the oldest parts of the country, there still exist "old families" and "old money" but there is not unified aristocracy, a titled elite where privilege is passed down through the generations. There are, however, varying levels of status. Today's elite is based on education and achievement. To quote David Brooks again, "genius and geniality" are replacing "noble birth and breeding".[8]

---

[7] Laura Tiffany, "If the Name Fits", *Entrepreneur* magazine, March 2000, http://www.entrepreneneur.com, printed 1/12/01
[8] David Brooks: 14

Today's elite is

Whether this equality is technically true or not, it is important to acknowledge and respect this ideal during business dealings. Treat everyone with the same measure of respect and remember you cannot tell if the person in casual clothes is responsible for photocopying or negotiating contracts.

Moreover, Americans prefer not to acknowledge differences in status. For example, business cards with today's creative titles may not help sort out the hierarchy. Is the Master of Mischief a deal maker or not? Also they will seldom include a person's educational level. Your host may hold a doctorate in microbiology but you won't know that from their business card.

Another distinguishing feature of the US is the idea and the real possibility of being able to move within the society – to grow up poor and end up educated, wealthy and well regarded. Well known examples of this range from Abraham Lincoln to Bill Clinton. But it isn't just at the famous level that this possibility exists. It's seen in the person who moves from washing dishes in a restaurant kitchen to owning a restaurant, in the secretary who becomes president of her own company. People discover and create their own opportunities with headlines or without.

based on education and achievement

WORDS TO LIVE BY

"") Mistakes are a part of life; you can't avoid them. All you can hope is that they won't be too expensive and you don't make the same mistake twice. **Lee Iacoca**

"") Even a mistake may turn out to be the one thing necessary to a worthwhile achievement. **Henry Ford**

"") I always tried to turn every disaster into an opportunity.
John D. Rockefeller

"") This is America. You can do anything here. **Robert Edward (Ted) Turner**

"") Those who deny freedom to others deserve it not for themselves, and, under a just God, cannot long retain it. **Abraham Lincoln**

"") Only our individual faith in freedom can keep us free.
Dwight D. Eisenhower

"") Freedom is not worth having if it does not connote freedom to err.
Mahatma Gandhi

"") Freedom rings where opinions clash. **Adlai E. Stevenson**

"") Those who expect to reap the blessings of freedom, must, like men, undergo the fatigues of supporting it. **Thomas Paine**

2:

open space (we've got lots) or big is better

INTRODUCTION

People are said to be the product of their upbringing and their environment. The very particular environment of the size and history of the United States has had a profound influence on the thinking and activities of today's business people.

WHAT YOU'LL LEARN

➡ There are certain natural endowments that have laid the foundation for the vibrant American economy.

➡ The size of the US has shaped behaviours in a number of ways.

➡ The abundance of natural resources and a general perception that there's "plenty to go around" means that Americans have been able to develop a "win/win" philosophy unlike some European business cultures (UK) which exhibit "win/lose" attitudes evolved partly as a function of sharing scarce resources.

Situation

In a recent conversation the director of a Paris based company starting a new operation in the US said: "We are still surprised at how big America and the marketplace are!" He continued to explain that they were surprised by the variety and the size of everything, including the portions of food in a restaurant. Coming from Paris, he was amazed to discover large blocks of office space, with parking, easy to find.

You start to plan a business trip to see the winemaking areas of the country and you find out that you can't limit your trip to California. Wine is made in New York, Oregon, Washington, Hawaii, Virginia and Texas, thousands of miles and many time zones apart.

On a more negative note, Germans with their strict packaging laws, and emphasis on a green environment, are amazed to discover that few Americans actively recycle. Land is still dedicated to landfills even though more and more communities debate their expansion. Size and abundance have not always been positive influences on America's living patterns.

Explanation

How big is it?

The US has a population totalling 281,421,906 people[1] and an area of 3,717,796 square miles[2] – three times the combined size of the EU 15.[3] Further it is 3,199 miles across, east to west, and 1,775 miles north to south.[4]

But size in terms of land mass and population are not the only factors that are significant when it comes to economic development. According to Jeffrey Sachs, Director of the Center for International Development at Harvard University, there are *four geographic factors* that can influence economic development.[5] America is well endowed

[1] US Census Bureau Quick Facts,http://quickfacts.census.gov/qfd/states/36000.html, printed 15/9/01
[2] Microsoft Encarta Interactive World Atlas 2000
[3] European Union in the US Facts & Figures, http://www.eurunion.org/profile/facts.htm, printed 8/9/01
[4] Encarta
[5] Jeffrey Sachs, "Notes on a New Sociology of Economic Development", *Culture Matters* (New York, 2000): 31

in all four areas, establishing a foundation for a growing economy. First, is its significant *size*. Next, the entire continental United States enjoys a temperate *climate* and provides an abundance of *natural resources*. Finally, there are extensive *transportation routes*. The country is bounded by oceans on both coasts and has navigable rivers enabling a flow of commerce both internally and externally. Combine all these elements of geography and you have the foundation for a large and dynamic economy.

The 9,629.047 square km[6] includes 50 states, plus a federal district that is home to the Capitol in Washington DC (District of Columbia). As big as the US is, it is not the largest country in the world; it is half the size of Russia but $2\frac{1}{2}$ times larger than Western Europe.[7]

To get a sense of the size, think about distance in terms of aeroplane and train travel. How much time do you allow to travel for a meeting? By air, an hour from Los Angeles takes you to another city in California. In contrast, an hour by air from London takes you to another country. It takes five hours to fly from New York to Los Angeles, about the same time as a flight from Paris to Moscow. A train ride from Chicago, in the middle of the country, to Seattle in the West takes almost three days. By train, you can cross all of France faster than you can go from Los Angeles to San Francisco.

Although the US is not the largest country in terms of physical size or population, it does rank first by other measures.[8] For example:

➡ It has more than $2\frac{1}{2}$ times as many airports with paved runways (5,174) as France, Japan, Germany, Italy, Brazil and the United Kingdom combined (2,039).

[6] Encarta
[7] Encarta
[8] CIA Worldfactbook Country Listings, http://www.cia.gov/cia/publications/factbookindex.html, printed 15/11/01

Los Angeles would be the world's

- In 2000, it led the world in terms of ISP providers with a total of 7,800 compared to the UK with 245, France 128, Germany 123, Japan 73, Russia 35, Argentine 33 and China 3.

- The network of paved highways is extensive. The US has 5,733,028 km, which is over six times the number in China and 30 times that of Argentina. (Other comparisons include: France 892,900 km, Russia 752,000, Germany 656,140 and UK 371,603.)

- In 2000, US GDP was more than $2 billion larger than the GDP for the EU 15 combined.[9]

- America covers six time zones as follows: Eastern, Central, Mountain, Pacific, Alaska and Hawaiian times. If it's noon in Paris and 11:00 a.m. in London it's midnight in Honolulu, Hawaii, 2:00 a.m. in Anchorage, Alaska, 3:00 a.m. in San Francisco, 4:00 a.m. in Denver, Colorado, 5:00 a.m. in Chicago and 6:00 a.m. in Miami and New York. (How would you schedule a videoconference that includes people in all those cities?) To check the time before you go, consult www.timeanddate.com.

[9] European Union in the US Facts & Figures, Basic Statistics 2000, http://www.eurunion.org/profile/facts/htm, printed 8/9/01

listed as No. 16 in economies if counted as a separate nation

Even at the state level, the US has a formidable economy. For the year 2000, California, if considered a separate country, based on its gross state product, would be the fifth largest country in the world, ranking before France which would be number six.[10] The same *Los Angeles Times* articles tell us that, according to the LA County Economic Development Corporation,[11] the city of Los Angeles itself would be listed as No. 16 in the world's economies if counted as a separate nation.

Within the country there are, of course, variations in physical features, temperature and ethnic make-up. Other chapters will address these differences but in this section we treat the US as a united whole.

Go West young man

The popular view of American history has been heavily shaped by the movie and television versions of the western expansion. These usually depict the West as raw territory that pits man against man and man against untamed nature. It was a "landscape that demanded great

---

[10] Karen Robinson-Jacobs, "Take That France" (*Los Angeles Times* 14 June 2001): C1
[11] Karen Robinson-Jacobs: C1

If life doesn't work

bravery and suffering".[12] The territory was big, open, unexplored with great open skies and room for everyone. Originally "The West" was everything outside the original colonies. Over time the designation came to stand for all the lands west of the Mississippi river.

Our view of US history tells us that the country we know today was originally explored, developed and built by people who thought boldly, took big risks, sought challenges and were brave and hard working. According to Michael Bond, in an article in the *Financial Times*, "People in the US remember the taming of the landscape as people in Europe might remember the wartime heroics of their own grandparents."[13]

This desire to explore, to find new challenges continues today. One measure of this can be found in the adventure travel business. According to a recent article in *Travel + Leisure* magazine more than 45 million Americans took vacations that were "to do more than just lie in a hammock".[14] They are searching for challenges and excitement.

Tied to the idea of vast space and brave people is the concept that the country is big enough for everyone. If the line so favoured by old western movies "This town isn't big enough for the two of us" was true, a person could always move on, find a new place to be. This

---

[12] Michael Bond, "Had the Wild West Already Been Tamed?" *Financial Times*, 30 June 2001: VIII

[13] Michael Bond: VIII

[14] Jeff Wise, "Spies Like Us", *Travel + Leisure*, September 2001, p. 50

here it will work somewhere else

attitude, that if life doesn't work here it will work somewhere else, that we can change our environment and in so doing succeed, is still part of the American outlook. This idea of vast open space also lends itself to the belief that there is always another boundary to be crossed, a new fork in the road to be explored. When Americans ran out of room, they went to the moon!

We thought we were safe

Before 11 September 2001 most Americans had a sense of invincibility that was not shared by people everywhere. Set aside all the issues of urban crime and look more broadly. Even today, post 11 September, most Americans will tell you there has never been a war fought on American soil.

This of course, isn't entirely true. To start, we had the Revolutionary War and there were ongoing clashes with the Native American tribes. But the war that still holds most importance, the one that took place in America when the country was less than 100 years old, was the Civil War (1860–1865) fought between North and South, the war to end slavery. Still researched, studied, remembered, it ended almost 150 years ago. Fought in the south-eastern states, you can still see the physical signs of the war, visit monuments and battlefields and even take organized tours of the areas. While it is said that the war is still fought in some parts of the south, on a day-to-day basis, most of the American population doesn't remember that it happened.

World War I didn't touch our boundaries, and unless you visit Hawaii and the Pearl Harbor memorial, it's hard to remember that World War II reached American shores. In the capital, Washington DC, you'll find monuments to wars past, to the soldiers who fought. But our landscape has not been touched. We experienced none of the devastation known in England, France, Japan and Germany. No houses or churches bombed, no tanks in the streets. We were big, safe and secure.

Although this vision has been shattered with the attacks at the World Trade Center and the Pentagon, it is still important to note the way it has shaped American behaviour toward the rest of the world. The American perspective was: We saved the world, kept it free. Afterwards helped rebuild Europe and Japan. Victors, heroes, we know how to do things.

At the time of writing, you might describe the new attitude as: big, anxious and in transition. The economy is a major concern as is a worry about further terrorist attacks. The trend appears to be towards an era of "Comfort and Connection"[15] where people stay home more, looking for comfort foods, comfortable clothes and connections with people. This trend pre-dates the attacks but has since gained momentum. How it will evolve is unclear. Americans are known for their short-term focus and we will have to watch to see if the sense of insecurity is long-lasting and truly modifies long-term behaviour or if there is a shift again in the next 12 months.

It's all here: attitude and the economy

The sheer size of America, the abundance of its resources, and the ability to move freely have contributed not only to the economic

---

[15] J. Walker Smith, "Weighing Anchor", A Yankelovich Monitor Perspective, 15 November 2001

growth of the country but also shaped the thinking of its people in ways that influence business today.

Grounded in a history filled with images of openness, encompassing vast areas for exploration, Americans developed a highly optimistic point of view, a conviction that there were opportunities and plenty of everything for everyone. Americans believed that they had everything and then alternated between two different views of their relationship with the rest of the world: either that they needed no one at all, or they could and should care for the entire world.

Historically all the resources needed were available locally: land, fuel, water, room for people, and room to grow food to feed them. America was virtually self-sufficient. Although this was never *entirely* true, it was a pervasive enough view to influence the perspective of the population. Today this is clearly not the reality. But attitudes don't change easily. Some Americans tend to hold on to their isolationist view that "we don't need anyone else" even though the trade statistics prove otherwise. Despite the fact that Americans imported $1,414,441,000 worth of foreign goods and services in 2000,[16] relatively few of them travel to where the goods are made.

While Americans guard a vision of themselves as intrepid explorers, conquerors of the West, they have not been frequent travellers beyond their own borders. According to a study for the British travel industry, only 18 per cent of the US population holds a current passport.[17] One reason has been the size and variety of the offerings within the US. For the tourist, plenty to explore at home. You can holiday in the desert or climb mountains. Skiers have lots of choices: Vermont, Colorado, Washington or California. Surfers choose waves in California and Hawaii. Museums and restaurants? New York, San Francisco, Chicago,

[16] Bureau of Economic Analysis International Accounts Data, http://www.bea.doc.gov/bea/di/tradgs-ct.htm, printed 12/11/01
[17] Marketing Intelligence US, http://travelbritain.org, printed 12/11/01, p. 2

Dallas to name just a few possibilities. Ocean beaches: take your pick, Atlantic or Pacific, or there's the Gulf of Mexico. Hot or cold, city hotel or country cabin – it's all available. Travel in the US is relatively easy. You can fly, take a train, or drive. You don't need to get a passport, learn a new language, cope with strange money or customs.

Business people have traditionally also been content to stay at home. Until recently business enjoyed a national market that provided seemingly unending opportunities. The growing population provided plenty of buyers for your product or service. Common currency and increasingly similar laws encouraged commerce. There was room to expand. There was little reason to take on the complexities of entering another country.

However, as the local markets became saturated, companies increasingly looked outside the United States in order to continue to grow. Probably the most well known are the food chains: McDonald's, Pizza Hut and KFC. Even though they were not the first American corporations to become global, they are better recognized as American companies than GE, GM or Citibank to name three that were global before it was trendy. No one has missed the march of the Gap, Nike, Toys R Us and Wal-Mart to new locations. Saturated local markets, the drive to provide growth for stakeholders, and the connectivity of the internet have all fuelled the escalation in global expansion.

The spirit of exploration revived?

Today everyone with internet access can connect with someone in another country. They can see and learn about distant places without leaving home. Tom Friedman tells a story in his book *The Lexus and the Olive Tree* about his 79-year-old mother playing bridge on the internet with people in France and Siberia.[18] We are connecting.

[18] Thomas Friedman, *The Lexus and the Olive Tree* (Anchor Books, New York, 2000): xix

But connecting virtually does not seem to be enough. Americans are travelling more, and increasingly outside the US. In the year 2000 Americans took 26,853,000 international trips which means that approximately 10 per cent of the population travelled outside the borders for business, education or pleasure.

Possibly more interesting, as an indicator that value is being placed on international experience, is the increase in American students studying abroad. According to the Open Doors 2001 report which included data from 2,700 accredited US institutions of higher education, the number of participants in study abroad programmes has increased 61 per cent over the past five years and has measured year-to-year double digit for the past four years.[19] The spirit of exploration may take us to new places.

The idea of size expresses itself in a number of ways

The idea of endless space, room to grow, translated from geography to personal patterns, is deeply embedded in the US psyche. Described below are some ways in which you will see this as you work with Americans.

Shout it out!

What is more famous than the image of the American tourist, in tennis shoes, having a private conversation that can be heard by everyone in the immediate vicinity? Americans don't know they're being loud and rude. Used to open spaces, loud voices are accepted, even encouraged. Americans tell their children: Speak up. Don't whisper!

---

[19] Todd Davis, Director of the Institute of International Education Resource Group, address @ National Press Club, Washington DC, 13 November 2001

The idea of endless space, from geography to personal

According to an observer, the volume can be startling. A Parisian staying at a small hotel in Switzerland recounts that when an American couple came into the breakfast room and greeted their travelling companions with a hearty "Good Morning" the other guests literally jumped in their chairs!

Privacy please and a place of my own

A five-year-old says to her grandmother "I need some privacy please" and shuts the door to her room. Americans value privacy, the ability to be separate, alone. This is a characteristic of an individualist culture; where people tend to segment their lives, keeping relationships, especially business and personal ones, separate.

Fortunately, the physical size of the US has allowed people to express this in their housing. By the standards of other countries, American living space is exceptionally large. Historically, as in European cities, people lived in apartments above the stores. Over time, with increased wealth and new highways, housing moved outside the commercial areas, to the suburbs. The 1950s post-war period saw the great expansion of the single-family dwelling.

A house with bedrooms for every child, and a backyard for family barbeques is still the American goal. Not only does the house fill an

room to grow, translated patterns, is deeply embedded in the US psyche

emotional desire, to put down roots, but it is also a driver of the American economy. Tax policy has been developed to essentially subsidize the purchase of homes by allowing the deduction of interest. Although it sounds faintly paternalistic, the government supporting home purchases in an economy strongly tied to consumer spending, is in the economic interests of both the state and federal governments. Home owners buy things for their homes. If you have any doubts, walk through a Home Depot, Sears or Wal-Mart, the home owner's speciality stores!

Personal space

"You're joking aren't you? This isn't really my room is it?" Overheard by a fellow new US arrival at a London hotel. It's always a shock to a traveller, how big the US hotel rooms are or how small the European ones seem. Americans' expectations are for space, and lots of it, all the time.

"People just bump into you. They're so rude." Another quote from a traveller. Americans don't realize they take up lots of space. They swing their arms as they walk and want space between themselves and everyone else. Emily Emerson, an American writer who lives in France, said that she found herself tilting back at about a 45-degree angle when she talked to a French person in an effort to create some comfortable physical space. She added "Americans like room around themselves, air between themselves and the nearest person."[20] For a culture that values its privacy and space, the change to open-plan offices has been a true shock. More than a dozen years after they were introduced people still resist them and companies still seek ways to make them current and appealing.

Caution: The bathrooms may surprise you. They are much less private than those in major European offices. Rather than private rooms there are stalls of metal dividers that do not extend floor to ceiling. If you walk in you can observe a row of feet.

Big food: all you can eat

Even the food is big. The US is the home of the hamburger called The Whopper, and All You Can Eat (for a fixed price) Buffets. There are even contests to see who can eat the most hot dogs in the shortest amount of time. Portions in restaurants have been called "huge", "generous" or "ridiculous" depending on your point of view. There does not seem to be a small size of anything anymore unless it is for children. Drinks come in medium, large and extra large. Or at a convenience store you can get a Big Gulp that is a very large 32 ounces. At Starbucks coffee shops drinks come tall, grand or venti at a full 20 ounces.

Size is often equated with value. Fast food restaurants have used this knowledge to create special "meals" with extra large servings at a price only slightly more than the regular size. The customer is happy because they "got their money's worth", at perceived good value.

Big cars: the gas guzzler

A famous American image from the 1950s is a Cadillac with fenders that looked like fins of a fish. The car was both long and wide.

---

[20] Emily Emerson, "Personal Space, French Style: Ooh La La!" *Bonjour Paris* newsletter, August 2001, www.bparis.com, printed 4/9/01

Americans then flirted with the VW bug in the 1960s but were much more passionate about the famous Volkswagen Van. This was the counter-culture car, famous for its "hippie" connection.

In the past 40 years Americans have incorporated the small, usually imported, car into their lives but for many the favourite remains the big car. The current favourites are a Van, although much more luxurious than its ancestor from the 1960s, or an SUV (Sports Utility Vehicle). Considering the number of these vehicles on the roads you would think that the entire population goes to the mountains instead of to Wal-Mart every week.

A nation of drivers, of commuters, with the largest amount of paved highways in the world, Americans have a well documented love affair with their cars. In California a car is your status accessory, often more important than your house. Gas prices go up, roads are crowded but people still buy big cars. Big is better.

Big business

Americans have a tendency to grow big businesses. Of the *Fortune* magazine Global 500: World's Largest Corporations for the year 2000, eight of the top 20, including numbers one to four are American companies (Exxon Mobil, Wal-Mart stores, General Motors and Ford Motor).[21] The fifth is Daimler Chrysler and is the result of a merger of two companies with one of the partners being American.

In the retail sector, a very American Wal-Mart is the biggest. In retailing, seven of the top ten are US based companies. The world's largest restaurant chain is McDonald's. Whether you like its food or not, it is the "largest global food-service retailer with more than 28,000 restaurants in 120 countries serving 45 million people daily".[22]

[21] Global 500 The World's Largest Corporations, *Fortune*.com, www.fortune.com, printed 26/8/01

Given American history and geography this tendency to bigness in business is not surprising. However, according to the well known management guru Peter Drucker "Size is often confused with importance."[23] There is always talk about efficiencies, synergies, the need for growth, to find new markets, serve more customers, but you can make an argument that as a nation Americans simply think: Big is Better.

WORDS TO LIVE BY

«» This is America. You can do anything here. **Robert Edward (Ted) Turner III**

«» Big companies are small companies that succeeded. **Robert Townsend**

«» If you can build a business up big enough, it's respectable. **Will Rogers**

«» My favourite thing is to go where I've never been. **Diane Arbus**

«» America is rather like life. You can usually find in it what you look for … It will probably be interesting and it is sure to be large. **E.M. Forster**

[22] "McAtlas Shrugged", Foreign Policy May/June 2001, p. 30
[23] Erick Schonfeld, "The Guru's Guru", *Business2.0* October 2001, http://ww.business2.com/articles, printed 22/10/01

we the people

INTRODUCTION

When terrorists attacked the World Trade Center, their goal was the death and destruction of Americans and American institutions. But they got it wrong: the charred ruins of the WTC became a global grave impacting businesses and professionals around the world, not just those in the US.

From Caribbean immigrant workers in the Towers' restaurants to British traders in its Wall Street firms – and dozens of fire fighters and police officers of Irish stock – those who worked and died in the WTC reflected America's melting pot. But the melting pot doesn't mean we're all the same, homogenized and bland. There are no cookie cutter Americans.

Indeed, regional differences abound. New Yorkers spread cream cheese on bagels for breakfast, while modest Midwesterners eat a bowl of oatmeal. Southerners dig into grits and biscuits, instead of hash browns and toast. A brash Texan might feel out of place in straight-laced Boston.

To be sure, there is a sense of unity, patriotism and a desire to "fit in" in America. Look what happened after the terrorist attacks on 11 September: sales of American merchandise soared. The country wrapped itself in a communal national spirit – regardless of whether your parents had arrived from Afghanistan or Zaire, if you wore a suit or turban or worshipped in a church or synagogue.

Immigrants preserve their cultural traditions, but also strive to assimilate and be "American". As American journalist Robert L. Barley wrote recently, "the ability to assimilate is the heart of the American genius, precisely the trait that sets the United States off from other nations".[1]

WHAT YOU'LL LEARN

➡ Americans are proud and patriotic, although everyone comes from somewhere else. They feel and look American, and sound American, but also cling to their Korean, Chinese, Irish or Indian heritage, describing themselves as "Irish American" or "Asian American".

➡ Immigrants built America. The Chinese laid the railway lines. Eastern Europeans helped create Hollywood. Their roots might have been in the old sod of Ireland, but here they have worked hard to build a new life and fit into the fabric of society.

➡ America is a big country, and there are marked regional differences and habits. California is a long, long way from South Dakota. A Floridian lifestyle would be mocked in Illinois. Few people have ever met someone from Montana. What ties them together: a common destiny of being "American".

➡ Americans laugh about their differences, but also relish the special things about their city or region, be it a plate of Boston baked beans or President George W. Bush's passion for clearing brush on his Texas ranch.

[1] *Wall Street Journal Europe*, © Dow Jones, 4 July 2001

Immigrants preserve but also strive to

Situation

Your New York colleague seems very different to your Los Angeles colleague. They both also seem very different from the folks in your Atlanta office. In the week you've spent flying around the country, you have been struck by their attitudes, the pace of the meetings, and their hospitality – or distinct lack of it. Now, as you head to your next meeting in Chicago, you wonder whether it will be more like Atlanta or New York – or perhaps an entirely new experience altogether.

Explanation

Immigration historically and today

"Give me your tired, your poor, your huddled masses yearning to breathe free, the wretched refuse of your teeming shore."

These moving words, written by poet Emma Lazarus, are inscribed on the base of the Statue of Liberty. She herself was an immigrant (gifted to the US from France) and, in many ways, her words are emblematic of this nation of immigrants.

As already mentioned in Chapter 1, for decades Europeans have looked to America and the "New World" for salvation. There were the

their cultural traditions, assimilate and be "American"

"To emphasize our commitment to diversity, I'd like to remind you that Mr. Denton is three inches taller than the rest of us."

Irish, devastated by the potato famine. There were Jews, seeking refuge from the Nazis. In later years, Cubans came to escape Castro. Indians from the subcontinent arrived in the 1970s and later in the 1990s. Vietnamese and other southeast Asians arrived after war ravaged their parts of the world. Mexicans and other Latin Americans

There are many regional

have been trickling in for years, and building a vibrant Hispanic Diaspora.

According to the latest US Census findings,[2] there were 26.4 million people – about 10 per cent of the population in America – who were foreign born. Among them, about half are from Latin America, and a quarter from Asia, while just over 16 per cent are from Europe.

How are they different?

Immigration patterns influence regional behaviour, and to do business in heavily Hispanic Austin, Texas is not the same as in the bustling Asian communities of San Francisco and Los Angeles. So, who are the new immigrants?

Today's immigrants are likely to be married and live in urban areas. They concentrate in certain regions: 48 per cent of Caribbean immigrants, for example, reside in the Northeast. The air crash in November 2001 of an American Airlines plane bound for the Dominican Republic from New York devastated that city's Dominican community.

Generally speaking, today's immigrants tend to have larger families, and less education than do native-born Americans. But that doesn't

[2] www.census.com, Census 2000 tables of foreign-born Americans

commonly accepted character traits

mean they're not hard working, smart or aspirational. On the contrary, most immigrants strive to improve their lot and the lives of their families. They push their kids to study harder, they open small shops and businesses, and display an entrepreneurial flair.

In New York and Los Angeles, Koreans are the greengrocers. In Silicon Valley, Indians power software development. The Irish swell the ranks of police and fire departments. Russian taxi drivers abound in New York. It's not always a land of milk and honey: many immigrants don't make it beyond poverty. Yet, there are the obvious success stories like Andy Grove, a Hungarian immigrant who founded chip giant Intel and became a billionaire.

Business is regional

"The business of America is business," as the saying goes. But that doesn't mean business is done the same way everywhere.

There are many commonly accepted regional character traits, and Americans love joking about them. Woody Allen, the quintessential New Yorker, once chided West Coasters by saying "the only advantage of living in California is being able to make a right turn on a red light".

Here are some other astute general observations about the regionalism of US business (they might help avert a deal-breaking faux pas, such as putting mayonnaise on your corned beef sandwich in New York):

⇒ New Yorkers are "competitive, in-your-face and argumentative, but will go out of their way to help you," says Helen Allen, a San Diego based executive working regularly with businesses from this global city. New Yorkers literally live on an island, and as the famous Saul Steinberg cartoon illustrates – with its portrayal of Manhattan as the centre of the universe – they can't see much beyond the Hudson River.

The pace of business in New York can be frantic; after all, this is the throbbing heart of the American market economy – at least that's what New Yorkers will tell you. There's Wall Street, media empires, Broadway and Madison Avenue. Anyone who doesn't keep up is labelled an "out-of-towner" who is "moving in second gear".

New York is also very ethnic: ever eat Cuban-Asian food? With its large Jewish population, be prepared to nosh on a latke and pepper your language with Yiddish expressions. New Yorkers like to kvetch but hate schlepping (Yiddish for "complain" and "hiking long distances" respectively).

⇒ Texans are also go-getters, and are often seen as showy loudmouths eager to impress with big ranches, big cattle, flashy cars and gushing oil wells. Remember a frequently heard factoid (thanks to CNN for this word): Texas is bigger than France. Be ready to discuss deals over a beef barbecue at a colleague's ranch, and don't forget to bring along your boots and an oversized cowboy hat. Got a saddle?

⇒ Further out West, Californians are fitness freaks and scoff at flabby, pasty faced foreigners who don't spend enough time at the beach or with a guru perfecting their karma. In the Northwest, home to Boeing and Microsoft, hard work is the norm, but outsiders are sometimes suspect. Several years ago, when too many new arrivals were upsetting the citizens of Oregon, a popular bumper sticker said "don't Californi-cate Oregon!"

➡ In the genteel South, there's still an unhurried, William Faulkner-esque way of life. Hospitality is generous and the pace of business is decidedly slower – like the way people speak in a syrupy drawl. Personal relationships are highly valued, and business often involves food and lengthy dinners.

➡ Some say the most "normal" Americans hail from the heartland of the Midwest. This is flat, farm country, where "the corn is as high as an elephant's eye", as the song from the musical Oklahoma goes. But there are also booming, powerhouse cities like Chicago, home to the nation's largest commodities exchange and a major financial and cultural centre. Regarded as reliable and honest, Midwesterners have the flattest, least nasal or offending accents in America. That's why a significant number of telemarketers have set up shop in the Midwest – rather than in Brooklyn.

Regions within regions

To make matters more complicated, there are further subdivisions among regional attitudes.

Modern "New South" cities like Atlanta identify more with big cities like Chicago or New York, and pride themselves on racial tolerance and reversing the ugly legacy of slavery and the Civil War. But in New Orleans, society is more traditional and insular, both economically and socially.

Bostonians can be preppy, stuffy and introverted, but its northeast neighbour New York prides itself on being pushy. San Franciscans consider themselves elitists and culturally superior – rather than

The lifestyle, fashion, trends more often

experimental and alternative – which is the more accepted view of Californians.

There are even differences within individual states. Houston is more freewheeling – home of the oil industry, a cafe society and a large gay community – while Dallas, home to banks and insurance companies, is more staid.

Stories from the left coast

As mentioned in Chapter 2, the latest statistic from the Governor's office of the State of California ranks this single (nation) state as the fifth largest global economy – which if allowed to join the G7, would displace Canada. The city of Los Angeles alone is the world's 16th largest economy,[3] ahead of Russia.

Besides hosting the wine, technology and entertainment industries (there does seem to be *some* synergy in this mix), aerospace and agriculture are also significant contributors to its GNP. Not only does the year-round fine weather attract millions of businesses and residents, but so does the promise of a lost identity and the reinvention of a new one with freedom and relative anonymity.

[3] Los Angeles Office of Economic Development, August 2001

legal and business than not begin in California

The lifestyle, fashion, legal and business trends more often than not begin in California – what starts West, drifts East. Market researchers usually test market any new product or service in California first, knowing it's the market for "early adopters" – those willing to try anything new.

The "dress down Fridays" office policy began here, telecommuting and flexitime began here (due to the incredible road traffic problems resulting from very poor public transportation infrastructures), "nouvelle cuisine" healthy eating began here, and "no win, no fee" personal injury lawyers advertising on TV began here.

WORDS TO LIVE BY

"" You ask the New Yorker to speak a little bit slower, and he tells you "you're just listening too slow!"

"" You can always tell a Texan, but not very much.

"" How do you know you're at a formal dinner party in California? The guests are wearing socks.

"" You know you are in California when:

➡ You make over $250,000 and still can't afford a house.

➡ You take a bus and are shocked at two people carrying on a conversation in English.

➡ Your child's 3rd grade teacher has purple hair, a nose ring, and is named Breeze.

➡ You have a very strong opinion about where your coffee beans are grown and can taste the difference between Sumatran and Ethiopian.

➡ A really great parking space can move you to tears.

➡ You have to leave the big company meeting early because Billy Blanks himself is teaching the 4:00 Tae Bo class.

➡ Your paper boy has a two-picture deal.

➡ The weatherman talks about the weather in other parts of the country, as if we really care.

4: everyone knows

INTRODUCTION

To understand a culture, you must understand its values. Americans in business, are, thankfully, a straightforward group, especially helpful when trying to work out what makes them tick. True to the national constitution, there are three things held dear in pursuit of the almighty business deal: life (read: having fun at work), liberty (read: having control and freedom over the work we do) and the pursuit of happiness (read: money).

What is astounding is the consistency of the business values in the US today – stable for the past few decades – flavoured and integrated with the national values and cultures brought by the waves of immigrants starting their new lives in the country.

Everyone in the US knows that "time is money", everyone knows that you've got to "speculate to accumulate", and everyone knows that "the early bird gets the worm". Everyone also knows that what enables these activities and business achievements to be open to anyone is the value Americans place on equality, freedom and the meritocratic distribution of the fruits of their labours.

WHAT YOU'LL LEARN

➡ There are a variety of values and attitudes which you should be aware of when considering the ways business is conducted in the US, some of which are laudatory, some of which are unattractive.

➡ By learning what "everyone knows", you can more quickly understand your American counterpart and link your business propositions to what they value, and therefore be more confident and prepared in your negotiations.

Situation

You've been working since 6:30 this morning in that climate-controlled office, and you can't wait to grab a decent lunch. Shouting down the hall for you is your colleague Bob, who says "why don't we go to lunch now? I could murder a pastrami on rye, how about you?" Bounding out of your chair, you head together to the nearby deli, sit down at the leatherette booth only to be barked at by the surly waiter. "You can't sit here – I'm not workin' this station today!" After moving tables to where the waiter points you, and finishing the sandwich, Bob leaves a $5 tip. "That's a bit excessive don't you think, given his attitude?" you remark. Bob shrugs and says "yeah, but you never know. He might be my boss one day – what goes around comes around!"

Explanation

Anything is possible

Americans generally believe that if you really want to pursue a business idea, it's possible to make it happen, and it's even possible you'll make good money trying. How will you recognize this? Because no matter how ludicrous an idea you present to your American boss or colleagues, it'll be given time and treated with respect. And we know from the history of business successes in the US (look at the success of pet rocks about 15 years ago, and 3M's Post-It™ notes), some of the wackiest ideas really make it to the big time. The downside of this positive and optimistic outlook however, is that those who raise concerns or reservations are sometimes viewed as negative, destructive and unhelpful. Tact and well-structured, objective arguments against will go a long way towards avoiding this perception.

Americans generally really want to pursue it's possible to

Competition

There is a shared understanding that competition raises the stakes of the game, and that winning brings sweet rewards. It is akin to playing tennis with a better player because you know you rise to their level. American business language often looks to competitive sports for its inspiration: slam dunk, home run, left field. The love of rankings is an indicator too of the spirit of competition that exists in the business world: The Fortune 100, The 100 Best Companies to Work for in America, The Best Bosses, The Best Business Schools.

Information is free

Telephone any American company for your market research exercise, and they'll usually not only answer your questions, but also route you to additional information sources. You're unlikely to be asked why you want to know, and you won't be grilled about who you are or any ulterior motives you might have. Most American companies know that if *they* don't tell you the information about themselves, you *will* find the information elsewhere – such as via the internet – and at least if you've gained the information from them, they are controlling the messages and the content. This openness and lack of suspicion comes

believe that if you a business idea, make it happen

from the belief that it's not what you know or who you know, it's how you've used what you know. In Europe, on the other hand, companies are highly suspicious of the motives of any researcher or enquirer (and even customers!) since power is derived from what you know and who you know it from.

Liberty and justice for all

This phrase, recited daily in American classrooms as part of the "pledge of allegiance", reflects the meritocratic, "all men are created equal" ethos that runs through the business culture. People really do believe that even those from the most humble beginnings can become business success stories – a belief which is reinforced regularly by the appearance of rags to riches stories in publications such as the *New York Times*, *Wall Street Journal*, *Fortune* and *Business Week*. Which partly explains why everyone's ideas and opinions count – because you don't know from where the next "killer app" might come. Calling the boss by her first name, wearing the same "smart casual" attire as the post room clerk, washing up your own coffee cup regardless of your job title, not listing academic qualifications on business cards are all indications of the value placed on equality at work and the desire for equal treatment. It's even possible your boss is significantly younger than everyone else in the company (Steve Jobs from Apple, Jeff Bezos at Amazon, Bill Gates at Microsoft).

A win/win approach

This is one of the best and most productive approaches to most business opportunities, since it works on the basis that both parties to a business deal emerge victorious. The rules of the American business game are clear: make as much money as you can, as fast as you can. This game theory approach perhaps comes from the economics of abundance rather than the economics of scarcity and invasions, so well known in Asia and Europe. It's apparent in the language of business negotiations, with phrases such as "how can we both make this work?" and "we're really excited about working with you on this!" The downside of this approach, however, is the assumption by Americans in business that cash is the universal motivator and language of business. Appreciating that in most business cultures with whom Americans work, winning is measured in more rounded ways (such as social inclusion, access to exclusive information) is not one of the stronger skills of US business people.

Live to work

Generally, your occupation defines who you are in the US, and gives you a branding and positioning despite your best efforts. Renowned for the 60 hour week, Americans in the world of business relish the satisfaction that comes from a good day's work – a sort of cleansing of the spirit, answering that Puritan calling. One way you can recognize this tendency towards overachievement is by the display of trophies, diplomas, sports medals and awards in the offices of your US colleagues, demonstrating their love of work and reinforcing the ethos that hard work pays off. Another clue is a recent statistic that 83 per cent of US office workers who went on a summer holiday for a week or more stayed in touch with their offices while away, usually by phone or e-mail.[1]

Transactions rule

Doing the deal is more important than building relationships and getting to know the other parties to the deal. This is apparent when beginning negotiations with your American colleagues who may neglect to offer you tea or coffee – since the transaction is foremost in their mind. The small talk that comes with relationship building is usually saved for the end of the negotiations. After all, "time is money", and transactions not only give more immediate rewards (a high return on time), they also deliver short-term positive commercial results at a faster pace than do relationships. Which *is* at odds with the usual American focus on all things to do with the future.

Young at heart

The aspiration to look and stay young can be seen in a general enthusiasm for attending training programmes and learning new and better ways of doing the job, regardless of age. The erosion of a mandatory retirement age demonstrates that many companies increasingly want employees to stay until they no longer wish to work. Encouraging this practice is the Department of Social Security, which increases payments if workers stay in employment until the age of 70. Even the corporate hospitality events of US companies are youthful: hot air ballooning, white water rafting, outdoor adventure trips, rather than the opera, ballet and boating events which many European companies favour.

[1] Accenture, "Study of US employees staying connected on vacation", August 2000

The attitude towards of doing business is

Insular

In part because the number of weeks allowed for annual holidays in the US is low relative to other countries (4–6 weeks in Europe), true insights, empathy and understanding of other national and business cultures is very weak. The negotiating power and confidence of non-Americans when striking a deal with a US partner is underpinned by the simple fact that they are likely to know less about your country and business culture than you already know about theirs – partly as a result of the pervasive distribution of American TV, films and books (remember Michael Douglas' character, Gordon Gecko, in the film *Wall Street*?). The attitude towards non-American ways of doing business is generally intolerant: "That's different, so that's wrong. It's not the way we do it at home." Speaking languages for business other than English and possibly Spanish is extremely rare, and most Americans in business who do venture to foreign climes seek out local and familiar destinations: US hotel and car rental chains and US food chains. It's borne from the belief that anything you could possibly want materially is already found in America, so why look elsewhere? Tip for your next US meeting: bring a map of your region and show your colleagues where your London and other offices are, explaining that the region is not like a United States of Europe but rather richer for its histories and cultures.

non-American ways generally intolerant

Welcoming

Despite the insularity of Americans in business, their openness, informality, optimism, humour, curiosity and friendliness instantly puts most people at ease. This is especially helpful when coming from business cultures with steep class hierarchies and formal rituals. Humour is a tool subconsciously used to relax the mood and build an atmosphere of friendliness and informality. Because of the belief that anything *is* possible in American business, this optimism carries over to your relationship too: the glass will be half full rather than half empty. Don't be surprised if your colleague suggests that the "problems" you foresee are actually "opportunities".

Ethical

Because the business culture (and national culture) values each person as a unique individual, the idea that any supplier or customer should get unusual preferential treatment is totally unethical and considered bad practice. US companies and business people are shocked by offers of bribes or kickbacks – since that would be rigging the rules of the game, and the rules apply to everyone. Even the practice of cause related marketing (companies doing good works in their communities) has gained momentum in the past few years as a result of the fashion for fair play and the ethics of giving something back to the community that helped create your success.

Masculine

In a recent study by culture guru Hofstede,[2] the US ranks 15th out of 50 as one of the more masculine cultures, with Japan at the top of the charts, and Sweden the most feminine. The value placed on personal achievement, challenges, material possessions which display the achievements, and the direct/assertive communication style all support this finding. Unlike many Asian and Latin cultures, the US does not have the masculine concept of "saving face". The results orientation and emphasis on decisive action often makes the US business culture unfriendly for women, who are inherently nurturers and relationship builders. However, in order to retain their large pools of female talent US companies are trying to nurture more feminine environments by adopting a more co-operative style and developing an awareness of lifestyle issues.

WORDS TO LIVE BY

"" If it ain't broke don't fix it. **Bert Lance, member of Jimmy Carter's cabinet, 1977**

"" A life spent in making mistakes is not only more honourable but more useful than a life spent doing nothing. **George Bernard Shaw**

"" The cream always rises to the top.

"" What goes around, comes around.

"" Winning isn't everything, it's the only thing. **Vince Lombardi, coach, Green Bay Packers football team**

[2] *Cultures and Organizations*, p. 84

part

foundations

do it now

INTRODUCTION

People's concept of time is a fundamental component of their definition of appropriate business and personal conduct. In this chapter we look at two significantly different ways of considering time. Although these guide our actions most people are not aware that they exist – they only know there is their way, and the wrong way. Understanding the different ways in which we view time and how this affects the way Americans behave in their business dealings is critical to building productive relationships and achieving success.

WHAT YOU'LL LEARN

➡ What drives the Americans' obsession with time (it's not just money!)?

➡ Why it's important to be on time and what is a reasonable response time.

➡ Factors that contribute to the impression of Americans being rushed and exhausted, which can be exhausting to work with.

Situation

You are a new employee with an American company. Your immediate supervisor tells you your work is excellent and that she is glad you're on the team. The next day Human Resources calls you to their office to counsel you about your record of tardiness. What's happening?

You begin to think something's wrong with your watch. No matter how many times you set it, check it, it seems to be running slow. You know this because the watches of all your colleagues seem to be ten minutes faster than yours. You finally ask and find out they all set them fast to be sure to be on time.

You arrive 20 minutes late to meet a friend for lunch and they've left the restaurant, leaving a message saying they couldn't wait any longer. Why?

"Hey, what are *you* doing at work so early?"

Explanation

Time: scarce or bountiful?

Time, is it scarce or bountiful? This question itself, although we are unlikely to raise it, illuminates the two schools of thought.

Scarce or bountiful? Do I have lots of time or am I always rushed? Can I spend a little extra time with a friend, interrupt a project or must I finish a task and meet a deadline? And the answer is: Yes, scarce. Yes, bountiful. Depending on your culture, your understanding of the world, either answer is true.

Overall, the world's cultures divide into two distinct approaches to understanding and using time. One approach, or system, is called monochronic, with an emphasis on tasks and schedules. The other is polychronic, where relationships outweigh the rule of the clock.[1]

Monochronic:

Some key characteristics:

➡ Time is a tangible thing. It can be spent, saved, lost, wasted.

➡ Time is linear.

➡ Do one thing at a time, sequentially.

➡ Tasks take precedence over people.

➡ Interruptions are not welcome.

➡ Relic of the industrial revolution.[2]

Countries considered to follow this system include: America, Switzerland, Germany, Canada and Northern European countries.

---

[1] Edward T. Hall and Mildred Reed Hall, *Understanding Cultural Differences* (Intercultural Press, 1990)

[2] Hall and Hall: 14

Americans simply relationships

Polychronic

Some key characteristics:

➡ Pre-industrial, seasonal, lunar, from agricultural base.

➡ Time is bountiful and ongoing, flowing, a river.

➡ People before task.

➡ Simultaneous activities possible.

➡ Interruptions acceptable.

Countries represented: everywhere not named above.

Simply stated, people in one group believe time is infinite, unending, impossible to use up and the other is certain that time is limited, finite, a disappearing resource.

Absolutely monochronic

Americans are probably best known for their focus on time, schedules and deadlines. Stories abound of negotiations adjusted, deals lost, misunderstandings created because American business people stuck to their schedules without regard to other events. The clock is the master.

This attitude about time is deeply ingrained, passed down through the generations as it is in all countries, all cultures. The founding fathers were immigrants from Northern Europe and they brought

believe that creating will wait

with them the influence of the industrial revolution, the schedules of the factory.

This focus on time and task contributes to Americans' reputation as alternately warm, friendly and then aloof, cool, unfriendly and direct. With the emphasis on "getting things done", it appears they're un-interested in you and the people involved. These problems arise because it never really occurs to the American that this could be insulting.

Absolutely monochronic, convinced that time is a non-renewable resource, they are certain that everyone will understand that keeping to schedule is critically important. Americans simply believe that creating relationships will wait. It is understood in the business culture that you can only do one thing at a time. A colleague talks about leaving "place markers" with her friends. That translates to sending brief e-mails, leaving voice mail messages to tell people she's thinking about them but is too pressed to see them or even have a serious conversation. Then when the deadline is passed she will take her "place" and in a sense re-enter their lives.

Since Americans usually work mainly with Americans, this mindset works. As with the colleague above, no one is insulted when a social engagement is cancelled due to a looming deadline, or when a call is cut short with the announcement "Got to run. Working on a big project. Catch you later." Time slips away. Use it or lose it!

Is the focus forward or backward?

Another important aspect of people's view of time is whether their focus is on the past, present or future. Is today the best, was yesterday, or will it be tomorrow?

For Americans the answer is "It's the future." From the founding fathers of history to the most recent arrivals, this is a country where people left their past to come to a strange place, to create something new, something better. Their actions clearly stated their belief in the future.

Although today you can read studies that indicate Americans are now less positive that tomorrow will always be better than today, the overall orientation of the culture still remains focused on the present and the future. Our connections to the past are limited.

A hallmark of future oriented cultures such as the US is a widely shared optimism that things can be changed for the better. A favourite American saying is "The best is yet to come." This optimism, in a business sense, is a driver of innovation and experimentation. A "dynamic perception of the future"[3] leads to planning, building, creating what comes next. One could say this is a necessary (but not sufficient) condition for economic development.

The focus on time and the future can be a powerful but sometimes problematic driver of US business. In this rush forward, Americans are sometimes accused of not thinking carefully, of proceeding in a way described as "Ready, Fire, Aim". From either perspective, under-standing the American attitude about time is key to understanding how they work at work.

As the following story shows, Americans do not view deadlines as flexible.

[3] *Culture Matters*: 68

The former vice-president of store planning for a European upscale men's retailer tells a story about her experience of opening a flagship store in New York City. The store had to open by mid-November in order to take advantage of the key retail season – Christmas. This was to be their first store in the US.

The store was designed to achieve the look of a fine, traditional men's store that meant fixtures, flooring and cabinetry in wood. They selected a small firm in Europe to handle the majority of the cabinetry. This firm had the expertise to do the job, experience with the client, and could obtain the specific materials they required. They signed a contract.

But one problem appeared – the deadline. The cabinetmakers informed their client, the retailers, that they would have to work weekends to meet the contracted deadline. But they didn't work weekends, so they couldn't meet the deadline. They were sorry. But the work could be done by early December and that wouldn't be too much of a delay as the store could simply open a few weeks later.

Telling the story, at least four years after the event, Meg is still incredulous. How could they not understand? A deadline is a deadline. It's a commitment. Once you agree you move "heaven and earth" to do "whatever it takes". Work weekends. Work nights. Hire more people. What were they thinking? Miss the Christmas season – don't be crazy!

In this case, retailer and supplier were able to resolve the issue (they worked those weekends), the contract went ahead and the store opened. At least this time there was a happy ending.

A deadline, a due date, is more than a goal – it is a promise, and Americans learn as children that you must keep a promise once it's made. Your honour is "on the line". So if you find yourself in a position

A deadline, a due a goal –

where you cannot meet a deadline agreed to with an American, tell them!

Don't attempt to hide the fact, to delay sharing the bad news. Americans do not respond well to bad news when it's a surprise, especially if it's received too late to correct the problem.

If you announce in advance that a problem has emerged you can take advantage of another American characteristic, the love of solving problems. Overall Americans enjoy a challenge, trying to find a way to do something other people think is impossible. If asked to paint the Golden Gate Bridge in San Francisco purple in two weeks some people would say "Ridiculous" but others would start lists of what would need to be done and create a project schedule.

Time considered in several ways

The key to working with monochronic people is to be sensitive to their view of time.

Punctuality

➡ Be on time. Being late equates to wasting other people's time.

➡ It's good to arrive five minutes early and wait. (A contrast to France where it's best to arrive five minutes late.)

date, is more than it is a promise

- ➡ Call if you're going to be more than five minutes late (use that mobile phone).

- ➡ Always apologize if late, even five minutes or less.

- ➡ For social occasions, dinner at someone's home, it is acceptable to arrive ten minutes after the appointed time. Being early is not good nor is being much later.

- ➡ If meeting at a restaurant, even for a social event, be on time.

Meetings

- ➡ Expect meetings to start on time.

- ➡ Stick to the agenda in a meeting; don't stray from the topics stated (that's wasting time).

Normal business hours

As with what to wear, you have to ask your colleagues to be sure of the best time.

Each part of the country has its own variation of normal hours and preferred time to meet. As a general rule, businesses start between 8:30 and 9:00 a.m. and end between 5:00 and 6:00 p.m.

Lunch is usually an hour beginning between noon and 12:30, sometimes as late as 1:00 p.m. and ending an hour later. Often people will skip a formal lunch and simply eat a sandwich in the office or at their desk.

When setting an appointment, Monday is the least desirable day to request – people tend to use that day to organize their week, start projects.

"You think 24/7 is bad – try 56/12."

The day has been extended: it's 24/7 and convenience

We are seeing an emergence of stores that are open 24/7 reflecting changes in people's work schedules and demands on their time. In major cities you can find restaurants, grocery stores and pharmacies open day and night. Home Depot, the large home improvement retail chain, keeps select stores open 24 hours a day, seven days a week. No matter what time you shop, you'll find people in the store. You can find food, buy plants or hardware, and pick up a prescription any time you wish.

Most retailers are open on Sunday although their hours may be shorter than on weekdays. However, during the Christmas holiday season, retailers may extend their hours from 7:00 a.m. to 11:00 p.m. (as opposed to the standard 10:00 a.m. to 7:00 p.m.). *The exceptions are:* Thanksgiving (third Thursday in November), Christmas Day and Easter Sunday. On these three days even the major retail stores close, however, some restaurants and most cinemas will be open.

Holidays

There are ten legal holidays when the banks, post office and businesses (except some retail and restaurants) are closed. Some are fixed to a specific date, for example 1 January, and others are a set day within a month, such as Veterans Day which is the second Monday of November. The ten days are as follows:

New Years Day	1 January
Martin Luther King Day	Third Monday of January
Washington's Birthday/ Presidents Day	Third Monday of February
Memorial Day	Fourth Monday of May
Independence Day	4 July
Labor Day	First Monday of September
Columbus Day	Second Monday of October
Veterans Day	Second Monday of November
Thanksgiving	Fourth Thursday of November
Christmas	25 December

Americans envy colleagues' extended

Plus: Easter Sunday, which is not counted as a federal holiday but along with Thanksgiving and Christmas is a day when most businesses are closed.

Response time

You need it when? Yesterday? OK, no problem. A joke that's almost serious. Americans seem to want everything instantly. Information. Deliveries. You name it.

The general rule for replying to phone messages and e-mail is no more than 24 hours, maybe 48 if you're travelling. If you are an American, waiting for an answer, a day or two seems reasonable. After that, unless you've been forewarned, the response time seems slow (translation may be the person is not interested, slow, lazy, not "with it", not professional). In Europe, a week may be a satisfactory time, in Asia even longer but not so in America.

But if you cannot reply promptly (American time) then tell your American colleague and indicate when they can expect a response: three days, a week, two weeks? If you will not be able to meet a target date, speak up, tell someone. People will let you know if that causes a problem and they will generally help find a solution but unexpected missed deadlines, or worse yet, unending silence, can precipitate a disaster. As one Senior Credit Officer at Citibank said "There is more focus on the time crunch. We want results daily. Every minute counts!"

their European summer holidays

Holidays

Americans envy their European colleagues' extended summer holidays. Three or four consecutive weeks holiday is almost unheard of in the States. In fact, the trend is toward shorter holidays, made to feel even shorter thanks to e-mail and mobile phones. According to an Accenture survey[4] over 80 per cent of US workers stay in touch with the office during holidays. Even President Bush was questioned (criticized) at one time for his decision to spend a month in Texas on a "working holiday".

Most industrialized countries (European, Japan, Australia) by law give employees four to six weeks annual paid leave. However, US labour laws do not obligate companies to give staff holidays. Holidays are part of many union contracts and are given to non-union workers by custom, but at the discretion of each company. Holiday time is allotted according to length of service with a company, varying from one week after one year to three (maybe four) weeks after ten years.

Currently US workers average nine days after one year. But as the trend toward contract and part-time work (free agency) increases, more people find it difficult to take holidays.

---

[4] "Accenture survey finds 83% of American workers stay connected on vacation", http://www.accenture/fi. printed 8/12/01

Possibly reflecting the fact that 78 per cent of Americans want to reduce stress in their lives[5] there has emerged a movement called Work To Live. The organization founded by Joe Robinson,[6] a California based writer, recently sent Congress a petition with 40,000 signatures seeking to change the federal Fair Labor Standards Act to give everyone who works for at least one year three weeks leave and four weeks holiday after three years of work.

Too much to do

You're in a hurry. You learned as a child that it's important to "Do something. Don't just sit there." But today, you're an adult and you are – busy, rushed.

Hurry, hurry. The message is everywhere:

⇒ A June 2001 McDonald's advertisement promises: "30 second drive thru or it's free."

⇒ Le Cordon Bleu (with cooking schools in London and Paris) ran an advertisement in *Gourmet*, an American magazine, with the headline: "Short on time, long on ambition?"

Although some studies indicate working hours have been reduced, the feelings of being rushed and stressed are increasing. People now have multiple roles in life. As adults we want to have a "well rounded" life: work, sports, friends, community activity and relationships. Faith Popcorn calls it the trend of "99 Lives". Men and women, single and married, juggle multiple roles or "Lives".

Additionally, it's not just vacations when we stay connected. Schedules are stretched. We check the e-mail at 5 a.m. before working out and at 10 p.m. after putting the children to bed, then maybe communicate

---

[5] Faith Popcorn, "99 Lives", www.faithpopcorn.com/trens/99_lives.htm, printed 8/9/01
[6] Susan Carpenter, "Don't We All Deserve a Month's Vacation", *Los Angeles Times*, 13 August 2001: E1

with the boss via e-mail. For all the complaints, it's worth noting that in some circles "busyness" ranks with money as a sign of status, success and importance.

In response to the difficulties of these demands we are seeing some women leave the workforce for a period of time to re-enter when their children are older. This is enough of a trend to have been given a name – the "Mommy track". Men can now take paternity leave. Neither of these trends is fully integrated into acceptable working practice yet. But keep watching.

WORDS TO LIVE BY

"" Everything comes to him who hustles while he waits. **Thomas A. Edison**

"" Next week there can't be any crisis. My schedule is already full.
Henry A. Kissinger

"" Someday is not a day of the week.

"" Time waste differs from material waste in that there can be no salvage. **Henry Ford**

"" Remember that time is money. **Benjamin Franklin**

"" Effective managers live in the present but concentrate on the future.
James L. Hayes

"" Lost time is never found again. **John H. Aughey**

"" Lost, yesterday, somewhere between sunrise and sunset, two golden hours, each set with sixty diamond minutes. No reward is offered for they are gone forever. **Horace Mann**

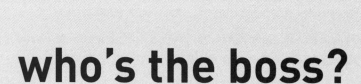

6: who's the boss?

INTRODUCTION

What do Americans mean by "the boss" today? Is it the venture capitalists who call the shots and give you the money? Is it the CEO? Is it the vice-president of the Knowledge Management department? Is it the Chief Marketing Officer, or maybe all of these simultaneously in a matrix organization structure?

A literal definition, according to the American Heritage Dictionary of the English Language,[1] is *"an employer or a supervisor, one who makes decisions or exercises authority"*. Of course, you could opt for their alternative definition as *"a circular protuberance or knoblike swelling, as on the horns of certain animals"*.

These masters, authorities, directors find themselves now in the most uncertain and fast moving business environment experienced at any time in US history. The challenges they face include such tasks as retaining talented people who'd rather be paid less to own their own lives, keeping a voracious financial community fed with news and ever improving results, and compressing five year plans into one year because as the boss you may not be around longer than this to see it through. With forecasts so unreliable that budgeting and planning must be done weekly, it's a stressful time!

[1] © Houghton Mifflin, 2000

But, let's go back to some fundamentals about leading and managing in America. Abraham Maslow's observations in the mid-1950s – that people have a "hierarchy of needs", each level of which comes into play once the subordinate need has been met – shaped the agenda for American business leaders and managers to allow those they lead to "self-actualize" (meaning to know, understand, systematize, organize and construct a system of values) in the workplace. This could *only* happen once their physiological needs (water coolers, coffee machines, staff toilets), safety needs (ensuring that the ceiling over their desks isn't going to collapse), and social needs (recognizing them with "employee of the month" awards) were met, in this sequence.

Also to be taken into account are the various shapes that corporate structures have taken over the past ten years – like watching amoebas on slides regularly changing their shapes. The steep, multi-layered pyramids that dominated the landscape until fairly recently have now been flattened significantly. In their place are virtual, matrix structured teams, committees, working groups and task forces that allow for immediate, fluid communication and action (and a lot less hierarchy thankfully too!).

The matrix organization – first installed in top US companies by management consulting firm McKinsey in the 1960s – which aligned employees to two bosses [one for their functional team (e.g. Marketing, Finance, Engineering, etc.) and one for their product or service team], meant that bosses had promiscuous servants: two allegiances (and sometimes more) instead of one.

Moving from these historical shapers to the capabilities needed in the future in order to run and lead corporate America, these leaders/chiefs will be expected to be great communicators, entrepreneurs, change agents and compromisers. Given that a large chunk of their salaries will be linked to meeting strategic and operational goals, they'll be zealous in ensuring they are around to see their plans bear fruit.

→ The American boss now plays many roles inside an organization, not just those of the traditional resource controller and team leader.

→ Many forces are shaping what American companies' leaders and bosses now actually do.

→ Situational leadership styles – varying the style with the situation – for effective US corporate bosses fall into a number of different categories.

→ The CEO and managers perform a more complicated juggling act than ever before, with a variety of global economic events and domestic industrial restructurings and process revolutions shaping their activities.

Situation

Despite your regular quarterly review meetings with the CEO at your headquarters in St Louis, he still doesn't seem to pay attention to your warnings that the international business is under threat: the euro currency, grey imports from outside the European Union, the vigilante customer making ever more sophisticated demands means that the international division needs some attention. But how can you focus the Chief Executive on these international events which *you* think are important? Why can't he seem to respond to these urgent issues?

Chief Executives of
are now earning

Explanation

What to call the boss

Spurred on by the creative titles to be found in the dot com economy, traditional American corporates are increasingly using newfangled titles of their own. According to a recent article in *Business Week*,[2] modern job titles include "Chief Talent Scout" used by a Florida software company to describe their head of recruitment, "Director of Consumer Delight and Loyalty" hired by a San Francisco dot com, and "Chief Experience Officer", a title developed by US headhunter Russell Reynolds Associates.

Regardless of their exact job title, what is clear is that American bosses are being labelled with new names, and are playing a number of new roles – often schizophrenically – because of the uncertain, fast changing times in which US companies now exist. In theory, this fluid boss can play the role of manager, leader, mentor, coach, strategist or even cheerleader – all at the same time.

[2] 28 August 2000 issue, *Business Week Online*, © McGraw-Hill, "Write Your Own Job Title", Michelle Conlin

large US companies close to $2 million per year on average

You might also call the boss "rich". According to US consulting firm Towers Perrin,[3] Chief Executives of large US companies are now earning close to $2 million per year on average. Of the 26 countries surveyed, Argentina ($879,068) and Mexico ($866,883) hold second and third places respectively. In Europe, Belgian bosses are the highest paid ($696,697) followed by UK Chief Executives ($668,526).

Attitudes toward women bosses have also changed and the stigma of working for a woman has more or less gone. According to a recent Gallup poll,[4] only 48 per cent of Americans prefer a male boss, 22 per cent prefer a female, and 28 per cent don't seem to care either way. A far cry from 1953, when 66 per cent of Americans preferred a male boss.

What does the boss do: lead or manage?

According to John Kotter,[5] an author of many works on leadership and a former Harvard Business School professor of organizational

---

[3] *Financial Times*, 13 December 2001, "Working Briefs" column
[4] The Gallup Organization, US poll conducted 2-4 December 2000, "Would you prefer to work for a man or a woman?"
[5] *Harvard Business Review*, © HBS Press, December 2001, "Best of HBR: What Leaders Really Do", John P. Kotter

behaviour, *management* is about coping with complexity, keeping chaos under control with order and consistency. *Leadership* is about coping with and initiating change. Both functions involve three types of activities: deciding what needs to be done, accomplishing an agenda and ensuring people actually implement that agenda. Distilling his ideas into the table below, you can see these two roles have different emphases when applied to a typical US boss.

Emphasis:	Manager	Leader
What needs to be done	Planning and budgeting	Setting a direction
Accomplishing the agenda	Organizing and staffing	Aligning committed people to the vision and forming coalitions
Ensuring people implement the agenda	Controlling and problem solving	Motivating and inspiring

Regardless of which specific roles your American boss plays, all bosses are affected today by a number of ever changing challenges, some of which include the following:

➡ Globalization: which is forcing US companies to not only serve many markets simultaneously, each at a different marketing and economic stage, but also try to serve these markets with an offering that doesn't reinvent the wheel every time.

➡ Initiative overload: too many change programmes under way at the same time [Six Sigma, Total Quality Management (TQM), Customer Relationship Marketing (CRM), restructuring the organization, strategic alliances/joint ventures, etc.].

➡ Hypercompetition: characterized by accelerated product and industry life cycles and the rapid entry and demise of competitors in an industry.

➡ A workforce seeking more meaning, fulfilment, community and spirituality and employer loyalty during their time spent at work.

➡ "New and improved" management trends touted by any of a number of rock star-like gurus as the latest cure-all (in the first global ranking of the 50 most influential business thinkers, the Thinkers50,[6] only ten are non-American!).

Follow the leader

A more sardonic view about leaders comes from Dilbert,[7] a popular American comic strip cult-hero created by Scott Adams. "Leadership skills are quite different from management skills. When you 'manage', by definition, you're trying to distribute resources where they will do the company the most good. When you 'lead', by definition, you're trying to get those resources distributed to yourself. Obviously, leadership is a better way to go. It's easier too."

[6] www.FTDynamo.com, created by Suntop Media © 2001
[7] *Dogbert's Top Secret Management Handbook*, Scott Adams, © 1996 HarperCollins

Effective bosses vary

Thankfully, this opinion has not influenced best or mass practice – much. A recent survey of American executives[8] suggests *effective* bosses vary their style depending on the situation. Six distinct leadership styles were identified:

➡ **Do what I tell you.** The "coercive" style, and the least effective of the six. Nobody likes to be bossed around, though in a crisis it mobilizes people quickly.

➡ **Do as I do, now.** The "pacesetting" style and second least effective. This leader is obsessed with doing things better, faster, but doesn't make expectations completely clear. "If I have to tell you, you're wrong for the job." Responsibility and initiative evaporate because people focus on second guessing the leader's expectations. Pacesetting can be effective with highly motivated, competent teams, however, if used with other styles.

➡ **Try this.** This "coaching" style of leadership helps employees identify their strengths and weaknesses, by offering feedback and delegating tough assignments to help people grow. While the leader's focus is on long-term results (the employee's growth), coaching delivers solid short-term pay-offs because employees tend to rise to the level of the boss's expectations.

---

[8] "Leadership That Gets Results", Daniel Goleman, *Harvard Business Review*, March–April 2000

their style depending on the situation

➡ **What do you think?** The "democratic" style which builds trust and commitment by soliciting people's ideas and opinions. Not surprisingly, morale and productivity rise, but it can take a fair bit of extra time to build consensus. The downside is if it is used to avoid decision making.

➡ **How do you feel?** Goleman labels this the "affiliative" style, where the leader appeals to the employees' emotional concerns, offers ample praise, and gives them greater freedom in doing their jobs, with intense loyalty the biggest benefit. This style is effective for rebuilding teamwork, morale and trust. It *can* leave some feeling rudderless, so best used in combination with the authoritative style.

➡ **Let's do this together.** The "authoritative" (not authoritarian) style states a clear vision for people and motivates them by making it clear how their work contributes to the vision. Staff see why their work matters, and are given flexibility in achieving their goals. This is the most positive style and works in most situations – unless the leader has less experience than his followers.

Looking at international leadership styles, author Richard Lewis[9] suggests the American style is built for "structured individualism, speed, drive".

[9] *When Cultures Collide*, Nicholas Brealey Publishing © 2000

Never has a more uncertain business these American

Tips for American leaders

According to America's most worshipped boss, Jack Welch, leaders should heed these tips:

1 There is only one way – the straight way. It sets the tone of the organization.

2 Get the right people in the right jobs – it is more important than developing a strategy.

3 Be open to the best of what everyone, everywhere, has to offer. Transfer learning across the organization.

4 An informal atmosphere is a competitive advantage.

5 Make sure everybody counts and everybody knows they count.

6 Legitimate self-confidence is a winner – the true test of self-confidence is the courage to be open.

7 Business has to be fun – celebrations energize an organization.

8 Never underestimate the other guy.

9 Understand where real value is added and put your best people there.

10 Know when to meddle and when to let go – this is pure instinct.

turbulent and climate existed for executives

Troop leader: the CEO

Usually the corporate leader in the US is the Chief Executive Officer, who is also often the company's President. Never has a more turbulent and uncertain business climate existed for these American executives than now. Consider the juggling balls now on their desks:

➡ Succession planning. Two-thirds of all major companies worldwide have replaced their CEO at least once since 1995, according to a recent survey by executive search firm Drake Beam Morin. More than 1,000 US CEOs left office in the 12 months of 2000, with one in three of those leaving in the last four months of that year.[10] Not only does this lack of continuity force share price fluctuations, but more fundamentally often means the outgoing Chief Executive takes a significant bit of knowledge and corporate history with them, information which may not have been logged or captured adequately before departure.

➡ Unrealistic expectations. These have been steadily inflating, coming from investors, employees, suppliers, customers and the media. According to Harvard Business School professor Rakesh Khurana, now writing a book on American CEOs: "We've made this a super-hero job. Boards look at the CEO as a panacea and get fixated on

[10] *Business Week* magazine, McGraw-Hill, 11 December 2000 issue, "The CEO Trap"

the idea that one single individual will solve all of the company's problems."[11]

➡ Business complexity. Compared to even five years ago, the US business climate is more intensely competitive. This involves looking for and applying new technologies, fine-tuning to achieve ever higher stock prices, and getting involved in lots of other aspects of business operations about which the CEO is expected to be expert.

➡ The CEO's role. Many ideas are now being entertained in American boardrooms about whether the CEO should be matched with a nonexecutive chairman who can mentor and manage the board, which is a long-standing British practice taken up by the dot com, biotech and even old tech companies such as General Motors Corporation (GM). It may not take root, however, given the typical American CEO's aspiration to "have it all" – act as Chief Executive, President and Chairman.

The manager's role

Looking at John Kotter's view of the three key roles of the manager – planning and budgeting, organizing and staffing, controlling and problem solving – it appears this boss has a more tactical focus on getting things done. Corporate objectives are usually achieved by cascading down to subordinates or teams of subordinates some group goals, i.e. taking Peter Drucker's advice for managing by objectives to get the most buy-in and enthusiasm.

Since this is the age of the matrix organization, many of the boss's team are most likely reporting to many bosses at once and getting a decent share of their attention can be a challenge. US managers are increasingly turning to HR practices such as the four step "performance

[11] Ibid.

management" method to help detail what's to be achieved (planning performance), tracking it as it happens (measuring performance), assessing how well it happens (reviewing performance), and rewarding those that achieve (rewarding performance).

Where "rewarding" performance used to be a fairly straightforward activity in the US – more cash or salary – now today's employees want "high peace" instead of "high pace" according to recent studies by market research bureau Roper Starch in the US. Since money can't buy quality of life, it isn't everything it used to be. Time is now one of the most effective incentives in the manager's bag.

The growing use of "hard" approaches (performance management) and "soft" approaches (getting employee behaviour to mesh with corporate objectives via communicating visions and strategies) when managing people is helping make American managers more ambidextrous and flexible. Given the high rates of staff burnout in the 24/7/365 American business climate, managers are having to apply more creative ways to elicit the performance they need.

Furthermore, a manager's performance and creativity is also most likely being assessed – by his/her own teams. Increasingly US bosses are turning to "360 degree feedback" approaches to allow staff to evaluate the boss's performance in order to integrate the goals of the manager and the managed more effectively.

Some memorable bosses...

➡ **Richard Brown**, CEO and Chairman of Ross Perot's company, EDS, flew recently to Bahrain and the United Arab Emirates despite his security team at HQ in Plano, Texas warning that the trip was risky because of the US and British bombing raids on Afghanistan begun earlier that day (prompted by the events of 11 September). Despite the UAE's support for the Taliban regime in

Afghanistan, the in-flight satellite phone malfunctioning, the former Israeli Prime Minister Ehud Barak appointed as Mr Brown's special adviser days before the 11 September events, Mr Brown himself felt compelled to continue his Middle East trip. "I knew my family didn't feel very good about it, and I didn't feel very good about that, but how would I tell my EDS people it's too risky for the Chairman to go, but it's not too risky for you to stay in the region?"[12]

➡ **Herb Kelleher**, Chief Executive of Southwest Airlines (the first and still leading US "no-frills" airline), believes work can be fun and makes it part of the company's culture by explicitly stating as one of its 11 primary values "have fun at work" along with "irreverence is OK", "it is OK to be yourself" and "take competition seriously, but not yourself". A few years ago, US carrier Northwest claimed to be ranked number one for customer satisfaction, and Kelleher rose to the bait. In a newspaper advertisement placed within days of Northwest's announcement, Kelleher writes *"After lengthy deliberation at the highest levels, and extensive consultation with our legal department, we have arrived at an official corporate response to Northwest Airline's claim to be Number One in Customer Satisfaction: Liar, Liar. Pants on fire."*

And in the future...

In 20 years, American CEOs will look and act differently from today. *Business Week*[13] predicts that US Chief Executives will:

➡ more likely be women, minorities, younger and older people

➡ be paid with a bigger share of their total salaries as stock options,

---

[12] *Wall Street Journal Europe*, 12 October 2001, Kevin Delaney, "As the Bombing Began, EDS Chief Debated: Do We Fly On to Bahrain?"

[13] 28 August 2000 issue, *Business Week Online*, © McGraw-Hill, "Now and Then: How CEO's Will Change Over The Next 20 Years", Anthony Bianco

now dependent on achieving staff retention targets and successful business partnerships

⇒ get about one year to show tangible results

⇒ be more consensus building and manage many teams

⇒ put more emphasis on forming alliances.

JOKE

The American boss is given two cows. He sells one, leases it back to himself, does an IPO on the second one. He forces the two cows to produce the milk of four cows. He's surprised when one cow drops dead. He spins an announcement to the analysts that he has reduced his expenses. His stock price goes up. The French boss has two cows. He goes on strike because he wants three cows. He goes to lunch. Life is good. The Japanese boss has two cows. He redesigns them so they are one-tenth the size of an ordinary cow and produce 20 times the amount of milk. The cows learn to travel on unbelievably crowded trains. Most are at the top of their class at cow school. The Swiss boss has 5,000 cows, none of which belong to him. He charges for storing them for others. If they give milk, he tells no one. The Italian boss has two cows but doesn't know where they are. While ambling around, he sees a beautiful woman. He breaks for lunch. Life is good.

WORDS TO LIVE BY

❝❞ Managers are people who do things right, while leaders are people who do the right thing. **Warren Bennis**

❝❞ Seek first to understand, and then to be understood. **Dr Steven Covey**

"") It's not the critic who counts, not the one who points out how the strong man stumbled or how the doer of deeds might have done them better. The credit belongs to the man who is actually in the arena; whose face is marred with the sweat and dust and blood; who strives valiantly; who errs and comes up short again and again; who knows the great enthusiasms, the great devotions and spends himself in a worthy cause and who, at best knows the triumph of high achievement and who at worst, if he fails, at least fails while daring greatly so that his place shall never be with those cold and timid souls who know neither victory nor defeat. **Theodore Roosevelt, 23 April 1923**

"") If you don't agree with me it means you haven't been listening.
Sam Markewich

"") The world is divided into people who do things, and people who get the credit. Try, if you can, to belong to the first class. There's far less competition. **Dwight Morrow, 1935**

"") The best way to have a good idea is to have lots of ideas. **Linus Pauling**

"") Managers are people who never put off until tomorrow what they can get somebody else to do today.

"") One of the tests of leadership is the ability to recognize a problem before it becomes an emergency. **Arnold Glasgow**

"") The ultimate leader is one who is willing to develop people to the point that they eventually surpass him or her in knowledge and ability.
Fred A. Maske, Jr

"") Leadership is a combination of strategy and character. If you must be without one, be without the strategy. **Gen. H. Norman Schwarzkopf**

7:

i'll do it myself

INTRODUCTION

The power of one person. Every American knows they are unique, special. Based on that certainty they are convinced that they can achieve their dreams and change things they don't like ("we never say something is impossible"[1]). If plans don't evolve as conceived, one can learn more, adapt, create a new plan, work hard and achieve *your* goals.

The whole notion of the importance of the individual, of one person's value, and focus on their growth is fundamental to American culture. It influences how people behave in all facets of their lives. It is particularly obvious in American marketing and human resource policies, two issues which broadly touch every facet of business.

WHAT YOU'LL LEARN

⇒ Americans are intensely, stunningly independent.

⇒ Given that Americans are taught to make personal choices early in life, it's no surprise that they grow up to expect personalized service and recognition in all aspects of their life, hence the expression "The Customer is King!"

⇒ Americans love challenges or often simply the idea of challenges whether they take them up or not.

⇒ For more and more Americans it's attitude not age that counts when it comes to how they work, live and dress.

[1] Quote overheard during a meeting. Source: Nancy Solin, IT Dept, Fashion Institute of Design & Merchandising, LA

Situation

Your friend has been laid off for the second time. A graduate of the Fashion Institute of Technology with an MBA from Duke, she combined her creative and practical education working for Ralph Lauren, VF Corporation and Donna Karan. She helped start several online retailers before taking a top job at gap.com. Now it's over. Determined to control her own destiny, she's called you to see if you want to back her new venture. She plans to start a new line of clothing for people who cook at home. She'll use special stain resistant fabrics and make colourful, comfortable "chef-wear" for the man, woman or child who loves to cook. She's already got a tie-in with a cookery book author and amazon.com. All she needs is some seed money. Can you give her $20,000 and do you have five friends who can also help? Her business plan says you'll be repaid in two years with interest, plus all the cook's clothing you can wear. She's sure that retailer Target will feature her line since it will be as stylish as their Michael Graves tea kettles. She's sure she'll make a fortune, have fun and wants to share it all with you. What's your answer?

Scene from the street: American walking briskly toward an unknown destination carrying his Dell laptop that he designed himself, wearing his Levi Original Spin jeans made just for him. On his way he stops at Starbucks to order a double latte low fat, double shot of espresso grande. The server calls his name, not a number, when his order is ready. My way, all the way.

Explanation

I not we

The American culture is above all individualistic, the focus on one person rather than a group of people. A clear explanation from Gary

The American

Ferraro's book *The Cultural Dimension of International Business* reads as follows: "The value of the individual is supreme and it is the individual who has the capacity to shape his/her own destiny. Furthermore, the individual is the source of moral power, totally competent to assess the effects of his or her own actions as well as to be responsible for those actions. Society is seen as an instrument for satisfying the needs of the individual."[2] (When asked, "Who comes first, me or the group?" Americans will most often answer "Me, of course".)

This attitude is in vivid contrast to that of people from many other countries. The majority of the world's population lives in cultures that are collectivist, where the group is more important than the individual. Members of a collectivist culture are, beginning almost at birth, integrated into strong, cohesive groups, for lifetime membership.[3] In contrast, Americans, in their strongly individualistic and highly mobile culture, change groups, jobs and relationships throughout their lives.

Even compared to other countries with individualistic orientations, Americans stand out. For example, Americans separate themselves from the group (I am Me) while the English value the eccentric within the group.[4]

[2] Gary P. Ferraro, *The Cultural Dimension of International Business* (Prentice Hall, 1994): 88
[3] Geert Hofstede, *Cultures and Organizations* (McGraw-Hill, 1997): 58
[4] Dean Foster, *The Global Etiquette Guide to Europe* (John Wiley & Sons, 2000): 14

culture is above all individualistic

The source

This strong individualism can be traced back to the Pilgrims, the founders of the United States. Then, as now, the majority of the population was Protestant and, according to their religious beliefs, each person had an individual relationship with God. Moreover, they had "contracts with God and each other for which they were personally responsible".[5]

This belief clearly holds that each individual is sufficiently meaningful to allow him or her to "speak" directly to God. But speaking for oneself is not sufficient. Each person has responsibility for his or her own actions. One can see a link between these two ideas and the American outlook that all people are created equal and that they should be responsible for themselves with minimal interference from government. These ideas were codified into laws with the writing of the Bill of Rights and the Constitution, the documents which guide the country even today.

Inseparable from the belief that all people are equal and responsible is the matter of freedom for the individual: freedom of speech, religion and of the press (which provides information to each individual), freedom to carry weapons, to congregate, to travel and to vote. All

[5] Fons Trompenaars and Charles Hampden-Turner, *Riding the Waves of Culture* (McGraw-Hill, 1998): 53

freedoms are granted to one person, the individual, so that they can conduct their lives as they choose. As a result of amendments to the Constitution, legislation and court rulings these freedoms have survived and in some cases expanded during the past 225 years.

Although these freedoms are a matter of law, clearly stated and protected, Americans continue to be intent on guarding these rights. They have not only brought lawsuits when it appeared their rights had been violated, but also created organizations to be "watchdogs", to protect individuals and groups. Probably the best known is the American Civil Liberties Union (ACLU) that was founded in 1920 and which in 2001 had over 300,000 members. The main focus of the ACLU is to safeguard what are referred to as First Amendment Rights, which give Americans the right of free speech.

It seems almost inevitable that the ACLU at times finds itself defending minority groups with opinions that are, at best, considered unpopular.

"Hi. I'm Dad and I'll be your server this evening. With tonight's meal you have a choice of tender green peas or no TV."

So, in the past, they have defended the right of people to oppose the Vietnam War and the Ku Klux Klan. The ACLU defends these opinions on the grounds that dissent is required in order to ensure an open society and to maintain freedom for all points of view to be heard. As new legislation emerges in the US to combat terrorism, it is anticipated that the ACLU will be active in assessing the impact on personal freedom.

It starts early

Children are encouraged to express their opinions and preferences almost before they can speak. Parents will ask a child to choose one of two toys when they can only point and make sounds. Americans learn early that they can have an opinion, make a decision and get what they want.

This early development sets the stage for an education that is designed to enable a child to take his/her place in a society of individuals. One goal of education is to help children learn "how to learn" because the assumption is that learning in life never ends. This attitude contrasts with collectivists, where learning is about what is necessary to be an acceptable group member.[6]

By learning to learn, it is more likely that people will be prepared to cope with new, unknown, unforeseen situations, and be able to adapt.

Boys and girls, men and women receive the same education in the United States. They attend school together, unless parents elect to send them to private same-sex schools, and participate in group activities from the time they start kindergarten (at age five) until they complete their education. Educated equally, sharing the same experiences, they naturally also expect equality in the workplace.

[6] Geert Hofstede: 63

Unlike many other cultures, children, boys and girls, are expected to move out, to live alone or with friends, after the basic schooling is completed. This is seen as a sign of independent development: a healthy person not dependent on a group (the family). It is important to be self-reliant.

In recent years this has become more complicated. Housing is increasingly expensive. Young people, starting their first jobs, often share apartments rather than live at home with the family. Some parents even subsidize the expenses of the children so that they can make this move. This trend may not be simply to encourage the child's development but may be connected to the parent's desire to be independent, free of familial responsibility also.

I am Me

As discussed later in this book (Chapters 9 and 17), knowledge of a country's vocabulary can help you understand its culture. From that perspective it is useful to note that the capital letter "I" is one of the most used capitals in the English language.[7] Today, even in a time when "Mass Customization" is a popular business expression, we see this focus on "I" reinforced in unexpected ways. For example:

➡ Levis will make jeans to individual order. The programme is called Original Spin and in only two weeks you can get jeans made just for you.[8]

➡ Starbucks lets you dictate what you drink. It's not simply coffee: it's the double latte, light with an extra shot of espresso, tall. Rather than having your order identified by number, or type, your name is put on the cup. It's your order, your drink. To deliver it, your name is announced.

[7] Fons Trompenaars and Charles Hampden-Turner: 53
[8] Gina Imperator, "Jean Machine", *Fast Company*, October 2001: 56

➡ Burger King is known for a slogan, "we do it YOUR way". Let it be clear whose desires are important.

In the tourist industry a new mini trend has surfaced. It's the highly personalized, private holiday. No longer content to join a tour, "baby boomers raised to believe they're special, accustomed to instant gratification"[9] want the perfect holiday. This has led to a growth industry in private tours, rentals of special homes and island retreats where the holidaymaker can have an "exclusive" individualized, private experience.[10]

Marketing the idea of the "I" is not just for food and fun. The government uses this message too. The US Army recruiting efforts have used different slogans to touch this idea. First was "Be All You Can Be!" Then in January 2001, "An Army of One" replaced that slogan. I am the army. I am unique, an army of one. The focus is on me, even though there are 1,045,690 soldiers.[11] This new slogan captures another theme basic to the American view of the world: I can and do make a difference. Who I am and what I do is important.

The many versions of me

For all the talk of Americans as one group, with one set of attitudes, it is important to note that the variations (which do exist) are not just regional but also experiential. Researchers use years of birth to segment these groups and thereby identify the experiences that define these clusters (sometimes called cohorts).

Some common divisions are: the Matures (1930–1946), the Boomers (1946–1964), Gen X (1965–1976) and Gen Y (1977–1994). Different researchers vary the division and names and some further divide the

[9] Michael Gross, "Pursuit of Privacy", *Travel+Leisure*, September 2001: 49
[10] Ibid.
[11] http://www.cnn.com, 10 January 2001

I can and do make
Who I am and what

groups.[12] The Yankelovich Monitor MindBase lists eight major market segments all of which can be divided into at least three additional groups all with specific characteristics.[13] The American individual comes in many forms. We will look at these groups further (particularly in Chapter 14), but for here suffice it to say, each group, every one within the groups, thinks they are special, knowledgeable and expect to have a voice, a choice in all facets of their life. Informed, educated, proactive, potentially self-actualized individuals.

Self-actualization: the top of the pyramid

"What a human can be, they must be." These words are taken from the work of Abraham Maslow an American psychologist known for defining human behaviour in terms of motivations and the subsequent efforts to satisfy needs.

He defined and organized these physical and emotional needs into five sets, ranked them and expressed their relationship to each other in the form of a pyramid labelled a Hierarchy of Needs.[14]

---

[12] DGA Consulting 1999

[13] Yankelovich Monitor MindBase, http://secure.yankelovich.com/solutions/mindbase.asp, printed 15/12/01

[14] Dr C. George Boeree, "Personality Theories: Abraham Maslow", http://www.ship.edu-cgboeree/ maslow.html, printed 18/10/01

a difference.
I do is important

The expression "Maslow's Hierarchy" has become part of the business management vocabulary and is used as a short way of expressing his entire idea, described below.

The hierarchy, or pyramid of needs, begins at the base with issues of survival and moves to the peak where we find self-actualization or the growth motivation. The breakdown is as follows:

Survival:	*Food, water, shelter, sex*
Security:	*Structure, rule of law, limits, protector*
Social acceptance:	*Affection place in a group, family, friends, love*
Self-esteem:	*Self-respect, dignity, appreciation, freedom, independence*
Self-actualization:	*Growth, being true to one's own nature, meaningfulness*

It is thought that these needs are universal without regard to geography, culture, age or education.

Each set of needs must be satisfied before one can move up a step in the pyramid. You must be fed before you can worry about organizing a group and you must have a sense of family, of belonging, before you can move toward self-esteem. The highest level, the concern for developing your full potential, to focus on personal growth, comes only after all the other needs are fulfilled.

It is this highest rank, of personal growth or self-actualization, that is increasingly important in today's business world. Today's employees want jobs that allow them to grow, to learn, and to do something considered meaningful and valuable. As a very general statement one can propose that the majority of Americans in today's workforce have always had their basic needs, the survival and security steps of the pyramid, satisfied. They, and their parents and likely their grandparents, have had food, shelter and money to provide for clothes and for education. They grew up safely in a society with a strong rule of law.

Given that perspective, they are likely to move quickly to the social acceptance and self-esteem steps. Companies are expected to support an employee's efforts to satisfy these needs and to facilitate the move toward self-actualization. And if not to help, to understand and support the individual employee's efforts to get there. The influence of these ideas can be seen in the many articles written today in the US about what employees want in the workplace, touching on such issues as social acceptance, achievement, self-respect, appreciation, and dignity. In the area of self-actualization, Americans are increasingly seeking meaningful work, that represents who they are, and that marks their contribution to the world.

Don't like it? Change it!

Self-actualization and the American dream

Although studies vary, even post 11 September 2001, Americans are generally optimistic and believe that you can create your own destiny, achieve the life, the future that you want. You can become that self-actualized person or simply rich and famous. The choice is yours. According to a University of Michigan study, one reason that Americans can hold this concept is that they believe that inequality is temporary. Look to the future, define your goal, work hard and you can succeed.

Americans even have a short way to express this concept. We simply say, "We believe in the Horatio Alger story." Horatio Alger was a writer in the late 1800s who wrote over 100 books telling the story of poor young boys who grew beyond their beginnings and achieved success. That story, told and retold, is alive to this day and children and adults can cite examples to prove it's true.

A popular historical case is Abraham Lincoln, the 16th President, who grew up in a log cabin, learned to read by candlelight, became a lawyer, went on to be elected President and guided the nation through the Civil War. Today, there is a Horatio Alger society that annually recognizes Americans who personify that story. Included in the list are such well known names as Colin Powell, Oprah Winfrey, Sam Walton (founder of Wal-Mart) and Gordon Moore (co-founder of Intel).

It isn't only the famous names that keep the dream alive. It's the local heroes who are publicized locally and every city has its stories. Recently the *Los Angeles Times* featured the story of Peggy and Andrew Chang.[15] They started with a single suburban restaurant and have built a chain that now numbers over 400 locations in 34 states. This restaurant empire was started by two immigrants who met when they came to the US to go to college. Thirty years later, they are that Horatio Alger story updated for today's business world.

Tied to this idea of endless possibilities, is the concept of personal responsibility. You can create the life you want but it's up to you to discover what you want and how to get there. If you aren't sure how to do this, many resources exist. Every book shop has shelves of "Self-help" books. Dating back to 1759 and Ben Franklin's *Poor Richard's Almanac* there have been books providing advice on how to do things

---

[15] James Flanigan, "Cooking Up a Powerhouse of Chinese Fast Food", *Los Angeles Times*, 8 October 2001: C1

Americans, always youthfulness, are now and what you can do

better. Today Amazon.com includes more than 19,000 books under the heading of "Self-help". Moreover, an entire industry has developed to help you. There are seminars, classes and personal coaches all to help you "be all that you can be".

There is no age limit, no completion point for this idea of creating or re-creating who you are. Faith Popcorn, a popular trend adviser and author, has labelled one trend "Down Aging" where the idea is that a person is "Never too old to start something new".[16] Americans, always fascinated by youthfulness, are now redefining what's old and what you can do at varying stages of your life. Can you wear jeans at 50? 60? Learn to skydive at 15 or 65? Graduate from college at 22 or 82? Retirement may not mean endless days on the golf course but new experiences, new learning and new careers.

[16] Faith Popcorn: 260

fascinated by redefining what's old at varying stages of your life

Independent in business too

This independent attitude, however, may reveal itself in business as stubbornness, a certainty that one knows the answers and insistence on doing things "my way". American business culture "puts a premium on confidence, leadership and self-assertion".[17] This emphasis can cause difficulties in certain business situations.

Jobs in America tend to be structured around the idea of the individual (independence). Often included when people are asked to describe their jobs is "other duties as defined". This phrase, taken from standard job descriptions, is intended to allow changes to be made to a person's responsibilities, and also implies that people are expected to be flexible, handle change, the unexpected. All marks of an independent, self-reliant employee.

[17] Sheida Hodge: 81

Alex Tattersall, a European executive who has lived in the United States and is now based in Switzerland, replied as follows when asked: "What advice would you give a colleague doing business for the first time with Americans?" "Americans are proud of themselves and their country. They have a problem admitting they do not (fully) understand something that is being discussed. Rather than express this, you are likely to hear that 'all is clear'. The result being that either things go wrong, or nothing happens and (only if you offer to do so) you have to explain it again."

Echoing this observation are the comments of Tad Bobak, a Polish born, retired IBM executive who now lives in Paris. During his 40 years with IBM, Mr Bobak had extensive experience working with Americans. His postings included a period at headquarters in New York, as well as assignments in San Francisco, Paris, Brazil, Germany and Russia. When asked what one should know about working with Americans he said:

"Know that Americans above all are individuals, independent. They must be in charge. They will learn eventually but not easily. When coming to Europe, Brazil or Russia and starting something new they will say to you: in Kentucky we are prosperous and we don't do it that way. We must do things the way we do in Kentucky. [Which for an American is amusing since Kentucky is not thought of as one of the most progressive places.]

"Americans must be 'behind the wheel', think they are in charge. Have patience. They will learn. They are smart. Clever. It may take them six months to understand this is not Kentucky, but they will learn."

WORDS TO LIVE BY

" We work to become, not to acquire. **Elbert Hubard**

" To be what we are, and to become what we are capable of becoming is the only end of life. **Robert Louis Stevenson**

" When you cease to make a contribution you begin to die.
Eleanor Roosevelt

" Don't compromise yourself. You are all you've got. **Janis Joplin**

" It's kind of fun to do the impossible. **Walt Disney**

" When fate hands us a lemon, let's try to make lemonade. **Dale Carnegie**

" If opportunity doesn't knock, build a door. **Milton Berle**

hi, my name is Jason

INTRODUCTION

People say Americans rush to do business before they know you, that an American's informality and directness have more than once been interpreted as rudeness. Also, their casual friendliness is often seen as superficial. Americans find these observations surprising and unsettling. They want to be friends, to do business together and are unhappy to hear they insult people. In this chapter we focus on rules about friendship and business relationships. You'll find other areas of American style etiquette covered throughout the book.

WHAT YOU'LL LEARN

- ➡ There is a link between informality and equality.
- ➡ Americans want to be friends and there is a reason for their seemingly contradictory behaviour, sometimes warm, sometimes cold.
- ➡ General rules of relationships American-style.
- ➡ Why Americans are always smiling.

Situation

You attend a seminar and enjoy a conversation with another attendee. Before leaving you exchange business cards and he shakes hands, expresses a desire to follow up on the conversation and says, "I'll give you a call and we'll do lunch." Then no call. What should you do? What does it mean?

Your American friend tells you she's having problems with her car and she may miss an important meeting because she's not sure she can get her car fixed in time. You offer to lend her your car but she declines and asks if you'll drop her off to pick up a rental. What's this about? Why pay money when it would be no problem for her to take your car?

Explanation

Forget the formalities

Americans are known for their informality, casual approach to friendships, their avoidance of formal ceremony and apparent lack of rules of behaviour. To understand this preference for informality, it helps to look back at the history of the country. For our purpose we can describe American history in a way that is familiar from films and television. This view, the popular story, is as follows:

Brave people setting out to create a wonderful new world with equal opportunity for everyone built America from nothing. Their survival depended on their own hard work and ability to move quickly to overcome challenges and take advantage of opportunities as they appeared.

The rush to survive, to create farms, communities, safety and shelter meant there was little time for formality, ceremony and social rules.

"Just Do It", Nike's well known marketing slogan, is illustrative of the attitude of the pioneers.

Even more important than the survival imperative was the concept of the equality of all people. To underscore that belief the founders eliminated many traditional, formal rules that were reminders of royalty, courts and the rigid class systems that they had left behind. Not only was informality symbolic of that basic American ideal – equality – but it also served as a way to blend a population with a variety of backgrounds. They created their own rules for behaviour in their new place.

This is not to say that Americans are unconcerned about social behaviour, or do not care about knowing the appropriate ways to behave. The earliest books on that topic date from the 1800s and today Barnes & Noble.com. lists more than 1,900 titles under the heading "Etiquette".

Looking for friends

Generally we want people to like us and we announce this fact by our welcoming smile. For us, especially on the West Coast, in the South, it is part of an appropriate, polite greeting. A smile indicates that you are friendly, happy and open to meeting people. Children are told to "smile at the nice lady", "smile at the camera". A smile means friendliness.

For many Americans making new friends is an ongoing necessity rather than an interesting option. Although there are Americans who live in one area for their entire lives, for many life is a series of moves, transitions, new places and new people. America has a highly mobile society where 15.9 per cent of the population, a total of 42.6 million

America has a highly

people, moved in the span of 1998–1999.[1] Given these numbers, you can understand why Americans are sometimes called "a nation of strangers". They move from state to state, city to city and place to place within a city. They move from one company to another. New, in a new place, you have to find your way, learn to meet people.

The American idea that friendships can be casual and flexible may, at least in part, reflect the mobility of the population. An individual has the right to agree to be a friend for an ongoing or specific period of time. It is understood between the parties that they are not necessarily linked for ever but by agreement for as long as they wish.

For example, friends may change to match your differing interests at different stages of life, and as you move to different locations. You grow up in Seattle, attend college in Boston, begin working in Atlanta and finally settle, raising your family in Los Angeles. You will build relationships; make close friends in each place, connected to what you are doing at the time. With luck, you will stay connected to some of those people in each place.

Do not think that Americans have no long-standing relationships. We know people who regularly see their friends from grammar school and others who share an annual weekend holiday with college room-mates 15 years after graduation. But it is important to recognize that Americans may have a variety of friends and continue to build new friendships throughout their lives.

[1] Cheryl Russell, *Demographics of the United States* (New Strategist Publication, 2000)

mobile society

Warm on the outside, cold on the inside

Unfortunately, others do not easily understand the American approach to friendship. With their ready smiles, informal greetings, quick use of first names and sharing of information others consider private, they seem open and accessible, friendly to all. However, after the initial involvement they may seem remote, unreachable and surprisingly private. Hence the description, "Warm on the outside, cold on the inside".

As odd and contradictory as these behaviours seem, they can be explained. Kurt Lewin a German-American psychologist provides us with useful imagery to help us understand.[2] He states that people everywhere, regardless of their culture, form relationships with varying degrees of intimacy and describes these relationships and levels of intimacy using the terms "public space" and "private space". The "public space" is what we easily share about ourselves with relative strangers. The "private space" is what we hold back, reserve for those with whom we share a more intimate relationship. Each culture, each person defines "public" and "private" differently. The impression that Americans seem warm but are cool links directly with such an interpretation of relationships – described in terms of open (public) and limited access (private) space.

To illustrate Lewin's ideas about the American division of space we can use the analogy of a convention exhibit hall. To gain entrance all

---

[2] Fons Trompenaars and Charles Hampden-Turner, *Riding the Waves of Culture* (McGraw-Hill, 1998): 84

one requires is a badge that serves as your basic introduction to everyone else. The space is large and people move around freely. There are warm greetings, smiles, quick, informal introductions. You're in easily.

You are at the convention for several days and have multiple conversations with other attendees sharing stories of your work, your family, your city and experiences. The large American space includes not only people but also an extensive number of topics available for sharing. Americans will talk easily about where they are from, what they do, their families and their activities. However, if in your culture public space is comparatively smaller, maybe the size of a hotel suite rather than the convention centre, some of the conversational topics will be surprising and may make you uncomfortable. Where are the lines and what topics are acceptable? Do family, religion, problems and pleasures fall into the public domain or not? For Americans they can all fall into the public category. There may be some limitations but the general topics are acceptable. It's no wonder that Americans can be perceived as rude when they jump into areas others consider private.

But even in the open space of an exhibition hall there are sections and boundaries. Areas for exhibitors, some open to all, others not. The same is true for an American's relationship space. The large public space has divisions and boundaries. Are you connected to each other through work? Through your children's activities? Do you take a class together? Your shared activities and level of intimacy may be restricted to things that flow from a specific relationship. Now we have an open space that's not entirely open where movement may be restricted to certain areas.

Then we move on to private space where there is very limited access. In our conference metaphor this is the suite you can only get into with a personal invitation. It's space reserved for a few, close friends who are an "inner circle". They may move through multiple sections in the public space unlike others with limited access. It is with this small group that one shares opinions that may be controversial, the most personal information, one's hopes and dreams.

While the downside of this large open space is unintentional rudeness, it also sets up the problem of "Warm outside, cold inside". Because the American's public area includes areas (subjects for discussion) that would be labelled private for people in other cultures he/she can mistakenly convey the impression that the relationship is one that is private and special. Friends and colleagues have described their surprise and dismay at realizing the friendship they believed they had with a colleague was really warm acquaintanceship.

However, Americans can be confusing to Americans too! The following is a story from a friend.

"When I first started making my way up the corporate ranks, I had trouble differentiating between levels of 'friendship'. I remember being hurt because a woman I was friendly with at work didn't ever invite me to her monthly card game when she invited others from the office. Finally one of my bosses explained to me that there were levels of friendship, and a certain appropriateness of relationship that accompanied each level. I 'knew' that on some level, but had never really considered how it applied to the people in my life. When I looked at all the people I knew, I could see how there was in fact more than just 'friend' and 'not friend', including a few levels in between and that was OK. Later, when I became a manager myself, I helped some of my own staff work through this issue."

My friend George

We use the word "friend" so easily. How is it correctly defined? According to *Merriam-Webster's Collegiate Dictionary,*[3] a *friend* is:

> One attached to another by affection or esteem; a favored companion; acquaintance; one that is not hostile.

From the same source:

> *Acquaintance:* a person who one knows but who is not a particularly close friend (lacks a certain level of attachment).

Some American friendships fall between these definitions, others fit the conventional understanding of "friend" or are the traditional "acquaintance" but generally we call them all "friends". There are other words: buddy, pal, companion, and even the British word mate is slipping into the vocabulary. We may define a relationship further by referring to someone as my "best friend" but there is nothing in the language that approaches the clarity of the French form of address "tu" and "vous" to indicate the intimacy of the connection.

According to Edward T. Hall, American friendship "depends more on common interests and congeniality than on shared philosophical beliefs".[4] This sharing may be limited to a specific activity: working out at the gym, playing basketball or participating in a book club. For other people it is understood that friendship is a relationship that forms over time through mutually shared experiences. In France one "becomes" a friend.

Americans, on the other hand, talk about "my friend George at the gym". He is called our friend, notwithstanding that we have only a

[3] Merriam-Webster's Collegiate Dictionary, http://www.m-w.com/cgi-bin/dictionary, printed 8/12/01
[4] Edward T. Hall and Mildred Reed Hall, *Understanding Cultural Differences* (Intercultural Press, 1990): 153

vague idea of George's last name or where he lives. It is likely that we know what he does and his entire workout and diet regime along with his favourite sports team. We see him frequently, but only at the gym. He is our "friend" by being there, simply sharing in the event of working out whenever we appear.

Americans are willing to include many people as friends, in different parts of their life; however, there may be no overlap between these people.

For example, I was one of four acquaintances who hosted a party to celebrate a milestone birthday of someone we each counted as a friend. We all represented specific segments of her life: school years, volunteer activities, teaching or consulting.

Each of the hosts invited people known to themselves and the guest of honour. We four knew each other but none of the people the others were inviting. At the party, the four groups didn't mingle very much. A few people introduced themselves but not many. Each group was separate connected only to their host and to the guest of honour. In a sense there were four parties happening simultaneously! The birthday person was surprised but happy to see friends from the many parts of her life assembled together for the first time ever.

Friendship has rules

The rules of friendship which seem quite obscure may be easier to understand if you think of them as linked concepts of privacy, segments of life, value of time and self-reliance. There is even a subtle suggestion of a contractual arrangement governing time and activities.

Americans value as individuals and

Famous phrases

Famous phrases that can be confusing:

> Give me a call
>
> Let's get together
>
> We must have lunch

All are said with great enthusiasm and sincerity but there's no follow-up, no date is set to get together. Don't be insulted if this happens to you. You can take the initiative and set a date or ignore the suggestion, as you wish. It's possible to see someone monthly at a meeting, discuss getting together at each gathering and not actually do it for a year! Think back to the idea of segmented lives.

Privacy

One facet of the independent American character is the desire for privacy. We do not like drop in guests, interruptions in activities or conversation. This is true in both our business and personal lives. A friend who drops in unexpectedly might be welcomed nicely, but for most people their arrival is not a happy event. Americans value their time alone both as individuals and family units. They all have schedules, plans that an unexpected visitor changes. Do not be fooled by the American invitation to "Drop by anytime". The invitation is

their time alone both family units

real but it is assumed you will follow the American rules and call in advance.

Variety

No matter how much you enjoy sharing a dinner, an evening at the theatre, or watching a children's soccer game together, do not expect to share a wide variety of events with an American friend. This does happen, though very rarely. Even close friends who regularly travel together often have other friends who share other activities. Remember Americans divide their time and attention. It isn't that they don't want to include you; they just assume you have other people in your life as they do. The saying that best explains this: "Variety is the spice of life".

Reciprocity

With each relationship there is an idea of reciprocity and exchange. Invited to dinner? Return the invitation. Gifts given? Give in return. This issue can be particularly challenging at holiday time. Do your friends celebrate Christmas, Chanukah or Kwanzaa? Will they give to me? Shall I give to them? Everyone has stories of the unexpected gift received, the rush to find something in return. It is difficult for

Americans to receive something, express thanks and simply wait for an opportunity to return the favour. We feel there should be an immediate, even exchange.

If invited to dinner you need not instantly return the invitation, but do note that a dinner or some other invitation is "owed". Sometimes the "payment" is not exactly in kind. If you are invited to a fund-raising dinner for your client's favourite charity, you may show your appreciation by making a donation in his or her honour. You can be creative in your expression but a return gesture is expected.

"Hi, I'm Alan, and I'm ranked in the sixtieth percentile of somewhat attractive male B-school graduates."

Asking for help

Self-reliant and independent can translate to refusing help even when there is a problem. You may see your friend coping with a problem, big or small, and offer to help only to be refused. Americans are raised with the ethic "take care of yourself". It is difficult for most people to accept assistance. In other cultures it is assumed your friends will step in, do what is necessary and you will welcome, even expect, their help. Not so in the US. Ask before you rush to assist. In addition, Americans are often reluctant to ask for fear of "bothering" someone, upsetting their schedule, imposing on them.

Something to note: If you need help, you can ask. Americans will be very cautious about offering to help, not wanting to appear to interfere or imply they doubt your ability to cope. But Americans do like to help, to fix problems, to be friends. Just remember that this desire to "be the good guy" will also be tempered by their focus on schedules and desire for privacy. Assuming that you really want to solve your problem yourself they may offer advice rather than practical assistance. Touching again on the example at the beginning of this chapter, if your car is out of service they may tell you how to rent a car, even take you to pick up the rental, rather than lend you their car.

Hi I'm Jason

In both your business and personal life, it is acceptable to introduce yourself. You do not need a referral to request an appointment or to introduce yourself at a business gathering. Americans find themselves in new places frequently. Out of necessity this informal, direct pattern has developed. Not only can you introduce yourself, but you can also expect to move quickly to the use of first names. The idea "all men are created equal" means titles, even honorifics, are not important once you are past the initial introduction. (See Chapter 16 for a guide to American introductions.) Although there are instances where titles are used (for example a student may call a teacher, Mr/Mrs/Dr/ Professor), these situations are limited. Although there are some regional variations – for example Southerners may be more formal than people in Southern California – you can expect to be addressed

People working with startled by the easy

by your first name. The practice is so omnipresent that even waiters in a restaurant will introduce themselves with their first name!

Informality of address really moved into the workplace in the 1960s and has advanced ever since, especially as organizations have down-sized or "flattened". Most companies encourage the use of first names to foster a sense of connection, teamwork and corporate spirit. Jack Welch, former Chairman of GE, is referred to by millions of Americans as Jack which is the title of his biography. We talk about Michael (Jordan) and Madonna as though we see them daily.

Unfortunately, people working with Americans are often startled by the easy informality of their American colleagues. Expressions vary along the lines of "Taken aback". "Offended". Americans do not intend to offend. They are just behaving in the democratic manner they know.

People may learn this pattern early. In some families, children are on a first name basis with adults. Pre-school children (up to three years old) are taught to call the parents of their friends "Lisa", "Peter" or "Kathy" rather than using the honorific "Mrs" coupled with their family name. If you've been raised this way, you will be uncomfortable being addressed as Mr or Mrs or heaven forbid, Madame! These titles

Americans are often informality of their American colleagues

are usually reserved for "senior citizens" and we know Americans don't want to be considered old.

Business relationship

To understand how much the idea of informality is seen as key to today's business success consider the statement in General Electric's annual report for the year 2000. Included in the nine stated GE Values is the following: "All of us ... always with unyielding integrity ... will work to 'Create an environment of "stretch"', excitement, *informality* and trust...." At that time General Electric ranked number 8 of *Fortune* magazine's Global 500 with revenues in excess of $129.9 billion.

Americans do build ongoing business relationships. Just as they want to be liked, to be friends, they want to do business with people they like and trust. They can be patient in building these connections. The beginnings can be in a shared project or as the result of networking.

Networking is a popular activity. Originally popularized as a way to find a job, it has evolved into a way to find jobs, customers, partners and information. Books are written, speeches given, newsletters created to help people build their networks. Among Americans, the

A business relationship, is not immediately

most famous network builder is former President Clinton, known for his most extensive Rolodex™ and the diverse group of people counted as "FOB" or Friends of Bill.

A business relationship, no matter its genesis, is not immediately a social friendship but is one that often develops out of working together on a specific project or transaction. The activities and conversations are often limited to topics from "public space". People will happily socialize with their business colleagues, even invite them to their homes for dinner. But, there will remain a certain limit in the relationship. A level of distance that may be sensed as coolness or result in surprise when the relationship doesn't expand. Business relationships often don't.

Indeed, these relationships are often active for the duration of a specific project but become dormant once it's over only to revive later with the advent of another project. For example, you may talk to someone daily, dine together regularly for a year. Then suddenly the building is finished, the sale made and everyone moves on. Conversations become quarterly. E-mail goes from daily to occasionally forwarding jokes. Cards are exchanged at the holidays. Then, a new project, a reunion and the cycle starts again as if there hadn't been a lapse. Business friends – connected but flexible about the connections.

no matter its genesis, a social friendship

WORDS TO LIVE BY

- " " If the house is on fire, forget the china, silver and wedding album – grab the Rolodex. **Harvey MacKay**

- " " People's lives change. To keep all your old friends is like keeping all your old clothes – pretty soon your closet is so jammed and everything so crushed you can't find anything to wear. Help these friends when they need you; bless the years and happy times when you meant a lot to each other, but try not to have the guilts if new people mean more to you now. **Helen Gurley Brown**

9:

send me a memo

INTRODUCTION

Before we consider how to communicate it's important to examine our goal when communicating. Our first thought is that we want to ensure that our message gets through, that the recipient understands the meaning spoken or written. However, in his book *Understanding Cultural Differences*, Edward T. Hall is perhaps more accurate when he proposes that effective communication "has more to do with releasing the right responses than sending the 'right' messages".[1]

In a business context the "right response" can range from something as simple as an agreement to set an appointment or as complex as entering into a strategic alliance. To obtain the response you want, you need to understand how people best receive information and in order to grasp the full meaning of their reply, you need to know how they prefer to transmit information.

WHAT YOU'LL LEARN

⇒ Why your American colleagues rely on memos and contracts, insist on having detailed information, and love statistics.

⇒ There are two basic, significantly different communication styles in our world and each is deeply embedded in one's culture. The difficulties that arise, misunderstandings, insults that are perceived often derive from the differences in the delivery of a message rather than its content.

---

[1] Edward T. Hall and Mildred Reed Hall, *Understanding Cultural Differences* (Intercultural Press, 1990): 4

➡ To understand their communication styles, it's necessary to be aware of the American attitude to time.

➡ Americans can be considered emotional and volatile or cool and rational depending on your culture's view of which feelings should or should not be expressed.

Situation

A conversation overheard in an office in Chicago. "It takes those guys in Paris *forever* to get back to me on anything. I've been waiting for two days. All I need is a 'yes' or 'no'. Can't they just send a quick e-mail. Does everything have to be a mini novel?"

You can't imagine why your counterpart in Dallas keeps asking for memos recapping your most recent meetings with a client. You already talked about it. Isn't that enough?

Those Americans don't know how to have a conversation! There's no flow, no interaction and then they never stop! It's so frustrating.

Explanation

Two ways in the world

High context: we already know

Communication styles throughout the world can generally be divided into two patterns each closely linked to a culture's concept of time (is it scarce or bountiful?) and its views on the balance between the individual and the group. Cultural researchers have labelled these differing styles as "high context" and "low context" communication. Context, in this sense, is the information surrounding an event, the background or the knowledge that one has about people, places and activities.

High context is the pattern common throughout most of the world. It relies upon the existence of close connections with a variety of people, and ongoing relationships with an emphasis on groups rather than individuals. One distinctive feature of this pattern is that "the information already resides within the person".[2] Thanks to extensive ongoing relationships, people approach each situation with prior knowledge applicable to the event, people involved or question under consideration.

"Would you prefer to receive messages by yelling or sticky note?"

[2] Hall and Hall: 6

Americans are famous for time and tasks

Linked to the polychronic view of time, with its emphasis on relationships and a sense that time flows endlessly, there is time for those extra minutes of conversation that can offer information. How many times have you had a casual chat that provides key information you would otherwise have missed?

This does not mean direct, explicit communication does not exist. It does. However, non-verbal clues are important and are generally observed and understood by the participants. Meaning can be conveyed indirectly and subtly, including being inferred by who is delivering the message. Is it the chairman of the board or the newest person on the staff? How is the request phrased? How formal is the language? A person from a low context culture can easily miss these subtle signals thereby blurring the message sent and reducing the possibility for the desired response.

Low context: no time to talk, I need it in writing

You can already guess that this is the style of the Americans! Often counted in this group are the British, Germans and Canadians. As with other definitions, no culture or country *always* follows exactly one style but the tendency, the overall style, will be recognizable.

Americans are famous for their emphasis on schedules, time and tasks rather than people. Their relationships are transitory, connected to projects and places. Comparatively, they move frequently and are forced to build new connections wherever they go. Their lives are

their emphasis on schedules, rather than people

segmented. As a consequence they often lack long-standing, close, information-bearing networks and therefore they have fewer opportunities to obtain information informally.

Since their focus is on time and schedules, dealing with the next deadline, they are not likely to take time for spontaneous conversations – thereby missing opportunities for gathering information. It's often said that Americans like their communications in "sound bites" – broken into pieces of information that are easy to digest and understand. In some ways this relates to the focus on the I, the Individual. It's my schedule; tell me in a way that's convenient for me!

Due to this focus on time and the limited use of networks, in low context cultures the words must carry all the meaning to be conveyed.[3] One cannot rely on body language and situation to make the meaning clear. Matters need to be spelt out, written, clearly stated, in a precise and concise manner.

As the world of business becomes increasingly interconnected, styles of communication are changing. Even two countries both considered low context do exhibit differences. Comparatively, the British are more high context than the Americans. Their use of understatement, implied ideas and qualified statements are more "high" than "low".

While the lines may blur, communication patterns are culturally

[3] Hall and Hall: 6

based. The underlying values of time, people and task stay in place. Our natural inclination will favour one form over another.

The problem is

In their effort to "stick to the facts", to "keep it short and simple" Americans can seem rude, blunt, aggressive and impatient to people accustomed to a more leisurely, subtle conversational style. Conversely Americans think time spent in social conversation, the slow building of relationships, allowing the transfer of information, is a waste of time. They say: "It takes too long! Can't they just say it and get on with it?"

Overall women in business are considered better communicators than men, leaning more toward a high context pattern. Their style is generally less direct, more tactful and they are more adept at relationship building. But be careful of your assumptions. The magazine *Business 2.0* recently ran an article about "Bully Broads", women whose style is so forceful they are enrolled in special training to develop softer, gentler communication skills![4]

Just the facts

As renowned as they are for their style of speech, Americans are equally famous for their preference for written communication, for memos, meeting agendas, taking minutes to recap what was said, and especially for detailed contracts. They look for numbers, hard data, facts stated clearly and concisely.

A business letter, American style, is usually limited to one page with a brief opening, a direct statement of the issue at hand and a closing "Very Truly Yours".

[4] Colleen O'Connor, "Finishing School", *Business 2.0*, April 2000, www.business2.com/articles/mag, printed 29/8/2001

A French public relations executive, Jacques, tells us about an exchange of letters that illustrates the problems that can arise between people accustomed to different communication styles.

Jacques was working with an American colleague, Dan, on the launch of a new product in France. They had worked together on other projects, and liked and respected each other. After a series of meetings in Paris they agreed the details of the product launch, their individual responsibilities, timing and budget. Dan returned to San Francisco and, as was his normal procedure, wrote a memo confirming their plans and sent a copy to Jacques.

When he received the memo, Jacques was surprised and insulted. "We had an agreement. Didn't he think I'd remember, honour it? The memo didn't say anything new that I could find. Why did he send it?"

Jacques first assumed there would be another message, subtly conveyed within the memo. "If I was writing, and the *only reason I would write* would be to include something that had been left out or changed, I would most likely include that new information in the third or fourth paragraph without fuss so as not to be too obvious that something was different." Having satisfied himself that there was no hidden message, he prepared a reply.

Imagine Dan's surprise when a four-page response arrived, acknowledging the memo but filled with allusions to history, literature and other plans that made no sense to him. Puzzled and aggravated he called Jacques and asked, "What did your letter mean? What do you want me to do?"

In the end they agreed that neither would write again. They would talk on the phone, meet regularly, work together, but no more American memos or long French replies.

The American style makes e-mail

You've got mail and messages

The American style of communicating makes e-mail a natural choice. It lends itself to messages that are kept short and direct.

Americans send e-mail and expect an almost instant reply. There is an unstated rule that e-mail messages and phone calls should be returned or acknowledged within 24 hours. If you are waiting for a response from someone in the US it's worth noting that there are six time zones in the United States, four within the continental states alone. When people in New York are having breakfast, those in Seattle may still be asleep.

It is also important to remember that, even though e-mail appears to be a medium for private conversation, that privacy is far from guaranteed. E-mail can be printed and distributed or simply forwarded. It is always advisable to write as if your mail will be posted on the canteen message board for everyone in the company to read.

In fact, some American companies use software that allows them to review the e-mail of their employees as well as to track their internet activity. E-mails that are perceived to create a "hostile work environment", broadly defined as one where employees could be "uncomfortable", can result in reprimands and even dismissal. E-mail in the office is one area where sharing humour can lead to difficulties, even in the typical American environment known to encourage humour and fun.

# of communicating
a natural choice

Telephone calls, like e-mail, should be returned within 24 hours or a business day (not counting weekends). Some people are quite adept at returning calls when they know the caller won't be in, e.g. at 5:00 a.m. Then they have returned the call, but have avoided engaging in a conversation. Pay attention to these small details and learn about your colleagues. Is the best time to get them at noon since they always have lunch at their desk? Do they arrive early or leave late?

Be cool

Communication is not simply words written and spoken, direct versus indirect, high context and low context. When we consider how we connect with each other, share information and elicit responses it's necessary to consider the emotional content of the messages and more particularly the amount of emotion that it is considered appropriate to reveal.

Fons Trompenaars and Charles Hampden-Turner cover this subject in detail in their book *Riding the Waves of Culture* where they describe two distinct cultural patterns: *Affective* (expressive) and *Neutral* (controlled, less outward display). As measured on their Affective/Neutral scale, Americans tend toward a middle ranking making them more expressive than the Japanese, but not as expressive as Italians.[5]

[5] Fons Trompenaars and Charles Hampden-Turner, *Riding the Waves of Culture* (McGraw-Hill, 1998): 71

Intense expressions acceptable in most

This matter of emotional display is important in understanding how people view each other. Neutrals can see Affectives as too emotional, not serious. Affectives may see Neutrals as cold or indifferent.

Americans do show their emotions, they may yell and scream, laugh out loud, jump for joy, but seldom in the office. They can be emotional, yell about something, "rant and rave", but then state "it's not personal, I wasn't yelling at you, I was just expressing myself, letting off steam". But such intense expressions of emotion are not acceptable in most corporate environments. Returning to the Trompenaars-Hampden-Turner scale, the generally acceptable behaviour is toward Neutral.

It's not only the words, but also the tone and volume of voice that matter. Yelling or raising your voice is counted as unprofessional, a serious breach of office protocol. This of course varies from office to office because what for one person is shouting to another is expressing enthusiasm and intensity. But in most places you can laugh out loud, call loudly to someone, but yelling when you are angry, never. Be cool.

of emotion are not corporate environments

WORDS TO LIVE BY

"" Say what you mean and mean what you say.

"" It is a luxury to be understood. **Ralph Waldo Emerson**

"" To improve communications, work not on the utterer, but the recipient. **Peter Drucker**

"" Speech is civilization itself. The word ... preserves contact – it is silence which isolates. **Thomas Mann**

part

3

business

10:

if it's new, it's great: innovation and entrepreneurship

INTRODUCTION

If you visit a favourite American supermarket about six months after the last trip, you are likely to feel confused and amazed at the same time. Not only will most of the aisles have been moved, but the number of new and updated products on the shelves will be significant, not to mention those that are no longer even there.

Innovations of the most subtle kind assault your senses while pushing your shopping trolley around the store: why do I smell chocolate when I pull the dry cake mix off the shelf? Is it the scent-strip laid down under the row of boxes on the shelf surrounding me with nanocapsules to deliver a true chocolate sensory experience? Why are the little red flashing lights on that coupon dispenser on the nearby shelf beckoning me near, then sensing I'm close enough so it can tell me "today only, buy two and get the third free"?

The belief that anyone in the US can legitimately try their hand at creating an innovation is widely held in the country. The US Patent and Trademark Office grants on average 150,000 patents every year, which is equal to one patent for about every 1,900 US residents – and that's not counting the number of applications which were *denied*. Of those granted, one in four was to an independent inventor as opposed to a corporation. However, of all these, only about 3 per cent become commercially viable products.[1]

[1] www.abcnews.com, WolfFiles, Buck Wolf, December 2001

The US Patent and grants on average

Another measure of the American entrepreneurial climate is the high ranking of Amazon.com's best-selling business books on corporate innovation and creating risk-taking climates. Evidence that the US is gripped now more than ever by trying to create innovative, entrepreneurial cultures can be seen in the proportion of books on this theme in the Top 10 (at the time of writing, December 2001):

➡ *Who Moved My Cheese* (Spencer Johnson and Kenneth H. Blanchard)

➡ *Straight from the Gut* (Jack Welch and John A. Byrne)

➡ *Good to Great: Why Some Companies Make the Leap and Others Don't* (James C. Collins and Jim Collins)

➡ *Gung Ho! Turn On the People in Any Organization* (Sheldon Bowles)

➡ *First, Break All The Rules: What the World's Greatest Managers Do Differently* (Marcus Buckingham and Curt Coffman)

WHAT YOU'LL LEARN

➡ There are many American business values that celebrate the entrepreneur.

➡ Why organizational structures have changed to allow more innovative, entrepreneurial activity.

Trademark Office 150,000 patents every year

→ A barometer of current American business thinking, such as Amazon.com's best-selling business books, can give a quick snapshot of the current issues of interest to corporate leaders.

Situation

Sitting in the Frankfurt office of your US-parent's subsidiary, you are debating how best to get funding from the bosses in San Francisco for your new idea that you know will revolutionize offices around the world: the talking stapler. Asked to present your proposal at the next international product development meeting in California, you're worried they won't give you the time or budget to take it beyond the prototype stage. How likely are they to support your innovation?

Explanation

There appears to be a national hunger in the US for innovations that serve up anything "new and improved". There are many likely drivers of this desire, starting with the Manifest Destiny wagon trains of the 1800s urging ordinary Americans to "claim as much land as you can, as fast as you can". Anyone could share some of this abundant

There appears to be the US for innovations

resource, provided your wagon train was fast enough and agile enough to navigate the mountainous impediments along the way.

This drive by the wagon train entrepreneurs to acquire more, better, faster is alive and well in American business today. A characteristic impatience – originally born of a new life started in a new, young, richly resourced country – helps too. It's easy to understand, given this history of converting raw prairies into fertile farms, how "new" and "better" have evolved to become synonymous.

In European business cultures, the image of an entrepreneur and innovator is less positive. The entrepreneur is typically seen as a casual risk taker whose bets rarely if ever pay off, daring to put his head above the parapet, break out of the mould of his social class, and even risking his professional reputation in the process (take British innovator Freddie Laker whose no-frills airline died a death in the 1970s).

Structures

Corporate structures that encourage employees to take calculated risks, innovate and become "intrapreneurs" are now becoming commonplace across all business sectors in the US. Many credible

a national hunger in that serve up anything "new and improved"

articles have appeared in publications such as the *Harvard Business Review*, written by gurus expounding the merits of nimble, virtual, delayered organizations. Because of their sleek design, these organizations are capable of inviting and acting on ideas from anywhere: suppliers, customers, strategic alliance partners, venture capitalists, incubators or business angels. All these ideas are then screened in a transparent, meritocratic way: how risky is the new concept, when will it deliver a payback, and does it build on the company's sustainable competitive advantages?

Management experts Michael Malone and William Davidow foretold in 1992 that the American organization of the future "will appear almost edgeless, with permeable and continuously changing interfaces among company, supplier and customers. From inside the firm, the view will be no less amorphous with traditional offices, departments and operating divisions constantly re-forming according to need." [2]

Processes

One of the best known experts on the links between structure, process and innovation is Rosabeth Moss-Kanter, the Harvard

[2] *The Virtual Corporation*, © 1992 Harper Business, New York

Business School professor who has analyzed companies that have successfully installed entrepreneurial cultures. In her book *When Giants Learn to Dance* (Simon & Schuster, 1989), she describes this type of company as representing: "a triumph of process over structure. That is, relationships and communication and the flexibility to temporarily combine resources are more important than the 'formal' channels and reporting relationships represented on an organizational chart ... The post-entrepreneurial corporation is created by a three-part mix: by the context set at the top, the values and goals emanating from top management; by the channels, forums, programs and relationships designed in the middle to support those values and goals; and by the project ideas bubbling up from below – ideas for new ventures or technological innovations or better ways to serve customers."

The results of such a bubbling up from below can give birth to fantastic innovations, such as the Post-It Note™, where, to 3M's credit, the inventor and his team were allowed to continue their development work despite negative internal sentiment about the product's commercial chances. Encouraging managers, teams and the organization to take calculated risks, encouraging failure and learning from such failures, is fundamental to American innovation and the health of corporate R&D pipelines. One Silicon Valley technology forecaster in a recent interview says "failure is an essential part of our ecosystem. It's like a forest fire burning space for new growth."[3]

Not only does this corporate attitude encourage a flow of employee-inventor's ideas, but it also fosters a working environment in which it is easier for managers to delegate and encourage staff to take initiatives forward without needing explicit permission. This is a characteristic found in the more entrepreneurial corporate cultures,

---

[3] "Down in the Valley" article, Louise Kehoe, *Financial Times*, 12 December 2001

fuelled by hypercompetition and accelerated R&D cycles in which most US business sectors now find themselves.

Role models

So who are some of America's entrepreneurial and intrapreneurial heroes? There are several recent ones, including Michael Dell of Dell Computers, Herb Kelleher of Southwest Airlines, Howard Schultz of Starbucks, Steve Case of AOL, Steve Jobs of Apple Computer, Bill Gates of Microsoft, Barry Diller of US Networks, Jack Welch of GE, Michael Ovitz of Disney and Creative Artists Agency fame, venture capitalist Esther Dyson or any of the other monthly heroes featured in *Fast Company*, *Red Herring*, *Business 2.0* and *Entrepreneur* magazines.

Some *places* serve as role models too, such as Silicon Valley, whose culture and business climate have inspired similar models around the globe, aiming to recreate this locale's legendary ability to incubate the paper multibillionaires of the future. In the UK alone, there's Silicon Glen in the Scottish Highlands, Silicon Fen near Cambridge, and the Thames Valley just an hour from London – all aiming to mimic the cocktail of connections that create fantastic start-ups.

Innovation infrastructure

Besides a US company's structures, processes and cultures that support innovation and entrepreneurialism, a host of other players contribute to make real the dreams of these corporates. Venture capital companies such as Kleiner Perkins, corporate venturing departments of big companies such as IBM, the management consulting firms' own venture operations such as Bainlab and McKinsey's Accelerator, and even specialist incubators such as the Women's Technology Cluster in San Francisco all mentor the people and their ideas along the commercialization chain. And these partners are chosen carefully based on what they bring to the party: cash, office space, introductions, management talent and sometimes all of the above.

Only in America: some wacky innovations

Should the well of ideas for a new business venture run dry, Americans might turn to *Entrepreneur* magazine's website for inspiration, which suggests hot business trends including personalization, ethnic foods, boomburbs, anything to do with India and "Boomer Menopause", i.e. anything to do with the aging baby boomers who are now in their sixties – with time and money on their hands.[4]

Or, you could monitor a website that tracks wacky inventions[5] and discover some of the patents granted to America's stranger product concepts. The "Panty Hose X 3" is a 3-legged pair which means you can rotate legs should a ladder develop in one of them. Or there's the "Toilet Landing Lights" which help you find the seat in the dark.

What about the "Hospital Happiness" modesty flap for the back of the hospital gown to protect your modesty when guests come for a visit? Or the baby nappy alarm that flashes when wet, alerting parents a change is needed without needing to tuck your finger inside it?

[4] www.entrepreneur.com , "Sweat Rewards" feature, December 2001 issue
[5] www.totallyabsurd.com

WORDS TO LIVE BY

" Ignore the people who tell you it won't work, and hire people who embrace your vision. **Michael Dell**

" He who asks the questions is in control.

" I have a dream... **Martin Luther King**

" Genius is one percent inspiration and ninety nine percent perspiration. **Thomas Edison**

11:

professional advisers

INTRODUCTION

Although the US has only 5 per cent of the world's population, it has 70 per cent of the world's lawyers[1] – about 1 million according to the American Bar Association, the US legal industry regulating body. Seven out of ten of these are in private practice, while the remainder are found in public sector or in-house counsel roles. Typically US lawyers are addressed by the term "Esquire" after their name, and you will often see the abbreviation "JD" on their business cards – "Juris Doctor", the name of the law degree granted in the US. However, the American lawyer is likely to be a specialist, belonging to one or more of about 100 specialist categories – from insurance defence litigator to probate lawyer. Like most other countries, the first (highest) level of classification is criminal or civil, with the many subcategories that follow. Unlike other British-style environments that differentiate between those who can procure business – solicitors – and those who can only represent the client in the courtroom – barristers, the US system makes no such distinction, with lawyers playing both roles.

Accountants are typically classified as either financial or management accountants, with far fewer specialist categories than the legal profession. Qualified financial accountants are referred to as "CPAs" or Certified Public Accountants, who number about the same as lawyers: 1,080,000[2] in 1998, with one in ten self-employed.

[1] www.refdesk.com, 19 November 2001
[2] US Bureau of Labor Statistics website, 19 November 2001

There is

As for the consultants, there were approximately 350,000 in 1998, 55 per cent of them self-employed,[3] and there are at least as many subcategories as there are consultants, depending on their functional roots (manufacturing, marketing, sales, finance, etc.) and methodological church (qualitative research, business process re-engineering, total quality management, etc.).

So in total about 1 per cent of the *entire* US population works in one of these three professions!

One thing is certain: these three groups of professional advisers are either loved or hated, and most Americans in business have a view of their usefulness one way or the other – there is no neutral ground. It's no wonder there are so many websites dedicated to chronicling the jokes and client stories about these advisers (especially lawyers).

According to a recent telephone Harris Poll[4] asking Americans which occupations in their eyes had "very great prestige", lawyers have lost the most ground over the years, falling from 36 per cent of the "vote" in 1977, to only 18 per cent in 2001. Well below the lawyers are accountants, with only 15 per cent believing this occupation has "very great prestige", and business people winning over only 12 per cent of Americans. All three professions are well below scientists (53 per cent) and members of Congress (24 per cent).

[3] US Bureau of Labor Statistics website, 19 November 2001
[4] Harris Poll 50, 10 October 2001

a definite need
for these advisers

However, there *is* a definite need for these advisers and there is no doubt that they can and do perform a valuable role within the corporate structure. Such professionals do add value when they are properly managed by their clients.

WHAT YOU'LL LEARN

➡ How the advisers work with clients.

➡ When and how to use a professional adviser.

➡ How to get the most from your relationship.

➡ Inventions and methodologies devised by US advisers.

Situation

You need a variety of types of advice on the ground in the US for your American business plans to succeed, and have a choice of local experts who can help – all add an essential perspective and dimension, but your budget *isn't* endless. Because you've heard stories about expert advisers costing companies millions of dollars, without always giving them the kind of help they need, you're worried about how to find and manage these experts. What should you do?

Explanation

When and why to use an adviser

American expert advisers (often referred to as "guides" in the US) are used in a variety of ways, depending on what the client wants them to achieve. It's not unknown for them to have multiple roles, including acting as advocate, internal lobbyist, coach, teacher, shrink, hatchet man, friend, confidant, giver of a "seal of approval", informant, data provider, researcher and/or plug-in source of expertise.

You might want to use any of the three groups of professional advisers (i.e. lawyers, accountants, consultants) to give you a form of insurance, perhaps in relation to a strategic decision to be made, or to compensate for areas where your firm has management or skills gaps or planning routines that could be improved. You might find these experts serve as useful catalysts during your company's US restructuring, or during the pursuit of alliances or acquisitions. They can also give you confidence or teach your team a new skill or build their knowledge base – all of which should bolster your US pursuits.

There are other valuable roles that an adviser might perform including benchmarking your company against the best in class, providing facts or industry intelligence you can't readily get on your own and helping you prove your business case.

Recognizing these advisers are experts, independent, objective, have dedicated time to help you, and are a flexible resource without a long-term commitment means you can focus this concentrated brainpower on specific management areas. If your need is immediate and well defined, you are likely to find the costs of hiring an employee with this legal, accounting or management expertise – whether found in the US or in your local market – are lower than taking on a full-time employee as the costs of private healthcare plans, holidays, 401k plans (the shorthand US term for a pension plan), and other benefits for such a full-time resource can be high.

The analytical tools, methodologies, audits and insights which these apolitical, objective advisers bring to companies doing business in the US can be invaluable, *provided* you manage your advisers well.

How professional advisers work with clients

It is clear that these advisers serve many purposes, but knowing what you want them to do, and recognizing when they are no longer doing it is key. (Their hourly fee levels are usually in the $350 per hour category for the most senior of partners in any of these professional services companies.)

"Your chiropractor, your acupuncturist, your t'ai chi instructor, your nutritionist, your feng shui consultant and your pet psychologist called. I've cleared your work schedule for the week."

There are as many specialist types of US consultants, lawyers and accountants as there are variety of business tasks – rather like doctors, they specialize in helping their patients depending on the ailment the patient thinks he/she has. The diagnoses will vary depending on the specialist's own areas of expertise, so try and ensure *your* diagnosis is the right one.

If an adviser misdiagnoses or offers the wrong treatment, you will – if you're like an American client – seek damages in the courts. Lawsuits against these advisers have grown massively in recent years. Professional indemnity insurance is now a standard part of being a practitioner, especially in the management consulting profession, unlike a decade ago. Typically you'll find two types of clauses in the contracts of most, if not all, of these practitioners:

⇒ Liability limits: capping how much money you can claim back for mistakes or bad advice.

⇒ One year statute of limitations: limiting the time to one year after the advice has been given that you can raise a lawsuit.

Interestingly, management consultants are the only professionals of these three types of adviser who are only *voluntarily* regulated or licensed. The American Bar Association (ABA) governs lawyers, the American Institute of Certified Public Accountants (AICPA) governs accountants, and there is a *voluntary* body, the Institute of Management Consultants (IMC), for consultants.

Lawsuits against grown massively

Most of the larger firms of accountants, lawyers and consultants have an international presence: international offices, mostly established in the past 20 years, and usually staffed by local nationals. This drive for internationalization has been fuelled by their clients wanting the convenience of a "one-stop shop" rather than having to find local experts in these foreign countries. Of these three professions, the lawyers have been the slowest to open overseas offices to capture this demand for a seamless, international service.

Finally, it is worth noting that these outside experts are usually among the first to feel the effects of economic downturns, leading to late payments, frozen or cancelled projects, and lay-offs, since their clients see their use as a discretionary spend.

Getting the most from your relationship

Key to having the most satisfying and cost-effective relationship with your US advisers is knowing what motivates them: money, knowing they've given you a good service, and the promise of repeat business from you and/or referrals.

Other tips for enjoying even more benefits from this professional relationship include:

➡ Ask for introductions to others in the advisers' networks of clients, prospects, contacts and/or internal colleagues.

➡ Brief clearly and well, with clear terms of engagement, clear

these advisers have

in recent years

Be aware of the US large companies to

deliverables, specific and measurable objectives. By managing and controlling your advisers, recognizing that they need input from you to do well, both of you should get what you're expecting.

➡ Allow for qualitative analysis and decisions, not just analyzing numbers. There is a tendency in the US to focus too heavily on the bottom line (of the income statement) impact of decisions (in fact, an often heard expression in any meeting will be "what's the bottom line?") which can lead to you possibly making a bad decision. Witness consulting firm McKinsey & Co.'s advice to the conglomerate Cadbury some years ago, suggested they get rid of facilities that weren't "revenue generating". The result was poor staff morale and higher employee turnover since the company became a less attractive place to work with the removal of non-revenue generating aspects of the business including the staff library along with many other amenities.

➡ Apply the "WYSIWYG" approach (what-you-see-is-what-you-get) to ensure that those business developers who presented the proposed projects to you are **also** the workers on these projects. It's better to pay $350 an hour and have something done by an expert than $200 per hour and the job take three hours.

tendency for most hire advisers in their own image

➡ Don't look to long-running TV shows such as *LA Law*, *Judge Judy* or *Court TV* as typical of these professions. Most of the work is office based, dependent on PC tools and heavy analysis, infrequently allowing these "super brains" to leave their desks.

➡ Expect to be asked more questions at the start of your relationship than given answers, in part because it's the American conversational style, and because your answers make it easier to accurately diagnose the scope of the work the practitioners will be doing.

➡ Know that the "win/win" game theory is the *modus operandi* not only in contractual, expert-input relationships but in most, if not all, US business relationships.

➡ Know the value to you of having these business, legal or accounting questions answered so that you recognize you're getting something of value when it's given to you.

➡ Bear in mind that implementation is not always the advisers' strongest suit – developing worthwhile strategies usually is.

➡ Know the advisers' American clients already have an expectation for speedy responses, accelerated deadlines and excellent project management skills.

➡ Don't be afraid to use super specialists (which may mean hiring a no-brand firm of advisers) instead of the large, generic corporates as they usually have more in-depth expertise and are very often more cost-effective than the large, well-branded firms.

➡ Be aware of the US tendency for most large companies to hire advisers in their own image who aren't always necessarily the best experts in a particular area. It's rare for a large corporate to hire a small, no-brand specialist adviser as the US company and that decision maker may well be using the adviser not so much for their competence as for what that brand communicates internally. As one well known European corporate tells us, "no one here gets fired for using McKinsey".

➡ Stay close to their projects so you know when the advisers are beyond their area(s) of expertise, and you know when a project is completed.

➡ Control the number of practitioners working in your organization as there is a tendency (if they're not closely managed) to multiply and spread teams throughout the company – this means controlling their agendas and time sheets appropriately.

Inventions and methodologies

There are a number of well known and packaged methodologies that have been devised by US professional advisers over the years to help add value within a client company, a few of which include:

➡ 5 Forces Model: developed by Harvard Business School professor and founder of management consulting firm Monitor Company, Michael Porter, this approach helps analyze an industry along five dimensions – the power of buyers, suppliers, substitutes, technology and competitors.

➡ The Balanced Scorecard: another Harvard Business School professor Robert Kaplan posits that companies should monitor a wider range of performance indicators than they typically do to ensure that the bottom line bias is balanced by a focus on other equally important indicators of corporate health, such as market shares, customer satisfaction and retention rates, among others.

➡ Business Process Re-engineering (BPR): a generic term for the reorganization of company internal structures, reporting lines and business processes to better serve internal and external customers – in terms of cost, quality and speed.

➡ Customer Relationship Management (CRM): a concept first posited by Peppers & Rogers Group that one-to-one marketing nets higher returns on investment in marketing, HR, IT and other functional areas. This is now being turned on its side with the growing number of followers of "CMR" – customer managed relationships – whereby customers permit and control the relationship your company has with them.

➡ Brand valuation: accountants are now increasingly urging clients to include the value of brands in the financial statements since this is a tangible investment that generates goodwill for the company and all of its activities.

➡ Litigation: not a new development in the legal realm, but one that is instigated at the earliest point of conflict between two parties. The courts are used in the US as interpreters of contract law, and seen as a credible reference point for dispute resolution.

➡ Management by Objectives (MBO): a practice which allows employees to suggest their own job objectives which are subsequently agreed with their managers. This is seen as a tool to empower the employee since they will feel a strong sense of ownership of the objective if it is they who crafted it.

➡ Strategic Business Unit (SBU): a concept originating from the 1960s US management consulting firms that recommends a conglomerate's businesses be tightly organized as profit or cost centres around which company resources are allocated.

➡ Total Quality Management (TQM): a form of company audit to identify ways for organizational processes to be better aligned with business opportunities.

The fact that these methodologies are so well known throughout Europe also (and elsewhere in the world) is testament to the effectiveness of American professional advisers. It is they who have spread this intellectual property so fast, so well and so profitably.

JOKES

Accountants

– What's an extroverted accountant? One who looks at your shoes instead of his own while he's talking to you.

– Why did the auditor cross the road? Because he looked in the file and that's what they did last year.

– What's the definition of an accountant? Someone who solves a problem you didn't know you had in a way you don't understand.

Lawyers

– In the US, everything that is not prohibited by law is permitted. In Germany, everything that is not permitted by law is prohibited. In Russia, everything is prohibited, even if permitted by law. In France, everything is permitted, even if prohibited by law. In Switzerland, everything that is not prohibited by law is obligatory.

– What's wrong with lawyer jokes? Lawyers don't think they're funny, and nobody else thinks they're jokes.

Consultants

How many management consultants does it take to change a light bulb?

Multiple answers:

1 How many did it take last year?

2 It depends – how much money is in your budget...?

3 None. A consultant would recommend replacing the light fixture.

4 None. Consultants don't know how to do anything; they can just tell you how you should do it.

5 One partner. He holds on to the bulb and the whole world revolves around him. (Contributed by Andrew Clark.)

6 That's difficult to say. First, we need to do a study to see if you really need light in that area, determine historically why the light burned out, and an analysis to determine whether it's the right kind of light anyway. Then, maybe, we can recommend appropriate action – although we may need to do additional studies to determine the light sensitivity of employees visiting the area. After that, we can: develop RFPs and RFQs, evaluate the abilities of various maintenance

workers to perform the task, recommend personnel selection, and supervise the activity.

7 Have you thought about rewiring your whole house recently?

WORDS TO LIVE BY

"" No one here gets fired for using McKinsey (substitute Baker & McKenzie for lawyers, PricewaterhouseCoopers for accountants).

"" Bigger does not mean better.

"" Advice giving is an art, not a science. **David Maister**

"" Advisers advise. Ministers decide. **Margaret Thatcher**

"" Give me reasons, not just instructions. **David Maister**

"" The sign of a truly educated man is to be deeply moved by statistics. **George Bernard Shaw**

12:

fight or flight

INTRODUCTION

Here's a question: what slogan best describes American business today? An obvious choice is the ominous "sue the bastard!" – a threat heard across America every day. Many believe it was coined by an irate businessman, an angry consumer or an excited lawyer. But in fact, litigation is now such an integral part of American life and business that just about anyone with a grievance – however slight – is likely to threaten to go to their nearest lawyer.

WHAT YOU'LL LEARN

➡ To an observer, it seems Americans *love* litigation. Going to court is as natural for Americans as stopping by Starbucks for coffee. And it all harks back to the inherent American sense of justice and individual rights, borne of the country's rebellious history.

➡ That's the bad news. The good news: American businesses often sue or threaten to sue as a tactical move to reach an amicable, out-of-court settlement or financial payment. It's simply part of the pushy way American business is conducted. However, there are ways to avoid a courtroom drama through independent arbitration or mediation, which is a much less painful way to get results.

➡ Foreign companies are likely targets. Newcomers who don't know the lie of the land, how contracts are structured or the peculiarities of workplace harassment legislation – in this age of rampant political correctness – can get burned.

➡ A contract isn't watertight. And an American contract is more complex and detailed than a European one. The moral is this: if you're doing business with Americans, have in your corporate arsenal a savvy, tough-as-nails lawyer who understands your business and who can ensure that your business partners aren't climbing the learning curve about your industry and organization at *your* expense.

Situation

Imagine you are a franchisee of an American fast food company in Hungary. Market research shows there's a big market among Magyars for cheeseburgers, as they're fond of meat and cheese and all things American. As part of the deal, the contract says your staff must also look the part – with red, white and blue uniforms and American flag pins on their lapels. One day, the American boss arrives and sees that the guy flipping burgers is wearing a Che Guevara t-shirt. "Get rid of him," shouts the American manager. What can you do?

Explanation

Who sues whom?

Anyone is fair game. Employees sue employers after they are dismissed. Investors sue financial advisers when the stock market dips; activist shareholders take on company management if performance slumps. More recently, a company was sued when an employee had a car accident while doing business on a mobile phone.

Outraged consumers are frequent litigants. They sue fast food chains and consumer goods giants over supposedly faulty products, like the woman who successfully took on McDonald's after she was scalded by hot coffee. Prisoners even sue the prison system. Children sue

America must the world's most

their schools for poor test performances and educational standards. And the government gets in on the act too, taking on corporate giants like Microsoft for alleged monopolistic behaviour.

Ever heard of religious harassment? The Civil Rights Act of 1964 offers broad protection to the religious. And the courts have been equally dogged about not allowing any employee to create a hostile work environment by harassing colleagues about their religious beliefs.

Many cases appear frivolous, but some lawsuits are deadly serious. Think Big Tobacco, gun manufacturers, asbestos makers and medical device manufacturers: all have been embroiled for decades in complex legal actions aimed at improving or safeguarding public health.

The statistics are certainly staggering. More than 260,000 civil cases were filed in 2000 in federal courts, according to the Administrative Office for US Courts. But that pales in comparison to the 15.1 million civil filings in federal courts in 1999 – that's a whopping 32 per cent rise from 1984.

Why Americans sue

America must certainly be the world's most litigious nation. Many of us grew up watching television shows like Perry Mason, which showcased a tenacious lawyer, but perhaps it's also because there are *so many* lawyers – over 1 million in 2000, according to the American

certainly be litigious nation

Bar Association – who are forever chasing ambulances and stalking courtroom corridors.

But it's not just the legions of lawyers who fuel the litigation bandwagon. Some suggest it's the American craving for individual freedom – along with an inflated sense of self – that prompts usually sane people to seek remedies in a court of law for anything that appears to violate their rights. After all, lawsuits rack up hefty legal bills and drain management time.

According to one expert, Philip K. Howard,[1] the urge to sue reflects Americans' preoccupation with the rights of the individual. After all, America's birth followed the rejection of a higher – at the time, royal – authority. This has fostered a cult of individualism and the quest to ensure that "personal" rights aren't violated.

Another factor: numerous laws enacted after the 1960s, including those guaranteeing civil and consumer rights, opened up an entire new legal battlefield of class action suits. The idea is that when you sue as a group there is strength in numbers.

Why others don't sue

Other countries resolve disputes differently. The stereotypes are as follows: the British prefer writing erudite letters to *The Times*, orderly

---

[1] *The Lost Art of Drawing the Line*, Philip K. Howard, Random House

Germans form committees and eventually reach a reasonable compromise after considerable intellectual debate, and the French prefer settling problems personally, over a bottle of Bordeaux. In fact, Great Britain is becoming much more of a litigation culture, and people everywhere are becoming more litigious by nature.

There's a more serious reason why the US has so many lawsuits: sympathetic juries hand out big cash settlements. Quite often the sum is substantially reduced during the appeals process, or in an out-of-court settlement. Even so the prospect of winning billions – like the bill Big Tobacco is often threatened with – is an incentive to lawyers or companies seeking redress for alleged damages.

One can walk away with a bundle: jury awards are increasing exponentially, according to the US Chamber Institute for Law Reform. The top ten jury awards in 1999 increased more than 1,200 per cent over the previous year to total over $9 billion. In Europe, by comparison, where there's no right to a jury trial in most civil cases, settlements are much smaller.

How the legal system works

American law derives from the British common law system (except in the state of Louisiana, which is based on the French civil code). While American lawyers don't wear wigs and gowns like British barristers, there are similarities in the legal structure.

Courts operate on various levels. The state supreme court is the ultimate arbiter, subject of course to legislative changes. Lawyers are licensed by state bars, not the federal government; each state has its own civil codes, which is why you can buy alcohol in some states on a Sunday but not in others.

Then comes the mighty US Supreme Court, with its seven members nominated by the President, which has the final say on all federal law and constitutional issues.

The US Constitution, frequently debated and only rarely altered, is regarded as holy. It holds sway over all other laws, providing a framework for how the country is governed. It defines the powers and limits of government, and dictates how the law is applied equally to all citizens.

Remember that the law is always in flux. The law shapes itself to take into account how the nation thinks and feels, scientific and technological advances and shifts in public opinion and morality. The internet, cloning and the terrorist attacks on New York and Washington – which led to tighter anti-terrorist laws – are good examples of how the law isn't divorced from reality.

Ethics

Cynics say lawyers have no ethics. But that's too harsh. While the profession has its share of swashbucklers, there are strict codes of ethics promoted by the American Bar Association and by state bars.

Lawyers get into trouble too – don't forget former President Bill Clinton. After the Monica Lewinsky shenanigans, he lost his Arkansas law licence for five years and was barred from practising law before the US Supreme Court.

American lawyers also act as advisers in business dealings. In fact, it's a good idea to use them, according to James Drew Lawson, a Los Angeles-based lawyer, who calls this type of legal advice "preventive law". That means using lawyers to give advice and help structure a deal before it's inked; hopefully, that will ward off problems later.

The overwhelming law-suits are not

How to find a good lawyer

Bad lawyers are easy to find: just follow an ambulance. Unfortunately, lawyers sometimes get a raw deal, and in America they are often the butt of jokes by late night television comics – and distinguished judges. "Lawyers spend a great deal of their time shovelling smoke," quipped Oliver Wendell Holmes Jr, the Supreme Court judge.

Good lawyers used to be difficult to find, like doctors. In the old days, established law firms protected their exclusivity, and their services were inherited by families or companies from one generation to another.

But the age of the internet has changed all that: you can find a reliable lawyer online at one of the most respected legal directories, www.martindale.com. Or just check the legal advertisements. Following legal changes in the 1970s, law firms won the right to advertise their services, like companies selling soap powder. It's probably best, though, to find a lawyer by recommendation from a trusted friend or business associate.

If you are sued...

First of all, don't panic. Consider this: the overwhelming majority of commercial lawsuits are not decided in the courts, mainly because the process can be long and legal fees are exorbitant. The parties usually

majority of commercial decided in the courts

settle cases after the lawsuit has begun. The strategy is more likely aimed at extracting a concession.

Our Hungarian fast food franchisee is a good example. The contract states that staff should be swathed head to toe in Americana – that's part of the deal. The boss's exhortations are really aimed at seeing more red, white and blue. That's because Americans like to play by the rules, and they're offended when others don't. "The American mindset is to follow the law," says lawyer James Drew Lawson.

There are ways to settle a dispute without resorting to a court appearance. Americans love direct confrontation and straight talking, which is why President George W. Bush's vow to "smoke out" terrorists after 11 September was cheered across the land. So it's worth trying to discuss and hopefully, resolve the dispute without dragging in lawyers.

Another option: dispute resolution services including conciliation, mediation or arbitration. Basically, you agree to try to work out the problem amicably for everyone's benefit.

Broadly defined, conciliation means facilitating communication between the feuding parties to informally resolve a dispute. Mediation goes a step further, adding a professionally trained mediator to the group who guides the parties to a solution. If all that fails, an arbitration hearing is called before an impartial third party – hopefully, before the fists start flying.

A contract with an will be as

Contracts

Contracts are made to be broken, the saying goes. But you should still cherish that trusty piece of paper if something does go wrong.

Americans have faith in contracts. That's why a contract with an American company will be as voluminous as a phone book. There will be appendixes and attachments. There will be lists of assets and regulatory filings. The idea? To pre-empt the unexpected.

"If anything goes wrong, there will be a system in the contract to solve the problem," explains Colin Buckley, an American corporate lawyer based in London. "The contract will say what could go wrong and how to deal with it."

Europeans view contracts altogether differently. In Europe, a contract is a simple, stripped down document, largely because lawyers in Europe play a smaller role in corporate affairs than in America.

Another warning: Europeans favour signing contracts on each page on the bottom right, while trustworthy Americans affix their names only at the end. Don't be afraid to ask for initials on every page though – **it's just as important that Americans learn other protocols too**.

American company voluminous as a phone book

WORDS TO LIVE BY

" The law isn't justice. It's a very imperfect mechanism. If you press exactly the right buttons and are also lucky, justice may show up in the answer. A mechanism is all the law was ever intended to be.

Raymond Chandler

" A court is a place where what was confused before becomes more unsettled than ever. **Henry Waldorf Francis**

" A jury consists of twelve persons chosen to decide who has the better lawyer. **Robert Frost**

13:

let's make a plan

INTRODUCTION

"Planning" is such a widely practised, celebrated event in the US that even Microsoft has decided to get in on the act: its Office2000 Pro software version comes pre-packaged with the integrated *Microsoft Business Planner* tool, which implies that their US customers expect this as part of any computer package, whether you use your computer for business applications or even leisure pursuits! Planning is one way of controlling the "ready, fire, aim" tendencies, for which American business is renowned, especially when planning forays into international markets. And now *hyperplanning* in most US organizations is becoming an even more widespread practice following the random acts of terrorism on New York City and the Pentagon on 11 September 2001. Where once an annual operating or business plan sufficed, quarterly detailed plans are now routinely written and revised in an effort to readjust strategies more often and more accurately.

WHAT YOU'LL LEARN

➡ Americans see planning as an inalienable right: it's in the blood of every American, or American-educated, business professional because time must be conquered, the future must be created, the forces of business must be controlled, new lives must be built . . . recalling the original settlers, once again.

➡ Planning has a language of its own, borne from the constructive, action-oriented event, delivering substantive results, business cases, solutions, returns on investment and clear closure rather than unguided, seat-of-the-pants, meandering, unsatisfying arguments with no clear outcomes for controlling the future.

Fatalism is determinism

➡ The process of planning usually varies from team to team, company to company, and tries to control dissent while simultaneously "firing up" the planning teams so that the objectives can be accomplished and the strategies implemented.

Situation

Imagine this situation: you're meeting with some US colleagues who ask you "what's your plan for lunch today?" You realize you don't have a *plan* for lunch – in fact, you'll eat when you're hungry! Why does everyone expect you to have a plan?

Explanation

The urge to plan

The American focus on controlling the future and what happens – in the office, at home, at the son's Little League baseball games – points to the fact that a favoured tool for control is planning – as the proverb goes, "If you fail to plan, you plan to fail."

This urge is probably most closely linked to the American heritage: the immigrants who left behind their economies of scarcity. More recent trends that have added weight to the importance of planning and the need to blueprint our futures, include the disappearance of the job for life, the receding social security nets to look after employees in their golden years, and of course unpredictable acts of

the old world;
is the new

terrorism. Where a few decades ago the optimism of US business was rooted in a belief that life would still get even better, we now live in a more sober era of downsizing, restructuring and unpredictability.

The general perception in the US is that if you're not first in the race to conquer your environment, to stake your claim in the Manifest Destiny, it's not worth doing. The pace of commerce is fast, and the frontier spirit is alive and well. Mastering one's destiny is a shared cultural view, an insight into our deterministic culture: we believe we *do* control most (if not all) of our environment – and through planning of any kind, you *can* master most of the elements in your environment. Fatalism is the old world; determinism is the new.

Why we plan

According to one cross-cultural commentator, Richard Lewis,[1] the American business philosophy is plain: to make as much money as fast as you can. And one of the best ways of doing so is through lots of very good planning. Everything in the American business culture is goal-oriented, action-oriented, with a perceived meritocratic pay-off of rewards based entirely on results. To ensure the effective workings of a true meritocracy it is necessary to track the achievement of the goals – which planning allows (assuming the goals have been clearly articulated).

[1] Richard Lewis, *When Cultures Collide*, Nicholas Brealey Publishing © 2000, p. 167

179

When Americans acknowledge the construction of plans as a valued behaviour in their culture, they are not saying that *not* planning is destructive, but it is viewed as being poorly organized and a signal that winning the race is not that important to you.

Another driver of planning in US companies is the linkage of personal performance to organizational performance – a management practice known as "performance management". By ensuring company goals (a by-product of the planning process) and individual goals are interdependent, US enterprises try to ensure individual acknowledgement and rewards stay merit-based. For some companies, planning for performance is about planning for fun. In a recent US magazine interview[2] Mona Cabler, Director of Fun at telecomms company Sprint asserts that "fun and work are mutually reinforcing". She goes on to say "when [US] companies say they're employee centred, they usually mean centred on helping employees achieve the company's goals. We emphasize helping individuals achieve their personal goals."

Accelerating decision making is a favourite pastime in the US business world since this fuels an ingrained need to take action, to *do* things. Sports company Nike's long-serving strapline "Just Do It" is evidence of this strong need, communicated very well.

Other motives for planning include avoidance of the accusation that anyone is following a "seat-of-the-pants" strategy – an irresponsible, profligate, unfocused, unmethodical set of steps towards pursuing the holy grail of business: profits. Planning is also viewed as necessary when allocating corporate resources, be they human, cash or intellectual property, in order for it to be done in a responsible and considerate way. The planning process is also thought to minimize

---

[2] *Fast Company* magazine, issue 12, p. 74

the risk of becoming just another statistic in the graveyard of failed corporate missions – the "plan or die" ethos must prevail.

The prioritizations which result from planning – making and communicating choices – are ingrained in Americans in business early on. We're taught these skills early in life, and to believe decisiveness means proactiveness, that indecision brings the loss of control. With decisiveness comes a perception of self-reliance and independence. "The buck stops here" religion reveals the importance Americans attach to making independent decisions, whether for business or private life.

It is also important to plan – alone or with a team – in order to construct the business case that will win budgets, increased territory, authority and recognition from peers. He who crafts the plan usually controls the resource purse.

Types of planning

The variety of categories of plans in current use reveals the pervasiveness of the practice throughout American life. Strategic, operational, contingency, business and financial plans are all eagerly propounded by the Entrepreneur (patron saint of business). Planning permeates every aspect of life at work and at home; when not planning what to do for lunch, Americans will plan their holidays, investment strategies, careers, parties and even their whole life. As if further evidence is needed, an entire industry has emerged in the US over the past few years, "Life Planning", with counsellors helping busy workforces to juggle the demands of home and work, helping prioritize life's demands for a happier, healthier, shinier, longer existence.

There's a relatively new category posited by US calendar manufacturer Franklin Covey, called the "personal productivity planner"

With decisiveness of self-reliance

which allows you to plan gift-giving occasions using their online reminder service. Covey, one of the leading personal desktop calendar manufacturers, conducted research in the past few years[3] to better understand how Americans plan: it found over 50 per cent use a calendar, 30 per cent notebook-style organizers, and over 80 per cent make lists. Nearly 75 per cent say they "always or frequently" know what they want to accomplish in life, nearly 40 per cent have written financial goals, and about 33 per cent have written career goals.

The most prevalent category of plan you are likely to come across is the *strategic* category, peppering most business meetings, and which disaggregates into "action plans" for realizing the overall, big-picture vision.

The technology of planning

Knowing the types and drivers of planning is very helpful, but also being aware of the planning industry is important as well. Besides the hardware of Franklin Covey organizers, Filofax, PalmPilots and Blackberry, there's the planning software such as project managers *FastTrack Schedule, Microsoft Project,* the contact planners *ACT!, Goldmine* and *Now Contact,* and the business planning software of *Business Plan Pro,* to name but a few.

---

[3] www.franklincovey.com/about/press/1998

comes a perception and independence

The language of planning

When Americans talk about planning they often use the vocabulary of battle: getting armed or equipped; leading or defending; attacking competitors; winning customers; slaughtering the competition; winning the war. Whatever strategy is employed, clear winners and losers are likely to emerge. There are also the planning acronyms: MBO (management by objectives), SWOT (strengths/weaknesses/opportunities/threats) and STEP analysis (sociocultural/technological/economic/political).

Another phrase that's successfully taken root, thanks to the best-selling Stephen Covey book *7 Habits of Highly Effective People,* is that we should "begin with the end in mind" – a plea to visualize the prize that comes with good planning. But to seize the prize, a well constructed *business case* – an often heard phrase – best shows how the 'ROI' (return on investment) can be achieved.

Who does all this planning?

Planning is typically an event, a project undertaken in purposefully formed teams whose prime source of cohesion is the need to complete the planning task at hand. There's no real need to get to know one another, just to collaborate on the planning event to produce a

"So then Mr Hotchkiss was all, 'Shall we discuss the new budgetary guidelines?' and Ms Putney was like, 'Perhaps the latest marketing figures will be of interest,' and Mr Meecham was all, 'I expect to have those figures later today,' and then ..."

lucid series of arguments to support the business case. If true friendship results, then that is a fantastic bonus.

Usually junior level management and above, across all functional departments and SBUs (strategic business units), participate on a planning team of one sort or another. Often the group is managed like a sports team which can alienate those women members not familiar with the locker room pep talks or sports analogies.

It is often an impersonal, routine activity, usually quarterly – borne out of a cultural need for independence and objectivity – but one which often hinders the creation of true teamwork. The schism between self-reliant, independent professionalism and wanting to be popular with the planning team is often a challenge, as most individuals are either task leaders or emotional leaders but very rarely both.

Even the best laid plans...

... do go wrong. Especially when it comes to US companies trying to grow in overseas territories. Despite an intense hunger for factoids, figures and almanac trivia, the carrying out of in-country research abroad is an often neglected part of the planning activities. It is rare to find anyone employed by the US company physically sited within the 50 states who speaks the local language, or understands the local culture. It's often felt to be just too difficult to plan for more substantive information gathering in any real depth.

This unwillingness to carry out proper research abroad has resulted in some real marketing clangers: Chevrolet "Nova" automobiles become "Doesn't Go" in Spanish-speaking markets, Kentucky Fried Chicken's long-term strapline "Finger Lickin' Good" becomes "So Good You'll Suck Your Fingers Off" in China, to name just two.

Thus, the American company will often assume overseas territories must be a lot like America, and will enter and grow that market accordingly. These frequent approaches are what keep the business consultants, accountants and lawyers a very happy and profitable group of advisers.

Decision making

Planning the "attack" on the market is the front-end of the business cycle; selling it internally to decision-making colleagues is the critical, implementational part of the planning process which allows business professionals to demonstrate their acute "action" skills. This hunting/ gathering view of business planning encourages the masculine, macho behaviours often seen during this cycle of business activity.

According to some keen observations put forward in a *Harvard Business Review* article on decision making,[4] most US business

---

[4] HBR article, September 2001 issue, "What You Don't Know about Decision Making" by David Garvin and Michael Roberto (© 2001 Harvard Business School Press)

Most US business planning as an event, to a collaborative

professionals see planning as an event, a contest, as opposed to a collaborative problem-solving process – with team discussions serving as a platform for demonstrating personal skills in persuasion and lobbying.

The team members charged with making the decisions about a plan typically play the role of spokesmen, advocating a clear position, aiming to convert the rest of the organization, defending their collective point of view and playing down any weaknesses in their arguments. While minority views are tolerated, they're usually discouraged or dismissed. The result: clearly identifiable winners and losers emerge as a result of the decision as opposed to a cadre of winners who share collective ownership. Because planning is a one-off event, it minimizes the *quality* of decision making by ensuring it is not an ongoing, iterative process. Instead, the event, with its finite start/stop, can take on a significance, drama and status all of its own.

The resistance to overt conflict means decisions are often less well informed of all possible routes, scenarios or options as they will not have been debated by the team. Once a decision is made, rarely is it re-examined during the fiscal year as this could imply possible mistakes or omissions, and loss of face and embarrassment for those who made the decision. After all, there are reputations to uphold.

professionals see a contest, as opposed problem-solving process

The American business view that dissent is often destructive means that there's a bias in favour of those who support a team decision and advocate it. Members who question a decision and the assumptions it is built upon are viewed as negative, unhelpful, politically motivated, subjective and are often unpopular as future team members.

What is surprising is that given the volume of US business experts writing on decision making and planning, and the number of MBA programmes that preach best practice, there is no widely-accepted procedure for making decisions – each team often has its own approach, based on the team's leader and his/her abilities of persuasion – so within one company, it is common to find many teams using many different procedures.

In an attempt to raise the level of sophistication of decision making, labels have been given to the various *types* of decision makers:[5] economic buyer, user buyer, technical buyer and coach (this last one helps other decision makers to understand and navigate the internal decision selling processes).

[5] *Strategic Selling*, Miller, Heiman and Tuleja © 1991 Kogan Page

WORDS TO LIVE BY

" Never put off until tomorrow what you can do today.

" It's better to be first than best.

" Paralysis by analysis.

" Begin with the end in mind. **Stephen Covey**

" If you fail to plan, you plan to fail.

" You don't have to focus on everything to be successful. But you do have to focus on something. **Al Ries**

" Plans are nothing; planning is everything. **Dwight D. Eisenhower**

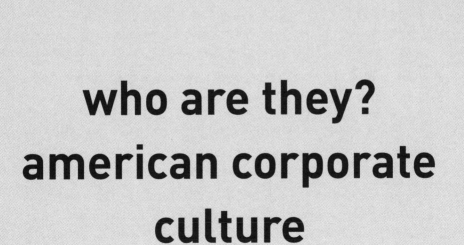

14:

who are they? american corporate culture

INTRODUCTION

One reason US corporate cultures are so often studied and judged by both non-American and American business professionals is because of their substantial power to motivate, retain and attract talent as well as fuel outstanding organizational performance in "better" companies.

The "way we do things around here" is at its heart – how a company treats customers, staff, suppliers, investors, its philosophy about the right and wrong ways to pursue profits.

The power of a strong, healthy, motivating company culture is demonstrated by the number of hours Americans are prepared to give to their employers: 46 hours each week *on average*,[1] which means there's a significant number who give their companies much more than this. Nearly 40 per cent in every age category described themselves as workaholics.

Besides a culture that encourages the workaholics, a company's culture can also be very powerful in winning over those who aren't completely satisfied with other aspects of their jobs. A significant number of Americans are not *completely* satisfied with their levels of stress at work (79 per cent), their pay (77 per cent), their opportunities to get promoted (68 per cent) or their company's recognition of their job achievements (62 per cent).

[1] Gallup "Job Satisfaction" poll, 3 September 1999

With 14 days per year the typical annual holiday allowance, and 21 days for very senior management, it's no wonder a long distance holiday to a distant land is nearly impossible to enjoy, especially after accounting for recovering from jet lag once you have arrived. It's hardly surprising that with the propensity to work, work, work, and limited holiday allowances, the American business culture is insular.

WHAT YOU'LL LEARN

➡ What is "corporate culture"?

➡ Why understanding a US company's culture is important.

➡ What to look for when assessing a US company culture.

➡ Typical characteristics of US company cultures.

➡ What are the shapers of American corporate culture?

➡ Case studies.

Situation

You are on the plane heading for your company's annual sales conference at the US headquarters, where your American vice-president of sales, vice-president of marketing and CEO will be sharing the platform to get you "pumped up" for next year's fantastic business prospects waiting to be converted – the low-hanging fruit. But how should you interpret the messages they're delivering? Why are your American colleagues so energized by this overzealous mania, this glorified evangelical sermon?

Explanation

What is "corporate culture"?

One of the most straightforward definitions comes from American

A company's culture indicator of its

change management consulting firm Senn-Delaney,[2] which suggests corporate culture is a composite of:

➡ Beliefs – how we think things should be done.

➡ Shared values – what we think is important.

➡ Heroes – the people who personify our corporate culture.

➡ Behaviours – the way we do things around here.

➡ Systems – our written and unwritten policies and procedures.

They espouse that these are created through the interaction of the key shapers of culture, which include:

➡ Leadership style

➡ Employees

➡ Organizational tasks

➡ Industry and environment

➡ Regional differences.

Why understanding a US company's culture is important

Understanding the US company's culture means there will be some clarity about the implied "contract" between your opposite numbers and their organization. It tells you what behaviours, actions, tasks

[2] *In the Eye of the Storm: Reengineering Corporate Culture*, John Childress and Larry Senn, Leadership Press, California 1995

serves as a leading business performance

they will likely perform to achieve the company's (and hopefully their own) business objectives. By understanding the culture of the American company with which you are working, you can adjust your own behaviours, messages and approaches in order to mesh, or conflict, with their own attitudes, values and ways of working.

Another reason for studying the quality of a company's culture is it serves as a leading indicator of its business performance. Empirical evidence supports the conclusion that companies with extremely well-defined cultures are far more likely to support the achievement of strategic objectives than those with very poorly defined cultures.[3] And the achievement of strategic objectives usually translates to ... business results.

In the "talent war" era in which most US companies now find themselves, the corporate culture is increasingly paraded as a differentiator (a "unique selling point") for attracting and retaining staff.

What to look for when assessing a US company culture

Lisa Carmichael, a partner with US management consulting firm Frontier Associates,[4] describe some ways to assess the US company's "corporate culture":

[3] "Driving Corporate Culture for Business Success" © Business Intelligence 1999
[4] Interview conducted October 2001

➡ **Read what they say.** Read the mission statements, values, corporate brochures and annual reports. Check for the stated goals and their current view of their own performance. What does success look like? Who are the people photographed in the corporate communications: Men? Women? Older or younger employees? Ethnically diverse? Does the board of directors look like the customers, or is it a panel of grey-haired white men? If there is a published mission and/or values statement, do people treat each other, and does the company treat its customers, in a manner consistent with these values? Are these values important and respected or just symbolic?

➡ **Look at the offices.** What does the office location communicate? Heart of the city or industrial area? Suburban office park or view of the beach? Look at the colours, the quality of furniture, the artwork (if any). Contemporary? Traditional? Expensive treasures? Flea market finds? Stylish but uncomfortable? Personal photos or memorabilia on desks or computer screens?

➡ **How people look.** Does everyone look alike? Is this a company where all the executives are the same size, are dressed alike? If there are variations, are the differences specific to a department? Is the corporate look a common uniform of suits and ties, or shorts and sandals?

➡ **How people are treated.** When sitting in the lobby, pay attention to the receptionist. How is the phone answered? How are people greeted?

➡ **Icons, words and symbols.** Is there a vocabulary, words and acronyms that only "insiders" understand? Who are the heroes and role models? Which people get promoted? Are there physical indicators that someone is doing well (size of office, window view, more equipment)?

"I think you know why I'm letting you go, Thorncroft."

➡ **Procedures.** In a meeting, watch the flow of conversation. Is there one person who everyone addresses, or is there an irregular flow back and forth involving everyone? How are tasks assigned and reports made? Does everyone speak? What is the mood – serious and quiet? Strained? Is there a light atmosphere with lots of jokes?

Typical characteristics of US company cultures

Regardless of the industry sector, you are likely to find the following generalizations hold true about what Americans are like to work with as a community of corporates:

➡ Amercian business professionals tend to be very focused on the endgame, the objectives and the transaction rather than the long-term, one-to-one relationship with you or your company. This is often evidenced by such mundane clues as the way you're announced by a receptionist at a company you're visiting, as we often find – "I have a 'Stewart-Allen' and a 'Denslow' in reception for you" – as if we're a new genus of *Homo sapiens* never before encountered!

➡ They tend to favour low context, direct messages that are to be taken at face value, and which are not mixed with deep irony or subtext (a challenge certainly for Europeans).

➡ There is often a swift response to market conditions and trends which is sometimes viewed by outside observers as knee-jerk (witness the massive hotel room rate and airline fares cuts across the US within hours of the 11 September 2001 terrorist attacks on New York).

➡ The generally accepted view is that it is better to do a job "right first time" than quickly but poorly.

➡ Building "fun" into one's company and one's job is important as it helps achieve organizational and personal goals simultaneously.

➡ There is a tendency towards micro-management: treating staff like children who need supervising while doing their homework – frequent "report backs" and meetings are the tools used by managers to monitor (not necessarily manage better) their staff.

➡ Most workplaces are high-feedback environments, where information about where you stand and how well you've performed is given freely and quickly in as much detail as you might want. Asking for feedback is an encouraged behaviour and a phrase often used in meetings is: "Hey Bob, can I get your feedback on ..."

➡ The more successful companies are run by accessible leaders and senior managers who encourage direct contact and feedback, usually "managing by walking around" (one of Peters and Waterman's findings of excellent managements[5]).

[5] Thomas Peters and Robert Waterman, *In Search of Excellence* (Warner Books, 1988)

➡ Businesses undertake a constant (if not regular) impact analysis of the operating environment so as not to be taken by surprise by events or be accused of slowness to respond to change.

➡ There are regular evangelical sessions ("love-fests") as a planned part of company-wide meetings, with senior leaders taking the role of "cheerleaders" to communicate and *control* the values and corporate culture.

➡ Lots of management time is spent in meetings rather than "doing" (part of the American belief that you can never *over*-communicate). The ritual of frequent meetings can be one of the more frustrating aspects of US company cultures.

➡ Status is usually granted by the deference and reference of others. Sometimes it can be inferred by where the senior manager sits in meetings (at the head of the table). At other times their position can be identified by whether they are interrupted infrequently or listened to frequently. However it is ascertained, it is certainly subtle in part because the "boss" often intentionally dresses like the rest of the staff to encourage a democratic, overtly low-status work environment.

➡ Conversations over the water cooler, in meetings or corridors, often seem to consist of a series of questions rather than statements or answers, which encourages the exchange of as much information as possible in the briefest amount of time.

➡ Information is seen as a freely accessible commodity rather than a status-determining one. It is freely given, taken and stored without an ego-driven sense of ownership.

➡ Overt disagreement in meetings or other public arenas with colleagues or managers is seen as shocking, surprising and something to be discouraged. Disagreement is seen as a destructive, unproductive behaviour that takes the focus off the

Humour

bottom-line, the tasks to be done. Usually disagreements are aired "off-line" in a more private setting.

→ Most US companies value "masculine" behaviours: quantitative analysis, task-oriented action, a focus on achievements, performance or results. Academics Fons Trompenaars and Charles Hampden-Turner describe American companies as having a "guided missile culture"[6] – heading towards a well-defined target (increased market share, higher ROI, better same store sales, being first or second in the market, reduced headcount, increased productivity).

→ "Command and control" management structures and styles are most common.

→ "Innovate or Die!" is a slogan often heard in management corridors. Cisco Systems CEO John Chambers is credited with saying "we're a company that reinvents itself constantly".[7] This ability to change, to adapt, is one of the characteristics of American culture. This capacity to reinvent, to believe that we can change our environment is key to both our national culture of determinism and corporate success.

→ Humour is often used as a management tool, as it helps offset the intense time pressures and goal orientations that are present in every American workplace. Even some job titles reflect this belief

[6] *Riding the Waves of Culture*, p. 177
[7] www.fortune.com, 19 February 2001 "How Long Can They Stay?", Diba and Munoz

is often used as a management tool

that humour is important,[8] including Minister of Comedy (at a major accounting firm), Manager of Mischief, Vice-president of Happiness and Director of Fun.

Shapers of American corporate culture

Understanding not only what is the American corporate culture generally, but also the shapers of that evolutionary culture is important in order to be able to predict where it's heading and thus best align yourself with it.

The US workforce in corporate America today[9] is a mix of Matures (born 1930–1946), Baby Boomers (born 1946–1964), X'ers (aka Generation X) (born 1965–1976) and Generation Y (born 1977–1994). Each place different types of demands on employers as a result of the eras that have shaped them.

US Baby Boomers want their companies to help them manage the Generation X and Y staff who report to them, as they grapple with the inexperience and confidence of these colleagues who expect immediate recognition for their successes. Happy with the notion of "paying your dues", they are puzzled by the way Gen X and Gen Y employees leave work exactly at 5:00 p.m., with not even a thought about doing overtime. To the Boomers this is slacking.

[8] *Fast Company* magazine article
[9] FT CareerPoint, 15 November 2001, "Generational Conflict: Algebra Lessons for Older Workers"

American women the same treatment

Generation X are resentful, achievement-oriented, individualist entrepreneurs raised in the downsizing era of the 1980s, nervous that their Generation Y colleagues will earn faster and better promotions than they will.

Generation Y wants the company that hires them to employ them on non-menial tasks that challenge them, and happily voice this demand. Used to getting what they want as cosseted children from time poor/materially rich households, they expect wealth and opportunity, and expect to achieve ambitious salaries early. Impatient, bright and frustrated, companies need to manage these multitaskers well, since this is the talent pool that is replacing the retiring Baby Boomers.

Both Generations X and Y are mystified by companies' tolerance of the "dead wood" – people who seem unproductive and incapable of achieving. What's important is making a difference to people's lives – working for the good of society instead of being a corporate slave to a bland mission statement. They value direct, upward communications, shun bureaucracy and politics and see work as allowing them to focus on other aspects of their lives. Clear goals, the right resources to do their jobs and being allowed to just "get on with it" is of great importance.

According to the authors of the book *It Takes a Prophet to Make a Profit*, US companies need to recognize that employing Gen X and Gen Y staff means allowing them to "feel they contribute meaningfully …

at work expect
as their male counterparts

People want to go home feeling good about themselves at the end of the day." This idea is echoed in David Brooks' book *Bobo's in Paradise* and contemporary business publications such as *Fast Company* magazine. Along with a sense of purpose, all generations want work to be fun, and to *have* fun while they work.

And those who contribute most to ensuring the culture is fun are the executive teams who should be (according to *Business Intelligence's*[10] research) the guardians and ambassadors of the culture – expected to walk the talk. As it is they who are expected to set the example for others to follow, better companies ensure that these enthusiasts are regularly on-message about "what's important around here".

As long as the business culture relies on traditional command and control approaches, men with more experience competing in sports and participating in goal-oriented teams are best prepared for success within these hierarchies. However, another significant driver of US corporate cultures is women, who make the cultures more qualitative, collaborative and communicative in general.

Women bring relationship orientations: collaboration, cooperation and creative problem solving. Increasingly as our knowledge-based economies move toward knowledge sharing and project teams, women's skills are more valued. According to Carl Steidtman: "As technology increases, the need for people within the organization to

---

[10] "Driving Corporate Culture for Business Success" © Business Intelligence 1999

be more sociable increases.[11] Women have a better understanding of nurturing, multitasking, and they speak a different vocabulary: cooperation not competition."[12] Although as of March 2000, 61 per cent of American women 16 years of age or older were members of the US workforce,[13] they are not yet represented in sufficient numbers within corporations to significantly alter the masculine cultures.

American women at work expect the same treatment as their male counterparts, the same status and the same tasks for the same pay. As often as not, she is a senior manager or team leader with significant power to make decisions and budgetary authority. Increasingly young women are participating in sports that teach them the competitive teamwork rules that most men have always known.[14]

Other shapers of the American corporate culture include:

➡ The US national culture and values of self-reliance, determinism, vocation as a calling and a belief in meritocratic and democratic processes.

➡ The heritage of the brands and what they stand for. Most Americans could accurately describe the culture of Ben & Jerry's ice cream, Amazon or even Federal Express!

➡ Explicit statements of the mission and values of the company which acts as a reference point for insiders and outsiders.

➡ Departmental orientations: Marketing has its focus on the customer, Finance has its eye on the best sources and uses of funds, while Engineering has its allegiance to the best form and function, each of which is a subculture of one form or another.

---

[11] Steidtman, Carl, "Notes from the Productivity Paradox: Loyalty, Gender and Generations, p. 2, check listing
[12] www.fortune.com, 19 February 2001 "How Long Can They Stay?", Diba and Munoz
[13] Steidtman, Carl, "Notes from the Productivity Paradox: Loyalty, Gender and Generations
[14] *New York Times* article, 4 November 2001, "Modernizing Economic Impact Of Women"

CASE STUDIES

Ernst & Young

Below is the "rocket" model of the company's culture showing how the vision derives from the company's characteristics, supported by competitive advantage, driven by the building blocks.

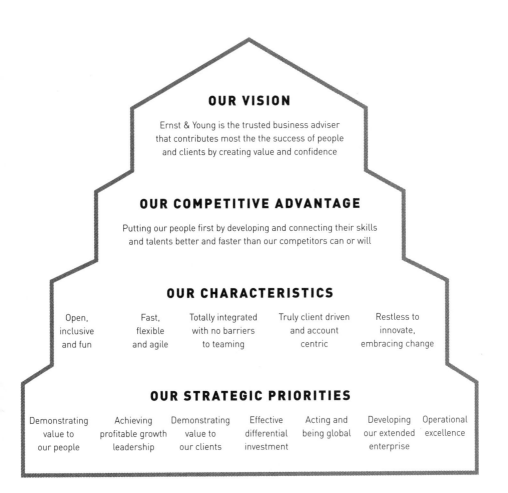

OUR VISION

Ernst & Young is the trusted business adviser that contributes most the the success of people and clients by creating value and confidence

OUR COMPETITIVE ADVANTAGE

Putting our people first by developing and connecting their skills and talents better and faster than our competitors can or will

OUR CHARACTERISTICS

| Open, inclusive and fun | Fast, flexible and agile | Totally integrated with no barriers to teaming | Truly client driven and account centric | Restless to innovate, embracing change |

OUR STRATEGIC PRIORITIES

| Demonstrating value to our people | Achieving profitable growth leadership | Demonstrating value to our clients | Effective differential investment | Acting and being global | Developing our extended enterprise | Operational excellence |

Smart is not enough: Microsoft

(extract from an article by Mark Gimein, www.Fortune.Com, 8 January 2001)

This description of life inside Microsoft is rich with the symbolism, behaviours and values that define a strong corporate culture.

Do you believe that there is justice in the next world? Do you believe that after your death you will stand in front of Saint Peter and be asked to account for yourself? Let us imagine that you do, and let us imagine that at the end of a full and constructive life you find yourself before the pearly gates, as Saint Peter stares into your eyes and barks out:

➡ "Why are manhole covers round?"

➡ "How many piano tuners are there in the world?"

➡ "Given a gold bar that can be cut exactly twice and a contractor who must be paid one-seventh of a gold bar a day for seven days, what do you do?"

If this sounds appealing to you, then consider moving to Seattle, Washington, or its immediate suburbs. If not, let's hope that getting into heaven is easier than getting a job at Microsoft.

You've heard, of course, that Bill Gates is supersmart and that everybody who works for him is supersmart too, but maybe not quite as smart as Bill. If by some chance you haven't heard this, then you won't have to spend long at Microsoft before someone sets you right. Microsoft employees will tell you this in any number of ways. They will say that their colleagues are "smart and passionate" or "smart and driven" or "smart and results-oriented", but each of these serves mainly to reinforce the point that they are ... smart. And so they are, at least in the kind of way that enables them to breeze through (or at least survive) Microsoft's "interview loop", a gruelling ritual in which job candidates are grilled by their future colleagues with the famous manhole cover question and the gold bar question and other brainteasers dreamed up by their incredibly smart interviewers.

Whether you believe that, taken as a whole, Microsoft employees are markedly smarter than the employees of any other company comes down to whether you believe that any group of 39,000 persons can be "smarter" in a meaningful way than any other similarly sized collection of souls. Maybe Microsoft employees are smarter, or maybe they're just better at puzzles. Ultimately, what you believe about this makes no difference, because what really matters is what the people at Microsoft believe. And what they believe is not only that Microsoft is different from other places but that they themselves are different from other people.

In November I spent several weeks trying to learn what it was like to work at Microsoft. I visited the company, and, at Microsoft's invitation, I spent time with the teams working on electronic books, or eBooks, and on the TabletPC, a flat pen-based computer that might be the Holy Grail of computer design and is a pet project of Bill Gates. I also spoke to researchers and programmers in other parts of the company, to so-called temporary workers, and to former employees as well.

This autumn seemed a particularly appropriate time to visit Redmond, Washington. "Microsoft" these days doesn't mean exactly what it meant five years ago. It's been battered by the Justice Department and nipped at by the "nya, nya, you don't control the world anymore" salvos of the West Coast's dot com princelings. And yet it's still the king of tech companies, the one company that can claim the kind of cultural significance that IBM had in 1965, or Ford in 1925. So this seemed the right time to see how Microsoft and, more to the point, its employees, were holding up.

It was early in my time at Microsoft that I was told about the interview loop, and I could not get it out of my mind in thinking about how Microsoft thinks of itself. Certainly, as with other institutions that are extraordinarily difficult to break into – Harvard University, McKinsey & Co., the State Department's Foreign Service and probably even the Ringling Brothers' Clown College – the mystique of the entrance exam fortifies Microsoft's *esprit de corps*. But the sense of electedness at Microsoft goes deeper. Over and over, people there told me a story that I came to think of as the story of the secret garden: Once I was lost, they said; I did not fit in; then I found the key to the magical garden of Microsoft, where I had belonged in the first place.

Saying that Microsoft is a country might be going a little far, but only a little. It still lacks its own language, but it undoubtedly has its own mores and values, all of which stem from the conviction of its citizens that they are part of a new, very special secular elect. Behind the door to the secret garden is a place designed to constantly reinforce the belief in its employees – in a way in which few corporations bother to anymore – that they are different. Almost all of Microsoft's employees have their own office, and the company can feel hushed in the way that one imagines the dusty hallways of the State Department must be hushed – only more so, because in this e-mail culture, the phones never ring. The public atriums are hung with contemporary paintings – not overly soothing "corporate" art or inspirational art, but real art that gets loaned to real museums. It is also, surprisingly, a place with a collegial (or, better, collegiate) sense of fun. When people go off on holiday, their colleagues take the trouble to welcome them back by filling their office with Styrofoam peanuts, covering it with spiders' webs, or even (as in one fairly recent Microsoft escapade) converting it into a miniature farm complete with pot-bellied pig.

All this emphasizes the distinction of working at Microsoft as opposed to working at either stodgy old-economy companies or the new-economy riffraff that happily pack their workers into "open offices", where they brush elbows as if at a crowded formal dinner. And yet strangely none of this veneer is central. It's just the icing on the cake of what anybody who spends much time at Microsoft, or talking in depth to people who work there, will recognize as the Microsoft way of thinking.

Life at Microsoft is all about the stock options. To a certain extent this is correct. Microsoft is a company of the post-loyalty economy, and its executives know that money matters. One former manager claims that the HR department kept a running chart of employee satisfaction vs the stock price. "When the stock was up," he quips, "human resources could turn off the ventilation and everybody would say they were happy. When the stock was down, we could give people massages and they would tell us that the massages were too hard." However, that so many employees are wealthy is hardly the distinguishing fact about the people of Microsoft. In Silicon Valley there are many high-tech companies in which a great proportion of employees has gotten rich, but unlike Microsoft employees these people don't think they are different from people elsewhere; they just know they are richer.

The other theory I had about Microsoft was the anthropomorphic theory: Microsoft is like Bill. Indeed, Bill is exceedingly present at Microsoft. Even ordinary employees can brag about having come this close to him. Maybe they didn't shoot Bill an e-mail, but – as happened with Chris Hahn, a young programmer I met who has been at Microsoft less than a year – they sent an e-mail to their manager, who forwarded it to his manager, who sent it to Bill, who returned it with comments, and, *voila*, they were part of an e-mail thread with the chairman. At the upper tiers of management, the weight attached to Bill's opinions is truly extraordinary. One manager I met likened an exhausting two-hour project review with Bill not just to sex but to "really good" sex.

It turns out that the more you talk to people at Microsoft, the more you find that these people who seem so spectacularly different on the surface all share a distinct ethos that transcends stock options or hours spent on their office couches or practical jokes or even the belief that Joe Klein is wrong. And, yup, this ethos is even more important to Microsoft than the average IQ of its employees. It embodies a few very big concepts about work and life. It's this set of values that is the key to understanding life in the innermost sanctum of the Information Age. And it's the evolution of these values that will define what Microsoft will become in the future.

The cornerstone of the Microsoft ethos is the unwavering belief in the moral value of zapping bugs and shipping products. Like other Brahmin societies, Microsoft (certainly the Brahmin society of the Information Age) puts a premium on doing things that are hard, and doing them the hard way; this makes one a better person and justifies one's place in the privileged class. The American upper class used to send its youth on freezing swims and mountaineering expeditions to build moral character. At Microsoft, moral fibre is believed to grow out of interminable discussion of the smallest details of software features, painful rounds of compromise, and unbelievably tedious sessions of categorizing hundreds of software bugs. Going through this process strengthens the intellect, hones the passions, and fortifies character.

The primary currency of prestige at Microsoft is the SHIP-IT plaque, given to every member of a team that has successfully shipped a product to the market. Outsiders who notice this – and virtually everyone does, in part because Microsoft's PR machinery points it out – generally use it as evidence of Microsoftian drive, resolve, go-getterhood, and all that good stuff.

Bert Keely, the prime technical visionary behind the TabletPC, sitting in an office filled with ebony cubes engraved with the titles of patents he's applied for at Microsoft, pooh-poohs the significance of the creative spark that other organizations value so highly. "Creativity is highly regarded for a very short time, but that's not how people rank each other," says Keely. "The primary thing is to ship a product. Before you've done it, you're suspect. It involves taking this passion of yours and running it through a humiliating, exhausting process. You can't believe how many ego-deflating compromises people have to make to get it out. Some have quit. Others have made lifelong enemies." We can safely assume that the ones who quit are, in the Microsoft cosmology, losers.

The second essential sentiment of the ethos is a belief that Microsoft wears the mantle of manifest destiny. Again, there's an obvious way to understand this, and a not so obvious one. The obvious one is that people at Microsoft think that they can change the world. This idea is shouted out by the company's recruitment advertisements, which cleverly repurpose its "Where do you want to go today?" advertising slogan. It is repeated ad infinitum in *Inside Out*, a big picture book of interviews with Microsoft employees that the company created for its 25th anniversary. And of course the current of manifest destiny runs powerfully through the pronouncements of senior executives explaining that, pace the Justice Department, Microsoft is just a bunch of nice people trying to make our lives better through technology.

The less obvious implication of manifest destiny, however, is the one that matters a lot more on a day-to-day level: Since you are changing the world, and since millions upon millions of people will use your products, your least consequential decisions have an outsized importance. Usually, these decisions are built (since it's taken for granted that tech-minded Microsofters themselves will be able to use any software, no matter how badly designed) around a basic unit of argumentation known as the "mom", as in "Will my mom understand how to use this?" Sometimes, says Cy Cedar, a program manager in the TabletPC group, "you have to fight like hell over whose mom will understand the product."

You can make fun of the constant resorts to mom (my problem with, say, Excel, has never been that my mom can't intuit how to use it, but that I can't), but the fact that people are willing to argue these points heatedly has helped give Microsoft its zing. But at their worst, the arguments can also be paralyzing. Explains Loeb: "People come to Microsoft because they want to change the world, so passions run really deep. There are days when you wish some of them came to Microsoft because they wanted to earn a few bucks that day."

WORDS TO LIVE BY

" You can't manage what you can't measure.

" I have four words for you: I-LOVE-THIS-COMPANY. **Steve Ballmer, President, Microsoft, staff meeting 2001**

" Leaders must create an atmosphere in which people understand that change is a continuous process, not an event. **Jack Welch**

" As we constantly see, nothing prevents autocratic companies from making money. **Ricardo Semler**

part 4

creating

connections

15:

how about those Mets

INTRODUCTION

In our own environment we are comfortable communicating, making conversation, knowing what to say and when to say it. Change the place, the people and it's not so easy. Read further to prepare yourself to participate in an American-style conversation, to enjoy the informality and avoid costly mistakes.

WHAT YOU'LL LEARN

➡ Topics favoured by your business colleagues and where to get the necessary up to date information about these topics.

➡ The potentially costly aspects of seemingly harmless humour.

Situation

You ask your American counterpart which is the best football team and they start talking about Super Bowl contenders not the World Cup.

When reviewing your standard interview questions with the director of human resources for the American company that is your partner, they are shocked to hear you ask about age and marital status, both of which are forbidden by US law.

They want lots of about everything,

Explanation

Wait your turn

An American conversation has been likened to a tennis match: back and forth, back and forth. Each party takes a turn serving (conversational tidbits) and returning the ball (replying). Interruptions are not appreciated. To a European accustomed to a more dynamic style of conversing, this American approach can be both fascinating and frustrating.

The directive "wait your turn to speak" learned by American children at an early age, seems strange and uncomfortable. Nevertheless, it is important to respect this formula. Americans do not like interruptions and consider people who do so to be rude and aggressive. A friend in Paris comments: "Americans don't like interruptions. They cannot stand the European form of conversation where everyone talks at the same time. Before they start talking they always ask: Are you finished?"

Patterns – overview

Casual conversation among friends and acquaintances may seem like an exchange of information (facts, data) rather than a serious

information, so that they can form their own opinion

discussion. Unlike the French, Americans do not generally engage in intellectual discussions. They do not enjoy participating in verbal debates for the pleasure of the exercise. In business the talk can be heavy on statistics and specific details about the subject. This may reflect another aspect of Americans' independent nature. They want lots of information, about everything, so that they can form their own opinion.

Directness is often valued over politeness, especially in business. This approach is connected to the American focus on schedules and emphasis on speed. Expressions such as "let's move things along" apply to conversation as well as activities.

In addition, speaking one's mind is considered a virtue and telling the truth (even if unpleasant) is a characteristic of a sincere and honest person.[1] Sorting out how much truth to tell can be complicated even for Americans. The amount of directness, or truthfulness, must be calibrated carefully. Generally there is a prohibition against making comments or asking questions that will make people "uncomfortable" (see the section headed "Speak with caution" on page 221).

[1] Geert Hofstede, *"Cultures and Organizations"* (McGraw-Hill, New York, 2000): 58

Both clarity and brevity (Get to the point! Stay focused!) are valued. Conversations filled with nuances and differing shades of meaning are less so. Business meetings are not the time to show that you are well read and broadly educated as literary allusions and historical comparisons may only confuse your audience.

Directness is valued not only in words, but also in the physical aspect of a conversation. "Look people in the eye when speaking" advises L. Baldridge in her book *New Complete Guide to Executive Manners*.[2] If you don't, it could be interpreted that "you are hiding something". You do not need to maintain eye contact throughout a conversation. It is acceptable to look away briefly but for most of the time you should look directly at the other person.

This is especially important in a situation such as a reception where there are many people and you move from conversation to conversation. It is considered rude to look away frequently, to appear to be scanning the group to pick someone else to meet. People want to know they have your full attention during a conversation. Looking at them confirms your interest.

The limits on directness extend to a dislike of overt confrontations or even debates. Accordingly the preferred topics are unlikely to elicit expressions of strong personal feelings. The exception is sport, a topic where people express great passion and often with noise and energy in startling contrast to their normal demeanour.

Americans dislike silence even more than they dislike arguments. To avoid it, they will fill time with unimportant conversation. Unlike cultures where your silences mean you are taking time to think about what the other person is saying, for Americans the lack of response is

---

[2] Letitia Baldridge, *New Complete Guide to Executive Manners* (Rawson Associates, New York, 1993): 122

equated with disinterest or disapproval or, according to author Sheida Hodge, deviousness.[3]

This distaste for silence may connect to the strongly individualistic culture of the United States and its monochronic orientation. Unlike members of collectivist cultures, Americans do not have extensive, long-standing networks that act as continuous sources of information and connection. Lacking this connectivity, Americans must continuously reach out with words to get information and to reassure themselves that they are connected.

Speak safely

Every place, every city, has its special topics. Traffic in Los Angeles. Weather in San Francisco. Commuting in New York. But aside from the local focus, Americans overall share a willingness to talk about:

⇒ Work

⇒ Sport

⇒ Weather

⇒ Restaurants

⇒ Food, diet, exercise

⇒ Films, theatre, clubs, music.

You can always ask:

⇒ What do you do?

⇒ Where do you live?

⇒ Where are you from?

⇒ What do you do when you're not at work? Hobbies?

[3] Sheida Hodge, *Global Smarts* (John Wiley & Sons, Inc., New York, 2000): 88

Americans appear

⟹ Have you seen any good films recently?

⟹ Where do you like to go on holiday?

⟹ What car do you drive? (In Los Angeles in particular this is a revealing symbol of your status.)

Sports, teams, favourites

In the business world, sport is often an easy conversation starter. The year is divided into sporting seasons:

Football (American)	August – January
Basketball	October – June
Baseball	March – October

As with so many other things, Americans have their own favourite sports: football American-style, basketball and baseball. There are also fans of soccer, hockey, tennis and golf. A wide audience follows the Olympics and the America's Cup.

People who understand cricket, rugby or hockey are hard to find. You'll have better luck with soccer and you'll occasionally discover Manchester United or Arsenal fans, but not many. Newsprint and reporting time mainly focus on the American favourites. Zidane's move to Real Madrid with a contract worth approximately $65

completely open, but they are not

million[4] made the papers, but that may have been more due to the size of the contract than general interest.

To see who's playing, who's on top, what the next major competition is and to identify current heroes, check the sports section of any major newspaper. Before you travel, read *USA Today* and *Sports Illustrated*. Sports are so much a part of business life that even the *Wall Street Journal* regularly provides news and analysis!

European sporting events get American coverage when Americans are involved: the Tour de France began to make the TV schedules with Greg LeMond and increased in the days of Lance Armstrong. Golf fans are passionate about the Ryder Cup. Tennis fans never miss Wimbledon. The America's Cup gets TV time, real time internet coverage and newsprint space.

Speak with caution

As mentioned earlier, it is risky to assume that the American reputation for openness and directness allows all matters to be discussed. If acted upon, this impulse can lead to embarrassment. Americans appear completely open, but they are not. They have

[4] BBC Sport "Zidane makes Real switch" 9 July 2001, http://news.bbc.co.uk/sport/hi/english/football/europe/newsid_1421000/1421741.stm, printed 26/11/2001

conversational limits with defined private areas. Be cautious in testing the boundaries. Avoid the following topics:

➡ Politics

➡ Religion

➡ Sex

A friend commented that in France it's okay to talk about sex not money. The reverse is true in the US! (In fact, although Americans are considered unbelievably focused on money, it is still a delicate topic. Do not ask what someone is paid or how much he or she paid for something. Generally if they want you to know they will tell you. Sometimes directly, sometimes indirectly.)

➡ Sexual orientation

➡ Age

➡ Salary.

Family

Do not ask about family until family has been mentioned. Generally if people are married or if they have children, they will tell you. The question of children can be especially sensitive. Notwithstanding the fact that life patterns have changed, some people decide to delay starting a family or not to have children at all, and there still is an unwritten expectation in the US that married people will have children. Recognizing that unstated pressure, it is best to leave the question unasked.

If people do have children that will often play a major part in their conversation. You will know without asking. Once the topic has been mentioned it is a good part of conversation and moves into the "Speak safely" category.

Starting points

In a business situation it is appropriate to introduce yourself and start a conversation with a stranger. The prohibitions about introducing yourself to someone you don't know are eliminated. This is especially true at semi-business events such as receptions or forums, when participating in volunteer activities or at official business activities such as conferences and meetings. The fact that you are both at a conference for IBM AS 400 Users establishes a common interest and serves as the basic introduction. You are therefore no longer strangers but colleagues sharing an experience. All you lack is the name of your new friend.

To know what to discuss after the introductions, a quick look at an *International Herald Tribune, USA Today* or the *New York Times* will give you an idea of what is considered important. Before travelling it is a good idea to take a look at the local paper (online or hard copy) to see the local events that may be important to the people you are meeting or that may affect your business. Are there rolling blackouts due to power shortages in California? Floods in Florida? Riots in Cleveland? State elections? It's useful to know.

Useful sources for finding such information include:

➡ Online editions of major newspapers.

➡ www.ceoexpress.com. (Provides links to many publications.)

➡ US editions of business magazines.

➡ CNN, CNBC, Bloomberg television.

➡ *The Economist* magazine and/or website.

Often the conversations will be about a person

Sad but true

Do not expect your American colleagues to know what is happening in your area. American newspapers and news programmes carry relatively little foreign news and Americans overall do not pay attention to international business or geopolitical events. Unless the news is on CNN or CNBC, unless it's a major disaster, it may not touch the American consciousness.

In London on May Day 2001, there were riots in the streets. A rampage on Oxford Street. Yet in the US there was no coverage all day about an important event happening in a major G7 city. The story did finally rate some coverage in local newspapers, two days later.

The major US television networks distill the international news into a one-minute evening spot. A study of television reporting content, *The Tyndall Report*, stated that in the year 2000, the three major US networks ran only 1,382 minutes of news from their foreign bureaus.[5] That is about 29 hours, or slightly more than two hours each month devoted to information about our increasingly connected, globalized world.

When you travel to the States it's easiest to keep up to date by reading your favourite paper online. You can find *The Economist* and the *Financial Times* at news-stands in major cities, but not always. You

[5] David Shaw, "Foreign News Shrinks in Era of Globalization", *Los Angeles Times*, 27 September 2001: A20

that go on around you rather than a topic

can find the information about events outside the US but you have to look carefully. However, it has been interesting to note recent reports from websites of overseas newspapers, especially the London based press, stating that their readership from the US has increased significantly. Americans increasingly appear to want another perspective on events.

Heroes: names to know

Often the conversations that go on around you will be about a person rather than a topic:

➡ What's happening with Michael Jordan's return to basketball?

➡ Will Al Gore (the former Vice-president) start raising money again for another run at the Presidency?

➡ Who will replace Alan Greenspan, Chairman of the Federal Reserve?

➡ Is Madonna doing a new album?

➡ Has Steve Jobs (Chairman of Apple Computer) started shaking up the company again?

➡ Is there a scandal? A new divorce?

➡ Which singers, actors or late night show hosts have made a hit film?

There are national names and local names. Read, listen and learn. It won't take long. As we said before, the American focus is often on an individual rather than a broader topic.

Heroes: the independent creators

The hero is often the entrepreneur, the self-made man, the doer not the thinker. Popular examples include Bill Gates, Steve Jobs and sports figures such as Michael Jordan and Tiger Woods. To these are often added names from music and films. Seldom do you hear of a writer, poet or artist.

People who have lived the American dream fascinate us: the idea that you can start from nothing and get to the top – from "Rags to Riches". You can be President of the US, start a company in a garage or on the road, or be a film star, rock star or sports superhero.

There is not a history of intellectuals, scientists and artists as heroes. Americans look for that "can do" idea, for personal improvement and talent. According to an article by Thaddeus Wawro in *Entrepreneur* magazine,[6] American heroes are typically "visionaries and dreamers, innovators and inventors, mavericks and rebels, trailblazers and pioneers". He goes on to say they are people who "knew how to use their talent, drive, ingenuity and desire to make dreams come true … and influence the course of history". An example from American history that fits his description is President Abraham Lincoln who lived in a log cabin, taught himself to read and rose to the position of President.

Americans love people who overcome adversity and modest backgrounds to excel. Lance Armstrong, the cyclist and cancer survivor, captured the imagination of the nation. You can do anything!

---

[6] Thaddeus Wawro, "Hero Worship", *Entrepreneur*, March 2000 http://www.entrepreneur.com/article/0,4621,233034,00.html. printed 2/12/01

In time of tragedy, war heroes appear. World War I and World War II gave us soldiers as heroes. On 11 September 2001 following the World Trade Center and Pentagon attacks it was firemen, policemen and citizens on airlines who earned that designation.

It's always business

Move quickly to the point. Don't waste time. If the purpose of the gathering is business, then get to the business! This approach can seem incredibly cold and rude, but to Americans it's normal. The focus is on time, tasks, projects and results. In meetings, beginnings are brief. There will be greetings, discussions of your travel, local or long distance, enquiries about your stay, but after cursory conversation you move to the business of the day. More extensive conversation is more likely to follow the business than precede it.

If the business is to be conducted with a meal, the rhythm will be somewhat altered. There will be general conversation first but earlier in the process than you might expect. As always, if you are a guest, the best rule is to let your host bring up the topic. As the host, best wait until everyone has ordered. Often, the conversation moves from general to specific business with the arrival of the main course. The French approach – never before the cheese – does not hold true here.

Europeans may find Americans impatient, especially if the meal is breakfast or lunch. The earlier in the day, the sooner you can start the business conversation. The staff may only have poured the first cup of coffee before "we can get down to business".

Generally, at social events "talking shop" in any detail is not acceptable. You can introduce yourself, talk about what you do if asked and then indicate that you will be in touch at a later time to talk business. You may exchange cards, even set a time to meet or follow up with a phone call.

Arranging a meeting

Americans are interested in establishing connections to extend their business activities and therefore are generally open to new opportunities. If you know someone who can arrange a meeting for you, introduce you to someone you want to meet, take advantage of the connection. However, if you do not, you can still proceed. To set a meeting, call or write and explain why you want to see someone. You do not risk being considered impolite. Overall, Americans like to help, to meet people, to say "yes" rather than "no".

As a colleague said, "There's no need to be 'placed', to have your credibility established by someone speaking for you. You simply are who you are and that's enough for setting up an appointment." This contrasts sharply with the French approach where every request needs validation and elicits the reply: "Please send me a fax stating your request and we'll consider it!" In this era of voice mail and e-mail, it's possible the person you want to see will reply personally to your request.

If you find yourself confronting a "gatekeeper", a receptionist or assistant who schedules appointments for the person you want to meet, don't despair. Simply recall some of the basic elements of the US value system: equality, lack of status, respect for all. Treat the "gatekeeper" as a colleague, a respected professional and you will increase your chances of getting that meeting.

Comments can be costly: sexual harassment

The issue of what you can say in the workplace has become sensitive and complicated. Mistakes in this area can be costly in financial and personal terms. Lawsuits have been prosecuted and awards from $50,000 to over $100 million have been granted to people involved in these cases. Accusations in this area have stymied careers. Jobs have been lost. Make no mistake: sexual harassment is a serious matter.

Initially, the label "sexual harassment" covered only the issue of demands for sexual favours by a superior to someone more junior. Over time the definition has expanded to include suggestive remarks, images and jokes.

According to Ron Ryan, Manager of Labor Strategy with a major California power company with over 12,000 employees, the definition has changed and broadened. The shift has been from specifically explicit sexual demands to any behaviour that creates a "hostile work environment", further defined as any "offensive behaviour that would make an employee uncomfortable and that interferes with their work performance".

Included in this definition are jokes with sexual or ethnic references. He advises if you are in a group and a person telling a joke is making a joke about their own heritage, you should not take it as permission to join in, adding to the stories. It is always possible that someone in the group, who may participate in the laughter, does not feel comfortable and will report the incident. The penalties can be severe, ending up in dismissal.

According to Ryan, even compliments can lead to complaints. Telling someone you like what he or she is wearing can be construed as inappropriate, unwelcome attention, and falls into the definition of hostile! When you don't know someone well, limit the remarks about their personal appearance in any form, sadly, even something positive.

Expanding the idea of a hostile workplace, no touching is allowed. A handshake is the limit. No hugs. No pat on the back, touch on the arm. Even with people who you know socially, where a hug and even a kiss is your normal greeting, in the workplace it's a handshake and a nod.

But it was funny

Humour is abundant and clearly evident in an American office. It's a tool used by people to communicate and relieve the stress of constant pressure. Unfortunately, the humour of one culture is not always clear to people from another – probably because the jokes usually develop from shared understandings and experiences. As frustrating as it may be, it is wise to be cautious in attempting to insert humour in a business setting. People may not understand and may be uncomfortable.

Equally, don't be surprised if you don't understand American humour, even after your colleague attempts to explain it. Time and exposure will provide the insights and lead to shared laughter.

WORDS TO LIVE BY

" Almost any game with any ball is a good game. **Robert Lynd**

" No man would listen to you talk if he didn't know it was his turn next. **Ed Howe**

" In Washington the first thing people tell you is what their job is. In Los Angeles you learn their star sign. In Houston you're told how rich they are. And in New York they tell you what their rent is. **Simon Hoggart**

" The only way to get the best of an argument is to avoid it. **Dale Carnegie**

"" The opposite of talking isn't listening. The opposite of talking is waiting. **Fran Lebowitz**

"" The safest words are always those which bring us most directly to facts. **Charles Parkhurst**

"" Without heroes, we are all plain people, and don't know how far we can go. **Bernard Malamud**

"" A difference of taste in jokes is a great strain on the affections. **George Eliot**

16:

let's do lunch

INTRODUCTION

We Do It Our Way. The typically independent attitude of Americans extends to all facets of their lives including their own definitions of appropriate behaviour. In this chapter we look at Americans' preference for building relationships by sharing activities, their approach to meeting people, and suggest some practical tips for being polite the American way.

WHAT YOU'LL LEARN

➡ Why Americans are known as "joiners par excellence".

➡ The role of philanthropy in American lives.

➡ Useful tips for adapting to American eating rituals.

➡ The complicated American views on food which take them from organic markets to fast food drive through lanes, from diet obsessions to food as an affordable indulgence.

Situation

You meet someone at a seminar and they suggest you get together to discuss areas of mutual interest. When they suggest breakfast you agree but are shocked to learn they mean breakfast at 7:00 a.m. Wanting to seem cooperative you agree. You arrive at 7:00, sit down

Individualist joiners

and before coffee is even poured your host starts talking about possible transactions. By 8:00 breakfast is over, you've mapped out a preliminary plan and set another date, but you barely know a thing about him. Is this normal? The deal sounds good, but who is he really?

You keep noticing the odd eating combinations. Why do people order a diet coke but eat pasta with a meat sauce and add lots of cheese? What are they thinking when insistent on saccharine for the coffee they are drinking with chocolate mousse cake? What's with Americans and food?

Explanation

Why rules?

Every society has sets of customs, rules that define proper behaviour, that explain how to conduct oneself in a variety of circumstances. We're taught these rules by direct instruction, experience and observation beginning at the same time as we learn to walk and to speak. Although the rules vary from society to society, they exist everywhere – giving structure and predictability to interpersonal encounters large and small.

These rules, sometimes referred to as rituals, etiquette or protocol, tend to develop around what Margaret Visser in *The Rituals of Dinners*

Americans are par excellence

calls "moments of transition".[1] These can be personal transitions such as graduation, moving, marriage or business related transitions such as retiring, changing companies or departments in a company, promotions, meeting new people, attending a conference.

As transitions inherently generate a level of stress, one role of these rules is to reduce uncertainty, to create a safe environment, where we know what to expect of other people and what is expected of us.

Where to meet - connecting through doing

Americans are justly known for behaving in ways that can be startling to people from other cultures. This is true when it comes to how Americans create relationships, meet and greet one another. Individualist Americans are joiners par excellence and have probably formed more voluntary associations than any other culture. But "*voluntary* association is the giveaway, because it states that in the beginning was the voluntary individual and then the group was formed from such people".[2]

Let us consider what happens when an American is suddenly in a situation where they no longer have an established circle of friends. In

[1] Margaret Visser, *The Rituals of Dinner* (HarperCollins Publishers, 1991): 21
[2] Fons Trompenaars and Charles Hampden-Turner, *Riding the Waves of Culture* (McGraw-Hill, 1998): 65

business it's a new city, new job, new industry. In one's private life it may be a new stage of life: first job, marriage, divorce, parenthood. All are occurrences that can require a person to develop new connections, new friendships. Building on their underlying traits of independence and informality, Americans have developed an approach to these situations that can be called "connecting through doing". In order to meet people who may share their interests they join organizations, take classes and participate in charitable activities. They perform a task (learning, giving, participating in activities) and in so doing meet others.

Because Americans move frequently, they often join groups that are nationwide, knowing they can participate in New York, St Louis, San Diego or Tucson. Whatever one's interest, with a little searching you can find a group. Some examples include Town Hall (known for outstanding speakers on business and current affairs), World Affairs Council, Rotary International, Women in International Trade, to name just a few. Every city has a Chamber of Commerce that draws local business leaders. There are college alumni groups and trade organizations, book clubs, sailing clubs and athletic clubs.

Americans also use their interest in learning, their idea that continuing to learn and improve oneself is necessary, as a vehicle for connecting. They take advantage of business seminars, classes at colleges and high schools, at wine shops and cooking schools, selecting a course for one evening or one year.

In each of these settings American directness and informality allows people to introduce themselves to people they want to meet. The sharing of tasks connected with the purpose of the organization or the school subject matter leads to new relationships. In a sense, the organization plays the role of another person, providing an intro-duction. In joining a group, enrolling in a class, you indicate your interest in the issue that brings the group together. This effectively announces something about you, providing the basic introduction of you as a "like-minded" person.

This activity is referred to as "networking", and many books are written and classes presented throughout the US every year to teach the skills required to build a network. This approach appears reasonable and straightforward to Americans but can be unseemly and false to people who expect the more widely held formula where a prior relationship is necessary to share activities.

Dan recently moved from New York to Los Angeles, a city where he had a new job and a cousin he didn't know well. But he was confident that new friends would welcome him because before the move, he transferred his membership in his favourite organization from New York to Los Angeles. (The organization being Company of Friends, for the readers of the magazine *Fast Company*.)

Dan was active in the New York group and knew that people who participated were interested in technology, change and the values expressed by the magazine. Likewise, simply by signing up, Dan introduced himself to the people in LA as being of a like mind, newly arrived. He expected to be welcomed and he was welcomed and put to work!

We like to help

Noted as being materialistic, Americans are also active donors to causes large and small. Active philanthropy responds to two aspects of the culture. On one hand *donating* money is a socially acceptable way of proclaiming your success, showing that you have sufficient resources to give some away. (Of course there is also the possibility of

Americans are active

reducing your tax burden, "writing off" part of the donation can be an incentive.)

No less important is the *participation* in philanthropic activities, the desire to "give back", to "do good" for your community, return some of what one has received and to aid those perceived as less fortunate. People give time over the weekends to staff food donation centres, devote countless hours to stage gala events in order to raise money for a charity, spend evenings teaching adults to read and weekends staffing Special Olympic competitions. Again, no matter what your interest, there is a choice of organizations to join and time to be spent participating. Give one evening a week, ten hours a month, a Saturday, three weeks as part of a holiday. As we have already seen, Americans value having choices and they exist in this area too.

This impulse to give was vividly illustrated by the American response to the attacks of 11 September. Within hours of the attacks, websites and phone banks were deluged with people wishing to help. Billions of dollars were raised by donations from corporations, individuals, children selling lemonade and their parents writing cheques, donating goods and services.

It is not only the well-established American businessperson who participates in volunteer activities. In April 2001 the *Los Angeles Times*

donors to causes large and small

ran an article titled "Unlikely Heroes of Nonprofits"[3] which told the stories of several university students who were donating their time and money to establish non-profit organizations to address issues they felt were not being well served through existing channels. This apparent trend touches not only the desire to "give back" but illustrates again the American urge to move forward, get things done, while retaining independence – "I'll Do It Myself".

Some rules of meeting and greeting

Although children are taught not to speak to strangers, that prohibition is eliminated for adults in business. At conferences men and women are encouraged to introduce themselves. If you want to do business with a particular company, it is acceptable to introduce yourself and your product. Sometimes these self-introductions occur in unexpected places. Our European friends are always startled when the waiter at a restaurant begins the evening by announcing, "Hi, I'm David and I'll be assisting you this evening." The sales staff in many retail stores wear name tags, effectively telling you their name (often only their first name) and encouraging you to use it. Informality and equality, whether one wishes it or not.

[3] Elizabeth Mehren, "Unlikely Heroes of Nonprofits", *Los Angeles Times*, 27 April 2001: A1

"Thanks, but I already know enough people."

One word of caution about starting conversations at conferences, parties, events where you don't know people. It's okay to join a group already together but don't add yourself to a conversation taking place between just two people. It's more likely that two people together will be having a private discussion. It's easier and wiser to head for the larger group, even though it may look more difficult.

Guidelines for introductions

Ever casual, Americans use informal language even for the formula of introductions. The traditional introduction: "May I present (name)" is often replaced by "I'd like you to meet (name)."

There are really no hard and fast rules about whether the most senior, oldest or most important person is mentioned first. In some cases the most important person is the client, bringing income to the firm. Her name is mentioned before the president of your company. "Joan Jones, I'd like to introduce you to Jason Green, president of our company. Jason, Joan is president of JJ Enterprises, our new client in New York." Rank rather than gender indicates who is named first. Note that some married women use their maiden name for business. This can complicate introductions a bit when their husband is being introduced. Be careful. Don't introduce Jill James's husband as Stephen James unless you're sure!

From an American perspective, more important than the order of naming is to remember that the purpose of an introduction is to connect people. A good introduction provides enough information so that the people involved understand why they're meeting and have some grounds to start a conversation. From that viewpoint it is acceptable to include some personal information about the people such as a common hobby (they paint, play golf), they attended the same university or recently travelled to China.

When you are introduced, stand up (if seated), look the person speaking in the eye, smile and shake hands firmly. Your response can be as simple as "how are you?" or "a pleasure". Then you move into a conversation.

Where to stand? Where to look?

Remember Americans like their privacy and this attitude influences how much space they want between themselves and another person when speaking. Generally, people are comfortable standing and talking with about two feet between them, i.e. an arm's length space, barely close enough to touch. If you observe people standing closer together it often indicates a private conversation between people who know each other well.

Distance is especially important at the ATM (cashpoint) line. It is the unwritten rule that you must stand approximately three feet, or more, behind and away from the person using the machine. A single line will form even if there are multiple machines, rather than individual lines at each terminal. Standing any closer will be considered frightening and an invasion of personal space. You'll note also there is little conversation between people waiting in line. People consider these transactions serious, somewhat risky and a time to be alert as to who is in the vicinity. (Every few months the newspapers print stories of robberies that take place at ATMs reinforcing people's sense of risk.)

The directness of language extends into the physical aspect of conversation. To be polite, look directly at the person you are addressing. In one book on executive manners, the section on communication includes a directive to "Look people in the eye when speaking, if not, you could be hiding something."[4] People have been known to comment, "Well, I just can't trust him or her. They never look at me when they talk to me!" Remember Americans want to feel that they are important to you, that you are paying attention to what they have to say and a simple way to communicate this is look at them when you are talking.

Your name is?

Everyone forgets sometimes. It's perfectly acceptable to ask "I believe we met at the dinner last week, can you remind me of your name?"

---

[4] Letitia Baldridge's *"New Complete Guide To Executive Manners"* (Rawson Associates, 1993): 122

"Hi, I'm Silvia Smith, I think we met at the alumni dinner last month." Make it easy for people. Most people are pleased that you recognize them and less concerned about whether you recall their name. When reintroducing yourself provide both your first and last name and in a business situation include the name of your company and describe your role.

Correcting your name: most important is not to embarrass the person handling the introductions. It is easy to create an opportunity to make the correction privately if there is anyone in the group who you want to connect with. You can correct the pronunciation the next time you meet.

Handshakes

This gesture can be traced to a time when all men carried arms and when battles were fought based on allegiance to a king or a duke. The question "Are you with me or with my enemy?" was answered by the style of the handshake. Firm and quick meant "we are together" but limp and slow suggested "look for another ally". Today we fight over market share and our weapons are advertising dollars not swords, but a handshake can still provide signals to sort out allies from false friends.

An American handshake is firm, quick and two pumps. Children are advised: neither limp fish-like nor bone crushing handshakes. The standard advice is, make it firm, quick and solid. Look directly at the person, make eye contact and smile. It is the accepted business greeting for both men and women.

Handshakes are exchanged as a normal part of introductions, to begin and end meetings when there are guests but seldom in a meeting with people who see each other regularly. Unlike the French, Americans do not shake hands in the office with their colleagues they see daily.

The other physical form of greeting is a hug, although given the concerns about sexual harassment, it is discouraged in most companies. It is more common in social or semi-social settings. For example business people at a trade show who haven't seen each other for some time may briefly embrace. It is quite unusual to see this between two men. Warmth of greeting is usually restricted to a handshake and a slap on the back.

The "air kiss" where people touch cheeks (almost) and kiss the air above the cheek is a popular social greeting that occasionally appears in business, mainly between women. No matter where it takes place, note that this is a single kiss on one cheek, unlike the multiple exchanges common in Europe. Be careful or your nose may get bumped!

Doors

The new rule is whoever gets there first, opens and holds the door for the other person, man or woman. Of course this rule is cancelled if the first person has their hands full carrying briefcase, computer and coffee. In lifts, ideally whoever is at the front gets out first and the others follow. In a more social setting, men still let women precede them through doors.

Business cards

Business meetings often open with an exchange of cards. In events that combine business and social elements, such as a conference, exchange of cards follows some conversation and an indication that further contact may occur. Don't rush to hand out your cards. It sometimes surprises people to see Americans using their business cards as note cards. Business networking guides encourage people to make notes on the back of cards to remember who they met and what they talked about. No offence is intended. This is simply a matter of efficiency, an aide to memory.

"Shall I beam you my information?" This is a recent addition to the business introduction conversation. What does it mean? Business card information can be stored on your PDA or Palm (the generic names for handheld personal organizers). The hipsters "beam" or electronically transfer the information from one device to another, completely eliminating paper business cards.

Gifts

Since the late 1980s many companies have had rules, limitations about what gifts employees can accept. Bankers complained that they could no longer let borrowers buy them lunch. Buyers in retail organizations note that $25 gift limits changed the face of Christmas holidays. Ask before you give or your gift may have to be returned.

Notwithstanding the above, taking someone to lunch or dinner is still a common way to thank them for assistance with your business. If you invite someone and their company has restrictions, they will tell you.

If you are invited to someone's home it is customary to bring a gift. Wine, flowers, chocolates are the usual choices, easy to acquire and generally well received. Caution: red roses are a symbol of romance and are to be avoided. Don't be insulted if you take wine and it is not opened. Your host may have selected a special wine to compliment the meal.

Now we eat

Following an initial meeting, eating together can provide a means to extend connections. Meal time sharing is a "bonding mechanism common to every human society".[5] When you consider a meal in terms of theatre with a beginning, middle and end, and a plot to "intrigue, stimulate, satisfy"[6] it expands our awareness of the richness of the experience.

Although Americans are known for the brevity of their meal times, "breaking bread" together is still an integral part of how we do business, discover opportunities, find jobs, move projects along. Seldom is there an activity that doesn't include a meal. Conference keynote speakers make their presentation at a lunch or dinner, volunteer organizations have board meetings at lunch or breakfast, corporate top performers are honoured at banquets, and interviews are conducted over coffee.

You seldom attend a meeting in a US company without being offered coffee or tea, although sometimes it only appears after the relevant business has been completed. It is worth noting that the one holiday that is particularly American, Thanksgiving, began as a harvest feast and to this day the celebration is built around a meal, planned to be bountiful and shared by as many people as can fit around an extended table.

When do we eat?

As a general rule:

➡ Breakfast meetings are popular, especially in the major cities. In Los Angeles it's not unusual for breakfast meetings to start between 7:00 and 7:30 a.m.

➡ Lunch in New York may not be until 1:00 p.m., while in Los Angeles it's between 12.00 and 12:30. As work schedules change, people eat lunch at any time between 11:30 a.m. and 2:00 p.m.

[5] Margaret Visser: 83
[6] Margaret Visser: 16

➡ Dinner can start as early as 6:00 p.m., a practice that is quite shocking to our friends in France. Starting times for business dinners vary from the very early 6:00 p.m. to 9:00 p.m. with most business events beginning between 7:00 and 8:00 p.m.

The duration of an American meal can be disconcerting. A three course dinner can be served and consumed in barely more than an hour and a two-hour dinner is considered very long. At lunch some restaurants guarantee you can be done in an hour or your meal is free.

People generally do not drink alcoholic beverages at lunch other than an occasional glass of wine during the holidays or if there is a reason for a celebration (birthday, contract signing, promotion).

A business meal will still be focused on business (there's that task emphasis again!) rather than being a leisurely way to build a relationship. When to start the business discussion varies. At breakfast, the topic may be broached as soon as the menus are taken away. At lunch, the main course may have been served.

Business dinners held in restaurants generally conclude at the end of the meal. People do not carry the conversation into the bar. If the dinner is at someone's home, people may linger. In that situation if you are uncertain whether to stay longer you can make a statement such as "This is a lovely evening but maybe I should be going...." The response will tell you whether to stay or go. If your host says, "Oh it has been a great evening and I hate to see you go but I have an early meeting," you know it's time to depart.

According to Scott Lomas, the Idea Shepherd (formerly known as the director of Business Development) for a Californian design company, D Zone Studios, the length and timing of a business meal reveals quite a lot about the business and the relationship between the parties. He goes on to say: "Breakfasts are short, business oriented, impersonal and easy to obtain. A dinner invitation, on the other hand, is a definite indication that you are 'in' with your contact. Lunch falls somewhere in between."

Where shall we eat?

Restaurants are the most popular venue for a business related meal, but once past the initial meetings don't be surprised if you are invited to someone's home for dinner. Americans like to invite people to their homes. According to an August 2001 article in the *Wall Street Journal*, "60 per cent of Americans either entertained or went to someone's house in the past month, making it the second most popular leisure activity after going to a restaurant".[7] Again, this is an area where the American way is quite distinctive.

The reasons the invitations are extended are several. First, the idea is that the meal will be less formal, more relaxed outside the structure of a restaurant. It is a way to show more about "who we are", what interests us. Also, Americans are proud of their homes often providing a tour, and not designating private or public space, a practice that can be disconcerting for newcomers.

One tradition that may surprise a visitor is that of the "potluck" meal, where guests are asked to bring a main course or another part of the

---

[7] Nancy Keates, "Guess Who's Bringing Dinner? Surprise, It Might Just Be You!", *Wall Street Journal*, http://www.wsj.com, 24 August 2001, printed 1/9/2001: 2

meal. The roots of this probably go back to the pioneers and church suppers. Food was limited and people brought something to share, knowing no one could manage to feed everyone. The tradition carries on today. One hostess said: "people tend to feel uncomfortable if they aren't contributing".[8] Whether this is true or not, don't be surprised. A simple bottle of wine, or dessert purchased at a bakery will serve well as the contribution to a shared meal.

Food: a complicated issue

A love of food is one thing the French have in common, that spans all the social classes.[9] Not so Americans, who exhibit conflicting attitudes towards food. One article talking about these attitudes summed this up, "People are obsessed with weight and diet and yet are the most overweight people in the world."[10]

As a conversational topic, food is as common as the weather. People compare restaurants, diets, recipes and grocery stores. Hundreds of websites exist, shelves are full of food related magazines, and you can watch cookery shows almost 24 hours a day on the Food Channel. We joke that people who travel may not know much about the culture of the countries they visit, but they will know which are the best restaurants in each city.

Judging by the increase in prepared meals sold from grocery stores, restaurant take away meals and speciality stores, Americans cook less every year. Notwithstanding all the interest in cooking and food, according to the book *Fast Food Nation* one out of every four Americans eats at a fast food restaurant every day.[11] But that's not the entire

---

[8] Nancy Keates: 3
[9] Jean-Louis Barsoux and Peter Lawrence: 121
[10] Josh Getlin, "To the Glutton, the Gold", *Los Angeles Times*, 28 May 2001: 1
[11] Eric Schlosser, *Fast Food Nation*, Houghton Mifflin Co. January 2001

Opinions vary
there is an

story. Farmers' markets, often featuring fresh produce are increasingly popular. According to the United States Department of Agriculture the number of farmers' markets grew by 63 per cent from 1994 to 2000 to a total of 2,800 operating as of June 2001.[12] On a busy day, lunch for some might combine French fries from McDonalds with organic fruit purchased at the neighbourhood farmers' market!

Opinions vary about whether there is an American cuisine. In many major cities there is an extensive selection of ethnic foods. There may be restaurants featuring foods from Poland, Ethiopia, Mexico or Spain. City guides list places for French, Italian, Persian, Chinese, Japanese, Korean or Greek cuisine. You can visit the restaurant or find the ingredients to prepare the meal at home.

But after sampling the variety available, for many Americans the favourite foods reflect their love of informality: the hamburgers, fried chicken, barbecues, food cooked over a fire. Americans are particularly attached to the idea of the backyard barbecue with friends and family. From April to September cooking magazines are filled with instructions for grilling and menus for that outdoor meal.

Another American favourite is ice cream – "world leaders in ice cream consumption". According to a recent *New York Times* article, Americans

[12] AMS Farmers' Markets, http://www.ams.usda.gov/farmersmarkets/facts.htm, printed 15/11/2001:1

about whether
American cuisine

consume 46 pints a person each year, more than twice as much as the Italians who lead the Europeans.[13]

> "There's no ice!" is a frequent lament of the American traveller. In the US, ice is everywhere. You are served a glass of ice water as soon as you sit down in a restaurant. Cold drinks come filled with more ice than liquid. Next to Coca-Cola, iced tea is America's best-known beverage. (It's hard to explain to an American tourist that they cannot order iced tea in London.)

The rules

At its most basic, the rules governing eating say that it should be noiseless and done cleanly and neatly.[14] But as we know, this is just a beginning. Children traditionally learned how to eat properly at the family table. Today, there are few families where everyone regularly eats together. Single parents may not have the time or energy for formal family meals. Parents travel. Children have sporting activities, classes, homework. After school are ballet classes and chess clubs at the time traditionally reserved for dinner. This has spawned an entire

[13] John Tagliabue, "In a Global Fight Sprinkles Are Extra", *New York Times*, 19 August 2001: 6
[14] Margaret Visser:17

industry teaching children, college students and working professionals the skills of dining.

At the table

Where to put your hands? At the table your wrists can rest on the table if you wish. American children are still admonished "No Elbows on the Table!" The general advice is to keep your hands in the lap when not eating (using your silverware, drinking).

Your napkin stays on the table until the host/hostess signals the start of the meal by placing his/her napkin on their lap. If you leave the table during the meal, place your napkin on your chair, a signal to the waiter that you will return. At the end of the meal the napkin is placed to the left of your plate.

Don't be surprised

Although the etiquette books (over 1,800 listed by Amazon.com) say it's not acceptable, Americans do use their fingers to eat a variety of foods. Most popular are French fries, even when served on a plate, at a sit down meal. Next are barbecue ribs and chicken, whether it's at a picnic or not. The one food that should always be eaten with your fingers, asparagus, is usually eaten with a knife and fork.

Sandwiches and pizza are eaten with your hands. From time to time you will see someone eating pizza with a fork in a more formal Italian restaurant but that can be considered quite "stuffy" or "fussy". At a business meeting where lunch is served in the office using a conference room as a place to eat, the meal may be served on paper plates and utensils will be plastic. Informal, casual, with roots in the outdoor lunch – the picnic.

Knife and fork

The way Americans use their utensils looks awkward by European standards: constantly picking them up, putting them down, and changing hands. For the Americans it's normal, natural. Don't worry about adapting to that style. Increasing numbers of Americans eat in the "continental" style. Just remember, neatness counts.

Who pays?

The general rule is that the person who extends the invitation pays the bill. Between friends it is normal to divide the bill no matter who has suggested getting together. Some mobile phones even have the facility to calculate the tip and divide the bill according to the number of people involved and tell you to the penny everyone's share. It is advisable to simply divide the bill by the number of people eating without considering what each person ordered. Often each person in the group will provide a credit card and ask that the waiter divide the bill among them. With two people this is acceptable but in a larger group it is preferable for one person to be responsible.

When calculating the amount to pay it is important to remember that a tip (gratuity) should be added to the total, as a service charge is not normally included. (Restaurants will include the tip for larger groups or clearly state their policies on the menu or when you make a reservation.) In other instances the question of how much to tip is left to the discretion of the diner. A general guideline is 15–20 per cent of the total bill, depending on the service and restaurant.

If you're not happy

If you don't like it, speak up! Americans will be quick to voice their complaints in a restaurant. This can be somewhat shocking.

Americans will send food back, request it be warmer, colder or different. The Customer is King and nowhere is this attitude more evident than in a restaurant. Sometimes a restaurant makes a mistake and there is a problem. If so, calling that to the attention of the staff is quite acceptable. A restaurant would prefer to know there is a problem and fix it than have a customer leave and never return. If you're not satisfied tell someone who can change things, not just your friends.

Forget smoking

Smoking is not allowed in most restaurants, public buildings or offices. Some bars do allow smoking. Each city and individual state has its own rules. In a social setting, always ask. Many people will be willing to share a cigarette with you in a bar but won't let you smoke in their car or in their home. It is a controversial topic on which everyone has a view.

Drinking (and not driving)

Wine, martini, beer and sake are all popular drinks. There are restaurants and shops where you can taste them, buy them, as well as drink them. What you drink is almost as popular a topic as what you eat. Wine is made in almost every state of the union. California and Oregon are the states most commonly associated with wine but you can also find wine made in New York, Texas and Hawaii. We have connoisseurs of wine, tequila, scotch and rum. But as with smoking, there are restrictions about drinking.

Remember this is the country that completely outlawed liquor at one time. The 18th amendment to the Constitution made alcohol consumption illegal. This lasted for more than 20 years ending with the ratification of the 21st amendment in 1933. (What a public way to admit a mistake, by amending the Constitution!)

Today, laws regulate the age at which you can drink, where you can drink and in some places where you can buy what you drink. The legal drinking age is 21 and prior to that one cannot drink or buy alcoholic beverages. There are serious penalties for bars, restaurants and stores if caught violating the law. But even all these restrictions are not sufficient to prevent drinking by some underage students in high school and college.

In addition to federal laws, the individual states regulate the sales of liquor. You will find varying hours for sales: some states prohibit sales on Sunday, others limit outlets to special state stores. In others you find wine and liquor available in the market near your fruit and vegetables.

For the businessperson, two issues related to alcohol are important. First, the matter of drinking and driving. The laws about drinking and driving differ from state to state but everywhere the penalties for drinking and driving "under the influence of alcohol" are becoming increasingly severe. Penalties include expensive monetary fines, revocation of a driver's licence and even jail sentences. It is increasingly common for one person in a group to be the "designated driver" and not consume any alcoholic beverages during an evening.

Additionally, if there is an accident related to drinking, the establishment or people serving the liquor to the person responsible can be sued for having provided the alcohol. Bars and restaurants do sometimes send patrons, judged too inebriated to drive, home in a taxi. A sushi bar in Southern California turned this problem into a way to build customer loyalty. They bought a limousine that can pick you up and take you home allowing everyone in the party to drink as they wish without having to select that "designated driver".

For more details

To learn more about the details of business etiquette we refer you to two popular books: *The Etiquette Advantage in Business,* Peggy Post and Peter Post and Letitia Baldridge's *New Complete Guide to Executive Manners.*

WORDS TO LIVE BY

" In general, mankind, since the improvement of cookery, eats twice as much as nature requires. **Benjamin Franklin**

" No man can be wise on an empty stomach. **George Eliot**

" Generosity is giving more than you can, and pride is taking less than you need. **Kahlil Gibran**

" To succeed in the world it is not enough to be stupid, you must also be well mannered. **Voltaire**

17:

what did you say?

INTRODUCTION

Language, spoken and written, is our primary means of communication. Listen carefully to the words people use. This tells us what is considered important to them. Develop an awareness of their vocabulary and you'll gain an insight into their thinking, clues that will help you understand how they conduct both their business and personal lives.

WHAT YOU'LL LEARN

➡ Even English speaking countries don't always understand each other. Australians, South Africans, New Zealanders, British and Canadians even have different business expressions that can be misunderstood by Americans and conversely they may miss the meaning of American expressions. If you learned British English, American English can be a surprise.

➡ American translations of common British English words.

➡ Language differences can lead to confusion in business matters even when arranging something as basic as the date and time for an appointment (read on to be prepared).

Situation

Your colleague tells you to meet him at two for a presentation that will be a slam dunk and after last week's bomb he's glad to have this one Blueberry'd.

You've just finished dinner at an American colleague's home and you ask if you can "wash up". Your colleague shows you to the bathroom not the kitchen! (In the US "wash up" is not often used but when it is, it means to wash your face and hands, not the dishes).[1]

Explanation

Words as windows

Language, especially the way in which it is spoken, fulfils several functions in both the business world and society as a whole:

➡ It is a window into the culture.

➡ It communicates information about past, present and future events.[2]

➡ It provides the "means by which cultural understanding is communicated from one generation to the next".[3]

Language reflects the realities and the priorities of a society. For example, by comparison Arabs have more words for camels than Eskimos who have more words for snow than Americans who generally have more words than either for cars and technology.

Generally, an American's vocabulary is filled with words from the business and sporting worlds while the French reveal a focus on food.

---

[1] Dileri Borunda Johnston, *Speak American* (Random House, 2000): 5
[2] Kenneth David and Vern Terpstra, *The Cultural Environment of International Business* (South-Western Publishing Co. 1991): 23
[3] Kenneth David and Vern Terpstra: 23

Communication is

Contrasting the French and the English, it has been said that the "French enjoy talking about food in much the same way as the British find diversion in the weather".[4] Our vocabularies reflect the topics that occupy our attention and further reveal what is important to us as a society.

By one count there are 3,000 mutually unintelligible languages in the world.[5] But, even if we all spoke the same language with simple differences in our vocabulary to reflect our culture, there would be difficulties communicating. Communication is not only a matter of words. Equally important is the method of delivering the message – something that significantly adds to the challenge of building effective communication across language barriers.

How Americans speak

When doing business with Americans it's important to bear in mind their style of communication and where it came from. Americans, known for their independence and their individualistic culture, communicate in ways that reflect those basic values. Their exchanges are direct, informal, transactional and factual. In business situations their conversations can vary from friendly and relaxed to "ruthlessly

[4] Jean-Louis Barsoux and Peter Lawrence, *French Management Elitism in Action* (Cassell, 1997): 121
[5] Gary P. Ferraro, *The Cultural Dimension of International Business* (Prentice-Hall, 1994): 60

not only a matter of words

focused".[6] Not part of extended networks, they require explicit information for effective communication. (This is known as low context communication and is covered in Chapter 9.) This style can be difficult, unsettling, for people in high context cultures where information is exchanged indirectly and more formally.

Americans are taught to be clear, direct and concise when speaking and writing. The focus is on clarity and brevity. The instructions, to children and adults alike, are: "Get to the point!" "Stay focused." "Don't ramble". To facilitate quick understanding they rely on abbreviations, acronyms and expressions that are generally understood. Some are familiar such as "FYI" = For Your Information, others like "In a New York minute" (a very short period of time, implying a rush, something that will pass quickly) may be more obscure. Some other examples include MBO = Management by Objectives, part of the emphasis on planning, and the expression to give someone a "411" which means to provide information. This expression comes from the phone number "411" which if dialled anywhere in the US will connect you to the information operator who can give you a telephone number.

[6] Sergy Frank, "Free-talking and fast results", *Financial Times*, 17 October 2001, www.ft.com, printed 15/11/01

The sounds of English

In addition to being quite direct, the volume of American conversation is considered by many non-Americans to be quite loud. Since everyone speaks at a similar volume people are not aware that they seem noisy. In fact, they often think they are speaking quietly when to a European ear it seems they are shouting.

Another point to bear in mind is that not all American English sounds alike. There are regional accents, expressions and patterns typical to a geographic area that can affect your understanding in certain situations. You won't be alone with that problem; there are times when even Americans don't understand each other!

Americans will tell you the following:

➡ People from New York speak fast; they're abrupt, rushed and rude.

➡ People from the south are slow and lazy in their speech.

➡ People from New England are reluctant to speak.

➡ People from California, especially Los Angeles, have limited vocabularies and say "Hey Dude" all the time!

There is, of course, some truth to all of the above. There are noticeable accents in the east (New York and New Jersey), in the south (Tennessee, Louisiana, Georgia, Mississippi), a different sound in New England (Maine, Rhode Island) and a distinctive twang in Texas. And in all parts of the country you can find differences in the choice of words rather than just the sound of the voice. The south, famous for its charm and hospitality, is best known for the phrase: "y'all come". Which translates roughly to "All of you please come and join us for ... (a visit or activity)."

Southerners still hold to some of the formalities and use the words "sir" and "ma'am" more than people elsewhere. Some of their colourful analogies also add to our perceptions of their quaintness, for example: "If you can't run with the big dogs, you better stay on the porch!"

What it's not

You will not find clues to the kind of relationship that exists between people by studying their forms of address. Unlike the French, for example, Americans do not have different forms of respectful address for children and adults or to measure the closeness of a friendship or the distance between ranks.

In the UK, although it is becoming less and less so, it is still the case that you can be judged on your accent. People still make assumptions about someone's social status based on the sound of their voice, their pronunciation of certain words. A friend says of her English husband: "Andy can tell if an English person is upper or lower class just by hearing him or her talk." This is not so in the US.

Why should we bother?

"Everyone speaks English don't they?" This commonly asked question reveals how ethno-centric Americans can be and is the usual justification given for their famous lack of interest in foreign languages. It is an eye-opener to most Americans when the response is "No, they don't."

There are several factors that contribute to this attitude:

⇒ The sheer size of the US both in physical and market terms mitigates against the learning of new languages. You can travel for days, do business for your entire career (until recently) and never hear another language. Therefore, no motivation existed; there appeared no necessity to learn another language.

The common key that allowed

→ The immigrants who first came to the US rushed to learn English to assimilate, to get ahead in this new country. The common language was the key that allowed people to realize the American dream. These were the parents, grandparents and great grandparents of today's business people. One way they expressed their pride in being part of this new country was to discourage the use of the language of their country of origin. Therefore, the succeeding generations received the message that only English was important.

→ Another (perhaps more tenuous) point of view, succinctly expressed by a multilingual European executive who has lived and worked with Americans, is that: "Americans are perfectionists. They can't stand making mistakes and having other people know it. There's no way to learn a language and avoid mistakes. So they can't tolerate the process."

As business becomes more interconnected, more global, English continues to grow as the language of business, and, of course, of the internet and there is even less urgency to learn another language. "English has become the tongue of management."[7] There are 372

[7] Felix G. Rohatyn, "US and Europe Can Do Business", *Wall Street Journal*, 11 July 2001: A22

language was the people to realize the American dream

million native English speakers[8] and 43 per cent of the 505 million people on the internet use the medium in English.[9] Notwithstanding the French efforts to keep their language pure, American business English even slips into the French business world with "le website".

A story recently heard tells how in Estonia, English has become the language for communication between the Estonians and the Russians. Neither will learn the language of the other for reasons tied to their history. Since most people know some English, it has become the neutral tool for communication.

So, don't be surprised when you travel around the States to see few international signs, even in the main airport. Everyone speaks English don't they?

This is not to say everyone in the US speaks only English. The Census for the year 2000 reports that approximately one in every seven people in the US speak a language other than English at home.[10] In

[8] Barbara Wallraff, "What Global Language?" The Atlantic online, November 2000, http://www.theatlantic.com/issues/2000/11/wallraff.htm, printed 16/11/01, p. 6
[9] Global Reach, "Global Internet Statistics (by Language), http://glreach.com/globstats/, printed 16/11/01, p. 3
[10] Wallraff, p. 3

Los Angeles where more than 50 per cent of the population is Hispanic, Spanish is widely spoken. Increasingly you can find Spanish language newspapers, television and radio stations and outdoor advertising signs.

Additionally there are areas with large Korean, Chinese or Vietnamese populations that are easily identifiable by the signage of buildings and billboards. Throughout the country in cities large and small you can hear a variety of languages spoken. However, it is still a minority of the population that speaks any language other than English.

Translations for daily life

Two areas that are critical to understand are time and date. For both, America has its own style.

What time is it?

Americans do not count time on a 24-hour basis. Generally, they cannot tell you where 1600 hours falls during a day. They divide time into "a.m." or morning (1200 hours) and "p.m." afternoon and evening (from 1200 to 2400). Thus a meeting scheduled for 1400 hours is set for 2:00 p.m. In the UK, the phrase "half nine" means half past nine, in Germany, "half nine" means "½ hour before nine" = 8:30 and in the US neither would be understood. In the US 30 minutes after the hour, 9:30, is stated as "nine thirty" followed by the designation "a.m." or "p.m.".

What day?

Dates are written in the order: month, day, year rather than day, month, year.

This can be especially confusing.

Exactly when?

If you tell an American, "We'll have that with you in a fortnight," they won't know when it will arrive – What's a fortnight? Sounds like a long time to us! Clearer, but still awkward: "I'll be there Tuesday week." Your American colleague will ask: Does that mean next Tuesday? (The first Tuesday following this week.) Or a week from next Tuesday? What's the exact date? Americans speak about days and weeks. Something will happen in two weeks, ten days, within a couple of days (which generally means two, no more than three).

Where is it?

On which floor is your company reception area? Where's your office? The first floor in the US is almost always at street level, except in an office building where street level is called the lobby. Often the next floor above street level will be the mezzanine, and thereafter, starting with floor 2, will be the offices. For retail stores and private residences, the first floor is always street level, and floors above begin with the 2nd floor.

Good or bad

Bad, unsuccessful:

➡ A bomb or to bomb in the US is a disaster, a big disaster or a failure of noticeable proportions. A Broadway play that closes after one performance is a bomb.

➡ Cratered

➡ Tanked

➡ Died.

Very good, successful:

➡ Home run

➡ Touchdown

➡ Score

➡ Slam dunk (also used to mean easy, simple to do. As in "That sale will be a slam dunk!")

➡ Insanely great.

Common UK expressions not used in the US

Some words are frequently used in the UK but not in the US:

➡ Keen

➡ Brilliant

➡ Chuffed

➡ Mind (as in mind the store; in the US you 'watch' the store)

➡ Smart (as in smart casual to describe a style of business dressing which Americans would call business casual or professional casual).

Expressions that reveal differences in outlook

Certain expressions reveal cultural/attitudinal differences between the UK and US:

➡ In America, one RUNS for office while in the UK, one STANDS for office.

The idea of running for (towards) something reflects Americans' focus on achieving goals, aggressively seeking to achieve what they want. They are willing to expose their strong desires and in politics it's important to demonstrate that you badly want the office. How much does he want it? Will he really run? – are frequent preliminary questions.

In the UK one presents oneself and then lets others decide, or so the words suggest. The notion of not indicating too strongly the importance of the race.

➡ "What goes around comes around" versus "Be nice to everyone on the way up because there's no telling who you'll meet on the way down."

The American expression presents the idea of a circle, a series of connections between people. It also suggests the idea of everything existing in the same plane, an important element in the modern organization. The second statement suggests the traditional hierarchical model with a ladder to be climbed up and possibly slid down at a later date.

Informal US expressions to be heard but not used

"Whatever" has become synonymous with "Who cares?" "I don't really care, you chose." "It's not worth going into the details." The 20 something work generation are becoming known in the American business vocabulary as the "Whatever Generation".[11] "Blah blah blah" is replacing "and so forth", "etc", "you fill in the blanks", "and he/she went on and on".

Some general differences in expressions

The table below lists some common British English words and the more favoured American equivalent.

American English	British English
Apartment	Flat
ATM	Cashpoint
Doctor's/dentist's office	Surgery
Drugstore/pharmacy	Chemist shop
Elevator	Lift

---

[11] *New York Times*, 2 September 2001

American English	British English
Friend	Mate
Homely (ugly)	Homely (pleasant, cosy)
Intermission (performance)	Interval
Lease/rent	To let
Liquor	Spirits
Mail	Post
Mutual fund	Unit trust
Parking lot	Car park
Raincheck	Postponement
Realtor	Estate agent
Schedule	Timetable
Second floor	First floor
Subway	Underground/Tube/Metro
Truck	Lorry
Two weeks	Fortnight
Vacation	Holiday
Zero	Nought
Zip code	Postal code
Food	
Cafeteria	Canteen
Candy	Sweets
Coffee with cream	White coffee
Cookie	Biscuit
Cracker	Biscuit
Dessert	Pudding
French fries	Chips
Hotdog bun	Bridge roll

American English	British English
Pit (fruit)	Stone
Potato chips	Crisps
Stand in line	Queue up
Take out	Take away
Clothing	
Bathrobe	Dressing gown
Custom made	Bespoke

Money

US paper money is called "bills" rather than notes and expressed as dollars. The most common denominations are one dollar (also called "a buck"), five, ten, twenty, fifty and 100 dollars. Coins are a penny – also called one-cent (100 = $1), a nickel (5 cents), a dime (10 cents) and a quarter (25 cents). Most ATMs (cash machines) give cash only in $20 bills.

When quoting prices, for example $1.50, they would say "a dollar fifty" or if the price is $5.99, the price is "five ninety-nine". Note that there is no reference to dollars or cents specifically, it is understood.

Temperature

When trying to ascertain whether the day will be warm or cold you may have to carry out some calculations because Americans use the Fahrenheit scale, rather than Celsius, to express temperature. To estimate closely enough to know if you need to wear an overcoat begin with the Fahrenheit temperature then subtract 32 and divide the answer in half. If the TV weather person says it will be 60 during the day, you'll know to expect approximately 14 degrees Celsius.

Americans do not

Weights and measures

It is highly unlikely that an American can tell you what a "stone" is or even a kilometre. Americans do not use the metric system. They measure weight in terms of pounds and ounces (multiply by .45 for a kilogram), and distance in miles (one square mile is about 2.6 square km), feet and inches.

When putting gas (not petrol) in your rental car it's useful to note that 2.64 gallons are the equivalent of 10 litres.

Paper (for copies)

When making copies or buying paper it is important to know that A4 does not exist. The two sizes in general use are letter-size, used for most business correspondence, measuring 8½ inches in width by 11 inches in length. The other size, used mainly for legal documents, is slightly larger measuring the same width but 14 inches in length. The sizes are simply called "letter" or "legal".

Greetings and responses

A standard greeting almost everywhere is "How are you?" In the US, especially in a business environment, the expected, polite answers are:

➡ Just fine

➡ Great

➡ Terrific

➡ Glad to be here.

use the metric system

Or similar words followed by the question: "How are you?" The answer is expected to be brief and positive. It is acceptable to say you are very busy, rushed or other words that imply you are busy and in demand but brevity is still required. Discussions of problems, illness or worries are not usual and should be reserved for conversations with close friends and colleagues.

WORDS TO LIVE BY

"" I don't care how much a man talks if he only says it in a few words.
Josh Billings

"" Speech is a mirror of the soul: as a man speaks, so he is. **Publilius Syrus**

"" One does not inhabit a country; one inhabits a language. That is our country, our fatherland and no other. **E.M. Cioran**

"" After all, when you come right down to it, how many people speak the same language, even when they speak the same language?
Russell Hoian

18:

you look wonderful darling

INTRODUCTION

How you look matters. In less than 30 seconds people form an impression about you. In that amazingly brief time, the only information they have about you is how you look, how you're groomed, what you're wearing. Packaging counts for people just as it does for products. In the US, where "The Brand is You", the packaging is what we wear.

WHAT YOU'LL LEARN

→ The basic purposes of clothing and a condensed history of what we wear and why.

→ How to answer the question: "What in the world should I wear for that meeting?"

→ How age intersects with dress.

→ Some indicators of status in a society known for its distaste of status and rank.

Situation

You are packing for a trip to meet a new client in the US. You've done all the research: what they do, who they count as competition, the history of the people you'll meet, but you still don't know what to put in the suitcase. How can you decide what to pack?

You arrive at a colleague's home to watch the Super Bowl. Your host told you it was "casual" so you arrive in jeans, trainers and a soccer shirt. All the other guests are in pressed khakis and golf shirts. What's casual?

Explanation

Why clothes?

We seldom reflect on the purpose of clothing. We are usually more concerned about what to wear for a specific event. But for a moment let's think about the purpose of clothing and some of the history behind what we wear today.

As far back as the 1600s there were three reasons for clothing: "decency, warmth and protection".[1] By the 1700s "convenience" was added as a requirement. Simple requirements but 400 years later we continue to debate the definition of "decency" in the workplace. Clothing evolves in relationship to the economy and politics of a society, it is a reflection of the lifestyle and culture of a nation.

In America fashion also served another purpose. It was an "aid for those newcomers to the US who sought assimilation and acceptance".[2] It has been said that "in the period from the 1890s to

---

[1] Christobel Williams–Mitchell, *Dressed for the Job – The Story of Occupational Costume* (Bland Press, 1982): 29

[2] Pia Nordlinger, "Dressing the Part of Ideal American", *Wall Street Journal*, 15 June 2001: W18

the 1930s (clothing) helped define what it meant to be an American".[3]

> Ever wondered about the origins of the dismissive phrase "blue-collar workers"? In the sixteenth century blue was the colour of the clothes worn by servants and other menials who worked in the household of nobles. The idea stuck. We still use blue, as in "blue-collar workers" to mean people who work with their hands not their heads. (*Dressed for the Job*, p. 29.)
>
> Not just colour but the type of collar also served as an indicator of status. If you wore a stiff collar you didn't do work that required you to bend over or lean down (manual labour). A stiff collar meant you read, stood up straight, sat at a desk. Thus the importance, status, of wearing a stiff starched collar that still influences a businessman's dress today. (*Dressed for the Job*, p. 102.)

Every period has its look, its style element. The styles of the 1920s came and went. The war years put women in trousers and peacetime moved them back into dresses. More enduring has been the influence of the "Youthquake" of the 1960s. This was the first time that young people were seen as trendsetters and when "fashion began to move from the street to the stores".[4] That trend continues today and is part of what created the form of business dressing known as business casual.

It's what I do, not how I look

The traditional thinking about dressing for business is that serious clothes are required for serious work. In the past few years, however,

---

[3] Nordlinger: W18
[4] Valerie Steele, *Fifty Years of Fashion, New Look to Now* (Yale University Press, 1997) :6

Americans have based on comfort, movement and

that attitude has been challenged and many US companies argue that comfortable clothes make more productive workers, the exact opposite of the serious clothes for serious business rules.[5] Casual dress, dressing down, business casual, whichever title you prefer, started as a weekly option for a few companies. By 2001, according to a recent Society for Human Resources Management survey, over 80 per cent of the companies surveyed allowed casual dress at least one day a week and more than 50 per cent allowed casual dress every day.[6]

Moreover, according to Marvin Piland, a personal clothier at Saks Fifth Avenue (an upmarket speciality store chain) in New York, "people do what they want"[7] or stated more bluntly by another person "Fashion today is a celebration of self."[8] It's how I want to look, not what I do that matters. One can view this focus on doing what I want, as consistent with Americans' basic values of individuality and insistence on personal choice.

Americans have defined a clear fashion style based on comfort, convenience, ease of movement and cleanliness. The influence comes

[5] Lisa Munoz, "The suit is back or is it?" *Fortune*, 25 June 2001: 202
[6] Ronald D. White, "Clashing Dress Styles", *Los Angeles Times*, 26 August 2001: W1
[7] Munoz: 202
[8] Nordlinger: W18

defined a fashion style convenience, ease of cleanliness

"My God, Ashton, didn't you get the memo?"

from sports, music and the street. It is not traditional fashion in the European sense. Cleanliness is not an issue usually coupled with the subject of clothing and fashion, but is an important one for Americans. In 1895 the issue of cleanliness, not freedom of movement, was an argument that was advanced in favour of shorter skirts,

279

a revolutionary idea at that time.[9] The importance of this issue continues today. Appropriate business attire means clean, pressed clothing; shiny, clean, well-cut hair for men and women; polished shoes and little ornamentation. Whether the attire is formal or casual, clean and neat are basic requirements. Our colleagues from the UK sometimes joke about jeans and tee shirts that are pressed and creased.

But, what do I wear? Check it out

How do you know what to wear? This was once a question only women asked. Now, everyone asks: "What are you wearing these days?" There are no easy answers.

Can casual be:

➡ Jeans and bare feet?

➡ Khaki slacks, blue Oxford button-down shirt and a navy blazer with loafers?

➡ Black slacks and a sweater set?

➡ Khaki trousers and a polo shirt?

➡ Skirt, shirt and jacket?

The answer is yes and no. From an American view, the first item is casual for personal time (or for the programmers of Silicon Valley). The other items fall into the category of "professional" or "business" casual. In business you'll see polo shirts with khaki trousers as casual wear. To make the look slightly more traditional (or formal), one adds a long sleeved shirt and a jacket (tie still not required). The fabric of the trousers or skirt might be wool not denim. The items are similar, the details are different.

[9] Nordlinger: W18

It's worthwhile noting that there still are some 20 per cent of companies in the Society of Human Resources Management survey who don't allow casual dress. The rules vary by city, industry, company and position within the company. In Portland, Oregon one major brokerage firm doesn't allow casual dressing, another does. Within a company, it is possible for one division to have casual dress, and others not.

Overall a general rule seems to be evolving. As one executive at a major Southern California company explained: "We tell our people to dress in a way that is appropriate to the work they are doing. More formal for client meetings, more casual for a day in the office." Other companies simply advise their staff to adapt to what the client wears, whether traditional suit or dress-down casual. There is no one answer that works every day, everywhere.

A senior marketer at Apple Computers says: "It's jeans, tee shirts, shorts. We're all very dressed down unless it's a client meeting. And people who come to Apple know the culture, and dress down. They know what our dress code is and they can wear whatever they want."

These informal rules can create unexpected problems:

➡ Where do you store that suit that you want to keep in the office for the unexpected client appointment?

➡ How to assess the cost of lost time for the employee who has to leave and buy shoes that he forgot to bring with the suit!

Recently a friend preparing for an interview asked four of her friends if she should wear trousers or a skirt with her jacket. Two voted for the skirt and two for trousers! (The financial services people voted for the skirt and the marketing people for trousers.)

Wearing a formal suit Microsoft will didn't

To get a sense of current trends look at the announcers on CNN and CNBC. Look at the photos in American business publications of people at work, not the people in TV advertisements. Check the websites of Banana Republic, Saks Fifth Avenue, Macy's or Bloomingdale's. The photos can give you some ideas. Visiting a new city? Try to look at the local magazine. Dallas, Atlanta, Los Angeles, New York and other cities all have magazines dedicated to local activities.

Also, you should know that as a visitor you are not expected to dress in exactly the same way as everyone else. No one expects someone from London to dress exactly as his or her colleagues in Houston, Texas. What you do want to try to match is the level of formality. Wearing a formal suit on your first visit to Microsoft will merely show that you didn't do your homework.

The best rules are – Pay attention to the industry. Keep your eyes open. Ask before you go.

It's regional too

Fashion, like food, has some regional characteristics:

➡ The coasts are more fashion conscious than the middle part of the US.

on your first visit to merely show that you do your homework

- Black is a favourite colour for women in New York, San Francisco and Los Angeles.
- You'll see bolder colours and more jewellery worn by women in the south – Atlanta, New Orleans, Texas.
- Men and women dress more formally in New York and San Francisco than in Los Angeles or San Diego.
- In Texas, cowboy boots are seen with traditional suits.

Womenswear

In order to move away from the traditional image of frivolity and fashion, to blend into the workplace, women entering the workforce in the 1970s and 1980s tended to dress in an imitation of the traditional suited look of men. As time passed, this approach to dressing shifted and by the 1990s women adopted a more individualized style. However, the question of what to wear is still more complicated for women than for men. Men can wear a blue shirt, khaki trousers and a navy blazer for years and be appropriately dressed. For women there still are more variables, more pressure to look "current". For women colours change, shoe styles change to say nothing of the length of skirts. But not all women respond to these variations. One acquaintance only ever wears navy or black trouser suits. No matter what the meeting, who is attending, that's her uniform. An independent American showing her individuality.

Today, the preferred outfit for a female professional is generally a trouser suit with a sweater or blouse. No matter where you work in the United States this combination seems to be acceptable. It even works for Americans who travel and work in other countries. A partner at PricewaterhouseCoopers working on a project in Switzerland says that her uniform, a trouser suit with a sweater, has served her well.

Colour is always important in women's clothing. Black continues as the strongest colour in most women's wardrobes. The famous "little black dress" always exists in some form and now the trouser suit mentioned above is often black. According to conventional wisdom the basic suits should be dark colours and other colours introduced in accessories. Overall you will find less colour worn in clothing and accessories in the major US cities than you will in major European cities.

Even once you have sorted out the basic question of what to wear, there are other matters to consider. Business dressing advisers suggest you limit the use of perfume, be sure clothing is not too long, nor too short, and not too revealing.

Who's too old? It's attitude, not age

Traditionally, the passages toward adulthood were marked by changes in clothing: short trousers to long, flat heeled shoes to exciting high heels, that first suit and tie. Children aspired to dress like their parents. Now, the lines have blurred again. Parents, grandparents, teens and children can all dress alike.

This recognizes a trend that Faith Popcorn calls *Down Aging* – "tossing away old ideas of what chronological age is and what it means".[10] In a time when people live longer, are more active, working and travelling into their nineties, they want to dress to reflect their attitude.

Where once a woman gave up jeans by the age of 40, today denim stylists struggle to make jeans that fit an 80-year-old. A study by IFM in Paris says that the junior market, which once was the early teenager, can now be interpreted to extend from under 12 to 35.[11] Another source, Worth Global Style Network based in London, says there is a trend to "Age Merge" – where diverse generations are merging and becoming more difficult to define. According to their Spring/Summer 2002 projection, the "youth market" now ranges from 15 to 50 years old![12]

It is worth it to the industry to try to accommodate this idea of attitude, not age. "In the $188 billion fashion industry, people over 34 account for over 50 per cent of the spending."[13] If people want to "Down Age", someone will ensure the look and the clothes fit.

Status

Although Americans play down the idea of status, it does exist. In a business environment clothes provide clues to status. This approach to determining rank and importance within an enterprise has historical roots: "A serf toiled in burlap while his master swanned around in velvets and brocade. You either worked the fields or you owned them."[14]

[10] Faith Popcorn and Lys Marigold, *Clicking* (HarperCollins Publishers, 1997): 263
[11] Patricia Romatet, "Teens generation: points de reperes", Institute Francais De La Mode, June 2001: 4
[12] Worth Global Style Network, "Age Merge", http://www.wgsn– edu/members/trends, printed 25/9/01
[13] Teri Agins, "Finally It Fits", *Wall Street Journal*, 17 August 2002:
[14] Donald A. Keeps, "Don't Cry For Me Valentino", *Fuse*, December 2000: 87

In a business clothes provide

What are the clues today? How can you tell who is the boss when everyone wears jeans? Clothing still provides clues. Are those khakis trousers Dockers or Armani? Look at labels, fabric and the colour. But more and more, in the world of jeans and polo shirts, look to accessories to tell the story. This topic was highlighted in the August 2001 issue of the magazine *GQ* in their article "What Sort of Man Are You? The Answer lies in your Accessories". Although the article was targeted toward men, its basic premise applies to both men and women. Status and attitude are shown in your shoes, belt, watch, jewellery, card case or briefcase. For women, add the handbag and for men it even extends to socks. One looks for brand names, shapes, good leather and above all the items must be well maintained, polished and neat.

Technology is included in the area of accessories. Are you wired? Do you have a pager, mobile phone, PDA? Palm Pilot or other? A Blackberry? As with clothing the importance of these items varies by industry, company and city. In some places you need to have them all, in others a simple mobile phone will do. And, if you think a mobile phone isn't an important accessory just check out Louis Vuitton, Longchamps and Coach, all makers of leather goods. They all now sell upmarket mobile phone cases to be worn around your neck or attached to your belt.

environment
clues to status

WORDS TO LIVE BY

"» Good clothes open all doors. **Thomas Fuller**

"» Like every good man, I strive for perfection, and, like every ordinary man, I have found that perfection is out of reach – but not the perfect suit. **Edward Tivnan**

"» Show me the clothes of a country and I can write its history. **Anatole France**

"» Age is not important, unless you're a cheese. **Helen Hayes**

"» To me, old age is always 15 years older than I am. **Bernard Baruch**

Suggested reading

Books

Andrews, R., *Cassell Dictionary of Contemporary Quotations*, Wellington House, London, 1996.

American English/English American, Abson Books, London, 1971.

Baldridge, L., *New Complete Guide to Executive Manners*, Rawson Assoc. Macmillan Publishing Co., 1993.

Barsoux, J. and Lawrence, P., *French Management Elitism in Action*, Cassell, London, 1997.

Beemer, C.B. and Shook, R., *It Takes a Prophet to Make a Profit*, Simon & Schuster, New York, 2001.

Brooks, D., *Bobos in Paradise*, Simon & Schuster, New York, 2000.

Cainer, S., *The Ultimate Book of Business Quotations*, Amacom, New York, 1998.

Carroll, R. *Cultural Misunderstandings*, The University of Chicago Press, Chicago, 1987.

Drucker, P., *Management Challenges for the 21st Century*, HarperCollins Publishers Inc., New York, 1999.

Ember, M. and Ember, C.R., Editors, *Countries and Their Cultures*, Volume 4, Macmillan Reference USA an imprint of Gale Group, New York, 2001.

Foster, D., *The Global Etiquette Guide to Europe*, John Wiley & Sons, New York, 2000.

Ferraro, G., *The Cultural Dimension of International Business*, Prentice-Hall, New York, 1994.

Friedman, T.L., *The Lexus and the Olive Tree*, Anchor Books a division of Random House, New York, 2000.

Hall, E. and Hall, M.R., *Understanding Cultural Differences*, Intercultural Press, Yarmouth, 1990.

Hammond, J. and Morrison, J., *The Stuff Americans Are Made Of*, Macmillan, New York, 1996.

Hampden-Turner, C., *Creating Corporate Culture*, Addison-Wesley Publishing Company, Inc., Reading, 1995.

Handy, C., *21 Ideas for managers*, Jossey-Bass, San Francisco, 2000.

Hodge, S., *Global Smarts*, John Wiley & Sons, Inc., New York, 2000.

Hofstede, G., *Cultures and Organizations*, McGraw-Hill, New York, 1997.

Hollander, A., *Sex and Suits, the Evolution of Modern Dress*, Alfred A. Knopf, Inc., New York, 1994.

Johnston Borunda, D., *Speak American*, Random House, New York, 2000.

Kohls, L.R., *Survival Kit for Overseas Living*, Nicholas Brealey Publishing, London with Intercultural Press, Inc., Maine, 2001.

Lewis, R., *When Cultures Collide*, Nicholas Brealey Publishing Limited, London, 1996.

Mattock, Guy, V. and Mattock, J., *The International Business Book*, NTC Business Books, Lincolnwood, 1995.

Mitchell-Williams, C., *Dressed for the Job, The Story of Occupational Costume*, Blandford Press, Poole, Dorset, 1982.

Mitchell, Susan, *American Attitudes 3rd Edition*, New Strategist Publications, Inc., New York, 2000.

Morrison, T., Conaway, W. and Robrden, G., *Kiss Bow & Shake Hands*, Bob Adams, Inc., Massachusetts, 1994.

Popcorn, F. and Marigold, Ly., *Clicking*, HarperCollins Publishers, New York, 1997.

Post, Peggy and Post, Peter, *The Etiquette Advantage in Business*, Harper Resource, 1999.

Russell, C., *Demographics of the United States*, New Strategist Publication, Inc., New York, 2000.

Sachs, J., "Notes on a New Sociology of Economic Development" pp. 29–43 *Culture Matters*, edited by Lawrence E. Harrison and Samuel P. Huntington, Basic Books, New York, 2000.

Schnurnberger, L., *Let There Be Clothes*, Workman Publishing, New York, 1991.

Sproles, G.B. and Burns, L.D., *Changing Appearances, Understanding Dress in Contemporary Society*, Fairchild Publications, New York, 1994.

Steele, V., *Fifty Years of Fashion, New Look to Now*, Yale University Press, Connecticut, 1997.

Terpstra, V. and David, K., *The Cultural Environment of International Business*, South-Western Publishing Co., Cincinnati, 1991.

Trompenaars, F. and Hampden-Turner, C., *Riding the Waves of Culture*, McGraw-Hill, New York, 1998.

Walmsley, J., *Brit-Think Ameri-Think*, Harrap Books Ltd., Bromley, Kent, 1988.

Wanning, Esther, *Culture Shock! USA*, Kuperard, London, 2000.

Wilen, T., *Europe for Women in Business*, Patsons Press, California, 1998.

Visser, M., *Much Depends on Dinner*, McClelland and Stewart Limited, Canada, 1986.

Visser, M., *The Rituals of Dinner*, HarperCollins Publishers, Toronto, Canada, 1991.

Magazines

Business 2.0, Colleen O'Connor, April 2000, "Finishing School", http://www.business2.com/articles/mag, printed 19/8/2001

Entrepreneur, Laura Tiffany, "If the Name Fits", March 2000, http:// www.entrepreneur.com

Entrepreneur, Thaddeus Wawro, "Hero Worship", March 2000, http:// www.entrepreneur.com

Fast Company, Gina Imperato, "Jean Machine", October 2001

Fast Company, FC: Learning, "The Brand Called You", Tom Peters (first in FC10, p. 83)

Foreign Policy, May/June 2001, "McAtlas Shrugged", pp. 26–37. FP Interview
  (no specific author named)
Fortune, Lisa Munoz, "The suit is back-or is it?", 25 June 2001. pp. 202–204
Fortune 19 February 2001, Ahmad Diba and Lisz Munoz, "How Long Can
  they Stay? www.fortune.com
Fuse, David A. Keeps, December 2000, p. 87
Gourmet, June 2001 (advertisement page not numbered)
GQ, August 2001, "What Sort of Man Are You?", p. 136
Time, Romesch Ratnesar, "Generation Europe", 2 April 2001, pp. 30–47
Travel + Leisure, September 2001, Michael Gross, "The Pursuit of Privacy",
  p. 49 and Jeff Wise, "New Classics The Adventure", p. 50
Wired, Sonia Zjawinski, "No More Fashion Victims", September 2001, p. 74

Newspapers

Financial Times, Weekend FT, Michael Bond, "Had the Wild West already been
  tamed?", 30 June/1 July 2001, VIII
Journal du Textile, No. 1668, Thomas Humery, "Les mythes americains
  retrouvent une nouvelle jeunesse", 11 June 2001, p. 62
Los Angeles Times, Karen Robinson-Jacobs, "Take That France", 14 June 2001,
  p. C1
Los Angeles Times, Josh Getlin, "To the Glutton, the Gold", 28 May 2001, p. 1
Los Angeles Times, Elizabeth Mehren, "Unlikely Heroes of Nonprofits", 27
  April 2001, pp. A1 and A24
Los Angeles Times, Ronald D. White, "Clashing Dress Styles", 26 August 2001,
  pp. W1 and W3
Los Angeles Times, David Shaw, "Foreign News Shrink in Era of Globalization",
  27 September 2001, p. A20
Los Angeles Times, James Flanigan, "Cooking Up a Powerhouse of Chinese Fast
  Food", 8 October 2001, pp. C1 and C5
New York Times, Suzanne Kapner, "From a British Chain, Lunch in a NY
  Minute", 29 July 2001, p. 4BU
New York Times, John Taglibue, "In a Global Fight, Sprinkles Are Extra",
  19 August 2001, p. 6
Wall Street Journal, Pia Nordlinger (book review of *A Perfect Fit*), 15 June 2001,
  p. W18
Wall Street Journal, "US and Europe Can do Business", Felix G. Rohatyn,
  11 July 2001, p. A22
Wall Street Journal Europe, Robert L. Barley, "Open Nafta Borders? Why Not?",
  4 July 2001, p. 8
Wall Street Journal, Nancy Keates, "Guess Who's Bringing Dinner, Surprise It
  Just Might Be You!", 24 August 2001.
  http:// interactive.wsj, www.wsj.com
Wall Street Journal, Holman W. Jenkins, Jr, "Uptight Is Back in Style",
  21 November 2001, p. A15
Wall Street Journal, Matt Murray, Thoms M. Burton and J. Lynn Lunsford,
  "Uncertainty Inc.", 16 October 2001, p. 1

Other

PricewaterhouseCoopers, *E-Retail Intelligence Report*, August 2001, "The
Productivity Paradox: Loyalty, Gender and Generations", pp. 1–3 by Carl
Steidtmann

US Census Bureau, US Dept of Commerce News, 15 March 2001, "US
Census Bureau Releases Profile of Nation's Women"
(www. census.gove/Press-Release/www./2001/cb01-49.html), 11/11/01

http://www.theatlantic.com/issues/2000/11/wallraff.htm, The Atlantic
Online, "What Global Language", Barbara Wallraff, November 2000,
printed 16/11/2000

http://glreach.com/globstats/, Global Reach, "Global Internets Statistics (by
Language)", printed 16/11/2001

The Top 100 Retailers Worldwide 2000, PricewaterhouseCoopers, Retail
Intelligence System, Critical Issues Series, August 2001

Statistical Abstract of US National Data Bank 2000, Hoovers Business Press,
US Dept. of Commerce, December 2000

CNN.com, January 2001

http://www.elderhostel.org, The Elder Hostel Fact Sheet

www.tinet.ita.doc/gove (ITA: Tourism Industries, govt. documents)

www.worldtrademag.com, article "global Online" 14 June 2001 (*World Trade
Magazine*)

"Common Law" Microsoft ® Encarta ® Online Encyclopedia 2001
http://encarta.msn.com (27 October 2001)

"Characteristic Features of Common Law, Civil Law" Infoplease.com,
http://In.infoplease.com/ce6/society/A0857483.html and A0813047.html
and A0857481.html (27 October 2001)

The Timetable of World Legal History, Lloyd Duhaime's Law Museum,
www.dhuhaime.org/hist.htm (27 October 2001)

FT.com, FT CareerPiont, "Free-talking and Fast Results", Sergey Frank,
17 October 2001, www.ft.com, printed 15/11/2001

AMS Farmers Markets, Farmers Markets Facts!,
http:// ww.ams.usda.gov/famersmarkets/facts.htm, printed 15/11/2001

Dr C. George Boeree, Personality Theories Abraham Maslow,
http://www.shi.edu/~cgboeree/maslow.html, printed 18/10/2001

Institute of International Education, Director of Higher Education Resource
Group, Todd Davis: Open Doors 2001,
http// www.opendoorsweb.com, printed 17/11/2001